W9-BTA-632

# ASPECTS

## OF

# VISUAL FORM PROCESSING

# ASPECTS

## OF

# VISUAL FORM PROCESSING

Edited by

### Carlo Arcelli
*Istituto di Cibernetica*
*Consiglio Nazionale delle Ricerche*
*Naples, Italy*

### Luigi P. Cordella
*Dipartimento di Informatica e Sistemistica*
*Università di Napoli Federico II*
*Naples, Italy*

### Gabriella Sanniti di Baja
*Istituto di Cibernetica*
*Consiglio Nazionale delle Ricerche*
*Naples, Italy*

**World Scientific**
*Singapore • New Jersey • London • Hong Kong*

*Published by*

World Scientific Publishing Co. Pte. Ltd.
P O Box 128, Farrer Road, Singapore 9128
*USA office:* Suite 1B, 1060 Main Street, River Edge, NJ 07661
*UK office:* 73 Lynton Mead, Totteridge, London N20 8DH

**ASPECTS OF VISUAL FORM PROCESSING**
**2nd International Workshop on Visual Form**

ISBN 981-02-2011-1

Printed in Singapore by Uto-Print

# PREFACE

This book contains the papers presented at the 2nd International Workshop on Visual Form (IWVF2), held in Capri, Italy, from May 30 to June 2, 1994. IWVF2 was sponsored by the International Association for Pattern Recognition, and jointly organized by the Dipartimento di Informatica e Sistemistica of the University of Naples and the Istituto di Cibernetica of the National Research Council of Italy.

Visual form plays a key role in computer vision and pattern recognition. The relevance of the topic encouraged the organizers to propose the second edition of the workshop, following the one held in 1991. During IWVF2, problems and prospects in 2D and 3D shape analysis and recognition were discussed extensively, so as to provide an updated description of the current research activity in the field.

The papers included in the book deal with theoretical and applicative aspects of visual form processing, with special reference to shape representation, decomposition, description and recognition. The papers cover important topics of current interest and constitute a collection of recent results achieved by leading academic and research groups from several countries. Contributed papers were reviewed by an international board of referees. Invited talks were given by Dana H. Ballard, Gunilla Borgefors, Jan-Olof Eklundh, Robert M. Haralick, Rangachar Kasturi, George Nagy, Theo Pavlidis, Shmuel Peleg, and Steve W. Zucker. The scientific contribution of the invited speakers, their presence and enthusiasm greatly favored the success of the meeting.

The interest of the participants in IWVF2 demonstrated that the research activity in visual form processing will certainly increase in the years to come.

*Carlo Arcelli*
*Luigi P. Cordella*
*Gabriella Sanniti di Baja*

June 1994

v

# ACKNOWLEDGMENTS

IWVF2 has been financially supported by the following organizations:

CNR - Comitati Nazionali
CNR - Gruppo Nazionale di Cibernetica e Biofisica
CNR - Istituto di Cibernetica
CRIAI
ELSAG Bailey S.p.A.
IBM Semea
Università degli Studi di Napoli Federico II
Università degli Studi di Salerno


The help of Mr. Salvatore Piantedosi in the preparation of this book is also gratefully acknowledged.

# LIST OF REVIEWERS

Abe, K.
Ablameyko, S.V.
Andersen, C. S.
Bårman, H.
Bruckstein, A.M.
Chetverikov, D.
Christensen, H.I.
Davis, L.
De Floriani, L.
Dorst, L.
Feng, L.
Ferretti, M.
Ferrie, F.
Gevers, T.
Granlund, G.
Granum, E.
Hall, R.W.
Kasvand, T.
Kimia, B.B.
Kirkeby, N.O.S.
Kittler, J.
Kropatsch, W.
Kübler, O.
Lam, L.
Larsen, O.V.
Legault, R.
Lemonnier, F.
Liu, K.
Madsen, C.D.
Maeder, A.J.

Manos, A.
Maragos, P.
Marcelli, A.
Marcotequi, B.
Melter, R.A.
Milios, E.
Mirzaian, A.
Montanvert, A.
O'Gorman, L.
Puppo, E.
Rosenfeld, A.
Samet, H.
Savini, M.
Serra, J.
Siddiqi, K.
Soille, P.
Sorrenti, D.
Stefanelli, R.
Strathy, N.W.
Suen, C.
Székely, G
Taddei C.
Tek, H.
Terzopoulos, D.
van den Boomgaard, R
Vento, M.
Vossepoel, A.M.
Weiss, I
Yacoob, Y.
Zamperoni, P.

# CONTENTS

# SHAPE PARTITION BY INTERACTION OF GROWING REGIONS

CARLO ARCELLI

*Istituto di Cibernetica, C.N.R., 80072 Arco Felice, Naples, Italy*

LUCA SERINO

*DIS, Facoltà di Ingegneria, Università di Napoli, 80125 Naples, Italy*

## ABSTRACT

Two types of feature sets related to shape are found in a pattern represented by its Distance Transform. The feature sets are expanded into elementary regions, which are possibly merged to create a number of pattern subsets constituting a partition. Depending on the different values chosen for the range of influence assigned to the feature sets, alternative partitions can be obtained. A criterion to identify the most significant partition is proposed, and experimental work addressing the issues of invariance, robustness and stability is briefly discussed.

## 1. Introduction

Describing a pattern in terms of parts is often a convenient way to approach a recognition task [1]. Parts are expected to have a shape easier to describe and, as a whole, should constitute a set which preserves its basic structure even if locally deformed. In particular, location and mutual relations of parts should not change if the parts are placed far from the portion of the pattern where deformation has occurred.

Different methods have been proposed for pattern decomposition [2]; we have followed one based on the exploitation of the shape properties characterizing the Distance Transform of the pattern [3]. Though the Distance Transform accounts for both contour information and region information, in this paper we focus basically on its capability to represent region information, and illustrate a procedure for partitioning a bidimensional pattern into parts, obtained by merging elementary regions grown from feature sets including centers of maximal discs. In this respect, our method is somehow related with the decomposition approach developed in the framework of Mathematical Morphology, e.g., [4,5]. The contribution of contour information to favor the partitioning process could also be taken explicitly into account, by suitably integrating the current procedure with previous work done to split clumps of touching or overlapping near-convex blobs, represented by their Distance Transform [6].

According to our model, partition is obtained by merging strongly adjacent elementary regions grown from feature sets interacting with each other. Interaction among the feature sets is evaluated by analysing, at different scales, the Reverse Distance Transform built from the feature sets themselves. Since a set of alternative pattern organizations into parts can be obtained, a criterion for the selection of the most significant one is presented. On the whole, the found organization behaves nicely with respect to translation, rotation and scale change of the pattern, and with respect to partial occlusion and slight contour deformations.

## 2. Distance Transforms and Feature Sets

Let F and B denote respectively the foreground and the background of a binary image. We assume that F is the pattern of interest and, for the sake of simplicity, that it consists of just one connected component, completely surrounded by B.

The Distance Transform of F with respect to B is the multi-valued set DT, which differs from F in having each pixel labeled with its distance from B, computed according a chosen distance function. We consider the weighted distance $d_w$ with weights $w_1 = 3$ and $w_2 = 4$, which is a quasi-Euclidean distance [7].

The structure of the DT can be expressed by the sets of pixels, called layers, placed within a given range of distances from B [8]. A pixel labeled p belongs to the j-th layer (equivalently, to the layer of order j) if $w_1 \cdot (j-1) < p \leq w_1 \cdot j$. A layer may have more than one component.

The set of layer components can be represented by a tree, where the root is the first layer, and the nodes and the arcs are respectively the layer components and their adjacency relations. Accordingly, the same terminology used for the elements of a tree (ancestor, father, son, descendant) can be used for the layer components.

We call n-type feature set any maximal subset of the DT bordered by a layer component, each descendant of which has at most one son and all its pixels are adjacent to the pixels of the son (if any).

In a layer with son(s), we call p-type feature set any proper layer subset whose pixels are not adjacent to the pixels of the son(s) and whose length is greater than a given threshold value $t$, $t \geq 0$. By length of a p-type feature set we mean the maximal linear extension of the set. In this paper, $t$ is chosen equal to 2.

Both types of feature set are related, by means of the Reverse Distance Transformation, to basic constituents of the pattern shape. In fact, an n-type feature set can be understood as the kernel of a non elongated near-convex region of F, and a p-type feature set as the kernel of a protrusion or of a neck.

For a pixel p labeled k, the Reverse Distance Transformation is the process building the open disc with radius $\lceil k/w_1 \rceil$ centered in p, and assigning to any pixel of the disc, say q, the label (k-distance(p,q)). The shape of the disc depends on the chosen distance function. For the chosen $d_w$, the shape varies as k increases and becomes octagonal as soon as k is great enough. Application of the Reverse Distance Transformation to any subset of the DT, allows one to obtain the union of the discs centered on the pixels of the subset.

## 3. Merging of Elementary Regions

The features sets are detected and individually labeled, then they are used as seeds for an expansion process that completely fills the space enclosed by the silhouette of F. As a result, the pattern is partitioned into a number of irregularly shaped tiles (called elementary regions), each one grown from a feature set. Information on the structure of F in terms of these tiles is collected in a Table where, in particular, for each tile the perimeter and the length of the common boundary shared with any adjacent tile is recorded. We omit the details of these processes as they can be found in [3], and focus on the mutual spatial relations among the elementary regions and among the feature sets.

The boundary of an elementary region is the set of crack-codes [9], separating the region from its complement. For every pair of adjacent regions X and Y, let $P_x$ and $P_y$ denote their perimeters, and $P_c$ the length of the common boundary they share. We say that X and Y are strongly adjacent if $\min(P_x/P_c, P_y/P_c)$ is less than a threshold value $t'$. In this paper, $t'$ is chosen equal to 5.

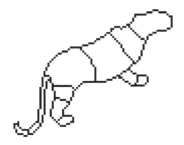

**Figure 1.** Partition in terms of elementary regions.

The elementary regions are generally too many for a significant partition of F, sometimes considerably more than in the example of Figure 1, so that possible merging of regions has to be checked. This check is performed by taking into account both the strength of adjacency between elementary regions and the spatial relations (precisely, whether interaction exists) among the feature sets. The latter are deduced from the structure of the Reverse Distance Transform (RDT, for short) built from the pixels of the feature sets.

For a more intuitive understanding of the structure of the RDT, we consider its version expressed in terms of layer labels instead of distance labels, and refer to the simple pattern shown in Figure 2, where the black regions denote the feature sets. The RDT can be interpreted as a set of sequences of expanding wave fronts, each one originated from a pixel in the feature sets and characterized by labels decreasing down to the value 1. Wave fronts collide if originated by pixels not too far apart. If not already labeled 1, after collision they merge and continue their propagation in the form of a single wave front until either label 1 is reached or some further collision possibly occurs.

The outermost layer in the RDT is labeled 1 and may have more than one component. In fact, the feature sets do not generally include all the centers of maximal discs, because of the exclusion from the p-type feature sets of the layer subsets with length less that $t$. Thus, it may happen that the RDT does not fully cover F and is constituted by more than one component.

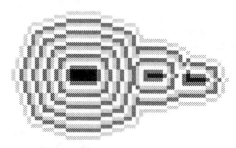

**Figure 2.** Layers of the RDT of a simple pattern. Black regions denote feature sets.

We are interested in investigating the possible interactions among the feature sets originating each component of the RDT. These are neighborhood relations that we will check on the tree representation of each component of the RDT, expressed in terms of its layer components. The tree is built by taking the outermost layer as the root, the layer components as nodes, and by defining the arcs in terms of the adjacency between layer components.

In Figure 3, the two components of the tree representation relative to the example in Figure 1 is shown. Squares are used to indicate the layer components including feature sets (denoted by lower-case letters), while circles indicate layer components not including feature sets.

Let us refer to a component of the RDT. Moreover, for simplicity, in the following let us mention as layer what may be properly a layer component.

We say that every feature set dominates the layer containing it as well as all the layers with smaller order surrounding it. Suppose now that the dominance of any feature set can be exerted only as far as the first r layers surrounding it. Then, two feature sets, belonging to layers $L_1$ and $L_2$, are said to interact within the range r if they dominate a same layer $L_3$, at most distant r from both of them. There are three possibilities: i) $L_1$ coincides with $L_2$ (so that $L_1=L_2=L_3$); ii) $L_3$ coincides with the layer with smaller order between $L_1$ and $L_2$; iii) $L_3$ has order smaller than both $L_1$ and $L_2$.

We call r the range of influence of the feature sets. Clearly, the possible number of interacting feature sets is controlled by the value of r, which can be any of the integers from 0 to the order of the innermost layer in the RDT (the latter being equal to the depth of the tree representing the RDT). Once r has been chosen, the interaction condition for two feature sets, respectively belonging to layers $L_1$ and $L_2$, is that there exists a layer $L_3$ such that $r \geq \max(O(L_1)-O(L_3), O(L_2)-O(L_3))$. Where $O(L_i)$ denotes the order of layer $L_i$. Only elementary regions grown from interacting feature sets will be accepted as candidates for merging.

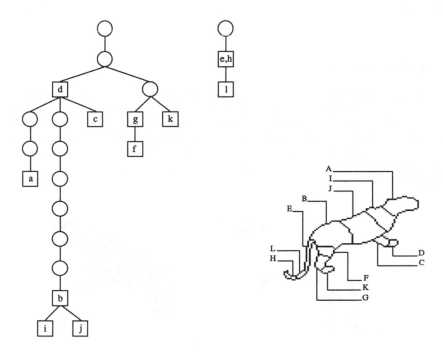

**Figure 3.** (Left) Tree representation of the RDT. Nodes depicted by squares refer to layer components including feature sets, denoted by lower-case letters. (Right) Capitals indicate regions grown from the feature sets denoted by the corresponding lower-case letters.

Let us consider the tree representation of the RDT, and let r be assigned a given value. If a node refers to a layer including more than one feature set, the node is called selfinteracting. Otherwise, let x and y be a pair of nodes, each including one or more feature sets. We say that x and y interact if either of the following occurs:

1) x can be reached from y by traversing the tree for a number of arcs not greater than r, either downwards or upwards.

2) there exists a branch node upwards of x and y, distant from each of them a number of arcs not greater than r.

Elementary regions grown from feature sets corresponding either to self interacting nodes or to pairs of interacting nodes are merged if they result strongly adjacent. Merging is accomplished by defining as equivalent the labels coloring the strongly adjacent regions.

When the RDT is represented by more than one tree, the same range r is taken into account for all the feature sets in the trees, to have consistent results.


## 4. Significant Partition

The possibility of merging adjacent regions is enhanced by increasing the value of r, since this causes also adjacent regions grown from feature sets more far apart to become candidates. Correspondingly, different pattern partitions into a smaller number of regions may originate. Obviously, if complete merging of the regions into the whole pattern is achieved for some value of r, that value of r and the higher ones are not of interest. In Figure 4, we show the partitions of the pattern in Figure 1, respectively obtained for r equal to 1 and 8.

**Figure 4.** Partitions for r=1 (left), and r=8 (right).

The value of r can be seen as the resolution unit adopted to analyse the set of layers grown from the feature sets and constituting the RDT. Thus, each value of r identifies the scale at which the spatial relations among the feature sets are checked, and one may talk of pattern partitions occurring at different scales. In the following we ignore the partition at r=0, since it often consists of a large number of regions, and consider the partitions originating when r varies from 1 to $r_{max}$, where $r_{max}$ is either the depth of the tree or a smaller value such that complete region merging is achieved at $r_{max}+1$.

The successive partitions are stored in a Table which has $r_{max}$ column entries in correspondence with the possible values of r, and a number of row entries equal to the number of distinct regions appearing in the set of partitions. Refer to Figure 5. Initially, the Table has the regions of the partition at r=1 as row entries. Then, the successive values of r are taken into account and a new row entry is started whenever two or more regions merge into one. Besides the regions of each partition, the Table allows one to know in correspondence of how many values of r a region is member of a partition.

A well-known criterion to find the most significant pattern organization in terms of appropriate subsets, when alternative organizations (obtained at different scales) are available, is to select the one showing a greater persistence through the scales [10]. We follow this criterion only if persistence of a given partition occurs at least $r_{max}/2$ times. When this is not the case, we assign the greatest significance to the organization consisting of the regions which individually appear more frequently along all the scales and, as a whole, constitute a partition of the pattern in the smallest number of parts.

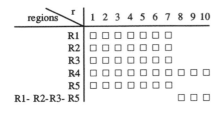
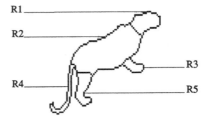

**Figure 5.** (Left) In each column, the □ indicate the regions of the partition obtained for a given value of r. (Right) Regions obtained for r=1.

In the case depicted in Figure 5, the most significant organization is given by any of the partitions obtained for r ranging from 1 to 7, since this organization persists more than $r_{max}/2$ times. Persistence is not so long for the pattern whose elementary regions are shown in Figure 6, whose possible partitions are illustrated in Figure 7. In this case the second part of the criterion is used to build the desired partition. Regions are accepted in order of decreasing occurrence and if an accepted region is the union of smaller regions, then its constituent regions are no longer considered as candidates. Similarly if an accepted region is part of a larger region (e.g., R3 is part of R2-R3-R4, but occurs more frequently) then the latter is no longer considered as candidate. The criterion returns as most significant organization the one made by regions R1, R2 union R4, R3, R5, and R6.

8

Since the elementary regions are grown from feature sets centrally located within the pattern, a partition including a region completely surrounded by another region cannot be originated. Any region, union of elementary regions, is adjacent to the background and is separated from the remaining portion of the pattern by subsets of its boundary, i.e., sequences of crack-codes, starting and ending in correspondence with the background. These subsets of the boundary play the same role as the part-lines characterizing a partitioning scheme [1].

**Figure 6.** Elementary regions.

For the partition corresponding to the most significant organization, we have carried out some experiments to check to which extent the partition enjoys the properties that, according to [1], should characterize a partitioning scheme: invariance, robustness and stability.

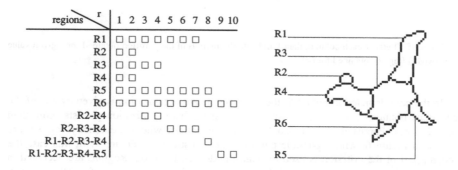

**Figure 7.** (Left) In each column, the □ indicate the regions of the partition obtained for a given value of r. (Right) Regions obtained for r=1.

Invariance, i.e., the property that "the part-lines are transformed in exactly the same manner when the pattern is transformed by a combination of translations, rotations and scalings", is enjoyed to a great extent, except for scaling (where some regions are not detected). The rationale is clear enough. Due to the quasi Euclidean metric used to compute the DT, the location of the centers of the maximal discs, hence of the feature sets, is sufficiently invariant under pattern rotation and translation, so that also the set of elementary regions is not significantly modified.

In case of scalings, the regions obtained at one scale are usually not in a 1-1 correspondence with those at another scale, since a coarser scale often implies the presence of only a subset of the set of centers of maximal discs found at a finer scale.

As for robustness, we have checked whether "deformation of the pattern due to partial occlusion or movement of some part, does not cause changes to the regions remote to such deformation". The results have been mostly satisfactory, and great modifications in the partition of the occluded pattern occurred only when the occlusion caused an appreciable change in the depth of the RDT tree. In Figure 8, the partitions obtained after different types of occlusion are shown.

**Figure 8.** Partitions obtained when the pattern is differently partially occluded.

In the case of movement of a portion of the pattern, the relations among the seeds, and among the elementary regions grown from them, change only slightly (since movement relates to rotation), except for the portion of the pattern playing the role of hinge. In proximity of the hinge, the strength of adjacency between neighboring regions may change in such a way to cause a local modification of the partition.

Finally, we have checked stability, i.e., that "slight changes in the contour of the pattern lead to slight changes in the regions and their relations". It is straightforward to note that if there are no modifications in the number and position of the seeds, there is also no change in the partition. Otherwise, elementary regions are grown also from the seeds created in correspondence with contour variations. These regions may be stable and persist, hence may influence the structure of the partition, if the range necessary to merge them with other regions is higher than the range necessary to cause merging of the other regions. This is the case for the pattern shown in Figure 9 (right), which has been slightly deformed in the bottom right portion with respect to the pattern shown in Figure 9 (left).

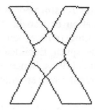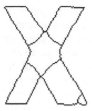

**Figure 9.** Different partitions may originate when the pattern contour is slightly modified.

The resulting partition includes a negligible region. Generally, these regions can be interpreted as of secondary importance in a hierarchical description of the partitioned pattern.

## 6. References

[1]     K.Siddiqi and B.B. Kimia, "Parts of visual form: computational aspects", *Proc. Int. Conf. on Computer Vision and Pattern Recognition*, New York, pp.75-81, 1993.

[2]     L.G.Shapiro, "Recent progress in shape decomposition and analysis", in *Progress in Pattern Recognition 2*, L.N. Kanal and A. Rosenfeld Eds., North Holland, Amsterdam, pp. 113-123, 1985.

[3]     C.Arcelli and L. Serino, "Shape features in distance transforms", in *Vision Geometry II*, R.A.Melter and A.Y.Wu Eds., SPIE Vol.2060, pp. 49-60, 1993.

[4]     I.Pitas and A.N. Venetsanopoulos, "Morphological shape decomposition", *IEEE Trans. on Pattern Analysis and Machine Intelligence,* vol. PAMI-12, 1, pp. 38-45, 1990.

[5]     A.Toet, "A hierarchical morphological image decomposition", *Pattern Recognition Letters*, 11, pp.267-274, 1990.

[6]     C.Arcelli and L. Serino, "Finding near-convex shapes in complex patterns", in *Advances in Structural and Syntactic Pattern Recognition*, H. Bunke Ed., World Scientific, Singapore, pp. 217-226, 1992.

[7]     G.Borgefors, "Distance transformations in arbitrary dimensions", *Computer Vision, Graphics and Image Processing,* 27, pp. 321-345, 1984.

[8]     C.Arcelli and G. Sanniti di Baja, "Weighted distance transforms: a characterization", in *Image Analysis and Processing II,* V. Cantoni *et al.* Eds., Plenum, New York, pp. 205 -211, 1988.

[9]     A.Rosenfeld and A.C. Kak, *Digital Picture Processing*, vol. 2, Academic Press, New York, 1982.

[10]    A.P.Witkin, "Scale-space filtering", *Proc. 8th Int. Joint Conf. on Artificial Intelligence*, Karlsruhe, pp.1019-1021, 1983.

# RECOGNITION OF GRAPHICAL OBJECTS FOR INTELLIGENT INTERPRETATION OF LINE DRAWINGS

JUAN F. ARIAS and RANGACHAR KASTURI

*Department of Computer Science and Engineering*
*The Pennsylvania State University, University Park, PA 16802, USA*

## ABSTRACT

One of the most challenging and important topics in document image analysis is the recognition and interpretation of line drawings. Although the dominant component of most paper documents is text, many documents contain some line art or graphics in addition to text. There are also those documents such as engineering drawings, electrical schematics, flow charts, utility company drawings, and maps which are predominantly graphics. Sometimes the graphical elements are used to interrelate the textual elements, as is the case in flow charts or tables. In other cases the textual elements are used to augment the information given by the graphical elements, as in maps, engineering drawings and utility company drawings. The main objectives of line drawing interpretation are to obtain a succinct description of the information content in documents and to create a representation that would facilitate efficient storage, retrieval, transmission and updating.

Graphical interpretation, as any other interpretation process, consists of three main levels of abstraction. In the lowest level the graphical primitives like line segments, curves, arrow heads or text, are recognized. In the next level the graphical primitives are related to form meaningful graphical objects like polygons, continuous lines, arrows, etc. In the highest level, by interrelating these objects, a description is extracted from the drawing. Most of the graphics recognition systems built to date perform the low and mid level interpretation tasks independent of the domain and use the domain dependent knowledge to guide the semantic analysis. Also the interpretation is done as a sequential bottom up process. In this paper, we emphasize the necessity of using domain specific knowledge in the three levels of the interpretation to improve the results. Likewise, the interpretation process has to be a combination of bottom-up and top-down approaches. We briefly describe some of the recent advances in this direction. We also present our recent research efforts in the area of utility company drawing interpretation along with some experimental results using real drawings to illustrate the capabilities and limitations of the methods.

## 1. Introduction

In recent years, the use of computer-based graphical systems has become widespread. Among these systems the most important we find are Computer Aided Design (CAD) systems and Geographical Information Systems (GIS). In general these systems allow to manage, using the computer, the information that previously was only handled by paper documents. The main bottleneck for increased use of such systems is that the vast majority of documents are still on paper and a large amount of new information is still being generated in the same manner. Manually performing the conversion is a slow and costly process and after many years of intense research, there are still no general purpose systems which can automatically convert the large variety of paper documents into computer readable form.

The input of a line drawing interpretation system is typically a raster image obtained from optically scanning the paper document. Such a document may contain text, block diagrams, tables, or graphical elements representing objects (e.g., roads in a map, different views of a mechanical part). The objective is then to extract the different elements and create a description of the drawing. This description must be at a level that facilitates the modification of the drawing and the interchange of information between various systems.

Something that any interpretation system has to do is the extraction of information at three different levels of abstraction. The lowest level corresponds to the graphical primitives, i.e., line segments, arcs, intersections, etc. The next level corresponds to graphical objects, i.e., boxes, lines, circles, etc. The highest level extracts information about the relation between these objects and gives meaning to the drawing. An analogy can be established between these levels and language compilation, with the levels corresponding to lexical, syntactic and semantic analysis respectively. Much work has been done in low and mid-level processing [17][26][40][47]. Some systems have been built with good performances up to the highest level of abstraction by limiting their application to specific domains [16][18][25][27]. The general characteristics of these systems is that the low and mid-level information is extracted independently from the domain, and the domain knowledge is used in the last stage of the information extraction process. Most of them take a bottom-up approach in the interpretation process.

In this paper we present an overview of recent research results in the interpretation of line drawings limited to specific domains. From the most recent developments in the area we can infer that a key aspect to the improvement in performance is the inclusion of domain specific knowledge in the three levels of recognition. Using a combination of bottom-up and top-down approaches the higher levels guide the extraction of information at the lower levels. Usually before processing a scanned paper document, some kind of preprocessing must be performed to enhance the information, i.e., removing noise, closing small gaps, etc. In Section 2 we describe some of these preprocessing techniques and give an overview of some commonly used low level information extraction methods. In section 3 some of the systems developed for recognition of diagrams are described. In Sections 4 and 5 we give brief overviews of the research in engineering drawing and map interpretation respectively, and finally, in Section 6 we describe recent results for utility company drawings interpretation. Parts of this paper were presented at earlier workshops [24]. A tutorial text on document image analysis with reprints of key papers has been scheduled for publication later this year [41].

## 2. Low Level Processing Techniques

The first steps in any document image analysis system are data capture and preprocessing. These steps comprise scanning [10][16][24], noise filtering, and thresholding [44] for converting the paper document into a binary-image with the least amount of noise possible and with the least amount of information loss as well. We will not discuss such techniques in this paper. This section will concentrate in the description of the most commonly used techniques for low level processing in line drawing interpretation.

A typical line drawing contains mixed elements of text and graphics. Usually, to interpret the drawing, it is advantageous to separate the text from the graphics elements. Fletcher and Kasturi [17] describe a Hough transform-based algorithm to extract text from a mixed text/graphics image. Using the Hough transform allows the method to extract text strings from skewed documents and in any orientation. The thresholds are determined adaptively, making the method invariant to change in size and font of the text. The method was enhanced to extract text connected to graphics [24]. Kida et al [29] use the neighborhood line density, which is a measure of the "complexity" of an image at every black pixel, to separate characters from graphics. Meynieux et al. [35] describe a method to segment long text strings by grouping nearby connected components into clusters. Sometimes, the presence of graphics elements can be used to detect the presence of text. Dori [13], for example, describes a syntactic/geometric approach for recognition of interpretation lines and associated components in engineering drawings. Arias et al [5] use the presence of line segments to extract single characters in the interpretation of manhole drawings.

Graphics in line drawings are usually composed of symbols and lines. Most of the symbols are composed of thin lines, and they are normally extracted at higher processing levels. Symbols such as arrowheads and diode symbols are filled regions instead. These symbols have to be extracted by low level techniques. One approach to detect solid regions is by erosion and dilation operations [19][25][36]. In this approach, the image is eroded by a predetermined number of pixels to completely remove all of the lines. The eroded image is then dilated back to its original dimension and a logical AND operation is performed to recover the solid symbols. The difference image, that is obtained by subtracting solid symbols from the original image, contains only lines. There are other methods which extract simultaneously the lines and boundaries of solid objects. Shih and Kasturi [46] have evaluated several picture decomposition algorithms for locating solid symbols. They also adapted the Maximal Square Moving algorithm [49], in which black pixel regions are represented as a union of the largest possible overlapping squares, for simultaneously locating the corelines of thin entities and boundaries of solid regions. This algorithm requires numerous data structures and pointers to obtain the required description.

With the solid regions extracted, the graphical elements left are composed purely by lines. One common step is to apply thinning to these elements. The goal of thinning is to keep a one pixel wide line per line present in the drawing. Traversing these single pixel wide lines makes it easier to find topological features. One common approach to thinning is to "peel" the region boundaries until the regions have been reduced to thin lines. Iteratively every image pixel is inspected within 3x3 windows, and single-pixel wide boundaries that are not required to maintain connectivity or endlines are erased. O'Gorman [40] proposes the kxk thinning method as a generalization of the 3x3 method.

Instead of erasing only one pixel on each iteration, k-2 x k-2 pixels can be erased, reducing the number of iterations required. Some methods have been proposed where the number of steps does not depend on the maximum line thickness [4]. In these methods, the skeletal points are estimated from distance measurements with respect to opposite boundary points of the regions. They are known as medial line extraction methods. The thinning methods usually create noisy junctions at corners, intersections and branches. The medial axis methods may fail to find the midpoint if they miss pairs of contour lines. Hori and Tanigawa [22] propose to use both methods simultaneously to create clean intersections. A good background on thinning techniques is given in [42].

After thinning, another popular low level technique is to extract connected chains of pixels. Harris et al [21] describe a method where the skeleton is coded with pixel values of 0, 1, 2, and 3 for background pixels, terminal (end of line) pixels, intermediate pixels, and junction pixels respectively. This, combined with chaining, allows line segments and their interconnections to be easily determined.

The chain code retains all the information in the thin line image and enables exact decoding of the curves. If exact decoding is not required, the image can be approximated by fitting line segments to the curves. This form of vectorization allows the image to be stored and accessed more easily. Such methods are specially useful when interpreting mechanical engineering drawings. Ramachandran [43] describes a vector extraction method that fits piece-wise linear segments to outlines of black pixels regions. Compression ratios of up to 35:1 have been reported for this. Bley [8] describes a picture decomposition algorithm for segmenting electrical schematics. In this algorithm black pixel regions are approximated by rectangular blocks that are then analyzed to segment lines and symbols. Watson et al. [50] describe a method for extracting lines from gray-level images of line drawings. The algorithm tracks the ridges of the gray-scale intensity surfaces, which are candidates for boundary regions between objects (lines) and background. Haralick et al. [20] describe a method for topographical labeling of gray scale image characteristics, such as peaks, ridges, valleys, etc., which can be applied to the line drawings to extract straight lines and curves.

These are some of the most popular techniques applied for low level information extraction. A more complete survey is given by O'Gorman and Kasturi in [26]. It should be emphasized that general low-level processing methods do not give good enough results to perform a complete interpretation of line drawings. One of the reasons for this is that most of these methods do not use domain knowledge. To increase the performance it is necessary to add domain knowledge to guide the extraction of the low level primitives. Some systems that apply this idea are described in subsequent sections.

## 3. Diagrams Understanding

One of the applications for a line drawing interpretation system is the recognition of diagrams, such as flow charts, tables, and other drawings in technical documents. One characteristic of these drawings is that they are usually composed of simple graphics like polygons, lines interrelating text blocks, points, etc.

Kasturi et al. [25] developed a system for the recognition of this type of line drawings. The system consists of four stages:

1) Separation of text strings from graphics.
2) Identification of line segments and their attributes.
3) Recognition of graphical primitives and their attributes.
4) Description of spatial relationships among primitives.

The first two stages are performed by applying some of the low level techniques described in the previous section. The output from the second step is a file describing the location and attributes of core-lines (for thin entities) and boundaries (for solid objects). Stages 3 and 4 perform higher level interpretation. The main objective is to obtain a succinct description of the contents of the graphics.

Futrelle et al. [18] describe a system which uses *graphics constraints grammars* for describing and analyzing diagrams and spatial indexing. This system was developed to understand diagrams in technical publications in biology. In this system, the organization of the diagrams is described with grammars. A grammar is a logical specification of a possible infinite set of structures. It specifies a set of objects, the objects' attributes, and their relations. In the graphics constraints grammars they developed, low level elements such as lines and polygons are objects. High level objects are more complex structures such as Data_points or Scale_lines. Each graphics constraint grammar is a set of rules comprising a production, a set of constraints, and a set of propagators:

- A production names the rule object as its left-hand side and the constituents of the object as its right-hand side.
- Constraints consist of spatial relations (such as Near, Horizontal, Aligned, etc.) as well as type of constraints, which require that an object be of certain type, such as a line or text.
- Propagators describe the relations between the attributes of the rule object and the attributes of the constituents.

For the recognition of tables, Chandran and Kasturi [11] describe a system for extraction of the structural information. The first step performed by the system is the identification of structural demarcations. This is done in a sequence of three steps. First, the horizontal and vertical lines in the image are identified. Second, these lines are used to identify the boundaries of the table. Any missing boundary demarcation is added to the list of identified demarcations. Finally, the vertical and horizontal demarcations represented by white streams are identified and added to the existing list of demarcations. To detect the horizontal lines a combination of brute force search for horizontal segments followed by a connectivity check is performed. A horizontal line segment is a group of consecutive black pixels exceeding the minimum line length threshold, along the same row. When the horizontal lines have been identified, the points of intersections with vertical lines are identified. These intersection points are grouped along vertical lines and the presence of the line is confirmed by checking selected columns. To detect the white streams demarcations, projection profiles are generated. In the case of vertical white streams, one projection profile is generated for each image segment that exists between two consecutive horizontal demarcations. This is followed by a codification of each of the histograms to separate text regions from the white streams. The white streams in each histogram are connected. Iterating over the histograms, all the vertical demarcations are recognized and saved as vertical line information. A similar procedure is used for the horizontal demarcations. Using the set of demarcations, each individual block is labeled as a heading, subheading, or an entry. A block is labeled as a heading if it has more than one child. It is a subheading if it is the first block with a single child, followed by a similar single child pattern. Figure 1 shows the steps.

## 4. Mechanical Engineering Drawing Interpretation

Mechanical engineering drawings are more complex than the diagrams considered in the previous section. This is due to the dual nature of the engineering drawings [14]. An engineering drawing is a mixture of two types of representation: the first is the actual object described by its orthographic projections, and the second, superimposed on the first, is the annotation —a formal, standard-based language that expresses dimensioning, toleranceing and manufacturing instructions and specifications. Some of the lines in the drawing reflect the shape of the desired object; others form large, complex symbols. Among these complex symbols, dimensioning is one of the most important. Dimensioning is a symbol consisting of text, leader, and witness lines. To interpret an engineering drawing, all the different levels of superimposed information must be extracted and understood.

Much work has been done in mechanical engineering drawing interpretation. Dori et al. [15] have described algorithms for the recognition of primitives in mechanical engineering drawings. By restricting the domain, the algorithms are capable of carrying out the recognition by examining a portion of the image pixels that is much smaller than the total pixel population. Straight line segments (bars) are detected first by sparsely screening the image and concentrating on black pixel areas. When a black pixel is found, the Orthogonal Zig-Zag (OZZ) routine is applied. The algorithm searches in both positive and negative directions of the axis perpendicular to the screening direction. It determines the direction of the 90° turn that would leave the screening within the area of black pixels. While the routine is periodically repeated, statistics are gathered about the average length of black runs parallel to each axis. When it is no longer possible to proceed in this manner, it assumes that the edge of the bar has been reached, and the same OZZ routine starts again from the first black pixel encountered towards the opposite direction. Next, the extracted bars, along with the original raster, serve as input to arc segmentation. This is done by finding chains of bars that may be a result of linear approximations of circular arcs. The two chain endpoints provide estimates for the two points on the presumed arc, and a third point is found by tracing through the perpendicular bisector of the line connecting these two points. The three points are used to compute the arc center, which is recursively refined, until an accuracy criterion is met. Finally, arrowheads are recognized through a two phase, semi-supervised pattern recognition process. In the first, the parameter learning phase, the values of arrowhead parameters are determined by sparsely examining a slot built around a sample of potential arrowheads. These values are used in the second, comprehensive search phase, to recognize the entire arrowhead population with a tighter set of parameter value that decreases the probability of error.

| Number | Start Type | End Type | Length | Direction |
|--------|-----------|----------|--------|-----------|
| 1 | Head | Branch | 4 | 62 |
| 2 | Branch | Node | 21 | 1 |
| 3 | Node | Node | 13 | 48 |
| 4 | Node | Node | 19 | 33 |
| 5 | Node | Loop | 14 | 17 |
| 6 | Head | Branch | 27 | 32 |
| 7 | Branch | Branch | 12 | 48 |
| 8 | Branch | Tail | 13 | 0 |
| 9 | Branch | Branch | 10 | 34 |
| 10 | Branch | Node | 11 | 48 |
| 11 | Node | Tail | 24 | 63 |
| 12 | Branch | Tail | 4 | 30 |
| 13 | Branch | Tail | 26 | 33 |

(a)

| Number | Start Type | End Type | Length | Direction |
|--------|-----------|----------|--------|-----------|
| 1 | Head | Branch | 4 | 62 |
| 2 | Branch | Node | 21 | 1 |
| 3 | Node | Node | 13 | 48 |
| 4 | Node | Node | 19 | 33 |
| 5 | Node | Loop | 14 | 17 |
| 6 | Head | Branch | 27 | 32 |
| 7 | Branch | Branch | 12 | 48 |
| 8 | Branch | Tail | 13 | 0 |
| 9 | Branch | Branch | 10 | 34 |
| 10 | Branch | Node | 11 | 48 |
| 11 | Node | Tail | 24 | 63 |
| 12 | Branch | Tail | 4 | 30 |
| 13 | Branch | Tail | 26 | 33 |

(b)

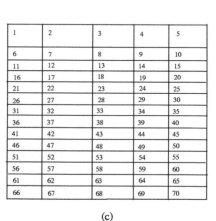

(c)

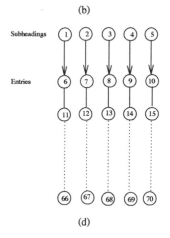

(d)

**Figure 1.** Table structure recognition: (a) Initial table, (b) recognized demarcations, (c) identified item blocks, and (d) recognized structure.

Dori [13] developed a methodology for recognizing dimensions in machine drawings that integrates a finite automaton and a look-up table with geometric, nonsyntactic pattern recognition techniques and syntactic ones. A dimension set is described as a (conceptual) web, whose nodes are alternating components and associators. The components are the graphic primitives composing the dimension-set, i.e. *Contour, Witness, Arrowhead, Text*, etc. An associator is the spatial relation between any pair of adjacent components, i.e. *Witness* guides to *Contour, Arrowhead* points at *Shape*, etc.

Lines have attributes that are expressed by their line descriptor. The expression <*blcn*>, for example, stands for a line whose geometry is *broken* (i.e., a chain of two or three vectors), long, continuous, and narrow. The Line Description Table is a look-up table that contains a line description for each object-similar component of each kind/type combination of dimension set. A deterministic finite automaton, the Dimension Set Profiler, is used to obtain a dimension-set profile that specifies the completeness, regularity, symmetry, and type of the dimension-set in question. The profile is used to get a sketch, which is converted into a conceptual web using the dimensioning grammar. A geometric web is obtained from the conceptual one by substituting the appropriate line descriptions for the components. The expected line descriptions are compared with the ones obtained from the actual drawing to verify the recognition.

Lai and Kasturi [30] also describe a system developed to recognize dimension-set components in engineering drawings. The system consists of three phases. The first phase is segmentation, which includes a new text/graphics separation algorithm. The second phase consists of the vectorization and feature extraction procedures which are used to detect text and graphics primitives. In the final phase arrowheads and leaders are detected, leader pairs are matched, witness lines are extracted, and the text blocks are associated with leaders to detect the dimension sets. Figure 2b shows the results of detecting the dimension sets in Fig. 2a.

They also describe some new methods for classifying object lines in mechanical part drawings [31]. These methods include section line detection, hidden line detection, centerline detection and object line extraction. Section (hatching) lines are detected by using an adaptive approach which includes a spacing estimation step and a recognition step. To estimate the spacing the ANSI drafting standards properties that these lines are uniformly spaced and at an angle of 45 degrees are used. This spacing is then used to determine whether potential section lines are hatching or not. Hidden lines and centerlines are represented by dashed patterns. These lines are detected using a general purpose algorithm [32] which not only detects dashed lines but also classifies them. After extracting dimension sets, section lines, hidden lines and centerlines, what is left are solid lines representing physical object lines and extraneous noise. Extraneous segments are usually due to unclassified segments belonging to dashed lines. They are discarded. The remaining vectorized graphics are the object lines. Several breaks may be present in the object lines because of witness lines which may intersect object lines and still preserve linearity, section lines which may be misclassified, and short common segments between dimensioning lines and object lines. These errors are corrected at this stage.

Vaxivière and Tombre [48] developed the Celesstin system. The first processing step of the system is the separation of text and dimensioning lines from pure graphics. The graphics are vectorized and the resulting lines are assembled into blocks. These blocks are closed polygons which are classified depending on a set of simple rules. These rules allow the system to formulate hypotheses about the blocks using their boundary line width and that of their neighbors. These rules propagate the labeling of all blocks to the whole drawing. The result is a complete decomposition of the drawing as a set of structures at a level higher than vectors. The next step is to create entities in two configurations: a set of blocks symmetrical with respect to a dot-dashed line and having the same shape and a set of blocks having the same hatching pattern. Higher level knowledge is then applied to these entities. A very strong technological rule used by Celesstin is that it must be possible to disassemble a mechanical setup.

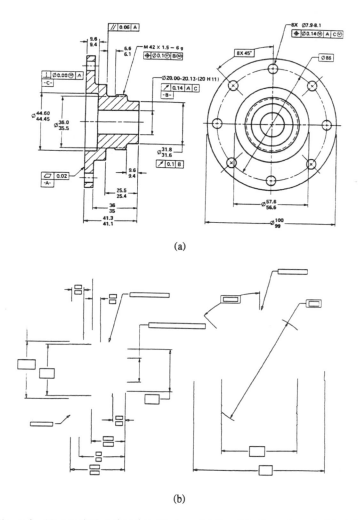

(a)

(b)

**Figure 2.** (a) A typical engineering drawing. (b) Complete dimension sets detected.

Joseph and Pridmore [23] developed Anon, a system that incorporates knowledge to help in the interpretation of mechanical drawings. The approach is based on a combination of the description of the prototypical drawing constructs with the library of low-level image analysis routines and a set of rules. The system combines bottom-up and top-down approaches. The prototypical drawing constructs are described by a set of schema classes. These are classes corresponding to solid, dashed, and chained lines, solid and dashed curves, cross hatching, physical outlines, text, witness and leader lines, and certain forms of dimensioning. The members of this set of schema (or schemata) are not isolated but form the nodes of a network in which arcs correspond to subpart and subclass relations. The schemata provide a common interface to Anon's library of image analysis routines. The functions in this library are divided into those that search the image for appropriately placed ink marks and others that use such marks as seed points for the development of low-level descriptive primitives. The control structure in Anon is modeled on the human "cycle of perception". The basis of this approach is a continuous loop in which a constantly changing world model directs perceptual exploration, determines how its findings are to be interpreted and is modified as a result. The control system consists of strategy rules written in the form of an LR(1) grammar and applied by a parser that is generated using the unix utility *yacc*. The rules specify strategies by which the various components of a drawing might be recognized.

Antoine et al [1] developed REDRAW, a prototype system for interpretation of technical documents. The system provides an integrated framework with low-level tools and an interpretation system driven by a structural model describing domain knowledge available for the document's type. They applied the system to the interpretation of dimensions in mechanical drawings and to the analysis of city maps. The domain knowledge is incorporated in the system by using a grammar. Typical knowledge rules are:
- dimension lines are thinner than drawing lines;
- the arrows' head is in contact with a line, witness or drawing line;
- two arrows that are in a same dimension have the same orientation and opposite directions; they can point "inwards" or "outwards" with respect to the dimension text;
- if two arrows point inward, they are connected to two different shape lines.

Many of the engineering drawing interpretation systems attempt to produce a 2D interpretation of mechanical drawings. Usually, mechanical drawings present multiple views of the represented objects. These multiple views contain adequate information to recreate 3D models of the objects. Automating such a recreation by integrating information from multiple views is a challenging research topic. Nagendra and Gudar [37] present a survey of some of the work done in this area. Wesley and Markowsky [51] developed a bottom-up approach for 3-D interpretation and Sakurai and Gossard [45] extended the work to include objects with curved surfaces. Nishihara and Ikeda [38] applied the bottom-up technique to interpret paper based drawings of polyhedral objects. An alternative approach was presented by Whitaker and Huhns [52], who developed a rule-based method to produce a wire frame interpretation.

Lysak and Kasturi [33] describe a system for the reconstruction of 3D objects from 2D orthographic projections by using a boundary representation model. Polyhedral objects and objects with spherical and cylindrical surfaces can be interpreted by their system. It is also capable of handling minor misalignments of views and missing information in one view if it can be determined by other views (this is a common occurrence in engineering drawings since the draftsperson takes liberty in leaving out redundant information to avoid clutter). The interpretation process is divided into three main procedures. First the views are identified. Then candidate sets of 3D vertices and edges are generated. Finally, the boundary representation is constructed. A boundary representation model, consisting of an enclosure assembled from a set of faces, is used to describe the object represented by the drawing. An enclosure may be described by a tree in which each node represents both a face and a (partial) enclosure. The root node represents a partial enclosure consisting of a single starting face. A subsequent node identifies a face which is added to the previous face to give a more complete enclosure. The process of generating possible enclosures starts by selecting some visible area of the root view, which is then used to create a set of possible visible faces. A face may be generated by taking a set of edges that correspond to the lines around the boundary of the visible area. Each such set of edges is considered to define a possible face. For each enclosure a certainty factor is computed based on how the visibility of the enclosure edges agrees with the input views of the drawing. Dempster's rule for combination of evidence is used to accumulate the evidence for or against a given enclosure based on a set of conditions. Figure 3 shows an example of different views of an object in a drawing and the corresponding enclosure trees.

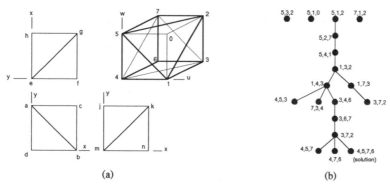

**Figure 3.** (a) Cube with a diagonal face. The thicker lines enclose the recognized cube. The thinner lines are used as intermediate hypothesis. (b) Enclosure trees.

## 5. Map Interpretation

Map interpretation is one of the most popular applications for line drawing interpretation. Maps contain several layers of information (parcels, buildings, roads, contour lines, rivers, text, etc.) usually overlapping each other. For example we can have a text string identifying a specific parcel on top of a hatching pattern used to identify parcels in general. The problems in the interpretation of maps differ depending on the scale. Cadastral maps, in scale range from 1:500 to 1:5000, represent buildings and parcels as closed polygons, roads are represented as parallel lines, etc. When we move to higher scales, the roads become single lines, the buildings become points or disappear entirely from the representation and rivers and elevation contour lines start to appear. Most of the research in map interpretation has been concentrated in cadastral maps.

Madej [34] describes a system to convert cadastral maps to CAD in an intelligent manner. The system developed uses a priori knowledge during different stages of low level processing, integrating the line approximation with the interpretation. Using knowledge based inference, the system makes preliminary assumptions of the possible line meanings. The knowledge is included in the form of rules. To reduce the processing time the system uses a Run Length Encoded (RLE) version of the input image.

Antoine [2] developed CIPLAN, a system that uses a priori knowledge about the representation of the objects at high level and low level to interpret French plats. The main goal of the use of knowledge is to reduce the number of entities to process at low level. The knowledge is represented in the form of a network, where the nodes represent entities of the model associated to a specific extraction process. The network is divided into four hierarchical levels. Once the entities of one level are extracted completely, the system proceeds to extract the entities at the next higher level. The lowest level contains buildings, covers, yards or gardens. The next level contains plots, which are represented by closed curves surrounding entities from the lowest level. The next level contains districts, surrounding neighboring plots from the previous level. The last level contains the roads, which are located between two neighboring districts. Once the system starts processing a new level, there are less graphical elements to process, because the search can be guided. This system is an improvement from REDRAW [1].

Ogier et al [39] describe a system for French map interpretation also. Their approach is the separation of the interpretation process into 3 levels, and the introduction of knowledge pertinent to each level. The first level (level 0) is related to the low level primitives. It concerns hatched areas, characters, arrows, and closed outlines. Level 1 constructs "non terminal" objects. Every attribute is preclassified into four classes: hatched areas, non hatched areas, roads, and residual areas. Level 2 constructs terminal objects and manages their consistency. A terminal object is consistent if all its neighboring objects are consistent at level 1. If there are inconsistencies at the higher level, the system tries to resolve them at the lower levels.

Boatto et al [9] developed a system for the automatic acquisition of land register maps. The system consists of four phases. In phase 1, the document is scanned and its graph-encoded binary image is produced. The result is an image decomposed into independent elements, namely, edges and nodes of the graph. In phase 2, each element of the image graph is classified as belonging to one of a set of basic categories such as continuous lines, dashed lines, symbols and shading patterns. Phase 3 provides proper descriptions of each labeled image piece, given its category. In these first three phases, the system builds a set of detailed descriptions of the individual geometric entities. Finally, in phase 4, the system establishes spatial and semantic relations among geometric entities and also recognizes high-level entities.

One of the early efforts in large scale map interpretation was performed by Kasturi and Alemany [27], who developed an intelligent system to automatically extract information from paper-based maps and answer queries related to spatial features and structure of geographical data. The system is designed to perform the same logical operations that a human would do to extract information from maps. For example, if a person wants to locate a city in a particular state, the sequence of steps performed are the following. First, read the state name and locate the state by identifying a closed contour that bounds the state. Then read the city names within the closed contour until the desired city is found. Finally, locate the symbol representing the city in the vicinity of the name. The corresponding steps that an automatic system should perform are then:

- Recognition of characters to locate names.
- Identification of the type of line that represents the state boundaries and the symbol that represents cities.
- Definition of a region in which the search for the state boundaries should be performed; this requires knowledge of at least one point inside the state, which is obtained by locating the state name.
- Search for a closed contour formed by the type of line which represent the state boundaries; if no close contour is found the system should define a larger area for search, which is done by returning to the previous step.
- Search for symbols which represent the cities near the city name and within a closed contour.

They developed several algorithms for interpretation of different types of lines in the map. The system was capable of automatically creating different information layers from composite maps. It also included a natural language interface for users to pose queries on the contents of a simple road map.

In [28], Kasturi et al describe the incorporation of information extracted from maps into GIS systems. They give a description of the typical GIS systems and give a survey of systems for automating the process of extracting information from maps for query processing in a GIS.

Recent research in the interpretation of large scale maps is limited to the reconstruction of road networks. Deseilligny et al [12] describe a system to reconstruct a road network map. The system uses a priori knowledge embedded into several rules. The rules represent the principles of global and local connectivity of the network, non redundancy, absence of dead ends, absence of curvature. These rules are used to compute the likelihood of adding a new edge to connect two open ends or the suppression of dangling edges from the vectorization process output.

Arai et al [3] also describe a system based in a neural net for map interpretation. In this system, the interaction between the system and the operator trains the neural net for the recognition process. As the system acquires more knowledge, the interaction with the operator decreases. The operator manually indicates the starting segment, the system calculates the probability of connecting a line end with each of the candidates and then decides whether to continue the automatic chasing or request the operator for an option. When the probability of connecting one arc is much more higher than all the others, automatic chasing is done. The neural network is initially loaded with some geometric information.

## 6. Utility Company Drawing Interpretation

Utility company drawings are one of the most complex line drawings to interpret. This is due to the amount of information that they usually contain. A typical utility company drawing consists of layers of information superimposed on a map. This information can correspond to electric power distribution, water pipelines, gas distribution, etc. Sometimes drawings which provide detailed information about the utility may lack the geographical information.

Not much research has been done to interpret these type of drawings. In recent years there has been a growing interest by utility companies to perform automatic interpretation of their drawings to incorporate them into computer databases.

Shimotsuji et al [47] developed a system to recognize drawings superimposed on a map. Their approach decomposes graphic and character regions into primitive lines, the definitions of which include their orientation and connectivity with other lines. Objects are extracted from these primitive lines based on recognition techniques that use shape and topological information to group them into meaningful sets such as character strings, symbols, and figure lines. To detect and identify symbols in the drawing, the system uses a model of graphic-symbol shapes. This model consists of two parts, one that describes the primitive elements composing the symbol, and the other defines the geometric relations between these primitive elements. To interpret the line they introduce a probability to assign to each line the appropriate meaning, (e.g., cable, road, pipeline, etc). Each probability regarding possible interpretations for the meaning of a line is successively updated by a relaxation method that lets the system decide on meaning from global information. The interpretation process attaches probabilities for possible meanings to each line. The initial probabilities are calculated based on connected symbols and characters. After adequate iteration, the meaning corresponding to the highest probability is selected for each line.

Arias et al [5] describe a system to interpret telephone system manhole drawings. A manhole drawing is shown in Fig. 4. The box made of thicker lines encloses the manhole. The lines represent cables carrying thousands of telephone pairs. The lines in the drawing are not completely connected due to noise, gaps to insert text, and gaps to reduce clutter. The system interprets the telephone network represented in the manhole by connecting the lines to extract the interconnections between the cables. The first step of the processing is to separate the text and graphic elements. Next, different graphical elements are extracted. Inside a manhole box three different types of graphical elements can be found. They are lines, dots and arrowheads. The lines correspond to the manhole box boundaries, the cables and the stubs. The dots indicate the splices, where the interconnections of the cables occur. The arrowheads differentiate an arrow from a cable. To extract the dots a circular template is used. For the arrowhead detection a model-based approach is used [30]. The lines are obtained through skeletonization and vectorization. The gaps left after extracting text are closed using the information about the presence of the text. Other gaps are closed using an iterative process over the line segments by using information about collinearity and proximity. Constraints such as any cable extending inside the manhole box must be connected to a splice or to a T junction (unused cables) are also used. With this information an output table like the one shown in Fig. 5 is constructed.

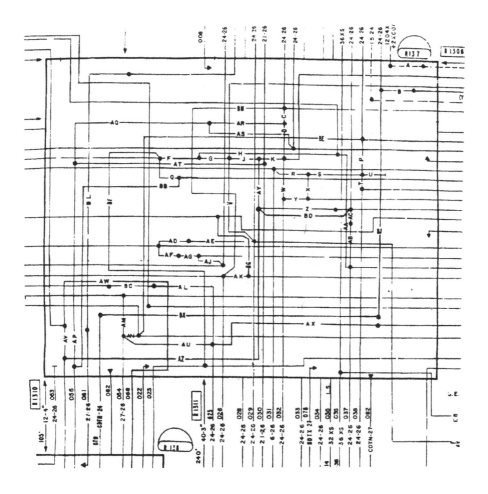

**Figure 4.** Section of a typical manhole drawing.

26

Cables and Stubs

| Line# | type | start_x | start_y | end_x | end_y | end_1 | end_2 |
|---|---|---|---|---|---|---|---|
| 1 | cable | 87 | 25 | 1299 | 581 | open | splice#44 |
| 2 | cable | 151 | 25 | 1383 | 205 | open | splice#47 |
| 3 | cable | 681 | 25 | 681 | 1137 | open | splice#20 |
| 4 | cable | 1253 | 25 | 1253 | 469 | open | splice#43 |
| 5 | cable | 590 | 27 | 590 | 1226 | open | splice#11 |
| 6 | cable | 900 | 27 | 900 | 889 | open | splice#30 |
| 7 | cable | 1032 | 27 | 1032 | 624 | open | splice#34 |
| 8 | cable | 1120 | 27 | 1120 | 911 | open | splice#37 |
| 9 | cable | 1169 | 27 | 1169 | 914 | open | splice#40 |
| 10 | cable | 1212 | 27 | 1212 | 403 | open | splice#42 |
| . | . | . | . | . | . | . | . |
| . | . | . | . | . | . | . | . |
| 71 | stub | 1383 | 205 | 1529 | 204 | splice#47 | splice#53 |
| 72 | stub | 1529 | 204 | 864 | 1067 | splice#53 | splice#27 |
| 73 | stub | 653 | 251 | 1565 | 247 | splice#18 | splice#54 |
| 74 | stub | 653 | 251 | 658 | 1094 | splice#18 | splice#19 |
| 75 | stub | 260 | 494 | 1402 | 305 | splice#3 | splice#49 |
| 76 | stub | 1337 | 364 | 1349 | 1616 | splice#45 | splice#46 |
| 77 | stub | 1212 | 403 | 1211 | 604 | splice#42 | splice#41 |
| 78 | stub | 1253 | 469 | 1431 | 470 | splice#43 | splice#51 |
| 79 | stub | 1431 | 470 | 1472 | 864 | splice#51 | splice#52 |
| 80 | stub | 1431 | 470 | 1429 | 536 | splice#51 | splice#50 |
| . | . | . | . | . | . | . | . |
| . | . | . | . | . | . | . | . |

Splices

| Splice# | coord_x | coord_y | junctions |
|---|---|---|---|
| 1 | 228 | 1672 | lines#: 61 115 |
| 2 | 230 | 1823 | lines#: 63 115 |
| 3 | 260 | 494 | lines#: 31 75 |
| 4 | 336 | 1630 | lines#: 60 113 114 |
| 5 | 339 | 1781 | lines#: 62 114 |
| 6 | 377 | 1584 | lines#: 57 58 |
| 7 | 415 | 1185 | lines#: 40 41 102 119 |
| 8 | 481 | 851 | lines#: 91 92 116 |
| 9 | 483 | 1184 | lines#: 92 102 103 |
| 10 | 550 | 1542 | lines#: 53 54 112 118 |
| 11 | 590 | 1226 | lines#: 5 42 43 91 |
| 12 | 616 | 1429 | lines#: 12 89 108 |
| 13 | 631 | 805 | lines#: 86 89 90 |
| 14 | 632 | 940 | lines#: 30 90 95 96 |
| 15 | 634 | 629 | lines#: 16 83 85 86 |
| . | . | . | . |
| . | . | . | . |

(b)

**Figure 5**. Output table after interpretation of manhole drawing in Fig. 4.

The manhole drawings are usually related to tables containing detailed information about the cables. The structure of these tables can be extracted with methods like the one described in section 3 [11]. The difficulty with these type of tables is with the special symbols that are used. When a section of the table is deleted, the corresponding entries are crossed-out by diagonal lines bounded by horizontal lines (A and B), and entries containing repeated text are indicated by ditto lines (C), as shown in Fig. 6a. Balasubramanian et al [7] describe a system to overcome these problems. The algorithm to detect crossed-out sections begins by calculating the length of the horizontal line bounding the table on the top or the bottom. A histogram of the distances between adjacent horizontal lines helps to locate all the horizontal lines which lie between lines forming rows of the table and which bound the diagonal lines. The maximum number of horizontal lines which have a particular inter-line spacing is determined. This number indicates that most of the rows in the table have that particular inter-line spacing. The minimum interline spacing is also determined. The image is then processed along the center line in a top-down manner, to locate the rows which have the minimum interline spacing. All the candidate lines obtained are paired if they are successive in terms of row locations and have almost identical lengths. Each pair of lines is then processed separately to verify existence of diagonal lines. If diagonal lines are not detected, each of the horizontal lines forming the pair is tested to check if it intersects text. The diagonal lines are detected by using a line tracking routine which starts at the starting point of the top horizontal line bounding the cross, traces the diagonal line until it reaches the bottom horizontal line bounding the cross, thus verifying that the pairs of lines do indeed bound diagonal lines. The line tracking routine utilizes the connectivity of pixels to track the line. Multiple entries are represented by vertical lines with demarcations (short horizontal segments) at regular intervals. These vertical lines start and end between horizontal lines forming the rows of the table and usually have a length greater than the average spacing between horizontal lines forming rows. The approach is to verify if the vertical line starts at a row value which lies between two lines forming the rows of the table. If the condition is satisfied, a mask is used to detect if the demarcation at regular intervals along the vertical line exist. The demarcations are usually located mid-distance between two adjacent horizontal lines. Hence the mask is used only for that part of the vertical line which is between the two adjacent horizontal lines. Once the demarcations are detected, all the item blocks which contain this vertical line are noted. Text in regions which are not crossed out is fed into an OCR system for further processing [6].

## 7. Summary and Conclusions

We have presented some of the most relevant recent work performed in the area of line drawing interpretation. First a short survey of the most common low level processing techniques was presented, followed by a description of the some of the most relevant systems developed for line drawing interpretation.

The systems were classified depending on the type of line drawings that they can interpret. Four classes are considered, diagrams, mechanical engineering drawings, maps, and utility company drawings. Diagrams are composed of simple graphics. Usually the systems built to interpret these drawings try to find known polygonal shapes after separating the text components. Mechanical engineering drawings contain two layers of superimposed information, the object described by its orthographic projections and the annotation. Much work in the interpretation of these drawing has been concentrated in extracting the dimension sets and the reconstruction of the 3D representation from the orthographic views. Maps contain several layers of superimposed information. This is one of the most popular areas of research. Most of the research in this area has been concentrated in the interpretation of cadastral maps. Systems that interpret maps usually classify the information in the map in layers and the extraction of information in one layer is helped by the already extracted information in the previous layer. The utility company drawings are usually composed of utility information superimposed on a map.

Not much work has been done in the interpretation of these drawings. Our effort in the interpretation of telephone company drawings was presented.

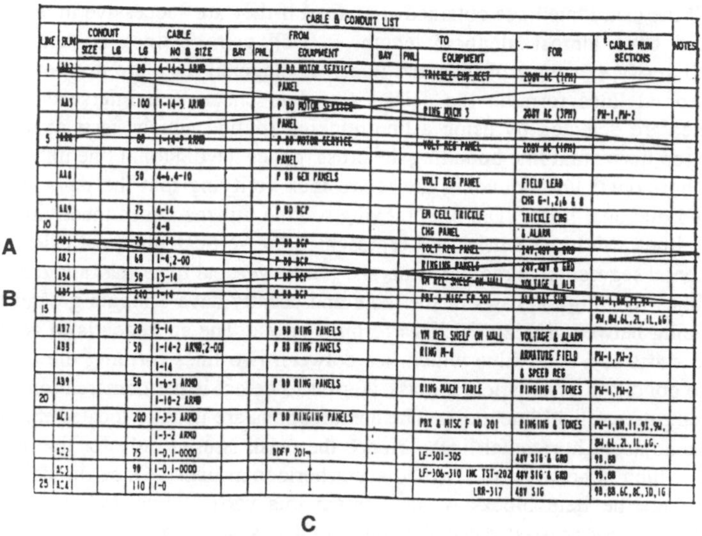

(a)

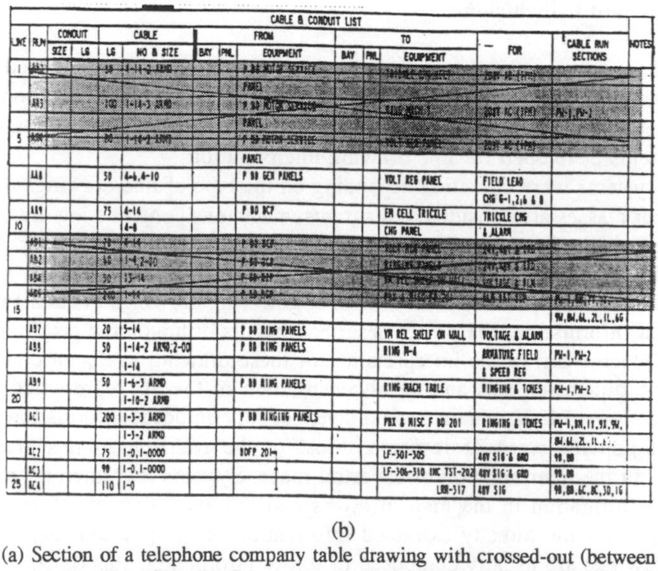

(b)

Figure 6. (a) Section of a telephone company table drawing with crossed-out (between A and B) and repeated entries (C). (b) Gray section indicates recognized crossed-out section.

One trend that can be noticed in the systems developed for line drawing interpretation is the inclusion of domain specific knowledge, which has shown to improve their performances. This knowledge has to be added not only in the higher level interpretation, but in the low level as well. A combination of bottom-up and top-down approaches in the interpretation process has also given some promising results.

## References

[1]   Antoine, D., S. Collin, and K. Tombre, "Analysis of technical documents: The REDRAW system," *Pre-Proc. IAPR workshop on Structural and Syntactic Pattern Recognition*, pp. 192-230, New Jersey, June 1990.

[2]   Antoine, D., "CIPLAN: A model-based system with original features for understanding french plats," *Proc. 1st ICDAR*, St. Malo, France, pp. 647-655, 1991.

[3]   Arai, H., S. Abe, and M. Nagura, "Intelligent interactive map recognition using neural networks," *Proc. 2nd ICDAR*, Tsukuba Science City, Japan, pp. 922-925, 1993.

[4]   Arcelli, C. and G. Sanniti di Baja, "A width-independent fast thinning algorithm," *IEEE Trans. PAMI*, 7(4):463-474, July 1985.

[5]   Arias, J.F., S. Chandran, R. Kasturi, and A. Chhabra, "Interpretation of telephone system manhole drawings," *Proc. 2nd ICDAR*, pp. 365-369, Tsukuba Science City, Japan, 1993.

[6]   Arias, J.F., S. Balasubramanian, A. Prasad, R. Kasturi, and A. Chhabra, "Information extraction from telephone company drawings," to appear in *Proc. CVPR*, Seattle, Washington, June 1994.

[7]   Balasubramanian, S., S. Chandran, J. Arias, R. Kasturi, and A. Chhabra, "Information extraction from tabular drawings," *Document Recognition, Proc. SPIE*, pp. 152-163, February 1994.

[8]   Bley, H., "Segmentation and preprocessing of electrical schematics using picture graphs," *Computer Graphics and Image Processing*, 28:271-228, 1984.

[9]   Boatto, L. et al., "An interpretation system for land register maps," *Computer*, 25(7):25-33, 1992.

[10]  Casey, R.G. and K.Y. Wong, *Document analysis systems and techniques in Image Analysis Applications*, R. Kasturi and M.M. Trivedi (eds), Marcel Dekker, 1990.

[11]  Chandran, S. and R. Kasturi, "Structural recognition of tabulated data," *Proc. 2nd ICDAR*, Tsukuba Science City, pp. 516-519, 1993.

[12]  Deseiglliny, M.P., H. Le Men, and G. Stamon, "Map understanding for GIS data capture: Algorithms for road network graph reconstruction," *Proc. 2nd ICDAR*, Tsukuba Science City, Japan, pp. 676-679, 1993.

[13]  Dori, D. "A syntactic/geometric approach to recognition of dimensions in engineering machine drawings," *Computer Vision, Graphics, and Image Processing*, 47(3):271-291, 1989.

[14]  Dori, D. and K. Tombre, "Paper drawings to 3D CAD: A proposed agenda," *Proc. 2nd ICDAR*, Tsukuba Science City, Japan, pp. 866-869, 1993.

[15]  Dori, D. Y. Liang, J. Dowell, and I. Chai, "Sparse-pixel recognition of primitives in engineering drawings," *Machine Vision and Applications*, 6(2-3):69-82, 1993.

[16]  Ejiri, M., S. Kakumoto, T. Miyatake, S. Shimada, and K. Iguamura, *Automatic recognition of engineering drawings and maps in Image Analysis Applications*, R. Kasturi and M.M. Trivedi, (eds), Marcel Dekker, 1990.

[17]  Fletcher, L.A. and R. Kasturi, "A robust algorithm for text string separation for mixed text/graphics image," *IEEE Trans. PAMI*, 10(6):910-918, November 1988.

[18]  Futrelle, R. P. et al, "Understanding diagrams in technical documents," *Computer*, 25(7):75-78, 1992.

[19]  Harada, H., Y. Itoh, and M. Ishii, "Recognition of free-hand drawings in chemical plant engineering," *Proc. IEEE Workshop on Computer Architecture for Pattern Analysis and Image Database Management*, pp. 146-153, 1985.

30

[20] Haralick, R.M., L.T. Watson, and T.J. Laffey, "The topographic primal sketch," *Int. J. Robotics Res.*, 2:50-72, 1983.

[21] Harris, J.F., J. Kittler, B. Llewellyn, and G. Preston, *A modular system for interpreting binary pixel representations of line-structured data* in *Pattern Recognition: Theory and Applications*, J. Kittler, K.S. Fu, and L.F. Pau (eds), D. Reidal Publishing Co., pp.311-351, 1982.

[22] Hori, O. and S. Tanigawa, "Raster-to-vector conversion by line fitting based on contours and skeletons," *Proc. 2nd ICDAR*, Tsukuba Science City, Japan, pp. 353-358, 1993.

[23] Joseph, S.H. and T.P. Pridmore, "Knowledge-directed interpretation of mechanical engineering drawings," *IEEE PAMI*, 14(9):928-940, 1992.

[24] Kasturi R., R. Raman, C. Chennubhotla, and L. O'Gorman, "Document Image Analysis: An overview of techniques for graphics recognition," *Pre-Proc. IAPR workshop on Structural and Syntactic Pattern Recognition*, pp. 192-230, New Jersey, June 1990.

[25] Kasturi, R., S.T. Bow, W. El-Masri, J. Shah, J. Gattiker, and U. Motake, "A system for interpretation of lines drawings," *IEEE Trans. PAMI*, 12(10):978-992, October 1990.

[26] Kasturi, R., S. Siva, and L. O'Gorman, "Techniques for line drawing interpretation: An overview," *IAPR workshop on Machine Vision and Applications*, pp. 151-160, Tokyo, November 1990.

[27] Kasturi, R. and J. Alemany, "Information extraction from images of paper-based maps for query processing," *IEEE TSE (special section on Image Databases)*, 14:671-675, 1988.

[28] Kasturi, R., R. Fernandez, M.L. Amlani, and W.-C. Feng, "Map data processing in geographic information systems," *IEEE Computer*, 22(12):10-21, 1989.

[29] Kida, H., O. Iwaki, and K. Kawada, "Document recognition system for office automation," *Proc. 8th ICPR*, pp.446-448, Paris, 1986.

[30] Lai, C.P. and R. Kasturi, "Detection of dimension sets in engineering drawings," to appear in *IEEE PAMI*, 1994.

[31] Lai, C.P. and R. Kasturi, "Extraction of object lines in engineering drawings," *Document Recognition, Proc. SPIE*, pp. 172-184, February 1994.

[32] Lai, C.P. and R. Kasturi, "Detection of dashed lines in engineering drawings and maps," *Proc. of 1st ICDAR*, St. Malo, France, pp. 507-515, 1991.

[33] Lysak, D.B. and R. Kasturi, "Interpretation of engineering drawings of polyhedral and non-polyhedral objects," *Proc. 1st ICDAR*, St. Malo, France, pp. 79-87, 1991.

[34] Madej, D., "An intelligent map-to-CAD conversion system," *Proc. 1st ICDAR*, St. Malo, France, pp.603-610, 1991.

[35] Meynieux, E., S. Seisen, and K. Tombre, "Bilevel information recognition and coding in office paper documents," *Proc. 8th ICPR*, pp. 442-445, Paris 1986.

[36] Nagasamy, V., and N.A. Langrana, "Engineering drawing processing and vectorization system," *Computer Vision, Graphics, and Image Processing*, 49:379-397, 1990.

[37] Nagendra, I.V. and U.G. Gujar, "3-D objects from 2-D orthographic views — a survey," *Computers & Graphics*, 12(1):111-114, 1988.

[38] Nishihara, S. and K. Ikeda, "Interpreting engineering drawings of polyhedrons," *Proc. 9th ICPR*, November, 1988.

[39] Ogier, J.M. J. Labiche, R. Mullot, and Y. Lecourtier, "Attributes extraction for french map interpretation," *Proc. 2nd ICDAR*, Tsukuba Science City, Japan,pp. 672-675, 1993.

[40] O'Gorman, L., "kxk Thinning," *Computer Vision, Graphics, and Image Processing*, 51:195-215, 1990.

[41] O'Gorman, L. and R. Kasturi, *Document Image Analysis*, IEEE Computer Society Press, a tutorial text schedule for publication in 1994.

[42] Pavlidis, T., *Algorithms for Graphics and Image Processing*, Computer Science Press, Rockville, Maryland, 1982.

[43] Ramachandran, K., "A coding method for vector representation of engineering drawings," *Proc. IEEE*, 68:813-817, 1980.

[44]  Sahoo, P.K., S. Soltani, A.K.C. Wong, and Y.C. Chen, "A survey of thresholding techniques," *Computer Vision, Graphics, and Image Processing*, 41(2):233-260, February 1988.

[45]  Sakurai, H. and D.C. Gossard, "Solid model input through orthographic views," *Computer Graphics*, 17(3):243-252, 1983.

[46]  Shih, C-.C. and R. Kasturi, "Extraction of graphic primitives from images of paper-based drawings," *Machine Vision and Applications*, 2:103-113, 1989.

[47]  Shimotsuji, S., O. Hori, M. Asano, K. Suzuki, and F. Hoshimo, "A robust recognition system for drawing superimposed on a map," *Computer*, 25(7):56-59, 1992.

[48]  Vaxivière, P. and K. Tombre, "Celesstin: CAD conversion of mechanical drawings," *Computer*, 25(7):46-54, 1992.

[49]  Wakayama, T., "A core line tracking algorithm based on maximal square moving," *IEEE Trans. PAMI*, 4(1):68-74, January 1982.

[50]  Watson, L.T., K. Arvind, R.W. Ehrich, R.M. Haralick, "Extraction of lines and drawings from grey tone line drawings images," *Pattern Recognition*, 17(5):493-507, 1984.

[51]  Wesley, M.A. and G. Markowsky, "Fleshing out projections," *IBM J. Res. Develop.*, 25(6):934-954, 1981.

[52]  Whitaker, E.T. and M.N. Huhns, "Rule-based geometric reasoning for the interpretation of line drawings," *Applications of Artificial Intelligence III, Proc. SPIE*, vol. 635, pp.621-627, 1986.

# SEMICONTINUOUS SKELETONS OF 2D AND 3D SHAPES

*Dominique ATTALI and Annick MONTANVERT*

*Groupe Infodis - Laboratoire TIMC-IMAG*
*CERMO BP 53, 38041 GRENOBLE Cedex 9, France*
*Email: Dominique.Attali@imag.fr - Annick.Montanvert@imag.fr*

### ABSTRACT

Some papers have proposed to approximate the skeleton of continuous shapes using the Voronoi graph of boundary points. Those approaches, referred to as semicontinuous approaches, generate noisy skeletons. In this paper, we present an efficient method to simplify semicontinuous skeletons of 2D and 3D shapes. The originality of our approach consists in simplifying the initial shape without modifying its topology and including these modifications on the skeleton.

In the 2D case, the proposed process is parametrizable with an angular threshold. Consequently, it does not depend on the size of the objects. We show how the simplified skeletons are related to discrete notions such as conditional bisectors and minimal skeletons. The latter are particularly representative of the initial shape.

In the 3D case, the simplified skeletons consist of pieces of planes and segments. One can preserve borders or force the skeleton to simplify into a wireframe figure. Thus, it is possible to adopt the simplification process to any case considered.

## 1. INTRODUCTION

The notion of skeleton was first introduced by Blum [5]. The skeleton of an object is a thin figure centered in the shape which summarizes its general form. It can be equivalent to the boundary representation but it allows an easier description of the shape. For this reason, the skeleton extraction is a well known transformation in image analysis.

Depending on how the initial object is discretized, two different approaches for skeleton extraction came out. On the one hand, discrete methods consist in redefining the skeleton in a discrete space and in handling discrete objects. Among these methods, some use an homotopic thinning or a medial line extraction from distance maps [2][9][16][20]. On the other hand, semicontinuous methods are justified by theoretical studies in continuous space. Lee has proved that the exact skeleton of a polygon is a subgraph of the generalized Voronoi graph of its boundary [10]. But computing the generalized Voronoi graph is a complex problem. Schmitt [15] has shown how the skeleton of a continuous shape is related to the Voronoi graph of its boundary points. Algorithms to compute the skeleton of continuous shapes have been proposed in [6][7]. Those methods work on a boundary representation which consists in a sampling of the boundary. The skeleton is approximated by taking a subgraph of the Voronoi graph of sampling boundary points.

In both the discrete and the continuous case, noise on the boundary makes some barbs appear in the computed skeleton, so that it no longer resembles the skeleton of the underlying continuous shape. The aim of this paper is to present an efficient method to simplify noisy skeletons provided by semicontinuous methods. After studying the two dimensional case, we present a 3D extension which enables 3D skeletons to be computed and simplified.

This paper is organized as follows. In Section 2, the definitions of the skeleton, the Voronoi graph and the Delaunay tessellation are recalled. In Section 3, a method to approximate the two dimensional skeleton is described. Although this method is not completely new, its presentation is absolutely necessary to understand our simplification method. Section 4 deals with the description of the simplification process. Finally, Section 5 is devoted to the 3D extension of the skeleton computation and simplification.

## 2. NOTATIONS AND DEFINITIONS

$R^n$ designates the Euclidean $n$-dimensional space and $d$ the Euclidean distance. For any set of points $A \in R^n$, $\partial A$ denotes its boundary. Note that the skeleton, the Voronoi graph and the Delaunay tessellation, whose definitions are recalled in the next paragraphs, are defined in a space of any dimension.

### 2.1 Skeleton

The skeleton $Sk(X)$ of an object $X \in R^n$ is the locus of the centers of the maximal balls included in $X$ [5]. A ball $B$ included in $X$ is said to be maximal if there exists no other ball included in $X$ and containing $B$.

### 2.2 Voronoi graph and Delaunay tessellation

Given that the computation of the Voronoi graph is the keystone of this paper, let us recall briefly its definition and its main properties. Let $E$ be a finite set of points in $R^n$ and $p$ a point of $E$. The Voronoi region of the point $p$ is defined as the set of points of $R^n$ closer to $p$ than to any other element of $E$. More formally :

$$V(p) = \left\{ m \in R^n, \ d(m,p) = d(m,E) \right\}$$

The Voronoi graph $V$ of $E$ consists of the boundaries of the Voronoi regions of $E$ :

$$V = \bigcup_{p \in E} \partial V(p)$$

A comprehensive treatment of the Voronoi graphs may be found in [13]. On the other hand, an incremental method to compute the 2D and 3D Voronoi graphs has been implemented by Bertin [4]. It has allowed us to use Voronoi graphs in practice.

The dual of the Voronoi graph is a tessellation of the convex hull of $E$ named the Delaunay tessellation. It is made up of simplexes (triangles in the plane and tetrehedra in the space) whose circumscribed balls contain no other points of $E$ [13].

In 2D space, the Voronoi regions are convex polygons. By duality, a Voronoi vertex is related to a Delaunay triangle, a Voronoi edge to a Delaunay edge and a Voronoi region to a point of $E$. In 3D space, the Voronoi regions are convex polyhedra. By duality, a Voronoi vertex is related to a Delaunay tetrahedron, a Voronoi edge to a Delaunay triangle, a Voronoi polygon to a Delaunay edge and a Voronoi region to a point of $E$. These duality relationships are used afterwards.

## 3. 2D APPROXIMATE SKELETON

In this section, we present a method to approximate skeletons of 2D continuous shapes that mixes up ideas due to Boissonnat [6] and to Brandt and Algazi [7].

Let $X \in R^2$ be a 2D continuous shape to skeletonize and $X^\sim$ a polygonal approximation of $X$. By polygonal approximation, we mean a bounded region of the plane whose boundary is the union of disconnected simple polygons (Figure 1). Each polygon is oriented, which enables regions to be disconnected or to have some holes. Furthermore, the vertices of the boundary polygons belong to $\partial X$. The more numerous these vertices, the more accurate the approximation. The *sampling density* $\omega$ of $X^\sim$ on $X$ allows the quality of the approximation to be estimated. It is the greatest number such that [15] :

$$\forall x \in \partial X, \exists s \text{ vertex of } \partial X^\sim, d(x,s) < \omega^{-1} \tag{1}$$

The sampling points can be boundary points of a discrete object (points of $N^2$) or the result of the evolution of a continuous deformable model [3] (points of $R^2$).

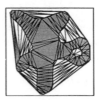

FIGURE 1. a) Polygonal approximation X ~ of a continuous shape X. b) Delaunay triangulation. c) Voronoi graph. The approximate skeleton (bold lines) is the dual of the inside Delaunay triangles (light grey triangles)

The Voronoi graph $V^\sim$ and the Delaunay triangulation $D^\sim$ of the boundary polygon vertices of $X^\sim$ are first computed. Then, the skeleton of $X$ is approximated by extracting a subgraph of $V^\sim$. The choice of this subgraph is guided by some properties we would like the approximate skeleton to satisfy. Firstly, the approximate skeleton should converge towards the exact skeleton as $X^\sim$ tends to $X$. Secondly, the approximate skeleton and $X$ must be homotopic, which means that they must have the same number of connected components and for each component, the same number of holes. Lastly, the process which computes the approximate skeleton should be reversible.

Boissonnat [6] was the first to notice that if the boundary of $X^\sim$ is included in the Delaunay triangulation $D^\sim$, then there exist only two types of triangles : inside triangles lying inside $X^\sim$ and partitioning $X^\sim$ and outside triangles lying outside $X^\sim$ (Figure 1). The demonstration of this property is provided in [1]. If one wants to approximate the skeleton, the best subgraph of $V^\sim$ is then the dual of inside triangles (Figure 1). Indeed, it can be proved that it has the three properties stated above. It converges towards the exact skeleton as $X^\sim$ tends to $X$, since Schmitt [15] has proved that Voronoi vertices tend to the skeleton and the exoskeleton. Moreover, it preserves homotopy and ensures reversibility. In what is to follow, the dual of inside triangles is denoted $Sk^\sim(X^\sim)$. We should note that

*Sk* ̃(*X* ̃) has no relation with the skeleton of *X* ̃ : *Sk*(*X* ̃) which consists of segments of straight lines and arcs of parabola.

The definition of the approximate skeleton *Sk* ̃(*X* ̃) has a meaning as long as the boundary of *X* ̃ is included in the Delaunay triangulation *D* ̃. Boissonnat refers to this condition as the *contour containment condition* [6]. One might think this is a restrictive condition. But, Brandt and Algazi have shown [7] that if the shape *X* to skeletonize is regular enough and if the sampling density ω of *X* ̃ is high enough, then the above condition is fulfilled. It is the case in the following.

## 4. SIMPLIFYING THE 2D APPROXIMATE SKELETON

The approximate skeleton defined in the previous section is very sensitive to noise on the boundary. It has barbs that are not characteristic of the underlying shape *X*. Simplifying *Sk* ̃(*X* ̃) is therefore necessary to obtain an efficient tool for shape description. Little research has been done on this subject in the case of semicontinuous methods. Let us quote another approach proposed by Ogniewicz [11][12]. He removes edges of the skeleton using lengths of pathes. We propose here a size invariant criterion.

### 4.1 Simplification process

By definition, the approximate skeleton *Sk* ̃(*X* ̃) is the dual of the polygonal shape *X* ̃. This duality suggests that one cannot simplify one without the other. Taking advantage of this remark, our simplification process prunes *Sk* ̃(*X* ̃) and simplifies *X* ̃ at the same time.

The extremities of the skeleton are sequentially removed according to an angular criterion. Each deletion affects the polygonal shape by removing an inside triangle from its initial partition.

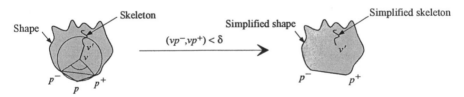

FIGURE 2. Removal of a skeleton extremity.

The decision to remove the barb [*vv′*] of the current skeleton where *v* designates an extremity depends on an angle calculated from *v* and local information (Figure 2). Let us denote (*p⁻pp⁺*) the dual inside triangle of *v*. Since *v* is an extremity, *p⁻* and *p⁺* are the neighbours of p on the current boundary. The barb [*vv′*] is removed if and only if the angle between the vector *vp⁻* and the vector *vp⁺* is less than a fixed threshold δ. In this case, the current polygonal shape is also simplified by removing from it the triangle (*p⁻pp⁺*). The major point is to preserve the duality between the current skeleton and the current polygonal shape.

The removal criterion is parametrized by an angle δ. As a result, a family of skeletons is increasingly simplified as δ increases from 0 to 2π is computed. The superposition of all those simplified skeletons leads to a hierarchical representation of $X$ (Figure 3), useful for shape description and pattern matching.

FIGURE 3. a) Initial polygonal shape. b) Superposition of the simplified skeletons. c) Superposition of the simplified polygonal shapes.

## 4.2 Interpretation

There exist two possible interpretations of the angle calculated during the simplification process. Firstly, one can note that $(pp^+,pp^-) = \pi - (vp^-,vp^+)/2$. Thus, an extremity $v$ of the skeleton is removed when its Delaunay triangle is not sufficiently pointed.

Secondly, it can be proved that the calculated angle approximates the angle formed by the center of a maximal ball and the contact points of this maximal ball with the boundary of the shape. This remark shows that the simplified skeleton of order δ is related to a discrete notion introduced by Meyer [16] : the *conditional bisector*. In the following paragraph, we examine in some detail different simplified skeletons and show how they can be related to known notions.

- Simplified skeleton of order 0 : It is no more than the approximate skeleton $Sk^{\sim}(X^{\sim})$ of Section 3, since the criterion is never verified (Figure 4).

- Simplified skeleton of order $2\pi^-$ : Every branch of the approximate skeleton is systematically removed. The result is an *homotopic marking* of $X$ as $X^{\sim}$ tends to $X$. First defined by Vincent for discrete objects [20], the homotopic marking of a shape $X$ is the smallest homotopic subset of its skeleton (Figure 4).

- Simplified skeleton of order $\pi$ : The simplified skeleton of order $\pi$ approximates the *minimal skeleton* of $X$. Defined by Meyer for discrete objects, it is the smallest homotopic subset of the skeleton which contains the *ultimate erosion* [16][19]. By construction, it is still homotopic to the initial shape $X$, but is more representative and allows a better description. Figure 4 shows the necessity of the simplification process and the quality of the minimal skeleton.

As a result of the use of an angular criterion, our method is independent of the size of the objects. It allows an efficient computation in $O(n \log n)$ where $n$ designates the number of vertices of $X\tilde{\ }$. Our work has already been applied in the frame of an European project (AIM program, IMPACT n°A2017 92-93) for the study of cell images [8].

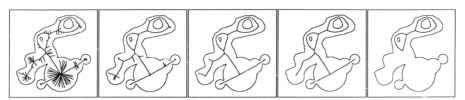

FIGURE 4. From left to right, simplified skeletons of order 0, $\pi/4$, $\pi/2$, $\pi$, $2\pi$.

## 5. 3D EXTENSION

3D extension of discrete methods have been proposed in numerous papers [14][17][18]. On the other hand, very few continuous methods have been generalized. Let quote [12] in which 3D simplified skeletons are used to describe the brain structure. In this section, we are interested in the 3D extension of our method.

### 5.1 3D approximate skeleton

Let $X \in R^3$ be a 3D shape to skeletonize. We have first to provide a representation of $X$. To do so, its boundary is decomposed into triangles, whose vertices belong to $\partial X$. This comes down to approximating $X$ with a polyhedral shape $X\tilde{\ }$. In practice, regular polygonal shapes are provided by a segmentation method using deformable surface models described in [3]. As in the 2D, the accuracy of the approximation is given by the sampling density $\omega$ defined by Eq. 1.

First, the Voronoi graph $V\tilde{\ }$ and the tetrahedronization $D\tilde{\ }$ of boundary polyhedron vertices of $X\tilde{\ }$ are computed with Bertin's algorithms [4]. We are looking for a subgraph of $V\tilde{\ }$ which will provide a good approximation of the exact skeleton of $X$.

Suppose that $X\tilde{\ }$ verifies the 3D extension of the contour containment condition defined in Section 3 ($\partial X\tilde{\ } \subset D\tilde{\ }$). Then, there exist only two types of tetrahedra : inside tetrahedra lying inside $X\tilde{\ }$ and partitioning $X\tilde{\ }$ and outside tetrahedra lying outside $X\tilde{\ }$. As in the 2D case, we define the approximate skeleton $Sk\tilde{\ }(X\tilde{\ })$ of $X$ as the dual of inside tetrahedra. It is a thin figure of 3D space composed of polygons and straight-line segments.

### 5.2 Simplifying the 3D approximate skeleton

In order to simplify the approximate skeleton, we are going to simplify its dual : the set of inside tetrahedra. By definition, the simplified skeleton is the dual of the remaining tetrahedra. In what is to follow, an inside (resp. boundary) face or edge designates a face or an edge included in (resp. on the boundary of) the union of current inside tetrahedra.

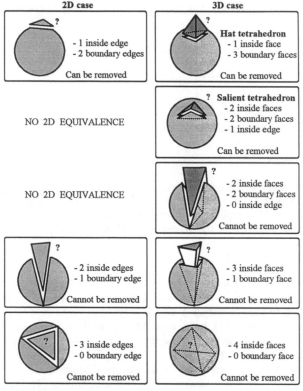

FIGURE 5. The simplification process consists in removing Delaunay simplexes (triangles in 2D and tetrahedra in 3D) providing it does not alter homotopy.

The main idea of the simplification process is to iteratively remove inside tetrahedra whose deletions do not alter the homotopy of the remaining set (Figure 5). Two types of inside tetrahedra hold this property.

- The first ones, called *hat tetrahedra*, have three boundary faces and an inside one. They are associated with extremities of the 3D skeleton. Their 2D equivalents are triangles associated with extremities of the skeleton. The consequence of their deletions is to shorten the skeleton.

- The second ones, called *salient tetrahedra*, have two boundary faces and an inside edge denoted [*ab*] in Figure 6. The deletion of the salient tetrahedra *T* leads to the removal of the associated Voronoi vertex $v$. Consequently, it opens the Voronoi polygon dual of $[ab]$ and may create new skeleton extremities.

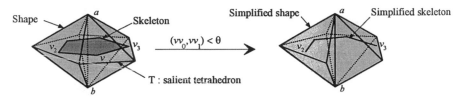

FIGURE 6. Removal of a salient tetrahedron.

Let us now consider on which condition hat and salient tetrahedra are effectively removed. Assume that the skeleton of X is not degenerated, which means it is formed of surfaces and contains no wireframe parts. In this case, hat tetrahedra must systematically be removed as they imply unidimensional parts in the skeleton. On the other hand, we decide to remove the salient tetrahedron $T$ if its two boundary faces form an almost obtuse angle. It is a natural extension of our 2D criterion which preserves pointed triangles. Formally, let $v$ be the dual of $T$. Let $v_0$ and $v_1$ be the two neighbouring outside vertices of $v$ and $\theta$ an angular threshold ; $T$ is removed if the angle between the vectors $vv_0$ and $vv_1$ is less than $\theta$ (Figure 6). The simplified skeleton is the dual of the remaining inside tetrahedra.

Figure 7 illustrates the necessity to simplify approximate skeletons and shows good simplified skeletons for a median value of $\theta$ (arccos(0.7)). The complexity is related to the complexity of the 3D Voronoi graph computation. Thus, it is $O(n^2)$ in the worst case and $O(n \log n)$ in the average case, where $n$ designates the number of vertices of $X^\sim$.

For shape having degenerated skeletons, another strategy is required and will be the subject of further researches. In this case, the systematic removal of salient tetrahedra is necessary to lead to an almost wireframe simplified skeleton. On the contrary, some hat tetrahedra must be preserved. A possible criterion could be for example to keep tetrahedra which contain their dual Voronoi vertices.

## 6. CONCLUSION

We have presented an efficient method for simplifying 2D and 3D skeletons with a semicontinuous approach. In the 2D case, the process is parametrized by an angle $\delta$ and thus is size invariant. The superposition of all the simplified skeletons leads to a hierarchical representation. Moreover, we have shown that the simplified skeleton of order $\delta$ is related to a discrete notion : the conditional bisector. In the 3D case, depending on the removal criterion, borders of the skeleton surface can be preserved, or on the contrary, removed so that an almost wireframe figure is obtained. The removal criterion can be adapted for different cases. 3D skeletons are promised to be useful for analysing 3D objects, for feature extraction and shape partitionning. Among the applications, one could be the computation of distance between selected sites in a chromosome provided by confocal images.

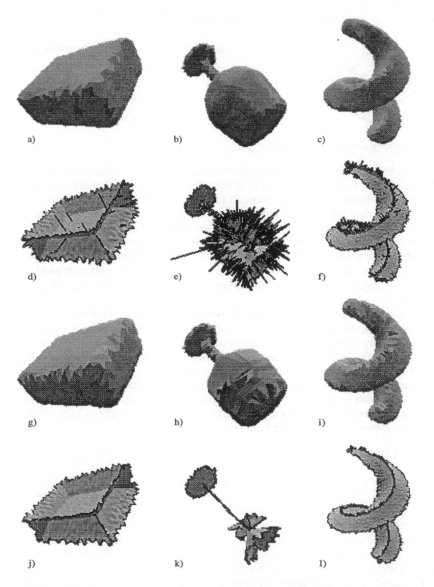

FIGURE 7. a) b) c) Polygonal shapes. d) e) f) Approximate skeletons. g) h) i) Simplified shapes of order $\theta / \cos \theta = 0.7$. j) k) l) Simplified skeletons of order $\theta / \cos \theta = 0.7$.

# 7. REFERENCES

[1]    D. Attali et A. Montanvert, "Squelettes et Diagrammes de Voronoi", *Rapport de recherche*, RR 922 - IMAG Grenoble, Juillet 1993.

[2]    C. Arcelli and M. Frucci, "Reversible skeletonization by (5,7,11)-erosion", *Proc. Visual Form Analysis and Recognition*, Capri, May 27-30, pp. 21-28, 1991.

[3]    E. Bainville, "Reconstruction d'objets tridimensionnels à partir de silhouettes", *Rapport de stage du DEA d'informatique fondamentale de l'ENS Lyon*, 1992.

[4]    E. Bertin et J.M. Chassery, "Diagramme de Voronoï 3D : Construction et applications en imagerie 3D", $8^{ème}$ *Congrès RFIA*, AFCET-INRIA ed., Lyon Villeurbanne, pp. 803-808, 1991.

[5]    H. Blum, "An associative machine for dealing with the visual field and some of its biological implications", *Biological Prototypes and synthetic systems*, Vol. 1, Proc. $2^{nd}$ Annual Bionics Symposium, Cornell Univ., 1961, E. E. Bernard and M. R. Kare eds., Plenum Press, New-York, pp. 244-260, 1962.

[6]    J.D. Boissonnat et B. Geiger, "Three dimensional reconstruction of complex shapes based on the Delaunay triangulation", *Rapport de Recherche N°1697*, Mai 1992.

[7]    J.W. Brandt and V.R. Algazi, "Continuous Skeleton Computation by Voronoi Diagram", *CVGIP : Image Understanding*, Volume 55, N°3, pp. 329-337, 1992.

[8]    G. Brugal, R. Dye, B. Krief, J.M. Chassery, H. Tanke and J.H. Tucker, "HOME: Highly Optimized Microscope Environment", *Cytometry*, 13, pp. 109-116, 1992.

[9]    J.M. Chassery et A. Montanvert, Géométrie discrète en analyse d'images, Editions Hermès, 1991.

[10]   D.T. Lee, "Medial axis Transformation of a Planar Shape", *IEEE Transactions on Pattern Analysis and Machine Intelligence*, Vol. PAMI-4, N°4, pp. 363-369, 1982.

[11]   R. Ogniewicz and M. Ilg, "Voronoi Skeletons : Theory and Applications", *IEEE Computer Vision and Pattern Recognition*, Champaign, Illinois, June 15-18, pp. 63-69, 1992.

[12]   R. Ogniewicz, G. Székely, M. Näf and O. Kübler, "Medial manifolds and hierarchical description of 2D and 3D objects with applications to MRI data of the humain brain", *Proc. 9th SCIA Conf.*, pp. 875-883, 1993.

[13]   F.P. Preparata, M.I. Shamos, Computational Geometry : an Introduction, Texts and Monographs in Computer Science, Springer-Verlag ed., 1988.

[14]   F. Rolland, J.M. Chassery and A. Montanvert, "3D Medial surfaces and 3D Skeletons", *Proc. Visual Form Analysis and Recognition*, Capri, May 27-30, pp. 443-450, 1991.

[15]   M. Schmitt, "Some examples of algorithms analysis in computational geometry by means of mathematical morphology techniques", *in Geometry and robotics* (J.D. Boissonnat and J.P. Laumond ed.), Lecture Notes in Computer Science, Vol. 391, Springer-Verlag, Berlin, pp. 225-246, 1989.

[16]   F. Meyer, "Skeletons and perceptual graphs", *Signal Processing*, 16(4) :335-363,1989.

[17]   J. Mukherjee, B.N. Chatterji, P.P. Das, "Thinning of 3-D images using the safe point thinning algorithm (SPTA)", *Pattern Recognition Letters*, 10, pp. 167-173, 1989.

[18]   P. Srisuresh, S.N. Srihari, "A shrinking algorithm for three dimensional objects", *Computer Vision and Pattern Recognition*, Washington DC, pp. 392-393, 1983.

[19]   H. Talbot and L. Vincent, "Euclidean Skeletons and Conditional bisectors", *Proc SPIE Visual Communications and Image Processing 1992*, Vol. 1818, Boston MA, November 1992.

[20]   L. Vincent, "Efficient computation of various types of skeletons", *Proc. SPIE's 1445 Medical Imaging V*, San Jose, CA, February 1991.

# Multiscale Spatial Filters for Visual Tasks and Object Recognition

Dana H. Ballard, Rajesh P.N. Rao and Garbis Salgian
Department of Computer Science
University of Rochester
Rochester, NY 14627, USA

### Abstract

In the active vision framework, vision is seen as subserving a larger context of the encompassing behaviors that the agent is engaged in. For these behaviors, it is often possible to use temporary, iconic descriptions of the scene. We describe an iconic method whereby points in a scene are associated with a characteristic vector ("zip code") comprised of the responses of a bank of steerable spatial filters tuned to a range of orientations and scales. The use of multiple scales renders the vector for each point unique for all practical purposes; it can thus be robustly matched to vectors for instances of the point in other possibly transformed images obtained after camera motion. The filterbank description is view-insensitive to a considerable extent and we present methods to make the recognition algorithm both rotation-invariant and occlusion-tolerant. We also present a method for coping with scale changes and suggest relatively simple strategies that exploit the multiscale structure of the zip code for tasks such as visual search using space-variant (log-polar) sensors and looming detection for obstacle avoidance.

## 1 Introduction

Visual tasks often require only temporary, iconic descriptions of the scene which are only relatively insensitive to variations in the view. For example, image color as a measure of surface albedo is relatively insensitive to variations in viewing direction. Swain used color for object recognition problems by exploiting properties of the color histogram [33, 34].

Our approach to the recognition problem is based on the use of photometric features that behave very much like color. In particular, these features are obtained by taking the responses of different order derivative of Gaussian filters (which are *steerable* [10]) at a range of orientations and scales. Such filters are a way of describing the

| Computing Methodology | Problem Being Solved | References |
|---|---|---|
| Calculus of | Optic Flow | [13] |
| Variations | Shape from Shading | [14] |
| Filters at | Brightness Edge | [12] |
| Single Scale | Detection | [7] |
| | Curved Line | [28] |
| | Grouping | [22] |
| Filters at | Optic Flow | [1],[11],[36] |
| Multiple Scales | Shape from Shading | [29],[30] |
| | Texture Segmentation | [19],[23] |
| | Stereo Correspondence | [18],[16] |
| | Scene Interpretation | [38],[20] |
| | Biometric Signatures | [9] |

Table 1: The trend from variational methods towards the use of filters for solving specific problems in computer vision.

intensities near a given point and have recently been used for wide variety of problems ranging from stereo correspondence [16] to texture segmentation [23]. Indeed, there appears to have been a silent revolution in the use of filters for proto-visual analysis and as computing machinery for solving complex vision-related problems which previously had been tackled, albeit not totally satisfactorily, by variational methods. This historic trend is depicted in Table 1.

It is clear that the filters will depend on the choice of the coordinate system; however, there is a normalization procedure that makes them invariant to rotations about the view vector. This means that an index can be constructed that almost uniquely describes the local intensity variations about a point. This description is in the form of a 45 element vector or *zip-code* of filter responses at different scales. The relatively large number of measurements at a point makes the point's zip code vector practically unique and its location can be thus recovered by the process of backprojection, or comparing a model response vector to the response vectors of all image locations. For rotations about axes other than the viewing axis, the success of the descriptors depends on their view insensitivity. Our experiments using backprojection indicate that the filters are insensitive to three-dimensional rotations of 25-45° at radial distances of 5 feet or more from the focal point.

Besides exhibiting rotational invariance about the view axis and robustness in the presence of 3D view variations, the method can also be extended to handle the case where the area near the point is partially occluded. This strategy uses a description of the occluder in the form of a template which can be obtained via active vision systems.

We also present a method for coping with scale variations and suggest relatively simple strategies that exploit the multiscale structure of the zip code for tasks such as visual search using space-variant (log-polar) sensors and looming detection for obstacle avoidance.

## 1.1 Steerable Filters

Steerable filters are a set of oriented basis filters with the important property that the response of a filter at an arbitrary orientation can be synthesized from linear combinations of the basis filters. It is well known ([10]) that using a circularly symmetric Gaussian function in Cartesian coordinates (with scale and normalization factors set to 1 here for convenience):

$$G(x,y) = e^{-(x^2+y^2)}$$

we can define two first order basis filters $G_1^0$ and $G_1^{\pi/2}$ as:

$$G_1^0 = \tfrac{\partial}{\partial x}G(x,y) = -2xe^{-(x^2+y^2)}$$

and

$$G_1^{\pi/2} = \tfrac{\partial}{\partial y}G(x,y) = -2ye^{-(x^2+y^2)}$$

such that the directional derivative in an arbitrary direction $\theta$ can be synthesized as:

$$G_1^\theta = \cos(\theta)G_1^0 + \sin(\theta)G_1^{\pi/2}.$$

Higher order filters at arbitrary orientations can be synthesized analogous to the first order case by using basis functions denoted by:

$$G_n^{\theta_n}, n = 1, 2, 3, \theta_n = 0, \ldots, k\pi/(n+1), k = 1, \ldots, n,$$

where $n$ denotes the order of the filter and $\theta_n$ the orientation of the filter. Figure 1 shows these filters for a particular scale $\sigma$ (standard deviation of the Gaussian). Different interpolation functions are needed to *steer* the different order Gaussian filters, as shown by Freeman and Adelson [10]. The number of the interpolation functions that are needed for steering is one more than the filter order. So, for example, the first-order filters can be steered with two interpolation functions given basis measurements at 0° and 90°, the second-order filters can be steered with three functions given basis measurements at 0°, 60°, and 120°, and so on. In particular,

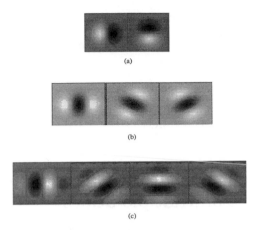

(a)

(b)

(c)

Figure 1: The nine different filters that comprise the steerable filters up to the third-order for $\sigma = 6.5$. (a) $G_1$; (b) $G_2$; (c) $G_3$.

$$G_n(\theta) = \sum_{i=1}^{n+1} G_n^{(i-1)\pi/(n+1)} k_{in}(\theta),$$

where the first-order interpolants ($n = 1$) are given by,

$$k_{i1}(\theta) = \left[\cos(\theta - (i-1)\pi/2)\right], i = 1, 2.$$

For $n = 2$, we have

$$k_{i2}(\theta) = \tfrac{1}{3}\left[1 + 2\cos(2(\theta - (i-1)\pi/3))\right], i = 1, 2, 3,$$

and for $n = 3$,

$$k_{i3}(\theta) = \tfrac{1}{4}\left[2\cos(\theta - (i-1)\pi/4) + 2\cos(3(\theta - (i-1)\pi/4))\right], i = 1, 2, 3, 4.$$

## 1.2  The Multiple-Scale Index or Zip-Code

Combining the responses from all the filters from different orders provides nine independent measures at each image point. This can be augmented further by using the filters at different image scales. To handle variations in scale, it is best to make the scales sufficiently close together so as to be able to interpolate between scales. In practice, this means choosing image domains that are multiples of two in area, or $\sqrt{2}$ in linear dimension. Since there are nine measurements per scale, there are $9 \times$ (the number of scales) total measurements. For the experiments, five different scales are used, for a total of forty-five measurements per point.

The different responses at different scales are sensitive to the width of the templates, so the responses, to be comparable across scales, have to be normalized. The easiest way to do this is to divide by the filter energy defined as:

$$e_i = \iint G_i^0(x,y)^2 dx\, dy, i = 1, 2, 3.$$

Now define the normalized response of a set of filters to the area surrounding a specific point in the image as the vector (zip code)

$$\mathbf{z} = (r_{i,j,s}), i = 1, 2, 3; j = 1, \ldots, f(i); s = s_{min}, \ldots, s_{max},$$

where $r_{i,j,s}$ denotes the response of a filter with the index $i$ denoting the order of the filter, $j$ denoting the number of filters per order ($f(i) = i + 1$), and $s$ denoting the number of different scales.

# 2   The Favorable Properties of Long Vectors and the Importance of Multiple Scales

Pentti Kanerva was among the first to realize the advantages of very long vectors as a representation medium. In his book [17], he convincingly demonstrates the usefulness of very long (binary) vectors in formulating a sparse distributed memory system that mimics the human memory system in many ways. For example, by approximating the binomial distribution (distances between points) of the space $\{0, 1\}^n$ by the normal distribution with mean $n/2$ and standard deviation $\sqrt{n}/2$, Kanerva shows that most of the space is orthogonal (or "indifferent") to any given point; in other words, most of the space lies at approximately the mean distance $n/2$ from a point, with only a minute fraction closer or further away (distances being measured in terms of the Hamming distance). The result is that if we are trying to determine whether a particular vector belongs to a specific class of similar vectors, the likelihood that it does increases rapidly as the vector approaches one of the vectors from the class only slightly. This property is experimentally confirmed in [4] and is a key cause of the uniqueness of matches and the robustness of the matching process.

Summarizing his views on the sensory interface with memory, Kanerva notes ([17] p. 119):

> The memory works with features and creates internal objects and individuals by chunking together things that are similar in terms of those features. In order for those internal objects to match objects of the world, the system's sensors must transform raw input from the world into features that are relatively invariant over small perturbations of objects.

and concludes by asserting that

> ... artificial intelligence methods need to be augmented with mathematical and statistical methods of dealing with representations in high-dimensional spaces.

| Number of Filters | Rank of Matching Point | Difference in Distance |
|:---:|:---:|:---:|
| 9 | 18.3 | -8.1 |
| 18 | 4.3 | -6.3 |
| 27 | 1.3 | 1.0 |
| 36 | 1 | 5.6 |
| 45 | 1 | 10.8 |

Table 2: Sensitivity of the match value to the length of the vector (= number of scales used ×
nine). The figures shown are the average of the results for three pairs of corresponding points.

In this regard, the multiscale response vector forms an effective representation
medium for vision-related computations in that it is both relatively invariant to minor
disturbances in the environment and retains the attractive matching properties of long
vectors.

Besides facilitating simple strategies for visual tasks such as space-variant sensing
(Section 7) and handling scale variations (Section 6), the use of filters at multiple
scales (in addition to the use of nine different filters at one scale) generates a longer
vector than one obtained by using filters at a single scale; this in turn helps to make
the matching process more robust. In order to experimentally verify the effectiveness
of multiscale templates over single scale ones, the match values of corresponding
points in 2D rotated and unrotated images of Section 4 were tested as a function of
the number of scales used. Table 2 shows these results. With less than three scales,
the matching point is not the best point selected. However, with three or more scales
it is ranked the best. The third column compares the distance measures used in the
match of the best and second-best point in the case where the matching point is
ranked first. In the case where the matching point is not the best the distance is that
of the best minus that of the matching point. This column shows that even after
the matching point is the best, its perspicuity continues to improve with additional
scales.

# 3    The Location-Identification Dichotomy

There is a growing belief that general image interpretation, the problem of associating
many models with many components of an image simultaneously, is either too hard or
unnecessary, or both. Evidence for such a belief comes from many fronts. First, there
exist convincing arguments that the segmentation problem, a precursor to most scene
interpretation strategies, is in general intractable [35]. In addition, a strong hint that
general scene interpretation may be infeasible comes from biological studies [24] that
seem to indicate that the primate visual cortex is organized into separate specialized
modules subserving the two complementary functions of directing eyes to new target

| | | Stored Model Object | |
|---|---|---|---|
| | | *One* | *Many* |
| **Image Components** | *One* | Manipulation: Handling an object whose location and identity are known. | Identification: Recovering the identity of an object whose location is currently being fixated. |
| | *Many* | Location: Finding a known object in the current image. | Image Interpretation: May be too difficult. |

Table 3: The Location-Identification Dichotomy of Visual Scene Interpretation (adapted from [5]).

locations and analyzing the currently foveated area. This suggests a "What versus Where" dichotomy in the scene interpretation problem, as depicted in Table 3, where the "What" component corresponds to the problem of identification of a foveated point and the "Where" component corresponds to the problem of locating a point of interest in the current image.

While the reduction of the recognition problem to the complementary problems of location and identification decreases the complexity of the problem to a considerable extent, the problems of location and identification themselves need to be solved. In the following, we develop efficient algorithms for both of these problems.

We first need to describe the match between two zip codes, one from a model point and one from an image point. Denote the zip code from an image point as $\mathbf{z^i}$ and that from a model point as $\mathbf{z^m}$. Then the distance between them is simply the Euclidean distance $d_{im} = \|\mathbf{z^i} - \mathbf{z^m}\|$.

## 3.1   The Backprojection Algorithm for Location

The localization algorithm crucially depends on the fact that only a single model is matched to an image at any instant. Let us denote this model as

$$M = \{\mathbf{z^m}, m = 1, \ldots, m_{max}\}.$$

The backprojection algorithm in its most general form proceeds as follows:

1. For each zip code representing some model point $m$, create a backprojected distance image $I_m$ defined by

$$I_m(x, y) = min[I_{max} - \beta d_{im}, 0]$$

where $\beta$ is a suitably chosen constant (this makes the best matching point the brightest spot in the image).

2. Find the best match point $(x_{b_m}, y_{b_m})$ in the image for each $m$ using the relation $(x_{b_m}, y_{b_m}) = argmax\{I_m(x, y)\}$.

3. Construct a binary "salience" image $S(x, y)$ where

$$S(x, y) = \begin{cases} 1 & \text{if } (x, y) \in \{(x_{b_m}, y_{b_m})\}, m = 1, \ldots, m_{max} \\ 0 & \text{otherwise} \end{cases}$$

4. Output the location of the object in the current image as $(x_b, y_b)$ where

$$(x_b, y_b) = argmax\{S(x, y) * B(x, y)\}$$

and $B$ is an appropriate blurring (local averaging) function whose size is usually known in active vision environments.

For the sake of convenience and clarity in understanding the performance of the algorithms, we present our results in terms the distance image rather than the results after applying the blurring operation.

## 3.2  The Identification Algorithm

In the general case, more than one model object can share the same zip code. Let $M(\mathbf{z}^{\mathbf{m}})$ denote the set of models (represented by their labels) that have $\mathbf{z}^{\mathbf{m}}$ as part of their set of zip codes.

The identification algorithm proceeds as follows:

1. First obtain for each chosen zip code on the object to be identified the model zip codes $\mathbf{z}^{\mathbf{m}}$ such that $d_{im} \leq T$, where $T$ is a prechosen threshold.

2. For each model $M_i$, initialize the "evidence" array $E(M_i)$ to 0.

3. For each $\mathbf{z}^{\mathbf{m}}$ from step 1 and each model $M_i \in M(\mathbf{z}^{\mathbf{m}})$, set $E(M_i) := E(M_i) + 1$.

4. Output the model label $M$ such that $E(M) = max\{A(M_i)\}$.

# 4  Coping with 2D Rotations

In two dimensions, the difference between an image point and a model point is limited to a rotation and scale. Assume that the scale is fixed. To normalize for the rotation about the viewing axis, one strategy is to select the orientation of the first-order filters as a reference. This is a good strategy for two reasons: (1) the orientation can be computed directly from the filter responses, and (2) these filter responses are usually the most stable.

Thus the orientation is computed as

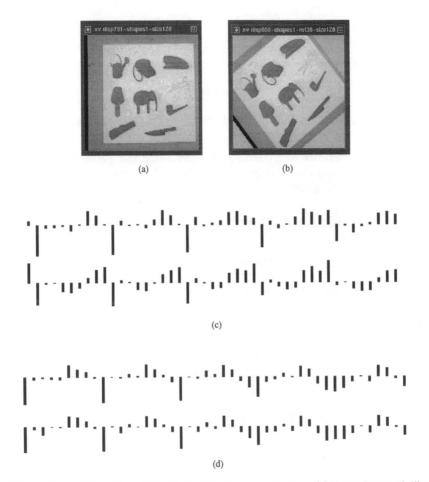

Figure 2: An illustration of the effect of rotation normalization. (a) A test image of silhouettes; (b) The test image rotated 38° counterclockwise; (c) the zip codes for corresponding points near the elephant's mouth in the two images before normalization; (d) the zip codes after normalization.

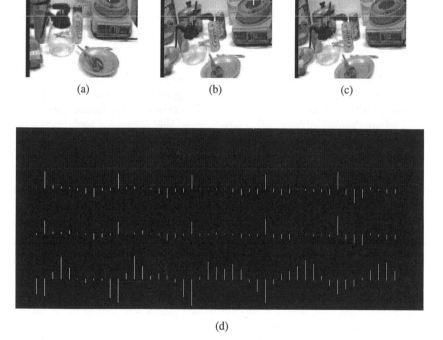

(a)    (b)    (c)

(d)

Figure 3: A demonstration of view insensitivity. (a) A point on the original image; (b) the same point correctly located by the algorithm in a second image with a $22.5^0$ 3-D rotation; (c) an unrelated point in the rotated image for the purpose of comparison; (d) the 45 filter responses for the point in (a) (top), the point in (b) (middle) and the point in (c) (bottom).

$$\alpha = tan^{-1}(r_{1,1,s_{max}}, r_{1,2,s_{max}})$$

and then the filter responses are rotated using the steering formulae to a canonical direction (horizontal), i.e.,

$$r'_{i,j,s} = Rot(\alpha, r_{i,j,s}).$$

Note that this normalization makes the matching process more powerful than that produced with rotation invariant templates. The latter sacrifice variability in the angular direction. Instead the filters capture the variations in angle, and preserve it in their components. Another feature of the normalization process is that it can be done without additional convolutions; the interpolation properties of the existing filters allow it to be carried out with a single basis set of convolutions. Figure 2 illustrates the rotation normalization procedure. It is clear that the procedure has rendered the two previously uncorrelated zip codes of the same point to be almost identical.

Rotations about an image plane axis are ameliorated in two ways. First, the algorithms for identification and location work as long as there is a useful subset of filter responses; all the responses do not have to be correct. More importantly, the filter responses are dominated by a cosine envelope, so that there is a useful range of rotations for which the responses will be effectively invariant. This fact is illustrated in the example shown in Figure 3.

## 5  Coping with Occlusion

The basic backprojection algorithm compares the filter responses with every point with those of a prototype. This algorithm will fail when the prototype is occluded if nothing is done as the occluder will distort the filter responses. Interestingly, humans have a similar problem. Figure 4 shows the experimental setup designed by Nakayama and Shimojo [26] to test subjects' ability to identify faces in the presence of positive occlusion cues. In one instance the face is painted on a picket fence; in the other it is behind the picket fence. The results show that identification is improved in the latter case. This observation forms the inspiration for our solution [3].

Suppose that an active imaging system is used [5]. As a consequence we can assume that the occluder can be detected by a method such as disparity filtering [8]. Disparity filtering is a way of creating a filter that only passes image energy in the horopter. Ideally one can create a template $T(x, y)$ such that $T(x, y) = 1$ for material in the horopter and $T(x, y) = 0$ otherwise. We assume the existence of such a template for our subsequent calculations.

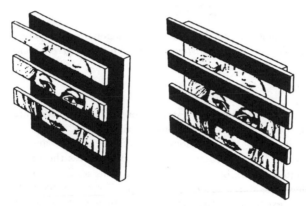

Figure 4: Nakayama and Shimojo's demonstration that recognition performance depends on whether or not the occluded is positive.

## 5.1 Occlusion Algorithm

The filter responses are the responses for a set of basis functions. As a consequence the image intensities near every point can be reconstructed by appropriately combining the responses and filter functions. As the functions are not orthogonal, a pseudo-inverse must be used to do this [16].

Any spatial filter with a finite impulse response can be represented as an $n \times 1$ vector $F_i$, $n$ = number of pixels in the support of the filter and $i = 1 \ldots 45$. A set of such filters can be stacked side by side to form a $45 \times n$ matrix $F$. For an image patch represented as an $n \times 1$ vector $I$, the $45 \times 1$ response vector (zip code) is

$$z = F^T I$$

Applying *singular value decomposition* [32] to $F^T$, we get

$$F^T = U \Sigma V^T$$

where $U$ is a $45 \times 45$ orthogonal matrix , $\Sigma$ is $45 \times n$ diagonal matrix, and $V^T$ is $n \times n$ orthogonal matrix. We can now *reconstruct* an image patch given a zip code $z$ by using the relation

$$I' = V \Sigma^{-1} U^T z$$

where $\Sigma^{-1}$ denotes an $n \times 45$ diagonal matrix whose diagonal entries are the multiplicative inverses of the corresponding diagonal entries of $\Sigma^{-1}$.

Note that the matrix $V \Sigma^{-1} U^T$ is independent of the zip code and hence can be precomputed and stored. Reconstruction then merely involves the multiplication of an $n \times 45$ precomputed matrix by a $45 \times 1$ vector. This ability to reconstruct the local intensities allows the stored prototype to be made comparable to the occluded image responses. For every point, the reconstructed image intensities are appropriately masked using the occluding template. A similar process is done to the incoming image. Thus the masked reconstructed image and the masked input image are now in the same coordinate system and can be compared by differencing their filter responses. This is formalized in the following algorithm for occlusion near a point $(x_0, y_0)$:

### Occlusion Algorithm

1. Use model zip code to reconstruct the local image patch, $I'(x_0, y_0)$.

2. For every point $(x, y)$ in the image do:
Compute $I''(x, y) = T(x, y)I(x, y)$ for all $(x, y)$ in a local domain of appropriate size.
Compute new filter responses $f''$ from $I''$.
Compare those with the filter responses $f$ computed from $I'(x_0, y_0)T(x_0, y_0)$ to compute $d(x', y')$.

3. The sought after point is given by argmin $d(x', y')$.

To demonstrate the occlusion algorithm, we created a face image similar to that of Figure 4. Figure 5 shows the results of using the occlusion algorithm on the face image. Just to make the obvious point, if the raw filter responses in the occluded image are compared to the previous point, then, as they are not comparable, the best match is not correct. This computation is shown in Figure 5 (e).

The occlusion strategy could be used in a more complicated graph-matching strategy such as that of [38], which also uses multi-resolution filters (Gabor filters in particular), but that would require additional computational machinery.

# 6   Scale Changes and Looming Detection

In order to be successful in a dynamic environment, a recognition mechanism must have the ability to handle scale changes in the projection of an object in an image usually caused by motion of the camera towards or away from the object. Our experiments seem to indicate that the backprojection and identfication algorithms can handle about 5-10% variations in scale but larger scale changes distort the filter responses causing the algorithms to fail.

However, this problem can be tackled in at least three ways. First, since the approximate distances are usually known by the perceiver, and the dimensions of the viewed object are usually small compared to the viewing distance, the scale can be pre-adjusted prior to the matching process. Second, a strategy such as that used by Murase and Nayar [25] for scale normalization by subsampling or oversampling the image of an object to a canonical size can be adopted but this assumes segmentation into object and background regions, an assumption that we question for general cases (see [35] for an argument that the general segmentation problem is intractable). We suggest the following more feasible but nevertheless effective strategy for handling scale changes that exploits the multiscale structure of zip codes. Since the responses of the filters will usually vary smoothly between scales, it should be possible to establish

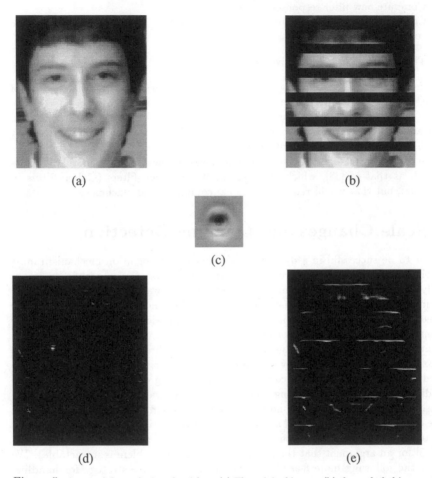

Figure 5: A test of the occlusion algorithm. (a) The original image; (b) the occluded image; (c) the reconstructed patch of the left eye (unmasked); (d) the distance image showing the left eye correctly located by using responses from the masked eye patch; (e) the result of directly comparing the unoccluded responses from (c) with those from the occluded image. (Face image courtesy Lambert Wixson, Sarnoff Research Center)

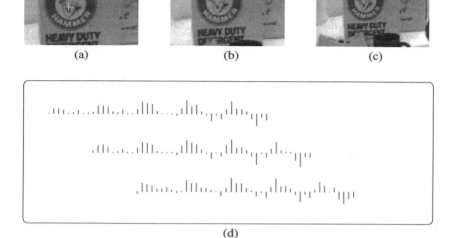

(a)    (b)    (c)

(d)

Figure 6: Handling changes in scale. (a), (b), and (c) are images of an object at three different scales, with 10% reduction in scale from the previous image. (d) depicts the process of shifting and matching zip codes (for the point marked by '+') across scales.

a correspondence between the two zip codes of the same point on an object imaged at different scales by using a simple *shift-and-compare* scale matching strategy: in addition to comparing an image zip code and a model zip code directly as outlined in Section 3, shifted versions of the image zip code are also compared with the model zip code i.e. image responses are compared with model responses at second, third, ... scales, then with model responses at third, fourth, ... scales, and so on upto some threshold scale. This procedure is illustrated in Figure 6. Note that this strategy also yields the % change in scale from the original model scale as a by-product of the matching procedure and could thus be used in estimating current distance from the point in the 3D environment.

Visual looming, or the expansion of the projection of an approaching object in the retina, is an important cue in the human reflex for obstacle avoidance [6]. Numerous approaches such as using flow field divergence [27], measuring optic flow via correlation [2], and computing the relative change in texture density [15] have been explored. The scale matching strategy introduced above suggests a natural and extremely simple strategy for tackling this problem. At any given point, if an object is approaching the camera, the filter responses at a coarse scale at time $t + \Delta t$ will roughly match those at a finer scale from time $t$. Thus, looming detection can be achieved by comparing the zip codes extracted from points near the center of gaze from one frame to zip codes (shifted to various degrees) extracted from the same points in the successive frame(s) as seen in Figure 6 for receding object. The time-to-contact (or time-to-collision [21]) can also be estimated by measuring the scale change (amount of shift yielding the best match) induced by motion of the object; a scale interpolation technique for estimating responses for scales lying between those used in zip codes would be useful in this regard.

# 7 Visual Search using Space-Variant Sensors

Active vision systems faced with the problem of searching for targets in natural scenes are finding wide field-of-view (FOV) sensors increasingly important. However, such systems also require good resolution to facilitate precise recognition. The simultaneous need for wide FOV and good resolution is realized in space-variant sensors (see [31] for example). A popular class of space-variant sensors are those based on the structure of the primate retina: they have a small area near the optical axis of greatly increased resolution (the fovea) coupled with a logarithmic falloff in resolution as one moves radially towards the periphery.

Since high acuity is restricted to the foveal region, a mechanism is required for moving the point of gaze. In the case of the human visual system, this is accomplished by a special targeting mechanism termed *saccades* [39]. There has been recent interest in active vision systems that search large areas using space-variant sensors that have variable resolution characteristics similar to the retina [31]. Such systems will require gaze targeting mechanisms for targeting the optical axis and the fovea to different points of interest in the visual world. The multiscale zip code description of points lends itself naturally to a robust and efficient paradigm for achieving foveal targeting of a space-variant sensor. Since decreasing radial resolution results in an effective reduction in scale of previously foveated regions as they move towards the periphery, the shift-and-compare scale matching strategy of the previous section can once again be applied to find previously foveated (and remembered) points on the current image. This is illustrated in Figure 7. The sequence of images (a) through (f) were obtained by passing appropriate portions of an original image through a log-polar mapping [37], with an effective radial drop-off rate (geometric) of 1.075 pixels of the original image per pixel of the new image. The resulting sequence simulates the effect of moving a log-polar space-variant sensor from a point of foveation at the point marked by '+' (Figure 7 (a)) towards the right. (g) illustrates the scale matching strategy of shifting and comparing the zip codes.

The figure suggests that more filter responses at higher scales may need to be stored in the zip code of foveated points in order for matching to be successful at point locations further away from the center. In this example, the images were chosen such that the drop-off in resolution was matched by a corresponding reduction in scale of

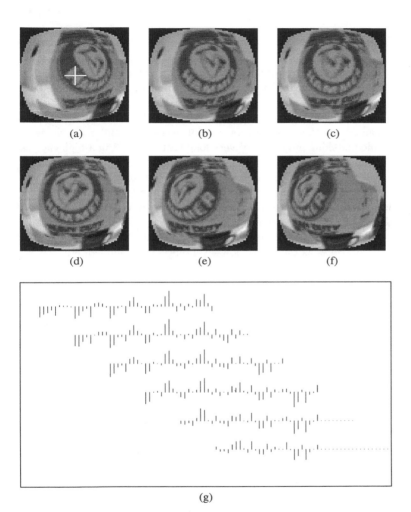

(a)  (b)  (c)

(d)  (e)  (f)

(g)

Figure 7: Using zip codes with a log-polar sensor. (a) through (f) represent a sequence of images obtained by movement of the sensor from a point of foveation (marked by '+') towards the right. (g) depicts the process of shifting and matching zip codes of the same point as it moves towards the periphery of the sensor.

$\sqrt{2}$ in order to illustrate the matching strategy. For the more general case, we can rely on a scale interpolation technique to effectively obtain a continuum of responses across scales.

# 8 Conclusion

In summary, the success of our approach can perhaps be attributed to three primary factors. First, the complexity of the scene interpretation problem is handled by reducing it to the two complementary and more manageable problems of location and identification. Second, the method is capable of coping with the problems of view variations, rotations about the view vectors, partial occlusions, and scale changes. Third, the favorable matching properties of very long vectors result in a high success rate during matching.

The use of a vector of filter responses as the representation medium for vision algorithms appears to hold much promise, as has been demonstrated by ourselves in this paper for object identification and localization, and by others (see Table 1, and [18, 16, 23, 36] in particular) for problems ranging from stereo matching to optic flow. We believe that this rich set of techniques could prove useful in building an integrated vision system with zip-codes as their basic low-level representation medium.

# References

[1] Edward H. Adelson and James Bergen. Spatiotemporal energy models for the perception of motion. *J. Opt. Soc. Am.*, 2(2):284–299, 1985.

[2] Nicola Ancona and Tomaso Poggio. Optic flow from 1d correlation: Application to a simple time-to-crash detector. AI Memo 1375, MIT AI Lab, October 1993.

[3] Dana H. Ballard and Rajesh P.N. Rao. Seeing behind occlusions. In *Proceedings of the Third European Conference on Computer Vision (ECCV), Stockholm, Sweden*, May 1994. To appear.

[4] Dana H. Ballard and Lambert E. Wixson. Object recognition using steerable filters at multiple scales. In *Proceedings of the IEEE Workshop on Qualitative Vision*, 1993.

[5] D.H. Ballard. Animate vision. *Artificial Intelligence*, 48:57–86, 1991.

[6] P.J. Beek. Perception-action coupling in the young infant: An appraisal of von hofsten's research programme. In *Motor Development in Children: Aspects of Coordination and Control*, pages 187–196. Dordrecht, Netherlands: Martinus-Nijhoff, 1986.

[7] Thomas O. Binford. Inferring surfaces from images. *Artificial Intelligence*, 17:205–244, 1981.

[8] D.J. Coombs and C.M. Brown. Real-time smooth pursuit tracking for a moving binocular head. In *IEEE Conference on Computer Vision and Pattern Recognition*, pages 23–38, June 1992.

[9] John Daugman. Biometric signature security system. January 1990.

[10] William T. Freeman and Edward H. Adelson. The design and use of steerable filters. *IEEE Transactions on Pattern Analysis and Machine Intelligence*, 13(9):891–906, September 1991.

[11] D. Heeger. Optic flow using spatiotemporal filters. *International Journal of Computer Vision*, 1(4):279–302, 1987.

[12] Berthold K.P. Horn. The Binford-Horn linefinder. AI Technical Report 285, MIT AI Lab, 1971.

[13] Berthold K.P. Horn and Brain G. Schunck. Determining optical flow. *Artificial Intelligence*, 17:185–203, 1981.

[14] Katsushi Ikeuchi and Berthold K.P. Horn. Numerical shape from shading and occluding boundaries. *Artificial Intelligence*, 17:141–184, 1981.

[15] Kunal Joarder and Daniel Raviv. A new method to calculate looming for autonomous obstacle avoidance. In *IEEE Conference on Computer Vision and Pattern Recognition*, 1994. To appear.

[16] David G. Jones and Jitendra Malik. A computational framework for determining stereo correspondence from a set of linear spatial filters. In *Proceedings of the Second European Conference on Computer Vision*, 1992.

[17] P. Kanerva. *Sparse Distributed Memory*. Bradford Books, Cambridge, MA, 1988.

[18] Michael Kass. Computing visual correspondence. In *Proceedings of the DARPA Image Understanding Workshop*, pages 54–60, 1983.

[19] H. Knuttson and G.H. Granlund. Texture analysis using two-dimensional quadrature filters. In *IEEE Workshop on Computer Architecture for Pattern Analysis and Image Database Management*, pages 206–213, 1983.

[20] M. Lades, J.C. Vorbruggen, J. Buhmann, J. Lange, C. von der Malsburg, R.P. Wurtz, and W. Konen. Distortion invariant object recognition in the dynamic link architecture. Technical report, Inst. fur Neuroinformatik, Ruhr-Universitat Bochum, August 1991.

[21] D.N. Lee. A theory of visual control of braking based on information about time-to-collision. *Perception*, 5:437–459, 1976.

[22] Jitendra Malik and Ziv Gigus. A model for curvilinear segregation. *Invest. Ophthalmol. Vis. Sci. (Supplement)*, 32(4):715, 1991.

[23] Jitendra Malik and Pietro Perona. A computational model of texture segmentation. In *IEEE Conference on Computer Vision and Pattern Recognition*, pages 326–332, June 1989.

[24] John H.R. Maunsell and William T. Newsome. Visual processing in monkey extrastriate cortex. *Annual Review of Neuroscience*, 10:363–401, 1987.

[25] Hiroshi Murase and Shree K. Nayar. Learning and recognition of 3d objects from appearance. In *IEEE Workshop on Qualitative Vision*, pages 39–50, 1993.

[26] K. Nakayama and S. Shimojo. Towards a neural understanding of visual surface representation. *Cold Spring Harbor Symp. on Quantitative Biology, Vol. 55, The Brain, edited by T. Sejnowski, E.R. Kandel, C.F. Stevens, and J.D. Watson*, 1990.

[27] Randal C. Nelson and John (Yiannis) Aloimonos. Using flow field divergence for obstacle avoidance in visual navigation. *IEEE Transactions on Pattern Analysis and Machine Intelligence*, 11(10):1102–1106, 1989.

[28] Pierre Parent and Steven Zucker. Trace inference, curvature consistency, and curve detection. *IEEE Transactions on Pattern Analysis and Machine Intelligence*, 11(8):823–839, 1989.

[29] Alex P. Pentland. Shape information from shading: A theory of human perception. In *Proceedings of the 2nd International Conference on Computer Vision, Tampa, FL, Dec. 3-8*, pages 404–412, 1988.

[30] Alex P. Pentland. From 2-D images to 3-D models. In K.N. Leibovic, editor, *Science of Vision*, pages 422–438. New York: Springer-Verlag, 1990.

[31] G. Sandini and V. Tagliasco. An anthropomorphic retina-like structure for scene analysis. *Computer Vision, Graphics, and Image Processing*, 14:365–372, 1980.

[32] Gilbert Strang. *Linear Algebra and its Applications (Third Edition)*. San Diego, CA: Harcourt Brace Jovanovich, 1988.

[33] Michael J. Swain. Color indexing. Technical Report 360, University of Rochester Computer Science Dept., 1990.

[34] Michael J. Swain and Dana H. Ballard. Color indexing. *International Journal of Computer Vision*, 7:11–32, November 1991.

[35] J.K. Tsotsos. The complexity of perceptual search tasks. In *Eleventh International Joint Conference on Artificial Intelligence*, August 1989.

[36] Joseph W. Weber and Jitendra Malik. Robust computation of optical flow in a multi-scale differential framework. Technical Report 709, Dept. of Electrical Engineering and Computer Science, University of California at Berkeley, November 1992.

[37] C.F.R. Weiman and G. Chaikin. Logarithmic spiral grids for image processing and display. *Computer Graphics and Image Processing*, 11:197–226, 1979.

[38] L. Wiskott and C. von der Malsburg. A neural system for the recognition of partially occluded objects in cluttered scenes. Technical report, Inst. fur Neuroinformatik, Ruhr-Universitat Bochum, 1992.

[39] A.L. Yarbus. *Eye Movements and Vision*. Plenum Press, 1967.

# IN-FORM-ATION

JÖRG D. BECKER

*ET / Physik, Universität der Bundeswehr München, D - 85577 Neubiberg*
*and*
*ICAS, Institute for Cybernetic Anthropology Starnberg, D - 82319 Starnberg*

## ABSTRACT

The fact that the word "form" is contained in "in-form-ation" must have some significance: at least it tells us that information is not only contained in symbolic representations. We take information as a measure for accuracy or success and discuss various definitions. Since information is always context dependent there are many of them.

In the second part we argue that forms have not only geometrical features but must be seen together with their proper functionals, like norms, information, and the like. The representation of forms as objects prevents us from confusions, helps us to ask the right questions, and sheds some light on the connection of representation and meaning.

Finally we present some ideas of pattern synthesis with evolutionary processes which can be seen properly as an in-form-ation of ideas. We discuss two mechanisms, namely synthesis by direct "bending" of forms, and synthesis by form generation through a dynamical process.

## 1. Information: from Hartley to pragmatic information

If we have a system with N states of which we want to locate one, according to Hartley the necessary information is given by

$$S = \text{ld } N \tag{1}$$

(Note that the dual logarithm ld measures information in bits, the decimal logarithm measures in digits, etc.) Thus we may state

Def. 1:     Information is the *precision* to which a given object is located in a given search space.

For later purposes we shall reformulate this definition in another way:

Def. 2:     Information is the *success* with which we can locate a given object in a given search space.

The innocent looking formula (1) is the foundation of information theory. To give a feeling for the power hidden in this concept we should like to give some examples:

i) Efficiency: Imagine that you have a system with n elements and N states. We may then define efficiency $\eta$ by $\eta := \partial S / \partial n$. This definition may be motivated e.g. from Laser theory (cf. Haken [8]) if you consider n as input and S as output; or from the considerations that led Caianiello [5] to the theory of Hierarchical Modular Systems.

ii) Chaos and causality: Chaotic systems are characterized by a loss of information which on the average is equal to the Lyapunov exponent $\lambda$ (cf. e. g. Schuster [14], $\langle \partial S / \partial t \rangle = - \lambda$. We are now in the position to define strong causality:

Def. 3:        A system is called *strongly causal* if and only if
               information is conserved, i. e. $\partial S / \partial t = 0$.

Note that chaotic systems are not causal in this sense. But this definition covers also systems where information is gained, $\partial S / \partial t > 0$, such as learning or evolutionary systems. Uncertainty relations, time horizons etc. apply to both cases.

iii) Fractal dimensions are also related to the localization of points in a search space.

iv) Shannon's information: Suppose that a we have some a priory knowledge about the relative frequencies $n_k/n = p_k$ with which a system can be found in a particular state k. Then

$$S_k = ld\ (n) - ld\ (n_k) = - ld\ (n_k / n) = - ld\ p_k \qquad (2)$$

is the information we gain if somebody tells us that the system is in the state k. The Shannon information is the statistical mean of the distribution $S_k$ of informations over the states. According to the rules of statistics, we have

$$\langle S \rangle = \sum_{k=1}^{N} p_k S_k = - \sum_{k=1}^{N} p_k\ ld\ p_k \qquad (3)$$

which is the Shannon formula. We use the notation $\langle S \rangle$ in order to remind ourselves that the Shannon information is a statistical average.

More general definitions of information based on the Shannon case can be found in Jumarie [11].

v) Kullback-Leibler and Jeffrey information, Fisher metric: For a continous parametrized distribution $\rho(z;c)$, z the system state, c the parameter, we may define the Kullback-Leibler information which is a measure for a change in information if the parameter c is changed from $c_0$ to $c_1$ (both z and c may be vectors):

$$S_{01} := \int \rho(z;c_1) \log (\rho(z;c_1) / \rho(z;c_0)) \, dz. \tag{4}$$

Haken [9] uses the Kullback-Leibler information in an attempt to define the information gain in a neural net. Let $f(z)$ describe the form of an input pattern to a neural net, and let $\tilde{f}(z)$ be the output pattern of the net; then we may set

$$\Delta S \, (f; \tilde{f}) := \int f(z) \log (f(z) / \tilde{f}(z)) \, dz. \tag{5}$$

For neural net purposes other than pattern recognition, however, this definition does not meet our intuitive understanding of information.

We may symmetrize the Kullback-Leibler information and get the Jeffrey information $J \, (c_0, c_1) := S_{01} + S_{10}$. An infinitesimal change in the control parameter c may be expressed by a metric tensor $g_{ik}$ (which usually is non-Euclidean),

$$J \, (c, c+dc) = g_{ik} \, dc^i \, dc^k \quad \text{with} \tag{6}$$

$$g_{ik} = \int \rho(z;c) \cdot \frac{\partial}{\partial c_i} \log \rho(z;c) \cdot \frac{\partial}{\partial c_k} \log \rho(z;c) \, dz. \tag{7}$$

$g_{ik}$ is called the Fisher metric. A discussion for possible implications of this approach may be found in Caianiello [6].

vi) Pragmatic information: The term *pragmatic information* has been coined by E. U. v. Weizsäcker [15]. We use the term in the same spirit but with a slightly different concept. Imagine you want to teach your robot to paint like Botticelli. If we call $\psi$ the Botticelli pattern, and $\phi$ the pattern that the robot has produced, we may define pragmatic information by $S = - \log \|\psi - \phi\|$ where $\| \cdot \|$ denotes a suitable norm on the space of patterns. Thus we are back to our original interpretations: information as a measure of *precision* or *success*. Thus, we may enlarge our definition of information:

Def. 4:        Information is a measure for the success
with which a certain goal is reached.

To conclude we may state that there are so many different definitions of information because it is always context-dependent, and even subjective.

## 2. Form and norm

Some prerequisites have to be met before we can even define information in a decent way.

First of all we should like to point out that with forms one can per-form operations which are not possible with other objects, like words or symbols: Forms may be superimposed; and forms allow for a continuous de-form-ation. This has to be seen in analogy with the relationship between quantum physics, where spatial states are described by forms, and classical physics where particles are described as points.

Superposition means that for two forms f and g also the sum f + g is a form. The + sign may have different meanings; if f and g are graphs or trajectories it simply refers to addition of the functions describing them, thus leading to the structure of a vector space; if they represent pixel patterns it refers to visual superposition of such patterns, thus leading to the structure of a semi-ring; etc.

Also continuity calls for a structure which may be a norm; in fact, continuity is the most important property of mathematical norms. It reads $\|f+g\| \leq \|f\| + \|g\|$ which means, e.g., that f is changed only little by superposition with g provided that g itself is small. (This will be important for the evolution of forms, as we shall argue below.) But again we have the choice between different norms, such as $L_1$, $L_2$, maximum norm, and the like. It is not arbitrary which mathematical structures we use to describe forms. (For more mathematics cf. Roman [12].)

i) Let $\rho$ (x) be a positive definite distribution (e. g., of masses, of pixels, or of frequencies). Its $L_1$ norm $m = \int \rho(x)\, dx$ is its total mass (or the number of events). We must require that m is finite. Hence, we may consider $\rho$ to be an element of $L_1$. Its normalized moments are given by

$$<x^n> \; = \; \frac{\int x^n\, \rho(x)\, dx}{\int \rho(x)\, dx} \tag{8}$$

For any function $\in L_1$, the Fourier transform $\tilde{\rho}$ (k) $:= \int \rho(x)\, e^{ikx}\, dx$ exists. **Note that the $L_1$ norm is not invariant under Fourier transformation.**

Even if the widths $\Delta x$ and $\Delta k$ may be defined by $(\Delta x)^2 := <x^2> - <x>^2$ and $(\Delta k)^2 := <k^2> - <k>^2$ we cannot expect the ordinary uncertainty relations to hold in this case.

ii) Let $A(t)$ be the (possibly complex) amplitude of a time signal. Its energy content is $E \sim \int A^*(t) A(t) \, dt$. This is the $L_2$ norm of $A$. Since we want energy to be finite we have to require that $A \in L_2$. Signals form the entire $L_2$ space because they can be superimposed arbitrarily. For an $L_2$ function, the Fourier transform $\tilde{A}(\omega) = \int A(t) \cdot e^{i\omega t} \, dt$ exists (almost everywhere). The $L_2$ norm is invariant under Fourier transformation, i.e. $\int A^*(t)A(t)dt = \int \tilde{A}^*(\omega)\tilde{A}(\omega)d\omega/2\pi$. We may define the moments,

$$<t^n> := \frac{\int A^*(t) \, t^n \, A(t) \, dt}{\int A^*(t) \, A(t) \, dt} \tag{9}$$

$$<\omega^n> := \frac{\int \tilde{A}^*(\omega) \, \omega^n \, \tilde{A}(\omega) \, d\omega/2\pi}{\int \tilde{A}^*(\omega) \, \tilde{A}(\omega) \, d\omega/2\pi} \equiv \frac{(-i)^n \int A^*(t) \, (d/dt)^n \, A(t) \, dt}{\int A^*(t) \, A(t) \, dt} \tag{10}$$

The difference between the $L_1$ and $L_2$ case may be expressed mathematically. Let $\rho = A^*A$. Then $\int \rho'' = \int (A^*A)'' = \int ( A^{*''} A + 2 A^{*'} A' + A^* A'' )$ yields $\Delta k$ in the $L_1$ case, whereas the $L_2$ case involves only $<A, K^2 A> \sim \int A^* A''$.

**Only for $L_2$ case** the following uncertainty relations hold (see e.g. Heisenberg [10]): $\Delta t \, \Delta \omega \geq 1/2$ (or $\Delta x \, \Delta k \geq 1/2$ for forms living in configuration space). If we have a form living in $L_2$ we may utilize the uncertainty relation to give one definition of the information content of a form. Again this relates to the concept of localization since $\Delta x$ is essentially the size of the form in search space and $\delta x := 1/\Delta k$ is the necessary granularity to locate a detailed feature of the form (i. e. the required precision):

$$S = \log (\Delta x \, \Delta k) = \log \Delta x + \log \Delta k = \log \Delta x - \log \delta x = \log (\Delta x/\delta x). \tag{11}$$

We have argued that a form may be seen as an object, consisting of
☐ a data structure (a vector, a function or the like) which describes the visual aspects of the form,
☐ a list of properties (or object-owned methods to compute them), like its norm, its width, its uncertainty product $\Delta x \, \Delta k$, its pragmatic information in a given context etc.

We see that the formation of an object from a geometrical data structure is not unique. One and the same function may form different objects, according to the choice of norm, of width, of pragmatic information, etc. This choice has a physical significance.

## 3. Evolution of forms

Recently we have investigated the synthesis of forms with the help of evolutionary strategies and genetic algorithms. The task is to find a form which meets certain requirements. In particular, we have studied the following cases:

i) Find a form that solves a system of nonlinear equations (such as the coupled equations of Poisson and Schrödinger which describe electrons in a quantum well, or the node potential analysis of nonlinear circuits; see Becker [1] and Gerlach [7]). The problem can formally be written as $P(F) = 0$ where F is the form to be determined, and P is some operator. If we don't know F we can have a guess G. In general, $P(G) \neq 0$; instead, $P(G) = D$, where D is called the discrepancy.

The pragmatic information of a guess G may be defined as $S := -\log \|D\|$ where $\|\cdot\|$ is a suitable norm on the space of forms. The mathematical properties of the norm guarantee (among other properties) continuity and additivity of S. Then we perform the evolutionary algorithm: start with a population of guesses - now called genes -, select the best ones with respect to their pragmatic information, perform genetic operations, like recombination and mutation, together with propagation to fill up the population again. (A mutation may be written $G \rightarrow G + \delta G$). Repeat the process until the pragmatic information ($\equiv$ localization of a form in a given space of forms) is satisfactory.

Two requirements are important for the success of the game: first, the continuity property of the norm $\|D\|$ is vital for learning and evolution (you can only learn if evaluation is continuous, at least piecewise); second, the mutations must be adequate for the problem. For instance, if F is supposed to be smooth then $\delta G$ should behave well, i. e. its own information content $\log(\Delta x \, \Delta k)$ should be small. Candidates for $\delta G$ are forms like Gaussian $*$ sine or Gaussian $*$ polynomial. In the case of discontinuous forms F other choices may be better, such as wavelets (cf. Bertoluzza [4]).

Note that here we do evolution on the form itself, the form represents both genotype and phenotype simultaneously. In such cases we speak of an evolutionary strategy.

In fig. 1 we give two examples of mutation of the Gabor type, i. e. $\delta G$ is of the form Gaussian $*$ sine. The parameters (width and centre of the Gaussian, frequency and phase of the sine, amplitude) are choosen at random from some reasaonable set. It is like asking some children to bend pieces of wire.

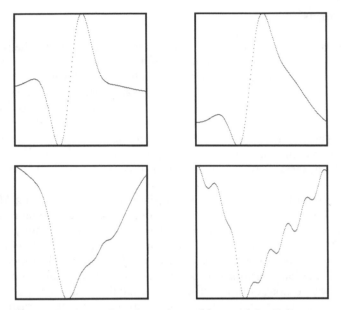

Fig. 1: Two examples of mutations of forms of the Gabor type

ii) Imagine a nonlinear (possibly chaotic) dynamical process which generates a pattern, such as

$$x_{n+1} = f_x (x_n, y_n, c_x) \; ; \qquad y_{n+1} = fy (x_n, y_n, cy) \qquad (12)$$

$x_n$ and $y_n$ are interpreted as points in the plane which form the pattern; $c_x$ and $c_y$ are sets of control parameters. If we change the control parameters the pattern may turn from a Botticelli into a Picasso.

Let us suppose that the task is to find a setting for the control parameters such that the pattern reproduces a given one (e. g. a portrait by Botticelli). Here we distinguish between the genotype, represented by the set of control parameters on which the evolutionary operations act, and the phenotype, represented by the pattern generated from this set of control parameters on which evaluation and selection act. In such cases we speak of genetic algorithms. Let us add that in dynamical pattern generation there are usually many sets of control parameters leading to the same pattern (Becker [3]).

A similar approach could be based on the skeleton description of forms (cf. Sanniti di Baja and Thiel [13]) where the centres and radii of the circles could be viewed as genes.

To give a concrete example, we use the following set of nonlinear difference equations,

$$\left.\begin{array}{l} x_{n+1} := x_n + (a_0 + a_1 x_n + a_2 y_n + a_3 x_n{}^2 + a_4 y_n{}^2 + a_5 x_n y_n) \\[2mm] y_{n+1} := y_n + (b_0 + b_1 y_n + b_2 x_n + b_3 y_n{}^2 + b_4 x_n{}^2 + b_5 x_n y_n) \end{array}\right\} \quad (13)$$

The pairs $\{x_n, y_n\}$ are interpreted as points in the plane, the time series generated by (13) is interpreted as a pattern in the plane, and the coefficients $a_k$, $b_k$ are control parameters which are subject to mutation. Lines, circles, spirals, and strange attractors (such as the Hénon attractor) may easily be generated. Most patterns generated at random are "uninteresting", but there is still a large number of "interesting" patterns. Evolution prefers "interesting" patterns, as we have seen in many simulations. Another interesting question is how the system (13) can cope with patterns which are not contained in the set of patterns which the system (13) can produce. As an example, we consider the letter "A" which due to the composite nature of its form cannot be generated in a single "stroke".

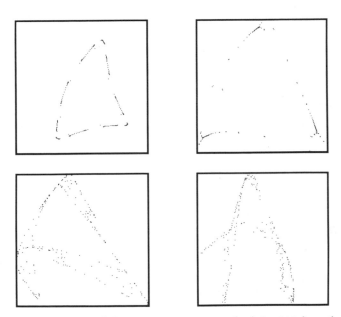

Fig. 2: Some "artistic" attempts to generate the letter "A" from the nonlinear dynamical series (13)

Let us conclude with some remarks:

☐ Evolutionary methods allow for complicated evaluation functions including constraints, additional conditions, and the like.

☐ If the evaluation function itself belongs to an $L_2$ space then its uncertainty product $\Delta x \cdot \Delta k$ should be a measure of complexity for the problem. It should thus provide an upper bound for the learning speed.

☐ Evolutionary methods provide fast solutions for problems with an evaluation function which is neither too simple (Gaussian) nor too complicated (random).

☐ Evolution is much better than negentropy production (cf. Becker [2]).

☐ More elaborate methods for synthesis of patterns are under consideration.

## 4. References

[1] J. Becker, "Learning as gain of information", in G. Dalenoort (Ed.), *The paradigm of self-organization II*, Gordon & Breach 1993

[2] J. Becker, "Entropy and evolution", in H. Atmanspacher (Ed.), *Inside and outside*, Plenum 1993

[3] J. Becker, "On the creativity of evolutionary processes", to be published in: J. Becker, I. Eisele, F. Mündemann (Eds.), *WOPPLOT 92*. Springer

[4] S. Bertoluzza, "Some error estimates for wavelet expansions", in *Math. Models and Methods in Appl. Sciences* **2**, 489-506, 1992

[5] E. R. Caianiello, "Some remarks on organization and structure", in *Biol. Cybernetics* **26**, 151, 1977

[6] E. R. Caianiello, "Systems and uncertainty", in J. Becker, I. Eisele, F. Mündemann (Eds.), *Parallelism, Learning, Evolution*, Springer 1991

[7] H. Gerlach, "The solution of nonlinear systems of equations by evolutionary strategies", to be published in: J. Becker, I. Eisele, F. Mündemann (Eds.), *WOPPLOT 92*, Springer

[8] H. Haken, *Synergetics*, Springer, 1978

[9] H. Haken, *Information and self-organization*, Springer, 1988

[10] W. Heisenberg, *Physikalische Prinzipien der Quantenphysik*. Bibliographisches Institut Mannheim, 1958

[11] G. Jumarie, *Relative information*, Springer, 1990

[12] P. Roman, *Some modern mathematics for physicists and other outsiders*, vol II., Pergamon, 1975

[13] G. Sanniti di Baja, E. Thiel, "A multiresolution shape description algorithm", in D. Chetverikov, W. Kropatsch (Eds.), *Computer analysis of images and patterns*, Springer, 1993

[14] H. Schuster, *Deterministic chaos*, VCH Verlagsgesellschaft, 1988

[15] E. U. v. Weizsäcker, *Offene Systeme I: Beiträge zur Zeitstruktur von Information, Entropie und Evolution*, pp. 82-113, Klett, 1985

# MULTIRESOLUTION REPRESENTATION OF VOLUME DATA THROUGH HIERARCHICAL SIMPLICIAL COMPLEXES

MICHELA BERTOLOTTO    LEILA DE FLORIANI

*Department of Computer and Information Sciences, University of Genova,*
*Viale Benedetto XV, 3 - 16132 Genova, Italy*

ELISABETTA BRUZZONE

*Elsag Bailey, Research and Development,*
*Via Puccini, 2 - 16154 Genova, Italy*

and

ENRICO PUPPO

*Institute for the Applied Mathematics - C.N.R.*
*Via De Marini, 6 (Torre di Francia) - 16149 Genova, Italy*

## ABSTRACT

We propose a new hierarchical model for multiresolution representation of a scalar field in the three-dimensional space, which finds applications in volume data visualization. The model is based on a hierarchy of three-dimensional simplicial complexes. We present an algorithm for building an approximated model, based on a sequence of tolerance values, as well as an algorithm for extracting isosurfaces from such model at any predefined level of accuracy.

## 1. Introduction

Several important applications in biomedical engineering, electromagnetics, fluidodynamics, chemistry, etc. need reconstructing, analyzing, and visualizing scalar fields. Examples are medical images from CT and MR, data from finite element analysis of electromagnetic systems, aircrafts, cars, and mechanical parts, simulations of molecular structures.

*Volume data* give a discrete description of a scalar field, usually in the form of a set of points located in space, with a field value attached to each point. In order to support data visualization and analysis, a finite, continuous representation of the scalar field over the domain spanned by volume data must be reconstructed. Depending on the sampling process, volume data can be either unstructured, or implicitly structured into regular or deformed grids.

Unstructured data are irregularly distributed, and are usually quite sparse; thus, building a structure on them is a non-trivial task. On the other hand, structured data are usually quite dense: therefore, obtaining a compact representation involves extracting relevant information, while dropping unnecessary data. Since the distribution of relevant data depends on the underlying function, adaptive techniques are often used for data compaction, that produce irregular structures. In any case, when the dataset is large, it can be useful to build approximations of the hypersurface represented by the scalar field at different levels of accuracy in order to allow multiresolution analysis as well as focusing on regions of interest.

A tetrahedral mesh connecting the data points is a structure for the representation of irregular volume data, that is suitable for efficient isosurface construction, and has also been successfully employed recently for direct volume rendering [3,6]. Among all possible tetrahedral meshes, the Delaunay tetrahedralization offers good properties, such as the relative equiangularity of its cells (that is important for numerical interpolation), and the visibility ordering of cells (that is required by certain visualization techniques) [5].

The main contribution of this paper is in the definition of a new hierarchical model for representing hypersurfaces in 3D space, that is based on a hierarchy of Delaunay simplicial complexes, and provides a multiresolution description of a hypersurface. Our model is adaptive, it supports explicit multiresolution based on a decreasing sequence of tolerance values, it can be built from both regularly and irregularly distributed data, and it allows focusing on local areas of interest. Moreover, Delaunay hierarchical simplicial complexes in any dimension can be ordered back to front at any level of precision and with respect to any viewpoint [1].

We present an algorithm for building a hierarchical hypersurface model approximating volume data at different levels of detail, which makes use of a top-down refinement technique that adds points on the boundary and/or inside each tetrahedron. Furthermore, we propose an algorithm for extracting isosurfaces from the hierarchical model at any predefined level of accuracy. Notice that the possibility to extract information directly from the hierarchical model allows producing sequences of isosurfaces at increasingly finer levels of resolution.

Our model and algorithms are mainly intended for applications to multiresolution visualization of volume data. However, isosurfaces are also an useful tool for data analysis. For instance, since different values are associated with different tissues in a CT image, isosurfaces at certain levels will correspond to meaningful contours in the image (e.g., skin, bone, muscle, tumor). The combined use of such properties and of the hierarchical data organization in our structure could help in both interactive and automatic data analysis.

## 2. Hierarchical Tetrahedralizations

A $d$-simplex is the convex linear combination of $d + 1$ affinely independent points in $\mathbb{E}^n$, with $d \leq n$. Thus, a 0-simplex is a vertex, a 1-simplex a segment, a 2-simplex a triangle, etc. Any $s$-simplex $f$, with $0 \leq s \leq d$, which is generated by a subset of $s + 1$ vertices of $\sigma$, is called an $s$-face of $\sigma$. If $s < d$, then $f$ is a *proper face* of $\sigma$.

A collection $\Sigma$ of simplices is called a *d-simplicial complex* (or, simply, a *d-complex*) in $\mathbb{E}^n$ when the following conditions hold:

- for each simplex $\sigma \in \Sigma$, all the faces of $\sigma$ belong to $\Sigma$;

- for each pair of simplices $\sigma, \tau \in \Sigma$, either $\sigma \cap \tau = \emptyset$ or $\sigma \cap \tau$ is a proper face of both $\sigma$ and $\tau$;

- $d$ is the maximum of the orders of the simplices belonging to $\Sigma$ ($d$ is called the *order* of $\Sigma$).

The union of all $s$-simplices of $\Sigma$, with $0 \leq s \leq d$, regarded as point sets, is called the *domain* of $\Sigma$, and denoted $D(\Sigma)$; any proper face of a simplex of $\Sigma$ is called a *boundary face* if it belongs to the boundary of $D(\Sigma)$, an *internal face* otherwise.

A $d$-complex $\Sigma$ is *regular* if and only if for each $s$-simplex $\sigma$, with $s < d$, there exists a $d$-simplex $\sigma'$ such that $\sigma$ is a proper face of $\sigma'$. Notice that a regular $d$-complex $\Sigma$ is uniquely characterized by the collection of its $d$-simplices, since all other $s$-simplices, for $s < d$, can be obtained as linear convex combination of vertices of $d$-simplices. Here, we consider only regular 3-simplicial complexes (i.e., tetrahedralizations) and regular 2-simplicial complexes (i.e., triangulations) whose domains are connected sets in $\mathbb{E}^3$.

A hierarchical 3-simplicial complex is defined by applying the concept of recursive refinement to a tetrahedralization. Given a tetrahedralization $\Sigma$, each tetrahedron $\sigma$ of $\Sigma$ can be refined into a tetrahedralization $\Sigma_\sigma$, whose domain covers $\sigma$, by adding new vertices either inside $\sigma$ or on its faces. The recursive application of the refinement process results in a hierarchy of tetrahedralizations.

Formally, let $\mathcal{T} = \{\Sigma_0, \ldots, \Sigma_h\}$ be a collection of tetrahedralizations such that $\forall j = 0, \ldots, h$, $T_j$ is the set of tetrahedra of $\Sigma_j$, with $\#T_j > 1$, and $\forall j > 0$, there exists exactly one $\sigma_j \in T_i$, for some $i < j$, such that $\sigma_j \equiv D(\Sigma_j)$. A *hierarchical 3-simplicial complex* is described by a triple $\mathcal{H} = (\mathcal{T}, \mathcal{E}, \ell)$, where

$$\mathcal{E} = \{(\Sigma_i, \Sigma_j) \mid \Sigma_i, \Sigma_j \in \mathcal{T}, \exists \sigma_j \in T_i, \ \sigma_j \equiv D(\Sigma_j)\}, \text{ and}$$

$$\ell : \mathcal{E} \longrightarrow \cup_{i=0}^h T_i \text{ is such that } \ell(\Sigma_i, \Sigma_j) = \sigma_j \Leftrightarrow \sigma_j \in T_i \text{ and } \sigma_j \equiv D(\Sigma_j).$$

For each $(\Sigma_i, \Sigma_j) \in \mathcal{E}$, $\ell(\Sigma_i, \Sigma_j)$ is called the *label* of $(\Sigma_i, \Sigma_j)$, and the tetrahedra in $\ell(\mathcal{E})$ are called *macrotetrahedra*, while the remaining ones are called *simple* tetrahedra. $\mathcal{H}$ can be regarded as a tree with labeled arcs, having $\mathcal{T}$ as its set of nodes.

Since any non-boundary face $t$ is shared by exactly two adjacent tetrahedra, we investigate the effect on $\mathcal{H}$ of refining face $t$. To this aim, we introduce the following definitions: two tetrahedralizations $\Sigma_i, \Sigma_j \in \mathcal{T}$ are said to be *adjacent* along a face $t$ if their domains intersect only along $t$; $\Sigma_i$ and $\Sigma_j$ are said to be *matching* along $t$ if they are adjacent along $t$ and if the triangulations induced on $t$ by $\Sigma_i$ and $\Sigma_j$ are coincident.

Our purpose is to use a hierarchy $\mathcal{H}$ as an approximating model of a scalar field (see Section 3); thus, any two adjacent tetrahedra must always be refined by inserting the same vertices on their common face $t$, and by triangulating $t$ in the same way, to preserve the continuity of the approximation. To this aim, we introduce the following rule, that we call *matching rule*:

(i) every pair $\Sigma_q$ and $\Sigma_k$ of tetrahedralizations belonging to $\mathcal{T}$, adjacent along a face $t$, with $V_q$ and $V_k$ sets of vertices of $\Sigma_q$ and $\Sigma_k$, respectively, must satisfy one of the following conditions:

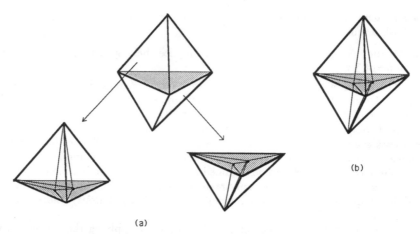

(b)

(a)

Figure 1: (a) An example of a hierarchical matching tetrahedralization. (b) Expanded tetrahedralization associated with the HMT in (a).

- $\Sigma_q$ and $\Sigma_k$ are matching along $t$;
- $t \cap V_q \subset t \cap V_k$ and there exists a descendant of $\Sigma_q$ which is matching with $\Sigma_k$ along $t$;
- $t \cap V_k \subset t \cap V_q$ and there exists a descendant of $\Sigma_k$ which is matching with $\Sigma_q$ along $t$;

(ii) for every $\sigma_j$ simple tetrahedron of $\Sigma_i \in \mathcal{T}$, the faces of $\sigma_j$ are never refined further in the hierarchy.

The matching rule ensures that any face of a tetrahedralization $\Sigma_i$ of $\mathcal{T}$ is always refined consistently in the subtree rooted at $\Sigma_i$ (see Figure 1(a) for an example). We call a hierarchical tetrahedralization satisfying the matching rule a *Hierarchical Matching Tetrahedralization (HMT)*.

By applying a recursive expansion process that replaces each macrotetrahedron $\sigma$ in an HMT $\mathcal{H}$ with the tetrahedralization refining it, we obtain a tessellation $\mathcal{H}_E$ that covers $D(\Sigma_0)$ and is composed of all simple tetrahedra of $\mathcal{H}$; $\mathcal{H}_E$ is called the *expanded tetrahedralization* associated with $\mathcal{H}$ (see Figure 1(b)).

We will consider a special class of HMTs, i.e., those based on Delaunay tetrahedralizations. A Delaunay 3-complex $\Sigma$ of a set of points $V \in \mathbb{E}^3$ is a regular, convex, 2-connected tetrahedralization of $V$ such that the circumsphere of any tetrahedron $\sigma \in \Sigma$ does not contain any point of $V$ inside. Such complexes are important because, if the components of a hierarchical tetrahedralization are all Delaunay tetrahedralizations, the matching rule is satisfied if and only if, for each pair of tetrahedra $\sigma_i$ and $\sigma_j$ adjacent along a face $t$, the same vertices are inserted on $t$ in the refinement of $\sigma_i$ and $\sigma_j$.

An HMT $\mathcal{H} = (\mathcal{T}, \mathcal{E}, \ell)$ is encoded in a data structure combining individual data structures representing the tetrahedralizations of $\mathcal{T}$, information describing the hierarchy links defined by $\mathcal{E}$, and information needed to maintain matching between adjacent tetrahedralizations [2].

## 3. Hierarchical Hypersurface Model

We consider a domain $\Omega \subseteq \mathbb{R}^3$, and a function $f : \Omega \to \mathbb{R}$ which describes a hypersurface over $\Omega$. Let $S = \{s_1, \ldots, s_n\}$ be a finite subset of $\Omega$ at which $f$ is known. We call the pair $\mathcal{M}_S = (S, f|_S)$ a *sampled model* (of $f$). An approximation of $\mathcal{M}_S$ can be obtained by tesselating $\Omega$ into simplices and by describing the hypersurface through a function over each such simplex. To this aim, we define a *tetrahedral model* as a pair $\phi = (\Sigma, F)$, where $F = \{f_1, f_2, \ldots, f_m\}$, with $m$ number of simplices of $\Sigma$, such that each function $f_i$ is defined over a simplex $\sigma_i$ of $\Sigma$. If $f$ represents a continuous function, all $f_i$'s will coincide on the common faces of adjacent simplices.

Given a sampled model $\mathcal{M}_S$ and a tetrahedral model $\phi = (\Sigma, F)$, the error in approximating $\mathcal{M}_S$ with $\phi = (\Sigma, F)$ is measured by defining an *error function* $E$ as follows: for each 3-simplex $\sigma_i \in \Sigma$, $E(\sigma_i) = max_{\sigma_i \cap S}|f - f_i|$. Then, $E(\Sigma) = max_{i=1}^m E(\sigma_i)$. A tetrahedral model $\phi = (\Sigma, F)$ is thus said to *approximate a sampled model* $\mathcal{M}_S$ *at level* $\varepsilon$ *of accuracy* if and only if $E(\Sigma) \leq \varepsilon$. In the following, if no ambiguity arises, we will use $\Sigma$ and $\phi$ interchangeably. In this paper, we consider only tetrahedral models $\phi = (\Sigma, F)$ approximating sampled models $\mathcal{M}_S$ whose vertex set $V$ is always a subset of $S$. Moreover, all functions of $F$ will be linear interpolants of $f$ at the vertices of $V$: thus, all such functions are uniquely defined by the values of $f$ on $V$, that we denote $f(V)$.

The concepts of tetrahedral model and of hierarchical matching tetrahedralization are combined together in order to define a hierarchical hypersurface model. Let $\mathcal{H} = (\mathcal{T}, \mathcal{E}, \ell)$ be an HMT such that $\mathcal{T} = \{\Sigma_0, \Sigma_1, \ldots, \Sigma_h\}$ and let $f : \Omega \longrightarrow \mathbb{R}$ be a three-dimensional scalar field defined over a compact connected set $\Omega \subset \mathbb{E}^3$. We assume that $f$ is sampled at a finite set of points $S$ of $\mathbb{E}^3$ and that $V \subseteq S$ is the set of vertices of the expanded tetrahedralization associated with $\mathcal{H}$. For each $\Sigma_i \in \mathcal{T}$, let $\phi_i = (\Sigma_i, F_i)$ be the tetrahedral model approximating $f$ over $D(\Sigma_i)$. If $\mathcal{F} = \{F_0, F_1, \ldots, F_h\}$, then $\mathcal{H}_\phi = (\mathcal{H}, \mathcal{F})$ is called a *hierarchical (hypersurface) model* of $f$. Furthermore, a *Delaunay hierarchical (hypersurface) model* is a hierarchical model $\mathcal{H}_\phi = (\mathcal{H}, \mathcal{F})$ such that $\mathcal{H}$ is composed of Delaunay tetrahedralizations. In the following, if no ambiguity arises, we will refer to $\mathcal{H}$ instead of $\mathcal{H}_\phi$.

We are interested in building a hierarchical model of $f$ at different levels of resolution by extracting its vertices from the set of sampled points $S$. Given a descreasing sequence of positive real values $\{\varepsilon_0, \varepsilon_1, \ldots, \varepsilon_k\}$, called *tolerances*, the hierarchical hypersurface model $\mathcal{H}$ defined by such a sequence has the following structure:

- if $\Sigma_0$ is the root of $\mathcal{H}$, then $E(\Sigma_0) \leq \varepsilon_0$

- if $\Sigma_j \in \mathcal{T}$ and $\varepsilon_{i+1} < E(\Sigma_j) \leq \varepsilon_i$, then for each $p$ such that $\Sigma_p$ is child of $\Sigma_j$, $E(\Sigma_p) \leq \varepsilon_{i+1}$

- for each $r$ such that $\Sigma_r$ is a leaf node of $\mathcal{H}$, then $E(\Sigma_r) \leq \varepsilon_k$

A hierarchical model $\mathcal{H}$ for $f$ is built according to a top-down strategy: first, an initial tetrahedralization $\Sigma_0$ approximating $f$ over the whole domain at level $\varepsilon_0$ of accuracy is computed. Then, for all tetrahedra of $\Sigma_0$ that do not satisfy precision $\varepsilon_1$, the tetrahedralizations refining them are computed in such a way that they satisfy $\varepsilon_1$. Such refinement process is performed at any generic step to produce the tetrahedralizations at level $\varepsilon_{i+1}$ of accuracy from those at level $\varepsilon_i$ and is repeated until the maximum precision $\varepsilon_k$ is reached.

Our algorithm is based on a selection criterion, called the *Delaunay selector*, that refines an existing Delaunay complex by inserting at each iteration the point that causes the maximum error in the approximation and updating the complex until the required precision is met (see [2] for more details). In the context of the hierarchical model, the Delaunay selector is used to compute the refinement of macrotetrahedra.

While all tetrahedra of a tetrahedralization $\Sigma$ are refined independently, some vertices introduced when refining a tetrahedron $\sigma$ could lie on its faces and edges. Matching between two tetrahedralizations adjacent along a face is guaranteed if the triangulations on the shared face are the same in both tetrahedralizations; in the case of tetrahedralizations sharing an edge, the common edge must be subdivided in the same way in all of them (i.e., the same vertices must be inserted on such edge). Thus, the refinement procedure must select points on a shared entity independently of the points inserted inside the entities sharing it. In order to achieve such result, we perform refinement through the following steps:

*Edge refinement*: for each edge $e$ of $\Sigma$ that needs to be refined, $e$ is subdivided by adding new points on it; thus, a chain $\Sigma_e$ of segments is obtained that approximates the field $f$ along $e$ at level $\varepsilon_i$ of accuracy;

*Triangle refinement*: for each triangle $t$ of $\Sigma$ that needs to be refined,

- a Delaunay triangulation $\Sigma_t$ of the set $V_t$, formed by the vertices of $t$ plus the points added on its edges, is computed;

- a selection criterion is applied to refine triangulation $\Sigma_t$ in such a way that the resulting Delaunay triangulation approximates $f$ on $t$ at level $\varepsilon_i$ of accuracy;

*Tetrahedron refinement*: for each tetrahedron $\sigma$ of $\Sigma$ that needs to be refined,

- a Delaunay tetrahedralization $\Sigma_\sigma$ of the set $V_\sigma$, formed by the vertices of $\sigma$ plus the points added on its faces, is computed;

- a selection criterion is applied to refine tetrahedralization $\Sigma_\sigma$ in such a way that the resulting Delaunay tetrahedralization approximates $f$ on $\sigma$ at level $\varepsilon_i$ of accuracy.

The above refinement technique guarantees that the matching rule is always satisfied, i.e., a hierarchical matching tetrahedralization is produced.

## 4. Isosurface Extraction from a Hierarchical Hypersurface Model

In this Section, we define the concepts of isosurface in a tetrahedral model and in a hierarchical model, and we present an algorithm for computing isosurfaces at a given level of accuracy $\varepsilon_i$, directly from the hierarchical model $\mathcal{H}$.

Let $f : \Omega \longrightarrow \mathbb{R}$ be a continuous scalar field on a compact and connected domain $\Omega \subseteq \mathbb{E}^3$; let $q$ be a real positive value. Let $\mathcal{M}_S$ be a sampled model for $f$ and let $\phi = (\Sigma, F)$ be a tetrahedral model approximating $\mathcal{M}_S$ such that the set $V$ of vertices of $\Sigma$ is a subset of $S$ and the functions in $F$ are linear interpolants of $f$ on $V$. For each tetrahedron $\sigma_j$ in $\Sigma$, let $f_j$ be the linear function approximating $f$ over $\sigma_j$. Inside each tetrahedron $\sigma_j$ of $\Sigma$, the scalar field is approximated by a tetrahedral patch in the four-dimensional space, corresponding to the graph of function $f_j$.

We define $S^{f_j, q} = \{p \in \sigma_j \mid f_j(p) = q\}$ as the *set of isosurfaces of $\sigma_j$ at level $q$*. If $S^{f_j, q}$ is non-empty, then it can either be a triangle or a quadrilateral (that can be in turn represented by two adjacent triangles), since $f_j$ is a linear function and the set $S^{f_j, q}$ is computed by intersecting the hyperplane $w = q$ with the tetrahedral patch associated with $\sigma_j$. We call $S^{\Sigma, q} = \cup_{\sigma_j \in \Sigma} S^{f_j, q}$ the *set of isosurfaces of $\Sigma$ at level $q$*. $S^{\Sigma, q}$ is a set of triangulations in $\mathbb{E}^3$, because, for each pair of tetrahedra $\sigma$ and $\sigma'$ of $\Sigma$ sharing a face $t$, the isosurface patches crossing $\sigma$ and $\sigma'$ through $t$ (if any) will match on $t$. The connected components $S_1^{\Sigma, q}, \ldots, S_p^{\Sigma, q}$ of $S^{\Sigma, q}$ can be either closed or open surfaces in the 3D space. The boundary of each open component is a closed chain of straight-line segments on the boundary of $D(\Sigma)$.

If we consider a hierarchical hypersurface model $\mathcal{H}$ for the scalar field $f$ defined by the sequence $\{\varepsilon_0, \ldots, \varepsilon_k\}$, the set of isosurfaces at level $q$ of $\mathcal{H}$ with precision $\varepsilon_i$ is the set of isosurfaces at level $q$ of the tetrahedral model of $f$ corresponding to the expansion of the subtree of $\mathcal{H}$ defined by the sequence $\{\varepsilon_0, \ldots, \varepsilon_i\}$.

In the following, we first describe how to extract isosurfaces from a tetrahedral model $\Sigma$, and next we generalize such an algorithm to extract isosurfaces at precision $\varepsilon_i$ from a hierarchical model $\mathcal{H}$. For the sake of simplicity, we assume that only one isosurface at level $q$ is considered at a time, although the algorithm could be easily extended in order to handle several levels.

Our method follows the technique proposed in [4]. To determine how an isosurface intersects a tetrahedron, its four vertices are marked with a Boolean label. A label equal to one is assigned to a vertex $v$ if the field value of $v$ exceeds (or is equal to) the value $q$ of the isosurface to be constructed. These vertices are inside (or on) the surface. Vertices with field values below the surface receive a label equal to zero and are outside the surface. The isosurface intersects those edges where one vertex is outside the isosurface (labeled one) and the other one is inside it (labeled zero).

After computing the various portions of the isosurface inside each tetrahedron $\sigma$ of $\Sigma$, we need a further step to reconstruct the complete isosurface on $\Sigma$ by merging the various pieces together. All internal faces of $\Sigma$ are considered in sequence, and, for each internal face $t$ crossing the isosurface, the two isosurface patches incident into $t$ from opposite sides are connected, by identifying the two corresponding edges which have been associated with $t$ during the extraction of the isosurface from the two tetrahedra sharing $t$.

Thus, given a tetrahedralization $\Sigma$ and a real positive value $q$, the algorithm for extracting isosurfaces from $\Sigma$ at level $q$ returns the set of triangulations $S_1^{\Sigma,q}, \ldots, S_k^{\Sigma,q}$ corresponding to the connected components of the isosurface $S^{\Sigma,q}$ at level $q$ of $\Sigma$.

If $D(\Sigma)$ is a tetrahedral volume, we can also encode information about the boundary of isosurfaces of $S^{\Sigma,q}$ as follows: we store four sequences of straight-line segments, one for each face of $D(\Sigma)$. Each segment is a boundary edge of an open component of $S^{\Sigma,q}$; each sequence is sorted according to the order of the corresponding list of boundary faces in the data structure encoding $\Sigma$. Boundary information will be used in the algorithm for the hierarchical case to merge isosurfaces extracted through the expansions of adjacent tetrahedra.

The algorithm for extracting isosurfaces at a given level of accuracy $\varepsilon_i$ (where $\varepsilon_i \in \{\varepsilon_0, \ldots, \varepsilon_k\}$) from a hierarchical model $\mathcal{H}$ is an extension of the algorithm outlined above, and works directly on the hierarchical model. The approach we follow is recursive. At a given recursion step, a tetrahedralization $\Sigma$ is considered, and is processed in three steps:

1. *Recursive extraction of isosurfaces from tetrahedra*: for each tetrahedron $\sigma$ of $\Sigma$, if $E(\sigma) \leq \varepsilon_i$, the isosurface inside $\sigma$ is computed and a set $S^{\sigma,q}$, composed of one or two triangles (composing a quadrilateral) contained inside $\sigma$, is returned together with four sets of edges, each containing at most one element. If $E(\sigma) > \varepsilon_i$, the procedure is recursively activated on the tetrahedralization expanding $\sigma$, and the following information is returned:

   - the set $S^{\sigma,q}$ of isosurfaces contained inside the tetrahedral volume corresponding to $\sigma$;
   - for each triangular face $t$ of $\sigma$, a sequence of segments belonging to the boundaries of the isosurfaces crossing $t$; each sequence is sorted as described before.

   Note that, for each internal face $t$ of $\Sigma$, two sequences of segments, relative to tetrahedra $\sigma_0$ and $\sigma_1$ sharing $t$, are computed. The refinements of $\sigma_0$ and $\sigma_1$ considered for extracting the isosurfaces will belong both to level $\varepsilon_i$. Thus, the matching rule guarantees that such refinements will match along $t$. Matching of triangulations refining $t$ guarantees that also the two sequences of segments associated with $t$ will be matching (see Figure 2).

2. *Isosurface merging*: for each internal face $t$, the isosurfaces crossing $t$ are merged by identifying corresponding segments bounding triangular patches that are incident into $t$ from opposite sides (i.e., from the tetrahedra adjacent along $t$). This "sewing" operation is performed sequentially on all internal faces of the tetrahedralization by parallel scanning the two lists of edges attached to

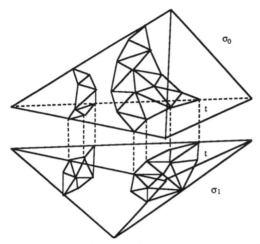

Figure 2: Merging the two sequences of segments associated with face $t$.

such faces and by identifying the corresponding edges (i.e., setting adjacencies between adjacent triangles of the isosurface).

3. *Boundary reconstruction*: boundary faces of $\Sigma$ are scanned, and, for every face $t$, the sequence of segments, attached to $t$, is added to the list of segments relative to the face of $D(\Sigma)$ containing $t$. Notice that, since boundary faces of $\Sigma$ are scanned in the same order according to which they are sorted, the resulting lists of segments will be naturally sorted in the same order, thus guaranteeing matching at the upper level of recursion.

At the end of the recursion step, the result obtained is $S^{\Sigma, q}$. Thus, the complete set of isosurfaces of $\mathcal{H}$ at precision $\varepsilon_i$ is obtained by applying the algorithm starting from the root tetrahedralization $\Sigma_0$.

## 5. Conclusions

We have presented a hierarchical model for representing scalar fields in three dimensions, that is suitable for multiresolution volume data representation and visualization. We are currently working on the implementation of a kernel system that includes the data structure and accessing algorithms for encoding and manipulating the model, the construction algorithm, the algorithm for expanding the model at a given level of accuracy, and the algorithm for extracting isosurfaces. Further developments of our work will also include algorithms for direct volume rendering based on our hierarchical structure.

Interactive analysis of volume data is supported by our model and algorithms, since identification of relevant zones (e.g., relative extrema for finite element analysis;

special tissues for medical data), and focusing on areas of interest are made easy and efficient through our multiresolution approach.

Problems in automatic analysis and recognition of relevant shapes in three-dimensional scalar fields could be also faced using our model. In this case, invariant properties (features), that usually depend on the differential structure either of the whole hypersurface, or of an isosurface of special interest, should be extracted. Anyway, in order to achieve this goal, the scalar field should be better approximated in the model through higher order interpolants over each tetrahedral element. The differential analysis of the hypersurface (or surface) could then be performed independently over each tetrahedral (triangular) cell. Again, the hierarchical structure could favor a top-down technique that handles, at each level, a restricted number of cells, while refining the analysis only in areas where features are expected.

## 6. References

[1] M. Bertolotto, E. Bruzzone, L. De Floriani, "Acyclic Hierarchical Cell Complexes", *Proceedings Fifth Canadian Conference on Computational Geometry*, pp. 279-284 , Waterloo, Ontario, Canada (August 1993).

[2] M. Bertolotto, E. Bruzzone, L. De Floriani, E. Puppo, "Multiresolution Representation of Volume Data through Hierarchical Simplicial Complexes", *Technical Report IMA-CNR n.13/93* (1993).

[3] M.P. Garrity, "Raytracing irregular volume data", *ACM Computer Graphics*, 24(5), pp.35-40, 1990.

[4] W.E. Lorensen, H.E. Cline, "Marching cubes: a high resolution 3D surface construction algorithm", *Computer Graphics* (1987).

[5] J. Wilhelms, A.A. Van Gelder "A coherent projection approach for direct volume rendering", *Computer Graphics*, 25, 4, (ACM SIGGRAPH), pp. 275-284 (July 1991).

[6] P.L. Williams, "Interactive splatting of nonrectilinear volumes", in *Proceedings IEEE Visualization '92*, A.E. Kaufman and G.M. Nielson, Eds., pp.37-45, 1992.

# APPLICATIONS USING DISTANCE TRANSFORMS

GUNILLA BORGEFORS

*Centre for Image Analysis*
*Swedish University of Agricultural Sciences*
*Lägerhyddvägen 17, S-752 37 Uppsala, Sweden*
*e-mail: gunilla@cb.uu.se*

## ABSTRACT

Digital shape is a fundamental concept in digital image analysis. In many applications shape is edited, recognised, stored, and reconstructed. For all these tasks, distance transforms are excellent tools. Here examples are given where distance transforms are used for morphological operations, compression, skeletonizing, Dirichlet tessellations, path finding, and template matching. Different distance transforms have different properties. Therefore, the first part of the paper gives an overview of available distance transforms and their properties.

## 1. Introduction

The purpose of a distance transform is to determine the distance between each individual pixel in one set of pixels to the nearest pixel in another set of pixels. This concept was introduced already in the mid 1960s, but for a long time only the simple type of distance transforms represented by the city block and chessboard distances were used. These distance are easy and efficient to compute, but have the disadvantage of being quite direction dependent. Thus, results for a specific shape will be very different for different orientations. In the mid 1980s weighted distance transforms were introduced, that are much less direction dependent. At about the same time people began using the (almost) true Euclidean distance transform. Today we have a good selection of distance transforms available. The most important ones and their main properties are presented in Section 2, together with the basic sequential and parallel computation algorithms.

Analysing digital shape using distance transforms can be efficient substitutes for iterative processes, as the distance transforms contains all distance information in a single image. Typical examples are the fundamental morphological operations, see Section 3. The same is true for skeletonizing algorithms. Instead of removing external pixels layer by layer, the skeletal pixels can be identified directly in the distance transform of the shape. Skeletonizing and related subjects are treated in Section 4. Another use of distance transforms is the computation of Dirichlet tessellations. The distance is computed from each seed, and the closest seed defines to which tile each seed belongs. When the seeds are not single points, but shapes in themselves, this approach is preferable to the standard "geometric" one, see Section 5. Constrained distance transforms can be used for finding the shortest path between two points in an image where there are obstacles that cannot be passed, see Section 6. Finally, distance transforms can also be used for very robust template matching. As the measure of the quality of the match is integrated along the whole template the matching is successful even in the presence of significant noise levels, see Section 7.

## 2. A Pride of Distance Transforms

### 2.1. Definitions

Denote a digital shape $F$, and the complement of the shape $\overline{F}$. Unless clearly stated, it is not assumed that $F$ or $\overline{F}$ are connected. A distance transformation, denoted DT, converts the binary image to a distance image, or distance transform. In the distance transform each pixel has a value measuring the distance to the closest pixel in $\overline{F}$. Thus, the pixels in $\overline{F}$ has value zero and the pixels in $F$ has positive values.

The basic idea utilised for most DTs is to approximate the global Euclidean distance by propagation of local distances, i.e., distances between neighbouring pixels. This idea was probably first presented by Rosenfeld and Pfaltz in 1966, [33]. The reason is ease of computation. In sequential computation only a small area of the image is available at the same time. In massively parallel computation each pixel has access only to its immediate neighbours.

A good underlying concept for all digital distances is the one proposed by Yamashita and Ibaraki, [39]:

> The distance between two points $\vec{x}$ and $\vec{y}$ is the length of the shortest path connecting $\vec{x}$ to $\vec{y}$ in an appropriate graph.

They proved that any distance is definable in the above manner, by choosing an appropriate neighbourhood relation and an appropriate definition of path length.

A convenient way to illustrate a DT is a "mask", where each pixel in the neighbourhood is marked by its local distance. Fig. 1 depict the $5 \times 5$ (and $3 \times 3$) masks. The "+" sign and the fact that some numbers are in italics has to do with the computation of the DT, described later. Using a $3 \times 3$ neighbourhood means that the distance between two pixels in an image is defined by the length of a minimal path between them, consisting of horizontal, vertical, and diagonal steps. Increasing the neighbourhood size to $5 \times 5$ means adding the "knight" step.

**Definition 1** *The distance transform (DT) of a binary image, where the pixel values are $DT(i, j)$, is defined as:*

$$DT(i,j) = \min_{(k,l) \in \overline{F}} \{ D(\max\{|i-k|, |j-l|\}, \min\{|i-k|, |j-l|\}) \},$$

| | +c | | +c | |
|---|---|---|---|---|
| +c | +b | +a | +b | +c |
| | +a | +0 | +a | |
| +c | +b | +a | +b | +c |
| | +c | | +c | |

Figure 1: Mask for $5 \times 5$ WDTs, where $a$ and $b$ are defined as in the $3 \times 3$ case, and $c$ is the "knight's move" distance.

*where $\overline{F}$ is the set from which the distances are measured, and $D(\cdot, \cdot)$ is the distance between two pixels defined by a minimal path between them.*

Due to symmetry, it is enough to consider distances from the origin to a point $(i, j)$ in the 45° wedge $0 \leq j \leq i$. To make the expressions for the different distances general the following notation is used:

$$\xi = \max\{|i - k|, |j - l|\} \quad \text{and} \quad \eta = \min\{|i - k|, |j - l|\}, \tag{1}$$

where $(i, j)$ and $(k, l)$ are two arbitrary points. (Cf. Definition 1.) We have $0 \leq \eta \leq \xi$.

The work on DTs early split in two directions. In the first direction the only value considered for the local distances where 1. The variable was the size of the neighbourhood. These DTs are closely related to connectedness. The second direction concentrates on the DT's ability to approximate the Euclidean distance transform, (denoted EDT). Therefore, other values of $a$, $b$, (and $c$) were soon considered. In 1968 Montanari published a paper, [27], on "Quasi-Euclidean" DTs. Here the local distances where set to their equivalent Euclidean values, i.e., $a = 1$, $b = \sqrt{2}$. This naturally makes the approximation to Euclidean distance much better, but – perhaps surprisingly – these values are not optimal using any of a number of optimality criteria. The other contribution of this paper, that was left unattended until 1986, see [14], was the suggestion of using larger neighbourhoods than $3 \times 3$. In this way, much better approximations to the Euclidean distance can be made, with reasonable effort. The first to suggest, but perhaps not to use, integer values that are scaled approximations of "optimal" real-valued local distances was probably Hilditch and Rutovitz in 1969, [24]. They suggest $a = 2$, $b = 3$ as an approximation of local distances $a = 1$, $b = \sqrt{2}$.

*2.2. Distance Transforms in 2D*

In the *city block* DT $a = 1$, see Fig. 1. Only horizontal and vertical steps are allowed in the minimal path between pixels. The city block distance is often denoted $D^4$ (or $d_4$), because it uses 4-connected paths between pixels. It is a metric, ([33, footnote 4]). The city block distance is computed as

$$D^4 = \xi + \eta. \tag{2}$$

Note that $\text{DT}^4(\xi, \eta) \geq \text{EDT}(\xi, \eta) \; \forall \; (\xi, \eta)$.

The city block DT, together with an efficient sequential algorithm for computing it, was first presented by Rosenfeld and Pfaltz in 1966, [33], (although not yet by that name). In 1968 they published a more thorough investigation of the city block distance, together with a parallel algorithm for it, [34]. Melter has published some geometric characterisations of this distance, [26].

In the *chessboard* DT $a = b = 1$, see Fig. 1. It is often denoted $D^8$ (or $d_8$), as it uses 8-connected paths between pixels. This DT was also introduced by Rosenfeld and Pfaltz, [34], who proved it is a metric, [34, Corollary to Proposition 2]. The chessboard distance between the two pixels is computed as

$$D^8 = \xi. \tag{3}$$

Note that $\text{DT}^8(\xi, \eta) \leq \text{EDT}(\xi, \eta) \; \forall \; (\xi, \eta)$.

The city block DT gives too large distance values and the chessboard DT gives too small distance values. Using them *alternatively* would result in a much better approximation of the Euclidean distance. When finding the minimal path between two pixels diagonal steps are allowed only every *even* step. The resulting DT, called an *octagonal* DT, together with a parallel algorithm for computing it, was first presented by Rosenfeld and Pfaltz in 1968, [34], who proved it is a metric, [34, Corollary to Proposition 5]. In our notation, (1), the octagonal distance becomes:

$$D^{oct} = \max\left\{ \xi, \; \left\lfloor \frac{2}{3}(\xi + \eta + 1) \right\rfloor \right\} \tag{4}$$

where $\lfloor x \rfloor$ denotes the greatest integer not exceeding $x$.

When computing the octagonal DT $a = 1$. The value of $b$ depends on the value $v$ of the pixel in the DT image it covers: $b = 1$ if $v$ is odd and $b = \infty$ if $v$ is even (including zero). The computation is simple when using parallel algorithms, but rather harder to perform efficiently sequentially.

Measuring the distance between the pixels using *weighted* local distances is equivalent to finding a minimal path between them using horizontal steps of length $a$, diagonal steps of length $b$, (and knight steps on length $c$,) Fig. 1, were the step lengths can have other values than 1. However, these lengths cannot be arbitrary if the distances are to "make sense". One way to determine the relations between the local distances is to use the following definition.

**Definition 2** *Consider two pixels that can be connected by a straight line, i.e., by using only one type of step. If that line defines the distance between the pixels, i.e., is a minimal path, then the resulting DT is* **semi-regular**. *If there are no other minimal paths, then the DT is* **regular**.

In the $3 \times 3$ neighbourhood case, the weighted DT (WDT) is regular if

$$a < b < 2a, \tag{5}$$

and semi-regular if at least one of the inequalities is replaced by equality. It can be proved that a regular or semi-regular $3 \times 3$ WDT is a metric. It is also worth noting that both the city block and chessboard DTs are semi-regular, but not regular.

The regular weighted $3 \times 3$ distance between two pixels is computed as (using (1))

$$D^{ab} = (\xi - \eta) \cdot a + \eta \cdot b. \tag{6}$$

The distance transform of a binary image is then computed using Definition 1.

If optimality is defined as minimising the maximum difference between the computed DT and the true Euclidean DT, then the optimal $a$ and $b$ in the $3 \times 3$ neighborhood case becomes, (see [14]),

$$\begin{aligned} a_{opt} &= \tfrac{1}{2}(\sqrt{2\sqrt{2} - 2} + 1) \approx 0.95509, \\ b_{opt} &= \sqrt{2} + \tfrac{1}{2}(\sqrt{2\sqrt{2} - 2} - 1) \approx 1.36930. \end{aligned} \tag{7}$$

Weighted distance transforms using the $5 \times 5$ neighbourhood were introduced in [14], and further investigated in [16]. A $5 \times 5$ WDT is regular, Definition 2, if

$$c > 2a, \quad 2c > 3b, \quad \text{and} \quad c < a + b. \tag{8}$$

and semi-regular if any of the inequalities is replaced by equality. The inequalities define a cone in $a, b, c$-space. The regularity conditions ensure that the minimal path consists of at most two types of steps, because any combination of $a$- and $b$-steps is always longer than a path containing some $c$-steps (the last inequality). The distance between two pixels becomes (using (1)):

$$D^{abc} = \begin{cases} \eta(c - 2a) + \xi a & \text{for } 0 \le \eta \le \xi/2 \\ \eta(2b - c) + \xi(c - b) & \text{for } \xi/2 \le \eta \le \xi \end{cases} \tag{9}$$

The $5 \times 5$ WDT of a binary image is then computed using Definition 1. The optimal local distances in this case becomes ([16])

$$\begin{aligned} a_{opt} &= \tfrac{1}{2} + \sqrt{\sqrt{5} - 2} \approx 0.98587, \\ b_{opt}^{min} &= \sqrt{2} - \tfrac{1}{2} + \sqrt{\sqrt{5} - 2} \approx 1.40018 \\ b_{opt}^{max} &= \tfrac{1}{10}(7c_{opt} - \sqrt{5} + 4\sqrt{\sqrt{5}c_{opt} - c_{opt}^2}) \approx 1.42178 \\ c_{opt} &= \sqrt{5} - 1 + 2\sqrt{\sqrt{5} - 2} \approx 2.20780. \end{aligned} \tag{10}$$

The value of $b$ can thus vary within a small interval, without increasing the maximum error. One attractive choice within the interval is of course $b = \sqrt{2}$.

It should be noted that other optimality criteria can and have been used, see, e.g., [22], [39]. The difference between optimal local distances computed according to different optimality critera is surprisingly small.

Using real valued local distances is generally not computationally desirable. Candidate integer approximations of the optimal values, denoted $A$, $B$, and $C$, are found by multiplying the optimal local distances by an integer scale factor and rounding to the nearest integer. Then the maximal errors are computed (all equations are available from the computations of the optimal local distances), to check the approximations. In the $3 \times 3$ case, $a = 2, b = 3$, $a = 3, b = 4$, and $a = 5, b = 7$, are all reasonable approximations. In the $5 \times 5$ case the integer approximation $a = 5, b = 7, c = 11$, is so good that no other values are worthy of consideration.

Vossepoel suggested a method for getting even better approximations to the EDT using (almost) integer arithmetic, [37]. The idea is to first compute an integer WDT, but then rescale the resulting values by a real valued scale factor, $r$. In the $3 \times 3$ case this can result in significant improvements. The best example is the 2-3 WDT, were multiplying the final results with $r = 0.94118$ reduces the maximum different from the EDT to less than half the original one. In the $5 \times 5$ case the 5-7-11 WDT is already so near the optimal solution that rescaling has no real effect.

The Euclidean DT can also be computed using local neighbourhoods. In that case, the pixel values in the image are *vectors*, rather than single values, at least during the computation process. In each pixel the number of horizontal and vertical steps to the nearest background pixel are stored. The local distances become: $a = (0, 1)$ or $(0, 1)$, and $b = (1, 1)$. Thus, we can not work within the original image as before, but must use twice the memory. Only integers are used, until the final step, where the actual EDT values are computed from the vector stored in each pixel.

When constructing a better parallel EDT algorithm Yamada suggested using *signed* vectors in the EDT computation, [38]. This idea was later taken up by Ye, [40], as an excellent tool in itself. The big advantage using the signed EDT is that each pixel not only stores the distance to the nearest $\overline{F}$ pixel, but also points to exactly the $\overline{F}$ pixel from which the distance is computed. The local distances become: $a = (0, \pm 1)$ or $(0, \pm 1)$, and $b = (\pm 1, \pm 1)$. Ragnemalm's thesis contains a wealth of practical knowledge about the EDT and some of its applications, [30]. Part of these results are published in [29] and [31].

One convenient way to compare different distances is to compute the "circle" for each distance, i.e., the points equidistant from a single centre point. The circles for some of the DTs discussed in this section are found in Fig. 2. The radii of the circles is considered large, so that all "jaggedness" is invisible. The circle for the city block distance is a diamond, and the circle for the chessboard distance is a square. The circle for the octagonal distance (which explains its name) is an octagon with

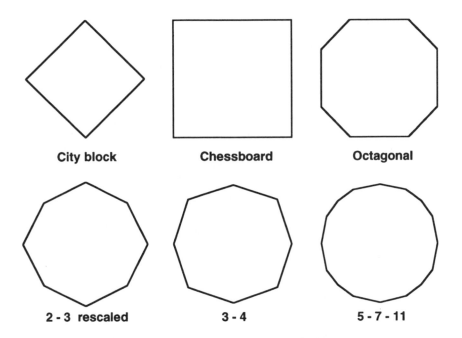

**City block**  **Chessboard**  **Octagonal**

**2 - 3 rescaled**  **3 - 4**  **5 - 7 - 11**

Figure 2: The circles for some DTs.

one side "up". Its character as a mix of the city block and chessboard distances is easily visible. The circles for regular $3 \times 3$ WDTs are also octagons. This is natural, as the mimimal paths can expand in eight different directions. The circles for the 3–4 DT and the rescaled 2–3 DT are found in Fig. 2. The circles for regular $5 \times 5$ WDTs are hexadecagons, i.e., have sixteen sides. The circle for the 5–7–11 WDT is also found in Fig. 2.

## 2.3. Distance Transforms in 3D

Distance transforms can be extended to 3D voxel imagery, where cubic *voxels* (volume elements) correspond to the square pixels. A good overview of this subject is found in the early, but incomplete, paper [12], together with the later refinements in [36] and [10].

In 3D there are three distances corresponding to the city block and chessboard ones. The first one uses only steps that connects the area neighbours (the 6 closest neighbours). The second uses steps both to the area and edge neighbours (the 18 closest neighbours). The third uses steps to all close neighbours, including the point neighbours (the 26 closest neighbours). The distances are denoted $D^6$, $D^{18}$, and $D^{26}$. Using the convention in Definition 1 extended to 3D, i.e., $0 \leq \zeta \leq \eta \leq \xi$, the three

DTs are computed as

$$D^6 = \xi + \eta + \zeta, \tag{11}$$

$$D^{18} = \xi + \max\left\{0, \left\lfloor \frac{\zeta+\eta-\xi+1}{2} \right\rfloor\right\}, \tag{12}$$

$$D^{26} = \xi. \tag{13}$$

The concept of regularity, Definition 2 is valid and useful also in 3D. It gives rather strict limits to the possible values of the local distances $\alpha, \beta$, and $\gamma$ (defining the distances to area, edge, and point neighbours respectively). To be regular, the local distances of a $3 \times 3 \times 3$ weighted DT must fulfil

$$\alpha < \beta < 2\alpha \quad \text{and} \quad \beta < \gamma < \frac{3}{2}\beta. \tag{14}$$

It can be shown that DT$^6$ and DT$^{26}$ are semi-regular, whereas DT$^{18}$ is not regular at all.

The optimal local distances in 3D are (see [12])

$$\alpha_{opt} = \frac{1}{2}\left(1 + \sqrt{2\sqrt{2}(1+\sqrt{3}) - 7}\right) \approx 0.92644,$$

$$\beta_{opt} = \frac{1}{2}\left(2\sqrt{2} - 1 + \sqrt{2\sqrt{2}(1+\sqrt{3}) - 7}\right) \approx 1.34065, \tag{15}$$

$$\gamma_{opt} = \frac{1}{2}\left(2\sqrt{3} - 1 + \sqrt{2\sqrt{2}(1+\sqrt{3}) - 7}\right) \approx 1.65849.$$

A good integer approximation of the optimal local distances is $\alpha = 3$, $\beta = 4$, $\gamma = 5$.

It is of course possible to use larger neighbourhoods also in 3D, but the computational complexity increases rather heavily. (There are 125 neighbours in the $5 \times 5 \times 5$ neighbourhood.) The EDT can also be computed in 3D, using 3D vectors as local distances, e.g. $\alpha = (1,0,0), (0,1,0)$, or $(0,0,1)$. Unfortunately, sequential computation is rather more demanding than one would at first guess.

The 3D DTs can be characterised by their associated spheres, just as the 2D DTs are characterised by their circles. The DT$^6$ sphere is an octahedron, the DT$^{18}$ sphere is a cubeoctahedron (or dymaxion), and the DT$^{26}$ sphere is a cube. The spheres for the regular weighted DTs are polyhedrons where the projection to any coordinate plane is an octaeder.

## 2.4. Computation

The question whether to compute a DT sequentially or in parallel is easy to answer. The sequential algorithms are superior unless you use a massively parallel architecture. Both sequential and parallel DT computation start by initializing the image. Pixels in $\overline{F}$ are set to zero and pixels in $F$ to infinity, i.e., a suitable large number.

All DTs using a constant neighbourhood can be *sequentially* computed using only two raster scans over the initial image, independently of the size of the neighbourhood and of the size and shape of $F$. The neighbourhood mask, see Fig. 1, is split into a forward mask, consisting of all pixels already visited in a forward raster scan, and a backward mask, consisting of all pixels already visited in a backward raster scan. In Fig. 1 the forward mask-pixels are boldface and the backward mask-pixels are italic. At each step, the mask is placed over the central pixel, the sum of all image pixels and the corresponding mask values are computed and the central pixel is set to the minimum of these sums. The algorithm in pseudo-code becomes:

> Forward pass:
>> for $i = q,\ q+1,\ ...,$ lines do
>>> for $j = q,\ q+1,\ ...,$ columns do
>>>> $v_{i,j}^1 = \min_{(k,l) \in \text{f-mask}} \{ v_{i+k, j+l}^0 + z(k, l) \}$

$$(16)$$

> Backward pass:
>> for $i =$ lines, lines$-1,\ ...,\ 1$ do
>>> for $j =$ columns, columns$-1,\ ...,\ 1$ do
>>>> $v_{i,j}^2 = \min_{(k,l) \in \text{b-mask}} \{ v_{i+k, j+l}^1 + z(k, l) \}$

where $q = \frac{1}{2}(m+1)$ for an $m \times m$ neighbourhood mask and $z(k, l)$ is the local distance at mask pixel $(k, l)$. Note that the central pixel itself can be excluded from the forward mask (but not from the backward one). We either have infinity, in which case the minimum must occur for one of the other mask-pixels, or we have zero, which cannot be improved upon. The DT values are here "exposed" by removing the too high initial values. The process was likened to chamfering in wood-working by Barrow et. al., [9], and the term "chamfer distance" has since then been extensively used for DTs computed using this two-pass method.

The octagonal DT can *not* be computed using only two raster scans over the image. Instead, four scans are necessary. These four scans can be organised in several ways. Danielsson, [21], suggests a version where the four scans are organised into two "super scans".

A worse problem is that the EDT can not be computed using only two passes over the image. This is not really surprising, as the minimal path is a single straight line that can have *any* direction. (In the $3 \times 3$ neighbourhood case there are eight directions and in the $5 \times 5$ neighbourhood case there are sixteen directions.) Danielsson, [21], suggested a four-pass algorithm for the EDT and the signed EDT. The four masks for the signed EDT are found in Fig. 3. The image is initialized by setting the $\overline{F}$ pixels to $(0, 0)$ and the $F$ pixels to $(\infty, \infty)$. The first five-pixel mask is moved over a line, then the second two-pixel mask is moved backwards on the same line. The process is repeated for each line, and then from bottom to top. At each pixel $(i, j)$

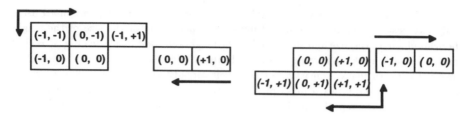

Figure 3: Masks for sequential computation of the signed Euclidean DT.

the value $\vec{v}^{\,t}_{(i,j)}$ is updated as:

$$\vec{v}^{\,t}_{i,j} = \vec{v}^{\,t-1}_{i+k,\,j+l} + (\hat{k}, \hat{l}), \quad \text{for } (\hat{k}, \hat{l}) \text{ such that}$$

$$|\vec{v}^{\,t-1}_{i+k,\,j+l} + (\hat{k}, \hat{l})|^2 = \min_{(k,l)\in\text{mask}}\{|\vec{v}^{\,t-1}_{i+k,\,j+l} + (k,l)|^2\}, \tag{17}$$

where $t \in \{1,2,3,4\}$ and $k,l \in \{-1,0+1\}$. The only difference between the EDT and the signed EDT is that $k$ and $l$ are signed in the latter case. After the four passes the actual distance values are computed as $EDT(i,j) = |\vec{v}^{\,t}_{i,j}|$. The time-consuming square root is computed only at the end. A way to avoid the square root entirely is to use a look-up table, where the Euclidean distances are stored for all vectors that can occur in the images.

Unfortunately, sequential computation algorithms based on the mask in Fig. 3 does not give the correct EDT values for all possible object pixel configurations. This was pointed out already by Danielsson, [21], and further investigated by Yamada, [38]. However, the errors are always small and do not increase with the size of the image. Danielsson's paper, [21], gives the upper bound of the errors as 0.09 pixels. Using a larger EDT mask is not the solution to this problem. Forchhammer, [23], has pointed out that no matter how big the mask is, one can always construct an example where there is an error, even though the errors become progressively smaller. The masks in Fig. 3 can be split in other ways. Ragnemalm has shown, [30], that only three scans are necessary and sufficient, but then one scan must go up or down along columns, rather than along rows. A more complex, but completely error free sequential algorithm can be found in [30].

For *parallel* computation we will assume a SIMD architecture where each pixel has its own processing element and where each processing element is connected to its edge- and point-neighbours. The traditional way to implement a DT on a parallel machine is the following, see e.g. [27], [14]. Initialize in the usual way. Then

$$v^t_{i,j} = \min_{(k,l)\in\text{mask}} \left\{ v^{t-1}_{i+k,j+l} + z(k,l) \right\}, \tag{18}$$

where $v^t$ is the pixel value at iteration $t$, $(k,l)$ is the position in the mask, and $z(k,l)$ is the local distance at that position. Note that the first value less than infinity a pixel gets is not necessarily the correct one! The iterations continue until no pixel changes its value. The number of iterations is proportional to the longest distance occurring in the image.

This approach yields the correct DT values for *all* DTs for which masks can be defined, including the octagonal one (where $b = 1$ when the underlying pixel value is even and $b = \infty$ when it is odd). However, when using a larger neighbourhood than $3 \times 3$, the values of pixels further away must be accessed, which is often not convenient in a SIMD architecture. Therefore, the $5 \times 5$ WDTs can not be efficiently computed in parallel. In the special case of $3 \times 3$ neighbourhood DTs with integer local distances, a much more efficient parallel algorithm is available, see [18]. The number of iterations is the same, but it uses *no arithmetic* (except a counter), only checks for equality.

The EDT can be computed using a algorithm similar to the one in (18), using the updating scheme of (17). Note, however, that using the unsigned EDT would result in the same small errors as in the sequential case. Yamada proved that using the signed EDT does give correct values in all situations, [38, Section 5].

The above algorithms for DT computation can in almost all cases be easily extended to 3D. The exceptions are the octagonal DT and EDT, that needs special care, see [32] for details.

## 2.5. *Choosing the Best Distance Transform*

After all the discussions in this paper the natural question to ask is: What is the best DT to use? That question is impossible to answer. The "best" DT must be chosen according to the application. But it is important to remember that there *is* a choice to be made! And that choosing badly may seriously affect the results of the application in which the DT is used.

In Table 1 the discussed DTs together with their maximum difference from the true Euclidean distance (maxdiff) are listed. The differences are proportional to the largest distance in the image, and occurs in different directions for different DTs.

In Table 2 the recommended DTs in 2D are listed, with indications of their strengths and weaknesses. In the first column we have the DT, and the following columns denote: suitability for sequential processing; suitability for parallel processing (on a massively parallel SIMD architecture); possibility of using integer arithmetic; memory requirements; approximation to the EDT (which indicates rotation independence); and preservation of the direction from which the distance originated. The notation should be obvious.

Table 1: Some distance transforms and their maximum errors.

| dim. | DT | maxdiff | remark |
|------|-----|---------|--------|
| **2D** | DT$^4$ | 58.58% | |
| | DT$^8$ | 41.42% | |
| | Octagonal | 41.42% | for dist. $< 5$ |
| | | 11.80% | for dist. $\geq 5$ |
| | 2–3 | 13.40% | |
| | 2–3 | 5.88% | rescaled, $r = 0.9412$ |
| | 3–4 | 8.09% | |
| | $3 \times 3$ WDT | 4.49% | optimal local distances |
| | 5–7–11 | 2.02% | |
| | $5 \times 5$ WDT | 1.41% | optimal local distances |
| **3D** | DT$^6$ | 126.80% | |
| | DT$^{18}$ | 41.42% | |
| | DT$^{26}$ | 73.20% | |
| | 3–4–5 | 11.81% | |
| | $3 \times 3 \times 3$ WDT | 7.36% | optimal local distances |

Table 2: Some DTs and their properties.

| DT | Seq. | Paral. | Integer | Memory | Approx. | Direction |
|-----|------|--------|---------|--------|---------|-----------|
| DT$^4$ | +++ | +++ | + | + | −− | − |
| DT$^8$ | ++ | ++ | + | + | −− | − |
| Octagonal | ± | ++ | + | + | ± | − |
| 3–4 | ++ | ++ | + | + | + | − |
| 2–3 rescaled | ++ | ++ | ± | + | + | − |
| 5–7–11 | + | −− | + | + | ++ | − |
| EDT | ± | + | ± | ± | +++ | − |
| signed EDT | ± | + | ± | ± | +++ | + |

## 3. Basic Morphology

First, some definitions.

**Definition 3** *A* **shrink** *operation changes all F-pixels within a given distance* $\Delta$ *($\Delta \geq 0$) from the background to $\overline{F}$-pixels. It is denoted $S_\Delta$. An* **expand** *operation changes all $\overline{F}$-pixels within a given distance* $\Delta$ *($\Delta \geq 0$) from the shape to F-pixels. It is denoted $\mathcal{E}_\Delta$.*

A shrink operation thus removes the outer "layers" of the shape, whereas the expand operation adds layers to it. Combining $S$ and $\mathcal{E}$ in various sequences can result in efficient shape editing algorithms. If a shape is first expanded and then shrunk, small holes and dents will disappear, while the overall shape is unaffected. On the other hand, if the shape is first shrunk and then expanded, thin protrusions will disappear.

**Definition 4** *The combination of an expand followed by a shrink, $S_\Delta \circ \mathcal{E}_\Delta$, is called a* **closing** *operation, denoted $\mathcal{C}_\Delta$. The combination of shrink followed by an expand, $\mathcal{E}_\Delta \circ S_\Delta$, is called an* **opening** *operation, denoted $\mathcal{O}_\Delta$.*

Traditionally the operations in Definitions 3 and 4 use iterated algorithms, where each pixel is inspected and removed/added if it is an edge- or point-neighbour of the shape/background. If more than a few layers are involved, i.e., if $\Delta \gg 1$, then this approach becomes very inefficient. A better approach is to use the DT. When the DT of the shape has been computed, it is simply thresholded at the appropriate value. A $S_7$ operation is equivalent to thresholding the DT of $F$ at value 7 (or $7 \cdot a$ for the WDTs or $7^2$ for the EDT). A $\mathcal{E}_7$ operation is equivalent to thresholding the DT of $\overline{F}$ at the same value. The first to suggest the use of DTs in this context, were all layers are simultaneously available, was probably Rosenfeld and Pfaltz, [34]. They suggested the use of $DT^4$ and $DT^8$. If these DTs are used, their direction dependence will lend its characteristics to the results. For example, in the extreme case, where only one pixel remains after the shrink, the result of the opening operation is a diamond (square), for the $DT^4$ ($DT^8$). If the shapes in the image *are* noisy diamonds (squares) this is perfect, but otherwise it may be better to use another DT. In Fig. 4 three tiny examples are given. To the left is the result of closing the amoeba-like shape, distance one ($\mathcal{C}_1$). In the middle is the result of opening the shape ($\mathcal{O}_3$), using the city block DT. Only the central "body" remains. On the right is the result of the same operation, using the 3–4 WDT. If the remaining blobs are compared, the diamond shape of the city block circle can be seen to influence the result in the centre figure.

The computations for repeated $S$ and $\mathcal{E}$ operations soon become lengthy. Arcelli and Sanniti di Baja has pointed out, [6], that the DTs for both $F$ and $\overline{F}$ can be computed simultaneously, and then they can both be thresholded at the same time. In this way, efficient smoothing can be achieved in only three sequential scans (two for the DT, one for the thresholding). Examples of quite complex shape editing

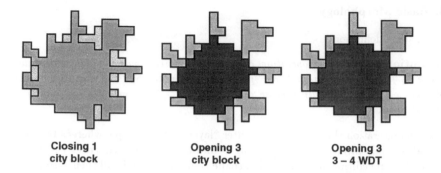

| Closing 1 | Opening 3 | Opening 3 |
| city block | city block | 3 – 4 WDT |

Figure 4: Examples of morphological operations on a shape (medium grey). Added pixels are light, remaining pixels are dark.

operations, that efficiently utilises morphological operations and skeletons (see next section) based on DTs can be found in [1].

## 4. Skeletonization and Reconstruction

Here the subject of skeletonization will be approached in a rather unusual way. First we will define layers on the DTs. Then we will find the centres of maximal discs, that contains the information necessary to reconstruct the shape. Finally, we will link these pixels to form skeletons.

### 4.1. Layers

The distance transformation can be interpreted as a propagation with constant speed from the outside towards the interior of a shape $F$. Pixels reached at the same instant of time are labelled with the same value. In $DT^4$ ($DT^8$) the layers are point-connected (edge-connected) curves, consisting of equi-labelled pixels. The layers in the WDTs and EDT do not have a unique type of connectedness. Both point- and edge-connected layers generally exist. Moreover, pixels in the same layer have different labels. A general layer definition is:

**Definition 5** *A* **layer** *is defined as a subset of the DT consisting of the pixels which receive distance information through the pixels in the previous (more external) layer, and through which distance information is propagated to the pixels in the next (more internal) layer. No distance information is propagated from a pixel of a given layer to another pixel in the same layer.*

This definition constrains the maximal label difference between two pixels in the same layer. It must be less than the minimal distance between any two neighbouring pixels.

In the DTs based on connectedness ($DT^4$, $DT^8$, octagonal) a layer is simply all pixels having the same label. In the WDT case, the minimal distance between neighbouring pixels is the local distance $a$ (between edge-neighbours). Thus, the first layer consists of all pixels with value $v$, where $0 < v \le a$. The second layer consists of all pixels with value $a < v \le 2a$, and so on. In general the $k$-th layer consists of all pixels valued

$$(k-1)a < v \le ka, \quad k = 1, 2, 3, \ldots. \tag{19}$$

Condition (19) is valid for all WDTs, independent of the neighbourhood size. It is, in fact, also valid for $DT^4$ and $DT^8$.

On the EDT the minimal distance between two neighbouring pixels is one. A pixel with value $v$ belongs to the $n$-th layer of the EDT, if and only if

$$(k-1)^2 < v \le k^2, \quad k = 1, 2, 3, \ldots \tag{20}$$

The layers in a quarter disc (the digital Euclidean disc with radius 9.5) for a number DTs are shown in Fig. 5. Odd layers are underlined, even layers are in outlined characters.

Shape information concerning $F$ can be derived from the DT layers. For instance, the existence of pixels of the $k$-th layer that have two unconnected components of pixels belonging to the $(k-1)$-th layer in their $3 \times 3$ neighbourhood reveals the existence of a neck in $F$.

## 4.2. Centres of Maximal Discs

A digital disc consists of all pixels that have a distance less than a certain value (radius) to a central pixel, using the appropriate DT. Among the discs centred on pixels in the shape $F$, that are included in $F$, the *maximal* ones are defined as follows.

**Definition 6** *A disc is* **maximal** *if it is not completely covered by any single other disc in the shape.*

Detection of the centres of the maximal discs, henceforth denoted CMD, is useful for compression and/or decomposition purposes. From the definition of the maximal discs it follows that *the union of the maximal discs in $F$ coincides exactly with $F$.* Thus, the set of CMDs, together with their radius values, contain enough information to exactly reconstruct the original shape.

Algorithms for extracting the CMDs have to be tailored to each specific DT. In $DT^4$ and $DT^8$, the CMDs coincide with the local maxima. A local maximum is a pixel with value $v_c$, where $v_c \ge v_n$ for all its neighbours $v_n$. Neighbour is in each case defined as pixels having distance one to the central pixel. In Fig. 5 the CMDs for the $DT^4$ and $DT^8$ are marked with circles.

The term "local maximum" has been used to denote the centre of a maximal disc also when referring to other DTs, even though a CMD might here have neighbours

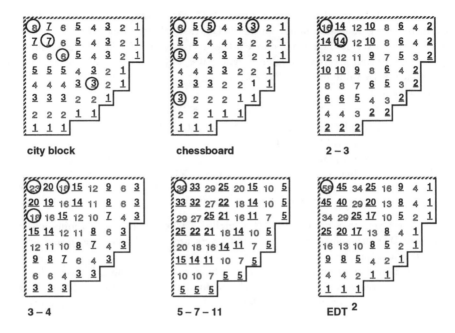

Figure 5: Layers and centres of maximal discs for six DTs. Only a quarter of each circular patch is shown. Odd layers are underlined boldface, even layers are outlined.

with higher values. The definition of CMDs, Definition 6, does ensure that they *act* as local maxima. In the continuous plane they would be local maxima, but that is not the case in discrete space, (not even – or rather especially not – for the EDT).

The CMDs for $3 \times 3$ neighbourhood WDTs have been identified by Arcelli and Sanniti di Baja, [5]. The definition is simple, except for a few small DT values.

**Definition 7** *A pixel in an a–b WDT valued $v_c$, where $v_c \geq V$, is a CDM if $v_e < v_c + a$ for all edge-neighbours $v_e$ and $v_p < v_c + b$ for all point-neighbours $v_p$, where $V$ is a unique value associated with a and b. For $v_c < V$, $v_c$ must be replaced by an "equivalent label", according to rules specific for each WDT.*

(Note that this definition is also valid for DT⁴ ($a = 1$, $b = \infty$) and DT⁸ ($a = b = 1$).) The equivalent labels are linked to non-occurring values in the DTs. For the 2–3 WDT we have $V = 3$, and label $v_c = 2$ should be replaced by $v_c = 1$ (the value 1 does not occur in this DT). For the 3–4 WDT we have $V = 7$, label 3 should be replaced by 1 and label 6 should be replaced by 5 (values 1 and 5 do not occur). In fact, each label should be replaced by a lower non-existent label, if possible. It has been proved,

Table 3: Tables for computing centres of maximal discs in the 5–7–11 WDT and EDT. ($v_c$ denotes centre pixel, $v_e$ denotes edge-neighbour, $v_p$ denotes point-neighbour, and $v_k$ denotes knight-neighbour)

| 5–7–11 DT | | | | | EDT | | |
|---|---|---|---|---|---|---|---|
| $v_c$ | $v_e$ | $v_p$ | $v_k$ | | $v_c$ | $v_e$ | $v_p$ |
| 5 | 7 | 10 | 14 | | 1 | 2 | 4 |
| 7 | 11 | 14 | 18 | | 2 | 5 | 8 |
| 10 | 14 | 15 | 20 | | 4 | 8 | 9 |
| 11 | 16 | 18 | 22 | | 5 | 10 | 13 |
| 14 | 18 | 20 | 25 | | 8 | 13 | 16 |
| 15 | 20 | 22 | 26 | | 9 | 16 | 20 |
| 16 | 21 | 22 | 27 | | 10 | 17 | 20 |
| 18 | 22 | 25 | 28 | | 13 | 18 | 25 |
| 20 | 25 | 26 | 30 | | 16 | 25 | 26 |
| 21 | 26 | 27 | 32 | | 17 | 26 | 29 |
| 22 | 27 | 29 | 33 | | 18 | 29 | 32 |
| 25 | 28 | 30 | 35 | | 20 | 29 | 34 |

[18, Theorem 5] that the largest value that can not occur in an integer $A$–$B$ WDT is $[(B - 1) \cdot A - B]$. The CMDs for the $2 - 3$ and 3–4 WDTs are marked in Fig. 5.

The CMDs for the $5 \times 5$ WDTs can also be computed using Definition 7, for all values $v_c$ above a certain limit, if knight-neighbours are added to the checks. However, for small $v_c$ the situation is more complex, and definition of equivalence classes are not enough. The important 5–7–11 is not regular until $v_c = 61$, see [17] for a thorough investigation. A look-up table should be used to find the CMDs in this case. The first entries in this table is found in Table 3. A pixel with value $v_c$ is a CMD if edge-neighbours have values less than $v_e$, point-neighbours have values less than $v_p$ and knight-neighbours have values less than $v_k$. The only CMD for the 5–7–11 WDT is marked in Fig. 5.

In the EDT the situation is even more complex. Details on how to identify the CMDs in this case are found in [19] and [20]. It is necessary to pre-compute tables containing *all* possible EDT values (that are identified as ($v_c = I^2 + J^2$), for non-negative integers $I$ and $J$). To each such value two other values are associated, one for edge-neighbours and one for point-neighbours. If all the neighbours around a pixel has lower values than those in the tables, then the pixel is a CMD. The first twelve entries are found in Table 3.

If the original shape is to be reconstructed from the CMDs a *reverse* DT, [5], [19], is used. A start image is constructed by putting the CMD values at the CMD positions. The reverse DT is computed in the same mask based fashion as the DT, except that the local distances are *subtracted* from the image value and the *maximum* value is chosen as the new centre pixel value. When the reverse DT has been computed all pixels with positive values coincide exactly with the original shape. Note, however, that the reverse DT may have other pixel values than the "direct" DT computed from the back-ground.

### 4.3. Skeletons

There is some confusion in the literature regarding the definitions of *skeleton* and *medial axis* or *MAT* (the T is for Transform). Here the following definition is used.

**Definition 8** *The skeleton of a connected digital shape F*
1. *Is centred within F and have the same topology.*
2. *Is a thin subset of F.*
3. *Allows reconstruction of F.*

Complete recovery and unit width can seldom be accomplished simultaneously. The skeleton computed by most skeletonization algorithms are two pixels wide in regions of $F$ having even width. Thinning the skeleton to unit width is easy, but then some border pixels of $F$ will be lost when the shape is reconstructed from the skeleton. The MAT is often defined as the set of CMDs (even though that name might not be explicitly used), which means that the MAT has property 3) and the first half of property 1) in the definition. However, there are other definitions of MAT in the literature, where the MAT fulfils conditions 1) and 2) instead. In any case, skeletons are good representations of digital shapes, and can be used for storage, shape editing, and shape analysis.

The classical approach to skeletonization is to see it as an iterated compression process. At every iteration all contour pixels are tested, and if certain removal criteria are satisfied, the contour pixels are deleted. This process is obviously unsuitable for sequential processing, unless the shape $F$ is very thin to begin with. The iterated procedure does generally not leave enough information to allow reconstruction of the original shape. Therefore, a new approach to skeletonization has been proposed, that uses distance transforms. Rather than iteratively removing contour pixels, the skeletal pixels are identified in the DT. This is possible, since successive contours, or rather layers, are simultaneously available. All CMDs should belong to the skeleton, but as we saw in Fig. 5, the set of CMDs is usually not connected. Other, "linking", pixels must be added, to give the skeleton the correct topological properties.

It is usually desirable that the same shape has roughly the same skeleton independent on its rotation. This means that the DT used should be rotation independent, or, expressed differently, its circle should be as round as possible. This may not be important for very thin shapes, but then the DT based approach is doubtful in any case. The DT based skeletonization can be outlined in the following steps

1. Compute the DT for the shape
2. Identify the CMDs
3. Identify linking pixels

Only the third step is dependent on the DT chosen. Generally, some sort of gradient following approach is used, until linking is achieved. If sequential computation is used, the DT uses two raster scans and the identification of the CMDs some linking pixels one raster scan. Identifying the rest of the linking pixels may need some path following. If parallel computation is used, the DT computation uses a number of iterations proportional to the longest distance, the CMDs and some linking pixels are found in one iteration, and the rest of the linking pixels in a number of iterations proportional to the longest path that needs to be filled.

Efficient skeleton extraction based on the city block DT is found in [7]. For skeletons based on the chessboard DT, see [3]. This early paper is probably contains the first efficient DT based skeleton, and has been the inspiration for much of the subsequent work. For WDTs some specific skeletonization algorithms have been published. Sanniti di Baja has thoroughly investigated 3–4 skeletons, [35]. A good skeleton for the 5–7–11 by Arcelli and Frucci is found in [2]. There have been several attempts to construct skeletons from the EDT. Many of the published papers yields results that do not fulfil the three skeleton conditions, so some care is needed. The most common failing is that the skeleton is not topologically correct, e.g. is not connected or contains loops that should not be there. Danielsson, [21], presents a skeleton that is not connected, but perfect for reconstruction. The skeleton by Klein and Kubler is correct, [25], but computational efficiency requires special hardware. The best effort so far seems to be the one by Arcelli and Sanniti di Baja, [8], even though perfect reconstruction is not guaranteed.

In Fig. 6 the $DT^4$, $DT^8$ and 3–4 skeletons for a square in two orientations are found. The "correct" skeleton would be a cross from corner to corner in all cases.

## 5. Dirichlet Tessellations

**Definition 9** *Assume a finite set $P = \{p_1, p_2, ..., p_m\}$ of points in the plane. The* **Dirichlet tessellation** *associates to each point $p_i$ the region of the plane that is closer to that point than to any other point $p_j$, $j \neq i$. The $p_i$ are called seed points.*

This definition is valid both in the continuous plane (where the tiles are convex polygons) and in the discreet plane, where each pixel is associated to the point closest to its centre. Of course, closeness can be determined by any metric. The definition can also be extended, so that the seeds are objects, rather points. In this case, the tiles can have any shape, even in the continuous plane.

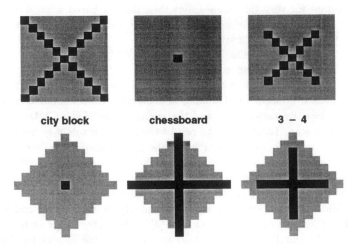

Figure 6: Skeletons pixels for square and diamond, based on three different distance transforms.

Computing the Dirichlet tessellation based on a DT is simple, although not easy to do efficiently. The naive approach is to mark each seed point or object with a distinct label, and then use an auxiliary image. In this image the label of the neighbour in the DT mask from which the distance is measured is entered, each time a distance value less than infinity is put in the distance transform. This approach was used in [14], where the main purpose was to show the effects of using different distances for the computation. When the signed EDT is used, the Dirichlet tessellation is almost automatically computed, [40]. Remember that in each pixel a signed vector pointing to the closest pixel is stored. The only operation necessary is to segment the DT according to vector directions.

The edges between the tiles in a Dirichlet tessellation is called the *Voronoi diagram*. Voronoi diagrams are sometimes used for shape and texture analysis. An efficient algorithm for computing the Voronoi diagram for arbitrarily shaped seeds is found in [4]. It requires five scans over the image, and uses no auxiliary image.

In Fig. 7 the Dirichlet tessellations and Voronoi diagrams are shown for an example, where there are three objects (dark grey) in the binary image. The cross-hatched pixels are equally close to at least two objects. Even in this diminutive example, there are quite large differences between the $DT^4$, $DT^8$, and the more exact 3–4 WDT and EDT.

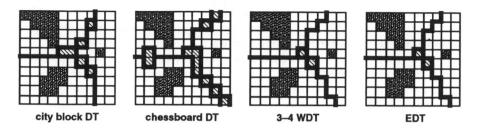

**city block DT**     **chessboard DT**     **3–4 WDT**     **EDT**

Figure 7: Dirichlet tessellations and Voronoi diagrams for a binary image, based on four different distances. The cross-hatched pixels are equally close to at least two objects.

## 6. Path finding

Distance transforms can be used for path finding. Consider a ternary image, consisting of free space ($F$), start position ($\overline{F}$), goal position, and obstacle areas that can not be passed. The objective is to compute the DT in the free space, from the start position, while not passing the obstacles. This situation is denoted *constrained* DT, [28]. Once the DT is computed, the value of the goal pixel denotes the shortest path and following the DT backwards in the direction of lower vales computes the actual path. A small example is found in Fig. 8.

Note that using constrained DTs to find short, smooth paths can be extended to many situations, and are not only useful in the image plane. Navigating robots

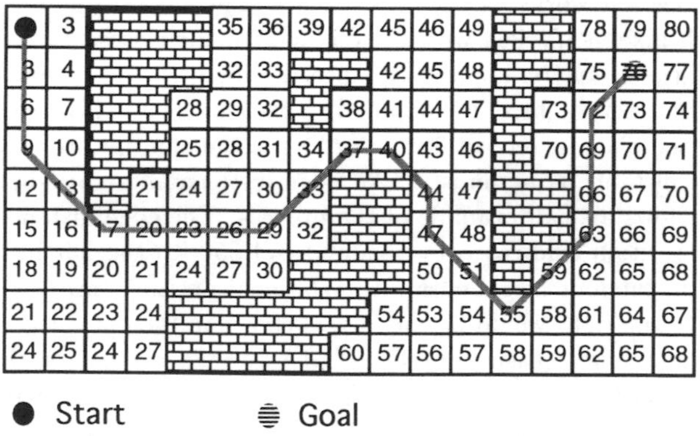

| ● | 3 | | | 35 | 36 | 39 | 42 | 45 | 46 | 49 | | | 78 | 79 | 80 |
|---|---|---|---|----|----|----|----|----|----|----|---|----|----|----|----|
| 3 | 4 | | | 32 | 33 | | | 42 | 45 | 48 | | | 75 | 76 | 77 |
| 6 | 7 | | 28 | 29 | 32 | | 38 | 41 | 44 | 47 | | 73 | 72 | 73 | 74 |
| 9 | 10 | | 25 | 28 | 31 | 34 | 37 | 40 | 43 | 46 | | 70 | 69 | 70 | 71 |
| 12 | 13 | | 21 | 24 | 27 | 30 | 33 | | 44 | 47 | | | 66 | 67 | 70 |
| 15 | 16 | 17 | 20 | 23 | 26 | 29 | 32 | | 47 | 48 | | | 63 | 66 | 69 |
| 18 | 19 | 20 | 21 | 24 | 27 | 30 | | | 50 | 51 | | 59 | 62 | 65 | 68 |
| 21 | 22 | 23 | 24 | | | | 54 | 53 | 54 | 55 | 58 | 61 | 64 | 67 |
| 24 | 25 | 24 | 27 | | | 60 | 57 | 56 | 57 | 58 | 59 | 62 | 65 | 68 |

**● Start**     **≡ Goal**

Figure 8: Constrained distance transform. The line marks the shortest path from the start to the goal, using 3–4 DT.

can include rotation in the possible movements by adding a rotation dimension. The state space of a robot arm can be discretized, forbidden states are obstacles, and a path can be found from one position to another.

The computation of constrained DTs is simple if a straightforward approach is used. The algorithms from Section 2.4 only need to be modified so that mask pixels over obstacles are ignored. Using parallel computation there are indeed no problems. However, using sequential raster scans, two scans may be far from enough. The distance can no longer spread in all directions. Raster scans in opposite directions must continue until no further changes occur. In fact, cases can be constructed where only a single pixel gets a new value in each raster scan (spiral channels facing the "wrong" way). Straightforward sequential computation of constrained DTs is thus not a good idea. If sequential computers are used, contour processing, where a list of the "active" contour is processed rather than the whole image, should be used, see, e.g., [28].

## 7. Matching

Another application of DTs is pattern matching. The so called "chamfer matching" algorithm, that matches edges using chamfer distances, was first published in 1977, [9]. The algorithm was improved, and made to function in a resolution pyramid in 1988, [15]. The new algorithm is known as the **H**ierarchical **C**hamfer **M**atching **A**lgorithm, HCMA. The latest development is to use stochastic optimization to speed up the search for the best match, [11].

The HCMA matches a set of feature points, usually edge points, to similar points in an image. It works basically as follows. The edge image is converted to a DT, where each pixel is marked with the distance to the closest edge pixel. The set of edge points, the *template,* is projected into the image, and the root mean square average of all the pixels it "hits" is computed. This average is called the *edge distance.* By moving the template incrementally, according to the appropriate parametric equations, the edge distance is minimised. An edge distance of zero indicates a perfect match. Fig. 9 shows a small example of the process. The edge distance for the edge in the current position (indicated by shadow) is 1.85. To the left in the figure the edge distances in the four neighbouring translational positions are indicated. In this case, one step to the right would be the logical choice in the optimization procedure.

As the matching measure in the HCMA is an average over the whole edge template, the algorithm becomes unusually robust. It gives good results even in the presence of much (random) noise. As the algorithm is parametric it can handle all distortions between template and image that can be described by parametric equations. One example is the rectification of satellite imagery, where the image edges are matched to a map. In this case six parameters are necessary: translation, rotation, scale, and perspective. To speed up the algorithm, the computations should

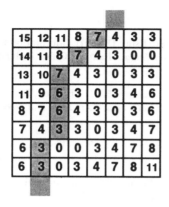
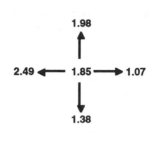

Figure 9: Computation of edge distance. The figures on the right indicate the edge distances for the current and neighbouring positions of the template (shaded).

start at a low resolution level in a resolution pyramid. The "best" positions for each level becomes the start positions in the next level. For details on how to determine start positions, step lengths in the parameters, rejection criteria for bad positions, etc., see [15].

In principle, the EDT would be the best DT for the HCMA. However, edge detection algorithms are seldom perfect, and computing exact distances from inexact edges is seldom useful. In fact, a small investigation, [13], compared the city block DT, the 3–4 WDT, and the EDT. The result was that the 3–4 distance was a good enough approximation of the ED, whereas the city block distance was not.

## 8. Conclusion

In this paper the useful distance transforms that are available has been presented. They have different properties and some care should be spent of which one to chose for a specific application. Table 2 can be used as a quick reference to an informed choice. In the rest of the paper some of the many uses of distance transforms have been briefly outlined. The idea is to make a survey of possible uses, rather than giving detailed algorithm descriptions. These can be found in the references. Distance transforms for 3D imagery has been summarily covered. No 3D applications have been explicitly listed. However, in most cases the extension from 2D to 3D in the applications is straightforward.

## References

[1] S Ablameyko, C Arcelli, and G Sanniti di Baja: Using Distance Information for Editing Binary Pictures, *Proc. 6th Scand. Conf. on Image Analysis*, Oulu, Finland, 1989, pp. 401–407.

[2] C Arcelli and M Frucci: Reversible Skeletonization by (5,7,11)-Erosion, In: C Arcelli, L P Cordella and G Sanniti di Baja, Ed., *Visual Form - Analysis and Recognition*, Plenum Press, New York 1992, pp. 21–28.

[3] C Arcelli and G Sanniti di Baja: A Width-Independent Fast Thinning Algorithm, *IEEE Trans. Pattern Analysis Machine Intelligence* **PAMI-7**, 1985, pp. 463–474.

[4] C Arcelli and G Sanniti di Baja: Computing Voronoi Diagrams in Digital Pictures, *Pattern Recognition Letters* **4**, 1986, pp. 383–389.

[5] C Arcelli and G Sanniti di Baja: Finding Local Maxima in a Pseudo-Euclidean Distance Transform, *Computer Vision, Graphics and Image Processing* **43**, 1988, pp. 361–367.

[6] C Arcelli and G Sanniti di Baja: Picture Editing by Simultaneously Smoothing Figure Protrosions and Dents, *Proc. 9th International Conference on Pattern Recognition*, Rom, Italy, 1988, pp. 948–950.

[7] C Arcelli and G Sanniti di Baja: A One-Pass Two-Operation Process to Detect the Skeletal Pixels on the 4-Distance Transform, *IEEE Trans. Pattern Analysis Machine Intelligence* **PAMI-11**, 1989, pp. 411–414.

[8] C Arcelli and G Sanniti di Baja: Ridge Points in Euclidean Distance Maps, *Pattern Recognition Letters* **13**, 1992, pp. 237–243.

[9] H G Barrow, J M Tenenbaum, R C Bolles and H C Wolf: Parametric Correspondence and Chamfer Matching: Two New Techniques for Image Matching, *Proc. 5th Int. Joint Conf. Artificial Intelligence*, Cambridge, USA, 1977, pp. 659–663.

[10] A L D Beckers and A W M Smeulders: Optimization of Length Measurements for Isotropic Distance Transformations in Three Dimension, *CVGIP: Image Understanding* **55**, 1992, pp. 296–306.

[11] M Bengtsson: Stochastic Optimization Algorithms - an application to Pattern Matching, *Pattern Recognition Letters* **11**, 1990, pp. 717–724.

[12] G Borgefors: Distance Transformations in Arbitrary Dimensions, *Computer Vision, Graphics and Image Processing* **27**, 1984, pp. 321–345.

[13] G Borgefors: An Improved Version of the Chamfer Matching Algorithm, *Proc. 7th Int. Conf. on Pattern Recognition*, Montreal, Canada, 1984, pp. 1175-1177.

[14] G Borgefors: Distance Transformations in Digital Images, *Computer Vision, Graphics and Image Processing* **34**, 1986, pp. 344–371.

[15] G Borgefors: Hierarchical Chamfer Matching: A Parametric Edge Matching Algorithm, *IEEE Trans. Pattern Analysis Machine Intelligence* **PAMI-10**, 1988, pp. 849–865.

[16] G Borgefors: Another Comment on 'A Note on "Distance Transformations in Digital Images"', *Computer Vision, Graphics and Image Processing* **54**, 1991, pp. 301–306.

[17] G Borgefors: Centres of Maximal Discs in the 5-7-11 Distance Transform, *Proc. 8th Scand. Conf. on Image Analysis,* Tromsø, Norway, 1993, pp. 105-111.

[18] G Borgefors, T Hartmann and S L Tanimoto: Parallel Distance Transforms on Pyramid Machines: Theory and Implementation, *Signal Processing* **21**, 1990, pp. 61–86.

[19] G Borgefors, I Ragnemalm, and G Sanniti di Baja: The Euclidean Distance Transform: Finding the Local Maxima and Reconstructing the Shape, *Proc. 7th Scand. Conf. on Image Analysis*, Aalborg, Denmark, 1991, pp. 974–981.

[20] G Borgefors, I Ragnemalm, and G Sanniti di Baja: Feature Extraction on the Euclidean Distance Transform, In: V Cantoni et al., ed., *Progress in Image Analysis and Processing II*, World Scientific, Singapore 1992, pp. 115–122.

[21] P-E Danielsson: Euclidean Distance Mapping, *Computer Vision, Graphics and Image Processing* **14**, 1980, pp. 227–248.

[22] L Dorst: Discrete Straight Line Segments: Parameters, Primitives and Properties, Ph. D. Thesis, Delft University of Technology, Delft, The Netherlands, June 1986.

[23] S Forchhammer: Euclidean Distances from Chamfer Distances for Limited Distances, *Proc. 6th Scand. Conf. on Image Analysis*, Oulu, Finland, 1989, pp. 393–400.

[24] J Hilditch and D Rutovitz: Chromosome Recognition, *Annals New York Academy of Sciences* **157**, 1969, pp. 339–364.

[25] F Klein and O Kübler: Euclidean Distance Transformations and Model Guided Image Interpretation, *Pattern Recognition Letters* **5**, 1987, pp. 19–29.

[26] R A Melter: Some Characterizations of City Block Distance, *Pattern Recognition Letters* **6**, 1987, pp. 235–240.

[27] U Montanari: A Method for Obtaining Skeletons Using a Quasi-Euclidean Distance, *J. Assoc. Computing Machinery* **15**, 1968, pp. 600–624.

[28] J Piper and E Granum: Computing Distance Transformations in Convex and Non-Convex Domains, *Pattern Recognition* **20**,1987, pp. 599–615.

[29] I Ragnemalm: The Euclidean Distance Transform and Its Implementation on SIMD Architectures, *Proc. 6th Scand. Conf. on Image Analysis*, Oulu, Finland, 1989, pp. 379–384.

[30] I Ragnemalm: Generation of Euclidean Distance Maps, Linköping Studies in Science and Technology, Thesis No 206, Linköping University, Linköping, Sweden, 1990.

[31] I Ragnemalm: Neighborhoods for Distance Transformations Using Ordered Propagation, *CVGIP: Image Understanding* **56**, 1992, pp. 399–409.

[32] I Ragnemalm: The Euclidean Distance Transform in Abritrary Dimensions, *Pattern Recognition Letters* **14**, 1993, pp. 883–888.

[33] A Rosenfeld and J L Pfaltz: Sequential Operations in Digital Picture Processing, *J. Assoc. Computing Machinery* **13**, 1966, pp. 471–494.

[34] A Rosenfeld and J L Pfaltz: Distance Functions on Digital Pictures, *Pattern Recognition* **1**, 1968, pp. 33–61.

[35] G Sanniti di Baja: Well-shaped, stable, and reversible skeletons from the (3,4)-Distance Transform, *Journal of Visual Communiation and Image Representation*, **5**, 1994, pp. 107-115.

[36] B J H Verwer: Local distances for distance transformations in two and three dimensions, *Pattern Recognition Letters* **12**, 1991, pp. 671–682.

[37] A M Vossepoel: A Note on: 'Distance Transformations in Digital Images', *Computer Vision, Graphics and Image Processing* **43**, 1988, pp. 88–97.

[38] H Yamada: Complete Euclidean Distance Mapping, *Proc. 7th Int. Conf. Pattern Recognition*, Montreal, Canada, 1984, pp. 69–71.

[39] M Yamashita and T Ibaraki: Distance Defined by Neighborhood Sequences, *Pattern Recognition* **19**, 1986, pp. 237–246.

[40] Q-Z Ye: The Signed Euclidean Distance Transform and Its Applications, *Proc. 9th Int. Conf. Pattern Recognition*, Rome, Italy, 1988, pp. 495–499.

# PROJECTIVE INVARIANT SMOOTHING AND EVOLUTIONS OF PLANAR CURVES

ALFRED M. BRUCKSTEIN

*Department of Computer Science*
*Technion-I.I.T., Haifa 32000, Israel*

and

DORON SHAKED

*Department of Electrical Engineering*
*Technion-I.I.T., Haifa 32000, Israel*

## ABSTRACT

Several recently introduced and studied planar curve evolution equations turn out to be iterative smoothing procedures that are invariant under the actions of the Euclidean and affine groups of continuous transformations. This paper discusses possible ways to extend these results to the projective group of transformations.

## 1. Introduction

Smoothing of planar curves - boundaries of 2-D shapes - is an often necessary, basic operation in shape analysis and recognition. Researchers even proposed to describe planar shapes and curves using hierarchical, multiscale representations. In such representations a parameterized set of shapes is associated with any given shape, the scale-parameter quantifying the degree of smoothing. Moving to coarser scales, i.e., increasing the scale parameter, implies producing smoother versions of the shape. Multiscale descriptions should enable robust shape analysis and recognition in cases where, due to noise and quantization, the object instances to be processed are significantly degraded. There exists yet another type of distortion that is common in image acquisition: the distortion due to the viewing geometry. Viewing transformations, i.e., the Euclidean, similarity, affine and projective maps, always affect the objects to be analyzed by computers. Hence, in performing smoothings of shapes, it is necessary to ensure invariance of the smoothing process under the viewing transformation expected to be in effect.

By invariance to the viewing transformation we mean the following: A shape $S$ may be smoothed to obtain a new (hopefully smoother) shape $T_S(S)$. The shape may also be transformed by some viewing transformation obtaining $T_V(S)$. The smoothing process $T_S$ is invariant under a group $\mathcal{V}$ of viewing transformations, if for every viewing transformation $T_V \in \mathcal{V}$ and for every shape $S$

$$T_V(T_S(S)) = T_S(T_V(S)) \tag{1}$$

There are many shape smoothing techniques and scale space approaches. We shall consider the curve evolution approach, that was recently introduced to computer vision. A shape is represented by its boundary curve $C$, which in turn, is represented as a 2-D parametric function $C(p) = [x(p), y(p)]^T$. The curve evolution is described via a partial differential equation determining the manner in which a shape deforms in time. To describe the time dependence we add the time parameter $\tau$ and denote a curve family by $\mathbf{C}(p, \tau)$. General curve evolutions may be described via $\frac{\partial \mathbf{C}(p,\tau)}{\partial \tau} = \alpha(p, \tau)\vec{T} + \beta(p, \tau)\vec{N}$ where $\vec{N}$ and $\vec{T}$ are the local unit tangent and normal to $\mathbf{C}(p, \tau)$ at the corresponding point in space and time. In the sequel we often refer to the following result by Epstein and Gage [8]: Consider all evolutions of the same initial curve with the same normal velocity component $\beta$, dependent only on the geometry of $\mathbf{C}$ at parameters $p, \tau$ and not on the parameterization of the curve. All such evolutions are geometrically equivalent in the sense that the images of the evolved curves are the same.

The simplest group of viewing transformations is the Euclidean group, under which planar shapes are translated and rotated in the image plane. The basic (Euclidean invariant) smoothing curve evolution is the equation known as the curve shortening evolution,

$$\frac{\partial \mathbf{C}}{\partial t} = \kappa \vec{N} \qquad (2)$$

postulating that each point on the curve moves in the direction of the local normal $\vec{N}$ to the curve, with a velocity proportional to the local curvature $\kappa$ of the curve.

The curve shortening evolution has many attractive smoothing properties. Under curve shortening, a curve behaves like an elastic band in heavy syrup. It first looses small, narrow and edgy features. Only later when changes accumulate does it affect the larger, more significant features. Gage, Hamilton and Grayson proved that every simple curve evolves under Eq. 2 to a vanishing circular point [9] [10].

Recently the very natural subject of invariance to more general viewing transformation groups was raised. In [14] and [1] it was shown that the following evolution is affine invariant.

$$\frac{\partial \mathbf{C}}{\partial t} = \kappa^{1/3} \vec{N} \qquad (3)$$

Similar to the Euclidean evolution equation Eq. 2 all simple initial shapes become convex, and tend to a vanishing elliptical point [14].

Equation Eq. 2 can be also formulated as something that looks like the classical heat equation (and was hence named the geometric heat equation)

$$\frac{\partial \mathbf{C}}{\partial t} = \frac{\partial^2 \mathbf{C}}{\partial s_e^2}$$

with $s_e$ the Euclidean arc length.

An affine equivalent to the Euclidean arc length was found at the beginning of this century by Blaschke [3] [11]. The affine arc length $s_a$ is a parameterization invariant to the group of affine transformations. It can be shown that the evolution of a boundary curve via Eq. 3 is the same as the evolution via

$$\frac{\partial \mathbf{C}}{\partial t} = \frac{\partial^2 \mathbf{C}}{\partial s_a{}^2}$$

The question that arises is: Can we do the same for every transformation group? This question is seemingly connected to the possibility of obtaining generalized invariant "arc-length"-reparameterizations under the groups in question. In fact, the theory of differential invariants for continuous groups of transformation, a theory developed by mathematicians about 100 years ago, yields such reparameterizations [17] [11] [5] [6] [4]. Those were recently found useful in deriving invariant signatures for recognizing partially occluded planar shapes, see [5] [6]. From the above description it seems, that it would be possible to find an invariant smoothing evolution for every transformation group.

Indeed one could follow that line of thought and define a similarity invariant smoothing process, using the similarity invariant arc length $s_s$ [4] to get

$$\frac{\partial \mathbf{C}}{\partial t} = \frac{\partial^2 \mathbf{C}}{\partial s_s{}^2} = \frac{1}{\kappa} \vec{N} \tag{4}$$

Unfortunately the above equation may develop shocks, and seems to behave differently from its predecessors Eq. 2 and Eq. 3. A little comfort may be found in the fact that negating the evolution direction one may show [2] [15] that $\frac{\partial \mathbf{C}}{\partial t} = -\frac{1}{\kappa} \vec{N}$ with a strictly convex initial curve, behaves similar to Eq. 2 and Eq. 3. Every strictly convex curve blows up, its shape tending to a circle.

The last example is a sign that things may not be as simple as one may extrapolate from the Euclidean and affine invariant examples. In an attempt to clarify the subject, we suggest in this paper a new approach that motivates the use of the heat-equation-like evolutions for invariant smoothings.

Our approach motivates heat-equation-like smoothing, as the limit of a discrete series of averaging steps performed on a curve. It is easy to show that the heat equation is the limit of many discrete averaging processes. To obtain an invariant process one has to use averagings based on invariant metrics on the curve. This we show leads to all the heat-equation-like equations presented above. In the projective case, however, there is a severe complication, since the mere action of averaging is not projective invariant. We propose to solve this problem using some alternative operators as candidates for the projective invariant averaging process. An amazing fact that emerges is that all the projective invariant averages considered, result in the same heat-equation-like geometric curve evolution.

As mentioned before, the basic practical question remains: Do all heat-equation-like evolutions perform invariant smoothings? The similarity example discussed above shows that the straight forward answer is No. In the sequel we also show that one may use different invariant metrics for the averaging, which implies that although for one invariant metric things go wrong there may be other better ones. The proof that an evolution is indeed a smoothing evolution is complicated [2] [9] [10] [14], and out of the scope of this paper. We hope that this paper may motivate others to find different, provable invariant smoothing evolutions of the type suggested here.

In the next section we introduce our basic approach in its simplest form, for 1-D functions. In this simplified form we introduce some of the ideas that will be used later in the more complicated 2-D case. In section 3 we introduce the 2-D case. In section 4 we discuss the special case of projective invariant averaging.

## 2. Invariant Smoothing of Functions

### 2.1. Smoothing Functions and the Heat Equation

Suppose we are given an already reasonably smooth function $f(x)$. A smoother version of $f(x)$ is obtained by convolving $f(x)$ with an averaging kernel $K(x; \tau)$, with width determined by $\tau$.

A multiscale or "scale space" representation of $f(x)$ is a continuum of functions $F(x; \tau)$ defined as (see Witkin, [18])

$$F(x; \tau) = f(x) * K(x; \tau) \tag{5}$$

for $\tau \in [0, \infty)$ where $*$ stands for convolution. Commonly used smoothing kernels are the Gaussian kernel $K_N(x; t) = \frac{1}{\sqrt{2\pi t}} e^{-x^2/2t}$, the uniform kernel $K_U(x; t) = \frac{1}{2\sqrt{3t}}$   $x \in [-\sqrt{3t}, \sqrt{3t}]$, and we shall also use $K_D(x; t) = \frac{1}{2}[\delta(x - \sqrt{t}) + \delta(x + \sqrt{t})]$ The width of the kernels is measured by their variance, chosen to be the same (Var $= t$) for all kernels defined above.

Let us consider the following discrete iterative smoothing process:

$$\tilde{F}(x, (n+1)\epsilon) = \tilde{F}(x, n\epsilon) * K(x, \epsilon) \qquad \tilde{F}(x, 0) = f(x) \tag{6}$$

This process generates a sequence of 1-D functions $\{\tilde{F}(x, n\epsilon), \ n = 1, 2, \ldots\}$, and we may ask what is the "multiscale representation" generated by this process as $\epsilon$ decreases to zero.

It is quite easy to see that for the kernels $K_U(x, \epsilon)$ and $K_D(x, \epsilon)$ we approach a continuous "scale space" representation defined by

$$\frac{\partial F(x, \tau)}{\partial \tau} = \frac{1}{2} \frac{\partial^2 F((x, \tau)}{\partial x^2} \qquad F(x, 0) = f(x) \tag{7}$$

This is, of course, the classical diffusion equation, the solution of which is Eq. 5.

The important fact for our purposes is that the iterative smoothing processes defined in Eq. 6 may be regarded as discrete approximations of the heat equation based smoothing process.

### 2.2. Invariant Smoothing

The smoothing processes discussed so far were shift-invariant and invariant to affine point transformations. We could, however, consider more general transformations like

$$T\{f(x)\} = f(m(x - \alpha)) \quad \text{or} \quad T\{f(x)\} = \frac{af(x) + b}{cf(x) + 1} \tag{8}$$

The question that arises in this context is whether we can develop smoothing processes invariant under such maps, i.e. transformations involving translation and scaling of the $x$-axis or nonlinear value transformations.

The basic idea in the sequel, is to adapt the smoothing span so as to achieve x-scaling invariance. If, for example, we use convolution smoothing like in Eq. 7, we should use a kernel $K(mx, \tau)$, but we do not know $m$. One way to solve the problem and to develop a scale-space with the desired properties is to do adaptive smoothing, i.e., let the signal itself set how far the smoothing windows used, e.g. $K_U$ or $K_D$, should extend.

We know that if we have $g(x) = f(m(x - \alpha))$, then $g'(x) = f'(m(x - \alpha)) \cdot m$, i.e. $|g'(x)|$ , if different from zero, could be used to set the span of the smoother since it scales proportionally with the parameter $m$. Hence, we are led to define the following diffusion type p.d.e.

$$\frac{\partial F(x, \tau)}{\partial \tau} = \frac{1}{2} \left( \frac{\partial F}{\partial x}(x, \tau) \right)^{-2} \cdot \frac{\partial^2}{\partial x^2} F(x, \tau) \tag{9}$$

If we want to develop smoothers that will be invariant to some nonlinear function transformations $T\{f(x)\}$ as in Eq. 8, then $T$ does not commute with the convolution smoother anymore. Hence we shall need to redefine the very meaning of averaging to an operation invariant to the desired nonlinear transformation.

Curve smoothing is much more complex than the 1-D function smoothing processes discussed in this section. The tools presented here serve, however, as a model for the curve smoothing processes presented next. The main ideas to remember are that for invariance under a linear group of transformations, one should adaptively control the smoothing span, and that in nonlinear cases one should look for nonlinear averaging operations.

## 3. Smoothing Planar Curves

We could smooth a planar curve $C(p) = [x(p), y(p)]^T$, $p \in [0, 1]$ by applying some averaging process to the functions $x(p)$ and $y(p)$ , extended periodically beyond $[0, 1]$. This was indeed proposed in some early work by Mackworth & Mokhtarian [12] and an iterative averaging process leads, as in the case of 1-D functions, to $\frac{\partial C(p, \tau)}{\partial \tau} = \frac{\partial^2 C(p, \tau)}{\partial p^2}$ with $C(p, 0) = C(p)$ We may regard $C(p, \tau)$ as a scale-space representation of $C(p)$. It is however clear that different reparameterization of the same geometric object, the image of $C(p)$, will lead to different scale-space representations. Hence, even the proposers of this approach Mackworth & Mokhtarian [13] realized that the smoothing process should be driven by some intrinsic properties of the curve.

## 3.1. Euclidean Invariant Smoothing

The first step in the direction of developing smoothing processes that would be geometric in nature, i.e, invariant under the Euclidean transformations is the invariant arc-length reparameterization of the curve to be smoothed. To maintain Euclidean invariance and the semigroup property we reparameterize the curve w.r.t. its own arclength at each step of the smoothing process. Considering the iterative process of smoothing as defined for 1-D functions with, say, the kernel $K_D(p,t)$, we must move the point $C(p)$ on the (arbitrarily parameterized) curve to the average of $C(p + p^f)$ and $C(p - p^b)$, so that the quantities $s_e^F = \int_p^{p^f} \sqrt{x'^2 + y'^2} d\xi$ and $s_e^B = \int_{p^b}^p \sqrt{x'^2 + y'^2} d\xi$ are set a-priori to say $s_e^F = s_e^B = \epsilon$. See Figure 1a. This leads to the smoothing process defined by

$$\frac{\partial \mathbf{C}(p,\tau)}{\partial \tau} = \frac{\partial^2 \mathbf{C}(p,\tau)}{\partial s_e^2} = \kappa(p)\vec{N} \qquad \mathbf{C}(p,0) = C(p)$$

This smoothing equation was already proposed by Mokhtarian and Mackworth [13] for shape boundary smoothing. In the mathematical literature [9] [10] it was proven that an arbitrary simple curve evolving under this evolution stays simple, becoming gradually smoother, in the sense that the number of its inflection points as well as its total curvature decrease monotonically. It was shown that any simple curve becomes convex, and finally shrinks to a vanishing circular point.

## 3.2. Similarity Invariant Smoothing

The similarity group of transformations is a slight generalization of the Euclidean group of motions, it allows uniform scaling of the $x$ and $y$ coordinates by a scale factor $m$. A Euclidean based similarity invariant arclength $ds_s$ would have to be

$$ds_s = \frac{1}{m} ds_e \tag{10}$$

Unfortunately $m$ is not known and we have to use some "adaptive" metric to compensate for the scale factor. Such a metric is, for example (see [4]).

$$ds_s = \frac{x'(p)y''(p) - x''(p)y'(p)}{x'(p)^2 + y'(p)^2} dp = \kappa ds_e \tag{11}$$

Indeed, $\kappa$ is inversely proportional to the radius of curvature, which in turn is proportional to $m$. As a matter of fact we can go on defining additional metrics like Eq. 11. Consider that if $\kappa$ is inversely proportional to $m$, so is $\partial^i \kappa / \partial s_s^i$. Now from Eq. 10 $\partial^i \kappa / \partial s_e^i$ is inversely proportional to $m^{i+1}$. Therefore, all of the following are also similarity invariant metrics. $ds_{s_i} = (\partial^i \kappa / \partial s_e^i)^{\frac{1}{i+1}} ds_e$.

Those metrics enable scale invariant evolutions. The corresponding invariant "scale spaces" will be generated by the equation

$$\frac{\partial \mathbf{C}_i(p,\tau)}{\partial \tau} = \frac{\partial^2}{\partial s_{s_i}^2}\mathbf{C}_i(p,\tau) \qquad \mathbf{C}_i(p,0) = C(p) \tag{12}$$

Or equivalently, using the result by Epstein and Gage [8], by $\partial^2 \mathbf{C}_i/\partial ds_{s_i}^2 = \kappa \cdot (\partial s_{s_i}/\partial s_e)^{-2} \cdot \vec{N}$. For example, for $i = 0$ we get $\frac{\partial \mathbf{C}}{\partial \tau} = \frac{1}{\kappa}\vec{N}$ This equation is problematic near the inflection points, where $\kappa$ is close to zero. As in th 1-D case, we can (at least partly) solve the problem by combining some metrics to create a new similarity invariant metric via say $d\hat{s}_s = (\kappa + \sqrt{\kappa'})ds_e$.

*3.3. Affine Invariant Smoothing*

Affine transformations are of the form $T_a : (x,y) \rightarrow (x,y)A + v$ where $A$ is a nonsingular $2 \times 2$ matrix. Also in this case we have several invariant metrics with which we can define a heat-equation-like evolution. However, the affine transformations group is larger than the similarity transformation group, and the invariant metrics are naturally more complex, see [4]. An interesting subgroup of the affine transformations is the area preserving or unimodular affine transformation group, for which $\det A = 1$, see [4]. For this group we have simpler invariants and the resulting heat-equation-like evolution is

$$\frac{\partial \mathbf{C}(p,\tau)}{\partial \tau} = \frac{\partial^2}{\partial s_A^{*2}}\mathbf{C}(p,\tau) \qquad \mathbf{C}(p,0) = C(p) \tag{13}$$

Equation Eq. 13 is the basis of the scale space representation proposed by Sapiro and Tannenbaum [14]. There it was proved that equation Eq. 13 is indeed the affine invariant equivalent of the Euclidean curve shortening process, and it smoothes curves shrinking arbitrary simple curves to elliptic points. Note however that if we insist on a truly affine invariant smoothing (i.e. not necessarily with $\det A = 1$), we are facing a situation similar to the attempt to extend the Euclidean results to the similarity group of transformations. One should carefully analyze those cases in order to see how the problem of unknown scale invariance could be dealt with.

# 4. Projective Invariant Smoothing

Projective transformations are much more challenging than the ones treated so far. Although the affine maps are often adequate approximations to the viewing projection (via a pinhole camera or the eye) the full mathematical description of the viewing transformations, when a planar object is imaged, is given by $T_p : (x,y) \rightarrow \frac{1}{z(x,y)}[(x,y)A + v]$ where $z(x,y) = (x,y) \cdot w + 1$, $w^T = (w,w_2)$.

This transformation is nonlinear hence we can expect the need for substantial departures from the relatively straightforward approaches to curve smoothing presented so far. Even if we manage to produce a projective invariant arclength, we cannot simply use the linear averaging procedures discussed in Sections 2-3 to derive the invariant smoothing process. Here as well, the problem is reduced to defining a good notion of projective invariant averaging.

Since a projective map takes line segments into line segments, the intersection of two line segments is invariant under projective transformation. With this idea in mind, and assuming we have reparameterized the curve $C(p)$ to $C(s_p)$ where $s_p$ is a projective invariant arclength yet to be determined, see [4]. Let us define the following projective invariant smoothing process:

Take points $A$, $B$, $C$, and $D$ equally spaced (in a projective invariant metric $s_p$) around $\mathbf{C}(s_p^0)$, as in Figure 1b. Denoting the projective center of $A$, $B$, $C$, and $D$ as $\mathbf{C}'(s_p^0)$, an iterative smoothing process can be defined as $\mathbf{C}(s_p^0) \longrightarrow \mathbf{C}'(s_p^0)$

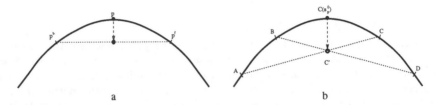

$$a \qquad\qquad\qquad\qquad\qquad b$$

Figure 1: Linear versus projective invariant averaging.

Having defined an iterative smoothing process, what is the corresponding differential equation, as $\epsilon$ decreases to zero? To derive the differential equation that governs the above smoothing process we should consider the projective invariant arclength reparameterization of $\mathbf{C}$ and write it as a series about a certain point $s_p$ the curve is then given by

$$\mathbf{C}(s_p + \delta) = \mathbf{C}(s_p) + \frac{\partial \mathbf{C}}{\partial s_p}\delta + \frac{\partial^2 \mathbf{C}}{\partial s_p^2}\frac{\delta^2}{2!} + \frac{\partial^3 \mathbf{C}}{\partial s_p^3}\frac{\delta^3}{3!} + \cdots \tag{14}$$

Carrying out the intersection of the line segments $AC$ and $BD$ in Figure 1b, and using Eq. 14 we get that

$$\mathbf{C}'(s_p) = \mathbf{C}(s_p) + \left( \frac{\partial^2}{\partial s_p^2}\mathbf{C}(s_p, n) - \frac{2}{3}W(s_p)\frac{\partial}{\partial s_p}\mathbf{C}(s_p, n) \right)\epsilon + O(\epsilon^2) \tag{15}$$

where: $W(s_p) = \frac{\det(\mathbf{C}', \mathbf{C}''')}{\det(\mathbf{C}', \mathbf{C}'')}$. (The computations are horrendous and were carried out using a symbolic mathematical software.) This result is not new: In connection with an iterative process of projective invariant polygon modification called the pentagram map, R. Schwartz [16] has obtained it as the limiting flow for parameterized curves.

Up to now we have suggested one projective invariant transformation as a candidate to replace linear averaging of points on the curve. There are however many alternatives one can think of, and the result obtained in Eq. 15 may not be unique. Therefore we tried several other projective invariant local transformations, depicted graphically in Figure 2. It turned out that all the projective invariant "averaging" alternatives we checked resulted in *the same limiting equations* Eq. 15 (possibly with a constant $\alpha$ multiplying the velocity term i.e. $\alpha\epsilon$ instead of $\epsilon$ in Eq. 15).

Figure 2: More projective invariant smoothing iterations.

This seems to suggest that the projective invariant smoothing flow is uniquely given by

$$\frac{\partial \mathbf{C}(p,\tau)}{\partial \tau} = \frac{\partial^2}{\partial s_p^2}\mathbf{C}(p,\tau) - \frac{2}{3}W(s_p)\frac{\partial}{\partial s_p}\mathbf{C}(p,\tau) \qquad (16)$$

where $s_p$ is a projective invariant arclength reparameterization, as discussed in [4].

Note that $\frac{\partial \mathbf{C}}{\partial p}$ is always tangent to the curve, independent of the parameterization $p$. Therefore, according to [8], the second term of the evolution in Eq. 16 is geometrically unimportant, and we arrive at

$$\frac{\partial \mathbf{C}(p,\tau)}{\partial \tau} = \frac{\partial^2}{\partial s_p^2}\mathbf{C}(p,\tau)$$

as a "geometric" projective invariant flow.

It is in our opinion quite amazing that, in spite of the nonlinearity of the projective transformation, this geometric evolution equation turns out to have the same form as the affine invariant one. There might be some deep reason for this that we do not yet understand. To substantiate the properties of this curve evolution a deep and probably difficult mathematical work still needs to be done. As exemplified by work done for the simpler transformations [9] [10] [2], the challenge is serious, and, as suggested by the similarity invariant case, positive results are not granted a-priori.

## 5. Concluding Remarks

We have attempted to outline a rather comprehensive theory of iterative invariant smoothings for planar curves, generalizing and extending some previous results. More details as well as extentions to invariant evolutions of polygons can be found in [7]. Many interesting questions remain open and we expect to address these in the near future.

118

# References

[1] L. Alvarez, F. Guichard, P. L. Lions, and J. M. Morel, "Axiomatisation et Equation Fondamentales du Traitement d'Images", *C. R. Acad. Sci Paris* Vol. 315, PP. 265–268, 1992.

[2] S. Angenent, "Parabolic Equations for Curves and Surfaces Part II. Intersections, Blow-up and Generalized Solutions", *Annals of Math.* Vol. 133, PP. 171–215, 1991.

[3] W. Blaschke, *Vorlesungen uber Differezialgeometrie II*, Verlag von Julius Springer, Berlin, 1923.

[4] A. M. Bruckstein, R. J. Holt, A. N. Netravali, and T. J. Richardson, "Invariant Signatures for Planar Shape Recognition under Partial Occlusion", *CVGIP Image Understanding*, Vol. 58, PP. 49–65, 1993.

[5] A. M. Bruckstein, N. Katzir, M. Lindenbaum, and M. Porat, "Similarity Invariant Recognition of Partly Occluded Planar Curves and Shapes", *Int. J. Comput. Vision*, Vol. 7, PP. 271–285, 1992.

[6] A. M. Bruckstein, and A. N. Netravali, "On Differential Invariants of Planar Curves and the Recognition of Partly Occluded Planar Shapes", AT&T Technical memo, July 1990; also in *Int. Workshop on Visual Form*, Capri, May 1992.

[7] A. M. Bruckstein, and D. Shaked, "On Projective Invariant Smoothing and Evolutions of Planar Curves and Polygons" *CIS Report No. 9328*, Computer Science Department, Technion, I.I.T., Haifa 32000, Israel, November, 1993.

[8] C. L. Epstein, and M. Gage, "The Curve Shortening Flow", in *Wave Motion*, Eds. A. J. Chorin, and A. J. Madja, Springer Verlag, 1987.

[9] M. Gage, and R. Hamilton, "The Shrinking of Convex Plane Curves by the Heat quation", *J. of Diff. Geometry*, Vol. 23, PP. 69–96, 1986.

[10] M. Grayson, "The Heat Equation Shrinks Embedded Plane Curves to Round Points," *J. of Diff. Geometry*, Vol. 26, PP. 285–314, 1987.

[11] E. P. Lane, *A Treatise on Projective Differential Geometry*, Univ. of Chicago Press, Chicago, 1941.

[12] F. Mokhtarian, and A. K. Mackworth, "Scale–Based Description and Recognition of Planar Curves and Two Dimensional Shapes", Planar Curves", *IEEE Trans. on PAMI*, Vol. 8, PP. 34–43, 1986.

[13] F. Mokhtarian, and A. K. Mackworth, "A Theory of Multiscale, Curvature-Based Shape Representation for Planar Curves", *IEEE Trans. on PAMI*, Vol. 14, PP. 789–805, 1992.

[14] G. Sapiro, and A. Tannenbaum, "Affine Invariant Scale-Space", *Int. J. of Computer Vision* Vol. 11, PP. 25–44, 1993.

[15] G. Sapiro, and A. Tannenbaum, "Area and Length Preserving Geometric Invariant Scale–Spaces", MIT-LIDS Report 2200, September 1993. Accepted for publication, *IEEE Trans. PAMI*.

[16] R. Schwartz, "The Pentagram Map", *Experimental Mathematics*, Vol. 1, PP. 71–81, 1992.

[17] E. J. Wilczynski *Projective Differential Geometry of Curves and Ruled Surfaces*, Teubner, Leipzig, 1906.

[18] A. P. Witkin, "Scale–Space Filtering", *Int. Joint Conf. Art. Intelligence*, PP. 1019–1021, 1983.

# LOCATION OF OBJECTS IN A CLUTTERED SCENE
# USING PROBABILISTIC RELAXATION

## W.J. CHRISTMAS, J. KITTLER, M. PETROU

*Department of Electronic and Electrical Engineering*
*University of Surrey, Guildford, Surrey, GU2 5XH, U.K.*

### ABSTRACT

In this paper, we show how a probabilistic relaxation algorithm can be used to locate a complex 2D object in a cluttered scene. The object model consists of a set of straight line segments that correspond to significant boundary segments of the object; these line segments and their relative positions and orientations are represented by an attributed relational graph. A similar graph is constructed from the scene after edge detection and line fitting. The model graph is matched to the scene graph by the method of probabilistic relaxation during which each model node is matched with a certain probability to each scene node. These probabilities are updated by the relaxation process using contextual information conveyed by the binary relations between the line segments. We demonstrate our method by applying it to the problem of identification of a certain shape in images of greeting cards.

## 1. Introduction

One of the most important cues of object recognition by the human visual system is the object shape. Thus for example in a shadow theatre people have no difficulty in recognising characters from their outlines only.

In machine vision, shape recognition is important in two ways. It can be used as a cue to 3D object recognition. For example, the identification of a certain arrangement of line segments in an image may invoke the hypothesis that a car is present in the scene. This hypothesis can be further tested by examining extra attributes of the object, or by focussing attention on it. In a second type of application, one may deal with 2D scenes only and be interested in identifying a certain shape in them. An example is the problem of accessing a database of images by content, as might happen in the case of a computerised catalogue of the contents of an art gallery or a greeting card manufacturer.

In this paper we present a robust algorithm appropriate for the identification of a certain shape in a 2D scene. The algorithm is so robust that the shape can be represented by a few line segments only, and the environment in which it resides could be very cluttered. In comparison with the popular shape detection alternative - the generalised Hough transform [1, 3, 5, 8] - its robustness is achieved by means of adopting a redundant shape representation. The main advantage over the Hough transform is that the approach does not require searching for local optima, and in this respect it is truly parallelisable.

The robustness of the algorithm stems from the inclusion of unary and binary relations between the segments that are to be matched. The line configuration we seek to identify is the scene, which is represented by an attributed relational graph where each node corresponds to a line segment and its attributes. A similar graph is constructed from the model, and thus the problem is reduced to that of subgraph matching. The initial correspondence of nodes and the probability of each possible match is decided on the basis of any unary information available, together with estimates of the prior probabilities. The contextual support for each possible match is then taken into consideration with the help of the binary relations. This results in a formula for the upgrading of the probabilities of the possible matches, which requires iterative implementation.

Our scheme converges very quickly, usually within one or two iterations. Furthermore the function that expresses the contextual support can be written as a product of functions that express pairwise dependencies, a fact that make the algorithm fast and efficient. The factorisation of the support function and the resulting efficiency in convergence of the algorithm are the major differences between the proposed scheme and that presented by Kittler *et al.* in [7]. Our application is also of a different type, in that in our case the scene is substantially larger than the model. Since this will mean that on convergence there will inevitably be many null matches, we can reflect this fact in our assumptions about the values of the prior probabilities.

The paper is organised as follows: In the next section we discuss how the attributed relational graphs are generated from edges extracted from the scene and model, and we summarise the derivation of the probabilistic relaxation rule. We present some experimental results in section 3 and we draw our conclusions in section 4.

## 2.  Theoretical framework for object labelling using Bayesian reasoning

In this section we state the problem of attributed relational graph matching in terms of Bayesian probability theory, and illustrate how the resulting Maximum A Posteriori expression can be expressed in terms of known quantities. The complete derivation of the algorithm that follows may be found in [2].

### 2.1.  *Generation of the attributed relational graphs*

The scene and model are each represented as an attributed relational graph, in which the nodes correspond to features extracted from the scene or model. In the application presented in this paper, the features used are straight line segments. We represent the nodes of the scene graph as a set of $N$ objects $\{a_1, \ldots, a_N\}$. We then assign to each object $a_i$ a label $\theta_i$, which may take as its value any of the $M + 1$ model node labels that form the set $\Omega = \{\omega_0, \omega_1, \ldots, \omega_M\}$, $\omega_0$ being the null label used to label objects for which no other label is appropriate. We use the notation $\omega_{\theta_i}$ to indicate that we specifically wish to associate a model label with a particular scene label $\theta_i$. We define two sets of indices, $N_0 \equiv \{1, \ldots, N\}$ and $N_i \equiv \{1, \ldots, i-1, i+1, \ldots, N\}$.

For each object $a_i$ there are $m_1$ attributes; these correspond to unary measurements $\mathbf{x}_i = \{x_i^{(1)}, \ldots, x_i^{(m_1)}\}$ made on the features. Since our features are line segments, the measurements could be one or more of the orientation, position and length of the segments. We use $\mathbf{x}_{i, i \in N_0}$ to denote the set $\{\mathbf{x}_1, \ldots, \mathbf{x}_N\}$. Similarly, for each pair of objects $a_i$ and $a_j$ we have a set of $m_2$ relations, corresponding to binary measurements $A_{ij} = \{A_{ij}^{(1)}, \ldots, A_{ij}^{(m_2)}\}$ which can be derived from the unary measurements $\mathbf{x}_i$ and $\mathbf{x}_j$. In our application we use:

$A_{ij}^{(1)}$ - the angle between line segments $a_i$ and $a_j$. Because the order of the objects $i$ and $j$ is significant, its value can range from $-90°$ to $+90°$.

$A_{ij}^{(2)}$, $A_{ij}^{(3)}$ - these measurements express the orientation $\alpha_{ij}$ and distance $d_{ij}$ of the midpoint of segment $j$ with respect to segment $i$. We could have used these measurements directly; however, the uncertainty in $\alpha_{ij}$ is highly dependent on the value of $d_{ij}$. In order to create a set of binary measurements that are independent, we derived a different pair of measurements:

$$A_{ij}^{(2)} = d_{ij} \cos(2\alpha_{ij})$$
$$A_{ij}^{(3)} = d_{ij} \sin(2\alpha_{ij})$$

The factor of 2 is included to express the 180° ambiguity in the line segment orientation.

$A_{ij}^{(4)}$ - the minimum distance between the end-points of line segments $a_i$ and $a_j$.

The abbreviation $A_{ij, j \in N_i} = \{A_{i1}, \ldots, A_{ii-1}, A_{ii+1}, \ldots, A_{iN}\}$ denotes all the binary measurements object $a_i$ has with the other objects in the set. The same classes of unary and binary measurements are also made on the model, to create the model graph: $\check{\mathbf{x}}_\alpha$ denotes the unary measurements of model label $\omega_\alpha$, and $\check{A}_{\alpha\beta}$ denotes the binary measurements between model labels $\omega_\alpha$ and $\omega_\beta$.

### 2.2. Description of the matching algorithm

We invoke the Maximum A Posteriori rule to state that the most appropriate label of object $a_i$ is $\omega_{\theta_i}$ satisfying:

$$P\left(\theta_i \leftarrow \omega_{\theta_i} \mid \mathbf{x}_{j, j \in N_0}, A_{ij, j \in N_i}\right) = \max_{\omega_\lambda \in \Omega} P\left(\theta_i \leftarrow \omega_\lambda \mid \mathbf{x}_{j, j \in N_0}, A_{ij, j \in N_i}\right) \quad (1)$$

We wish to express (1) in a form that is a function of terms derived from the measurements. To do this we make the following assumptions:

- The distribution of a unary measurement conditional on a given match is independent of all other measurements and matches.

- The distribution of a given binary measurement $A_{ij}$ conditional on a given pair of matches $\theta_i \leftarrow \omega_\alpha$ and $\theta_j \leftarrow \omega_\beta$ is independent of all other binary measurements in the set $A_{ij,j \in N_i}$ and all other matches.

- The unconditional match probabilities are mutually independent.

Then by repeated application of Bayes's rule and the theorem of total probability we can expand the expression on the right-hand size of (1) as follows:

$$P(\theta_i \leftarrow \omega_\lambda \mid \mathbf{x}_{j,j \in N_0}, A_{ij,j \in N_i}) = \frac{P(\theta_i \leftarrow \omega_\lambda \mid \mathbf{x}_i) Q(\theta_i \leftarrow \omega_\lambda)}{\sum_{\omega_\alpha \in \Omega} P(\theta_i \leftarrow \omega_\alpha \mid \mathbf{x}_i) Q(\theta_i \leftarrow \omega_\alpha)} \tag{2}$$

where

$$Q(\theta_i \leftarrow \omega_\alpha) = \prod_{j \in N_i} \sum_{\omega_\beta \in \Omega} P(\theta_j \leftarrow \omega_\beta \mid \mathbf{x}_j) p(A_{ij} \mid \theta_j \leftarrow \omega_\beta, \theta_i \leftarrow \omega_\alpha) \tag{3}$$

Clearly the last term in (3) is a quantity that is known to us at the outset of the matching process; hence the equations effectively tell us how to update the probabilities $P(\theta_i \leftarrow \omega_{\theta_i} \mid \mathbf{x}_i)$ given information about the binary measurements. This suggests that the desired solution to the problem of labelling, as defined by (1), can be obtained by combining (2) and (3) in an iterative scheme where the probabilities $P(\theta_i \leftarrow \omega_{\theta_i} \mid \mathbf{x}_i)$ are those calculated at one level (level $n$, say) of the iteration process, and the probabilities $P(\theta_i \leftarrow \omega_{\theta_i} \mid \mathbf{x}_{j,j \in N_0}, A_{ij,j \in N_i})$ are the updated probabilities of a match at level $n+1$ (*c.f.* [4, 6]):

$$P^{(n+1)}(\theta_i \leftarrow \omega_{\theta_i}) = \frac{P^{(n)}(\theta_i \leftarrow \omega_{\theta_i}) Q^{(n)}(\theta_i \leftarrow \omega_{\theta_i})}{\sum_{\omega_\lambda \in \Omega} P^{(n)}(\theta_i \leftarrow \omega_\lambda) Q^{(n)}(\theta_i \leftarrow \omega_\lambda)} \tag{4}$$

where

$$Q^{(n)}(\theta_i \leftarrow \omega_\alpha) = \prod_{j \in N_i} \sum_{\omega_\beta \in \Omega} P^{(n)}(\theta_j \leftarrow \omega_\beta) p(A_{ij} \mid \theta_j \leftarrow \omega_\beta, \theta_i \leftarrow \omega_\alpha) \tag{5}$$

The quantity $Q^{(n)}(\theta_i \leftarrow \omega_\alpha)$ expresses the support the match $\theta_i \leftarrow \omega_\alpha$ receives at the $n^{th}$ iteration step from the other objects in the scene, taking into consideration the binary relations that exist between them and object $a_i$. The density function $p(A_{ij} \mid \theta_i \leftarrow \omega_\alpha, \theta_j \leftarrow \omega_\beta)$ corresponds to the compatibility coefficients of other methods (*e.g.* [4, 9]); that is, it quantifies the compatibility between the match $\theta_j \leftarrow \omega_\beta$ and a neighbouring match $\theta_i \leftarrow \omega_\alpha$.

The iteration scheme can be initialised by considering as $P^{(0)}(\theta_i \leftarrow \omega_\alpha)$ the probabilities computed by using the unary attributes only, *i.e.*

$$\begin{aligned} P^{(0)}(\theta_i \leftarrow \omega_\alpha) &= P(\theta_i \leftarrow \omega_\alpha \mid \mathbf{x}_i) \\ &= \frac{p(\mathbf{x}_i \mid \theta_i \leftarrow \omega_\alpha) P(\theta_i \leftarrow \omega_\alpha)}{\sum_{\omega_\lambda \in \Omega} p(\mathbf{x}_i \mid \theta_i \leftarrow \omega_\lambda) P(\theta_i \leftarrow \omega_\lambda)} \end{aligned} \tag{6}$$

Ideally the process would terminate when an unambiguous labelling is reached, that is when each object is assigned one label only with probability 1, the probabilities for all other labels for that particular object being zero. Since the form of updating rule that we have derived approaches the state of unambiguous labelling asymptotically, in practice we terminate the algorithm if any one of the following conditions is true:

- For each scene node one of the match probabilities exceeds $1 - \epsilon_1$, where $\epsilon_1 \ll 1$ (we set the value of $\epsilon_1$ to 0.1).

- In the last iteration, none of the probabilities changed by more than $\epsilon_2$, where $\epsilon_2 \ll 1$ (we set the value of $\epsilon_2$ to $10^{-9}$).

- The number of iterations has exceeded some large limit (200, say).

We then use (1) to determine the actual match.


## 2.3. Evaluating the terms in the relaxation formula

The evaluation of (4) and (5) requires the calculation of various match probabilities and density functions. The prior probabilities $P(\theta_i \leftarrow \omega_\alpha)$ are defined thus: we estimate the prior probability of the null label to be some value $\zeta$, based on any knowledge we may have of the application; the prior probabilities of all other labels are then set equal to each other. When the size of the scene node set is larger than that of the model (as is the case in the examples in section 3), we assume that the difference in the set sizes reflects the number of null matches. If we had no means of estimating a possible value of $\zeta$, all prior probabilities would be set equal.

In evaluating the density functions for the binary measurements, $p(A_{ij} \mid \theta_i \leftarrow \omega_\alpha, \theta_j \leftarrow \omega_\beta)$, we first consider the general case, in which neither $a_i$ nor $a_j$ is matched to the null label $\omega_0$; in this case, because the density function is conditional on both matches, there is an associated set of model measurements $\check{A}_{\alpha\beta}$. We assume that the noise in the binary measurements $A_{ij}$ can be approximated by a Gaussian:

$$p\left(A_{ij} \mid \theta_i \leftarrow \omega_\alpha, \theta_j \leftarrow \omega_\beta\right) = \mathcal{N}_{A_{ij}}\left(\check{A}_{\alpha\beta}, \Sigma_2\right) \qquad (7)$$

where $\Sigma_2$ is the covariance matrix for the binary measurements $A_{ij}$.

In the remaining cases, in which at least one out of $a_i$ and $a_j$ is matched to the null node, we assumed that they are uniformly distributed. Assuming each measurement $A_{ij}^{(k)}$ has a range of possible values whose width is $\rho^{(k)}$, and denoting the overall range of $A_{ij}$ by $\mathcal{D}$, then

$$p\left(A_{ij} \mid \theta_i \leftarrow \omega_\alpha, \theta_j \leftarrow \omega_0\right) = \begin{cases} \dfrac{1}{\prod_{k=1}^{m_2} \rho^{(k)}} & \text{if } A_{ij} \in \mathcal{D}, \\ 0 & \text{otherwise.} \end{cases} \qquad (8)$$

Because this null match density represents a neutral value, it is convenient to use it as a normalising factor for the compatibility coefficients. Then, coefficients greater than 1 can be thought of as indicating that the match $\theta_i \leftarrow \omega_\alpha$ is supported by the match $\theta_j \leftarrow \omega_\beta$, while coefficients in the range $0 \ldots 1$ indicate the reverse.

We use a similar reasoning to determine density functions for the unary measurements $p(\mathbf{x}_i \mid \theta_i \leftarrow \omega_\alpha)$.

## 3. Experimental results

We demonstrate our method using two hand-painted scenes. The first (fig. 1a) shows a panda surrounded and partially obscured by a bamboo forest. The task was to find and indicate where and in which orientation the model panda (fig. 1b) was in the scene. Line segments were extracted from the scene and model, segments shorter than 32 pixels being discarded in order to keep the problem size within reasonable bounds. These were then used to generate the respective attributed relational graphs. The scene graph consisted of 167 nodes and the model graph 32 nodes (including the null node). Thus in the matching process there were 5344 possible matches to be considered, and about $3 \times 10^7$ compatibility coefficients to be calculated. We chose values for the standard deviations of the relational measurements as follows:

$$\sigma_1 = 10°$$

$$\sigma_2 = 5 \text{ pixels}$$

$$\sigma_3 = 5 \text{ pixels}$$

$$\sigma_4 = 5 \text{ pixels}$$

The distributions of the attribute measurements were considered to be uniform over the whole range of possible values in this application The relaxation process was deemed to have converged when each model node was matched to some scene node with a probability of at least 0.9 ($\epsilon_1 = 0.1$ in section 2.2).

The results can be seen in fig. 2, in which the line segments corresponding to the graph nodes are shown overlaid on the images. The matching line segments are shown in white, and the unmatched ones in black. The white pointer in the scene shows the position of the centre of the model, the arrow of the pointer indicating the orientation of the vertical axis of the model in the scene. These results clearly indicate that the correct match was found. Varying the measurement standard deviations within reasonable limits (*e.g.* doubling them) did not significantly change the results. Although individual nodes were then occasionally mismatched, the position of the panda was always correctly identified.

Using the above parameters, the result was obtained in 2 iterations, and took about 20s on a Sparc10 processor. Most of the execution time (about 90%) was spent computing the compatibility coefficients. Clearly the execution time and storage requirements for the compatibility coefficients are highly dependent on the problem size:

(a) scene                    (b) model

Figure 1: Panda scene and model

reducing the number of nodes in the graphs by a factor of two would decrease them by a factor of 16. There is therefore a compromise to be made between having enough graph nodes to adequately represent the structures of the scene and model, while containing the execution time and memory requirements within reasonable bounds.

The second scene consists of a landscape including two flying birds (fig. 3a). The model to be located in this case was one of the birds (fig. 3b).[1] Line segments shorter than 15 pixels were excluded. Although the model in this example is not occluded, the ratio of scene graph nodes (224) to model nodes (15) was substantially higher. There were thus 3360 possible matches, and about $10^7$ compatibility coefficients to be calculated. Again the correct match was established, also within two iterations. The execution time in this case was 8s.

## 4. Conclusions

In this paper we have presented a method for the matching of attributed relational graphs using probabilistic relaxation, based on the ideas presented in [7]. The principal difference between the approach described here and that of [7] is that in this

---

[1] Here the model is shown rotated though 90°, to emphasise the insensitivity of the matching process to the relative orientation of the model with respect to the scene.

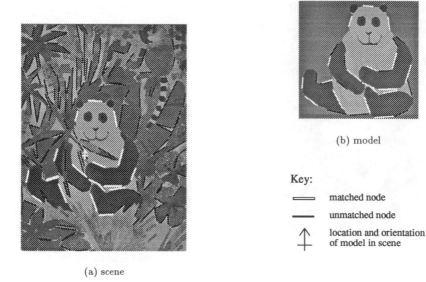

(b) model

Key:

═══ matched node

─── unmatched node

location and orientation
of model in scene

(a) scene

Figure 2: Panda scene and model, showing matched nodes

paper we have avoided the need to assume that the contextual information in the attributed relational graph is small. Since this assumption is frequently not correct in many matching applications, the algorithm presented here is far more robust; in addition it converges to a stable solution extremely rapidly, typically after one or two iterations.

The method readily lends itself to a parallel implementation. In practice, because of the rapid convergence of the algorithm, most of the computation time is spent in the calculation of the compatibility coefficients. Since these calculations are for the most part identical in nature, and are all independent from each other, parallelisation on either SIMD, MIMD or vector machines is straightforward. In this respect the proposed approach has the advantage over the generalised Hough transform in which vote accumulation may easily be parallelised but the search for local maxima is inherently a global process.

An additional benefit of our scheme for shape detection and localisation is its robustness which is achieved by means of adopting a redundant representation for the model shape. The robustness facilitates the detection and localisation of the model shape even in highly cluttered scenes.

(b) model

Key:

⇒ matched node

— unmatched node

⊥ location and orientation
of model in scene

(a) scene

Figure 3: Birds scene and model, showing matched nodes

## 5. References

[1] A. Califano and R. Mohan. Multidimensional indexing for recognising visual shapes. *Conference on Computer Vision and Pattern Recognition*, pages 28–34, 1991.

[2] W.J. Christmas, J. Kittler, and M. Petrou. Matching in computer vision using probabilistic relaxation. Submitted to *IEEE Trans. on Pattern Analysis and Machine Intelligence*.

[3] D.H.Ballard. Generalising the hough transform to detect arbitrary shapes. *Pattern Recognition*, 13(2):111–122, 1981.

[4] R.A. Hummel and S.W. Zucker. On the foundations of relaxation labeling process. *IEEE Trans. Pattern Analysis and Machine Intelligence*, 5(3):267–286, May 1983.

[5] J. Illingworth and J. Kittler. A survey of the hough transform. *Computer Vision, Graphics and Image Processing*, 44:87–116, 1988.

[6] J. Kittler and E.R. Hancock. Combining evidence in probabilistic relaxation. *International Journal of Pattern Recognition and Artificial Intelligence*, 3:29–51, 1989.

128

[7] J. Kittler, M. Petrou, and W.J. Christmas. Probabilistic relaxation for matching problems in computer vision. In *Proceedings of the Fourth International Conference on Computer Vision*, pages 666–673, Berlin, 1993.

[8] H.M. Lee, J. Kittler, and K.C. Wong. Generalised hough transorm in object recognition. In *11th International Conference on Pattern Recognition*, pages 285–289, 1992.

[9] A. Rosenfeld, R. Hummel, and S. Zucker. Scene labeling by relaxation operations. *IEEE Trans. Systems, Man, and Cybernetics*, 6:420–433, June 1976.

# SHAPE DESCRIPTION THROUGH LINE DECOMPOSITION

L.P. CORDELLA, F. TORTORELLA, M. VENTO

*Dipartimento di Informatica e Sistemistica*
*Universita' di Napoli "Federico II"*
*Via Claudio 21, 80125, Napoli, Italy*

ABSTRACT

Representing ribbon-like figures by means of simple primitives is a desirable result in fields such as OCR and document interpretation. We discuss a method which allows the decomposition of ribbon-like shapes into pieces assimilable to circular arcs, starting from the polygonal approximation of the skeleton of the ribbon. The fitting criterion, used to find the best arc approximating a given set of segments, obviously depends on the error norm used to measure the similarity between an arc of circle and a polygonal. According to the scope and to the semantics of the ribbon shape, different error norms can be used, attaining representations with different geometric properties. Two error norms, based on the $L_2$ and $L_\infty$ metrics, are described; the results, obtained using a database containing figures from different documents, are discussed.

## 1. Introduction

In the framework of structural methods for the recognition of shapes, one of the approaches followed by many authors [1-4] is based on the decomposition of an initial representation into simply describable parts. In this way a shape is transformed into a structure made of a set of elementary components interrelated by more or less complex links.

Whenever the shapes of interest can be thought of as ribbons evolving and intersecting in a 2D space (characters, line drawings, etc), the most convenient initial representation seems to be a thin line, centered within the strokes and then called Medial Axis Transform (MAT) [4-6]. Alternative thinning techniques have also been used [7].

We illustrate a method especially tailored for decomposing characters, either handprinted or printed, into strokes. The method can be easily adapted to the case of different classes of ribbon like shapes.

The MAT is chosen as the initial ribbon representation. It is known [8,9] that Medial Axis Transformations may give place to distorted representations of the shape of the strokes they should describe. We use a preprocessing [10] that allows to correct MAT disortions without producing unwanted side effects. The preprocessing also transforms the MAT into a polygonal line which is successively either suitably broken or unfolded in correspondence to crossings or junctions. The actual representation we start from is

130

thus a set made of one or a few polygonal lines that guarantee an adequate preservation of the shape of the characters (see Fig. 1).

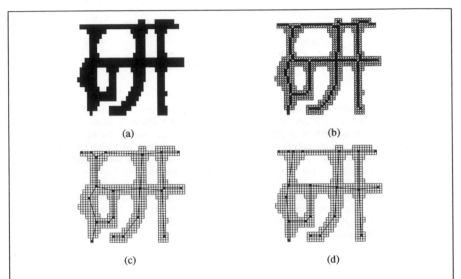

(a)

(b)

(c)

(d)

Fig. 1. The bit map of a kanji character (a), its MAT (b) and the corresponding polygonal approximation before (c) and after (d) correcting shape distortions introduced by the thinning process.

The next step in the process is that of decomposing the mentioned lines into pieces in such a way that each piece can be simply described and at the same time represents a perceptively significant feature of the character. This problem has been faced by many authors [e.g., 11-13].

The shape of unconstrained handprinted characters produced by a large number of writers shows an extreme variability. Recognition has thus to be based on singling out features as much as possible invariant within any given class.

We believe that instead to rely on local features [e.g., 14,15] which, although carefully selected, could be missing or could vary in shape and position, it is better to attempt to single out and describe larger pieces of lines, through a suitable integration process, so as to obtain more general descriptions which absorb local variability.

The task is anything but trivial since it implies a compromise between conflicting aims: to reabsorb variability within each class and not to destroy information necessary to discriminate among the different classes.

It can be noted that lines representing both printed and handprinted characters can be effectively represented in terms of sequences of conic arcs and straight segments.

However, in the universe of latin characters, different types of arcs appear to have the same semantic value, especially if the context in which they are embedded is considered. Experiments have shown that the circular arc has enough descriptive power to substitute curves of different shape, but having the same semantic value, without destroying discriminant features. Our algorithm decomposes the lines representing a character into circular arcs (arcs by now on) of different radius of curvature; straight segments are considered as the limit case of an arc. Conceptually the algorithm is based on some a priori knowledge about the way characters are drawn. Arcs are then used as primitive components for the description.

## 2. The Method

The aim of our algorithm for fitting circular arcs to polygonal lines is to obtain an heuristically optimal compromise between "faithful reproduction" of character shape and "adequate tolerance" with respect to not significant shape variations. As it is well known [16], curve fitting implies two problems: first, how to fit a given curve to a set of input data, second, how to decide that the fitting (i.e. the approximation) is satisfactory.
To face the former problem, we first transform the polygonal line in the $(x,y)$ plane into a set of horizontal segments (a stepwise function) in a $(l,\alpha)$ plane, where $l$ is the distance of points along the polygonal from a reference point (curvilinear abscissa), and $\alpha$ is the angle between each segment of the polygonal and a starting segment (see Fig. 2).

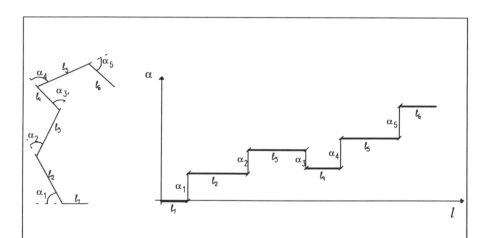

Fig. 2. A polygonal line in the $(x,y)$ plane (left) and its representation in the $(l,\alpha)$ plane (right). Counterclockwise angles are positive.

If continuous curves instead of polygonals were considered, circular arcs in the (x,y) plane would be transformed into straight segments in the $(l,\alpha)$ plane. Similar representations have been used elsewere [17-19].

A fitting criterion should be based on an error norm that allows to measure the similarity between a circular arc and a polygonal, in order to find the best arc that approximates a given set of segments. The adopted representation allows to transform this problem into that of best approximating a stepwise function by a straight line.

More formally, the problem of decomposing a given shape represented by a polygonal P can be stated as finding the set $\Gamma$ of circular arcs such that:

$$\|P - \Gamma\| < E$$

where E is the maximum allowable error made by the approximation and $\|\bullet\|$ is the norm used to measure the shape distance between the two curves.

This task, particularly heavy from a computational point of view if performed in the (x,y) plane, is much easier to tackle in the $(l,\alpha)$ plane. In this case, in fact, we have to approximate a staircase function (representing the polygonal) with a set of straight segments (each representing a circular arc of a certain radius of curvature): in other words, we deal with first order curves instead of second order ones.

According to the scope and the semantics of the ribbon shape, different error norms can be used, so attaining representations with different geometric and topological properties. For our purposes, the error norms based on the $L_2$ and $L_\infty$ metrics [20] are particularly significant. Given two curves $C_1$ and $C_2$, represented in the $(l,\alpha)$ plane, two shape distances between them can be consequently defined:

$$E_2 = \sqrt{\int \left| \alpha_1(l) - \alpha_2(l) \right|^2 dl}$$

$$E_\infty = \max_l \left| \alpha_1(l) - \alpha_2(l) \right|$$

where $\alpha_i(l)$ is the angle between the tangent to $C_i$ in the point of curvilinear abscissa $l$ and a reference direction.

Depending on the metric employed, the circular arc best fitting a piece of polygonal can be obtained by calculating, in the $(l,\alpha)$ plane, the straight segment which minimizes, respectively, the integral square error $E_2$ or the maximum error $E_\infty$.

Both parameters can be evaluated by measuring the difference between the $\alpha$ coordinates of points of equal curvilinear abscissa, belonging respectively to the stepwise function and to its approximating straight line. In order to find the straight line minimizing the value of the approximation errors, in case of $E_2$ we use the least square method, while for $E_\infty$ we use the one-point exchange algorithm [21]. Note that, in the first case, the contribution given by any segment of the polygonal depends on its length.

This is reasonable because long segments should give a greater contribution than short ones to the determination of the approximating arc.

Once the arc best approximating a given piece of polygonal has been determined, it is necessary to verify if it can be actually assumed to stand for the original polygonal line, i.e., if its shape is not "too" different from that of the polygonal. This is achieved by comparing the obtained value of the approximation error with a dinamically evaluated threshold value that represents the error that would be made when approximating with a circular arc a portion of a k-side polygon having the same angular span of the approximated polygonal. The value attributed to k allows to control the degree of approximation (see Fig. 3).

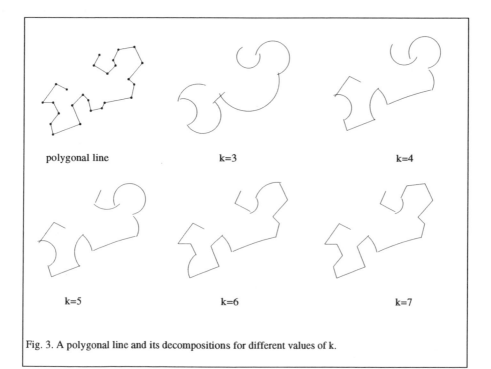

Fig. 3. A polygonal line and its decompositions for different values of k.

Note that the $(l,\alpha)$ transforms are position and rotation invariant; the representations are also normalized in order to become size invariant. Invariance with respect to the mentioned transformations is an important and wanted feature of the representation since it is needed both to correctly apply the acceptance criterion and to cancel some types of not significant variations among characters belonging to the same class.

Another important feature of a curve decomposition technique is the strategy according to which the segments of the polygonal are considered for grouping them together in order to determine the set of circular arcs fitting the polygonal.

A first strategy we adopted is based on merging: successive segments of the polygonal are grouped and approximated with the arc which minimizes the chosen shape distance. The grouping proceeds until the approximation is considered acceptable; the segment on which the approximation has failed is assumed as the starting segment of a further polygonal piece to be approximated.

A splitting scheme has been considered too. The whole polygonal is approximated with a single arc and, if the distance between the approximating arc and the polygonal is over a dinamically evaluated threshold, the polygonal is split at the segment for which the approximation error was the highest. The process is then iterated until the error is below the threshold for every achieved polygonal piece.

The above strategies when combined with the already mentioned error norms give place to decompositions schemes having some different properties which will be discussed in the following.

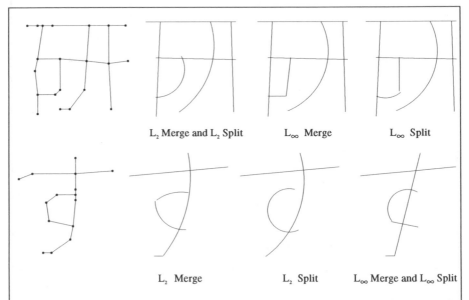

$L_2$ Merge and $L_2$ Split    $L_\infty$ Merge    $L_\infty$ Split

$L_2$ Merge    $L_2$ Split    $L_\infty$ Merge and $L_\infty$ Split

Fig. 4. The polygonal lines representing two kanji characters and their decompositions using the various combinations of strategies and of error norms. The results refer to k=5.

## 3. Discussion

The decomposition schemes have been tested on characters (latin and kanji) and on line drawings: the obtained results allow to outline some different features of the considered schemes.

Splitting schemes allow to fit particular segment configurations with less arcs than merging schemes, so giving place to more synthetic decompositions. In these cases, in fact, merging schemes lead to overcome the dynamic error threshold during the sequential grouping of segments (so producing more than one arc) even though the whole piece could be approximated with one single arc, because the overall approximation error is below the dynamic threshold.

On the other hand, splitting schemes exhibited some drawbacks for other peculiar configurations of the polygonal line, independently of the adopted error norm. In particular, when the segments of the polygonal line could be grouped in two clusters having opposite concavities (see the top character in Fig. 5), the corresponding $(l,\alpha)$ transform has the aspect shown in Fig. 5. According to splitting schemes, the first step of the fitting process tries to find the circular arc best approximating the whole piece of polygonal and evaluates the committed approximation error. If the approximation error is overcome, the polygonal is split at the segment giving the highest contribution to the error. In the considered case, the highest relative error values are generally obtained at the extremes of the considered piece and at the segment in which the polygonal changes its concavity. If, among these values, the maximum is reached for one of the extreme segments, the split strategy will generate two clusters, one containing only the extreme segment, and the other containing the remaining segments of the polygonal line. In a similar way, the successive step of the split process isolates once again the last polygonal segment, holding all the remaining ones together. This situation generally occurs until the change of concavity is reached; the final result is that one of the parts of the original piece of polygonal is decomposed into its component segments.

Similar problems arise when the polygonal line can be seen as made of two successive pieces having different curvature, as in the case of the bottom character of Fig. 5.

As for merging schemes, their main drawback is a side effect due to the way the grouping is performed: in fact, as already said, contiguous segments are grouped together until the error threshold is exceeded. If the remaining successive segments will be approximated by an arc with a low error value, it could happen that, moving the last segment from the first cluster to the successive one (so obtaining two new clusters), the error relative to the second cluster remains below the threshold, while the overall error on the two new clusters decreases. This process implies a more uniform redistribution of the approximation error over the various clusters and a decrease of the total error. In principle, more than one segment could be moved from a cluster to the successive one .

Starting from the above considerations, we have defined a simple but effective readjustment procedure involving a re-examination of the distribution of the segments among contiguous arcs, once the whole polygonal has been decomposed. In Fig. 6 the result of the readjustment procedure on a latin character is shown.

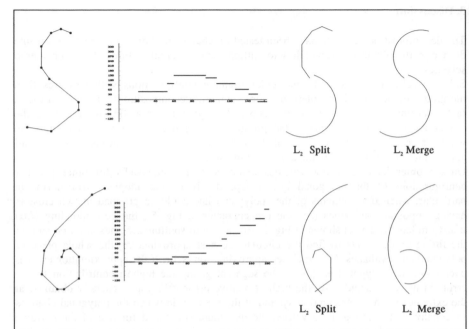

Fig. 5. The polygonal lines of two characters, the corresponding $(l,\alpha)$ transforms, and their decompositions obtained with both split and merge strategies (k=5).

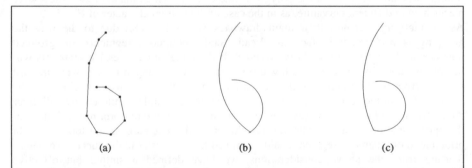

Fig. 6. A polygonal line (a) and its decomposition with the merge strategy (k=5) before (b) and after the knot readjustment procedure (c).

# 4. References

[1]     T. Pavlidis, *Structural Pattern Recognition*, Springer-Verlag, 1977.

[2]     T. Pavlidis, "A Vectorizer and Feature Extractor for Document Recognition", *Comput. Vision, Graphics, Image Processing*, vol. 35, pp. 111-127, 1986.

[3]     C.Y. Suen and R.I. Shillman, "Low Error Rate Optical Character Recognition of Unconstrained Handprinted Letters Based on a Model of Human Perception", *IEEE Trans. Syst., Man, Cybern.*, vol. SMC-7, pp. 491-495, 1977.

[4]     A. Rosenfeld and A.K. Kak, *Digital Picture Processing*, 2nd ed., Academic Press, 1982.

[5]     C. Arcelli, L.P. Cordella and S. Levialdi, "From Local Maxima to Connected Skeletons", *IEEE Trans. Pattern Anal. Machine Intell.*, vol. PAMI-3, pp. 134-143, 1981.

[6]     C. Arcelli and G. Sanniti di Baja, "A Width Independent Fast Thinning Algorithm", *IEEE Trans. Pattern Anal. Machine Intell.*, vol. 7, pp. 463-474, 1985.

[7]     L. Lam, S. Lee and C.Y. Suen, "Thinning Metodologies: A Comprehensive Survey", *IEEE Trans. Pattern Anal. Machine Intell.*, vol. 14, pp. 869-885, 1992.

[8]     S. Mori, K. Yamamoto and M. Yasuda, "Research on Machine Recognition of Handprinted Characters", *IEEE Trans. Pattern Anal. Machine Intell.*, vol. PAMI-6, pp. 386-405, 1984.

[9]     O. Hori and S. Tanigawa, "Raster-to-Vector Conversion by Line Fitting Based on Contours and Skeletons", *Proc. of 2nd Int. Conf. on Document Analysis and Recognition*, Tsukuba Science City (Japan), pp. 353-356, 1993.

[10]    L.P. Cordella and A. Marcelli, "Normalization and Decomposition of Thin Lines Representing Handprinted Characters", *Proc. of 8th Int. Conf. on Pattern Recogn.*, Paris, pp. 723-725, 1986.

[11]    G.A.W. West and P.L. Rosin, "Techniques for Segmenting Image Curves into Meaningful Descriptions", *Pattern Recognition*, vol. 24, pp. 643-652, 1991.

[12]    D.M. Wuescher and K.L. Boyer, "Robust Contour Decomposition Using a Constant Curvature Criterion", *IEEE Trans. Pattern Anal. Machine Intell.*, vol. 13, pp. 41-51, 1991.

[13]    M.A. Fischler and H.C. Wolf, "Locating Perceptually Salient Points on Planar Curves", *IEEE Trans. Pattern Anal. Machine Intell.*, vol. 16, pp. 113-129, 1994.

[14]    K. Kobayashi et al., "Recognition of Handprinted Kanji Characters by the Stroke Matching Method", *Pattern Recognition Letters*, vol. 1, pp. 481-488, 1983.

[15]    T. Pavlidis and F. Ali, "A Hierarchical Syntactic Shape Analyzer", *IEEE Trans. Pattern Anal. Machine Intell.*, vol. PAMI-1, pp. 2-9, 1979.

[16]    T. Pavlidis, "Curve Fitting As a Pattern Recognition Problem", *Proc. of 6th Int. Conf. on Pattern Recogn.*, Munich, pp. 853-859, 1982.

[17]    W.A. Perkins, "A Model-based Vision System For Industrial Parts", *IEEE Trans. Comput.*, vol. 27, pp. 126-143, 1978.

138

[18]   V.S. Nalwa and E. Pauchon, "Edgel Aggregation and Edge Description", *Comput. Vision, Graphics, Image Processing*, vol. 40, pp. 79-94, 1987.

[19]   E.M. Arkin, L.P. Chew, D.P. Huttenlocher, K. Kedem and J.S.B. Mitchell, "An Efficiently Computable Metric for Comparing Polygonal Shapes", *IEEE Trans. Pattern Anal. Machine Intell.*, vol. 13, pp. 209-215, 1991.

[20]   W. Rudin, *Real and Complex Analysis*, McGraw-Hill, New York, 1970.

[21]   J.L. Buchanan and P.R. Turner, *Numerical Methods and Analysis*, McGraw-Hill, New York, 1992.

# Multiscale Contour Approximation Based on Scale Space Analysis with A Stable Gaussian Smoothing

Koichiro DEGUCHI,    Hidekata HONTANI

Faculty of Engineering, University of Tokyo
Hongo, Bunkyo-ku, Tokyo 113 Japan

### Abstract

In this paper, a new contour figure approximation method for interpretation and recognition is proposed, where detail structures are blurred out by Gaussian filters and global structures remain clearly.

This approximation is based on scales, which are locally inherent sizes of structures at every point on the contour. The point by point local scales are extracted based on the scale space analysis. Then, the approximation is generated by using Gaussian filters having those individual scales for every point.

By this method, a series of limited number approximation figures were obtained. Furthermore, the series of approximations of an approximated figure is entirely included in the original series. These properties mean the the proposed approximation is useful for description of structures of contour figures.

## 1    Introduction

A contour shape is well characterized by approximating figures by blurring out its details with Gaussian filters. The result has smoother arcs than the original figure. But, for interpretation and recognition of the global figure, those arc curves must have proper "smoothness" locally point by point on the contour. We call these proper smoothness to characterize the original feature "the characteristic scales."

A Gaussian filter with a scale $t = \sigma^2$ blurs out smaller features of the contour than $\sigma$. For example, when the original contour is blurred by a Gaussian filter with $t_0 = \sigma_0^2$, convex or concave vertexes having smaller side-slopes than $\sigma_0$ are smoothed out. So that, we obtain an approximation which figures out global characteristics of the contour.

However, if we use a fixed scale $t_0$ for entire points on the contour, as in conventional methods, while detail local structures are smoothed out, even global structures will be deformed as the side effects. So, we must select suitable scale $t$ point by point on the contour. In this paper, we define and find such the inherent scales, which make global structures remain clearly, based on the scale space analysis of the second derivatives of the curvatures of the blurred figure.

When we are given a scale $t_0$, in this method, the suitable scales for every contour points are selected according that ;

- smaller structures which are smoothed out with $t_0$ and smaller scales should be smoothed out using the smallest possible scale,

- larger structures which remain in the blurring with $t_0$ should remain as it was without blurring at this scale.

To generate well characterizing approximations according to these policies, we must solve next two problems. Firstly, to employ different scales point by point to blur a figure, every individual point on the given original contour must be traced across the scale values. In other words, every points between blurred figures with different scales should maintain their respective correspondences.

Secondly, as shown in later, a series of limited number of approximated figures are obtained by this method. In this series, a strict inclusion must be hold. That is, the series of approximations of an approximated figure must be entirely included in the original series.

Theoretically, the Gaussian blurring process is considered to form a "semi-group", that is, blurring an original figure with $t_a = \sigma_a^2$ then with $t_b = \sigma_b^2$ should be equivalent to the blurring it with $t_c = t_a + t_b$. This is one of the good properties of the Gaussian blurring and necessary to maintain the correspondences and the inclusions. [1, 2, 5]. But, this is not achieved by conventional simple methods [3]. Recently, one method which coped with this problem was proposed by Makhtarian *et al.* [1]. In our approximation, we follow this method to construct a stable scale space.

It should be also noted that we have only small number of approximations, even if changing the value of $t_0$ in a wide range. It is shown that, by this method, the resulted figures characterize respectively the contour well reserving its global features.

In the followings, we describe the stable Gaussian blurring techniques and the extraction of the suitable scales for a given contour, then we propose the approximation method.

# 2   Gaussian Blurring and Scale Space Analysis

## 2.1   A Stable Gaussian Blurring

Firstly, we introduce a stable Gaussian blurring following Makhtarian *et al.* [1]. By this blurring, the point correspondences across the scale values can be maintained and the resulted scale space enables our multi-scale approximation.

Let us consider a contour represented as

$$\Gamma = \{(x(w), y(w)) | w \in [0, 1]\} \tag{1}$$

where $w$ is a parameter proportional to the arc length along the contour from a fixed point and normalized with its total length.

We blur a contour using the Gaussian filter having a scale $t = \sigma^2$ into

$$\Gamma_t = \{(X(u, t), Y(u, t)) | u \in [0, 1]\} \tag{2}$$

where

$$X(u, t) = x(u) * G(u, t) ,$$
$$Y(u, t) = y(u) * G(u, t) ,$$
$$\text{and} \quad G(u, t) = \frac{1}{\sqrt{2\pi t}} e^{\frac{-u^2}{2t}}$$

**Fig.1** shows an example of this Gaussian blurring.

By this operation, we obtain a smoothed figure whose smaller structures than $\sigma$ has been blurred out. The space $(u, t)$ is called a scale space, and analyzing the changes of figure in this space is called the scale space analysis.

It should be noted that the parameter $u$ of above $X(u, t)$ and $Y(u, t)$ will no longer be proportional to the arc length of $\Gamma_t$. Without some adjustments on the parameter $u$, this makes false traces of the corresponding contour points in the scale space to extract suitable scales for later analyses.

Theoretically, the operation of the Gaussian blurring forms a "semi-group" with respect to the scale parameter $t$. But it does not hold for *digital curves* if simply apply the operation next by next. That is, denoting the Gaussian blurring with the scale $t = \sigma^2$ by $\mathcal{G}_t$, the shape of $\mathcal{G}_{t_a+t_b}(\Gamma)$ does not necessarily equal to $\mathcal{G}_{t_b}(\mathcal{G}_{t_a}(\Gamma))$ $= \mathcal{G}_{t_b}(\Gamma_{t_a})$ as shown in **Fig.2** This is because the density of the digitized points will locally change after the blurring, and the number of the points will no longer correspond to the arc length of the blurred contour.

For our purpose of shape analysis, the series of blurred figure with respect to the scale values should have a strict order of smoothness, as shown in **Fig.3**.

To hold $\mathcal{G}_{t_a+t_b}(\Gamma) = \mathcal{G}_{t_b}(\mathcal{G}_{t_a}(\Gamma))$, it is concluded that the parameter $u$ should be always adjusted to be proportional to the arc length along the new blurred contour. This can be established as followings [1]:

Let a point on the blurred contour with the scale $t = \sigma^2$ be denoted with

$$\mathbf{R} = (X(W, t), Y(W, t)), \tag{3}$$

where the parameter $W = W(w, t)$ represents its arc length after blurring.

Because the Gaussian function is a Green function for a diffusion process,

$$\frac{\partial \mathbf{R}}{\partial t} = \kappa \mathbf{n}, \tag{4}$$

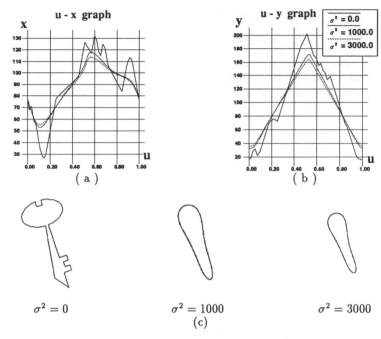

Figure 1: Smoothings of contour figures with simple Gaussian blurrings. (a), (b)X-
and Y-coordinates of contours obtained with $\sigma^2 = 0,\ 1000,\ 3000$. (c) Smoothed
figures with $\sigma^2 = 0,\ 1000,\ 3000$, respectively.

this means that by blurring a contour point moves with an amount of curvature $\kappa$
at the point in the normal direction $\boldsymbol{n}$ of the contour. Then,

$$\frac{\partial}{\partial t}\left|\frac{\partial \boldsymbol{R}}{\partial u}\right| = -\left|\frac{\partial \boldsymbol{R}}{\partial u}\right|\kappa^2. \tag{5}$$

So, denoting the total arc length with $L$,

$$\frac{\partial L}{\partial t} = -\int_0^L \frac{\partial}{\partial t}\left|\frac{\partial \boldsymbol{R}}{\partial u}\right|du = -\int_0^L \left|\frac{\partial \boldsymbol{R}}{\partial u}\right|\kappa^2 du. \tag{6}$$

This implies that

$$\frac{\partial W}{\partial t} = -\int_0^W \kappa^2(U,t)dU, \tag{7}$$

which means that, by blurring with $t = \sigma^2$, the local arc length will be shortened by
the amount of the integral of the square of its curvature. This can be rewritten as

$$W(w,t) = -\int_0^t\int_0^W \kappa^2(U,T)dU\,dT + w, \tag{8}$$

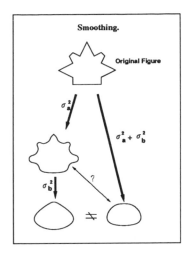

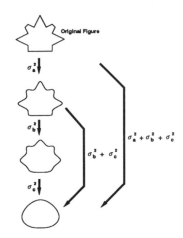

Figure 2: Blurring with $t_a = \sigma_a^2$ then with $t_b = \sigma_b^2$ does not necessarily equivalent to the blurring with $t_a + t_b$ in conventional scale space analyses.

Figure 3: Desired stable blurring and its resulted series of blurred figures.

where $W(w, 0) = w$ which is the original arc length.

Therefore, to hold the order of blurred figures just as mentioned above, a point on the blurred contour with $t = \sigma^2$ should always be represented with the parameter $W$ given as (8). However, the calculation of (8) is not easy, and here we employ an alternative method to maintain the parameter being proportional to the arc length.

**Fig.4** shows this adjustment process by re-sampling the points on the contour, schematically. To blur the contour with some total scale $t$, we repeat the blurring with small value $\Delta t$'s next by next, adjusting the sample points to hold even spacings for every time, until the total amount of the blurring reaches $t$. It has been proven [1] that this process is equivalent to the adjustment by (8) when $\Delta t \to 0$.

## 2.2 Determination of Local Scales Based on the Scale Space Analysis

Employing the blurring method just described in previous section, we can trace the corresponding points through the series of blurred figures.

Being applied the Gaussian blurring next by next, the curvature of the resulted figure becomes more even and constant, so that the blurred figure becomes circular as shown in Fig.1.

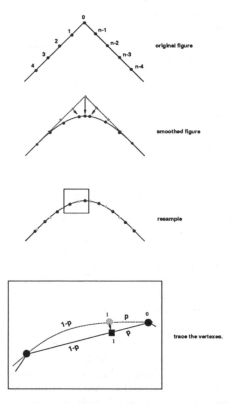

Figure 4: Parameter adjustment and tracing vertexes in the stable blurring for making correspondence to the arc length of contours.

When we plot the zero-crossings of the second derivatives of curvatures of blurred figures on the space of the scale $t$ and the original arc position $w$, which is the scale space, we obtain so-called "finger print" pattern. Examples are shown in **Fig.5** and **Fig.6**. It is shown that each of the plotting forms upward closure at some scale value [4, 5]. This is because the zero-crossing is considered as a boundary of a group of local contour structures having some common scale along the contour. The scale value with which some zero-crossing just closes upward and disappears is considered as that of the local structures. We can define local inherent scale of structures as the blurring scale when the zero-crossing just disappears.

We determine local scales of given contour by plotting the "finger print" pattern of zero-crossings of the second derivatives of the curvature and trace them increasing the scale value to find the point where they disappear.

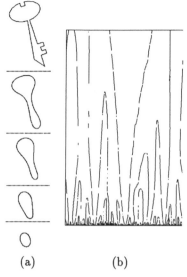

(a)                    (b)

Figure 5:
(a)An example of smoothed figures of "key" using modified Gaussian filter.(b)Obtained zero-crossings of second differentiated curvature.

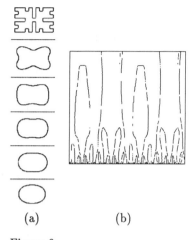

(a)                    (b)

Figure 6:
(a)Another example of smoothed figures of "crest" using modified Gaussian filter.(b)Obtained zero-crossings of second differentiated curvature.

# 3 Approximating Contour Figures Based on Curvature Scale Space Analysis

Now, we present the approximation procedure based on the just determined local scales. In this approximation for a given scale $t_0$, features with smaller scales than $t_0$ are smoothed out by the Gaussian filters having the smallest possible scales to blur them, but larger features remain as it was without blurring.

The total process for approximating the contour figures is summarized as:

1. Assume that we obtained a finger print map for a given contour figure in the scale space with an axis of original arc length $w$ and the scale value $t$, which is shown in **Fig.7**(a). Then we approximate this figure by deleting smaller detail structures than a given scale $t_0$.

2. Divide the scale space into two areas A and B with the boundary of the nearest small zero-crossing plot to $t = t_0$, as shown in Fig.7(b), where the area A includes $t = t_0$ and the area B is the region of smaller scales than the boundary. That is, given $t_0$, the boundary $t = t(w)$ is given as; i) $0 \leq t(w) < t_0$, ii) there

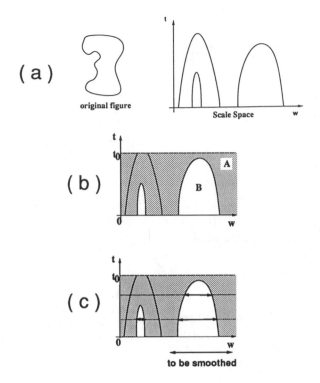

Figure 7: The proposed approximation method. (a) Original contour and its finger print map of curvature zero-crossings, (b) Area B shows the area of the structure whose scale is smaller than $t_0$. (c) At each scale, the area on the contour figure showed by Area B is smoothed.

is no *closed* zero-crossing plot between $t = t(w)$ and $t = t_0$, and iii) every part of $t = t(w)$ is either on a closed zero-crossing plot or $t = 0$.

3. Smoothen the given original contour figure by the Gaussian blurring with scales $t = t(w)$ at every respective contour point $w$, as shown in Fig.7(c).

By changing the base scale $t_0$, we have a finite number of approximations by this procedure. This is because, within an interval around a given $t_0$, we obtain same blurring scales of $t = t(w)$. The pattern of $t = t(w)$ for a given $t_0$ will only changes when the value $t_0$ crosses over some closing point of zero-crossing plot.

We will show some remarkable properties of this approximating method with experimental results in the next section.

# 4 Experimental Results of Approximations

**Fig.8** shows approximations of silhouette contours by proposed method.

Only detail local structures are deleted and global structures remain clearly with respect to every scales, which is evidently shown in (a) in comparison with Fig.1(c) or Fig.5(a).

It should be noted that the series of figures of (a) show all approximated figures obtained from the original contour, and no other type of approximation were obtained by the proposed method. Other examples shown in Fig.5 also have limited numbers of approximations just shown here.

We also show approximations of an approximated figure of (a) in Fig.5(b). This shows a series of approximations of an approximated figure is entirely included in the series of approximations of the original figure. This property of inclusion is important for discriminating the similarities of the shape of contour figures.

Fig.8(c) and (d) show the results for two figures which have common structures in their parts. These figures show that the same structure will be blurred similarly. This means the the proposed approximation is useful for description of structures of contour figures. This cannot be achieved by blurring with a fixed scale for entire figure.

# 5 Conclusions

In this paper, a new approximation method for contour figures is proposed, where detail structures are blurred out by Gaussian filters and global structures remain clearly.

This method has following properties: First, a limited number of approximated figures were obtained, each of which represent every local inherent scales. This means the the proposed approximation is useful for description of structures of contour figures. Next, a series of approximations of an approximated figure is entirely included in the series of approximations of the original figure. This property of inclusion is important for discriminating the similarities of the shape of contour figures. This promises a step of good recognition method for contour figures.

# References

[1] Mokhtarian, F. and K.Mackworth, A.: A Theory of Multiscale, Curvature-Based Shape Representation for Planar Curves, *IEEE Trans.* Vol. PAMI-14, No. 8, pp. 789–805 (1992).

[2] Lu, Y. and Jain, R. C.: Behavior of Edges in Scale Space, *IEEE Trans.*, Vol. PAMI-11, No. 4, pp. 337–356 (1989).

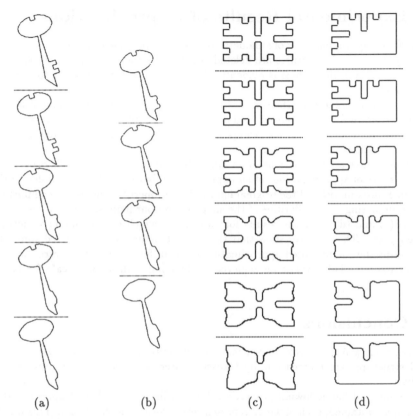

Figure 8: (a) Results of proposed approximation method for silhouette contour of a key, and (b) the approximation results for the figure of the middle of(a). (c) Approximations of an artificial contour figure, and (d) the results for figure which has the same structures in parts as (c).

[3] Mokhtarian, F. and K.Mackworth, A.: Scale-Based Description and Recognition of Planar Curves and Two-Dimensional Shapes, *IEEE Trans.*, Vol. PAMI-8, No. 1, pp. 34–43 (1986).

[4] Mokhtarian, F.: Fingerprint theorems for curvature and torsion zerocrossings, *Proc. IEEE CVPR(San Diego,CA)*, pp. 269–275 (1989).

[5] Yuille, A. L. and Poggio, T. A.: Scaling Theorems for Zero Crossings, *IEEE Trans.*, Vol. PAMI-8, No. 1, pp. 15–25 (1986).

[6] Bengtsson, , Eklundh, and Howako, : Shape Representation by Multiscale Contour Approximation, Dept. of Numerical Analysis and Computing Science TRITA-NA-8607, University of Stockholm, Sweden (1986).

# OCR by Elastic Digit Models

A. Del Bimbo, S. Santini

*Dipartimento di Sistemi e Informatica, Università di Firenze*
*50137 Firenze, Italy*
and

Jorge L. C. Sanz

*Department of Electrical and Computer Engineering*
*The University of Illinois at Urbana-Champaign*
*Urbana, IL*

### Abstract

In this paper we present a method for elastic pattern matching that we apply to segmentation-free OCR. We use a number of digit models (*templates*) that are allowed to undergo elastic deformation while trying to adapt to the digit image they are exposed to. Each template must satisfy two competing requirements: (1) it must match the image as much as possible and (2) it must keep its elastic deformation energy as little as possible. These two requirements can be expressed in the form of a variational problem, whose solution givesthe optimal deformation for a template. Once all the templates have been deformed, their elastic energy and match are measured to determine which of them obtained the best much with the lowest deformation energy.

## 1 Introduction

OCR spanned the life of pattern recognition research as the eternally almost-solved problem. From the days of the flying-spot scanner to the age of CCD devices ([3, 5, 10]), a number of people committed to solve this deceivingly simple problem.

In the last two decades, working systems have been presented – mainly for the recognition of printed characters – ranging from the high-cost, high-volume systems of some twenty years ago [7] to complete families of devices of varying cost and performance [2].

Yet, the "ultimate goal" is still to be reached. A number of documents, mainly handwritten or poorly scanned samples, still defy the ingenuity of OCR designers.

Several authors pointed out that the critical step in any OCR system is character segmentation (see, for instance, [4, 6, 8, 9, 11]). Segmentation, with the meaning this term assumes in OCR, comprises the separation of the characters from the background, as well as the separation of the characters from each other. The latter problem is most common when dealing with handwritten characters, although it is not unknown in printed characters. The former problem is relatively uncommon in office automation, but may be encountered fairly often in other contexts. The credit card slip of Figs. 1, for instance, is quite hard to segment due to the poor quality of the printing, while the slip in Fig. 2, although of good quality, may present segmentation problems because of the backgroung drawing. We argue that good recognition

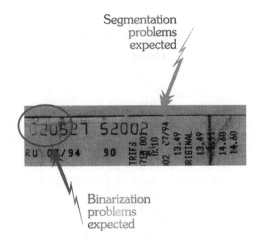

Figure 1: Image of a credit card slip from a receipt carbon copied by a manually operated printing machine. The pressure of the moving part often causes the ink to blur and to deposit outside the digit areas, giving the receipt the characteristic "dirty" aspect.

should be attained *without* segmentation; working directly on the gray level image. Moreover, we assume that vision character recognition be model-based.

Based on these assumptions, we develop a theory of *1D elastic templates* that provide a distortion-robust, segmentation-free method of recognition. We develop the theory for digit recognition.

## 2   Elastic Templates

Our theory is based on the superposition of a number of 1D templates to a digit image, each template representing the "ideal model" of a digit. We superimpose each template to the digit image and then start to deform it to find a better match

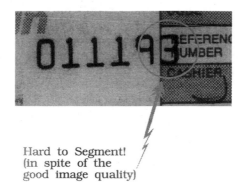

Hard to Segment!
(in spite of the
good image quality)

Figure 2: In this case, the inprint (which reports the purchase date) is of good quality, but the background drawing makes quite difficult to separate the digit.

between the template and the black areas on the image. We repeat this process for all the templates. Finally, er measure the match between the deformed template and the digit, as well as the energy of the elastic deformation of the template.

The model that was "close" to the image to begin with will have a smaller deformation and a higher match. Thus, the measurements can be given to a classifier that will tell which model better represents the digit in the image.

A *model template* is a curve $\tau : \mathbb{R} \mapsto \mathbb{R}^2$. In the following we will assume that all the templates are parametrized with respect to arc length $s$, and that the length is normalized to 1 (i.e. $s \in [0, 1]$).

When we try to match the template to the image $\mathcal{Q} : \mathbb{R}^2 \mapsto [0, 1]$, it undergoes a deformation $\theta$, resulting in a deformed template $\phi$, defined as:

$$\phi^\nu(s) = \tau^\nu(s) + \theta^\nu(s),$$

where $\nu = 1, 2$. While deforming the template, we must take into account to opposite requirements. The first is that the template must be as much as possible on the "black" areas of the image (i.e., on the digit). If the value 0 corresponds to the white and the value 1 coresponds to the black, we can measure the "blackness" of the portion of the image under the deformed template as:

$$\int_0^1 \mathcal{Q}(\phi(s))ds = \int_0^1 \mathcal{Q}(\tau(s) + \theta(s))ds. \tag{1}$$

The second requirement is on the deformation $\theta$. The amount of deformation necessary to achieve a good match is an indicator of how much the original template was close to the image. Note that the absolute value of $\theta$, by itself, is of no use. If

$\theta(s)$ is a constant function, then the deformation of the template is just a translation, something we don't want to count as dissimilarity.

We assume that the template is made of a weird sort of rubber, and that the shape $\tau$ corresponds to its undeformed state. Then we measure an approximation of the *elastic deformation* energy as:

$$\int_0^1 \alpha_1 \left[\left(\frac{d\theta^1}{ds}\right)^2 + \left(\frac{d\theta^2}{ds}\right)^2\right] + \alpha_2 \left[\left(\frac{d^2\theta^1}{ds^2}\right)^2 + \left(\frac{d^2\theta^2}{ds^2}\right)^2\right] ds. \qquad (2)$$

The quantity depending on the first derivatives is a measure of how the deformed template hs been (locally) stretched with respect to the rest state, while the quantity depending on the second derivatives is an approximate measure of the energy spent to bend locally the template.

Our goal is to maximize (1) and, in the same time, to minimize (2). We do this by minimizing the compound functional:

$$\int_0^1 \alpha_1 \left[\left(\frac{d\theta^1}{ds}\right)^2 + \left(\frac{d\theta^2}{ds}\right)^2\right] + \alpha_2 \left[\left(\frac{d^2\theta^1}{ds^2}\right)^2 + \left(\frac{d^2\theta^2}{ds^2}\right)^2\right] - Q(\tau(s) + \theta(s))ds. \qquad (3)$$

This is a variational problem regularized in the sense of Tihonov [12], whose solution $\theta$ is obtained as a solution of the Euler-Lagrange equations:

$$\alpha_2 \frac{d^4\theta^\nu}{ds^4} - \alpha_1 \frac{d^2\theta^\nu}{ds^2} = \left(\frac{\partial Q}{\partial \theta^\nu}\right)_{\theta+\tau} \qquad (4)$$

If we approximate the integral (1) with a sampled measure taken on $n$ points:

$$\sum_{i=1}^n Q\left(\tau(s_i) + \theta(s_i)\right) \qquad (5)$$

with $s_i = i/n$, then it is possible to show, in a way similar to [1], that the locally optimal solution is a spline function. Since eq. (4) involves fourth order derivatives of $\theta$, we must express $\theta$ as a spline functions of degree at least 5.

If the spline is expressed as:

$$\theta^\nu(s) = \sum_{\mu=-3}^{n+3} c_\mu^\nu B_\mu(s) \qquad (6)$$

– where $B_\mu$ are the components of the B-spline basis for the 5-th order splines – then the differential equation (4) can be translated into an algebraic non linear system in the unknowns $c_\mu^\nu$. Note that we added three nodes on each side of the interval [0,1], to avoid border effects.

Because of the linear nature of the differential operator:

$$D = \alpha_2 \frac{d^4}{ds^4} - \alpha_1 \frac{d^2}{ds^2} \qquad (7)$$

involved in the solution of (4), the only nonlinearity is given by the evaluation of the image $\mathcal{Q}$, and the algebraic system can be written as:

$$\mathbf{Ac} = \mathbf{b(c)} \tag{8}$$

where

$$\mathbf{A} = \{a_{\lambda\mu}\} \tag{9}$$

$$= \left\{ \alpha_2 \frac{d^4 B_\mu(s_\lambda)}{ds^4} - \alpha_1 \frac{d^2 B_\mu(s_\lambda)}{ds^2} \right\}, \ \mu = -3 \ldots N_\theta + 3, \ \lambda = -3 \ldots N_\theta + 3$$

and

$$\mathbf{b(c)} = \{b_\lambda(c)\} \tag{10}$$

$$= \left\{ \left( \frac{\partial \mathcal{Q}}{\partial \theta} \right)_{\theta(s_\lambda,\mathbf{c})+\tau(s_\lambda)} \right\} \ \lambda = -3 \ldots N_\theta + 3$$

Note that, because of the limited support of the B-spline basis, $A$ is a band matrix with only seven nonzero diagonals.

## 3 Measuring the Match

All the templates are deformed to find the optimal match with the input image. After they have reached an equilibrium, it is necessary to measure which one fits the image the better and with less deformation. To this end, we define a series of fitness measures.

So far, we have considered all the equations for a single template. in the following, however, we will need a notation to distinguish between the different templates that we match against the image. We suppose that the number of templates is $N_\tau$. We will use capital greek letters to index the different templates, so, $\tau_\Sigma$ is the undeformed version of the $\Sigma$-th template, and $\theta^{\Sigma;\mu}$ is the $\mu$-th component ($\mu = 1, 2$) of the $\Sigma$-th deformation.

The first quantities we use derive directly from eq. (3). For the $\Sigma$-th template, we measure the *Bending energy*:

$$B^\Sigma = \int_0^1 \left( \theta_{,2}^{\Sigma;\mu} \right)^2 ds \tag{11}$$

the *Strain Energy*:

$$S^\Sigma = \int_0^1 \left( \theta_{,1}^{\Sigma;\mu} \right)^2 ds \tag{12}$$

and the *Relative matching*:

$$\mathcal{M}^\Sigma = \int_0^1 [\beta(\tau(s) + \theta(s))]^r ds \tag{13}$$

154

The latter measure is called "relative" because it is normalized with respect to the length of the template. It measures how much "gray" there is under the template when the template is considered of unitary lenght. If we think for a moment in terms of black and white images, then $\mathcal{M}$ indicates which fraction of the template is on the black area.

This is a limitation of $\mathcal{M}$, as can be seen by observing the situation in Fig. 3. In

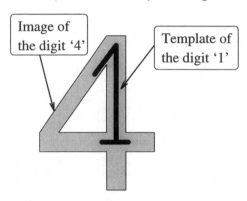

Figure 3: This is a situation in which the measure $\mathcal{M}$ fails. Since the template 1 is completely contained in the black area of the 4, it results $\mathcal{M} = 1$.

this case, the template of a "1" is superimposed to the image of a 4. Since all the template is contained in the black area of the image, we have $\mathcal{M} = 1$ that is, a perfect match, in spite of the fact that the "1" template covers only a part of the 4.

In order to discriminatein situations like this, we need another measure that takes into account the fraction of the image that is covered by the template. Since the image is two-dimensional and the template is one-dimensional, this fraction is, strictly speaking, zero. To obtain a significative value, consider the distance $\| \cdot \|_2$ in $\mathbb{R}^2$ and, for the deformed template $\phi$, the set:

$$Q_\rho(\phi) = \left\{ x \in \mathbb{R}^2 | \min_s \|x - \phi(s)\| \leq \rho \right\} \tag{14}$$

the *Absolute matching* is then defined as:

$$\mathcal{A}^\Sigma = \int_{Q_\rho(\tau^\Sigma + \theta^\Sigma)} \beta(x) dx \tag{15}$$

where the constant $\rho$ is chosen to be rougly the size of a pixel.

The four measures $\mathcal{B}^\Sigma$, $\mathcal{S}^\Sigma$, $\mathcal{M}^\Sigma$, $\mathcal{A}^\Sigma$ are used to determine the likelihood that the image is a realization of the template $\Sigma$.

# 4  An Example

We report here an example of application of the deformable templates to a credit card slip. Fig. 4 shows a digit with the ten templates deformed to fit it. The digit represented here is the first "2" in the slip of Fig. 1. Tab. 1 reports the measurements

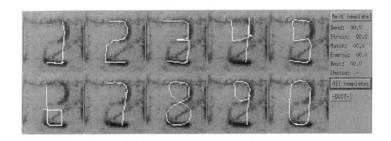

Figure 4: An example of image taken from a credit card slip.

obtained for the ten deformed templates of Fig. 4, and the output $\mathcal{C}$ of a simple linear classifier:

$$\mathcal{C} = w_1\mathcal{S} + w_2\mathcal{B} + w_3\mathcal{A} + w_4\mathcal{M} \tag{16}$$

trained to minimize a quadratic cost on 30 samples of credit card digits.

# References

[1] P. M. Anselone and P. J. Laurent. A general method for the construction of interpolating or smoothing spline-functions. *Numerische Matematik*, 12:66–82, 1968.

[2] Mindy Bokser. Omnidocument technologies. *Proceedings of the IEEE*, 80(7):1066–1078, July 1992.

| Measure | Digit | | | | |
|---|---|---|---|---|---|
| | 1 | 2 | 3 | 4 | 5 |
| $\mathcal{S}$ | 2.43 | 2.11 | 4.43 | 4.39 | 3.92 |
| $\mathcal{B}$ | 1.08 | 1.26 | 3.44 | 2.58 | 2.22 |
| $\mathcal{A}$ | 6.21 | 9.12 | 8.69 | 7.22 | 8.54 |
| $\mathcal{M}$ | 0.76 | 0.65 | 0.67 | 0.58 | 0.57 |
| $\mathcal{C}$ | 0.91 | 1.18 | 0 | 0 | 0 |
| | 6 | 7 | 8 | 9 | 0 |
| $\mathcal{S}$ | 2.04 | 5.73 | 2.67 | 11.28 | 2.44 |
| $\mathcal{B}$ | 1.21 | 2.39 | 1.99 | 2.69 | 1.41 |
| $\mathcal{A}$ | 6.59 | 6.54 | 11.59 | 7.51 | 10.15 |
| $\mathcal{M}$ | 0.69 | 0.65 | 0.60 | 0.71 | 0.63 |
| $\mathcal{C}$ | 0.87 | 0 | 0.2 | 0 | 0.95 |

Table 1: Fitness measures and classification output for a simple linear classifier and the image of Fig. 4.

[3] D. G. Elliman and I. T. Lancaster. A review of segmentation and contextual analysis techniques for text recognition. *Pattern Recognition*, 23(3/4):337–346, 1990.

[4] Hiromichi Fujisawa, Yasuaki Nakano, and Kiyomichi Kurino. Segmentation methods for character recognition: From segmentation to document structure analysis. *Proceedings of the IEEE*, 80(7):1079–1092, July 1992.

[5] V. K. Govindan and A. P. Shivaprasad. Character recognition – a review. *Pattern Recognition*, 23(7):671–683, 1990.

[6] Tin Kam Ho, Jonathan J. Hull, and Sargur N. Srihari. A computational model for recognition of multifont word images. *Machine Vision and Application*, 5:157–168, 1992.

[7] T. Iijima, S. Mori, H. Genchi, and K. Mori. Simulation for theory, design and tests of the ocr ASPET/71. In *AICA Symposium on Simulation of Complete Systems*, 1971.

[8] Jim Keeler and David E. Rumelhart. A self-organizing integrated segmentation and recognition neural net. In J. E. Moody, S. J. Hanson, and R. P. Lippmann, editors, *Advances in Neural Information Processing Systems, 4*. Morgan Kaufman, San Mateo, CA, 1992.

[9] Gale L. Martin and Mosfeq Rashid. Recognizing overlapping hand-printed characters by centered-object integrated segmentation and recognition. In J. E. Moody, S. J. Hanson, and R. P. Lippmann, editors, *Advances in Neural Information Processing Systems, 4*. Morgan Kaufman, San Mateo, CA, 1992.

[10] Shunji Mori, Ching Y. Suen, and Kazuro Yamamoto. Historical review of OCR research and development. *Proceedings of the IEEE*, 80(7):1029–1058, July 1992.

[11] Q. Tian, P. Zhang, T. Alexander, and Y. Kim. Survey: Omnifont character recognition. *Proceedings of SPIE: Visual Communications and Image Processing '91*, 1606:260–268, 1991.

[12] A. N. Tihonov. Regularization of incorrectly posed problems. *Soviet Mathematical Doklady*, 4:1624–1627, 1963.

158

# Constrained Recovery of Deformable Models from Range Data*

Sven J. Dickinson[†]    Dimitri Metaxas[‡]    Alex Pentland[§]

### Abstract

We present a technique that uses aspects to constrain the fitting of deformable models to range data. Unlike previous work in deformable model recovery from range data, the technique does not depend on accurate initial position and orientation of the model. Furthermore, occlusion is handled at segmentation time and does not complicate the fitting process, as only 3-D points known to belong to a part participate in the fitting of a model to the part. We present the approach in detail and apply it to the recovery of objects from range data.

## 1    Introduction

The recovery of volumetric shape descriptions from range data has drawn much attention in the literature, e.g., [15, 7, 12, 16, 13, 5]. While each of these approaches addresses the problem of recovering a deformable model, superquadric, or set of modes corresponding to a part, many avoid the issue of part segmentation. In some cases, either a single unoccluded object appears in the image or part segmentation is performed manually [13, 16]. In other cases, decomposition of the image into parts is integrated into the fitting process, resulting in a costly global optimization process [15, 12]. Furthermore, in many cases, the fitting process is sensitive to initial placement and orientation of the model. If its initial position is not inside the data or if

---

*The authors gratefully acknowledge the assistance of Dr. Tim Newman and Sharath Pankanti of the Michigan State University Pattern Recognition and Image Processing (PRIP) Laboratory, in providing both the range image segmentation code as well as the original images (originally captured by Pat Flynn). The authors would also like to thank Gene Amdur at the University of Toronto and Michael Chan at the University of Pennsylvania for their support and assistance in the implementation of this work. The second author was supported by an NSF-IRI-9309917 grant.

[†]Media Laboratory, Massachusetts Institute of Technology, and Department of Computer Science, University of Toronto.

[‡]Department of Computer and Information Science, University of Pennsylvania.

[§]Media Laboratory, Massachusetts Institute of Technology.

its $z$ axis is not closely aligned with the principal axis of the data, a canonical fit may not be achieved.

In this paper, we propose a novel two-step shape recovery process that decouples the tasks of segmenting a range image into parts and fitting deformable models to the parts. In the first step, the range image is segmented into a set of homogeneous regions. Next, the regions are grouped into aspects or views corresponding to a vocabulary of 3-D parts. For unambiguous views, this process yields the qualitative shape of the part, the qualitative orientation of the part through its aspect, and an exact mapping between the regions in the recovered aspect and the surfaces on the part. This information is used in the second stage to provide strong constraints on the fitting of a deformable model to the segmented range data. The 3-D data corresponding to the contours that define the recovered aspects are used to recover a part's global deformations, while the 3-D data corresponding to pixels bounded by aspect faces are used to recover a part's local deformations. Finally, the initial model can be specified in *any* initial size, position, and orientation with correct convergence guaranteed by the constraints.

Following the introduction, we review both our qualitative and quantitative shape representations. Next, we present our qualitative and quantitative shape recovery techniques. Finally, we apply the techniques to a set of range images and close with some conclusions and limitations.

# 2 Related Work

The qualitative and parametric approaches to representing shape have complementary properties. The qualitative representation of part structure has proven [4, 3] useful for segmentation and grouping, while the parametric representations have proven useful for recovering precise descriptions of shape [12, 13, 15, 16]. It is therefore natural to try to combine the strengths of the two approaches, using one for grouping and segmentation, and the other for fitting and description.

Some work has already proceeded along these lines. Using a part-based aspect approach to segmentation based on Dickinson et al. [4], Raja and Jain [14] segment a range image into parts corresponding to geons. In order to determine geon orientation, i.e., end vs. side faces, they fit a superquadric to the segmented part to determine the principal axis of the geon. The technique combines qualitative models for segmentation but does not attempt to recover a precise parametric model. Instead, the static superquadric fitting step is used only as an aid for geon labeling. Metaxas and Dickinson [10] present an approach in which recovered qualitative shape is used to constrain the recovery of a deformable model (global deformations only) from 2-D image data. This paper extends that approach to 3-D data and includes local deformation recovery.

# 3 Object Modeling

Our object representation integrates both qualitative and quantitative shape models. In the following sections, we briefly review these two components and how they have been extended to support shape recovery from range data. Further details can be found in [4, 3] and [16], respectively.

## 3.1 Qualitative Shape Modeling

To demonstrate our approach to shape recovery, we have selected an object representation similar to that used by Biederman [1], in which the Cartesian product of contrastive shape properties gives rise to a set of volumetric parts called geons. For our investigation, we have chosen three properties including cross-section shape, axis shape, and cross-section size variation (Dickinson, Pentland, and Rosenfeld [4]). The values of these properties give rise to a set of ten volumetric parts (a subset of Biederman's geons), shown in Figure 1(a). To construct objects, the volumes are attached to one another with the restriction that any junction of two volumes involves exactly one distinct surface from each volume.

Traditional aspect graph representations of 3-D objects model an entire object with a set of aspects, each defining a topologically distinct view of the object in terms of its visible surfaces (Koenderink and van Doorn [9]). Our approach differs in that we use aspects to represent a (typically small) set of volumetric parts from which each object in our database is constructed, rather than representing an entire object directly. Consequently, our goal is to use aspects to recover the 3-D volumetric parts that make up the object in order to carry out a recognition-by-parts procedure, rather than attempting to use aspects to recognize entire objects. Since the number of qualitatively different volumes is generally small, the number of possible aspects is limited and, more important, *independent* of the number of objects in the database. However, if a volume is occluded from a given 3-D viewpoint, its projected aspect in the image will also be occluded. We accommodate the matching of occluded aspects through the use of a hierarchical representation we call the *aspect hierarchy*.

The aspect hierarchy consists of three levels, including the set of *aspects* that model the chosen volumes, the set of component *faces* of the aspects, and the set of *boundary groups* representing all subsets of contours bounding the faces. Figure 1(b) illustrates a portion of the aspect hierarchy, along with a few of the volumes. The ambiguous mappings between the levels of the aspect hierarchy are captured in a set of conditional probabilities, mapping boundary groups to faces, faces to aspects, and aspects to volumes. These conditional probabilities result from a statistical analysis of a set of images approximating the set of *all* views of *all* the volumes.

The aspect hierarchy was originally introduced as a representation to support 3-D object recognition from 2-D images (Dickinson, Pentland, and Rosenfeld [4, 3]). With faces in the aspect hierarchy now representing 3-D surfaces instead of 2-D projections

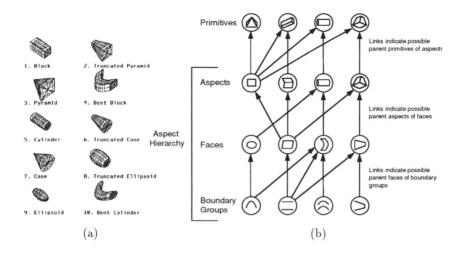

Figure 1: (a) The Ten Volumetric Modeling Parts (b) The Aspect Hierarchy

of 3-D surfaces, much of the ambiguity of the original aspect hierarchy has been removed. Adding face attributes such as Mean and Gaussian curvature can effectively prune many of the mappings from boundary groups to faces, faces to aspects, and aspects to volumes. However, for the experiments presented in this paper, the original aspect hierarchy has been used. For high probability views of volumes, there is little or no ambiguity in the mapping from aspects to volumes, providing a unique labeling of the object. In current work, we are constructing an aspect hierarchy which takes surface curvature into account.

## 3.2 Quantitative Shape Modeling

Geometrically, the models used in this paper [11] are closed surfaces in space whose intrinsic (material) coordinates are $u = (u, v)$, defined on a domain $\Omega$. The positions of points on the model relative to an inertial frame of reference $\Phi$ in space are given by a vector-valued, time-varying function of u:

$$\mathbf{x}(\mathbf{u}, t) = (x_1(\mathbf{u}, t), x_2(\mathbf{u}, t), x_3(\mathbf{u}, t))^\top \tag{1}$$

where $^\top$ is the transpose operator. We set up a noninertial, model-centered reference frame $\phi$, and express these positions as:

$$\mathbf{x} = \mathbf{c} + \mathbf{R}\mathbf{p}, \tag{2}$$

where $\mathbf{c}(t)$ is the origin of $\phi$ at the center of the model, and the orientation of $\phi$ is given by the rotation matrix $\mathbf{R}(t)$. Thus, $\mathbf{p}(\mathbf{u}, t)$ denotes the canonical positions of points on the model relative to the model frame. We further express $\mathbf{p}$ as the sum of a global reference shape $\mathbf{s}(\mathbf{u}, t)$ (global deformation) and a displacement function $\mathbf{d}(\mathbf{u}, t)$ (local deformation):

$$\mathbf{p} = \mathbf{s} + \mathbf{d}. \tag{3}$$

We define the global reference shape as

$$\mathbf{s} = \mathbf{T}(\mathbf{e}(\mathbf{u}; a_0, a_1, \ldots); b_0, b_1, \ldots). \tag{4}$$

Here, a geometric primitive $\mathbf{e}$, defined parametrically in $\mathbf{u}$ and parameterized by the variables $a_i$, is subjected to the *global deformation* $\mathbf{T}$ which depends on the parameters $b_i$. Although generally nonlinear, $\mathbf{e}$ and $\mathbf{T}$ are assumed to be differentiable (so that we may compute the Jacobian of $\mathbf{s}$) and $\mathbf{T}$ may be a composite sequence of primitive deformation functions $\mathbf{T}(\mathbf{e}) = \mathbf{T}_1(\mathbf{T}_2(\ldots \mathbf{T}_n(\mathbf{e})))$. We concatenate the global deformation parameters into the vector

$$\mathbf{q}_s = (a_0, a_1, \ldots, b_0, b_1, \ldots)^{\mathsf{T}}. \tag{5}$$

Even though our technique for defining $\mathbf{T}$ is independent of the primitive $\mathbf{e} = (e_1, e_2, e_3)^{\mathsf{T}}$ to which it is applied, we will use superquadric ellipsoid primitives, with linear tapering and bending global deformations [11].

For local deformations, we express the displacement $\mathbf{d}$, as a linear combination of finite element shape functions [8] and local deformation parameters:

$$\mathbf{d} = \mathbf{S}\mathbf{q}_d, \tag{6}$$

where $\mathbf{S}$ is a shape matrix whose entries are the shape functions and

$$\mathbf{q}_d = (\ldots, \mathbf{d}_i^{\mathsf{T}}, \ldots)^{\mathsf{T}} \tag{7}$$

is the vector of local deformation parameters [16].

## 4   Kinematics, Dynamics and Generalized Forces

Differentiating (2), the velocity of points on the model is given by:

$$\dot{\mathbf{x}} = [\mathbf{I} \ \mathbf{B} \ \mathbf{R}\mathbf{J} \ \mathbf{R}\mathbf{S}]\dot{\mathbf{q}} = \mathbf{L}\dot{\mathbf{q}}, \tag{8}$$

where $\mathbf{J}$ is the Jacobian of the reference shape with respect to the global deformation parameter vector, and $\mathbf{L}$ is the Jacobian matrix that converts $q$-dimensional vectors to 3-D vectors [11]. Here,

$$\mathbf{q} = (\mathbf{q}_c^{\mathsf{T}}, \mathbf{q}_\theta^{\mathsf{T}}, \mathbf{q}_s^{\mathsf{T}}, \mathbf{q}_d^{\mathsf{T}})^{\mathsf{T}}, \tag{9}$$

with $\mathbf{q}_c = \mathbf{c}$ and $\mathbf{q}_\theta = \boldsymbol{\theta}$, serves as the vector of generalized coordinates of the model.

When fitting the model to visual data, our goal is to recover $\mathbf{q}$, the vector of degrees of freedom of the model. We make the kinematic model dynamic based on the use of Lagrangian mechanics and appropriate simplifications suitable for static shape recovery [16, 11]. The dynamic equations of motion then take the form

$$\mathbf{D}\dot{\mathbf{q}} + \mathbf{K}\mathbf{q} = \mathbf{f}_q, \tag{10}$$

where $\mathbf{D}$ is the damping matrix and $\mathbf{K}$ is the stiffness matrix that defines the elastic properties of the model. $\mathbf{f}_q$ are the generalized external forces associated with the components of $\mathbf{q}$ and are computed using

$$\mathbf{f}_q = \int \mathbf{L}^\mathsf{T} \mathbf{f} \, du, \tag{11}$$

where $\mathbf{f}(u,t)$ is the force distribution applied to the model through our physics-based approach to visual estimation. The visual data are converted into traction forces that act on the dynamic model [16] by appropriately assigning data points to points on the model and exerting a force on the model which is proportional to the distance between them.

# 5   Shape Recovery

## 5.1   Qualitative Shape Recovery

From an input range image, we apply Flynn's range image region segmentation algorithm [6]. From the resulting 2-D region label image, we build a *region topology graph*, in which nodes represent regions and arcs specify region adjacencies. Each node (region) encodes the 2-D bounding contour of a region as well as a mask which specifies pixel membership in the region. From the region topology graph, each region is characterized according to the qualitative shapes of its bounding contours (see [2] for details). The result is a *region boundary graph* representation for a region, in which nodes represent bounding contours, and arcs represent pairwise nonaccidental relations between the contours.

Face labeling consists of matching a region boundary graph (and its subgraphs) to the graphs representing the model faces (and boundary groups) in the aspect hierarchy using an interpretation tree search. The result is a *face topology graph* in which each node contains a set of face labels (sorted by decreasing order of probability) associated with a given region.

In an unexpected object recognition domain, in which there is no a priori knowledge of scene content, we search through the space of groupings of regions into aspects. From a set of recovered aspects, we search through the space of volume interpretations that is consistent with the objects in a database (see [4, 3] for details). In an expected object recognition domain, in which we are searching for a particular object or part, we use the aspect hierarchy as an attention mechanism to focus the search for an aspect at appropriate regions in the image [2]. Moving down the aspect hierarchy, target objects map to target volumes which, in turn, map to target aspect predictions which, in turn, map to target face predictions. Those faces in the face topology graph whose labels match the target face prediction provide an ordered (by decreasing probability) set of ranked search positions at which the target aspect prediction can be verified If the mapping from a verified aspect to a target volume is ambiguous, this attention mechanism can be used to drive an active recognition system which moves the cameras to obtain a less ambiguous view of an object's part [2].

## 5.2 Quantitative Shape Recovery

In the dynamic model fitting process, the data are transformed into an externally applied force distribution $\mathbf{f}(u, t)$. We convert the external forces to generalized forces $\mathbf{f}_q$ which act on the generalized coordinates of the model [16, 11]. We apply forces to the model based on differences between the model's points and the 3-D data. Each of these forces is then converted to a generalized force $\mathbf{f}_q$ that, based on (10), modifies the appropriate generalized coordinate that has to be adapted so that the model fits the data.

Given that our vocabulary of volumes is limited, we devise a systematic way of computing the generalized forces for each volume. The computation depends on the influence of particular parts of the data to model degrees of freedom. Such parts correspond to the various regions making up the aspect used to identify the volume's coarse shape. From the correspondence between the the 3-D points which project to the bounding contours of each region in the recovered aspect and the corresponding points on the model, we use (11) to define forces that will affect the global deformations of the model. Next, from the correspondence between the 3-D points internal to a region and their nearest points on the model, we use (11) to define forces which will affect the local deformations of the model. In the case of occluded volumes, resulting in both occluded aspects and occluded faces, only those portions (boundary groups) of the faces used to define the faces exert external forces on the models.

### 5.2.1 Model Initialization

One of the major limitations of previous deformable model fitting approaches is their dependence on model initialization and prior segmentation [16, 13]. Using the qualitative shape recovery process as a front end, we first segment the data into parts, and for each part, we identify the relevant non-occluded data belonging to the part. In addition, the extracted qualitative volumes explicitly define a mapping between the image faces in their projected aspects and the 3-D surfaces on the quantitative models. Moreover, the extracted volumes can be used to immediately constrain many of the global deformation parameters. For example, from the qualitative shape classes, we know if a volume is bent, tapered, or has an elliptical cross-section. Finally, although the initial model can be specified at any position and orientation, the aspect that a volume encodes defines a qualitative orientation that can be exploited to speed

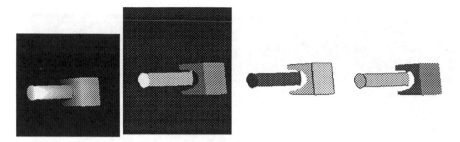

Figure 2: Left to right: range image, region segmentation, recovered qualitative block, and recovered qualitative cylinder

up the model fitting process. Sensitivity of the fitting process to model initialization is also overcome by independently solving for the degrees of freedom of the model. By allowing each face in an aspect to exert forces on only one model degree of freedom at a time, we remove local minima from the fitting process and ensure correct convergence of the model.

# 6 Results and Discussion

We demonstrate our approach by recovering the two parts in the range image shown in Figure 2(a)[1]; the region segmented image is shown in Figure 2(b). For this example, we invoked the expected object recognition mode to first search for the best instance of a block. Figure 2(c) shows the highlighted aspect recovered for the block; only those contours used to infer the block are highlighted in the image. Note that the most probable aspect for the block (containing three faces) was not recovered; however, the next most probably aspect (containing two faces) was recovered and used to locate the block. Figure 2(d) shows the highlighted aspect recovered for the cylinder.

For each of the two recovered qualitative volumes, we now proceed to show the results of using the recovered qualitative shape to constrain the fitting of a deformable model to the original range data. In Figures 3(a-c), we show the initial, an intermediate, and the final frame in the sequence of model deformations taking the initial model to its final shape describing the block. For clarity, only the recovered contours belonging to the block's recovered aspect are shown in the sequence. Next, in Figures 3(d-f), we show the initial, two intermediate, and the final frame in the sequence of model deformations taking the initial model to its final shape describing the cylinder. Finally, in Figure 3(h), we show the two fitted parts together from a different viewpoint.

---

[1]The image was captured using a Technical Arts Scanner at the Michigan State University's PRIP Laboratory.

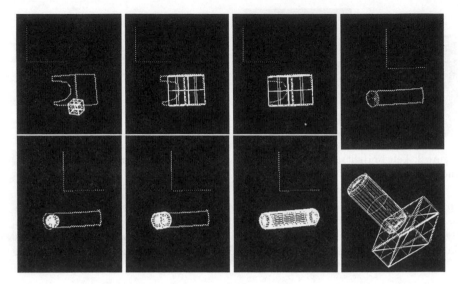

Figure 3: Selected Frames from the Part Fitting Sequence: (a) Initial Block Frame; (b) Intermediate Block Frame; (c) Final Block Frame; (d) Initial Cylinder Frame; (e) Intermediate Cylinder Frame; (f) Second Intermediate Cylinder Frame; (g) Final Cylinder Frame; (h) Recovered Object from a Different Viewpoint

The fitting constraints provided by the recovered qualitative shape means that the deformable model fitting process is invariant to initial position, orientation, and shape of the model. Unfortunately, relying on the correspondence between recovered image faces and model surfaces means that the recovery process is sensitive to region segmentation errors. However, by only allowing high-scoring volumes to constrain the fitting process, the chances of letting any region segmentation problems affect the fitting process is low. In fact, low-scoring volumes can be used to guide the sensor to acquire a higher-scoring volume.

In conclusion, by first recovering the coarse shape of an object's parts through a part-based aspect matching strategy, we not only address the part segmentation problem prior to fitting, but provide a powerful set of fitting constraints ensuring that convergence of the deformable model is invariant to initial size, position, or orientation of the model. Furthermore, we extend our previous method of shape recovery from 2-D data which recovered only global deformations to shape recovery from 3-D data which recovers both global and local deformations.

# References

[1] I. Biederman. Human image understanding: Recent research and a theory. *CVGIP:IU*,

32:29–73, 1985.

[2] S. Dickinson, H. Christensen, J. Tsotsos, and G. Olofsson. Active object recognition integrating attention and viewpoint control. In *Proceedings, ECCV '94*, Stockholm, May 1994.

[3] S. Dickinson, A. Pentland, and A. Rosenfeld. From volumes to views: An approach to 3-D object recognition. *CVGIP:IU*, 55(2):130–154, 1992.

[4] S. Dickinson, A. Pentland, and A. Rosenfeld. 3-D shape recovery using distributed aspect matching. *IEEE Transactions on PAMI*, 14(2):174–198, 1992.

[5] F. Ferrie, J. Lagarde, and P. Whaite. Darboux frames, snakes, and superquadrics. In *Proceedings, Workshop on Interpretation of 3D Scenes*, pages 170–176. IEEE Computer Society Press, 1989.

[6] P. Flynn. Cad-based computer vision: Modeling and recognition strategies. *Ph.D. thesis*, 1990.

[7] A. Gupta. Surface and volumetric segmentation of 3D objects using parametric shape models. Technical Report MS-CIS-91-45, GRASP LAB 128, University of Pennsylvania, Philadelphia, PA, 1991.

[8] K. Kardestuncer. *Finite Element Handbook*. McGraw–Hill, New York, 1987.

[9] J. Koenderink and A. van Doorn. The internal representation of solid shape with respect to vision. *Biological Cybernetics*, 32:211–216, 1979.

[10] D. Metaxas and S. Dickinson. Integration of quantitative and qualitative techniques for deformable model fitting from orthographic, perspective, and stereo projections. In *Proceedings, Fourth ICCV*, Berlin, May 1993.

[11] D. Metaxas and D. Terzopoulos. Shape and nonrigid motion estimation through physics-based synthesis. *IEEE PAMI, in press*, 1993.

[12] A. Pentland. Automatic extraction of deformable part models. *IJCV*, 4:107–126, 1990.

[13] A. Pentland and S. Sclaroff. Closed-form solutions for physically based shape modeling and recognition. *IEEE PAMI*, 13(7):715–729, 1991.

[14] N. Raja and A. Jain. Recognizing geons from superquadrics fitted to range data. *Image and Vision Computing*, 10(3):179–190, 1992.

[15] F. Solina and R. Bajcsy. Recovery of parametric models from range images: The case for superquadrics with global deformations. *IEEE PAMI*, 12(2):131–146, 1990.

[16] D. Terzopoulos and D. Metaxas. Dynamic 3D models with local and global deformations: Deformable superquadrics. *IEEE PAMI*, 13(7):703–714, 1991.

# FROM PIXELS TO EDGES IN MEDICAL RADIOGRAPHS:
# A PATTERN RECOGNITION APPROACH TO EDGE DETECTION

DOV DORI, GUSTAVO GAMBACH

*Faculty of Industrial Engineering and Management*
*Technion, Israel Institute of Technology*
*Haifa 32000, Israel*

and

ROBERT M. HARALICK

*Department of Electrical Engineering*
*University of Washington*
*Seattle, Washington 98195, USA*

## ABSTRACT

This work presents edge detection as a supervised pattern recognition problem, in which the edge is modeled as a linear combination of basis functions. The parameters of these basis functions are learned during the training phase, and the recognition phase uses these learned parameters to locate pixels that belong to edges. This modeling of edges is suitable to edges found in radiographs, which are more complex than step functions. Since edges may appear in any direction, we first show how to determine the gradient direction of the edge. We then present the basis functions selected for modeling edges in bone radiographs, show some of their characteristics and compute the relevant coefficients and parameters to be used for discriminating between edge and non-edge pixels.

## 1 Introduction

Physical edges of the objects are fundamental descriptions of physical objects as they relate to transitions in surface orientation or texture. Edge detection is the identification of the intensity changes corresponding to the underlying physical changes. Detecting edges in a radiograph is a first step in taking measurements. Edges in radiographs differ from "conventional" edges, because X rays, unlike visible light, are only partially absorbed by the object they hit. The physical properties of the object and the width the X rays must traverse before hitting the photographic film determine the brightness level of each point in the radiograph. Edges in radiographs have therefore pattern of edge function that is more complex than the step function that models edges in ordinary images. To achieve radiograph understanding, computer systems must relate the raw input data to the physical structure that cause it, i.e., the object being radiated.

Davis [2] provides a surevy of edge detection techniques prior to 1975. One of these methodes is the "gradient" operator $|g(i,j) - g(i+1, j+1)| + |g(i, j+1) - g(i+1, j)|$, proposed by Roberts [2]. It detects either a horizontal or a vertical edge, where $g(i,j)$ is the gray level at point $(i,j)$. Marr and Hildreth [4] proposed a scheme that has become a standard gauge against which other methods are compared. The basic approach is to convolve the image with a rotationally symmetric Laplacian of Gaussian and to locate zero crossings of the convolution. The Nevatia-Bavu technique

[5] consists of determining the edge magnitude and direction by convolving the image with a number of masks and thinning and thresholding these edge magnitudes. Torre and Poggio [7] poins out that better results may be obtained by using two directional filters with directional derivatives, especially in the neighborhood of corners. Haralick [3] locates edges at zero crossings of the second directional derivative in the direction of the gradient. Canny [1] defines certain desirable criteria for edge detection. He shows that in 1-D the optimal filter is a linear combination of four exponentials, well approximated by a first derivative of a Gaussian. In 2-D images he proposes to use a combination of such filters with varying length, width and orientation. Shen and Castan [6] propose a linear filter, in which images are convolved with the smoothing function $f(x) = -\frac{1}{2}\ln(b)b^{|x|}$ prior to differentiation.

## 2 Edge Detection as a Supervised Pattern-Recognition Problem

Since bone edges in radiographs present a more complicated problem than identifying a step function, we propose a pattern-recognition approach to detect these edges. Assuming an edge is perpendicular to the $x$ axis, the intensity of pixels of this edge can be represented analytically as a linear combination of $n$ basis functions as follows:

$$I(x) = \sum_{i=1}^{n} b_i B_i(x, \mathbf{P}_i) = (b_1, b_2, b_3 \ldots b_n) \left\{ \begin{array}{c} B_1(x, \mathbf{P}_1) \\ B_2(x, \mathbf{P}_2) \\ \vdots \\ B_n(x, \mathbf{P}_n) \end{array} \right\} = \mathbf{b}\mathbf{B}((x, \mathbf{P})) \tag{1}$$

Each $B_i(x)$ is a separate basis function evaluated at point $x$ with its coefficient $b_i$ and vector of parameters $\mathbf{P}_i = (P_1, P_2, \ldots P_{j_i})$, where $j_i$ is the number of parameters in the basis function $B_i$ used in the pattern recognition procedure.

Based on this formulation, edge detection is presented as a supervised pattern recognition problem, in which the parameters of the basis functions are learned and calibrated during the learning phase. During the recognition phase, these parameters provide for classifying each pixel as an edge or a non-edge pixel. Figure 1 represents schematically edge detection as a 2-dimensional pattern recognition decision problem. The training set is used to construct the border between edge and non-edge pixels based on the parameters $b_1$ and $b_2$. In the recognition phase, each pixel is classified as edge or non-edge according to its location in the $b_1 - b_2$ plane, i.e., its $(b_1, b_2)$ combination using Fisher linear discriminator.

Since edges may appear in any direction, we first develop the mathematical tools to determine the gradient direction of the edge. We then present the selected basis functions for the edge model and show some of their basic characteristics. Finally we devise the scheme for the pattern recognition based edge detection method.

Figure 2 depicts the edge model in 3-D, where $(r, c)$ is the image plane (rows and columns of pixels), while the third dimension is the image intensity for each pixel. Either the curve in the wall of the vertebrae or curvature in the spine may result in an alteration in the orientation, making an angle $\theta$ with the $r$ axis, as shown in Figure 3. By substituting $x = r\cos\theta + c\sin\theta$ in Equation 1 we generate a 3-D surface that sweeps the edge curve perpendicular to the gradient direction $\theta$, as shown in Figure 4 and expressed in Equation 2, where the parameter vectors $\mathbf{P}_i$ are ommitted for brevity.

$$I(r, c) = \sum_{i=1}^{n} b_i B_i(r\cos\theta + c\sin\theta) \tag{2}$$

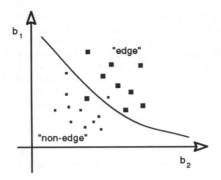

Figure 1: Discriminating between edge and non-edge pixels in a 2-D parameter space

The partial derivatives of $I$ with respect to $r$ and $c$ are

$$\frac{\partial I(r,c)}{\partial r} = \cos\theta \sum_{i=1}^{n} b_i B_i{}'(r\cos\theta + c\sin\theta) \text{ and } \frac{\partial I(r,c)}{\partial c} = \sin\theta \sum_{i=1}^{n} b_i B_i{}'(r\cos\theta + c\sin\theta).$$

A unit vector is:

$$\vec{g} = \frac{\begin{pmatrix} \frac{\partial I(r,c)}{\partial r} \\ \frac{\partial I(r,c)}{\partial c} \end{pmatrix}}{\sqrt{\left(\frac{\partial I(r,c)}{\partial r}\right)^2 + \left(\frac{\partial I(r,c)}{\partial c}\right)^2}} = \frac{\sum_{i=1}^{n} b_i B_i{}'(r\cos\theta + c\sin\theta) \begin{pmatrix} \cos\theta \\ \sin\theta \end{pmatrix}}{\sqrt{(\sum_{i=1}^{n} b_i B_i{}'(r\cos\theta + c\sin\theta))^2 (\cos^2\theta + \sin^2\theta)}} = \begin{pmatrix} \cos\theta \\ \sin\theta \end{pmatrix}$$

(3)

where the denominator was taken to be positive because the gradient direction is set to go upwards.

To estimate the edge direction, we assume that the neighborhood of a pixel can be approximated as a plane, described in Equation 4.

$$I(r,c) = \alpha r + \beta c + \gamma + \epsilon(r,c) \tag{4}$$

where $\epsilon(r,c)$ is the error function—the difference between the observed intensity values $I(r,c)$ and the expected ones. To minimize the error in the $(2m+1) \times (2m+1)$ neigborhood of the pixel $(r,c)$, we convert Equation 4 into a least-square problem:

$$\epsilon^2(r,c) = \sum_{r=-m}^{m} \sum_{c=-m}^{m} [I(r,c) - (\alpha r + \beta c + \gamma)]^2 \tag{5}$$

where $(-m,-m)$ and $(m,m)$ are the coordinates of the lower left and upper right corners of the $(2m+1) \times (2m+1)$ mask used as an approximation for the plane patch of the pixel under consideration,

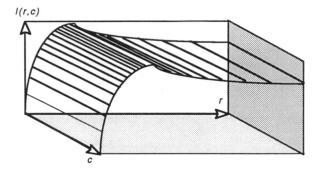

Figure 2: Radiation intensity through a schematic section of a bone

located at $(0,0)$. We are looking for $\alpha$, $\beta$ and $\gamma$ which minimize $\epsilon^2$. To find $\alpha$ that minimizes $\epsilon^2$ we take the partial derivative of $\epsilon^2$ with respect to $\alpha$ and equate it to zero.

$$\frac{\partial \epsilon^2}{\partial \alpha} = \sum_{r=-m}^{m} \sum_{c=-m}^{m} 2\left[I(r,c) - (\alpha r + \beta c + \gamma)\right](-r) = 0 \tag{6}$$

Opening parentheses, we get:

$$-\sum_{r,c} I(r,c)r + \sum_{r,c} \alpha r^2 + \sum_{r,c} \beta rc + \sum_{r,c} \gamma r = 0 \tag{7}$$

where $\sum_{r,c}$ is shorthand notation for $\sum_{r=-m}^{m} \sum_{c=-m}^{m}$. $\gamma$ is an even function since it is constant. $r$ is an odd function since it is a $45°$ line passing through the origin. Hence, $\gamma r$ is an odd function and $\sum_{r,c} \gamma r$ is an odd function taken over limits that are even (i.e., limits that are symmetric around the axes). Since the summation of an odd function taken over such even limits is identically zero, $\sum_{r,c} \gamma r = 0$. Equation 7 can therefore be written as follows:

$$\sum_{r,c} I(r,c)r = \sum_{r,c} \alpha r^2 + \sum_{r,c} \beta rc \tag{8}$$

The last term can be written as $\beta(\sum_{r=-m}^{m} r)(\sum_{c=-m}^{m} c)$, where the last two elements are identically zero, yielding

$$\alpha = \frac{\sum_{r,c} I(r,c)r}{\sum_{r,c} r^2} \tag{9}$$

where the denominator is a fixed number $2(2m+1)\sum_{k=1}^{m} k^2$ for a given $m$. For example, if $m = 2$ (a 5×5 mask), we have:

$$\alpha = \frac{3}{m(m+1)(2m+1)^2} \sum_{r=-m}^{m} \sum_{c=-m}^{m} I(r,c)r = \frac{1}{50} \sum_{r=-2}^{2} \sum_{c=-2}^{2} I(r,c)r \tag{10}$$

A similar development for $\beta$ yields

$$\beta = \frac{\sum_{r,c} I(r,c)c}{\sum_{r,c} c^2}. \tag{11}$$

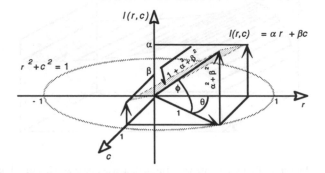

Figure 3: Inclination angle $\phi$ of the edge intensity plane (the gray parallelogram) and the angle $\theta$ of a unit vector in the gradient direction

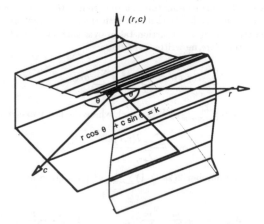

Figure 4: The intensity of a bone edge making an angle $\theta$ with the $c$ axis

Since $\gamma$ is the elevation of the plane, it may be taken as zero without loss of generality. To determine the relations between $\alpha$, $\beta$, $r$, and $c$ in the plane $I(r,c) = \alpha r + \beta c + \gamma$, we find $(r,c)$ such that $r^2 + c^2 = 1$ (a unit vector) which maximizes $I(r,c)$. The direction of the vector is the gradient direction. Figure 3 describes the intensity of the edge gradient making an angle $\theta$ with the $r$ axis.

Using Lagrange multipliers, we get: $e(r,c) = \alpha r + \beta c + \gamma - \lambda(r^2 + c^2 - 1)$. Differentiating, $\frac{\partial e}{\partial r} = \alpha - 2r\lambda = 0 \Rightarrow r = \frac{\alpha}{2\lambda}$, $\frac{\partial e}{\partial c} = \beta - 2c\lambda = 0 \Rightarrow c = \frac{\beta}{2\lambda}$ and $\frac{\partial e}{\partial \lambda} = r^2 + c^2 - 1 = 0$. Substituting $r$ and $c$ in $r^2 + c^2 = 1$, we get $(\frac{\alpha}{2\lambda})^2 + (\frac{\beta}{2\lambda})^2 = 1$, which yields $\lambda = \frac{1}{2}\sqrt{\alpha^2 + \beta^2}$, $r = \frac{\alpha}{\sqrt{\alpha^2 + \beta^2}}$, and $c = \frac{\beta}{\sqrt{\alpha^2 + \beta^2}}$. Substituting $r$ and $c$ in the plane $f(r,c) = \alpha r + \beta c + \gamma$ and taking $\gamma = 0$ we get $\frac{\alpha^2}{\sqrt{\alpha^2 + \beta^2}} + \frac{\beta^2}{\sqrt{\alpha^2 + \beta^2}} = \sqrt{\alpha^2 + \beta^2}$, which is the amount we rise by taking a unit step in the gradient direction, as can be seen in Figure 3. The actual way traversed (see Figure 3) is $\sqrt{1 + \alpha^2 + \beta^2}$ and the gradient direction is $\theta = \tan^{-1}\frac{\alpha}{\beta} = \tan^{-1}\frac{\sum_{r,c} I(r,c)r}{\sum_{r,c} I(r,c)c}$, while the angle of the plane of inclination is $\phi = \tan^{-1}\sqrt{\alpha^2 + \beta^2} = \tan^{-1}\sqrt{\left(\sum_{r,c} I(r,c)r\right)^2 + \left(\sum_{r,c} I(r,c)c\right)^2}$. Having found $\theta$, the adjustment of our edge model is done by using Equation 2 rather than Equation 1.

## 3 Basis Functions Specification

Following Equation 1, we model the edge of a bone as it appears in a radiograph as a linear combination of three basis functions: $I = k_f f(x) + k_g g(x) + k_h h(x)$, where $f(x)$ models the step function of the transition from bone to soft tissue, $g(x)$ models the fact that the bone is like a hollow pipe, and $h(x)$ is an adjustment constant. $k_f$, $k_g$ and $k_h$ are the constants of the linear combination.

The first basis function is a hyperbolic tangent, aimed at representing a smoothed step function that models the transition between two tissues with different response to X ray absorption.

$$f(x,t) = \frac{e^{tx} - e^{-tx}}{e^{tx} + e^{-tx}} \tag{12}$$

**Theorem 1** $t$ in Equation 12 is the slope of the hyperbolic tangent at $x = 0$.

**Proof** The first derivation of $f(x,t)$ with respect to $x$, yields

$$\frac{\partial f}{\partial x} = \frac{[e^{tx} + e^{-tx}][te^{tx} - (-t)e^{-tx}] - [e^{tx} - e^{-tx}][te^{tx} - te^{-tx}]}{[e^{tx} + e^{-tx}]^2}$$

At the point $x = 0$, $\frac{\partial f}{\partial x}\big|_{x=0} = \frac{2 \cdot 2t}{4} = t$. Thus, $t$ is the slope of the curve at $x = 0$. Q.E.D.

Since the edge can be tilted at any angle $\theta$, $x = r\cos\theta + c\sin\theta$, and Equation 12 becomes:

$$f(r,c,t,\theta) = \frac{e^{t(r\cos\theta + c\sin\theta)} - e^{-t(r\cos\theta + c\sin\theta)}}{e^{t(r\cos\theta + c\sin\theta)} + e^{-t(r\cos\theta + c\sin\theta)}} \tag{13}$$

**Theorem 2** $f(r,c,t,\theta)$ is an odd function with respect to the $(r,c)$ plane.

**Proof** We need to show that $f(r, c, t, \theta) = -f(-r, -c, t, \theta)$ for any point $(r, c)$.

$$f(-r, -c, t, \theta) = \frac{e^{t(-r \cos \theta - c \sin \theta)} - e^{-t(-r \cos \theta - c \sin \theta)}}{e^{t(-r \cos \theta - c \sin \theta)} + e^{-t(-r \cos \theta - c \sin \theta)}} =$$

$$\frac{e^{-t(r \cos \theta + c \sin \theta)} - e^{t(r \cos \theta + c \sin \theta)}}{e^{-t(r \cos \theta + c \sin \theta)} + e^{t(r \cos \theta + c \sin \theta)}} = -f(r, c, t, \theta) \tag{14}$$

Q.E.D.

**Theorem 3** The sum of the values of $f(r, c, t, \theta)$ over the $(2m + 1) \times (2m + 1)$ mask $(-m \ldots m) \times (-m \ldots m)$ is zero.

**Proof** We need to show

$$\sum_{r=-m}^{m} \sum_{c=-m}^{m} f(r, c, t, \theta) = 0. \tag{15}$$

We decompose the left-hand side of Equation 15 as follows:

$$\sum_{r=-m}^{m} \sum_{c=-m}^{m} f(r, c, t, \theta) = f(0, 0, t, \theta) + \sum_{r=1}^{m} \sum_{c=1}^{m} [f(-r, -c, t, \theta) + f(r, c, t, \theta)]$$

But $f(0, 0, t, \theta) = 0$ and, from Theorem 2, $\forall (r, c) : 1 \le r \le m$ and $1 \le c \le m$ it holds that $f(-r, -c, t, \theta) = -f(r, c, t, \theta) \Rightarrow f(-r, -c, t, \theta) + f(r, c, t, \theta) = 0.$ Q.E.D.

The motivation for Theorem 3 is that we want the basis functions to be pairwise orthogonal, i.e., the product of each function pair should be zero.

**Theorem 4** $t$ is the directional slope (with direction $\theta$) of the hyperbolic tangent function $f(r, c, t, \theta)$ at the point $x = 0$.

**Proof** We need to show that the directional derivative of function $f(r, c, t, \theta)$ with respect to the gradient direction $\theta$ at the point $x = 0$ is equal to $t$. Using $x(r, c) = r \cos \theta + c \sin \theta$, we compute $\frac{\partial f}{\partial r} \cos \theta + \frac{\partial f}{\partial c} \sin \theta$ at $x = r \cos \theta + c \sin \theta = 0$. Using $\frac{\partial x}{\partial r} = \cos \theta$, and $\frac{\partial x}{\partial c} = \sin \theta$, from Equation 12 we derive

$$\frac{\partial f}{\partial r} = \frac{\partial f}{\partial x} \frac{\partial x}{\partial r} = \frac{[te^{tx} - (-t)e^{-tx}][e^{tx} + e^{-tx}] - [te^{tx} + (-t)e^{-t}][e^{tx} - e^{-tx}]}{[e^{tx} + e^{-tx}]^2} \cdot \cos \theta \tag{16}$$

$$\frac{\partial f}{\partial c} = \frac{\partial f}{\partial x} \frac{\partial x}{\partial c} = \frac{[te^{tx} - (-t)e^{-tx}][e^{tx} + e^{-tx}] - [te^{tx} + (-t)e^{-t}][e^{tx} - e^{-tx}]}{[e^{tx} + e^{-tx}]^2} \cdot \sin \theta \tag{17}$$

Substituing $x = 0$ in equations 16 and 17, we obtain $\frac{\partial f}{\partial r}\big|_{x=0} = \frac{2t \cdot 2 \cdot \cos \theta}{4} = t \cos \theta$ and $\frac{\partial f}{\partial c}\big|_{x=0} = \frac{2t \cdot 2 \cdot \sin \theta}{4} = t \sin \theta$.
This yields $\frac{\partial f}{\partial r} \cos \theta + \frac{\partial f}{\partial c} \sin \theta \big|_{x=0} = t \cos \theta \cos \theta + t \sin \theta \sin \theta = t \cos^2 \theta + t \sin^2 \theta = t$ Q.E.D.

The second basis function is a shifted-down Gaussian, which models the fact that the bone can be considered a hollow pipe, causing the intensity near the edge to be higher than in the middle of the bone. Formally,

$$g(r, c, \sigma, \theta) = e^{-\left(\frac{r \cos \theta + c \sin \theta}{\sigma}\right)^2} - k, \tag{18}$$

where $\sigma$ is a parameter that controls the spread of the gaussian and $k$ is a down-shifting constant.

**Theorem 5** $g(r, c, \sigma, \theta)$ is an even function.

**Proof** We need to show that for any point $(r, c)$, $g(r, c, \sigma, \theta) = g(-r, -c, \sigma, \theta)$.
Starting with $g(-r, -c, \sigma, \theta)$, we can write

$$g(-r, -c, \sigma, \theta) = e^{-(\frac{-r\cos\theta - c\sin\theta}{\sigma})^2} - k = e^{-(\frac{r\cos\theta + c\sin\theta}{\sigma})^2} - k = g(r, c, \sigma, \theta) \qquad \text{Q.E.D.}$$

As with the hyperbolic tangent function, we want $g(r, c, \sigma, \theta)$ to sum to zero over the mask $(-m, \ldots, m) \times (-m, \ldots, m)$. Hence, $g(r, c, \sigma, \theta)$ is shifted down by $k$, such that for any such mask with a fixed $\sigma$ and the particular $\theta$ found for that mask it satisfies:

$$\sum_{r=-m}^{m} \sum_{c=-m}^{m} g(r, c, \sigma, \theta) = 0 \qquad (19)$$

The value of $k$ is set so as to make the area under the function $g$ be equal 0. For each mask we find a particular $k$ that satisfies Equation 19. By substituing Equation 18 in Equation 19 we get $\sum_{r=-m}^{m} \sum_{c=-m}^{m} [e^{-(\frac{r\cos\theta + c\sin\theta}{\sigma})^2} - k] = 0$. This yields

$$\sum_{r=-m}^{m} \sum_{c=-m}^{m} e^{-(\frac{r\cos\theta + c\sin\theta}{\sigma})^2} = \sum_{r=-m}^{m} \sum_{c=-m}^{m} k = (2m+1)^2 \cdot k$$

$$k = \frac{1}{(2m+1)^2} \sum_{r=-m}^{m} \sum_{c=-m}^{m} e^{-(\frac{r\cos\theta + c\sin\theta}{\sigma})^2} \qquad (20)$$

The third basis function, $h(x)$, is a normalized unit function, and is described by $h(r, c) = 1$. Being a constant function, $h(r, c)$ is obviously even, because $h(-r, -c) = h(r, c) = 1$

**Theorem 6** The basis functions $f(r, c, t, \theta)$ and $g(r, c, \sigma, \theta)$ are orthogonal.

**Proof** We need to show that $\sum_{r=-m}^{m} \sum_{c=-m}^{m} f(r, c, t, \theta) g(r, c, \sigma, \theta) = 0$. We divide the plane $(-m, \ldots, m) \times (-m, \ldots, m)$ into two sub-planes, $R$ and $R'$, which have just one common point—the point $(0, 0)$—such that for the set of points $R$, $R'$ is the reflection set of points, defined as follows. $R' = \{(r, c) \in (-m, \ldots, m) \times (-m, \ldots, m) | (-r, -c) \in R\}$, satisfying: (1) $R \cup R' = (-m, \ldots, m) \times (-m, \ldots, m)$, and (2) $R \cap R' = (0, 0)$. Using this definition, the above expression can be written as

$$\sum_{(r,c)\in R} f(r, c, t, \theta) g(r, c, \sigma, \theta) + \sum_{(r,c)\in R'} f(r, c, t, \theta) g(r, c, \sigma, \theta) - f(0, 0, t, \theta) g(0, 0, \sigma, \theta) = 0,$$

where the last term is subtracted because it appears twice, once in $R$ and once in $R'$. The last equality stems from the definitions of $R$ and $R'$ and from theorems 2 and 5, which state that $f(r, c, t, \theta)$ and $g(r, c, \sigma, \theta)$ are odd and even functions, respectively. \qquad Q.E.D.

**Theorem 7** The basis functions $f(r, c, t, \theta)$ and $h(r, c)$ are orthogonal.

**Proof** We need to show $\sum_{r=-m}^{m} \sum_{c=-m}^{m} f(r, c, t, \theta) h(r, c) = 0$. From the definition of $h(r, c)$, the last term can be written as $\sum_{r=-m}^{m} \sum_{c=-m}^{m} f(r, c, t, \theta) = 0$, which is true by Theorem 3. \qquad Q.E.D.

**Theorem 8** The basis functions $g(r, c, \sigma, \theta)$ and $h(r, c)$ are orthogonal.

**Proof** We need to show $\sum_{r=-m}^{m} \sum_{c=-m}^{m} g(r,c,t,\theta)h(r,c) = 0$. From the definition of $h(r,c)$, this expression can be written as: $\sum_{r=-m}^{m} \sum_{c=-m}^{m} g(r,c,t,\theta) = 0$. This is made true by setting the value of $k$ in the shifted Gaussian for the given mask, the parameter $\sigma$ and the precomputed value of $\theta$. Q.E.D.

Having selected the three basis functions, the squared error function becomes

$$\epsilon^2 = \sum_{r,c} \left[I(r,c) - k_f f(r,c,t,\theta) - k_g g(r,c,\sigma,\theta) - k_h h(r,c)\right]^2,$$

where $k_f$, $k_g$ and $k_h$ are the constants we want to find for the linear function combination. We find the three constants by setting the corresponding derivatives of $\epsilon^2$ equal to zero, as follows:

$$\frac{\partial \epsilon^2}{\partial k_f} = \sum_{r,c} 2 \left[I(r,c) - k_f f(r,c,t,\theta) - k_g g(r,c,\sigma,\theta) - k_h h(r,c)\right] \left[-f(r,c,t,\theta)\right] = 0.$$

Since $f$ and $g$ are orthogonal, $\sum_{r,c} \left[k_g g(r,c,\sigma,\theta)\right] \left[f(r,c,t,\theta)\right] = 0$. Similarly, since $f$ and $h$ are orthogonal, $\sum_{r,c} \left[k_h h(r,c)\right] \left[f(r,c,t,\theta)\right] = 0$.

Hence, $k_f = \frac{\sum_{r,c} [I(r,c) f(r,c,t,\theta)]}{\sum_{r,c} f^2(r,c,t,\theta)}$.

Similarly, $k_g = \frac{\sum_{r,c} [I(r,c) g(r,c,\sigma,\theta)]}{\sum_{r,c} g^2(r,c,\sigma,\theta)}$ and $k_h = \frac{\sum_{r,c} [I(r,c) h(r,c)]}{\sum_{r,c} h^2(r,c)} = \frac{\sum_{r,c} I(r,c)}{(2m+1)^2}$.

With the three basis parameters $k_f$, $k_g$ and $k_h$ we calculate $\sigma$ using the Fibbonacci search method, assuming the second squared error function $\epsilon^2$ is unimodal. The method consists of checking the values of the squared error function for pairs of values of $\sigma$. As an example, we take the range of sigmas between 1 and 21 of the Fibbonacci's numbers (1,1,3,5,8,13,21). If $\epsilon^2|_{\sigma=21} > \epsilon^2|_{\sigma=1}$ we reduce the interval to $[1,13]$ and continue the search in this way untill the $\sigma$ with the smallest $\epsilon^2$ is found.

## 4   Summary and Future work

We propose a notion of edge that is more general than a mere step function and suits the description of edges in radiographs. The pattern-based edge detection starts with supervised learning, in which the user teaches the system what are the pixels in the displayed radiograph that should be considered as edges by pointing at those pixels. The system analyses the selected image points and computes the values of the six parameters $t, \theta, \sigma, k_f, k_g, k_h$ according to the process described. The edge pixel sample size is determined by the variation of the values formed for each parameter. Having found the values of $t, \theta, \sigma, k_f, k_g, k_h$, we devise a method to answer the question: Given a pixel $(r,c)$ in the input image, does it belong to an edge or not?

The proposed procedure is as follows. (1) Find the six-dimensional classification function for any input pixel $(r,c)$, which classifies the pixel as "edge" or "non-edge". (2) Classify each pixel in the image as "edge" or "non-edge" according to the classification function.

Work must be done in order to adapt the discrimination function that fits the problem at hand. Human-machine interface for efficient learning should also be devised. Finally, the effectiveness of the method should be tested in practice. The detected edge points may serve a number of functions. First, they may as anchors for traditional orthopaedic measurements. The angle of curvature of the spine is one such measurement. Alternately, objective measurements such as cortical area of implants may made where previously subjective interpretation was thought to be adequate. In both cases, great precision is brought to bear upon the decision process. The numbers obtained from the computer radiograph may be at odds with those determined by the physician by hand. Hence, inter-observer variation will still exist. However, the issue of intra-observer variation is essentially eliminated.

## References

[1] Canny, J.F., Finding Edge and Lines in Images, *MIT Artificial Intelligence Lab. Tech. Reprot 720*, June 1983.

[2] Davis, L.S., Survey of Edge Detection Techniques, *Computer Graphics and Image Processing*, **4** pp. 248-270, 1975.

[3] Haralick, R.M., Zero-crossing of Second Directional Derivative Edge Operator, *IEEE Trans. Pattern Analysis and Machine Intelligence* **PAMI-6**, 1, pp. 58-68, 1984.

[4] Marr, D., Hildreth, H., Theory of Edge Detection,*Proc. Royal Society, London*, **B207**, pp.187-217, 1980.

[5] Nevatia, R., Bavu, K.R., Linear Feature Extraction and Description,*Computer Graphics and Image Processing*, **13**, pp.257-269, 1980.

[6] Shen, J., Castan, S., An Optimal Linear Operator for Edge Detection,*Proc. CVPR-86, Miami Beach,FL*, pp.109-114, 1986.

[7] Torre, V., Poggio, T., On Edge Detection,*IEEE Trans. Pattern Analysis and Machine Intelligence*,**PAMI-8**, pp.147-163, 1986.

# Two Dual Representations of Mathematical Morphology Based on the Parallel Normal Transport Property

Leo Dorst and Rein van den Boomgaard[*]
*Department of Mathematics and Computer Science*
*University of Amsterdam, The Netherlands*

### Abstract

A familiar way to describe shapes is through their behavior under the operations of mathematical morphology. We provide a *quantitative analysis* of the basic operation of mathematical morphology: *dilation*. This operation has the important property that it 'transports' points such that normals to surfaces are preserved. As a consequence, straight lines are eigenfunctions of morphology. We present two ways to convert the parallel normal transport property into a computational representation of dilation. One is the *slope transform*, designed for the dilation of functions, the other is the *normal transform* (appearing in this paper for the first time), designed for the dilation of geometrical objects. For both transforms, we show how *dilation* in the spatial domain becomes *addition* in the transformed domain (plain addition for the slope transform, radial harmonic addition for the normal transform). Though both representations are complete, there are applications in which one is preferable over the other - we give some recommendations for the selection.

## 1 Introduction

Mathematical morphology describes the contact of *sets*, and does so typically in an algebraic and set-theoretic notation. If one would like to use it for the description and analysis of the contact of *physical rigid bodies*, a more quantitative description is required. Such a representation can be based on the eigen-objects of morphology: the planes.

---

[*]Work done under NWO/SION project 612-322-205: Model-controlled Image Processing.

In previous papers [4][5], we have presented the *slope transform* of a function for precisely this purpose. The graph of any function can be represented as the caustic of its tangent planes, and these tangent planes can be characterized by their intercept with the value axis as a function of their slope. This representation is additive under dilation.[1] It is closely related to the Legendre transform of theoretical physics [1], the Young-Fenchel conjugate of convex analysis [8][11] and to the $\mathcal{A}$-transform [10].

Application of the slope transform to the contact of geometrical object surfaces (rather than to the morphology of signals) requires their representation by *functions*. This can be done locally in the standard way of differential geometry [12] as a height function in some chosen direction (Monge patches). However, it is unsatisfying to have to introduce a preferential axis to describe objects that are free to roam through space.

In this paper, we introduce a dual representation of morphology that is *isotropic*, and hence more suited for the description of the contacts of rigid objects. Just as the slope transform it is based on the representation of object surfaces by their tangent planes, since planes are the morphological eigenfunctions. The new element is that we characterize these tangent planes by projective covectors rather than by their slopes relative to some fiducial direction. The resulting transform we propose to call the *normal transform*; it is related to the Gauss map, but invertible (which the Gauss map is not). Under this normal transform, dilation of object surfaces becomes radial harmonic addition of their transforms.

# 2 Objects in Contact

Consider two object surfaces $A$ and $\check{B}$, both assumed to be smooth. Let $A$ and $\check{B}$ each be given a reference point, to keep track of their translations - we will not permit rotations. Bring $A$ and $\check{B}$ into contact by some translation, in all possible ways. The locus of all positions of the reference point of $\check{B}$ relative to that of $A$ forms an object surface called the *dilation result* of $A$ and $B$, denoted $A \oplus B$. (Here $\check{B}$ is the point-mirrored image of $B$ relative to its reference point, and so $B$ is the point-mirrored image of $\check{B}$ - we need this mirroring to correspond to the conventional notation of dilation based on Minkowski sums.) The dilation result is the separating surface between contact-free and overlapping relative positions of the objects. It is not necessarily smooth: at locations where $\check{B}$ has a multiple contact with $A$, a sharp non-differentiable edge appears in the dilation result.

If we assign local coordinate systems to $A$ and $B$ which permit us to describe part of the surface as a function (with the object below the graph, free-space above) , then

---

[1]There is a subtlety: dilation of differentiable functions or objects with differentiable boundaries leads to non-differentiable functions or object surfaces. In our work on the slope transform we extended the dilation to *tangential dilation* to retain differentiablility. The classical dilation is a subset of this dilation. We follow the same procedure in this paper.

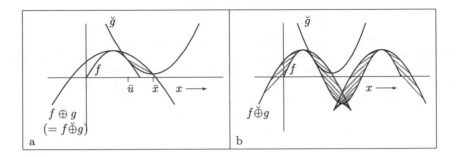

Figure 1: *Dilation and the slope theorem. (a) parallel transport of slope for convex functions; (b) tangential dilation: parallel transport everywhere.*

we can describe the operation as a *dilation* of functions (see e.g. [7]):

$$(f \oplus g)(x) = \sup_u [f(u) + g(x - u)]. \tag{1}$$

Here $f$ and $g$ are height functions on a domain $X$, such that $(x, f(x))$, for $x \in X$, is a patch of $A$, $(x, g(x))$, for $x \in X$, is a patch of $B$, and $(x, (f \oplus g)(x))$ is a patch of the dilation result. Note that the result is symmetrical in $A$ and $B$: it is invariant under the coordinate transformation $\bar{u} \mapsto x - \bar{u}$.

Let $\bar{u}$ be the value of $u$ for which the supremum is reached; it is the abscissa of the contact point in the coordinate system of the $B$-patch. At locations where all terms of the equation exist, we have an interesting equality of derivatives (noted in [9] and first proved in [2]):

$$\nabla(f \oplus g)(x) = \nabla g(x - \bar{u}) = \nabla f(\bar{u}) \tag{2}$$

**Derivation:** Immediate from differentiation of eq.(1) to $x$ and $\bar{u}$. $\square$
Geometrically, this means that dilation of two surface patches is a parallel transport of the tangent planes to that surface: the slopes of $f$ at $\bar{u}$, of $g$ at $\bar{x} - \bar{u}$ and of $f \oplus g$ at $\bar{x}$ are all equal (Fig.1a). For this reason we refer to eq.(2) as the *slope theorem*. Obviously, when the slopes in coordinate directions of the Monge patches are preserved, then so are the normals to the surfaces $A$, $B$ and $A \oplus B$.

We can use this property to define a generalization of the dilation which is more tractable, since it is differentiable everywhere if $f$ and $g$ are. This was done in [4], where it was called *tangential dilation*:

Given smooth surfaces $A$ and $B$ with reference points $o_A$ and $o_B$. Construct a surface $A \check{\oplus} B$ by the following procedure: for any point $p$ of $A$ (relative to $o_A$), determine the normal $n_p$ to $A$ at $p$. Find all points $q$ relative to $o_B$ such that the normal to $B$ at $q$ equals $n_p$ (or equivalently, the points $-q$ such that the normal to $\check{B}$ equals $-n_p$). Construct all points of $A\check{\oplus}B$ corresponding to this contact as: $p + q$, for all $q$.

The classical dilation result $A \oplus B$ is contained in $A\check{\oplus}B$, since the condition is satisfied at all differentiable points of the classical dilation by the slope theorem (Note that $p + q$ is indeed the correct result for the classical dilation of eq.(1): both the function values and their abscissae add up: $x = \bar{u} + (x - \bar{u})$ and $(f\check{\oplus}g)(x) = f(\bar{u}) + g(x - \bar{u})$.). But the tangential dilation also includes points that represent a contact in which $A$ and $\check{B}$ touch locally, but intersect somewhere else (Fig.1b). By including those points, the tangential dilation is a purely local operation, and this makes its analysis much more tractable.[2]

*Eigenfunctions* of an operation are those functions that do not change more than an 'amplitude' (appropriately defined) when the operations is applied, and retain their functional 'form'. Planar functions are the eigenfunctions of dilation. This can be seen easily as follows. A plane $n - 1$ dimensional surface $A$ has the same normal $\nu$ at any point. Under tangential dilation by a surface $B$, each point $p$ of $A$ translates by the same amount (according to the slope theorem), namely by $q$ such that the normal of $B$ at $q$ equals $\nu$. Therefore, the dilation result is also a plane (in general, a set of planes), with the same normal $\nu$. We have found: *an $n - 1$ dimensional plane surface is an eigenfunction of the tangential dilation in dimension $n$.*

Taking our cue from representation theory, we look for a representation of arbitrary surfaces in terms of these eigenfunctions. That should then form a representation in which the dilation operation is simple. We present two such representations: the *slope transform* (a generalization of the Legendre transform, introduced before in [4]) and the new *normal transform* (which is related to the Gauss map).

# 3   The Slope Transform

The results in this section are taken from [4] and [5].

Let a differentiable function $f : X \to \mathbb{R}$ be given. At a point $(x, f(x))$, the tangent plane is given by all points $(u, \nabla f(x) \cdot (u - x) + f(x))$, for $u \in X$. We can characterize this plane by the slope $\nabla f(x)$ and the intercept $f(x) - \nabla f(x) \cdot x$. Indeed, we may move to a dual representation in which $\omega = \nabla f(x)$ is the independent variable, and consider the intercept of the tangent plane as a function of $\omega$. This is the *slope transform* of $f$. We introduce the notation:

$$\text{stat}_x[f(x)] = \{f(u) \mid \nabla f(u) = 0, u \in X\} \tag{3}$$

---

[2]The term *tangential dilation* was coined in [4] for the local functional representation of surface patches as functions. In the present paper, we will move to the general geometrical representation, based on normal covectors or tangent 1-forms. Since these reside in the (co-)tangent space, we will stretch the original intended meaning of 'tangential dilation' and keep using the same term.

for the stationary values of a differentiable real-valued function $f$. Then we can compute the slope transform $\mathcal{S}[f]$ of $f$ as:

$$\mathcal{S}[f](\omega) = \text{stat}_x[f(x) - \omega \cdot x].$$ (4)

Note that the analytical evaluation of the slope transform involves inverse functions. The original function $f$ can be reconstructed from its slope transform by:

$$f(x) = \text{stat}_\omega[\mathcal{S}[f](\omega) + \omega \cdot x]$$ (5)

for a wide class of functions. The derivation, and the relationship to the Legendre transform [1], the Young-Fenchel conjugate of convex analysis [8][11], and the $\mathcal{A}$-transform of [10] can be found in [5].

The tangential dilation can be formulated using the 'stat' operator as:

$$(f \check{\oplus} g)(x) = \text{stat}_u[f(u) + g(x - u)].$$ (6)

It is straightforward to show that *tangential dilation of functions becomes addition of their slope transforms* [4] [5]:

$$\mathcal{S}[f \check{\oplus} g] = \mathcal{S}[f] + \mathcal{S}[g].$$ (7)

The slope transform thus indeed provides a simple representation of the dilation operation, namely as *addition*. There is a nice analogy to the way in which the Fourier transform represents convolution as multiplication [5].

# 4    The Normal Transform

The function representation of the slope transform is convenient for morphological processing of *signals*, but *not* the most natural representation for morphology on geometrical *objects*. The preferential treatment of the function value direction, and with it the use of the slope itself, will have to be replaced by an isotropic treatment of directions based on normals.

At any point $p$ of a differentiable surface $A$, we can set up a tangent plane to the surface. It is the best linear approximation to the surface at $p$. The orientation of this tangent plane can be specified by a 1-form (or co-vector) $\nu_p$ at $p$; a tangent vector $v$ in the plane is then characterized by $\nu_p(v) = 0$. Thus our use of the 1-form $\nu_p$ permits an undetermined scalar factor: $c\nu_p$ denotes the same tangent plane. (For readers unfamiliar with covectors: $\nu_p$ is like a vector $n_p$ normal to the surface at $p$, and $\nu_p(v)$ is like $n_p \cdot v$, the inner product of $n_p$ and $v$).

For the construction of the tangential dilation, we need to be able to find all points at which a certain tangent plane occurs; therefore we want a representation in which a covector yields a position vector. The object surface determines a relationship between position vectors and covectors, and is therefore an object in the cotangent bundle $T^*(X)$ of the base space $X$, a typical point being $(p, \nu_p)$. The cotangent bundle object is not unique, however, due to the projective freedom in the covectors indicating the same tangent plane: $(p, \nu_p)$ should be the same as $(p, c\nu_p)$. We can make it unique by the following procedure: we represent the pair $(p, \nu_p)$ by a pair $(p, \omega_p)$ such that $\omega_p = c\nu_p$ and $\omega_p(p) = 1$. (This is called a projectivization of the cotangent bundle, and it leads to a *contact manifold*, see [1].) Thus we have:

$$\omega_p = \frac{\nu_p}{\nu_p(p)}. \tag{8}$$

To obtain the desired map, we now consider the section $(p, \omega_p)$ for all $p$ not as providing $\omega_p$ given $p$, but as providing $p$ given $\omega_p$. (There is no problem switching to this dual point of view for Euclidean $X = E^n$; we will restrict ourselves to such spaces in this paper.) We call $\omega_p$ the *normal transform* of $p$. By performing the normal transform at all points of an object surface $A$, we obtain the normal transform $\mathcal{N}[A]$ of the object surface.

The surface $\mathcal{N}[A]$ constructed in this way has the interesting property that its normal at a point $\omega_p$ is proportional to $p$. Indeed, when we perform the normal transform on $\mathcal{N}[A]$, we obtain $A$ again. This means that the *normal transform is an involution* (an operation that is its own inverse). Notationally we have to be a bit careful, since the normal transform was only defined on $X$. Let us denote by $I$ the operation that converts covectors of the dual space into vectors of the base space $X$, and vice versa, so that we can indeed do the normal transform again (if we denote a point $p$ by an $n \times 1$ column vector, then $Ip$ is the $1 \times n$ row covector with corresponding coefficients). Then we can write the involution property as:

$$I\mathcal{N}[I\mathcal{N}[A]] = A. \tag{9}$$

**Derivation:** Let $p_i$ denote the $i$-th component of $p$, $\omega_i$ the $i$-th component of $\omega_p$. The identity $\omega_p(p) = 1$ is then written as $\omega_i p_i = 1$ (Einstein convention). Then $\dot{\omega}_i p_i + \omega_i \dot{p}_i = 0$. Since $\omega_p$ represents a tangent plane to the surface at $p$, we have $\omega_i \dot{p}_i = 0$, and it follows that $\dot{\omega}_i p_i = 0$. Therefore, $Icp$ represents a tangent plane to the dual surface point at $I\omega_p$ ($c$ any non-zero real). The transform of the dual surface point is hence $Icp_i/(cp_j\omega_j) = Ip_i$, and hence $I\mathcal{N}[A]$ transforms to $IA$. $\square$

It is instructive to verify this for a parametrized curve $p(t) = (p_1(t), p_2(t))^T$ in $E^2$. The (right-handed) normal to the curve at $p$ is the cotangent vector $(\nu_1, \nu_2)(t) = (-\dot{p}_2, \dot{p}_1)(t)$, so the transform at $p$ is

$$\begin{pmatrix} p_1 \\ p_2 \end{pmatrix}(t) \rightarrow (\omega_1, \omega_2)(t) = \frac{(-\dot{p}_2, \dot{p}_1)}{\dot{p}_1 p_2 - \dot{p}_2 p_1}(t). \tag{10}$$

Some algebraic manipulation demonstrates that the formula is invariant under the exchange of $p \leftrightarrow I\omega$. Therefore the transformation (including $I$) is an involution.

As a representation of the normals on the original surface, the normal transform is related to the *Gauss-map*. The Gauss-map image of a point $p$ with normal $n_p$ is the point $n_p/||n_p||$ on the unit sphere. Therefore the Gauss map contains directional information only, the position information is lost, and inversion has become impossible. The Gauss-map has been used by Ghosh to describe certain aspects of dilation [6]. Other mappings from differential geometry related to the normal transform are the *pedal* curve, $n_p(n_p.p)$, which is invertible but does not scale well, and the *dual curve* $(n_p, n_p.p)$ which is overdetermined [3]. To the best of our knowledge, the normal transform is new to mathematical morphology.

Tangential dilation has a simple representation in the normal transform. Let $p+q$ be a point of the surface $A \check{\oplus} B$, obtained by tangential dilation of $A$ at $p$ and $B$ at $q$. Let the normal covector at the considered points be $\nu$ (so $\nu = \nu_p = \nu_q = \nu_{p+q}$). Then the transform is:

$$\mathcal{N}[A \check{\oplus} B] : \quad \omega_{p+q} = \frac{\nu_{p+q}}{\nu_{p+q}(p+q)} = \frac{\nu}{\nu(p+q)} = \frac{\nu}{\nu(p) + \nu(q)}, \tag{11}$$

since covectors are linear. Thus the direction of $\omega_{p+q}$ is the same as that of $\omega_p$ and of $\omega_q$ (namely the direction of $\nu$), and the magnitude of $\omega_{p+q}$ is the harmonic sum of the magnitudes of $\omega_p$ and $\omega_q$:

$$\frac{1}{||\omega_{p+q}||} = \frac{1}{||\omega_p||} + \frac{1}{||\omega_q||}. \tag{12}$$

We will denote this by $\omega_{p+q} = \omega_p \,/\!/\, \omega_q$, or for the object surfaces $A$ and $B$ by:

$$\mathcal{N}[A \check{\oplus} B] = \mathcal{N}[A] \,/\!/\, \mathcal{N}[B]. \tag{13}$$

Compare this to eq.(7) for the the the slope transform.

Example: The dilation of two circles of radii $r_1$ and $r_2$ is a circle of radius $r_1 + r_2$. The transform of a circle of radius $r$ is a circle of radius $1/r$. So indeed the transform of the result equals the harmonic addition of the originals: $1/(1/r) = 1/(1/r_1) + 1/(1/r_2)$.

# 5   Comparison of the Two Dual Transforms

As an example of the use of the transformations, we describe the dilation of a parabola $y = \frac{1}{2a}x^2$ and the circle $x^2 + y^2 = r^2$, in both representations.

- *The Slope Transform View*
  The slope transform of $f(x) = \frac{1}{2a}x^2$ is $\mathcal{S}[f](\omega) = -\frac{a}{2}\omega^2$ (see [4]). A circle is represented by the set-valued function $g(x) = \pm\sqrt{r^2 - x^2}$, of which the slope transform is the two-sheeted hyperbola $\mathcal{S}[g](\omega) = \pm r\sqrt{1 + \omega^2}$. We need the upper half circle, which corresponds to the upper sheet of the hyperbola. These slope transforms are drawn in Fig.2b for $a = 1$, $r = 2$, as is their sum. The

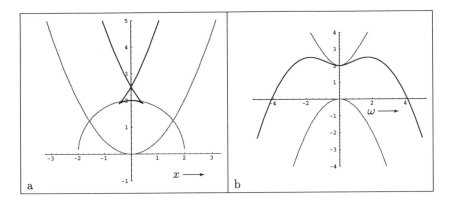

Figure 2: *The tangential dilation of a parabola $y = x^2/2$ and a circle with radius 2, in spatial domain (a) and slope domain (b), where it is addition.*

inverse slope transform of the sum (it requires the explicit solution of the equation $r\omega/\sqrt{1+w^2} - a\omega + x = 0$ for $\omega$) gives the tangential dilation of the two functions. The result is indicated in Fig.2a.

- *The Normal Transform View*
  The normal transform of the parabola $p_2 - \frac{1}{2a}p_1^2 = 0$ is $\omega_p = (\omega_1, \omega_2) = (2/p_1, -2a/p_1^2)$, so $a\omega_1^2/2 + \omega_2 = 0$. The normal transform of the circle $p_1^2 + p_2^2 = r^2$ is the circle $\omega_1^2 + \omega_2^2 = \frac{1}{r^2}$. To compute the harmonic sum we introduce polar coordinates, $\omega_1 = \rho \cos\phi$ and $\omega_2 = \rho \sin\phi$. The circle has $\rho(\phi) = \frac{1}{r}$, the parabola has: $\rho(\phi) = -\frac{2\sin\phi}{a\cos^2\phi}$. Thus the harmonic sum is: $\frac{1}{r - (a\cos^2\phi)/(2\sin\phi)}(\cos\phi, \sin\phi)$, and the inverse normal transform can be solved (use Mathematica !) to yield:

$$(\cot\phi(r\sin\phi - a), \frac{2a\cos^2\phi + 3r\sin\phi - r\sin 3\phi}{4\sin^2\phi})^T. \tag{14}$$

Fig.3 shows the plot of this solution.

The plots for the dilation results Figs.2a,3a are indeed identical, even though the computation of the dilation is performed in different dual domains. This example illustrates the fact that there is no *fundamental* reason why one should use one transform or the other. The only distinction between them is the assumed presentation of the mathematical objects they act on. As a rule, this distinction coincides with that between *signals* and *objects*:

- *Signals: Slope Transform*
  If a surface is obtained as a *signal*, namely as a real-valued function on some

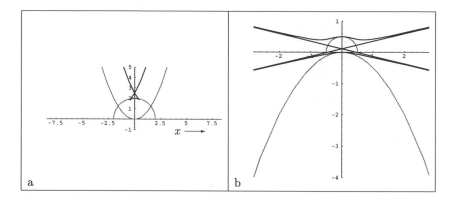

Figure 3: *The tangential dilation of a parabola $y = x^2/2$ and a circle with radius 2, in spatial domain (a) and normal domain (b), where it is harmonic addition (dark curve).*

$n$-dimensional space $X$, then one should use the *slope transform* to describe the morphology. This is especially so when there are symmetries in $X$ (such as translation invariance) that are not symmetries of $X \times \mathbb{R}$. In that case, the slope transform is the most natural representation of dilation. Such is the case in the processing of grey-valued images: the intensity dimension has properties rather different from the spatial dimensions. Thus in grey-value morphology, the slope transform should be used to analyze the effect of morphology on the images, and as a tool for filter design.

- *Objects: Normal Transform*
  If a surface is obtained as the boundary of an *object* in a uniform and isotropic space, then the *normal transform* should be used to describe the morphology. Thus in morphological processing on binary images of objects, one should use the normal transform for the analysis and design of filters.

There are of course situations that are ambiguous. One occurs in the scanning tunneling microscope, a morphological measurement instrument for atomic surfaces [9]. Here an atomic probe moves scanning in contact with an atomic surface, and the probe's height is measured as a signal. Thus one might use the slope transform; but since the signal is a height function, one may also view the result as an isotropic object representation and use the normal transform.

To conclude, note that both transforms convert the basic operation of dilation into a simple addition operation in the transformed domain. As such, they both are counterpart of the Fourier transform in linear filtering, which transforms the involved operation of convolution into the simple operation of multiplication. We believe that the two morphological transforms provide the analytical apparatus to develop a *morphological systems theory* with a power and rigor fully comparable to linear systems theory. If this succeeds, we will have two equally consistent theories of signal processing, each applicable to the analysis and control of different aspects of the natural world.

# References

[1] V.I. Arnold, *Mathematical Methods of Classical Mechanics*, Springer, New York, 1989.

[2] R. van den Boomgaard, *Mathematical Morphology - extensions towards computer vision*, Ph.D. Thesis University of Amsterdam, 1992, Chapter 8. To appear as *The Morphological Structure of Images: The differential equations of mathematical morphology*, IEEE-PAMI, 1994.

[3] J.W. Bruce, P.J. Giblin, *Curves and Singularities*, Cambridge Univ. Press, 1984.

[4] L. Dorst, R. van den Boomgaard, *An Analytical Theory of Mathematical Morphology*, Math. Morphology and its Applications to Signal Processing, Barcelona 1993, 245-250.

[5] L. Dorst, R. van den Boomgaard, *Morphological Signal Processing and the Slope Transform*, invited paper for Signal Processing, submitted 1993.

[6] P.K. Ghosh, *On Negative Shape*, NATO Workshop *Shape in Picture*, Driebergen, The Netherlands, September 1992.

[7] H.J.A.M Heijmans, *Mathematical Morphology: a Geometrical Approach in Image Processing*, Nieuw Archief voor Wiskunde, vol.10, 1992, 237-276.

[8] A.D.Ioffe, V.M.Tihomirov, *Theory of Extremal Problems*, North-Holland, Amsterdam, 1979.

[9] D. Keller, *Reconstruction of STM and AFM images distorted by finite-sized tips*, Surface Science 253 (1991), 353-364.

[10] P. Maragos, *Max-min Difference Equations and Recursive Morphological Systems*, Math. Morphology and its Applications to Signal Processing, Barcelona 1993, 168-173.

[11] J. Mattioli, *Differential Relations of Morphological Operators*, Mathematical Morphology and its Applications to Signal Processing, Barcelona 1993, 162-167.

[12] B. O'Neill, *Elementary Differential Geometry*, Academic Press, New York, 1966.

# Human Integration of Shape Primitives

Gregory Dudek
Center for Intelligent Machines
McGill University
Montreal, Canada H3A 2A7

Martin Arguin
Dept. de Psychologie
Univ. de Montrèal
Montreal, Canada H3A 2B4

Daniel Bub
Montreal Neurological Inst.
McGill University
Montreal, Canada H3A 2A7

### Abstract

This paper deals with human shape recognition. In particular, we present results relating the role of human inferior temporal cortex to the description and recognition of shapes using a parametric three-dimensional shape space.

In experiments with a patient with damaged IT cortex, we show that his inability to recognize or distinguish between members of a large family of simple shapes can be traced to an inability to simultaneously combine information related to multiple global shape dimensions. We have discovered that the relevant dimensions describing global object shape, in this case, are related to simple geometric deformations. When object recognition tasks involve multi-dimensional comparisons between potential targets our subjects have difficulty. This deficit is not related to early visual processing, but to an apparently higher-level processing stage.

We suggest that the role of IT cortex in combining shape dimensions may be related to its acknowledged role in the control of visual attention. This has implications for the construction of computer vision systems that recognize large ensembles of objects.

# 1 Introduction

This may be, in part, because there are multiple mechanisms that contribute to the concept of shape [5, 15]. The very power of the human shape recognition system and the multiple computations apparently involved have made it difficult to decompose functionally [13, 7, 8, are but a few examples]. In this paper we describe an approach to uncovering the mechanisms underlying human shape recognition by looking at the precise deficits that arise in the presence of localized damage to the human visual system. By observing the shape-specific deficits that occur as a result of localized brain damage, we believe important characteristics of the involved computations can be elucidated. In particular, although the specific deficit that we have examined occurs in only a small number of patients, the fact that similar functional deficits may be associated with different types of brain lesion suggests that the presence of the shape-processing characteristics we have discovered may have far-reaching implications.

Brain-damaged subjects with different types of high-level shape processing deficit are shown to be impaired in the integration of multiple shape primitives that appear to be used in object identification. One of these (who we will focus on in this paper) is a visual agnosic (suffers from an inability to recognize certain objects) while the other is an optic aphasic (suffers from a deficit in labelling visual objects with spared recognition if tested non-verbally). The first patient's impairment (subject ELM) is independent of either subject's ability to perform a wide range or visual tasks (including discrimination between the specified objects) at a perceptual level – that is, under simultaneous presentation. It is only when the object shape must be remembered and recalled that the deficit is apparent, and this deficit appears to be intimately associated with specific shape attributes of the objects involved. This patient's ability to only partially recover object shape information from memory following brain-damage implies that the representation of shape knowledge about objects in neurologically intact individuals itself based on a decomposition into discrete parameters (i.e. it is not an integral representation). Normal object recognition therefore requires these discretely stored shape primitives to be re-associated together via an integration mechanism.

## 2  Global Parametric Shape

The first patient, ELM, suffered bilateral posterior and inferior temporal lobe lesions. He shows no significant language impairment, no visual field deficit, no hemispatial neglect, no evidence for a perceptual encoding deficit, and he drives a car. Naming and recognition of line drawings of certain objects (for example many classes of biological objects) is severely impaired whereas performance is markedly higher for other groups of objects, for example man-made artefacts (Table 1 a and b). While the recovery of encyclopedic information about biological objects from their names is largely spared, recovery of visual properties is impaired (Table 1c). Stored knowledge of visual properties of objects that cannot be named (eg. biological objects) is not entirely inaccessible or compromised however, since word-to-picture matching errors for fruits and vegetables are shown to be determined by visual similarity (Table 1d).

We attempted to characterize the shape properties that specify the relationships between the objects that ELM fails to correctly identify. The morphologically simplest class of real objects for which ELM exhibits impaired recognition is fruits and vegetables (59 per cent errors in naming, as opposed to near perfect scores for normal observers). These can be described as a single component (in the sense of Hoffman and Richards [6]) that can be obtained through global deformations to an ellipsoid.

|  | Stimulus category | |
|---|---|---|
|  | Biological objects | Artefacts |
| Controls | 6% | 7% |
| ELM | 61% | 12% |

a) Naming

|  | Stimulus category | |
|---|---|---|
|  | Biological objects | Artefacts |
| ELM | 41% | 7% |

b) Object decision (ELM)

|  | Category of probe question | |
|---|---|---|
|  | Encyclopedic | Visual |
| Controls | 2% | 3% |
| ELM | 15% | 45% |

c) Knowledge recovery from animal names

| Word | Picture | | | | | |
|---|---|---|---|---|---|---|
|  | Banana | Carrot | Eggplant | Apple | Orange | Pumpkin |
| Cucumber | 80% | 60% | 40% | 0% | 0% | 0% |
| Tomato | 0% | 0% | 0% | 80% | 60% | 40% |

d) Sample of performance on word-to-picture matching (ELM)

Table 1: Summary of ELM's agnosia
a) Error rates shown by ELM and 10 matched controls in naming line drawings presented for an unlimited duration. These results represent performance on 66 pictures of biological objects (animals, birds, insects, and fruits and vegetables) and 80 pictures of artefacts. b) ELM's error rate in deciding whether pictures were of real or unreal animals (n=70) or artefacts (n=41). c) Error rates shown by ELM and 10 matched controls on two-alternative forced-choice probe questions about animals given their names. Encyclopedic questions (n=60) probed verbal knowledge about animals. Visual probe questions (n=78) concerned visual properties of the items. d) Representative subset of ELM's error rates in matching pictures of fruits and vegetables to names.

Through a careful examination of the identification errors for this and other subjects (using multi-dimensional analysis) we hypothesised three simple shape parameters that are implicated in the performance of ELM. These are:

- changes of elongation (ratio of minor to major axes for a defining ellipsoid),

- tapering along the major axis of the ellipsoid,

- and global curvature (bending) of the ellipsoid perpendicular to the major axis.

These were defined using sequential global transformations of the coordinate plane $(x,y)' = \vec{p'} = \hat{\Omega}(\vec{p})\vec{p} + \hat{T}(\vec{p})$. where $\vec{p}$ and $\vec{p'}$ are the initial and transformed points and $\hat{\Omega}()$ and $\hat{T}()$ are the rotation ans translation matrices. The transformation are

| Condition | Examples of test picture(s) | Percept. matching errors | Concept. matching errors |
|---|---|---|---|
| Positive trial |  | 9% | 23% |
| Shares 0/3 primitives with target |  | 0% | 8% |
| Share 1/3 primitives with target |  | 3% | 25% |
| Share 2/3 primitives with target |  | 10% | 44% |

Figure 1: Sample shapes.

Several of the sample shapes in the three-dimensional shape space. This figure illustrates the test pictures used when the target stimulus (picture or word) was 'banana'.

specified as follows (deformations are given below with respect to the $y$ axis, with full generality). For elongation by a factor $\alpha$ we have

$$\hat{\Omega}(\vec{p}) = \begin{bmatrix} 1 & 0 \\ 0 & \alpha \end{bmatrix}, \ \hat{T}(\vec{p}) = [0, 0]. \tag{1}$$

For tapering by a factor of $\gamma$ we have:

$$\hat{\Omega}(\vec{p}) = \begin{bmatrix} \gamma/(K-y) & 0 \\ 0 & 1 \end{bmatrix}, \ \hat{T}(\vec{p}) = [0, 0] \tag{2}$$

where $K$ is a constant larger that the maximum $y$ value of any shape of interest. For bending by a factor $\beta$, we have:

$$\hat{\Omega}(\vec{p}) = \begin{bmatrix} 1 & 0 \\ 0 & 1 \end{bmatrix}, \ T = [0, \beta|y|] \tag{3}$$

Some sample shapes are shown in Figure 1.

By parametrically combining deformations to a circle using these three indepen-dent dimensions, a surprisingly wide variety of candidate shapes can be synthesised. In particular, combinations of these three shape dimensions can define a wide vari-ety of shapes resembling fruits and vegetables. This has allowed use to examine the shape perception deficit of ELM, as observed in terms of simple biological forms, in the context of parametrically variable synthetic shapes. It is interesting to observe that these deformations are closely related to the "intuitive" parametric deformations typically associated with synthetic solid modelling (for example using Platonic solids or superquadrics) [1, 3, 11, 2, 12] as well as to the Lie groups often associated with motion processing. The stimuli used in the present experiments were filled blobs whose shapes were generated in terms of this three dimensional parameter space. In all experiments, orientation of the items on the picture plane was constantly varied and object length was held constant (we also considered, but rejected, holding other attributes such as object area constant).

# 3 Perceptual and Conceptual Processing

The experimental approach used was based on the synthesis of artificial shapes from this three dimensional parameter space. The experiments focussed the the ability of a subject to recognize one of these shapes with respect to an ensemble of objects seen previously. By associating these objects with familiar biological forms, a version of the experiment could be carried out that directly related to a pre-existing recognition deficit (as well as being a readily accessible and comprehensible task for naive subjects).

For unique identification of an arbitrary target shape defined within this space, the simultaneous consideration of multiple shape dimensions (in the sense described above) is required. The exposition to this point does not preclude the possibility that the actual measurement dimensions for shape used by humans are quite different from these three and hence the number of dimensions spanned by these target objects may be less than three. As it happens, there is a direct relationship between dimensionality of the ensemble in terms of the specific shape dimensions described above and the performance of our subjects.

Consider a simple shape recognition tasks with shapes labelled with respect to similar-looking fruits. Analysis of the elongation of an object may establish that it is either a banana or a cucumber but, to disambiguate between these alternatives, estimation of the global curvature of the object is also necessary (although perhaps not explicitly). One of our experiments was *word-to-picture matching*: a word and a filled blob were simultaneously presented and the subject had to simply indicate whether the two were consistent (i.e. was the word the correct label for the object). For the set of shapes we used, this task was extremely easy for normal observers.

The recognition impaired subject ELM consistently accepted pictures that only partially matched the shape primitives corresponding to the target words (Fig. 1). In particular, ELM would accept word-picture matches that were correct with respect to *at least one shape dimension* while ignoring the inconsistency in the other dimension(s). This suggested that ELM's visual inability to recognize objects may be determined by a failure to integrate or select specific shape properties, such that his responses are based on only partial shape information.

To precisely examine the distinction between perceptual and conceptual shape recognition as a function of the number of shape dimensions, we developed a more refined experiment, as follows. We compared subject's capacity for a) *perceptually encoding* shapes defined by combinations of shape dimensions (perceptual integration) *without* having to remember them except for a very brief delay, and b) recovering shapes (as a function of multiple properties) from memorized (i.e. stored) representations of objects that were previously viewed (*conceptual integration*). These tasks were based on the subject indicating whether or not a sample shape matched a target shape using either simultaneously presented stimuli or remembered stimuli. The two experiments conducted used the same design.

The target stimuli used were either filled blobs (perceptual matching) that could unambiguously be identified by normal observers as 'banana', 'carrot', 'cucumber', or 'eggplant', or the visually presented names of these items (conceptual matching). The present figure illustrates the test pictures used when the target stimulus (picture or word) was 'banana'.

On each perceptual matching trial, a target picture was presented for 2 sec., followed by a blank 1 sec. interval, and then by a test picture which remained visible until the subject responded. In conceptual matching, the target word and the test picture were presented simultaneously and remained on until the response. In both experiments, ELM indicated whether the test picture matched the target (yes/no).

On negative trials, the number of shape primitives the test-picture shared with either a previously presented target-picture (perceptual matching) or the shape corresponding to a simultaneously presented target-word (conceptual matching) was varied. If a match is performed on partial shape information, error rates on negative trials will increase with the number of shared primitives between the test-picture and the target. This effect occurred only in conceptual matching and ELM's error rates were notably greater in this task than in perceptual matching. This dissociation indicates a selective impairment for the conceptual integration of shape primitives. The results of these trials are summarized in Figure 1.

On negative trials, the test-picture had either zero, one, or two shape primitives in common with the target. If only a subset of the relevant shape primitives (elongation, curvature, and tapering) is considered to perform the match, error rates on negative trials will increase with the number of primitives the test-picture shares with the target. For instance, if only curvature is considered, the error rates on negative trials would be 0%, 33%, and 66% with zero, one, and two shared primitives, respectively. Overall, the error rate was much higher on conceptual than on perceptual matching $[c2(1) = 52.2; p < 0.001]$. On negative trials, the effect of number of shape primitives by which the test- picture differed from the target was highly significant in conceptual matching $[c2(2) = 18.5; p < 0.001]$ but not in perceptual matching $[c2(2) = 5.1;$ n.s.].

This integration impairment for shape primitives dissociates from both verbal and semantic processing. Thus, the experiment required no verbal mediation and did not refer to any semantic category. It therefore appears that ELM's impairment involves either

    i) the acquisition of shape information from the visual image or

    ii) the recovery of shape knowledge from memory.

    The learning of arbitrary shape-to-location associations was tested to determine whether ELM's recognition errors reflect a deficit in the integration or combination of a shape measurements. Shape contrasts between the items to be learned were defined over a single dimension (elongation or tapering) or over a conjunction of these dimensions (Fig. 2). The subject had to memorize the positions of four target shapes located at the corners of a rectangular layout. These targets were then removed and the subject had to point to the appropriate reference location for the corresponding target when a sample shape was presented (i.e. the corresponding corner of the now-invisible rectangular layout of targets). An increased error rate on the two-dimensional conjunction cases relative to the single-dimension sets would indicate a separable analysis of shape properties. This was exactly the case for ELM.

    Three sets of items differing from one another on a single dimension were constructed. The conjunction sets required the simultaneous consideration of two shape dimensions for unique identification. For example, for any item in the conjunction set there was another that had the same degree of elongation and yet another that had the same degree of tapering. Differences in elongation or tapering between items were *greater* in the conjunction condition than in the single-dimension conditions. Each stimulus set was tested in 10 consecutive blocks. Each block started with a learning trial where all items in a set were displayed simultaneously, each at its assigned location (corners of an imaginary square). Each shape was then shown twice, individually, and in a random order and the task was to point to its assigned location.

    The problem in combining individually solvable dimensions in a stimulus suggests that the computational process involved in recognizing these shapes is sensitive specifically to these dimensions. Further, it implies that because increased difficulty arises only when such stimulus dimensions must be extracted *simultaneously*, there must be some degree of separation in the way these individual shape parameters are extracted. We believe that the increased severity of ELM's visual agnosia when the contrast between items was defined over a *conjunction* of multiple shape dimensions indicates a deficit in the *integration* or *selection* of independent shape measurements. Perhaps most striking was the nature of the errors on the multi-dimensional stimuli: errors corresponded to an incorrect estimate of one of the shape parameters involved in the decision, but almost never two parameters simultaneously. In the conjunction condition only 4 per cent of his errors involved confusions between items that differed on *both* elongation and tapering.

    A non-agnosic brain-damaged control with a left-hemisphere lesion that includes area V4 showed *more* errors on *single-dimension* sets. Normals also find these single-dimension cases *more difficult* although their error rates are very low. In general,

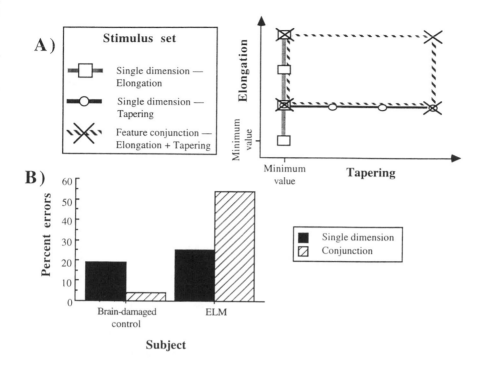

Figure 2: Results for shape identification task by pointing.
A) Positions in two dimensions of the shape shape described above of the stimuli used for testing the learning of shape-to-location association. Each axis represents values on a particular shape dimension. Each point represents a specific stimulus used in testing. For any item in the conjunction set, there was another that had the same degree of elongation and yet another that had the same degree of tapering.
B) Error rates shown by ELM and by a brain-damaged (left occipital lesion) non-agnosic control in the learning of arbitrary shape/location associations with single-dimension and conjunction sets. The control subject made fewer errors with the conjunction stimuli than with the single-dimension sets. The opposite result was found in ELM.

having additional shape characteristics available makes the task easier. In contrast, subject ELM was dramatically impaired on the conjunction set (Fig. 2). (Note that the dimensional parameterization of the shapes was not made explicit to the patient – this is an implicit characteristics of the ensemble of objects.)

In recent experiments, a second patient with with a left-hemisphere lesion that includes area V4 as well as lower visual areas unilaterally who suffers from a deficit related to naming objects has also shown a performance deficit that is directly related to the dimensionality of the task in sense described above. This this case preliminary data indicates that the patient can correctly localize shapes independent of their shape dimensions (unlike ELM) but his reaction time for uttering their names is reduced with the task involves multiple shape dimensions. The apparent significance of these shape dimensions in this rather different task suggest they may play a significant role of human shape processing.

Acquisition of structural information from the image was tested in a third experiment to rule out a deficit in the early vision system. It used the same stimuli as experiment 2 (i.e.blob/learning/pointing experiment) in a paradigm that emphasized a perceptual load as opposed to the memory load emphasized in the previous experiment, i.e. a perceptual matching task. A single shape (target) was presented for 1 sec. and the subject was asked to remember it. After a delay of 1 sec., the four shapes tested in a particular condition (conditions were tested in a single block and were presented in a random order) were shown simultaneously and the subject was asked to point to the target. In this experiment, both the brain -damaged control and ELM showed a better performance with the conjunction set of stimuli than with the single-dimension sets. Thus, with the conjunction set of stimuli, neither of the patients made a single error. In contrast, with the single-dimension sets, the control subject made 6.9% errors and ELM made 11.5% errors. In the case of ELM, the results indicate a cross-over interaction between experiments 2 and 3. In experiment 2, his error rate was markedly higher with conjunction stimuli whereas, in experiment 3, he showed more errors with the single-dimension sets. This, despite the fact that the perceptual discriminations that had to be performed in each experiment were identical. The perceptual matching results of experiment 3 therefore indicate that ELM's impairment with conjunction stimuli in a recognition task (experiment 2) cannot be due to a perceptual (early vision) failure. It is argued that ELM's visual recognition deficit can be attributed to an impairment in maintaining and/or retrieving shape knowledge about objects in memory. Furthermore, given that his impairment in shape-knowledge retrieval is specific to a task involving a conjunction set of stimuli, it can be concluded that this impairment is characterized by partial retrieval of shape information from memory.

# 4 Discussion and Conclusions

To summarize, an impairment specifically affecting the capacity of a subject to consider multiple shape primitives for object recognition was described. This impairment dissociates from verbal and semantic processes and from the perceptual integration of shape primitives in the image. The recognition deficit can therefore be attributed to a failure in the recovery of multiple properties from stored representations of structural knowledge, a process we called conceptual integration.

The effect of inferior temporal cortical brain-damage on a process of conceptual integration of shape features indicates that this operation contributes to object recognition in neurologically intact individuals. The requirement of conceptual integration in visual recognition has two related implications. First, it implies that visual knowledge about object shapes is decomposed into discrete features rather than as integral, picture-like representations. More fundamentally, it implies that visual recognition cannot merely be defined as a process by which perceptual information is mapped to stored structural representations. The present observations rather demonstrate that visual recognition also involves an assembly operation by which discretely stored primitives are conjoined.

The link between the role of inferior temporal cortex and spatial visual attention has been previously established[10, 4]. Likewise, it is well acknowledged that attention refers to a control of processing that can be applied to domain other than simply the spatial one (for example specific colors or sound pitches). It may be that the impairment in object recognition we have observed as a result of IT damage relates to a form of attentional control in the *feature* or *shape dimension* domain: that is, IT serves to direct a non-spatial aspect of attention to the correct shape attributes to be used in recognition and access to memory. This idea has interesting implications for the design of computational vision systems [14].

Although ELM's agnosic symptoms are category-specific (see above), the underlying impairment extends to the visual classification of arbitrary shapes that have no referential content. This raises the possibility that biological and man-made objects differ in the requirements they impose in terms of shape-knowledge recovery for unique identification.

These results suggest that human object representation involves the analysis of object shape with respect of distinct, separable shape attributes. More surprisingly, it also implies that shape recognition involves the use of an *incomplete subset* of the available shape dimensions. Further, the subset of shape dimensions used for a given recognition task appears to be highly context and task dependent. This may suggest that computational vision systems can also profit from such strategies. In fact, they have tantalizing similarities to existing (but far more restrictive) recognition approaches based on using "precompiled" strategies that are context sensetive.

# Acknowledgements

This research was supported by a fellowship from the Medical Research Council of Canada (MRC) to Martin Arguin, a grant from the MRC to Daniel Bub, and a grant from the Natural Sciences and Engineering Research Council of Canada to Gregory Dudek.

# References

[1] A. H. Barr. Superquadrics and angle-preserving transformations. *IEEE Comp. Graphics and Appl.*, 1:1–120 1–20, 1981.

[2] I. Biederman. Recognition by components. *Psychological Review*, 94:115–147, 1987.

[3] Rodney A. Brooks. Symbolic reasoning among 3-d models and 2-d images. *AI*, 17:285–348, 1981.

[4] Leonardo Chelazzi, Earl K. Miller, John Duncan, and Robert Desimone. A neural basis for visual search in inferior temporal cortex. *Nature*, 363:345–347, 27 May 1993.

[5] M. A. Fischler and R. C. Bolles. Perceptual organization and the curve partitioning problem. In *Proc. of the International Joint Conf. on Artificial Intel.*, pages 1014–1018, Karlsruhe, Germany, Aug. 1983.

[6] D. D. Hoffman and W. A. Richards. Parts of recognition. *Cognition*, 18:65–96, 1984.

[7] J. J. Koenderink and A. J. van Doorn. Dynamic shape. *Biological Cybernetics*, 53:383–396, 1986.

[8] M. Leyton. A process grammar for shape. *Artificial Intelligence*, 34(2):213–247, March 1988.

[9] S. Marshall. Review of shape coding techniques. *Image and Vision Computing*, 7(4):281–294, November 1989.

[10] Jeffrey Moran and Robert Desimone. Selective attention gates visual processing in the extrastriate cortex. *Science*, 229:782–784, August 1985.

[11] A. P. Pentland. On describing complex surface shapes. *Image and Vision Computing*, 3(4):153–162, 1985.

[12] Alex Pentland. Automatic extraction of deformable part models. Vision Sciences TR-104, MIT Media Lab, July 1988.

[13] R. N. Shepard. *J Exp. Psychology*, 3:287, 1966.

[14] John K. Tsotsos. Analysing vision at the complexity level. *Behavioral and Brain Sciences*, 13(3):423–496, 1990.

[15] Elizabeth K. Warrington and Angela M. Taylor. Two categorical stages of object recognition. *Perception*, 7:695–705, 1978.

# IRREDUCIBLE AND THIN BINARY SETS

ULRICH ECKHARDT

Institut für Angewandte Mathematik, Universität Hamburg,
Bundesstraße 55, D-20 146 Hamburg, Germany

LONGIN LATECKI

Fachbereich Informatik, Universität Hamburg,
Bodenstedtstraße 16, D-22 765 Hamburg, Germany

and

GERD MADERLECHNER

Siemens Corporate Research and Development,
Otto–Hahn–Ring 6, D-81 739 München, Germany

## ABSTRACT

Thinning algorithms are in wide use in binary picture processing. They are used for reducing the amount of data in a picture by replacing the objects contained in it by "thin" sets. Simultaneously, they are considered to conserve "essential" information contained in the objects, specifically topological properties and "form" properties are retained under thinning. On the other hand, it is known that there exist very "thick" sets having the property that they are irreducible, i.e. they cannot be thinned further. The first example of such a set was presented by C. Arcelli in 1981. In this paper we investigate the questions how such thick skeletons look like and under which conditions one can guarantee that the skeleton of a set is indeed a "thin" set.

## 1 Introduction

Thinning is a well–established method for preprocessing binary images. The goal of thinning a binary digital image is to reduce the amount of black points while retaining essential properties of the image. The remaining digital set, the so–called *skeleton* of the original objects should therefore posess some important properties to make the process meaningful and efficient. These properties are

- The skeleton should be indeed "thin". In the literature this property is often referred to as the requirement that the skeleton should be "one pixel thick". Ideally, the skeleton should have a "graph–like" structure, i.e. it should consist of a large number of "line points" having two neighbors each, a relatively small number of end points having one neighbor and bifurcation points having more than two neighbors each. In this case, the original set is segmented by the skeleton and the latter can be represented by a very efficient and convenient data structure.

- The skeleton should have the same topological structure as the original point set. This point is important since topological predicates are essential for the interpretation of images and on the other hand they are in some sense "hard" to verify in parallel [7].

- Yet more importantly, the skeleton should reflect in some sense the "shape" of the object. Since the notion of shape cannot be defined in a precise sense, one usually requires that the skeleton should possess a number of properties which are considered to be owned by the shape of an object. Such properties are typically invariance properties, but also the requirement that the object can be reconstructed from the skeleton and that the skeletonization process is well–defined.

Due to the importance of thinning algorithms, there exists a large amount of literature on them. Most of the authors in this area are concerned with practical problems, such as the performance of thinning algorithms, the "aesthetic" appearance of the skeletons and related questions. There is a surprising lack in *understanding* of the thinning process. We list some desiderata:

- The continuous concept underlying the idea of thinning is the medial axis of a set. There exists some theory (far from being complete) for the Euclidean norm. It is well–known that in polyhedral norms nearly all known assertions about medial axes are wrong. However, in the usual setting of digital geometry, the adequate norms are polyhedral ones. Even worse, the medial axis transform is known to be "incorrectly posed" in the Hausdorff metric for sets, which means that small changes of the original set can cause large changes in the medial axis of it (see [10]). This means that in using skeletons we literally rely on an instable foundation.

- Almost all thinning methods, whether they are intended for sequential or parallel implementation, proceed in a basically sequential way. Consequently, their results depend (more or less) for example on the orientation of the document to be processed. Bearing in mind the inherent instability of the thinning process, one might wonder how it is possible to draw any conclusions about form properties of the original object from the skeleton.

- Almost all authors claim that skeletonization results in "thin" skeletons (or even "one–pixel–thick" skeletons) without defining what this means. In 1981 Arcelli presented an example of a set which is not "thin" in any conceivable sense but nevertheless irreducible, i.e. its own skeleton. It appears miraculous that apparently nobody ever encountered such a set in practice!

In order to understand the skeletonization process, the authors attempted to make it mathematically tractable by imposing some rather natural requirements on it. These requirements were invariance (with respect to all motions of the digital plane) and well–definedness [2]. It turned out that these requirements ruled out most of the known approaches and led in a quite natural way to a specific method. More importantly, since the process was required to be well–defined, it became possible, to investigate it theoretically. Specifically, properties of the skeletons could be proved.

The aim of this paper is to present some results concerning properties of skeletons. Emphasis is given to the question, under which circumstances the skeleton will be thin and what this property actually means. It turns out, that "thin" skeletons are obtained if the underlying sets have certain properties.

## 2  Basic Definitions

The *digital plane* $\mathbb{Z}^2$ is the set of all points in the Euclidean plane having integer coordinates. A *digital set* is a subset of the digital plane.

Each point $P$ in the digital plane has eight *neighbors*, which are numbered 0 to 7 according to the following scheme

$$
\begin{array}{ccc}
N_3(P) & N_2(P) & N_1(P) \\
N_4(P) & P & N_0(P) \\
N_5(P) & N_6(P) & N_7(P)
\end{array}
$$

$\mathcal{N}(P)$ is the set of all neighbors of $P$ (without $P$ itself) and is termed the *neighborhood* of $P$. Neighbors with even numbers are *direct neighbors* of $P$ or *4–neighbors*; neighbors having odd numbers are *indirect neighbors* of $P$. All neighbors together are sometimes called *8–neighbors*. By means of the neighbor–relation we are able to define a 'topology' in the digital plane [9].

A point of a digital set $S$ having all four direct neighbors also in $S$ is an *interior point*. The set of all interior points of a set $S$ is termed the *kernel* of $S$. All points in $S$ which are not interior points are *boundary points*. Among the boundary points we distinguish between those having interior points as 4–neighbors, which we call *inner boundary points*, and boundary points having no interior points as direct neighbors. The set of all inner boundary points is the *inner boundary*.

A point $P$ on the inner boundary is termed *perfect* if a neighbor of $P$ which is opposite to an interior point directly neighboring $P$, is white (neighbor $N_i(P)$ is termed opposite to neighbor $N_j(P)$ if $j = (i + 4) \bmod 8$).

For a point $P$ in a digital set $S$ we define the 8–*connection number* $C_8(P)$ to be the number of 8–connected components in $\mathcal{N}(P) \cap S$. Similarly, the number of 4–connected components in $\mathcal{N}(P) \cap S$ which contain direct neighbors of $P$ is termed the 4–connection number $C_4(P)$ of $P$ in $S$.

A point in $S$ is termed (4/8–) *simple*, if it is a boundary point and if $C_{4/8}(P) = 1$ [9]. A 4/8–*end point* is a point in $S$ having only one 4/8–neighbor in $S$.

*Thinning* a digital set means application of an iterative procedure for removing simple points. A set is termed (4/8–) *irreducible* if it does not contain any (4/8–) simple points with exception of end points. For a topological motivation of the special role played by end ponts, see [2].

A digital set it is called *p–irreducible* if it does not contain any simple and perfect points. When only simple and perfect points are used for thinning, then a thinning method is obtained which is inherently parallel and invariant with respect to motions of the digital plane [2]. We note that the following implications hold for a point in a digital set:

$$8\text{–simple and perfect} \implies 4\text{–simple} \implies 8\text{–simple}.$$

Here we consider exclusively sequential methods for thinning. This means that the assertions concerning p–irreducible sets should be taken with some care.

During this text we denote for illustration purposes the different types of points by the following symbols: '$\bullet$' denotes a black point, 'o' a white point, '$\blacksquare$' an interior point and '·' a point of either color.

## 3 Irreducible Sets

In this paragraph we investigate the kernel sets of irreducible sets. It will turn out that the inner boundary of an irreducible set has a remarkably simple structure.

We define: A point $P$ on the inner boundary is a *sharp vertex* if it has two neighbors on the inner boundary and if all these three points have an interior point as a common direct neighbor.

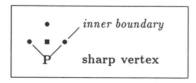
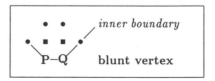

A pair $P$, $Q$ of points on the inner boundary is said to form a *blunt vertex* if the following conditions are true:

- $P$ and $Q$ are direct neighbors,

- There exists exactly one direct neighbor of $P$ which is an interior point and exactly one direct neighbor of $Q$ which is an interior point and these two interior points are direct neighbors of each other,

**Theorem 1** *The 8–connected components of the kernel of an 8–irreducible set are 4–connected and simply connected digital sets (i.e. they contain no holes). They consist of parallelepipeds whose sides are diagonal lines in the digital plane. The sides are joined together by sharp or blunt vertices.*

**Proof** The Theorem can be proved by straightforward (but rather tedious) elimination of all possible cases. For details the reader is referred to [2]. Here we give only a sketch of the proof.

For proving the Theorem we investigate *kernel–boundary points*, i.e. points of the kernel having at least one direct neighbor not belonging to the kernel. It can easily be shown by enumeration of all possible cases that it is not possible to have more than two successive kernel–boundary points on a horizontal or vertical line without generating a (4–) simple point. Thus we can conclude that only the two types of vertices mentioned above can appear. In contrast, arbitrarily long diagonal runs of kernel–boundary points are possible for 8–irreducible sets.

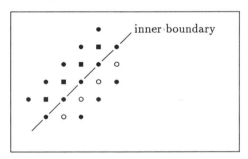

Observing that diagonal runs and vertices can only be joined in such a way that an acute angle of the kernel–boundary is formed, the assertion about the form of the kernel components of an irreducible set is obtained.

The remaining assertions now become obvious. □

In the next section we apply Theorem 1 for investigation of "thick" sets.

## 4 Arcelli–Sets

There exist sets without 8–simple points which are not "thin". The first example of such a set was published by Arcelli in 1981 [1]. Theorem 1 states that *all* 8–irreducible sets have the same structure as Arcelli's example. For this reason we term those sets Arcelli sets.

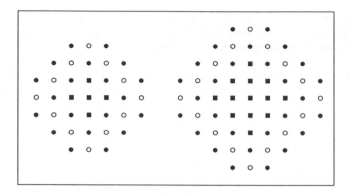

Figure 1: Arcelli–sets $A_3$ and $A_4$

The $n-th$ *Arcelli set* $A_n$ is defined for $n = 2, 3, 4, \cdots$ by

$$A_n = \left\{ \begin{pmatrix} i \\ j \end{pmatrix} \in \mathbb{Z}^2 \;\middle|\; |i| + |j| < n \quad \text{or} \quad |i| + |j| = n + 1, \quad |i|, |j| \neq n + 1 \right\}.$$

**Theorem 2** *$A_n$ is an 8–irreducible set.*

*$A_n$ consists of $2n^2 + 2n + 1$ points. $2n^2 - 6n + 5$ of them are interior points and $8n - 4$ are boundary points.*

The proof of the Theorem is straightforward.

As an application of Theorem 2 we conclude that the relation of interior points to black points in $A_n$ approaches the value one for large $n$. This observation disproves a proposition in [8, Proposition 3, p. 140] stating that at most one third of all points of an irreducible set consists of interior points.

The set $A_3$ (see Figure 1) was originally used by Arcelli [1] as an example of an irreducible set having a nontrivial structure.

All irreducible sets having "large" kernel components necessarily contain "Arcelli–like" sets by Theorem 1. There exist also Arcelli–sets having blunt vertices (see Figure 2) and of course, sets having both possible types of vertices, but that is all what is possible.

## 5 Qualified Irreducible Sets

It can be shown that under certain conditions irreducible sets have a very simple structure. Specifically, "large" kernel components are not possible for such sets. There are mainly two such qualifying concepts for digital sets: Sets without 1–holes [4,5] and well–composed sets [6].

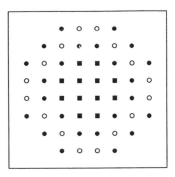

Figure 2: Arcelli–set having blunt vertices

We define: A 1–*hole* or *eye* of a digital set is a point in the complement of the set having all direct neighbors in the set:

A digital set is termed a *well–composed set* if the following *critical configuration* (an the configuration rotated by 90°) does not occur in it:

We note that under any thinning method (4–, 8– or p–thinning) the number of 1–holes never increases. The number of critical configurations is not influenced under sequential 4–thinning (and sequential p–thinning, of course) and is not decreased under all other thinning variants considered here.

Both qualifications can be checked by simple preprocessing the images under consideration. This is even possible in an obvious way by means of a local parallel algorithm which inspects $3 \times 3$–neighborhoods. If a set turns out to be not qualified in this sense, it can be easily "repaired".

We now state a Theorem about irreducible digital sets without 1–holes (see [5, Theorem 5.1])

**Theorem 3** *1. Given a digital set having no simple and perfect points and no 1–holes. Then the connected components of the kernel will have one of the following types (and those generated therefrom by 90° rotations; numbers in the upper left corners indicate the number of elements in the corresponding component):*

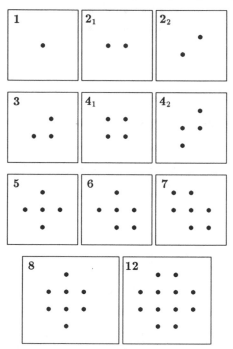

*2. If a digital set has no 1–holes and is 4–irreducible (i.e. it contains no 4–simple points except 4–end points) then its kernel components can only have one of the seven types 1, $2_1$, $2_2$, 3, $4_1$, $4_2$ or 5.*

*3. If a digital set has no 1–holes and is 8–irreducible (i.e. it contains no 8–simple points except 8–end points) then its kernel components can only have one of the four types 1, $2_1$, $2_2$ or 5.*

*For each of the kernel components mentioned, there exists a digital set having the appropriate irreducibility property and containing this specific kernel component.*

For a proof of part 1, see [2]; part 3, see [4]. Part 2 of the Theorem is proved analogously.

From the Theorem it becomes clear why Arcelli sets were apparently never observed in practice. Usually 1–holes will be considered as discretization errors and removed e.g. by median filtering in a preprocessing step.

As a consequence of the Theorem, the 8–irreducible sets are already quite close to be "one pixel thick" sets when we assume that no 1–holes are present. It is a remarkable fact that Arcelli's original set is not ruled out by Theorem 3 under all three thinning approaches considered here (configuration 5).

Quite recently it became possible to proceed one large step further [6]. If one considers sequential 4–thinning algorithms applied to well–composed sets, the only kernel components which are possible are isolated points (type 1 in Theorem 3).

**Theorem 4** *The kernel components of 4–irreducible well–composed digital sets consist of isolated points. This means that no interior point of such a set has an 8–neighbor which is an interior point. More precisely, interior points of 4–irreducible well–composed sets can only appear in the following context:*

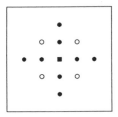

The proof for this Theorem can be found in [6, Theorem 6.1]. Under The assumptions of the Theorem the skeletons obtained are really 'one pixel thick'. The concept of 'thinness' of the skeleton can be made more precise. These results were published in [6].

# 6 Conclusions

In this paper, a partial answer to the question was given, how thick irreducible sets look like and under which conditions the skeleton of a set is indeed thin.

It is possible to prove further nice properties of skeletons, this was done elsewhere [6]. Specifically, the notion of a graph–like set can be given a precise meaning and it can be proved that under rather mild conditions the sets resulting from certain thinning procedures are indeed graph–like. Numerical experiments show that the skeletons obtained by applying invariant algorithms to realistic problems have only relatively few end points and bifurcation points and consist mainly of "line–points" having exactly two neighbors in the skeleton (see [2, Table 1]). That means at least that the description of skeletons as graphs is a realistic data structure.

These results are of practical importance since they indicate in which manner a digital set should be preprocessed in order to get *provable* decent results. A thinning philosophy based on these considerations was formulated in [6].

# References

[1] Carlo Arcelli, "Pattern thinning by contour tracing", *Computer Graphics and Image Processing*, vol. 17, pp. 130–144, 1981.

[2] Ulrich Eckhardt and Gerd Maderlechner, "Invariant thinning", *International Journal of Pattern Recognition and Artificial Intelligence), (Special Issue on Techniques for Thinning Digitized Patterns)*, vol. 7, pp. 1115–1144, 1993.

[3] Ulrich Eckhardt, "Anwendung der digitalen Topologie in der Binärbildverarbeitung", *Mitteilungen der Mathematischen Gesellschaft in Hamburg*, vol. XI/6, pp. 727–744, 1989.

[4] U. Eckhardt and G. Maderlechner, "The structure of irreducible digital sets obtained by thinning algorithms", *9th International Conference on Pattern Recognition, Rome, November 14–17,1988, Proceedings*, pp. 727–729. IEEE Computer Society Press, Washington, DC, 1988.

[5] Ulrich Eckhardt and Gerd Maderlechner, "Parallel reduction of digital sets", *Siemens Forsch.– u. Entwickl.–Ber.*, vol. 17, pp. 184–189, 1988.

[6] Longin Latecki, Ulrich Eckhardt and Azriel Rosenfeld, "Well–Composed Sets", *CVGIP: Graphical Models and Image Processing*, to appear.

[7] Marvin Minsky and Seymour Papert, *Perceptrons. An Introduction to Computational Geometry*, Expanded Edition, The MIT Press, Cambridge, Massachusetts, London, England, 1988.

[8] Theo Pavlidis, "An asynchronous thinning algorithm", *Computer Graphics and Image Processing*, vol. 20, pp. 133 – 157, 1982.

[9] Azriel Rosenfeld, "Digital topology", *American Mathematical Monthly*, vol. 86, pp. 621–630, 1979.

[10] Zhangzheng Yu, Christoph Conrad and Ulrich Eckhardt, "Regularization of the Medial Axis Transform", In Reinhard Klette and Walter G. Kropatsch, editors: *Theoretical Foundations of Computer Vision 1992, Proceedings of the V$^{th}$ Workshop 1992, Buckow (Märkische Schweiz), March 30–April 3, 1992, (Mathematical Research, Volume 69)*, pages 13–24, Akademie–Verlag, Berlin, 1992.

# REPRESENTING ORTHOGONAL MULTIDIMENSIONAL OBJECTS BY VERTEX LISTS [1]

CLAUDIO ESPERANÇA

*Computer Science Department, University of Maryland*
*College Park, Maryland 20742*

and

HANAN SAMET

*Computer Science Department and Center for Automation Research and*
*Institute for Advanced Computer Studies, University of Maryland*
*College Park, Maryland 20742*

## Abstract

A method is presented for representing multidimensional objects with orthogonal faces (i.e., collections of hyperrectangles or $n$-dimensional rasters) compactly by a vertex list. This is a list of points with their corresponding weights (collectively termed vertices). Algorithms for converting between rasters and vertex lists as well as performing set-theoretic operations on these structures are described and shown to execute in $O(N \cdot d)$ time, where $d$ is the dimension and $N$ is the number of vertices in the representation. Other applications of vertex lists are also discussed.

## 1 Introduction

The shape of objects can be represented by the interiors of the objects or by their boundaries. The most common interior-based representation is one that decomposes the object into a collection of cells all of whose sides are of unit length (termed *pixels* or *voxels* in two and three dimensions respectively). The elements of the this collection (i.e., the cells) are labeled with values or attributes and are frequently aggregated into subcollections of similarly-valued cells. The decomposition into a collection of uniform cells makes it very easy to calculate properties such as mass as well as determining the value associated with any point of the space covered by the cell.

On the other hand, boundary-based representations are more amenable to the calculation of properties pertaining to shape (e.g., perimeter, extent, etc.). In this case, we simply record the different boundary elements. We frequently make use of a similar technique to that of decomposing an object into a collection of unit-sized cells. The difference is that now we record their boundaries. Such methods are relatively

---

[1]The support of the National Science Foundation under Grant IRI-9017393 and of Conselho Nacional de Desenvolvimento Científico e Tecnológico (CNPQ) are gratefully acknowledged.

easy in two dimensions where the boundaries are lines. It is somewhat more difficult in three dimensions (and higher).

Both interior- and boundary-based representations can be made more compact by just recording the *change* in the values rather than the values themselves. For interior-based representations this technique is known as runlength encoding [3]. It aggregates identically valued cells into one-dimensional rectangles for which only the value and the length of the rectangle are recorded. The location of the cell can be computed by referring to the location of the starting position. This method is also applicable to data of higher dimensions. For boundary-based representations, an analogous effect can be achieved by use of chain codes [1]. This is a technique for representing the boundary of an object by a sequence of directional codes corresponding to unit steps in the four or eight principal directions. Unfortunately, it is difficult to extend this idea to dimensions higher than two as there is no natural order for traversing the boundaries of such objects.

Recently, Schechtman [7] introduced a mathematical concept called the *vertex algebra* for storing and processing VLSI masks. The vertex algebra is also based on recording changes in values rather than the values themselves. It is a combination of an interior and a boundary representation in the sense that both interiors and boundaries of regions are represented implicitly through the aid of a single vertex which is the tip of a "cone". The vertex algebra was originally presented primarily as an alternative model for two-dimensional data represented as lists of rectangles. Algorithms have been devised for a number of vertex algebra operations in two dimensions [7].

In this paper, we show how the vertex algebra can be extended to represent orthogonal objects in arbitrary dimensions, and present a number of algorithms for operations that are useful in computer vision and pattern recognition applications. Our algorithms assume that the vertices are stored in a list (termed a *vertex list*) although they could also be stored using other representations (e.g., a point variant of a quadtree). We do not address these other representations in this paper. The contribution of our work is the generality of the solutions that we obtain through the use of recursion to construct the representation in higher dimensions, as well as performing the operations on it. This is largely a result of the switch of the primitive unit to being a one-dimensional vertex list rather than a two-dimensional vertex list. This same principle was also used by us in developing a raster-to-vertex list conversion algorithm, reported here, which works in arbitrary dimensions.

The rest of this paper is organized as follows. Section 2 reviews the vertex algebra. Section 3 shows how to use this method to represent multidimensional objects with orthogonal faces (termed *orthogonal maps*). Section 4 introduces a data structure called a *vertex list* and several associated algorithms. Section 5 summarizes what is presently known about vertex representations and gives directions for further research.

## 2 Vertex Algebra

Let $p = (p_1, p_2 \cdots p_d)$ be a point in $\mathcal{R}^d$. We define the *cone* of $p$ as the scalar field $Q_p : \mathcal{R}^d \to \mathcal{Z}$ where:

$$Q_p(x) = \begin{cases} 1 & \text{if } x_1 \geq p_1 \wedge x_2 \geq p_2 \wedge \cdots \wedge x_d \geq p_d \\ 0 & \text{otherwise.} \end{cases}$$

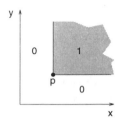

Figure 1: Cone of a point in $\mathcal{R}^2$.

In other words, the cone of $p$ maps to 1 all points inside a hyperrectangle with its minimum vertex at $p$ and extending to infinity in the positive directions of all axes, and maps to 0 all other points. Figure 1 illustrates the scalar field represented by the cone of one single point in $\mathcal{R}^2$.

A *vertex* is defined as a weighted point, that is, a point with an associated scalar value (a point can be thought of as a vertex with weight 1). The cone of a vertex $v = (p, \alpha)$, where $p$ is the *position* of $v$ and $\alpha$ is the *weight* of $v$, is a scalar field given by $Q_v = \alpha \cdot Q_p$. Thus $Q_v(x)$ is $\alpha$ for all points such that $Q_p(x) = 1$ and 0 otherwise. Similarly, the scalar field represented by a set of vertices $V = \{v_1, v_2 \cdots v_k\}$ is given by $Q_V = \sum_{i=1}^{k} Q_{v_i}$. Figure 2 shows an example of a scalar field in $\mathcal{R}^2$ given by a set of 3 vertices. The labeled black dots correspond to the positions of the vertices and their weights.

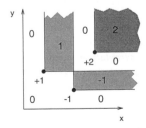

Figure 2: Scalar field represented by a set of vertices in $\mathcal{R}^2$.

It is useful to enumerate some properties of scalar fields expressed using the vertex algebra. Let $a$ and $b$ be vertices, $\alpha$ and $\beta$ be integers, and $Q_v$ denote the scalar field represented by vertex $v$. Then,

1. $\alpha Q_a + \beta Q_a = (\alpha + \beta)Q_a$.

2. $0Q_a = 0$.

3. If $\alpha Q_a + \beta Q_b + \cdots = 0$ and the positions of $a$, $b$ etc. are all distinct, then $\alpha = \beta = \cdots = 0$.

## 3  Orthogonal Maps and Polygons

In the following, we use the term *orthogonal map* to designate any scalar field that can be represented by a finite set of vertices. A set of vertices that represents an orthogonal map is termed a *vertex representation* and obeys the following rules:

1. No two vertices with the same positions are allowed. This is reasonable, since if $t = (p, \alpha)$ and $u = (p, \beta)$ are vertices in the set, then they can be replaced by vertex $v = (p, \alpha + \beta)$

2. Vertices with weight 0 are not allowed as they add no new information.

The main purpose of enforcing these rules on sets of vertices is to ensure uniqueness, i.e., that every orthogonal map has exactly *one* vertex representation.

We define an *orthogonal polygon* to be a special case of an orthogonal map where all points are mapped either to 0 or to 1. Those points that are mapped to 0 are said to be *outside* the polygon and those that are mapped to 1 are *inside* the polygon. If we restrict ourselves to $\mathcal{R}^2$, the class of orthogonal polygons closely resembles the class of ordinary polygons whose edges are parallel to one of the coordinate axes. In fact, given any such polygon, we can construct an equivalent vertex representation with the following algorithm. Since we have already used the term *vertex* to mean a point with an associated weight, we refer to the vertices of ordinary polygons as *articulation points*:

1. Select a *minimum* articulation point of the polygon and create a vertex with weight $+1$. A *minimum articulation point* is a point $(x_0, y_0)$ such that no other point $(x, y)$ on the boundary of the polygon has $x < x_0 \wedge y < y_0$. Note that more than one articulation point may satisfy these requirements.

2. Follow the boundary of the polygon starting from the minimum articulation point in a clockwise (or counterclockwise) direction. For each articulation point, create a vertex with weights alternating between $-1$ and $+1$, that is, $+1$ for point $(x_0, y_0)$, $-1$ for point $(x_1, y_1)$, $+1$ for point $(x_2, y_2)$, and so on.

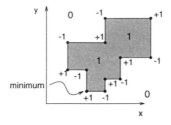

Figure 3: Vertex representation for an orthogonal polygon.

3. Stop when reaching the minimum articulation point again.

The labeling process is illustrated in Figure 3. Observe that the algorithm is only well-defined if in step 2 we know exactly which vertex/articulation point to visit next. In the case of self-intersecting polygons we have more than one choice at certain points and the resulting vertex representation may differ. This is illustrated in Figure 4. Notice that Figure 4(d) contains a vertex with weight 2, which is a result of visiting an articulation point twice while traversing the boundary of the polygon.

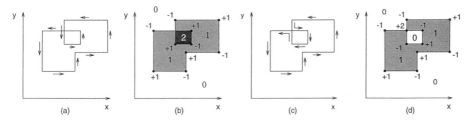

Figure 4: Two ways of building a vertex representation of a self-intersecting orthogonal polygon. Visiting the articulation points as in (a) yields the vertex representation given in (b), whereas visiting them as in (c) results in the vertex representation given in (d).

It is also possible to represent polygons with "holes". In this case, apply the algorithm to the boundary of each hole but label the starting minimum vertex with value $-1$ instead of $+1$. If we regard the example in Figure 4(a) as a polygon with one hole touching the outer boundary, then we would also get the vertex representation in Figure 4(d).

A similar construction algorithm may be devised for orthogonal polygons in any dimension. The task of selecting a minimum articulation point poses no difficulties. There is no obvious order, however, for traversing the articulation points. This doesn't matter at all since, at least for non-self-intersecting polygons, all that is needed is to assign opposite weights to any two vertices that share an edge.

## 4   Vertex Lists

Most algorithms on vertex representations use the plane-sweep paradigm [2]. Moreover, plane-sweep is frequently applied recursively, that is, the solution of a problem in $d$ dimensions is obtained by combining the partial solutions of many subproblems in $d - 1$ dimensions. This suggests that vertices should be organized as a list in reverse lexicographic order by dimension (termed a *vertex list*). For example, letting $((u_1, u_2 \cdots u_d), \alpha)$ and $((v_1, v_2 \cdots v_d), \beta)$ be vertices $u$ and $v$, respectively, we have that vertex $u$ appears before vertex $v$ in a vertex list if $u_d$ ($u$'s last coordinate value) is less than $v_d$. Similarly, if $u_d$ is greater than $v_d$ then $u$ appears after $v$. If $u_d = v_d$ then $u$ and $v$ are on the same hyperplane and the ordering between them is determined by the $d - 1$ remaining coordinate values, with coordinate value $d - 1$ being the most significant. If all coordinate values of $u$ and $v$ are equal, then $u$ and $v$ are in the same position and they may be replaced by one vertex whose weight is the sum of the weights of $u$ and $v$. For instance, the vertices $a = ((4,5),1)$, $b = ((3,2),2)$ and $c = ((4,2),-1)$ would appear in a vertex list in the order $b\ c\ a$.

In the remaining sections, vertex list algorithms are given using the following conventions. All parameters are call-by-value.

1. Uppercase letters such as $L$, $R$ and $S$ represent lists of vertices.
2. Lowercase letters from the end of the alphabet, such as $u$, $v$ and $w$ represent vertices.
3. Other lowercase letters, such as $i$, $j$ and $k$ represent integers.
4. $position(v)$ is the coordinate values of vertex $v$ or raster $v$.
5. $weight(v)$ is the weight of vertex $v$.
6. $value(v)$ is the value of raster $v$.
7. $head(L)$ is the first vertex of $L$.
8. $tail(L)$ is $L$ without its first vertex.
9. $concat(L, S)$ is list $L$ concatenated with list $S$.
10. $concat(L, v)$ is list $L$ concatenated with vertex $v$.
11. $\epsilon$ represents an empty list.
12. $dim(v)$ is the number of coordinates of $v$.
13. $weight(v)$ is the weight of $v$.
14. $coord(v, i)$ is the $i^{th}$ coordinate value of $v$.
15. $proj(v)$ is vertex $v$ with its last coordinate dropped.
16. $unproj(S, k)$ is the set $S$ of vertices with one additional coordinate with value $k$.
17. $precedes(u, v)$ is a Boolean function that is defined only if $dim(u) = dim(v)$. It returns *true* if $u < v$ in reverse lexicographic order, i.e.,
$$precedes(u, v) \Leftrightarrow \quad (coord(u, dim(u)) < coord(v, dim(v))) \lor$$
$$(coord(u, dim(u)) = coord(v, dim(v)) \land$$
$$precedes(proj(u), proj(v)))$$

## 4.1   Sum of Vertex Lists

Given two vertex lists $L$ and $S$ of the same dimension, their sum is a vertex list that represents the sum of their orthogonal maps, that is $Q_{L+S} = Q_L + Q_S$. This operation is achieved by merging vertex lists $L$ and $S$ adding the weights of vertices in the same position. Similarly, the multiplication of a vertex list by a scalar $\alpha$ is equivalent to multiplying the weight of each vertex in the list by $\alpha$.

Procedure *add*, given below, implements these operations. Given vertex lists $L$ and $S$ and a scalar $\alpha$, the algorithm returns the vertex list $L + \alpha S$ in vertex list $R$.

**procedure** *add*$(L, S, \alpha)$
   $R \leftarrow \epsilon$
   **while** $L \neq \epsilon \vee S \neq \epsilon$ **do**
      **if** $S = \epsilon \vee precedes(head(L), head(S))$ **then**
         $R \leftarrow concat(R, head(L))$
         $L \leftarrow tail(L)$
      **else if** $L = \epsilon \vee precedes(head(S), head(L))$ **then**
         $v \leftarrow head(S)$
         $weight(v) \leftarrow \alpha \cdot weight(v)$
         $R \leftarrow concat(R, v)$
         $S \leftarrow tail(S)$
      **else**
         $v \leftarrow head(L)$
         $weight(v) \leftarrow weight(v) + \alpha \cdot weight(head(S))$
         **if** $weight(v) > 0$ **then** $R \leftarrow concat(R, v)$
         $L \leftarrow tail(L)$
         $S \leftarrow tail(S)$
   **return** $R$

This algorithm is clearly linear in the total number of vertices in the two vertex lists, since at each iteration one vertex of $L$ or $S$ (or both) is removed and one (or none) is added to $R$. This claim can be contested on the grounds that comparing the positions of two $d$-dimensional points in space (as required by *precedes*) takes $O(d)$ time. Fortunately, though, the reverse lexicographic ordering of vertices in vertex lists enables this operation to be executed in $O(1)$ time.

## 4.2   Converting Rasters to Vertex Lists

A raster in $d$ dimensions is defined by the value associated with each of its cells. Let $extent(i)$ represent the range of the coordinate values of the raster in the $i^{th}$ dimension (assuming that they start at 1), and $F$ be a list of the raster's values stored in reverse lexicographic order. For instance, if the raster is a $2 \times 3$ matrix, then $extent(1)$ is 2, $extent(2)$ is 3, and the values would be stored in $F$ row-wise, i.e., first the element in row 1 column 1, then row 1 column 2, row 2 column 1, etc.

Each vertex represents the position in space where there is a change in value. We view the raster as an aggregation of one-dimensional rows stored in reverse lexicographic order. In one dimension, if two cells $a$ and $b$ with values $\alpha$ and $\beta$ are neighbors, then the change in value is given by $\beta - \alpha$; if $\alpha = \beta$, then no vertex is necessary to indicate the change from $a$ to $b$. Also, we assume that these changes are accumulated over an initial value of 0.

As an example, consider the one-dimensional raster given by values $\langle 5, 3, 3, 4 \rangle$: the corresponding vertex list is given by $\langle ((1), +5), ((2), -2), ((4), +1) \rangle$ (see Figure 5). Notice that the interval $(-\infty, 1)$ is assumed to be mapped to 0, while interval $[4, +\infty)$ is mapped to the last value in the raster (i.e., 4). This means that initially changes in value across different one-dimensional rows are not recorded. In other words, every one-dimensional row starts with the first non-zero location.

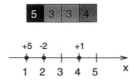

Figure 5: Conversion of a one-dimensional raster to a vertex list.

For higher dimensions the problem can be expressed as a combination of $extent(d)$ subproblems of dimension $d - 1$. First, we find the vertex list for each sub-raster corresponding to the hyperplanes perpendicular to the $d^{th}$ axis at coordinates $1, 2 \ldots extent(d)$. The vertex list for the $d$-dimensional raster is then computed by *subtracting* each previous vertex list from the current one. The rationale behind this procedure is that we are computing the *change* in value from one hyperplane to the next. Procedure *raster_to_vlist*, given below, implements this process and returns its result in vertex list $R$.

**procedure** *raster_to_vlist* $(d, L, extent)$
    $R \leftarrow \epsilon$
    **if** $d = 1$ **then**
        $j \leftarrow 0$
        **for** $i$ **in** $\{1 \ldots extent(1)\}$ **do**
            $k \leftarrow value(head(L))$
            $L \leftarrow tail(L)$
            **if** $k \neq j$ **then** $R \leftarrow concat(R, (position(head(L)), k - j))$
            $j \leftarrow k$
    **else**
        $S \leftarrow \epsilon$
        **for** $i$ **in** $\{1 \ldots extent(d)\}$ **do**
            $T \leftarrow raster\_to\_vlist\ (d - 1, L, extent)$
            $R \leftarrow concat(R, unproj(add(T, S, -1), i))$

$$S \leftarrow T$$
**return** $R$

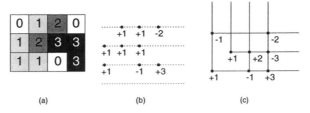

(a)        (b)        (c)

Figure 6: Converting a raster to a vertex representation. (a) A two-dimensional raster. Each raster line is converted to a one-dimensional vertex representation as given in (b). The subtraction of each pair of 1D vertex representations results in the 2D vertex representation given in (c).

Figure 6 shows an example in two dimensions. We can see that the algorithm reads each cell value exactly once and thus is linear in the number of cells. For a one-dimensional raster, the algorithm produces at most as many vertices as there are cells in the raster. This worst case corresponds to the case where each cell value is different from the previous one. For a $d$-dimensional raster, the algorithm outputs $extent(d)$ lists of vertices of dimension $d-1$, each with potentially as many as $extent(1) \times \ldots \times extent(d-1)$ vertices. Thus, given a raster with $N$ cells, the storage requirement is always $O(N)$. Also, each vertex list produced by the algorithm at dimension $i > 1$ results from the addition of two vertex lists, a process that is linear in the number of vertices. This is done once for all but the first dimension and thus the algorithm executes in $O(N \cdot d)$ time.

## 4.3 Transformations and Set Operations

A common operation on orthogonal maps is to compose them with a transformation function $f : \mathcal{Z} \to \mathcal{Z}$ Thus if $L$ is a vertex representation of a particular orthogonal map $Q_L$, then to apply $f$ on $L$ is equivalent to evaluating $f(Q_L)$.

One major application of transformations is to perform set-theoretic operations. For instance, consider two orthogonal polygons represented by their vertex representations $A$ and $B$. In the orthogonal map corresponding to the vertex representation $L = A + B$, those areas originally covered by either $A$ or $B$ are mapped to 1, while those areas covered by both $A$ and $B$ are mapped to 2. It is possible to obtain the *union* of $A$ and $B$ by applying to $L$ the transformation

$$f_\cup(x) = \begin{cases} 1 & \text{if } x > 0 \\ 0 & \text{otherwise.} \end{cases}$$

Similarly, the following transformation on $L$ may be used to obtain the *intersection* of $A$ and $B$:

$$f_\cap(x) = \begin{cases} 1 & \text{if } x > 1 \\ 0 & \text{otherwise.} \end{cases}$$

The *set difference* may be obtained by first subtracting $B$ from $A$ and then applying transformation $f_\cup$.

The algorithm to apply a transformation to a vertex representation implemented as a vertex list is similar to the raster-to-vertex list conversion algorithm. Once again, we recursively sweep hyperplanes of decreasing dimension. The problem that we must address is that the values stored in the vertices correspond to differences in the values of cones in space rooted at the vertices, while the transformation involves the application of a function to the actual values of the points in space. This is easy to overcome by recalculating the values of the points in space during the sweep. In algorithm *transform* below, $L$ is a vertex list of dimension $d$ and $f$ is a transformation. Variable $i$ contains the value of the $d^{th}$ coordinate for the current position of the sweeping hyperplane and $I$ is the list of vertices on it. $T'$ is the vertex list corresponding to the value of the orthogonal map of the sweeping hyperplane. $S$ and $T$ are transformed vertex lists of the prior and current sweeping hyperplanes, respectively.

**procedure** *transform* $(d, L, f)$
    $R \leftarrow \epsilon$
    **if** $d = 1$ **then**
        $j \leftarrow 0$
        **while** $L \neq \epsilon$ **do**
            $k \leftarrow weight(head(L)) + j$
            $L \leftarrow tail(L)$
            **if** $f(k) \neq f(j)$ **then** $R \leftarrow concat(R, (point(head(L)), f(k) - f(j)))$
            $j \leftarrow k$
    **else**
        $S \leftarrow \epsilon$
        $T' \leftarrow \epsilon$
        **while** $L \neq \epsilon$ **do**
            $i \leftarrow coord(head(L), d)$
            $I \leftarrow proj(ihead(L, i))$
            $T' \leftarrow add(T', I, +1)$
            $L \leftarrow itail(L, i)$
            $T \leftarrow transform(d - 1, T', f)$
            $R \leftarrow concat(R, unproj(add(T, S, -1), i))$
            $S \leftarrow T$
    **return** $R$

In procedure *transform*, function $ihead(L, i)$ returns the prefix of $L$ where all vertices have their last coordinate value equal to $i$, while $itail(L, i)$ returns the remainder of $L$ (i.e., $L$ with the vertices in $ihead(L, i)$ dropped). Figure 7 shows how a two-dimensional orthogonal map is transformed by $f_\cup$.

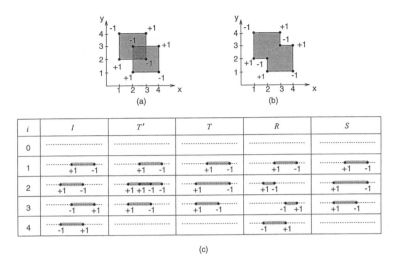

(a)  (b)

| $i$ | $I$ | $T'$ | $T$ | $R$ | $S$ |
|---|---|---|---|---|---|
| 0 | | | | | |
| 1 | +1   -1 | +1   -1 | +1   -1 | +1   -1 | +1   -1 |
| 2 | +1   -1 | +1 +1 -1 -1 | +1   -1 | +1 -1 | +1   -1 |
| 3 | -1   +1 | +1   -1 | +1   -1 | -1 +1 | +1   -1 |
| 4 | -1   +1 | | | -1   +1 | |

(c)

Figure 7: Example of a transformation applied to a two-dimensional orthogonal map. A call to procedure *transform* with list $L$ containing the vertices shown in (a) and $f = f_\cup$ results in the vertex representation given in (b), which is essentially $T - S$. Table (c) shows how $I$, $T'$, $T$, $R$, and $S$ vary with $i$.

The complexity analysis for *transform* follows the same reasoning as in the raster to vertex list conversion algorithm. For a vertex list with $N$ vertices of dimension $d$, the algorithm has a worst-case $O(N \cdot d)$ running time.

## 5 Concluding Remarks

A new approach to deal with orthogonal objects in arbitrary dimensions known as a vertex representation and implemented as a vertex list has been described. Although the basic idea has already been presented for two-dimensional data [7], our contribution has been the extension to higher dimensions. Its advantage lies in its compactness in comparison with more traditional representations such as rasters and collections of hyperrectangles (disjoint and non-disjoint). Unlike rasters, the storage required for vertex lists is proportional to the boundary of the represented objects and remains invariant under scaling. Also, normalized vertex representations have the property of being unique, a property that can be exploited in many ways (e.g., Santos [6] showed how vertex lists are useful for the recognition of circuit elements in VLSI design).

Vertex lists are similar in spirit to chain codes with the advantage that they are not restricted to two dimensions. In particular, the *precedes* relation imposes a total ordering on the vertices in the vertex list. For example, 3D objects are ordered by faces perpendicular to the $z$ axis. Algorithms have been given for converting between vertex lists and a conventional raster representation as well as set-theoretic transformations for the construction of more complicated objects. The same techniques can also be used to perform contraction and expansion. This means that operations such as skeletonization can be implemented easily.

In general, the vertex list implementation of a vertex representation is not appropriate for localized querying – for instance, the extraction of the value of a particular point in space requires the traversal of the entire vertex list. These operations can be performed better using other implementations of vertex representations or other data structures like rasters or hierarchical structures such as *quadtrees* [4, 5]. Conversion of vertex lists to these other forms of representations can be done with little difficulty.

## 6 Acknowledgements

We have benefitted from discussions with J. Schechtman, whose work sparked our interest in vertex representations.

## References

[1] H. Freeman. Computer processing of line-drawing images. *ACM Computing Surveys*, 6:57–97, March 1974.

[2] F. P. Preparata and M. I. Shamos. *Computational Geometry: An Introduction*. Springer-Verlag, New York, 1985.

[3] D. Rutovitz. Data structures for operations on digital images. In G. C. Cheng et al., editor, *Pictorial Pattern Recognition*, pages 105–133. Thompson Book Co., Washington DC, 1968.

[4] H. Samet. *Applications of Spatial Data Structures: Computer Graphics, Image Processing, and GIS*. Addison-Wesley, Reading, MA, 1990.

[5] H. Samet. *The Design and Analysis of Spatial Data Structures*. Addison-Wesley, Reading, MA, 1990.

[6] F. V. Santos. Extração de circuitos VLSI. Master's thesis, Eng. Elétrica, Universidade Federal do Rio de Janeiro, Rio de Janeiro, April 1991.

[7] J. Shechtman. Processamento geométrico de máscaras VLSI. Master's thesis, Eng. Elétrica, Universidade Federal do Rio de Janeiro, Rio de Janeiro, August 1992.

# EFFICIENT SKELETONIZATION OF BINARY FIGURES
# THROUGH (d₁,d₂)-EROSION AND DIRECTIONAL INFORMATION

Maria Frucci

Istituto di Cibernetica del C.N.R., Via Toiano, 2
80072 Arco Felice (NA), ITALY

and

Angelo Marcelli

Dipartimento di Informatica e Sistemistica
Universita' di Napoli "Federico II", Via Claudio, 21
80125 Naples, ITALY

ABSTRACT

An iterative algorithm to obtain the 8-connected labelled skeleton of a binary figure by performing the distance transformation and the erosion at the same time is presented. The algorithm accomplishes the task by adopting a $(d_1,d_2)$-distance and by using directional information to guide both the distance transformation and the erosion. It leads to a reversible skeleton which preserves the topology of the figure and is largely rotation invariant.

## 1. Introduction

Among the tools for shape description developed within the framework of structural pattern recognition, skeletons have received far more attention than any other one. Since when a skeleton model was suggested [1], a large number of algorithms have been developed in order to implement skeletonizing transformations in the digital plane, and there have been innumerable attempts to use the obtained skeletons for shape analysis and description. Although the desirable properties of a skeleton depend on the class of figures at hand, the specific application, and the use it is intended for, there appears to be a general agreement about a set of basic requirements any skeletonization algorithm should satisfy: reversibility, isotropy, preservation of topological and geometrical features, low computational cost [2]. Reversible skeletonization ensures that an appropriate set of pixels of the figure retains enough information to describe both the local thickness of the regions and their organization into the figure. Complete reconstruction of the original figure is ensured if all the centers of maximal discs inscribed into the figure are included in the skeleton [3]. Isotropy guarantees that the resulting skeleton is invariant under rotation of the figure with respect to the digital plane. Since the envelope of the union of the maximal discs coincides with the figure boundary, and because the actual boundary of a figure changes with its orientation, a different number of pixels, corresponding to the centers of the maximal discs, can be associated to rotated instances of the same figure, giving raise to different skeletons. Such a variation is negligible only if the disc is a polygon with a rather large number of sides [4]. The isotropism of the transformations also produces skeletons which are less sensitive to border noise. By preserving both geometric and topological features it is ensured that the skeleton of a connected figure is connected with the same multiplicity order of the original figure, and that its shape faithfully reflects the geometry of the original figure. Eventually, since skeletonization is very often an intermediate step toward recognition, a low computational cost is highly desirable.

Among these basic requirements, invariance under rotation and shape fidelity are the most difficult to meet, especially when computational cost issues are involved. This is basically due to the metric adopted to compute the distance transform and to the need of preserving all the centers of maximal discs to have a complete reversible transformations. Therefore, we have decided to explore a rather different approach to devise a novel criterion for selecting the skeletal pixels, i.e. the pixels forming the skeleton. Basically, skeletonization can be seen as an iterated and isotropic erosion of the figure, during which only certain pixels are preserved from deletion; in turn, erosion can be interpreted as a propagation of the background over the figure [5]. Hence, skeletal pixels are those pixels where different propagation fronts collide frontally, i.e. without any possibility of continuing their propagation toward pixels which have not been already reached by other fronts. This condition cannot be detected by using only distance information, because such a distance represents the length, computed according to a given metric, of a minimal path between the pixel and the background, and does not convey any information about the actual direction of the propagation. There are cases, vice versa, where although the wavefronts collide frontally, they have different intensity, that is they come from pixels having different labels, and therefore the propagation does not annihilate in it, but can continue toward inner pixels [6]. Therefore, only a combination of both, distance and propagation information, can be adopted to discriminate among skeletal and non skeletal pixels.

In the sequel we outline an iterative skeletonization algorithm which exploits simultaneously the information obtained by a $(d_1,d_2)$-distance transformation and that conveyed by a suitable propagation mechanism associated to any pixel of the figure, to perform an isotropic erosion of the figure itself. The algorithm leads to 8-connected labelled skeletons which allow the reconstruction of the original shape, exhibit a linear structure, and are largely invariant under rotation.

## 2. The method

Preliminarily to the description of the algorithm, let us introduce some notations used in the sequel of the paragraph and recall few basic notions.

### 2.1 Definitions

Let S be a binary picture, and let $F=\{1\}$ and $F'=\{0\}$ indicate the foreground and the background, respectively.

1) *($d_1,d_2$)- distance.* For any two pixels p and q in S, a path from p to q is a finite sequence of pixels starting from p and terminating in q, where each pixel is a neighbour of the preceding one. The length of a path is given by the sum of the distances relative to all the successive pairs of neighbours in the sequence. The values $d_1$ and $d_2$ are respectively adopted to weight the distance between any two horizontal/vertical and diagonal adjacent pixels. Such adjacent pixels will also be referred to as d-neighbours and i-neighbours, respectively. A path whose length is minimal is called a shortest path. The distance d(p,q) is the length of a shortest path from p to q.

2) *Labelling.* In this paper, the letter P is used to indicate the value of the pixel p in S. During the erosion process, some pixels of the figure are labelled with their distance from background. Thus, when P>1, P represents the distance d(p,0) of p from background and L(P) is the equivalent label of P, defined as in [7]. If P=1, p is a figure pixel not yet visited, while for P=0, p belongs to the current background.

3) *List of Directional Field.* A directional field of a pixel p is a pointer to a neighbour of p. During the erosion process, each addressed pixel p has an associated list of directional fields, LDF(p) for short, computed according to the masks of fig. 1. In this paper, the notation DF(p,j) is used to indicate the sub-list of LDF(p) constituted by the pointers of LDF(p) addressing neighbours of p at the distance $d_j$ from p.

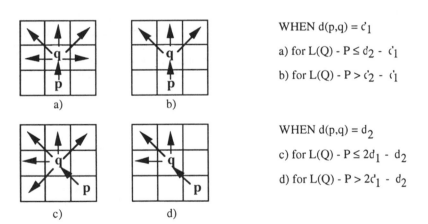

WHEN $d(p,q) = c_1$

a) for $L(Q) - P \leq d_2 - c_1$

b) for $L(Q) - P > c_2 - c_1$

WHEN $d(p,q) = d_2$

c) for $L(Q) - P \leq 2d_1 - d_2$

d) for $L(Q) - P > 2c_1 - d_2$

Figure 1. Propagation rules for a pixel q addressed by a pixel p with d(q,0)>d(p,0).

4) *Bucket.* A bucket $B_i$ is used to store the set of pixels at distance i in the form of an address field (coordinates) plus a list of directional fields.

5) *Basic skeletal pixel.* A pixel p is called non-propagating pixel if it does not exist a pointer of LDF(p) to a inner pixel. That is, p is a non-propagating pixel if LDF(p) is empty or for

each pixel q addressed by a pointer of LDF(p) it results $d(q,0) \leq d(p,0)$. A non-propagating pixel is assumed to be a basic skeletal pixel.

## 2.2 Algorithm

The skeletonization is performed in two phases, the first of which is concerned with the deletion of non skeletal pixels, while the second one is devoted to reduce the set of skeletal pixel to unitary width (thinning), and to remove the skeletal branches possibly originated in correspondence of not significant regions of the input shape (pruning).

Initially, the array S is scanned once and the pixels belonging to F' which are d-neighbours of F are identified and stored in the bucket $B_0$ with their pointers to pixels belonging to F. They constituted the list of directional fields associated to any pixel of $B_0$. No use of the directional fields is done at this moment.

Starting from $B_0$, successive buckets $B_i$ are built. For this purpose, the pixels of F are addressed in order of increasing distance. Specifically, the set of pixels at distance i from background is reached from (generated by) the sets at distance $(i-d_2)$ and $(i-d_1)$, respectively. We will describe the algorithm by considering separately the two cases, $i=d_j$ and $i \neq d_j$.

Let us refer first to the construction of buckets $B_i$, $i=d_j$, with $j=1,2$. The bucket $B_{i-d_j}$ (i.e. $B_0$) is visited to find the pixels which could generate the elements of $B_i$. Only the pixels p in the bucket $B_{i-d_j}$, whose sublist DF(p,j) is not empty, are checked. Let q be one of the neighbours addressed by a pointer of DF(p,j). If $Q=1$ (i.e. q has not been previously visited), q is labelled i in S and it is stored in $B_i$ with its list of directional fields computed by using one of the masks of fig.1, according to the values of L(Q) and P as well as to the position of q respect to p. Otherwise, the case $Q>1$ indicates that q has already been visited and stored in $B_Q$; hence only the updating of LDF(q) is required. This is achieved by selecting the proper mask associated to Q as before, and by ANDing such a mask with LDF(q). The case $Q \leq P$ is not possible, due to the way LDF(p) has been built. The bucket $B_0$ is deleted as soon as the construction of $B_{d_2}$ ends.

As for the construction of the bucket $B_i$, $i \neq d_j$, $B_{i-d_2}$ and $B_{i-d_1}$ are examined in succession. Only the pixels p in the buckets $B_{i-d_j}$ whose list of directional fields is not empty are checked. Suppose DF(p,j) is not empty. Let q be one of the neighbours addressed by p through a pointer of DF(p,j). If $Q \neq 1$ and $Q \leq P$, the directional field of p addressing q is deleted from LDF(p); thus, the resulting LDF(p) might be empty. If $Q=1$ $(Q>P)$, the same actions done to built (to update) $B_i$ ($B_Q$) when $i=d_j$, are repeated. However, differently from before, while $B_i$ is filled in ($B_Q$ is updated) by means of pixels of $B_{i-d_2}$, each pixel p in $B_{i-d_2}$ with the resulting not empty LDF(p) is deleted in S, provided that its presence is not required to maintain the connectedness of the figure currently eroded in S. As soon as p is deleted in S, all the information relative to p is removed from $B_{i-d_2}$ as p is no longer of interest.

The bucket construction process terminates when all the resulting lists of directional fields of the pixels belonging to the last constructed bucket are empty. At the end of the process, the pixels in the buckets are the skeletal pixels.

During the  second phase, the content of the buckets has to be examined again, starting from the bucket having the minimum index i. Topology preserving removal operations tailored to favour the well shapedness of the skeleton are applied if the set of the skeletal pixels does not have unitary width. Moreover, operation based on directional and distance information are applied to prune not significant branches of the skeleton. More precisely, the branches are followed and for each non-propagating pixel p the difference of the distance value between p and the successive pixel  on the current branch is computed. As soon as such a difference is not bigger than the difference $d_2-d_1$, the branch is recognized as significant. Otherwise, the pixels of the branch are removed from S and from the corresponding buckets. Note that, depending on the thickness of the resulting skeleton, at the most three inspections of the buckets are needed if both thinning and pruning have to be performed. This phase terminates when no pixel can be removed. In fig. 2 it is shown an example of propagation with $d_1=3$ and $d_2=4$ .

## 3. Concluding  remarks

In this paper we have presented a skeletonization algorithm which accomplishes the task by means of a repeated erosion of the figure. The novelty of the approach is that the selection of the skeletal pixels is  based on both distance and directional information, instead of using distance information only, as mostly done in literature. For this purpose, a propagation mechanism  which allows to associate to any pixel a list of directional fields conveying information about the direction of the background propagation has been defined.

The results provided by the algorithm are shown in figg. 3 and 4. They show how the use of a combination of both distance and directional information leads to reversible skeletons, whose structures can be considered, at least by a human being, a faithful representation of the original shapes. The proposed method also improves the efficiency of the computation, since it performs the distance transformation and the erosion at the same time. Moreover, the algorithm preserves all the significative centers of maximal discs, without requiring a specific test for them. This results in a lower computational cost, because there are not specific tests to do on each figure pixels to check whether or not it is a center of maximal disc, and also because very few spurious branches are generated, and therefore the pruning process, which is very simple and effective, will also require less processing time (fig. 5). Eventually, it is worthwhile to note that, as other recent algorithms based on contour generation, the processing time is directly proportional to the area of the object rather than to the size of the image containing the figure.

## Acknowledgements

This work has been supported by Ministero dell'Universita' e della Ricerca Scientifica e Tecnologica and by Consiglio Nazionale delle Ricerche. The help of Mr. Salvatore Piantedosi in preparing the illustrations is also gratefully acknowledged.

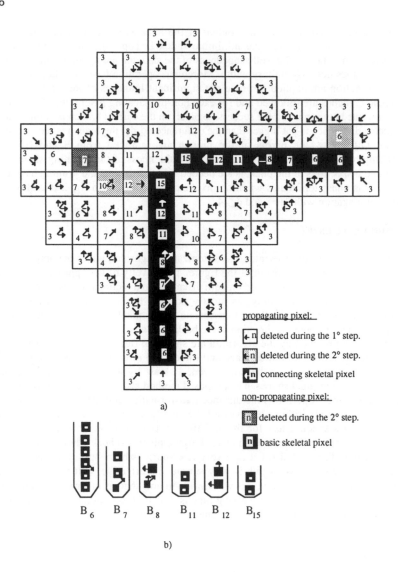

a)

b)

Figure 2. Example of propagation with $d_1$=3 and $d_2$=4. In fig. 2a, each pixel has associated its distance value. The arrows represent the directional fields of the propagating pixels. The skeleton is constituted by the set of black pixels. In fig. 2b, it is shown the content of the resulting buckets.

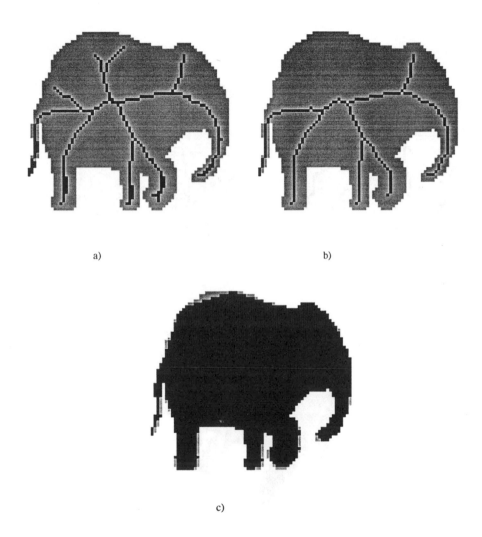

a)

b)

c)

Figure 3. The results of the proposed algorithm. a) the skeleton at the end of the first phase. b) the skeleton after the thinning and pruning operations. c) the reconstruction obtained by using the skeleton in b). The lighter pixels represent the only pixels of the figure not reconstructed.

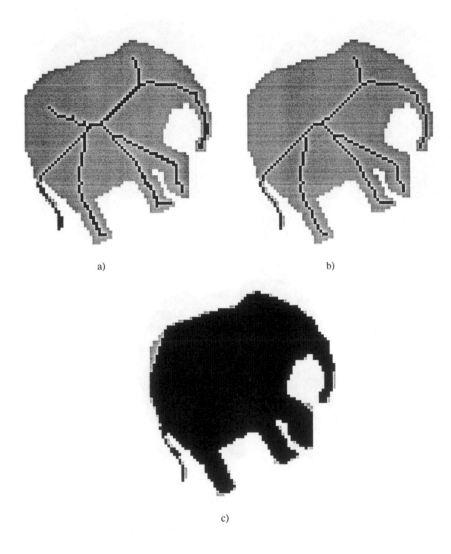

a)

b)

c)

Figure 4. The results on the same image of fig. 3, slightly rotated.

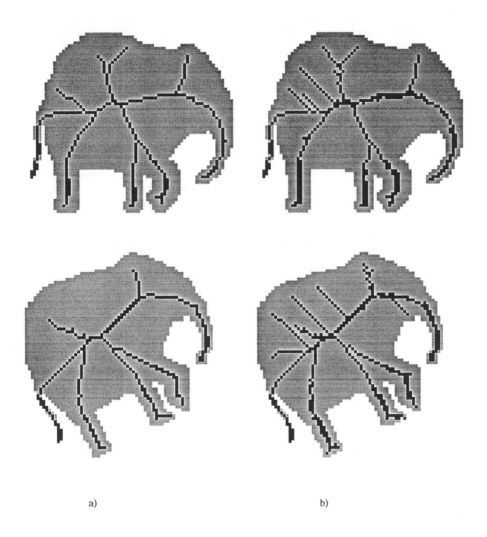

a)                                            b)

Figure 5. The comparision between the thick skeletons provided by the algorithm proposed in the paper (a) and the ones obtained by assuming all the centers of maximal discs as skeletal pixels (b).

230

References

[1] H. Blum, "A transformation for extracting new descriptors of shape", in *Models for the Perceptionof Speech and Visual Form*, W. Wathen-Dunn Ed., MIT Press, Cambridge, pp. 362-380, 1967.

[2] L. Lam, S. Lee, and C.Y. Suen, "Thinning methodologies - A comprehensive survey", *IEEE Trans. Pattern Analysis and Machine Intelligence*, vol. PAMI-14, pp. 869-885, 1992.

[3] A. Rosenfeld and J. L. Pfaltz, " Sequential operations in digital picture processing", *J. ACM*, vol. 13, no. 4, pp.471-494, 1966.

[4] C. Arcelli and M. Frucci, "Reversible skeletonization by (5,7,11)-erosion", in *Visual Form: Analysis and Recognition*, C. Arcelli, L.P. Cordella and G. Sanniti di Baja Eds., Plenum, New York, pp. 21-28, 1992.

[5] C.J. Hilditch, "Linear skeletons from square cupboards", in *Machine Intelligence IV*, B. Meltzer and D. Mitchie Eds., University Press, Edinburgh, pp. 403-420, 1969.

[6] M. Frucci and A. Marcelli, "Axial representation of shape", *in preparation*.

[7] C.Arcelli and G.Sanniti di Baja, "Finding local maxima in pseudo-Euclidean distance transform", *Computer Vision, Graphics, and Image Processing*, vol.43, pp. 361-367, 1988.

# REGULARIZATION OF LOW-LEVEL BINOCULAR STEREO VISION CONSIDERING SURFACE SMOOTHNESS AND DISSIMILARITY OF SUPERIMPOSED STEREO IMAGES

G. L. GIMEL'FARB

*Image Recognition Dept.,*
*V.M.Glushkov Institute of Cybernetics,*
*prosp. Akad. Glushkova 40,*
*Kiev-207, 252650 GSP, Ukraine*

## ABSTRACT

The intensity-based computational binocular stereo vision reconstructs a digital elevation model (DEM) of a continuous optical surface of the natural object (such as the Earth's surface) by matching directly the pixels in a given digital stereo pair of images. To regularize partially this ill-posed inverse optical problem a novel probabilistic geometric model describing more precisely a shape of the desired surface and supplementary measure of mutual distinctions between both stereo images superimposed by transforming in accordance with the DEM are proposed. The desired DEM is defined as a bundle of epipolar profiles of the surface. The geometric model describes the DEM as a sample of a Markov random field where each profile is considered as a Markov chain of admissible transitions between surface points described by a planar graph of possible variants of the profile. The chain has a stationary probability distribution of the states showing the binocular or only monocular visibility of the surface points. The regularization relies on assumptions about maximal smoothness of the surface to be reconstructed as the main feature of its shape and about minimal mismatches of the corresponding intensities between the superimposed stereo images. These assumptions make obvious changes in the probabilistic models of the DEM and stereo pair and can be readily taken into account in the previous symmetric dynamic programming stereo algorithms. Experiments with the real stereo images show the efficiency of such regularization.

## 1. Introduction

The shapes of the objects have obvious and unique formal descriptions only in specific areas of human activity where these objects are used for man-to-man or man-machine communication (texts and technical drawings) or obtained in a result of man-machine interaction (industrial structures and components). Such complex object can be decomposed into strictly defined 2D or 3D primitive ones with simple shapes (say, segments of straight lines, circles, patches of planes, spheres, quadrics) which are governed by self-consistent rules for their combination.

The directly opposite situation prevails for the shapes of natural (real-world) objects like the Earth's surface where the primitives and combining rules take mainly informal, or fuzzy definitions of a very general type like "a plain", "a flat slope", "a valley", "a ridge", etc. These natural primitives possess recurrent features which are typical to fractals [7]: any plain and flat slope of the valley or ridge of a certain scale have its own valleys and ridges of the less scale. Such inherent fuzziness of the surface shape and primitives inhibits the unique decomposition of the observed surface into the patches having strictly determined formal definitions.

Computational stereo vision is the main passive tool for collecting initial data to describe shapes of exterior surfaces of observed natural objects. There is rather high variety of possible solutions of the stereo vision problems (see, for example, [1-3]) but only a few of them explicitly take account of inherent ambiguities in reconstructing a digital elevation model (DEM) of the optical surface from stereo pairs of images [3, 5, 6]. These ambiguities are caused primarily by monocular sensing of some surface points due to occlusions or surface slopes. So any surface has at least one equivalent variant with only monocularly visible points which can form (under the particular coloring of its points) precisely the same stereo images [5]. To regularize this ill-posed problem in a rather reasonable way we are to represent the most distinctive features of the presumed surface shape and its stereo perception in the underlying signal models and algorithms.

We will consider the previously proposed symmetric probabilistic approach [2-4] which defines the presumed shape of the surface and admissible distortions of the stereo images in terms of local features of random fields describing the surface and image signals (intensities in the surface points and corresponding pixels of the images) and embeds these features into dynamic programming (DP) algorithms for reconstructing the DEM in a profile-by-profile mode. Each profile is to give the maximal similarity between the intensities estimated in the surface points and initial intensities in the corresponding pixels to within the allowable signal distortions for binocularly (BVP) and monocularly visible points (MVP) of the surface. These distortions preserve a given range of ratios between the corresponding intensity changes between the adjacent BVPs in both stereo images.

## 2. The symmetric approach to DEM reconstruction

The symmetric intensity-based binocular stereo vision reconstructs the DEM of the continuous optical surface from intensities obtained by epipolar raster scanning of the stereo pair of optical images and takes into account geometric and photometric symmetries of stereo channels, independent regular and random distortions of the intensities within the channels, and binocular or only monocular visibility of surface points due to surface slopes and occlusions [2-4]. The DEM is presented as a bundle of independent epipolar profiles. Each profile is considered as a sample of a Markov chain of points within a particular planar graph of variants of the profile (GVP).

Let us introduce the following notation:

$R_i = ((x_i, y_i): x_i = 0,...,M-1; y_i = 0,...,N-1)$ denotes raster with Cartesian coordinates $(x_i, y_i)$ of the pixels to represent the image $i = 1,2$ of the digital stereo pair; the epipolar scan lines in the optical stereo images which represent the same epipolar profile are defined as two corresponding x-lines in R1 and R2 with the same y-coordinate y1=y2=y of the pixels; M denotes the number of pixels in the corresponding lines; N denotes the number of the epipolar profiles in the DEM;

$C_i$ = (ci(xi,yi): (xi,yi) ∈Ri; v=ci(•,•)∈V) denotes the image i=1,2 of the stereo pair (C1,C2) where V is a scalar or vector set of intensity values; in the simplest case it is the integer set V = {0,1,...,vmax}; vmax > 0;

p = x1-x2 denotes the x-parallax of the corresponding pixels (x1,y) and (x2,y) which represent the same BVP in the images C1 and C2; this parallax determines uniquely the elevation of this BVP over the reference plane; the last one is parallel to the plane of stereo images and contains the base-line of the stereo channels linking their optical centers. The GVP-points form the lattice GVP(y) = ((x,p|s): x=xmin, xmin + 0.5, xmin + 1,..., xmax; p ∈ [pmin, pmax]; s ∈ {B, M1, M2}) in the coordinates (x, p) where x=(x1+x2)/2 is the x-coordinate of the surface point in the profile with the y-coordinate y within the DEM and p=x1-x2 is the x-parallax of the corresponding pixels (x1=x+p/2,y) and (x2=x-p/2,y) in both images [4, 5]. The points with integer (half-integer) x-coordinate have only even (only odd) values of the x-parallax. Symbols "min" and "max" indicate above the lowest and highest values of the variables. The state s of the GVP-point (x,p) shows its visibility in variants of the profile: the symbol "B" stands for the BVP and symbols "M1", "M2" - for the MVP observed only by the channel i=1 or i=2. The admissible profile variant is formed as a continuous sequence of straight-line local arcs (transitions) between the adjacent GVP-points having the proper states. Only the following local transitions from the current point (x,p|s) to the next ones are allowed (Fig.1):

$$(x,p|B) \rightarrow (x+1,p|B), (x+1,p|M1), (x+0.5,p-1|M2);$$

$$(x,p|M1) \rightarrow (x+0.5,p+1|B), (x+0.5,p+1|M1);$$

$$(x,p|M2) \rightarrow (x+1,p|B), (x+1,p|M1), (x+0.5,p-1|M2).$$

The difference probabilistic model of the stereo images introduced in [2, 3] reduce the a posteriori probability of any profile variant within the GVP to a monotone function of certain additive dissimilarity measure. This measure combines residual mismatches between the corresponding intensities c1(x1,y) and c2(x2,y) in the images and estimated ones c(x,p|s) = (c1(x1,y) + c2(x2, y))/2 in the GVP-points to within the allowable regular distortions of their local changes for the BVPs and extensions of such mismatches to the MVPs along the variant. The DP algorithm which realizes the simple Bayesian MAP-decision of the maximal a posteriori probability finds the profile giving the minimal dissimilarity by exhausting all possible variants of the profiles [2-4]. It can be shown that the compound Bayesian MSMAP-decision of the maximal sum of marginal a posteriori probabilities of the GVP-points for the desired DEM [3, 6] also is realized by the DP if the a posteriori probability model of the profiles under the given stereo images allows to compute directly or estimate these marginals.

234

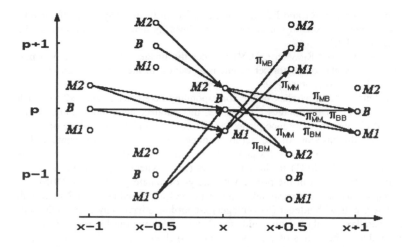

Fig.1. The fragment of the GVP

## 3. Dynamic programming MAP-reconstruction of the profile

The DP algorithms search for minimal total dissimilarity by running from the starting x-position x=xmin to the finishing one x=xmax and looking for any current position x=xmin, xmin+0.5, xmin+1, ..., xmax over all admissible GVP-points (x,p|s) with even or odd parallax values p in line with the integer or half-integer value of x. The parallax values vary within the bounds $pmin(x) \leq p \leq pmax(x)$ which depend on the current position x. For each current GVP-point (x,p|s) the transition to the nearest preceding point $(x^0, p^0|s^0)$ lying on the potentially optimal variant (POV) of the desired profile passing through the point (x,p|s) is stored.

Let us denote Pre(x,p|s) the set of the preceding points linked with the point (x,p|s) in the GVP (Fig.1) and let D(x,p|s) be the cumulative value of the dissimilarity measure for the POV passing the point (x,p|s) and d(x,p,s|x',p',s') be the local dissimilarity for the transition $(x', p'|s') \rightarrow (x,p|s)$ within the GVP. The POV-transition is determined as:

$$(x^0, p^0|s^0) = \underset{(x',p'|s') \in Pre(x,p|s)}{Argmin} \{D(x',p'|s') + d(x,p,s|x',p',s')\} \tag{1}$$

and the cumulative dissimilarity takes here the value:

$$D(x, p|s) = D(x^0, p^0|s^0) + d(x, p, s|x^0, p^0, s^0). \tag{2}$$

The dissimilarity d(x,p,s|x',p',s') is obtained from the probabilistic model of stereo images describing the mismatches between the intensities in the surface points and corresponding pixels by means of a random field which takes account of local signal changes along and across the profiles and their allowable distortions in the images [3, 4] and in a general way is to contain term describing the transition probabilities for the Markov chain which models the profile variant in the GVP. The oversimplified assumption which has been used previously in [2-4] about the equiprobable variants of the profile leads to the DEM with no a priori constraints on the surface shape and its smoothness.

We will describe below the shape of the surface to be reconstructed by a more general probabilistic model of the epipolar profiles. This model takes into account the a priori probabilities of transitions from a current binocularly visible surface point (BVP) or monocularly visible one (MVP) to the next BVP or MVP along the profile and binds their values with the initial probabilistic assumptions about the smoothness of the surface. The resulting dissimilarity measure allows to reconstruct the DEM by choosing the most smooth surface with the given local probabilistic features between the equivalent ones which have the least signal dissimilarity.

To regularize further such solution and bring it into a more close correspondence with the visually perceived surface we will supplement the measure d(x,p,s|x',p',s') with one more term r(x,p,s|x',p',s') which can be justified by an additional model of possible mutual distortions of the stereo images superposed under the given DEM:

$$dr(x,p,s|x',p',s') = (1-w) \cdot d(x,p,s|x',p',s') + w \cdot r(x,p,s|x',p',s') \qquad (3)$$

where w is a relative weight ($1 \geq w \geq 0$) of the term r(x,p,s|x',p',s') which describes the maximal mismatch between the intensities $c1(x1,y)$ and $c2(x2,y)$ in the pixels corresponding to the same point $(x,p)$ in the GVP(y) if one image of the stereo pair is transformed into another according to the DEM with due account of signals and signal distortions for the BVPs and their possible extensions to the occluded MVPs. Such regularization tends to suppress former equivalence of the profile variants by emphasizing the estimated dissimilarity for the ones which have long fragments containing only MVPs if the intensities corresponding to these fragments in both images have too different values.

## 4. Generating probabilistic model of the profile

Due to the spatial uniformity of the profile variants the transition probabilities $\pi(x,p,s|x',p',s')$ forming the profile as the Markov chain of the arcs between the adjacent GVP-points $(x',p'|s') \rightarrow (x,p|s)$ are to be held fixed for all positions $(x,p|s)$ within the GVP. Let us denote the transition probability $\pi_i(s|s')$ because the x-coordinate increment $i=x-x'$ and visibility states $s,s'$ determine unequivocally the next point $(x,p|s)$ relative to the current one $(x',p'|s')$.

These probabilities are governed by obvious equations:

$$\pi_1 (B|B) + \pi_1 (M1|B) + \pi_{0.5} (M2|B) = 1;$$
$$\pi_{0.5} (B|M1) + \pi_{0.5} (M1|M1) = 1;$$
$$\pi_1 (B|M2) + \pi_1 (M1|M2) + \pi_{0.5} (M2|M2) = 1. \tag{4}$$

Let us describe the profiles by marginal state probabilities P(B), P(M1), P(M2); P(B) + P(M1) + P(M2) = 1, because the spatial uniformity of the profiles leads to the probabilistic model of the stationary Markov chain of the GVP-transitions with the fixed marginal state probabilities for any GVP-point. This model introduces the following relations:

$$P(B) = P(B) \cdot \pi_1(B|B) + P(M1) \cdot \pi_{0.5}(B|M1) + P(M2) \cdot \pi_1(B|M2);$$
$$P(M1) = P(B) \cdot \pi_1(M1|B) + P(M1) \cdot \pi_{0.5}(M1|M1) + P(M2) \cdot \pi_1(M1|M2);$$
$$P(M2) = P(B) \cdot \pi_{0.5}(M2|B) + P(M2) \cdot \pi_{0.5}(M2|M2). \tag{5}$$

In such a case five variables can be given independently from the 11 ones $\pi_t(s|s')$, P(s). Uniformity and symmetry considerations allow to unite some of them in such a way:

$$P(B) = P_B; \quad P(M1) = P(M2) = P_M / 2; \quad \pi_1(B|B) = \pi_{BB};$$
$$\pi_{0.5}(B|M1) = \pi_1(B|M2) = \pi_{BM}; \quad \pi_{0.5}(M1|B) = \pi_{0.5}(M2|B) = \pi_{MB};$$
$$\pi_{0.5}(M1|M1) = \pi_{0.5}(M2|M2) = \pi_{MM}; \quad \pi_1(M1|M2) = \pi_{MM}^0. \tag{6}$$

After this symmetrization the model depends only on two parameters $\pi_{BB}$ and $\pi_{MM}$ as follows: $\pi_{MM}^0 = 0$ and

$$\pi_{BM} = 1 - \pi_{MM}; \quad \pi_{MB} = (1 - \pi_{BB}) / 2; \quad P_B = \xi / (1 + \xi); \quad P_M = 1 / (1 + \xi) \tag{7}$$

where $\xi = (1 - \pi_{MM})/(1 - \pi_{BB})$. By varying the parameter values $\pi_{BB}$, $\pi_{MM}$ one can change expected numbers of the BVPs and MVPs and expected local smoothness along the profile and generate the profiles with different shapes in the x-direction. If using $P_B$ and $\pi_{BB}$ as initial model parameters (under the obvious constraints $1/(2 - \pi_{BB}) \geq P_B \geq 0$ ) then $\pi_{MM}^0 = 0$, $P_M = 1 - P_B$ and $\pi_{BM} = \kappa$; $\pi_{BM} = (1 - \pi_{BB})/2$; $\pi_{MM} = 1 - \kappa$ where $\kappa = P_B (1 - \pi_{BB})/(1 - P_B); \quad 0 \leq \kappa \leq 1$.

For the equal parameter values $\pi_{BB} = \pi_{MM}$ the marginal state probabilities have the following values: P(B)=0.5; P(M1)=P(M2)=0.25 and the expected number of MVPs is equal to the number of BVPs. The smoothness of the profiles with such expected values of the BVPs and MVPs is decreasing and their shapes are changing from nearly plane to jagged ones when the transition probabilities $\pi_{BB} = \pi_{MM}$ are increasing from low (like 0.1 in Fig.2,a) to high values (0.9 in Fig.2,f); if these probabilities are over 0.95 the profiles take the pit-like (zigzag) forms (Fig.2,c with $\pi_{BB} = \pi_{MM} = 0.99$). When $\xi \gg 1$, or $\pi_{BB} \gg \pi_{MM}$, the generated profiles are comprised predominantly of the elongated straight horizontal segments (Fig.2,b with $\pi_{BB} = 0.9$; $\pi_{MM} = 0.1$). In the opposite case $(\pi_{BB} \ll \pi_{MM})$ the profiles contain predominantly long slopes (Fig.2,d and 2,e with $\pi_{BB} = 0.1\text{-}0.3$; $\pi_{MM} = 0.9$) and also acquire the zigzag forms for the $\pi_{MM} > 0.95$.

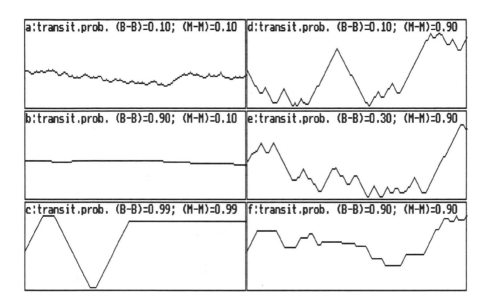

Fig.2. Examples of the profiles generated using
different transition probabilities

The a priori probability of the single profile variant is given by the product of the transition probabilities:

$$\alpha \cdot (\pi_{BB})^{N_{BB}} \cdot (\pi_{BM})^{N_{BM}} \cdot (\pi_{MB})^{N_{MB}} \cdot (\pi_{MM})^{N_{MM}} \qquad (8)$$

where $N_{ss'} \equiv N_{ss'}(y)$ is the number of transitions from the state s' to the state s along this variant and $\alpha$ is the a priori probability of the starting GVP-point (these points are assumed to be equiprobable for all admissible variants). By specifying these transition probabilities one can introduce a probabilistic ordering for the presumed profile shapes.

## 5. Experimental results and concluding remarks

In a simplified special case the local dissimilarity measure which can be derived approximately from the above models (1), (2) to be implemented for a causal profile-by-profile DEM reconstruction is presented as follows:

$$dr(x,p,s;x',p',s') = dr_s(x,p,s;x',p',s') + \sigma|\ln(\pi_{ss'})|;$$

$$D(x,p|s) = D(x^0,p^0|s^0) + dr(x,p,s|x^0,p^0,s^0). \tag{9}$$

Here $dr_s(x,p,s;x',p',s')$ denotes weighted sum of two local square mismatches $d_s$ ($\bullet$) and $r_s$ ($\bullet$): a) the basic mismatch $d_B$ ($\bullet$) of the intensities in the corresponding points for the BVP (x,p,s=B) by virtue of the random noise to within the admissible regular distortions of their differences or the corresponding estimate $d_M$ ($\bullet$) of the noise-like distortions extended to the MVP (x,p,s=M1, M2) and b) the regularizing maximal mismatch $r_B$ ($\bullet$), $r_M$ ($\bullet$) of the intensities in the same points for the transformed and superposed stereo images; $\sigma^2$ is the expected value of the random variable $d_B$ ($\bullet$). The mismatch $d_B$ ($\bullet$) can be computed by estimating the intensities in the BVPs and bringing them into the best agreement with the initial stereo images C1 and C2 to within the admissible regular distortions specified by the given bounds of the ratios between the corresponding intensity differences [3, 4].

Fig.3 shows the fragments 256 * 256 pixels of the aerial stereo pair of a highland (the symbols H-L, H-R denote its left and right images) and the close-range stereo pair of a Martian scene (M-L, M-R) taken from the images which have been received during NASA's Viking space mission and the reconstructed DEMs which are presented in a form of range images (with light ridges, or near points, and dark valleys, or distant points). These DEMs are reduced to the left stereo image. Both DEMs were reconstructed under the assumption about the rather smooth surface with more probable long chains of the same states M1-M1-M1-..., M2-M2-M2-..., and B-B-B-... along the profiles: $\pi_{BB} = 0.9$; $\pi_{MM} = 0.9$) and with the regularizing weight w=0.5. The proposed DP algorithm implemented using an IBM PC AT 386DX (40 MHz) spends approximately 3 s per a single profile with the following parameters: xmin=0, xmax=255, pmin=-40, pmax=40 (that is, 150 $\mu$s per a GVP-point). The DEMs presented in Fig.3 were smoothed after the DP reconstruction by means of a moving-inter-line-window median filtering to exclude possible local outliers.

The comparison of these and like experimental results with the ones obtained by the previous symmetrized algorithms described in [3, 4] shows that proposed regularization leads to substantially more robust and accurate reconstruction of the DEMs and perception of the desired shape of the observed natural surfaces.

The described algorithms take into account only the local smoothness of the surface in the x-direction and reconstruct the profiles independently. The experiments show that even under such simplification we can regularize (within certain limits) the ill-posed problem of the computational stereo vision and reduce enough the ambiguity of its solution.

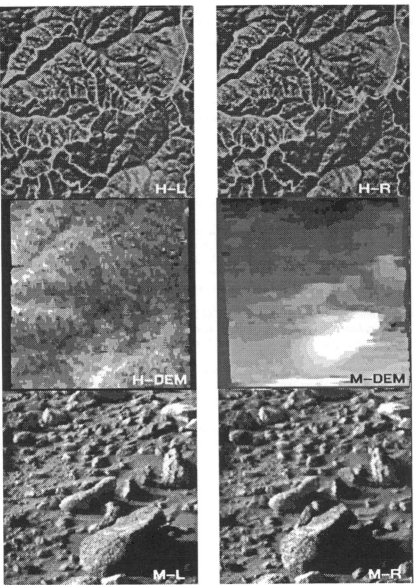

Fig.3. The initial stereo pairs and
the reconstructed DEMs as the range images

One might expect that a consideration of both x- and y-directed signal interactions in the image model will enhance further the stereo perception of the surface and simplify the following description of its shape but at the expense of greatly increased volume of computations.

## 6. Acknowlegements

The author would like to thank his collaborators Marina Grigorenko, Dmitry Kalmykov, and Boris Mikhalevich for their help in experiments and dr. Marina Kolesnik (Institute of Space Researches, Moscow, Russia) for the Martian stereo pair.

## 7. References

1. H.H.Baker, "Surfaces from mono and stereo images", *Photogrammetria*, vol. 39, no. 4-6, pp.217-237, 1984.
2. G.L.Gimel'farb, "Symmetrical approach to the problem of automating stereoscopic measurements in photogrammetry", *Kibernetika*, no. 2, pp. 73-82, 1979 [English transl.: *Cybernetics*, vol. 8, no. 2, pp. 311-322, 1979].
3. G.L.Gimel'farb, "Intensity-based computer binocular stereo vision: signal models and algorithms", *Int. Journal of Imaging Systems and Technology*, vol. 3, no. 3, pp. 189-200, 1991.
4. G.L.Gimel'farb, V.M.Krot, and M.V.Grigorenko, "Experiments with symmetrized intensity-based dynamic programming algorithms to reconstruct digital terrain model from a stereo pair of images", *Ibid*, vol. 4, no. 1, pp. 8-21, 1992.
5. V.R.Kyreitov, *Inverse Problems of Photometry*, Novosibirsk: Computing Center (Academy of Sciences of the USSR, Siberian Branch), 1983 (In Russian).
6. J.Marroquin, S.Mitter, and T.Poggio, "Probabilistic solution of ill-posed problems in computational vision", *Journal of the American Statistical Association*, vol. 82, no. 397, pp. 76-89, 1987.
7. A.P.Pentland, "Fractal-based description of natural scenes", *IEEE Trans. Pattern Anal. Machine Intell.*, vol. PAMI-6, no. 6, pp.661- 674, 1984.

# QUANTITATIVE COMPARISONS OF DIFFERENTIAL METHODS FOR MEASURING OF IMAGE VELOCITY

PETER HANDSCHACK

*ATIS Assmann, Fürstenwalder Damm 880, D-12589 Berlin*

and

REINHARD KLETTE

*Fachgebiet Computer Vision, Institut für Technische Informatik im FB 13*
*Technische Universität Berlin, Franklinstr. 28/29, D-10587 Berlin*

## ABSTRACT

For eight point-based differential methods of image velocity measurement, including two new methods, quantitative evaluations are reported based on synthetic images, and qualitative evaluations based on real images. A new method (*cluster method*) is characterized by the determination of the nearest point to all constraint lines, and the other (*Voss method*) by local approximation of the motion vector field. For six methods, solutions for algorithmic use are compiled, e.g. also iterative solutions for the Schunck and the Nagel constraint. The given quantitative evaluations may be used for characterizing situations where methods may be applied, and where not, and what parameters may be suggested.

## 1. Introduction

Results of image velocity measurement are often applied in modular, or integrative solutions for shape analysis or shape reconstruction, cp.[5, 9, 10]. This paper deals with point-based differential methods, cp. [4], for which it is assumed that spatial and time gradients of the image irradiance function E may be calculated. At first for some typical differential methods concrete formulae for algorithmic use are compiled. In some cases, such concrete specifications could not be found in literature, and they are given here for unique definition of the method as used for evaluation. Then, some general specifications for method evaluation are given and applied to the defined eight methods.

The Taylor expansion for the image irradiance $E = E(x, y, t)$ in its general form may be simplified if the approximation

$$\frac{dE}{dt} \approx \frac{\delta E}{\delta t}, \tag{1}$$

may be assumed for time gradients that may be calculated for a constant time interval $\delta t$ between two images of an image sequence. In the sense of this approximation, $\mathbf{u} = (u, v)^T = (\delta x, \delta y)^T \approx (dx, dy)^T$ denotes the *local displacement vector* (LDV) of a certain pixel position at times t+1 and t. A *local displacement vector field* (LDVF) is defined by LDV's in all, or at least several pixel positions of an image at time t. Unfortunately, the Taylor expansion is a non-linear equation for calculating vector's $\mathbf{u}(x,y)$. Difficulties with the non-linearity would increase with the application of additional solution conditions, as e.g. the smoothness constraint considered below. The "classical" Horn-Schunck constraint

$$\mathbf{u} \cdot \nabla E + E_t = 0, \tag{2}$$

is especially true for interior areas (i.e. no discontinuities as edges) of Lambertian surfaces.

## 2. Differential Methods for Optical Flow Computation

The Horn-Schunck constraint has some drawbacks as mentioned already by Horn and Schunck themselves, the *rotation problem* and the *uniqueness problem*. For $E_x \cdot E_y \neq 0$, the LDV **u** points to an unknown point on the constraint line. Unique solutions are possible for some very specific local functions E, cp. [12], so-called "gray value corners".

Certain additional constraints for the LDVF may be formulated and used for solving the uniqueness problem, or even uniqueness and rotation problem. The *simple smoothness constraint* of a "locally smooth LDVF" is formally defined by

$$\xi_{sm} = \left(\frac{\partial u}{\partial x}\right)^2 + \left(\frac{\partial u}{\partial y}\right)^2 + \left(\frac{\partial v}{\partial x}\right)^2 + \left(\frac{\partial v}{\partial y}\right)^2 \Rightarrow \text{minimum} . \tag{3}$$

Based on the Horn-Schunck constraint and the simple smoothness constraint, several methods may be suggested for computing LDVF's as methods (i)...(v) described below.

### 2.1. Algebraic Methods

Methods (i)...(iv) are based on the Horn-Schunck constraint and the simple smoothness constraint.

*(i) Pseudo-inverse method:* For n pixel positions (x1, y1), ..., (xn, yn) the simple smoothness constraint is assumed, i.e. the constraint lines of these n points should cross (nearly) in one point **u** = (u, v) defining the LDV. This point **u** may be calculated by solving

$$\left( E_{x1}, E_{y1}, E_{x2}, E_{y2}, \cdot, \cdot, \cdot, \cdot, E_{xn}, E_{yn} \right) \cdot \mathbf{u} = M \cdot \mathbf{u} = - \left( E_{t1}, E_{t2}, \cdot, \cdot, E_{tn} \right) = - E_t . \tag{4}$$

A solution $\mathbf{u} = - M' \cdot E_t$ is given by the pseudo-inverse $M' = (M^T M)^{-1} M^T$ of M, cp. [7].

*(ii) Method by Lucas and Kanade:* By Lucas and Kanade, certain refinements of the pseudo-inverse method as weighting of the point equations with respect to the distance of the point to the reference point by a Gaussian mask, were suggested, cp. [1].

*(iii) Cluster - method:* This new method is based on the assumption, that point **u** should be as close as possible to all the n constraint lines

$$r_i = u \cdot \cos \phi_i + v \cdot \sin \phi_i \quad \text{(Hessian normal form)} \tag{5}$$

of n pixel positions where the simple smoothness constraint may be applied. By LSE minimization, the solution $\mathbf{u} = (\xi, \eta)$ has to satisfy

$$S = \sum_i w_i \cdot ( \xi \cdot \cos \phi_i + \eta \cdot \sin \phi_i - r_i )^2 \Rightarrow \text{minimum}, \tag{6}$$

where the $w_i$'s are proportional to the inverse distance of the pixel position to the actual reference point. The solution $\mathbf{u} = (u, v)$ may be calculated by solving the equation system

$$\begin{pmatrix} \sum_i w_i \cdot \dfrac{E_x^2}{\sqrt{E_x^2 + E_y^2}} & \sum_i w_i \cdot \dfrac{E_x E_y}{\sqrt{E_x^2 + E_y^2}} \\[4mm] \sum_i w_i \cdot \dfrac{E_x E_y}{\sqrt{E_x^2 + E_y^2}} & \sum_i w_i \cdot \dfrac{E_y^2}{\sqrt{E_x^2 + E_y^2}} \end{pmatrix} \cdot \begin{pmatrix} u \\ v \end{pmatrix} = - \begin{pmatrix} \sum_i w_i \cdot \dfrac{E_x E_t}{\sqrt{E_x^2 + E_y^2}} \\[4mm] \sum_i w_i \cdot \dfrac{E_y E_t}{\sqrt{E_x^2 + E_y^2}} \end{pmatrix} . \tag{7}$$

*(iv) Method by Voss:* By Klaus Voss[1] it was suggested to use a local approximation (based on Taylor expansion of **u**) of the LDVF. Assuming the Horn-Schunck constraint and the

---

[1] personal communication

simple smoothness constraint in "small pixel environments" $U(p)$, with $p \in U(p)$, for point $p = (x, y)$ it is assumed that the LDV $\mathbf{u} = (u(p), v(p))$ satisfies

$$S = \sum_{q \in U(p)} w(q) \cdot ( E_x(q) \cdot u(q) + E_y(q) \cdot v(q) + E_t(q) )^2 \Rightarrow \text{ minimum.} \qquad (8)$$

Let

$$\overline{E_x E_y} = \sum_{q \in U(p)} w(q) \cdot E_x(q) \cdot E_y(q) . \qquad (9)$$

Following [16], the LDVF $\mathbf{u}$ may be approximated by a Taylor expansion with respect to points in $U(p)$. If only the first term $(u_{00}, v_{00})^T$ of this expansion is used as approximation of the desired solution $(u, v)$, then this leads to the equational system

$$\begin{pmatrix} \overline{E_x E_x} & \overline{E_x E_y} \\ \overline{E_x E_y} & \overline{E_y E_y} \end{pmatrix} \cdot \begin{pmatrix} u_{00} \\ v_{00} \end{pmatrix} = -\begin{pmatrix} \overline{E_t E_x} \\ \overline{E_t E_y} \end{pmatrix} . \qquad (10)$$

Assuming these simplification to the general Taylor expansion, this solution is formally nearly the same as the solution of the cluster - method. In the more general case of using also first order derivatives $(u_{10}, v_{10})^T$ and $(u_{01}, v_{01})^T$, the method leads to improved results but needs much computation time.

These methods (i)...(iv) could be represented in the evaluation typically just by one method for simplifying comparisons and figures.

### 2.2. Methods Based on Variation Calculus

Method (v) below may be called the *classical way* for measuring image velocity. Besides the Horn-Schunck constraint and the simple smoothness constraint as assumed for methods (i)...(v), also different constraints may be assumed for function E. Methods (v)... (viii) are based on the variation calculus, cp. [14]. Let $\xi_{2,b}$ be the error of the defining constraint with respect to $\mathbf{u}$, e.g. the Horn-Schunck constraint, and $\xi_{2,sm}$ the error of the smoothness constraint with respect to $\mathbf{u}$. Let $\alpha^2$ be a weight of the "smoothness strength". For solving the optimization problem

$$\xi^2 = \int \int (\alpha^2 \xi_{sm}^2 + \xi_b^2) \, dxdy \Rightarrow \text{ minimum}, \qquad (11)$$

in all relevant pixel positions $(x, y)$, certain Euler-Lagrange differential equations will be calculated as necessary condition that u determines such a minimum. In these equations, the Laplace operator $\nabla^2$ (it appears in the solution of the Schunck method), as first derivations $E_x$, $E_y$ or $E_t$ in the coefficients, may only be approximated for a discrete function $u(x,y)$, e.g. by

$$\nabla^2 u = 3 \cdot (\bar{u} - u), \qquad (12)$$

cp. [6]. This leads to an iterative solution. A solution of the system of Euler-Lagrange differential equations would be an alternative choice. Let $\mathbf{u}^{(i)} = (u^{(i)}, v^{(i)})^T$ be the solution in step i. For averaging and approximation of first and second derivations, common 3x3 ... 5x5 local operators were used.

*(v) Iterative method by Horn and Schunck:* In [6], the iterative solution for computing LDVF is based on $\xi_b^2 = (E_x u + E_y v + E_t)^2$ and $\xi_{sm}^2 = u_x^2 + u_y^2 + v_x^2 + v_y^2$. The iteration formulae are

$$u^{(i+1)} = \bar{u}^{(i)} - \frac{E_x \cdot ( E_x \bar{u}^{(i)} + E_y \bar{v}^{(i)} + E_t)}{\alpha^2 + E_x^2 + E_x^2} \quad \text{and}$$

$$v^{(i+1)} = \bar{v}^{(i)} - \frac{E_y \bullet (E_x \bar{u}^{(i)} + E_y \bar{v}^{(i)} + E_t)}{\alpha^2 + E_x^2 + E_x^2}. \tag{13}$$

*(vi) Iterative method for the Schunck constraint:* Schunck himself suggested in [15] the use of the following constraint,

$$\mathbf{u} \bullet \nabla E + E_t + E \bullet \nabla \mathbf{u} = 0. \tag{14}$$

By his opinion, the additional term should relax the rotation problem. No mathematical proof was given in [15] for this statement. For minimization of $\xi_b = E_x u + E_y v + E_t + Eu_x + Ev_y$ and applying the simple smoothness constraint, i.e. minimization of $\xi_{sm}^2 = u_x^2 + u_y^2 + v_x^2 + v_y^2$, no derivation of an iterative solution could be found in the literature. By applying the variation calculus, a necessary condition for a relative extreme of the function $\xi^2$ is given by the following Euler-Lagrange differential equations

$$E_{xx}u + Eu_{xx} + 2E_xu_x + E_xv_y + E_yv_x + E_{yx}v + Ev_{yx} + E_{tx} + \frac{\alpha^2}{E} \bullet \nabla^2 u = 0 \quad \text{and}$$

$$E_{yy}v + Ev_{yy} + 2E_yv_y + E_xu_y + E_yu_x + E_{xy}u + Eu_{xy} + E_{ty} + \frac{\alpha^2}{E} \bullet \nabla^2 v = 0. \tag{15}$$

The equation system

$$\left(\frac{\alpha^2}{E} - E_{xx}\right)u - E_{yx}v = A, \quad A = Eu_{xx} + 2E_xu_x + E_xv_y + E_yv_x + Ev_{yx} + E_{tx} + \frac{\alpha^2}{E} \bullet \bar{u},$$

$$-E_{xy}u + \left(\frac{\alpha^2}{E} - E_{yy}\right)v = B, \quad B = Ev_{yy} + 2E_yv_y + E_yu_x + E_xu_y + Eu_{xy} + E_{ty} + \frac{\alpha^2}{E} \bullet \bar{v} \tag{16}$$

leads to the iterative solution

$$u^{(i+1)} = \frac{A^{(i)} \bullet \left(\frac{\alpha^2}{E} - E_{yy}\right) + B^{(i)} \bullet E_{yx}}{\left(\frac{\alpha^2}{E} - E_{xx}\right)\left(\frac{\alpha^2}{E} - E_{yy}\right) - E_{xy}E_{yx}}, \quad v^{(i+1)} = \frac{B^{(i)} \bullet \left(\frac{\alpha^2}{E} - E_{xx}\right) + A^{(i)} \bullet E_{xy}}{\left(\frac{\alpha^2}{E} - E_{xx}\right)\left(\frac{\alpha^2}{E} - E_{yy}\right) - E_{xy}E_{yx}}. \tag{17}$$

*(vii) Iterative method for the Nagel constraint:* In [13], the Horn-Schunck constraint, which may be accepted in case of parallel projection, was modified by studying the impact of central projection on deriving a constraint from the Taylor expansion. Assume the camera-centered coordinate system in the 3D space, cp. [9]. For focal length b, point $P = (X, Y, Z)$ is mapped onto point $p = (x, y, b) = (bX/Z, bY/Z, b)$ in the picture plane $Z = b$. Let k be the unit vector in Z-direction, i.e. it holds that $k \bullet P = Z$. Assume a translation U of point P. In the *Nagel constraint*

$$\mathbf{u} \bullet \nabla E + E_t - 4E \bullet \left(\frac{k \bullet U}{k \bullet P} - \frac{P \bullet U}{P \bullet P}\right) = 0, \tag{18}$$

vectors P and U in 3D space are unknowns. Vector U is mapped onto vector $\mathbf{u} = (u, v, 0)^T$,

$$p = \frac{b}{k \bullet P} \bullet P \quad \text{and}$$

$$\mathbf{u} = \frac{b}{(k \bullet P)^2} \bullet k \times (U \times P) = \frac{b}{(k \bullet P)^2} \bullet ((k \bullet P) \bullet U - (k \bullet U) \bullet P). \tag{19}$$

Following [19], thus the Nagel constraint may be written as

$$E_xu + E_yv + E_t + 4E \bullet \frac{ux}{x^2 + y^2 + b^2} + 4E \bullet \frac{vy}{x^2 + y^2 + b^2} = Au + Bv + E_t = 0 \tag{20}$$

with

$$A = E_x + \frac{4E \bullet |x|}{x^2 + y^2 + b^2} \quad \text{and} \quad B = E_y + \frac{4E \bullet |y|}{x^2 + y^2 + b^2}. \tag{21}$$

For algorithmic use of this constraint, i.e. minimization of $\xi_b = Au + Bv + E_t$, and applying the simple smoothness constraint, i.e. minimization of $\xi_{sm}^2 = u_x^2 + u_y^2 + v_x^2 + v_y^2$, also here, a derivation of an iterative solution could not be found in the literature. By applying the variation calculus, the following iteration formula results,

$$\mathbf{u}^{(i+1)} = \bar{\mathbf{u}}^{(i)} - \frac{\begin{pmatrix} A \\ B \end{pmatrix} \cdot \bar{\mathbf{u}}^{(i)} + E_t}{\alpha^2 + A^2 + B^2} \cdot \begin{pmatrix} A \\ B \end{pmatrix}. \tag{22}$$

*(viii) Nagel-Enkelmann method:* The simple smoothness constraint as used so far may be refined in relation to local gradients of the irradiance function E. In [3, 11], the following *refined smoothness constraint* was suggested,

$$\xi_{sm}^2 = \frac{\alpha^2}{\text{trace}(F)} \cdot \text{trace}((\nabla^T \cdot \mathbf{u}^T)^T \cdot F \cdot (\nabla^T \cdot \mathbf{u}^T)) \Rightarrow \text{minimum}, \tag{23}$$

where in matrix

$$F = a^2 \cdot \begin{pmatrix} 1 & 0 \\ 0 & 1 \end{pmatrix} + b^2 \cdot \begin{pmatrix} E_y^2 & -E_x E_y \\ -E_x E_y & E_x^2 \end{pmatrix} + c^2 \cdot \begin{pmatrix} E_{yy}^2 + E_{xy}^2 & -E_{xy}(E_{yy} + E_{xx}) \\ -E_{xy}(E_{yy} + E_{xx}) & E_{xx}^2 + E_{xy}^2 \end{pmatrix} \tag{24}$$

the first summand corresponds to the simple smoothness constraint (with weight $a^2$), the second models smoothness orthogonal to the local gradient of irradiance function E (with weight $b^2$), and the third models smoothness orthogonal to the local main curvature of function E (with weight $c^2$). In this refined smoothness constraint, trace(F) is used for normalization. The simple smoothness constraint corresponds to $a^2 = 1$ and $b^2 = c^2 = 0$.

For an iterative solution $\mathbf{u}^{(i+1)} = \mathbf{u}^{(i)} + D_\mathbf{u}$ and $p = (x, y)$ let $E_1 = E(p - \mathbf{u}^{(i)}, t)$ and $E_2 = E(p, t + \delta t)$. The variation problem $\xi^2 \Rightarrow$ minimum, with

$$\xi^2 = \int \int \left[ (E_1 - E_2)^2 + \frac{\alpha^2}{\text{trace}(F)} \cdot \text{trace}((\nabla^T \cdot \mathbf{u}^T)^T \cdot F \cdot (\nabla^T \cdot \mathbf{u}^T)) \right] dxdy, \tag{25}$$

leads to the solution (m denotes an a-priori parameter)

$$\left( \begin{pmatrix} E_x^2 & E_x E_y \\ E_x E_y & E_y^2 \end{pmatrix} + \xi^2 \cdot \begin{pmatrix} E_{xx}^2 + E_{xy}^2 & E_{xy}(E_{yy} + E_{xx}) \\ E_{xy}(E_{yy} + E_{xx}) & E_{yy}^2 + E_{xy}^2 \end{pmatrix} + \alpha^2 \cdot m \cdot \begin{pmatrix} 1 & 0 \\ 0 & 1 \end{pmatrix} \right) \cdot D_\mathbf{u}$$

$$= -(\overline{E_2 - E_1}) \cdot \nabla E + \frac{\alpha^2}{\text{trace}(F)} \cdot \begin{pmatrix} \text{trace}(F \cdot \nabla^T \nabla u^{(i)}) \\ \text{trace}(F \cdot \nabla^T \nabla v^{(i)}) \end{pmatrix} \tag{26}$$

as proved in [3].

## 3. Evaluation and Comparison

In [8] a qualitative, theoretical analysis of error sources for point-based differential methods is given. In literature there are already some reports on quantitative evaluations of different approaches for motion measurement. For example, in [19] the absolute errors of the Horn-Schunck, the Schunck, and the Nagel constraint were computed for central projection of a sphere, i.e. these constraints are evaluated for a specific projection, but not certain methods for measuring image velocity. By these studies, some basic statements are possible: maximum errors appear at motion and image value edges, errors and their variance increase with motion speed, the Horn-Schunck constraint and the Nagel constraint lead to similar results, and the Schunck constraint increases the errors. For the first time it was studied in [1, 2, 18] how calculated LDVFs differ from the ideal LDVF.

### 3.1. Specifications for Evaluations

The synthetic images were selected for simulating translations and rotations of patterned (regular patterns, *wave images*) or textured (pseudo-random patterns, *texture images*) planes in 3D space. Wave images were generated for homogeneous motions of an object plane in XYZ-space, assumed to be parallel to the xy-image plane, with regular wave patterns in X- and/or Y-direction representing ideal waves of wave length $\lambda$. Texture images were generated also for object motions in this object plane. Each texture image contains a homogeneous textured background and at most one homogenous textured planar object region. The image resolution was 64x64, the focal length was assumed to be 100 pixel, and the distance of the object plane to the image plane was assumed to be 1000 pixel. Parallel lighting was assumed for the object plane. Translations in the object plane are specified by numbers of pixels (e.g., a 10 pixel translation in X-direction results in a 1 pixel translation in x-direction in the image plane), and rotations by degrees.

For evaluations on real objects, textured polyhedrons and cylinders and defined moves in front of a camera were used. In both the synthetic and the real cases, if textures were used, then these textures were generated by the autoreggressive method given in [17]. For the real objects, the textures were glued on the object surfaces. But, in this report quantitative analysis is restricted to synthetic images. For real images, only some qualitative evaluations were possible.

For the synthetic images, the correct LDVF $\mathbf{u}_m = (u_m, v_m)$ of the motion model could be used for comparison with the calculated image velocity $\mathbf{u}_c = (u_c, v_c)$. The normalized sum SRE of all relative errors in the measured LDVF is very sensitive to small translations but easy to interpret. In [1] it is suggested to use the normalized sum SAD of angular differences, i.e. of all arc-cos-values of angles between $(u_m, v_m, \delta t)$ and $(u_c, v_c, \delta t)$. This error measure SAD is not so sensitive to small translations, but has some other drawbacks (not a good evaluation of practical importance of a method, no reflection of errors at small or large speed etc.). Measure SAD may be at the right place if all absolute values of $\mathbf{u}_m$ are known to be quite small. In the following, the error measure SRE is used where image border points with some incomplete information were excluded from consideration in this measure.

At the algorithmic level, each method may be still realized in very different implementations, e.g. what operators are used for approximation of derivations. For Fig. 1 (above), a texture image was considered for different translations in the object plane (in X- or Y-direction). For each translation, the correct values of the LDVF $\mathbf{u}_m = (u_m, v_m)$ were used in the Horn-Schunck constraint, and the coefficients $E_x$, $E_y$ and $E_t$ were calculated with 3x3, 4x4 or 5x5 local operators. The absolute value of the resulting numeric expression was considered to be the error of the Horn-Schunck constraint. This method could also be used for the Taylor expansion up to the second order terms,

$$\frac{1}{2} E_{xx} u^2 + \frac{1}{2} E_{yy} v^2 + E_{xy} uv + (E_x + E_{xt})u + (E_y + E_{yt})v + (E_t + \frac{1}{2} E_{tt}) = 0, \tag{27}$$

and the errors for this case are shown in Fig. 1 (below). In general, the errors are not essentially reduced by using second order expansions, and especially for textured images also no systematic differences could be seen between 3x3-, 4x4- or 5x5-operators for calculating derivations. The reason should be that the discrete approximations of derivations are to rough anyway.

In the following experiments, first order expansions are used, and 3x3 local operators for calculating derivations. Only in the case of the Nagel-Enkelmann method, for some situations the results may be improved if 4x4 operators were used instead of 3x3.

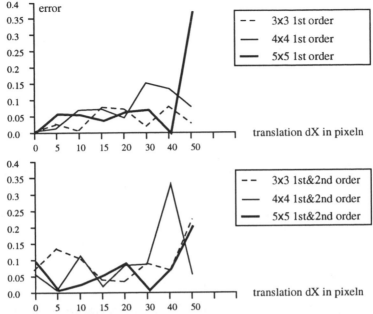

*Fig.1:* First and second order Taylor expansion with different local operators for a texture image.

For stopping the iteration processes, in general an approximation of the first derivation of the total differences between $\mathbf{u}^{(i)}$ and $\mathbf{u}^{(i+1)}$ was used in the implementations. The iteration stops if the absolute value of this derivation is below a given threshold, the *iteration threshold*, or after 64 iterations as upper limit (for the used 64x64 images). Proper start values would improve iterations, but $\mathbf{u}^{(0)} = (0, 0)^T$ was used here for method comparison. To improve the running time of the iterative procedures, an algebraic method as the pseudo-inverse method was also used to calculate start values. In image sequences, also the LDVF at time t may be used as initialization at time t+1. The parameters have influence on the quality of results and running time. The LDVF will change faster for small values of $\alpha^2$. But, for small values of $\alpha^2$ the errors of the LDVF will increase in general. So, as compromise the value of $\alpha^2$ may be increased during iterations. But, in practical experiments the benefit of such an approach of increasing $\alpha^2$ values was hard to recognize. In the performed experiments, the computing time was essentially increasing for $\alpha^2 > 100$, i.e. $\alpha^2 = 100$ may be considered as good compromise between acceptable computing time and good correctness (with the exception of the Schunck-method which needs very high $\alpha^2$ - values, say 8000, for best results). For the parameter m in the given solution of the Nagel-Enkelmann method, in [3, 11] the value m = 2/35 was given. In the performed experiments, this value proved to be to small. Best results with respect to low errors and low computing time were obtained for m = 1.5 ... 2.0.

For each computation of errors SRE, the values in all non-border image points were used, in general that means 62•62 = 3844 values, i.e. for each experiment, one image was used.

## 3.2. Synthetic Images

Here, (I) wave images, (II) textured images (just background) and (III) textured images with a circular textured object are considered for analyzing relations between minimum SRE errors of the different methods (very small iteration threshold, very large $\alpha^2$-value).

(I) In a certain interval of translations (e.g. 10...25 in object plane, i.e. 1...2.5 in image plane), the used 3x3 operators approximate the irradiance function quite well, and by the SRE-measure results of the differential methods are acceptable with the exception of the Schunck-method. So, all the other methods may be used for motion measurement for relatively small translations with respect to irradiance value patterns and used operator size. The Schunck-method leads to best results for larger translation distances (in the image plane greater than half of the operator size), but also these results are very inaccurate (SRE greater than 20%) such that they can not used practically. The results of the algebraic methods, as the pseudo-inverse, are not as good as Horn-Schunck, Nagel, or Nagel-Enkelmann method results, but may be fast calculated (the new method, called cluster-method, is suggested) and used as start values to speed-up the methods based on variation calculus.

In case of translations orthogonal to the image, i.e. in Z-direction, the Nagel-method and the Horn-Schunck method behave very similar. In general (also real images, complex motions) it holds that the value of the additional term introduced by Nagel into the Horn-Schunck constraint was typically close to zero in the experiments. In case of rotations of the object plane, the SRE measure of the Schunck-method typically leads to large values already for very small rotation angles, say 2 degrees. For the remaining methods, the SRE values for relatively small rotation angles seem to be acceptable, say below 7%.

In the case of textured or even real images, the errors increase in relation to these synthetic wave images. For different wave length, the algebraic methods and the Nagel-Enkelmann method were quite tolerant. In general, the behavior of the algebraic methods was slightly more worse than that of the Horn-Schunck, Nagel or Nagel-Enkelmann method. But, acceptable results of these three variation calculus based methods, which are called the *HSNE-methods* in the sequel, typically require a large number of iterations if no specific start values are used.

(II) In textured images, the irradiance function is discontinuous in comparison to the wave images. Thus errors in approximating derivations will increase. Again, the Schunck-method is out of question. For the Horn-Schunck and the Nagel-method, errors increase significantly in relation to the same translation of wave images, but the Nagel-Enkelmann method may lead to even improved results for certain textures. The similar behavior of Nagel and Horn-Schunck methods in general is experimentally verified here again. Both, as well as the algebraic method (but these at a higher SRE error level) react quite tolerant on the different texture structures. The Nagel-Enkelmann method, based on the adaptive smoothness constraint, leads to best results if the translation is orthogonal to edges in the irradiance function. The methods of Schunck and Nagel-Enkelmann react quite sensitively on the coarseness or value structure of the textures.

(III) Now, in the textured images a circular textured object was assumed in the object plane which is differently textured as the background. Then, the motion of the object (e.g. translation along Z-axis toward the image plane) and the motion of the textured object plane (e.g. translation along Z-axis away from image plane) were assumed to be directly inverse transforms in 3D space. This results in the LDVF into motion boundaries between the two inverse motions.

The pseudo-inverse method did lead to very good results (because of its robustness against discontinuities in the LDVF), and the Nagel-Enkelmann method, so far in general with best behavior of the HSNE-methods, did fail. The HSNE-methods have better accuracy as the algebraic methods for continuous LDVFs. But, by using the results of the pseudo-inverse method for the start values of the Nagel-Enkelmann method, this did lead to improved results of the pseudo-inverse method, and did reduce the computing time for the Nagel-Enkelmann method.

### 3.3. Real Images of 3D Objects

Quantitative evaluations of computer vision methods should always include studies for real images. For the evaluation of motion detection methods, a simple blocks world may be suggested. Between taking images, these textured polyhedrons or cylinders were moved on the table. Very small motions, say 1 mm, were realized. For these motions the results of the different methods were visualized (needle maps) and qualitatively compared. As for the synthetic images, the algebraic methods (all based on the Horn-Schunck assumption and using the simple smoothness constraint) did behave very similar. The Schunck method did not lead to any acceptable needle maps. The Horn-Schunck method and the Nagel method did lead to nearly the same results.

Vectors corresponding to a translation of some polyhedrons were best represented by the needle maps calculated with the Horn-Schunck method. The cluster method was still acceptable. Because of missing edges in textured surfaces of some moving polyhedron, the Nagel-Enkelmann method did fail. For translations of roughly textured polyhedrons the results of the Nagel-Enkelmann method did improve, but results by Horn-Schunck and cluster method still seemed to be better. Highlights on object surfaces did lead to local errors. Interreflections introduced by light surface patches increase the errors in general.

### 4. Summary

All the eight considered methods may detect only relatively small motions. The smoothness constraints solve the uniqueness problem, but lead to essential errors at pixel positions with abrupt changes in the LDVF. Motion orthogonal to object edges may be recognized by matching or optimization methods (regions or contours) as reported in [4], but not with point-based differential methods. In such regions, the LDVF is discontinuous, and the Taylor expansion approach fails with just a very few exceptions.

The introduction of the additional term of the Schunck constraint into the Horn-Schunck constraint did result in an increase of errors in nearly all experiments. The introduction of the additional term of the Nagel constraint into the Horn-Schunck constraint seems to be of theoretical interest only. Practically it makes no difference, and for non-synthetic images the values of P and U are also unknown. The improved smoothness constraint of the Nagel-Enkelmann method leads to better results in many cases in comparison to he Horn-Schunck method. The Nagel-Enkelmann method fails for some value structures in the irradiance function. An initialization of start values by an algebraic method may be suggested because of improving results, and reducing computing time. For real applications, such differential methods should be combined with (or integrated into) more complex methods for measuring image velocities.

### 5. References

[1]  J.L. Barron, D.J. Fleet and S.S. Beauchemin, "Performance of optical flow techniques", Report No. 299, Dept. of Computer Science, Univ. of Western Ontario, London, Ontario, July *1992*.

[2]   K. Daniilidis and H.-H. Nagel, "Analytical results on error sensitivity of motion estimation from two views", Image and Vision Computing 8 (*1990*), pp. *297-303*.

[3]   W. Enkelmann, "Investigations of multigrid algorithms for the estimation of optical flow fields in image sequences", CGVIP: Image understanding 43 (*1988*), pp. *150 - 177*.

[4]   D.J. Fleet, *Measurement of Image Velocity*, Kluwer, Boston *1992*.

[5]   R. M. Haralick, L. G. Shapiro, *Computer and Robot Vision*. Vol. II, Addison-Wesley, Reading *1993*.

[6]   B.K.P. Horn and B.G. Schunck, "Determining optical flow", Artificial Intelligence 17 (*1981*), pp. *185 - 203*.

[7]   B. Jähne, *Digitale Bildverarbeitung*, Springer, Berlin *1991*.

[8]   J.K. Kearny, W.B. Thompson and D.L. Boley, "Optical flow estimation: An error analysis of gradient-based methods with local optimization", IEEE Transact. PAMI 9 (*1987*), pp. *229 - 244*.

[9]   R. Klette and V. Rodehorst, "Algorithms for shape from shading, lighting direction and motion", Proceed. 5th Int. Conf. CAIP'93, Budapest, September *1993* (eds.: D. Chetverikov, W.G. Kropatsch), Springer, Lecture Notes in Computer Science 719, pp. *420 - 427*.

[10]  S. Maybank, *Theory of Reconstruction from Image Motion*, Springer, Berlin *1993*.

[11]  H.-H. Nagel and W. Enkelmann, "An investigation of smoothness constraints for the estimation of displacement vector fields from image sequences", IEEE Transact. PAMI 8 (*1986*), pp. *565 - 593*.

[12]  H.-H. Nagel, "On the estimation of optical flow: Relations between different approaches and some new results", Artificial Intelligence 33 (*1987*), pp. *299 - 324*.

[13]  H.-H. Nagel, "On a constraint equation for the estimation of displacement rates in image sequences", IEEE Transact. PAMI 11 (*1989*), pp. *13 - 30*.

[14]  F. Schlögl, "Randwertprobleme", in: Handbuch der Physik, Bd. I (Hrsg.: S. Flügge). Springer, Berlin *1956*, pp. *218 - 352*.

[15]  B.G. Schunck, "The motion constraint equation for optical flow", Proceed. ICPR, Montreal *1984*, pp. *20 - 22*.

[16]  K. Voss, "Differentialgeometrie und digitale Bildverarbeitung", Bild und Ton 43 (*1990*), pp. *165 - 170*.

[17]  K. Voss and H. Süsse, *Praktische Bildverarbeitung*, Hanser, München 1991.

[18]  A.M. Waxman and K.Y. Wohn, "Contour evolution, neighborhood, deformation, and global image flow: Planar surfaces in motion", Int. J. Robotics Research 4 (*1985*), pp. *95 - 108*.

[19]  D. Willick and Y.-H. Yang, "Experimental evaluation of motion constraint equations", CVGIP: Image Understanding 54 (*1992*), pp. *206 - 214*.

# APPROXIMATE CONVEXITY IN N-DIMENSIONS

ANDREAS HELD
*Shizuoka University*
*Graduate School of Electronic Science and Technology*
*3-5-1 Johoku*
*Hamamatsu, 432 Japan*

JIN JIA and KEIICHI ABE
*Shizuoka University, Dept. of Computer Science*
*3-5-1 Johoku*
*Hamamatsu, 432 Japan*

## ABSTRACT

A new measure which qualitatively expresses how much a given shape differs from its convex hull is proposed. Starting with a sound and intuitive definition of approximate convexity, this definition is first generalized to Euclidean $N$-space and then the general results are derived, using integral geometry. It is shown that in the most useful cases of two and three dimensional spaces, the general relation reduces to simple measurements on boundaries or surfaces, respectively. Further, how to transpose those results to discrete spaces is briefly outlined and optimal estimators for length measurements in two dimensions and surface measurements in three dimensions are given. In order to get an idea of the performance of the new measure, it is compared with several, previously proposed measures. It appears that the results obtained with the proposed approach are reasonable and because of its simplicity, the proposed measure might become a useful tool in many shape description or recognition systems.

## 1 Introduction

The concept of convexity plays an important role in various fields like computational geometry, computer graphics, image processing, etc. Convexity and its ramifications are well understood, thanks to its sound underpinnings from mathematics and geometry. Despite the mathematical and geometrical importance of convexity, convex sets are rarely encountered in nature. For many applications, particularly in image decomposition or recognition, it seems appropriate to relax the notion of convexity and to deal with sets that are almost convex or approximately convex. Such a notion of approximate convexity does not only allow to actively disregard effects of distortion and noise, but it also captures some perceptual notions about fuzziness of the appearance of shapes. Both of those points are important if we attempt to build a truly versatile vision system.

What we need for capturing this idea of approximate convexity is a measure that expresses how much a given shape differs from or resembles its convex hull. Ideally but not necessarily, such a measure should be obtained as a scalar in the range $[0 \ldots 1]$. In the literature not much work along those lines can be found. In the next section, we will mention three different approaches together with one approach as previously proposed by the authors. Next, we will attempt to give a complete theoretical treatment of approximate convexity in $n$-dimensional Euclidean space. We will show that it is possible to find a solution which is valid in Euclidean space of arbitrary dimensionality. Finally, we will mention some practical considerations on how to actually measure approximate convexity in discrete 2 or 3-dimensional spaces.

## 2 Convexity Measures

Scanning the literature, it is possible to find several papers that deal explicitly or implicitly with the problem of measuring approximate convexity. The first such approach is due to J. Sklansky [7] and is centered around the idea of *convex deficiency*. Sklansky actually defined two different measures: an area measure $S_a$ and a depth measure $S_d$. The area measure $S_a$ simply corresponds to the ratio of the area of the concavity to the area of the convex hull. The depth measure $S_d$ is given as the sum of weighted ratios of the depths of concavities to the width of the convex hull. Further work includes Stern's *polygonal entropy* [8] and Boxers's *Deviation from Convexity* [1], which, however, is subsumed by Sklansky's measure $S_d$, which can be viewed as a normalised version of Boxer's deviation measure.

A slightly different approach to the measurement of non-convexity was chosen by the authors in [4]. This work, which is the foundation for our present work, takes its ideas from geometrical probability. Unlike the other approaches which are defined over the family of polygons, our approach is defined using the language of set theory. Although this is not of practical importance, it allows us to obtain mathematically simple but strong results, which can be easily generalised to any dimensions.

In order to define approximate convexity, it is of advantage to start with a proper definition of convexity. There are several definitions possible, here we choose the following one:

**Definition 1** *A set of points $K$ is called convex if for each pair of points $A \in K$, $B \in K$ it is true that $AB \subset K$, where $AB$ is the line segment connecting $A$ with $B$.*

It can easily be seen that this definition is as such valid in Euclidean space of any dimensionality. Taking the above definition as a starting point, in the case of two dimensions, we defined approximate convexity as follows [4]:

**Definition 2** *The degree of approximate convexity of a set $X$ is defined to be the probability that an arbitrary line segment that intersects $X$ is convex, i.e., produces only one intersection.*

Again, this definition can be transposed to Euclidean spaces of arbitrary dimensionality without any changes. As we show in the next section, based on the above definition, it is possible to derive an equation that keeps its generality for $n$-dimensions, and that yields computationally simple results for the important cases of two and three dimensional spaces.

## 3 Derivation

### 3.1 Definitions

In the sequel, let us denote the set in question by $X$, and its convex hull is given as $C(X)$. Further we define the residue of $C(X)$ minus $X$

$$R(X) = C(X) \setminus X \tag{1}$$

that is, the set of concavities. Hence, $X \cup R(X) = C(X)$. Similarly we need the residue which can be defined using the boundaries of $C(X)$ and $R(X)$

$$Q(X) = B(C(X)) \cap B(R(X)) \tag{2}$$

where $B(X)$ denotes the boundary of the set $X$. In what follows, $Q(X)$ will sometimes be called the cover of $R(X)$, as it can be visualized as covering the hole created by the concavity. Note that if $X$ has a certain dimension $n$, then $Q(X)$ will have dimensionality $n - 1$.

In the next subsection we will try to obtain the most general result possible, based on the derivations in the Appendix. We can start by redefining approximate convexity in the more general setting:

**Definition 3** *The degree of approximate convexity of a set $X^n$ is defined to be the probability that the intersection of an arbitrary set $L^r$ ($r < n$) with $X^n$ is convex.*

where the superscript denotes the dimensionality of the set. We showed in [4] that the consideration of interactions between concavities introduces complications which make the problem almost intractable, although doing so does not change the result too much. Therefore, here as well, we will neglect any interactions between concavities and consider only the simple case.

According to the law of big numbers, we can obtain probabilities by observing and counting outcomes of experiments. In the case of Definition 3, this means, that we can count how many of the intersections of the probing set $L^r$ with the probed set $X^n$ are convex. However, as for instance the number of lines that intersect a given curve is infinite, we have to employ concepts from integral geometry, in particular the concept of a *measure* of a line or a hyper-plane. Therefore, instead of actually counting hyper-planes, we can work with the measures of those planes.

Instead of using the measure of the sets that give a convex intersection, it is actually easier to use the measure of all those sets $L^r$ whose intersection with $X$ is not convex (see Fig. 1). Let us denote the measure of all the sets $L^r$ that intersect $X$ by $m(L^r \mid L^r \cap C(X) \neq \emptyset)$. The measure of the sets $L^r$ that intersect $R(X)$ can then be written as $m(L^r \mid L^r \cap R(X) \neq \emptyset)$; clearly, all the non-convex intersections must be included in this measure. Actually, among all the sets $L^r$ intersecting $R(X)$, only those sets whose members are intersecting the associated cover of $R(X)$, namely $Q(X)$ are convex, hence the measure of the non-convex set is given by $m(L^r \mid L^r \cap R(X) \neq \emptyset) - m(L^r \mid L^r \cap Q(X) \neq \emptyset)$[1].

---

[1] As stated before, here we are neglecting the fact that all those sets $L^r$ which intersect more than one concavity are counted multiply. For an example of such a $L^r$ see line $l_4$ in Fig. 1

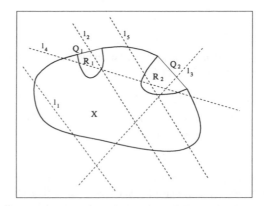

Figure 1: Random lines intersecting a set $X$: lines $l_1$, $l_2$, and $l_3$ are convex, whereas lines $l_4$ and $l_5$ are non-convex

The degree of approximate convexity can now easily be obtained by putting together all those fragments, namely

$$cv^{n[r]}(X) = 1 - \frac{m(L^r \mid L^r \cap R(X) \neq \emptyset) - m(L^r \mid L^r \cap Q(X) \neq \emptyset)}{m(L^r \mid L^r \cap C(X) \neq \emptyset)} \tag{3}$$

where $cv^{n[r]}$ denotes the approximate convexity of an $n$-dimensional set $X$ when using an $r$-dimensional set $L$ for probing. If we rephrase the above equation, then we have that the value for approximate convexity is one minus the probability that a set that intersects the $X$ is non-convex.

### 3.2   Approximate Convexity in N-Dimensions

As we have seen in Section 3.1, we need to calculate the measure for three different sets, which can actually be divided into two groups. To the first group there belong the convex hull of $X$, namely $C(X)$, and the concavities $R(X)$. Both sets are proper $n$-dimensional sets in $E^n$. The case is somewhat different for the third kind of set $Q(X)$, which is a boundary set, that is a $(n-1)$ dimensional set in $E^n$.

As already stated, we want to calculate the degree of approximate convexity for the set $X$ as given in Eq. 3. Some of the steps that lead to those results can be found in the appendix. The two measures $m(L^r \mid L^r \cap R(X) \neq \emptyset)$ and $m(L^r \mid L^r \cap C(X) \neq \emptyset)$ can readily be calculated from Eq. 24. For the calculation of $m(L^r \mid L^r \cap Q(X) \neq \emptyset)$, however, we have to employ Eq. 26, in connection with Eq. 24. Putting everything together, we can calculate $cv^{n[r]}(X)$ as follows

$$cv^{n[r]}(X) = 1 - \frac{W_r(R(X)) - \frac{\binom{n-1}{r-1}}{\binom{n}{r}} \frac{O_{r+1}}{O_r} W_{r-1}(Q(X))}{W_r(C(X))} \tag{4}$$

which is the most general solution possible. The notation of the above equation is according to the Appendix.

Intuitively, it appears best to use lines as the probing set $L^r$, that is, $r = 1$. Furthermore, in that case Eq. 4 can be given a particularly simple and concise form. Therefore, we obtain

$$cv^{n[1]} = 1 - \frac{F(R(X)) - 2V(Q(X))}{F(C(X))} \qquad (5)$$

where $F = nW_1$ is the area of the hyper-surface, and $V = W_0$ is the volume of the set in question.

## 4  Practical Considerations

The main problem that remains to be solved for an application of Eq. 5 in practice is how to estimate hyper-surface and volume of sets, particularly in 2D. For a digitized 2D shape we orient ourselves at the thorough work done by L. Dorst [2]. If we assume that the contour of a shape consists only of straight lines and circular arcs then Dorst gives several estimators of different complexity and accuracy. We will here only briefly describe one such estimator, which is simple to calculate and still yields remarkably accurate results.

The estimator we use here employs different weights for horizontal or vertical and for diagonal links, which for instance can be obtained from the chain-coded boundary. If we call the number of horizontal or vertical links as $n_e$ and the number of diagonal links as $n_o$, then the length estimator $L_K(n_e, n_o)$ that minimizes the expected error is given as [2]:

$$L_K(n_e, n_o) = 0.948 n_e + 1.343 n_o \qquad (6)$$

As can be seen from Eq. 5, we need to estimate three different entities: the perimeter of the convex hull of $X$, the perimeter of the concavities, and the length of the cover. The perimeter of the convex hull can readily be estimated from the boundary of the convex hull. For the perimeter of the concavities, however, we cannot simply use the perimeter of the set $C(X) \setminus X$, but we have to obtain the length of the boundary of pixels adjoining $Q(X)$ in $X$, in order to get a coherent estimator even for small concavities. Therefore we are using the set $(Q(X) \oplus D_1) \cap C(X)$, where $D_1$ is the diamond structuring element of size 1, or its boundary, for a proper estimate. The cover length is then obtained from the set $B((Q(X) \oplus D_1) \cap C(X)) \cap B(C(X))$. In practice, it is advisable to disregard small concavities of one pixel size. This can easily be done by a filtering of $Q(X)$.

Approximate convexity is a rather vague concept and thus is not easily analyzed. If we employ psycho-physical experiments for verifying concepts like approximate convexity then there remains always a doubt as to how far the subjects were influenced by the phrasing of the question and how strong individual differences are. As there exists no objective evaluation criterion it is finally left to each prospective applier of such a measure to select the measure which suits his or her needs best. Fig. 2 shows some shapes which were used for a comparative characterization. The values for Sklansky's two measures $S_a$ and $S_d$, Boxer's measure $pd$, and our degree of approximate convexity $cv$ are given in Table 1. For reference purposes we also included the commonly used measure of compactness $P^2/A$,

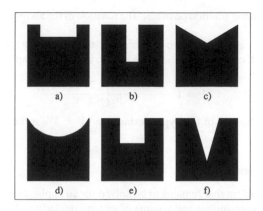

Figure 2: Shapes used for evaluation

| Figure | $S_a$ | $S_d$ | $pd$ | $cv$ | $P^2/A$ |
|--------|-------|-------|------|------|---------|
| a) | 0.88 | 0.8 | 8.5 | 0.9 | 21.89 |
| b) | 0.88 | 0.41 | 25.5 | 0.7 | 30.47 |
| c) | 0.85 | 0.7 | 13 | 0.96 | 20.47 |
| d) | 0.78 | 0.7 | 13 | 0.94 | 22.8 |
| e) | 0.84 | 0.6 | 17 | 0.8 | 27.2 |
| f) | 0.86 | 0.3 | 30 | 0.74 | 29.64 |

Table 1: Values for shapes in Fig. 2

where $P$ is the perimeter and $A$ is the area. Although Stern's polygonal entropy seems to yield results similar to ours, we still have no implementation available and therefore an accurate comparison is not possible.

The case in 3D is more complicated than the above calculation, because estimating the area of 3D digitized surfaces is more complicated. However, if we follow the thorough work by Mullikin and Verbeek [5], then it is as well possible to find a simple and sufficiently accurate estimate. Unlike the 2D case, in 3D three different situations have to be distinguished. This distinction is done according to the number of adjacent sides of a voxel that are exposed to the background. Neglecting the cases of lines or planes, only configurations of voxels with one, two, or three adjacent sides exposed to the background are possible. This roughly corresponds to voxels in planar areas, voxels in edges, and corner voxels. If we denote the number of those three types by $n_1$, $n_2$, and $n_3$, respectively, then the optimal estimator according to [5] is given as

$$F(n_1, n_2, n_3) = 0.894n_1 + 1.3409n_2 + 1.5879n_3 \qquad (7)$$

The actual derivation of the three entities used in Eq. 5 proceeds in an analogous way to the 2D case.

## 5 Conclusions

In this paper we proposed a new *degree of approximate convexity* and showed that this degree has a natural extension into Euclidean spaces of arbitrary dimensionality. We showed that the initial definition of approximate convexity, if some simplifying facts are assumed, resolves to simple measurements of hyper-surface and volume. Further, we outlined how such measurements could be carried out in discrete spaces of dimension two and three, that is, in spaces that are generally of interest. Due to its generality and its simplicity, we believe that our proposed degree of approximate convexity is a useful tool in many shape description tasks.

## Appendix

Here we will try to give a very simplified derivation of the equations used in Section 3. For a more complete treatment, the reader is referred to the books by Hadwiger [3] and Santaló [6].

Let us denote by $x = (x_1, x_2, \ldots, x_n)$ the coordinates of an $n$-dimensional space. The measure $m(X)$ of a set of points $X$ is defined as the integral over the set of a differential form $\omega = f(x_1, x_2, \ldots, x_n)dx_1 \wedge dx_2 \wedge \ldots \wedge dx_n$ (provided that integral exists in the Lebesgue sense), where the function $f(x_1, x_2, \ldots, x_n)$ is chosen so that the measure $m(X)$ is invariant under the group of motions in $n$-space.

A motion in Euclidean $n$-space is an affine transformation of $E^n$ onto itself such that distances are preserved. The motions form a subgroup $\mathcal{M}$ of the group of affine transformations, defined by

$$x' = Ax + B , \quad AA^t = I \tag{8}$$

where $I$ denotes the identity matrix of dimension $n$, and, therefore, $A$ is an orthogonal matrix.

Clearly, $A = (a_{ij})$ and $B = (b_i)$ are $n \times n$ and $n \times 1$ matrices respectively. Hence, if we set $A = (a_{ij})$, $B = (b_i)$, $A^{-1} = (\alpha_{ij})$, then we obtain

$$\omega_{ij} = \sum_{h=1}^{n} \alpha_{ih} da_{hj}$$

$$\omega_i = \sum_{h=1}^{n} \alpha_{ih} db_n \tag{9}$$

Consider a moving frame $(p; e_1, \ldots, e_n)$ composed of a point $p$ and $n$ independent unit vectors $e_i$. Using the relations $e_i \cdot e_j = \delta_{ij}$, $de_i \cdot e_j + e_i \cdot de_j = 0$, we have

$$\omega_i = dp \cdot e_i$$

$$\omega_{ji} = de_i \cdot e_j$$

$$\omega_{ji} + \omega_{ij} = 0 \tag{10}$$

Now, we want to define a density for $r$-dimensional planes $L^r$ in $E^n$, invariant under the group of motions. If we denote the group of motions in $E^n$ by $\mathcal{M}$, we can further denote by $\mathcal{H}^r$ the group of all motions that leave a fixed $L_0^r$ invariant. Clearly, there is a one-to-one correspondence between the $r$-planes of $E^n$ and the elements of the homogeneous space $\mathcal{M} \setminus \mathcal{H}^r$, which is the set of left cosets $g\mathcal{H}^r$, $g \in \mathcal{M}$. This means that each plane $L^r$ can be obtained from $L_0^r$ by some motion. Therefore, the problem of finding an invariant density for sets of $r$-planes is equivalent to that of finding an invariant density on $\mathcal{M} \setminus \mathcal{H}^r$.

It can be proved (see [6] for details) that

$$d(\mathcal{M} \setminus \mathcal{H}^k) = \omega_1 \wedge \ldots \wedge \omega_k \tag{11}$$

is invariant under $\mathcal{M}$, and up to a constant factor, is the unique form with this property.

In terms of our $r$-plane in $E^n$, the invariant density for $\mathcal{M} \setminus \mathcal{H}^r$ is therefore given by

$$dL^r = \bigwedge_{i,\beta} \omega_{i\beta} \wedge \bigwedge_{\alpha} \omega_\alpha \tag{12}$$

with $\alpha, \beta = r+1, \ldots, n$; $i = 1, \ldots, r$.

Let us next consider a $q$-dimensional plane $L_0^q$, fixed in $E^n$. Now, we are looking for the density of $r$-planes $L^r$ $(r > q)$ that contain $L_0^q$. With similar reasoning as above, the density for $r$-planes about $L_0^q$ becomes

$$dL^{r[q]} = \bigwedge_{h,i} \omega_{hi} \quad (h = r+1, \ldots, n; \ i = q+1, \ldots, r) \tag{13}$$

Let us now try to compute the measure of all $r$-planes $L^r$ about $L_0^q$. To this aim, we first consider the case where $q = 0$, that is, the group of rotations about the origin $p$ of the moving frame $(p; e_i)$. By rotation about $p$, the end points of the vectors $e_i$ move on the unit sphere $U_{n-1}$ centered at $p$. The scalar product $de_i \cdot e_j = \omega_{ji}$ is equal to the arc element on $U_{n-1}$ at the endpoint of $e_i$ in the direction of $e_j$, so that, denoting by $du_{n-1}$ the $(n-1)$-dimensional volume element of $U_{n-1}$ at the end point of $e_1$, we have

$$du_{n-1} = \omega_{21} \wedge \ldots \wedge \omega_{n1} \tag{14}$$

Therefore

$$du_{n-r} = \omega_{r+1,r} \wedge \ldots \wedge \omega_{n,r} \tag{15}$$

If $du_{r-1}$ denotes the volume element of the unit $(r-1)$-dimensional sphere in $L^{r[0]}$, then after some transformation, we obtain

$$dL^{r[0]} \wedge du_{r-1} = dL_{(n-1)}^{r-1[0]} \wedge du_{n-1} \tag{16}$$

By successive exterior multiplications and by integrating we get the total measure of $r$-planes of $E^n$ through a fixed point

$$\int dL^{r[0]} \wedge du_{r-1} \wedge \ldots \wedge du_1 = \int du_{n-1} \wedge \ldots \wedge du_{n-r} \tag{17}$$

Hence

$$m(G_{r,n-r}) = m(G_{n-r,r}) = \int_{G_{r,n-r}} dL^{r[0]} = \frac{O_{n-1}O_{n-2}\cdots O_{n-r}}{O_{r-1}O_{r-2}\cdots O_1 O_0} \tag{18}$$

where $O_i$ is the surface area of the $n$-dimensional unit sphere[2]

We have seen in Eq. 12, that $dL^r$ is given in terms of a point $p$ and $r$ orthonormal vectors $e_i$ contained in $L^r$. If we set $d\sigma_{n-r} = \omega_{r+1} \wedge \omega_{r+2} \wedge \ldots \wedge \omega_n$, then we get

$$dL^r = d\sigma_{n-r} \wedge dL^{r[0]} \tag{19}$$

such that $d\sigma_{n-r}$ is the volume element of $L^{n-r[0]}$ at $p$, as $\omega_{r+h} = dp \cdot e_{r+h}$ is the arc element of $L^{n-r[0]}$ at $p$ in direction $e_{r+h}$.

Let $K$ be a convex set and let $O$ be a fixed point in $E^n$. We consider all the $(n-r)$-dimensional planes $L^{n-r[O]}$ through $O$ and we let $K'^{m-r}$ be the orthogonal projection of $K$ onto $L^{n-r[o]}$. In other words, $K'^{m-r}$ denotes the convex set of all intersection points of $L^{n-r[o]}$ with the $r$-planes $L^r$ perpendicular to $L^{n-r[o]}$ through each point of $K$. Now, the mean value of the projected volumes $V(K'^{m-r})$ becomes

$$E(V(K'^{m-r})) = \frac{\int_{G_{n-r,r}} V(K'^{m-r}) dL^{r[O]}}{m(G_{n-r,r})} \tag{20}$$

The relation

$$I_r(K) = \int_{G_{n-r,r}} V(K'^{m-r}) dL^{r[O]} \tag{21}$$

is an important characteristic in integral geometry. $I_r(K)$ can be expressed in terms of the quermassintegrals $W_r(K)$ as introduced by Minkowski. We have

$$W_r(K) = \frac{(n-r)O_{r-1}\cdots O_0}{nO_{n-2}\cdots O_{n-r-1}} I_r(K) \tag{22}$$

In general, the following equalities hold for quermassintegrals

$$\begin{aligned} W_0 &= V \\ nW_1 &= F \\ nW_n &= O_{n-1} \end{aligned} \tag{23}$$

where $V$ is the volume, $F$ is the surface, and $O_{n-1}$ is the surface of the $n-1$-dimensional unit ball.

Integrating Eq. 19 and substituting Eq. 22 gives for the measure of the $r$-planes

$$\begin{aligned} m(L^r, L^r \cap K \neq \emptyset) &= \int_{L^r \cap K \neq \emptyset} dL^r = \int d\sigma^{n-r} \wedge dL^{r[0]} \\ &= \frac{nO_{n-2}\cdots O_{n-r-1}}{(n-r)O_{r-1}\cdots O_0} W_r(K) \end{aligned} \tag{24}$$

---

[2] The surface area of the $n$-dimensional unit sphere is given as $O_n = \frac{2\pi^{(n+1)/2}}{\Gamma(\frac{n+1}{2})}$.

Let $K^q$ be a convex body in the $q$-plane $L^q \subset E^n$. Further, let $W_r^{(q)}(K^q)$, $(r = 0, 1, \ldots, q)$ be the quermassintegrals of $K^q$ as a convex body of $L^q$. If we consider $K^q$ as a flattened convex body of $E^n$ $(n > q)$, the quermassintegrals $W_r^{(n)}(K^q)$ can be evaluated by considering first the quermassintegrals of the parallel convex body[3] $K_\rho{}^q$ and then taking the limit as $\rho \to 0$. The actual derivation and proof has been done by Hadwiger [3], here we will only give the results. As Hadwiger showed, if we assume that $q = n - 1$, then we have

$$W_r^{(n)}(K^{n-1}) = \frac{r}{n} \frac{O_{r+1}}{O_r} W_{r-1}^{(n-1)}(K^{n-1}) \tag{25}$$

Now, we can recursively apply Eq. 25 to obtain the quermassintegrals for any convex body $K^q$ of dimensionality $q$, such that $q < n$:

$$W_r^{(n)}(K^q) = \frac{\binom{q}{r-n+q}}{\binom{n}{r}} \frac{O_{r+1}}{O_{r-n+q+1}} W_{r-n+q}^{(q)}(K^q) \tag{26}$$

## Acknowledgements

This work was partially supported by a Grant-in-Aid for Priority Areas from the Ministry of Education, Science, and Culture, Japan (No. 05213204).

## 6 References

[1] L. Boxer, "Computing Deviations from Convexity in Polygons", *Pattern Recognition Letters*, vol. 14, pp. 163–167, 1993.

[2] L. Dorst and A.W.M. Smeulders, "Length Estimators for Digitized Contours", *Computer Vision, Graphics, and Image Processing*, vol. 40, pp. 311–333, 1987.

[3] H. Hadwiger, *Vorlesungen uber Inhalt, Oberflache und Isoperimetrie*, Springer, Berlin, 1957.

[4] A. Held and K. Abe, "On Approximate-Convexity", *Technical Report of IEICE*, vol. PRU92-53, November 1992, also to appear in *Pattern Recognition Letters*.

[5] J.C. Mullikin and P.W. Verbeek, "Surface Area Estimation of Digitized Planes", *Bioimaging*, vol. 1, no.1, pp. 6–16, 1993.

[6] L.A. Santaló, *Integral Geometry and Geometric Probability*, Addison-Wesley, Reading, 1976.

[7] J. Sklansky, "Measuring Concavity on a Rectangular Mosaic", *IEEE Trans. on Computers*, vol. C-21, no.12, pp. 1355–1364, 1972.

[8] H.I. Stern, "Polygonal Entropy: A Convexity Measure", *Pattern Recognition Letters*, vol. 10, pp. 229–235, 1989.

---

[3]The parallel body $K_\rho$ in the distance $\rho$ of a convex set $K$ is the union of all solid spheres of radius $\rho$, the centers of which are points of $K$.

# Quantitative Performance Evaluation of Thinning Algorithms in the presence of Noise

M. Y. Jaisimha, Robert M. Haralick and Dov Dori*

Dept. of Electrical Engineering,
University of Washington
Seattle, WA 98195
{jaisimha,haralick}@george.ee.washington.edu
*Faculty of Industrial Engineering and Management,
Technion, Israel Institute of Technology
Haifa 32000, Israel

## Abstract

Thinning algorithms are an important sub-component in the construction of OCR systems. In order to be able to make a choice of an appropriate thinning algorithm, it is important to be able to answer questions such as 1) How well does the thinning algorithm do relative to other algorithms under noise free-conditions for a given complexity of the input shape ? 2) How sensitive is the thinning algorithm to increasing complexity of the input shape ? 3) How sensitive is the thinning algorithm as the amount of noise present in the input image increases ? and so on. These questions must be answered in a precise fashion. In previous work, we introduced a methodology to quantitatively analyze the performance of thinning algorithms. In this paper we extend upon this methodology to answer these and other experimental questions of interest. We use a noise model that simulates the degradation introduced by the process of Xerographic copying and laser printing. We then design experiments that study how each of 16 popular thinning algorithms performs relative to the Blum ribbon gold standard and relative to itself as the amount of noise varies. We design statistical data analysis procedures for various performance comparisons. We present the results obtained from these comparisons and a discussion of their implications in this paper.

**Keywords:** Performance Evaluation, Thinning Algorithms.

# 1 Introduction

This paper presents a quantitative methodology for characterizing the performance of thinning algorithms. A large number of papers proposing thinning algorithms have been published in the literature. A comprehensive survey is given in [17]. A key issue in the performance evaluation of thinning algorithms is the choice of the "gold standard" or reference. The performance of the algorithm is quantified by studying how different the output of the algorithm is from the gold standard. Previous efforts to provide a quantitative performance measure have used a subjective "gold standard" provided by a "panel of experts." [18],[21]. One obvious limitation of this approach is the infeasibilty of conducting an exhaustive study/analysis of the performance over a wide range of operating conditions since the gold standard for each instance must be specified interactively by the expert. This is too expensive to do for large numbers of input images, leading to small sample sizes, which, in turn prevent us from being able to draw statistically significant conclusions from the data. In this investigation we propose to overcome the limitations of the expert approach in two ways. We first define an objective gold standard based on Blum ribbons, where the expected output of the ideal thinning algorithm is the spine of the ribbon. Since, one may argue that is not an appropriate gold standard, we propose an alternative method of comparison for the purposes of studying the noise sensitivity of the thinning algorithms. The alternative gold standard is the output of the thinning algorithm under noise free conditions. This is a reasonable choice, since any reasonable algorithm developer would proceed with the intent of producing a "perfect" output under noise free conditions. The performance of the thinning algorithm as a function of the amount of noise is studied relative to the output under noise-free conditions.

Since thinning forms an important component in many OCR systems, it is important to accurately estimate the performance of thinning algorithms. Also, all real-world document imagery is contaminated to a greater or lesser extent by random perturbations or noise. This noise influences the performance of OCR algorithms that have to operate on these images. It is important to choose a thinning algorithm that is relatively insensitive to noise or whose performance degrades relatively gracefully as the amount of noise in the input image increases. In addition, thinning algorithms may perform differently as the geometry of the input shapes change. It is therefore important to be able to choose thinning algorithms that are relatively insensitive to the geometry of the input shapes.

We first review the basic philosophy underlying quantitative performance characterization of algorithms in the following section. We then discuss briefly issues specific to the performance characterization of thinning algorithms in Section 3. Ribbons are an attractive model for the world of characters on which thinning algorithms operate. Blum ribbons are generated when a disk sweeps along a curve in two dimensions. We present the ideal world model for thinning based on Blum ribbons in Section 3.1.

Once an ideal world model for thinning has been introduced, the next task is to design a perturbation model that has a basis in reality. Kanungo et. al. [16] describe a degradation model that models the degradation of documents due to photocopying and printing. Since, printed/photocopied document images form a large fraction of the images input to a typical OCR system, we use this perturbation model in our investigation to introduce controlled perturbations in our input images and then study the performance of the thinning algorithms under noisy conditions. We briefly review the degradation model in Section 5. Next, we need to design an error criterion function that measures the deviation between the output of the thinning algorithm and the ideal expected results. The error criterion function is based on the Hausdorf distance and is described in Section 4. We present a brief review of the thinning algorithms evaluated in this paper in Section 7.3. The performance characterization experiments and the results obtained are described in Section 7. Finally, we present conclusions and further research directions in Section 8.

# 2   Performance Characterization and Evaluation

What does performance characterization of an algorithm entail ? Given a noise-free input the ideal algorithm would produce an ideal output. However, if the input image is contaminated by noise, the output of the algorithm too could deviate from the ideal output. Performance characterization is then defined as establishing the correspondence between the random perturbations and deviations on the input, and the random perturbations and deviations on the output. Sometimes (as is the case with thinning algorithms), the algorithms fail to produce the ideal output even under noise-free conditions. Given this, it would be useful to study in a controlled and quantitative manner how the output deviates from the ideal as the algorithm and image generation parameters are varied. This is referred to as Performance Characterization under the ideal case. Thus, it is obvious that in order to characterize or evaluate an algorithm or family of algorithms, one must first choose a world of ideal images to be input to the algorithm. Two choices present themselves at this stage - real or synthetic images. Quite often, we have to choose to use synthetic images that are based on real world images on which these algorithms operate. This is referred to as the Image Suitability criterion. The factors one has to consider in using synthetic imagery are the following: 1) The image generation can be controlled by a set of parameters and the algorithms can then be tested for sensitivity to changes in parameters or their combinations, 2) The random perturbations can be carefully controlled though much thought has to be given in choosing a random perturbation model that corresponds to reality, 3) We can generate a large number of representative images fairly easily by simply executing the image generation procedure under a variety of conditions, 4) We can analytically compute the output of the algorithm in the noise-free case.

Once a choice of input images has been made, we have to come up with a procedure of generating these images as specified by the image generation parameters. Since the number of parameters (and their values) that specify the population of input images may be fairly large, we can then use a Latin Square layout to span the space of input images. More formally, let $z_1 \cdots z_K$ be the parameters estimated from the images by the algorithm, let $w_1 \cdots w_M$ be the nuisance variables that provide for variation in the image and $y_1 \cdots y_J$ be the random perturbation parameters over which the performance is to be characterized. Given an image generation mechanism for the population of input images, one can analytically compute the ideal output of the algorithm under noise-free conditions. Alternatively, information of the ideal noise-free output may be available as part of the image generation process. In either case, once the ideal noise-free output is available, it is then important to define an error criterion, $e(\hat{z}_1, \cdots, \hat{z}_K, z_1, \cdots, z_K)$, that relates the estimates of the parameters under noisy conditions, $\hat{z}_1, \cdots, \hat{z}_K$ to the ideal estimates of the parameters $z_1, \cdots, z_K$.

The experimental component of performance evaluation consists of generating a representative set of input images according to an experimental protocol and then studying the variation of the error criterion function with respect to the values of the nuisance, perturbation and algorithm parameters. Further discussion of the philosophy and application of Performance Characterization and Evaluation to thinning algorithms is available in [13].

## 3 Performance Characterization of Thinning

Considering the difficulty of assigning ground truth to real world images (the "expert" approach), we use synthetic imagery for performance evaluation of thinning algorithms. Synthetic imagery permits us to carefully control the conditions under which the input images are generated and enables us to more accurately characterize or evaluate the performance of the algorithm. Once the choice of using synthetic imagery has been made, the next critical choice is the nature of the shapes to be used. It is important that the shapes under consideration should model the shapes that OCR algorithms operate on - namely characters (printed or handwritten) since that is one of the most popular application areas for thinning algorithms. It should be possible to analytically compute the skeleton of the input shape under noise-free conditions and the ideal output of the shape should fit commonly held notions of what a skeleton of a shape should be. Given all these criteria we choose ribbons (specifically Blum Ribbons) as our ideal world model for the world of thinning algorithms.

Blum ribbons are generated by sweeping a generating disk (whose radius might vary) along a two dimensional curve. The spine of the Blum ribbon (i.e. the two dimensional curve along which the generating disk is swept) is the "ideal" output of the thinning algorithm. The output of the thinning algorithm is compared against the spine to evaluate its performance. The generated ribbons have to fulfill certain shape constraints in order to serve as suitable inputs for the world of thinning algorithms. Given the fact that the skeleton captures global topological information, while many

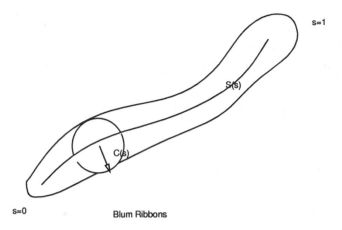

s=1

S(s)

C(s)

s=0

**Blum Ribbons**

Figure 1: Blum Ribbons

thinning algorithms in the literature are local in nature, we expect to find differences in performance to show up even when no noise is added to the ribbon images. When noise is added to the input images, we expect different thinning algorithms to respond differently as the amount of noise varies.

## 3.1   Blum Ribbons as an Ideal World Model

A ribbon can be qualitatively defined as the shape obtained when a shape referred to as the "generator" is swept along a curve. The generator can have any arbitrary shape and can make either a fixed or varying angle with the curve as the ribbon is generated. An ideal ribbon is constructed from a simple (one that does not self-intersect) bounded curvature arc which is the spine, specifying the medial axis of the ribbon and a cross-section function giving the ribbon's width at each point of the spine.

At any point of the the arc, the width of the ribbon is the length of the line segment defined by the intersection of the ribbon with a line perpendicular to the arc at the given arc point. The cross-section function has bounded first derivatives to keep the width from changing too fast. The width itself is also bounded from both sides, to prevent too narrow or too wide ribbons. Additionally, there is a relation between the maximum allowed curvature (minimum local radius) of the arc and the maximum allowed width of the ribbon, in order to prevent a case in which the combination of sharp curvature and large width at that point cause the ribbon to overlap itself. An ideal digital image is constructed from a scene of ribbons by tessellating the scene of ribbons into pixels.

In Blum's medial axis representation, called the "Blum ribbon," [6] the generator is a disk with its center on the spine. The Blum ribbon is illustrated in Figure 1. A constraint that fixes the angle that the bar makes with the spine gives rise to a "Brooks ribbon," while requiring that the bar make equal angles with the sides of the ribbon yields a "Brady ribbon." Rosenfeld [23] discusses these descriptions from the standpoint of both generation and recovery. He notes that Blum ribbons are both constructible and uniquely recoverable. These two features make this type of ribbon a natural choice for our purpose. In addition, Blum ribbons agree quite well with the "prairie fire" analogy for a skeleton. In this definition the skeleton of a shape is the set of quench points of a fire that is started simultaneously all around the boundary of the shape. It also agrees quite well with the concept of a medial axis. The medial axis of a shape is defined as the loci of the set of maximal inscribing disks into which a shape can be decomposed.

To avoid problems of instability when the slope of the spine approaches $90°$, and to enable self intersection of the spine, we adopt the following parametric description for the spine $S$.

$$S(s) = \begin{pmatrix} x(s) \\ y(s) \end{pmatrix}$$

The scalar function that describes the radius of the generating disc sweeping along $S$ is called the *contour function* and denoted by
$C(s)$.

The region contained by the Blum ribbon is defined as

$$R(s, \theta) = \{ \begin{pmatrix} x(s) \\ y(s) \end{pmatrix} \mid \begin{pmatrix} x(s) \\ y(s) \end{pmatrix} = S(s) + \lambda(\cos \theta \mathbf{t}(s) + \sin \theta \mathbf{n}(s)) \}$$

$$0 \le \theta \le 2\pi; \ 0 \le s \le 1; \ 0 \le \lambda \le C(s),$$

where

$$\mathbf{t}(s) = \dot{S}(s)/\|\dot{S}(s)\|$$

is a unit velocity vector tangent to the spine $S$, and

$$\mathbf{n}(s) = \begin{pmatrix} 0 & -1 \\ 1 & 0 \end{pmatrix} \mathbf{t}(s)$$

is a unit velocity vector normal to the spine. The boundary of the ribbon is given by its envelope, which is tangent to the curves $R(s, \theta)$ for every $s$. According to Faux [11], envelope points are characterized by

$$\frac{dS}{ds} \times \frac{dS}{d\theta} = 0$$

where $\times$ is the operator that associates to two vectors their determinant.

Ponce [22] uses this relation to derive the upper and lower contour functions $C_u$ and $C_l$ where

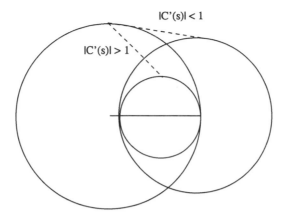

Figure 2: Slope Constraint on $C(s)$

$$C_u(s) = S(s) + C(s)(-C'(s)\mathbf{t} + \sqrt{1 - C'^2(s)}\mathbf{n})$$

and

$$C_l(s) = S(s) + C(s)(-C'(s)\mathbf{t} - \sqrt{1 - C'^2(s)}\mathbf{n})$$

This solution exists iff $|C'(s)| < 1$. The geometric interpretation of this result is that the radius of the disc must not change its value faster than the disc sweeps the spine S, for if this happens, the smaller disc will be entirely contained within the larger one, resulting in a discontinuity in the contours. In Figure 2 we illustrate this constraint.

In order for the ribbon to be useful in characterizing the performance of a thinning algorithm, the radius of the generator has to be small relative to the radius of curvature of the spine in order to prevent the ribbon from intersecting itself. We illustrate a situation in which self-intersection of the ribbon occurs in Figure 3.

Most (if not all) thinning algorithms would not produce the spine of the ribbon as their output in this case. In fact, given the nature of the shape it would be unreasonable for us to expect it to be so. Thus, we have to impose constraints that relate the value of the radius function to the radius of curvature of the spine in order to generate ribbons suitable for the characterization of thinning algorithm performance. We can see that if the maximum value of the radius function is less than the minimum value of the radius of curvature of the spine, this sort of situation can be avoided. Specifically, if

$$\rho_{max} < \frac{(\dot{x}^2 + \dot{y}^2)^{2/3}}{|\dot{x}\ddot{y} - \ddot{x}\dot{y}|}$$

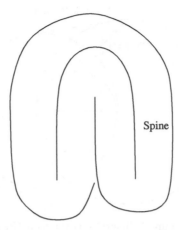

Figure 3: Curvature Constraint on $C(s)$

where $\rho_{max}$ is the maximum value of the radius function and the terms $\dot{x}$, $\dot{y}$, and $\ddot{x}$, $\ddot{y}$ are the first and second order derivatives of the $x$ and $y$ components of the spine. These components are expressed in parametric form parameterized by the arc length $s$. Then, $\rho_{max}$ is the minimum value of the radius of curvature of the spine. Once we assume a form for the functions $x(s)$, $y(s)$ and $C(s)$ (the contour function, which, in our case, is the radius function), the problem of generating a ribbon becomes one of choosing the parameters of the form such that the constraints mentioned above are satisfied. For the purposes of this study we assume that the spine polynomial components are of the form

$$x(s) = \sum_{i=0}^{i=3} a_i s^i$$

and

$$y(s) = \sum_{i=0}^{i=3} b_i s^i$$

Thus, the highest power of $s$ in either the $x$ or $y$ component is 3. Further, we assume that the radius function takes the form

$$C(s) = \sum_{i=0}^{i=2} c_i s^i$$

Generating a ribbon thus reduces to the problem of choosing the coefficients $a_i$, $b_i$ and $c_i$ to satisfy the constraints on the curvature of the spine relative to the value of the radius function. Two images are generated. One contains the discretized version of the spine and the other contains a discretized version of the ribbon. The ribbon is generated by stepping along the spine and rendering digital disks of a radius specified by the radius function.

# 4  Error Criterion Function

Thinning can have a variety of purposes such as the estimation of the analytic expression for the spine of the ribbon or the identification of the pixels through which the spine passes. In this discussion we take the purpose of thinning to be the identification of the pixels through which the spine passes. With this purpose in mind, the goal of any thinning algorithm is to erode all but the spine pixels. The measure of the algorithm's quality then inversely depends on the deviation of the resulting skeleton from the source spine. We use as the error criterion, a metric based on the Hausdorf distance [12]. Given two sets $A$ and $B$ and a distance metric $\rho$, the Hausdorf distance is given by

$$\max(\rho(A, B), \rho(B, A)) =$$

$$\max\{inf\{r | A \subseteq B \oplus disk(r)\}, \; inf \; \{r | B \subseteq A \oplus disk(r)\}\}$$

It has been shown in [12] that the Hausdorf distance has the properties of a metric (for example: that it satisfies the triangle inequality). Geometrically, we can visualize the Hausdorf distance in terms of the morphological operation of dilation. Given the sets $A$ and $B$, we first find the smallest disk such that $A$ dilated by the disk completely contains $B$. We next find the smallest disk such that $B$ dilated by the disk completely contains the set $A$. We then find the supremum of these two radii and assign the Hausdorf distance between the two sets to the larger of the two radii.

The Hausdorf distance provides a measure of the farthest distance between two sets. The Hausdorf distance measure does not have the disadvantage of other measures that compare two digital curves pointwise and computes average Euclidean distances between the two curves. These error measures are especially difficult to use in the context of thinning since the number of points in the output of the thinning algorithm is frequently different from that of the ideal skeleton.

In order to compute the Hausdorf distance between the two images - one the reference spine produced during the generation of the ribbon and the other the output of the thinning algorithm, we use the following procedure. Let

$A^c$ denote the complement of the image $A$ (obtained by inverting the image).

$d\{A\}$ denote the distance transform of image $A$ and $d\{A\}(r, c)$ denote the pixel in the distance transform image whose row coordinate is $r$ and column coordinate is $c$.

Let $\varrho_1$ be given by

$$\varrho_1 = \max_{(r,c) \in B} d\{A^c\}(r, c)$$

Let $\varrho_2$ be given by

$$\varrho_2 = \max_{(r,c) \in A} d\{B^c\}(r, c)$$

The Hausdorf distance $\varrho(A, B)$ between two images $A$ and $B$ is then given by

$$\varrho(A, B) = \max\{\varrho_1, \varrho_2\}$$

Computationally, the maximum value of the error criterion function is half the larger of the row or column size of the image.

The Hausdorf distance can also be alternately interpreted as the maximum of the shortest distances between every point on one curve and the second curve.

# 5   Noise Model

In this section we briefly review the noise model proposed in [16] that we use as a degradation model in our study. Degradations in bi-level document images consist of foreground pixels becoming background pixels and vice-versa. Briefly, the degradation model operates as follows:

- Compute the Euclidean distance transform $(d_F(r, c))$ ([12]) of each member of the foreground pixel set $I_F$ in the image $I(r, c)$ where $(r, c)$ are the row and column coordinates of the pixel. The set of foreground pixels is given by

$$I_F = \{(r, c) | I(r, c) = 1\}$$

- Compute the Euclidean distance transform $(d_B(r, c))$ of each member of the background pixel set $I_B$ in the image $I(r, c)$ where

$$I_B = \{(r, c) | I(r, c) = 0\}$$

- The probability of a pixel in $I_F$ at $(r, c)$ (denoted by $I_F(r, c)$) becoming a background pixel is given by $c_0 + \alpha_0 e^{-\alpha d_F^2(r,c)}$

- The probability of a pixel in $I_B$ at $(r, c)$ (denoted by $I_B(r, c)$) becoming a foreground pixel is given by $c_0 + \beta_0 e^{-\beta d_B^2(r,c)}$

- Correlation is then introduced in the degraded image by performing a binary morphological closing with a digital disk of diameter $K$.

The model is parameterized by $\alpha, \alpha_0, \beta, \beta_0$ and $c_0$. For the purposes of the experiment we hold the following values fixed : $c_0 = 0$, and $\alpha_0$ and $\beta_0$ take values from the set $\{0, 1\}$. We can see that values of $\alpha$ influence the amount of "thinning" of the foreground in the image that takes place while $\beta$ influences the "thickening" of the foreground. The higher the value of $\alpha$ (or $\beta$) the lower the amount of degradation introduced in the image.

# 6 Computational Procedure for Generating Ribbon Images

Once we assume a form for the functions $x(s)$, $y(s)$ and $C(s)$ (the radius function) the problem of generating a ribbon becomes one of choosing the parameters of the form such that the constraints mentioned above are satisfied (Section 3.1).

Generating a ribbon thus reduces to the problem of choosing the coefficients $a_i$, $b_i$ and $c_i$ to satisfy the constraints on the curvature of the spine relative to the value of the radius function. Two images are generated - one containing a discretized version of the spine and the other containing a discretized version of the ribbon.

The user supplies as input to the procedure the following inputs: Maximum degree of the spine polynomials for the $x$ and $y$ components, Maximum degree of the radius polynomial, Number of rows and columns in the image and the aspect value (this is the ratio of the length of the spine to the maximum value that the radius function can take).

The procedure for generating random ribbons has to pick coefficients for the radius and spine polynomials in such a way as to satisfy the given constraints. The procedure for picking coefficients is as follows -

1. Generate coefficients between -1.0 and +1.0 for each of the polynomial components of the spine. For the coefficient $a_i$ of the $x$ component we have

$$a_i \sim U(-1, 1)$$

where $U(-1, 1)$ is a uniformly distributed random variable on the interval $[-1, 1]$. The coefficients $b_i$ for the $y$ component are also given by

$$b_i \sim U(-1, 1)$$

2. Compute the minimum radius of curvature for the coefficients $a_i$ and $b_i$ for all values $t_j$ in the interval $(0, 1)$ where

$$t_j = j \times \delta, j = 1, \cdots, (1/\delta) - 1$$

and $\delta$ is the discretization increment in the value of the parameter $t$. Given the forms we have assumed for $x$ and $y$ we have

$$\dot{x}(t_j) = a_1 + (2 \times a_2 \times t_j) + (3 \times a_3 \times t_j^2)$$

and

$$\ddot{x}(t_j) = 2 \times a_2 + (6 \times a_3 \times t_j)$$

The values of $\dot{y}$ and $\ddot{y}$ are given in a similar fashion. These values are then used in the expression for the radius of curvature given in Section 3.1. The minimum value of the radius of curvature $r_{min}$ is given by

$$r_{min} = \min_{t_j} \left( \frac{(\dot{x}(t_j)^2 + \dot{y}(t_j)^2)^{3/2}}{|\dot{x}(t_j)\ddot{y}(t_j) - \ddot{x}(t_j)\dot{y}(t_j)|} \right)$$

3. Generate coefficients $c_i$ for the radius function using $c_0 \sim U(0.1, 1)$ and $c_i \sim U(0.0, 1.0)$ for $i > 0$ where $U(0, 1)$ is a uniformly distributed random variable in the interval $(0, 1)$. The coefficients are then scaled to satisfy the Blum ribbon generation condition given by $|C'(s)| < 1$

# 7 Experiments for Performance Characterization

In this section we describe in detail the experiments for performance characterization of the thinning algorithm under noisy conditions. We first describe the population of input images that we study in this investigation. The experiments for performance characterization are divided into two major sub-experiments - the first for performance characterization under noise-free conditions and the second for performance characterization under noisy conditions. For each of the sub-experiments we describe the various input images that we generate, the measurements that are made and the statistical data analysis procedures we employ.

## 7.1 Population of Input Images

We have to define populations of images based on the parameters used as input to the image generation process. We vary only the degree of $x$ and $y$ components of the spine polynomial and the degree of the radius function polynomial. We hold the image size fixed at $128 \times 128$ and the aspect value fixed at 5.0. Letting $d_x$ be the degree of the $x$ component of the spine polynomial, $d_y$ be the degree of the $y$ component of the spine polynomial and $d_r$ be the degree of the radius function we define six image populations by taking $d_x = 1$, $d_y = 0$, 1 or 2 and $d_r = 0$, 1 or 2. In Figure 4 we show an example Blum ribbon images with the spine overlaid on the ribbon.

## 7.2 Computation of the Error Criterion Function

As mentioned earlier, the Hausdorf distance takes values in the range 0 through to a maximum of half the larger of the row or column sizes of the input image. If the image is square (which is the case in our experiments), the maximum value of the Hausdorf distance is just half the number of rows (or columns) in the image. In order to normalize this quantity with respect to the size of the image, we divide the distance by half the number of rows in the image. Formally

$$\epsilon_1 = \varrho(S, T)/(N_{ROWS}/2)$$

where $\epsilon_1$ is the normalized error criterion function, $S$ is the spine of the Blum ribbon, $T$ is the output of the thinning algorithm and as before $\varrho(S, T)$ denotes the Hausdorf distance between the two.

## 7.3 Thinning Algorithms under Investigation

We evaluate sixteen thinning algorithms in this study. They are based on distance transform methods [4] (Algorithm 1), binary picture thinning by an iterative parallel two-subcycle operation [26] (Algorithm 2), two different distance transform based algorithms [27] (Algorithm 3 and 4), morphological thinning algorithm (does not give connected skeletons) [10] (Algorithm 5), Arcelli's Parallel Thinning algorithm (Algorithm 6) [1], Parallel thinning (Algorithm 7), Rutovitz Algorithm (Algorithm 8), [24] E.S. Deutsch's Algorithm (Algorithm 9) [9], Tamura's Algorithm (Algorithm 10) [28], Ma and Yudin Algorithm (Algorithm 11) [18], SPTA thinning (Algorithms 12 and 14) [20], Stefanelli and Rosenfeld (Algorithm 13) [25], Hilditch's algorithm (Algorithm 15) [14] and Zhang's algorithm [29].

## 7.4 Performance Characterization under Noise-Free Conditions

As we had mentioned in the Introduction, we expected differences in algorithm performance to show up even under noise-free conditions. Upon exhaustive experimentation we find that this is indeed the case. In this experiment we generate 250 images of each of the six combinations of the values of $d_y$ (the degree of the $y$ component of the spine polynomial) and $d_r$ (the degree of the radius function). Each of these images is then input to the sixteen thinning algorithms under investigation. We can compute the error criterion function relative to the Blum ribbon gold standard for each of the algorithm outputs. The following table (Table 1) presents the mean and the standard deviation for the Hausdorf component of the error criterion function.

To illustrate, the two entries in the upper left hand corner cell of Table 1 denote the mean (upper entry) and standard deviation (lower entry) of the normalized Hausdorf error criterion for Algorithm 1 where the input image population has $d_y = 1$ and $d_r = 0$.

### 7.4.1 Data Analysis and Results

From this table we can now design statistical data analysis procedures to draw conclusions about statistical hypotheses concerning the performance of thinning algorithms. We use a One-way Fixed effects ANOVA model ([19]) to analyze the effect the various factors have on the performance of the various thinning algorithms as quantified by the normalized Hausdorf distance. The null hypothesis for the first test is that the mean of the error criterion function is invariant with respect to the degree of the radius function $d_r$ when all other parameters are held fixed for each of the thinning algorithms.

The following table (Table 2) lists the P values obtained for each the 16 algorithms for $d_y = 2$ and $d_r$ takes values from the set $\{0, 1, 2\}$. The P value is the probability of the null hypothesis being true given the data.

Table 1: Mean and Standard Deviation of Error Criterion for Thinning Algorithms

|  | $d_y = 1$ $d_r = 0$ | $d_y = 1$ $d_r = 1$ | $d_y = 1$ $d_r = 2$ | $d_y = 2$ $d_r = 0$ | $d_y = 2$ $d_r = 1$ | $d_y = 2$ $d_r = 2$ |
|---|---|---|---|---|---|---|
| Alg. 1 | 0.127438 | 0.209000 | 0.235062 | 0.119062 | 0.171000 | 0.172750 |
|  | 0.083111 | 0.104458 | 0.103030 | 0.084966 | 0.107978 | 0.111849 |
| Alg. 2 | 0.031500 | 0.033625 | 0.029938 | 0.128625 | 0.167313 | 0.127562 |
|  | 0.062594 | 0.062486 | 0.012096 | 0.292012 | 0.327983 | 0.280542 |
| Alg. 3 | 0.168375 | 0.121750 | 0.104625 | 0.174437 | 0.137688 | 0.154375 |
|  | 0.181077 | 0.113416 | 0.073441 | 0.190659 | 0.149392 | 0.162911 |
| Alg. 4 | 0.039062 | 0.048188 | 0.045688 | 0.042000 | 0.054125 | 0.045125 |
|  | 0.029114 | 0.032770 | 0.029199 | 0.035944 | 0.046636 | 0.031326 |
| Alg. 5 | 0.092375 | 0.152688 | 0.172312 | 0.089313 | 0.139000 | 0.142625 |
|  | 0.059148 | 0.080675 | 0.082838 | 0.064361 | 0.089355 | 0.095460 |
| Alg. 6 | 0.030437 | 0.060875 | 0.037937 | 0.040750 | 0.061937 | 0.044250 |
|  | 0.011896 | 0.070751 | 0.023624 | 0.030896 | 0.066326 | 0.038413 |
| Alg. 7 | 0.042562 | 0.051250 | 0.047438 | 0.043625 | 0.060375 | 0.049063 |
|  | 0.028423 | 0.034307 | 0.029151 | 0.035276 | 0.049523 | 0.030905 |
| Alg. 8 | 0.060187 | 0.092625 | 0.102750 | 0.063625 | 0.098125 | 0.093938 |
|  | 0.047462 | 0.065896 | 0.071466 | 0.050322 | 0.073784 | 0.067398 |
| Alg. 9 | 0.025875 | 0.039500 | 0.033125 | 0.036312 | 0.049562 | 0.037125 |
|  | 0.009519 | 0.024899 | 0.015417 | 0.030306 | 0.045994 | 0.018960 |
| Alg. 10 | 0.043500 | 0.081188 | 0.053312 | 0.054063 | 0.079812 | 0.057375 |
|  | 0.014897 | 0.106856 | 0.031133 | 0.035731 | 0.072427 | 0.047293 |
| Alg. 11 | 0.058625 | 0.085000 | 0.065187 | 0.116062 | 0.165688 | 0.121437 |
|  | 0.063962 | 0.109691 | 0.065589 | 0.236628 | 0.274828 | 0.216384 |
| Alg. 12 | 0.090062 | 0.149750 | 0.164062 | 0.147250 | 0.218875 | 0.189750 |
|  | 0.059388 | 0.100390 | 0.086723 | 0.231767 | 0.258298 | 0.211009 |
| Alg. 13 | 0.076000 | 0.115813 | 0.113187 | 0.139375 | 0.201188 | 0.164625 |
|  | 0.065662 | 0.101022 | 0.077210 | 0.252716 | 0.284176 | 0.230433 |
| Alg. 14 | 0.093250 | 0.148438 | 0.166000 | 0.090563 | 0.138125 | 0.139125 |
|  | 0.058712 | 0.083860 | 0.085654 | 0.064679 | 0.091375 | 0.093591 |
| Alg. 15 | 0.086438 | 0.126438 | 0.142813 | 0.084250 | 0.126687 | 0.121750 |
|  | 0.065848 | 0.103932 | 0.103740 | 0.072383 | 0.103028 | 0.102470 |
| Alg. 16 | 0.044750 | 0.045063 | 0.040438 | 0.048000 | 0.056063 | 0.044750 |
|  | 0.055197 | 0.031370 | 0.023107 | 0.043215 | 0.048817 | 0.025809 |

Table 2: P values for 1-way ANOVA with $d_r$ as a factor

|        | P            |
|--------|--------------|
| Alg. 1 | 1.26104e-10  |
| Alg. 2 | 0.2431301    |
| Alg. 3 | 0.05138505   |
| Alg. 4 | 8.55982e-14  |
| Alg. 5 | 8.55982e-14  |
| Alg. 6 | 9.143812e-07 |
| Alg. 7 | 9.258232e-06 |
| Alg. 8 | 1.073249e-09 |
| Alg. 9 | 6.176975e-06 |
| Alg. 10 | 7.270414e-08 |
| Alg. 11 | 0.04479234   |
| Alg. 12 | 0.002871699  |
| Alg. 13 | 0.02609828   |
| Alg. 14 | 4.218959e-12 |
| Alg. 15 | 2.994326e-07 |
| Alg. 16 | 0.005863055  |

We can see that the null hypothesis (that the algorithms perform equally well at all three levels of $d_r$) can be rejected at a significance level of 0.05 for all but Algorithms 2 and 3. At a significance level of 0.005 we can accept the null hypothesis for Algorithms 11, 13 and 16 too. The higher the P value, the more sure we are that the null hypothesis is true.

Similarly we can now pose a null hypothesis relative to the value of $d_y$ when $d_r$ is held fixed. Alternatively, we can use a two-way fixed effects ANOVA model and explore interactions between the two factors $d_y$ and $d_r$ which are a measure of the complexity of the input shapes. We present the P values for each of the three factors ($d_y$ and $d_r$ and interactions) for each of the 16 algorithms in Table 3. The column $P_y$ contains the P values obtained for the factor $d_y$, $P_r$ is the P values obtained for factor $d_r$ and $P_{yr}$ is the P value obtained for the interaction of the two factors.

At a significance level of 5% we can reject the null hypothesis for the factor $d_y$ for all but Algorithms 4, 5 and 15. Algorithm 8 is clearly insensitive to the factor $d_y$ but is highly sensitive to the factor $d_r$. No algorithm is insensitive (i.e. has a P value high enough relative to the significance level to justify accepting the null hypothesis) to both factors. The only algorithms to show any significant interactions are Algorithms 1 and 5 (here the P value is lower than the significance level causing the null hypothesis to be rejected). An ideal algorithm (in terms of being invariant to the geometry or complexity of the input shape) would have have high P values for both factors and their interaction. Algorithm 1 is highly sensitive to the geometry

Table 3: P values for two way ANOVA with $d_y$ and $d_r$ as factors

|         | $P_y$      | $P_r$      | $P_{yr}$   |
|---------|------------|------------|------------|
| Alg. 1  | 0.000000   | 0.000000   | 0.000115   |
| Alg. 2  | 0.000000   | 0.203913   | 0.307711   |
| Alg. 3  | 0.002154   | 0.000003   | 0.055927   |
| Alg. 4  | 0.1221822  | 0.0000086  | 0.3334617  |
| Alg. 5  | 0.00017562 | 0.000000   | 0.02939563 |
| Alg. 6  | 0.0125985  | 0.00000    | 0.2762129  |
| Alg. 7  | 0.0310419  | 0.0000001  | 0.1317269  |
| Alg. 8  | 0.9898693  | 0.0000000  | 0.1570388  |
| Alg. 9  | 0.000000   | 0.000000   | 0.1051961  |
| Alg. 10 | 0.1520152  | 0.00000    | 0.2857383  |
| Alg. 11 | 0.000000   | 0.0018802  | 0.4886845  |
| Alg. 12 | 0.000000   | 0.000000   | 0.1317364  |
| Alg. 13 | 0.000000   | 0.0001265  | 0.3613095  |
| Alg. 14 | 0.00146164 | 0.000000   | 0.05356874 |
| Alg. 15 | 0.1118477  | 0.000000   | 0.1422055  |
| Alg. 16 | 0.0026202  | 0.0026202  | 0.2478276  |

of the input shape since the P value is lower than the significance level for all three factors. We see that the methodology is fairly powerful in that it permits us to study, compare and draw conclusions about the performance of thinning algorithms in a statistically sound fashion. We can also introduce noise in the input images and study how the various algorithms perform for different noise levels.

## 7.5  Performance Characterization under Noisy Conditions

In this experiment, we study the effects of noise on the performance of thinning algorithms. We saw earlier that the degradation model had two components - one that "thickened" the foreground and the other that "thinned" the foreground. We conduct three sub-experiments to study how each of these two kinds of degradation influence the performance of the thinning algorithms. In the first experiment, $\beta_0$ is set to 0, $\alpha_0 = 1$ and $\alpha$ takes values from the set $\{0.1, 0.2, 0.3, 0.4\}$. This has the effect of introducing only "thinning" degradation of the foreground. In the second experiment $\alpha_0 = 0$, $\beta_0 = 1$, and $\beta$ takes values from the set $\{0.1, 0.2, 0.3, 0.4\}$. This has the effect of introducing only "thickening" degradation of the foreground (in addition to adding disconnected foreground pixels in the background). In the third experiment, where we explore the effects of the interaction of the two types of noise on the performance, we set both $\alpha_0$ and $\beta_0$ to be 1 and $(\alpha, \beta)$ take the following sets of values $\{(0.1, 0.1), (0.2, 0.2), (0.3, 0.3), (0.4, 0.4)\}$.

Figure 4: Ribbon with $d_y = 2$, $d_r = 2$

Figure 5: Ribbon with noise

For each of these experiments we generate 250 ribbon and spine images for each of the six combinations of the values of $d_y$ and $d_r$. The noise-free images are first input to the sixteen thinning algorithms to produce thinning algorithm outputs. Noise is then added to the ribbon image and the noisy image is then input to the thinning algorithms. We then measure the Hausdorf distance between the output of the thinning algorithms under noisy conditions with respect to the Blum spine of the ribbon and the output of the thinning algorithm under noise-free conditions. In Figure 5 we show the ribbon of Figure 4 with noise added using the degradation model. Figure 6 shows the noise-free ribbon overlaid with the output of Algorithm 1 when the noise-free ribbon is used as input. Figure 7 shows the noisy ribbon overlaid with the output of Algorithm 1 when the noisy ribbon is used as input.

The three Hausdorf distances we can measure are between the noise-free output and the Blum spine, the noisy output and the Blum spine, and, the noisy output and the noise-free output. We can then use these measurements to characterize the performance of the algorithms. In order to illustrate the application of the methodology to the study of the noise sensitivity of the thinning algorithms we now present data analysis procedures and inferences for a sub-set of this rather large set of experiments.

### 7.5.1 Data Analysis and Results

In the first illustration we wish to answer two questions: 1) How do each of the algorithms perform in the presence of varying levels of "thickening" degradation ? 2) How does the choice of reference skeleton (Blum spine vs. noise-free algorithm output) influence the conclusions on algorithm performance ?

We use the one-way ANOVA model to analyze the results obtained. Table 4

Figure 6: Output of Algorithm 6 for noise-free ribbon

Figure 7: Output of Algorithm 6 for noisy ribbon

Table 4: P values for one way ANOVA with $\beta$ as a factor and Error criterion computed relative to the Blum spine

|         | P             |
|---------|---------------|
| Alg. 1  | 0.3793545     |
| Alg. 2  | 0.003407573   |
| Alg. 3  | 0.04085983    |
| Alg. 4  | 0.009665507   |
| Alg. 5  | 0.1717833     |
| Alg. 6  | 1.945989e-08  |
| Alg. 7  | 5.177823e-06  |
| Alg. 8  | 0.0192007     |
| Alg. 9  | 7.576562e-11  |
| Alg. 10 | 2.079902e-07  |
| Alg. 11 | 0.0008889729  |
| Alg. 12 | 0.0310366     |
| Alg. 13 | 0.0007498882  |
| Alg. 14 | 0.1761424     |
| Alg. 15 | 0.1821755     |
| Alg. 16 | 3.099773e-10  |

shows the P values for each of the 16 algorithms for $d_y = 2$ and $d_r = 2$ when the null hypothesis is that the mean values of the error criterion (Hausdorf distance measured with respect to the Blum spine) are equal for all four noise levels $\beta \in \{0.1, 0.2, 0.3, 0.4\}$. We can see that at a 5% significance level, we can accept the null hypothesis (that the algorithm performance does not greatly vary with noise level) for Algorithms 1, 5, 14 and 15. These algorithms exhibit performance that is relatively insensitive with respect to noise. The smaller the P value for an algorithm, the more variable the quality of the algorithm output is with respect to noise. Algorithm 9 and 16 are relatively sensitive with respect to the noise level for this image population.

Table 5 shows the P values for the same experiment when the error criterion is the Hausdorf distance is computed with reference to the noise-free output of the thinning algorithm. Clearly, the P values computed using this reference skeleton are different from those of Table 4. However, we find that at a 5% significance level we can accept the null hypothesis (of equal performance) for Algorithms 1, 5, 14 and 15 (as in the

Table 5: P values for one way ANOVA with $\beta$ as a factor and Error criterion computed relative to the noise-free thinning algorithm output

|          | P             |
|----------|---------------|
| Alg. 1   | 0.1591778     |
| Alg. 2   | 3.369093e-09  |
| Alg. 3   | 3.420988e-06  |
| Alg. 4   | 0.01325209    |
| Alg. 5   | 0.1493699     |
| Alg. 6   | 1.760964e-09  |
| Alg. 7   | 5.589675e-06  |
| Alg. 8   | 0.02541082    |
| Alg. 9   | 1.046807e-11  |
| Alg. 10  | 1.242838e-08  |
| Alg. 11  | 5.417444e-11  |
| Alg. 12  | 2.967738e-07  |
| Alg. 13  | 8.881784e-16  |
| Alg. 14  | 0.09592299    |
| Alg. 15  | 0.1007167     |
| Alg. 16  | 6.475187e-11  |

previous case). Once again, Algorithms 9 and 16 are the most sensitive to noise. Thus the inferences we can make from the data do not change based on what we use as the gold standard ! We have strong evidence to conclude that the Blum spine is a suitable gold standard for performance evaluation of thinning algorithms. Also, while the Blum spine may vary from what many algorithm developers may refer to as the ideal spine, the diagnostic efficiency (so to speak) of the Blum spine is high.

In the second sub-experiment we pose the null-hypothesis that all algorithms perform equally well for a particular image population $d_y = 1$ and $d_r = 0$, and $\alpha \in \{0.1, 0.2, 0.3, 0.4\}$ (when only "thinning" degradation is present). We once again use a One-way fixed effects ANOVA model where the factor being studied is the algorithm level. The null hypothesis can be restated as the mean value of the criterion function is the same for all algorithms. Table 6 shows the P values when the error is measured relative to the Blum spine. We can see that the null hypothesis (of all algorithms having the same level of performance) with respect to different noise levels is resoundingly rejected. Thus, we can conclude that algorithms do differ in performance. Once it is established that they do differ, we can postulate alternative null hypothesis with regard to the "ranking" of the various thinning algorithms and perform ANOVA analyses to verify these hypotheses.

In the third sub-experiment we study the performance of the the thinning algorithms when both varieties of degradation are present. The noise parameters we use

Table 6: P values for 1 way ANOVA with the Thinning Algorithm as a factor

|  | P |
|---|---|
| $\alpha = 0.1$ | 0.0 |
| $\alpha = 0.2$ | 0.0 |
| $\alpha = 0.3$ | 0.0 |
| $\alpha = 0.4$ | 0.0 |

Table 7: P values for 1 way ANOVA with both "thickening" and "thinning" noise

|  | P |
|---|---|
| Alg. 1 | 0.6720077 |
| Alg. 2 | 3.704943e-08 |
| Alg. 3 | 3.576554e-06 |
| Alg. 4 | 0.01325209 |
| Alg. 5 | 0.8422795 |
| Alg. 6 | 0.000000 |
| Alg. 7 | 1.171285e-13 |
| Alg. 8 | 0.03366714 |
| Alg. 9 | 0.00000 |
| Alg. 10 | 0.00000 |
| Alg. 11 | 7.796093e-09 |
| Alg. 12 | 0.01451161 |
| Alg. 13 | 3.29613e-08 |
| Alg. 14 | 0.8530453 |
| Alg. 15 | 0.7882021 |
| Alg. 16 | 0.000000 |

are $\alpha_0 = 1$, $beta_0 = 1$, $c_0 = 0.0$. The four noise levels we study have the following parameters - $\{\alpha = 0.1, \beta = 0.1\}$, $\{\alpha = 0.2, \beta = 0.2\}$, $\{\alpha = 0.3, \beta = 0.3\}$ and $\{\alpha = 0.4, \beta = 0.4\}$. We use a one-way ANOVA model to study the performance of the thinning algorithms for a particular image population $d_y = 2$ and $d_r = 1$. The null hypothesis under consideration is that the mean value of the error criterion function remains the same for different values of the noise level. The P values measured relative to the Blum ribbon are shown in Table 7. The null hypothesis can be accepted at a significance level of 5% for Algorithms 1, 5, 14 and 15. These results are identical to the conclusions drawn from Tables 4 and 5.

The ANOVA procedures described above show how invariant a given algorithm is with respect to a factor that affects its performance be it the amount of noise or the geometry of the input shape. Clearly, if an algorithm were to be invariant with respect to a factor while at the same time having a high mean error criterion value, that would be a wholly unsatisfactory state of affairs. In addition to invariance, we also need to study how the error criterion value varies over a population of input images. The graphs shown in Figure 8 and Figure 9 show the mean error criterion value versus noise level for each of the sixteen thinning algorithm for each of the six ribbon types. In this experiment, both "thinning" and "thickening" noise are present. So a noise level of 0.1 on the graph implies $\alpha = 0.1$ and $\beta = 0.1$. A noise level of 1.0 on the graph corresponds to the noise free case. The best algorithm at each noise level is the algorithm with the lowest mean error criterion function value. If one expected to operate in an environment where the noise level is expected to change from one level to another, our criterion for choosing an algorithm would be some combination of the P value over the various noise levels and the expected mean error criterion function value. At different noise levels we expect different algorithms to perform differently. Thus for example at high noise levels (0.1 and 0.2), Algorithm 10 performs better than all the other algorithms, but at a noise level of 0.4 Algorithm 9 becomes better than Algorithm 10. In the case of quadratic ribbons on the other hand, Algorithm 10 performs better than Algorithm 9 at a noise level of 0.4 but in the noise free case once again Algorithm 9 is the best. Thus in terms of having the lowest error criterion value, Algorithm 9 (Deutsch's algorithm) performs better than all the other algorithms for low levels of noise but at higher noise levels Algorithm 10 (Tamura's algorithm) is better.

# 8 Conclusions and Work in Progress

We have presented a methodology for the performance evaluation of thinning algorithms. We describe mechanisms to generate ideal world images based on the Blum ribbon model. We then used a degradation model that simulates perturbations found in real-life document images to introduce noise in the ideal world images. We designed experiments to study the performance of 16 thinning algorithms under different perturbations and image populations. We then use measurements of the Hausdorf error criterion function in conjunction with powerful statistical ANOVA tests to compare the performance of thinning algorithms. We are able to identify candidate algorithms whose performance is relatively insensitive to noise level and complexity of the input shape. For a given geometry we can also identify which algorithm is the best at a given noise level. Thus if we are provided with a description of the population of input images in terms of the geometry of the input shapes as well as the noise level, we can provide guidelines for the choice of an appropriate algorithm. We also show that the Blum ribbon permits us to make valid inferences about algorithm performance.

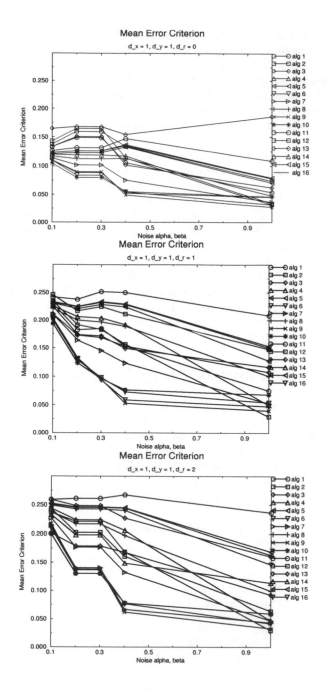

Figure 8: Mean error for linear ribbons

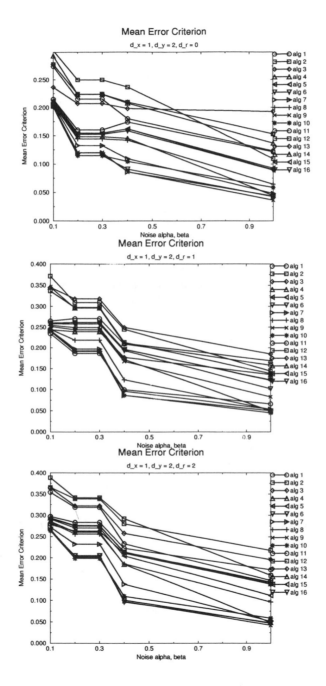

Figure 9: Mean error for quadratic ribbons

# References

[1] Arcelli, C., "Pattern Thinning by Contour Tracing," *Computer Graphics and Image Processing,* Vol. 17, 1981, pp. 130–44.

[2] Arcelli, C., L.P. Cordella, and S. Levialdi, "From Local Maxima to Connected Skeletons," *IEEE Transactions on Pattern Analysis and Machine Intelligence,* Vol. 3, 1981, pp. 134–43.

[3] Arcelli, C., and G. Sanniti di Baja, "A Width- Independent Fast Thinning Algorithm," *IEEE Transactions on Pattern Analysis and Machine Intelligence,* Vol. 7, 1985, pp. 463–74.

[4] Arcelli, C., and G. Sanniti di Baja, "A Width- Independent Fast Thinning Algorithm," *IEEE Transactions on Pattern Analysis and Machine Intelligence,* Vol. 7, 1989, pp. 463–74.

[5] Blum, H., "A Transformation for Extracting New Descriptors of Shape," in *Models for the Perception of Speech and Visual Form,* (W. Wathen-Dunn, Ed.), MIT Press, Cambridge, Mass., 1967, pp. 362–80.

[6] Blum, H., and R.N. Nagel, "Shape Description Unisg Weighted Symmetric Axis Features," *Pattern Recognition* 10, 1978, pp. 167–80.

[7] Brooks, A., Symbolic Reasoning among 3-D Models and 2-D Images, *Artificial Intelligence,* Vol. 17, 1981, pp. 185-348.

[8] Brady, J.M., and H. Asada, *Smoothed Local Symmetries and Their Implementation,* MIT Artificial Intelligence Laboratory Memo 757, Feb. 1984.

[9] Deutsch, E. S., "Preprocessing for character recognition," *Proc. IEE NPL Conference on Pattern Recognition,* Teddington, 1968, pp. 827-837.

[10] Giardina, C. R., and Dougherty E., "Morphological Methods in Image and Signal Processing," Prentice-Hall, 1988.

[11] Faux, I.D., and M.J. Pratt, *Computational Geometry for Design and Manufacture,* Ellis-Horwood, Chichester, UK, 1979.

[12] Haralick, R. M., and Shapiro, L. G., *Computer and Robot Vision,* Addison-Wesley Inc. 1992.

[13] Haralick, R. M., "Performance Characterization in Image Analysis - Thinning, a case in point", *Pattern Recognition Letters,* Vol. 13, 1992, pp. 5-12.

[14] Hilditch, C. J., "Linear skeletons from square cupboards," *Machine Intelligence Vol. 4,* American Elsevier Inc., New York, 1969, pp. 403-420.

[15] Jaisimha, M. Y., Haralick, R. M., and Dori, Dov M., "A Methodology for the Quantitative Performance Characterization of Thinning Algorithms," *Proc. Second International Conference on Document Analysis and Recognition*, October 1993, Tsukuba City, Japan.

[16] Kanungo, T., Haralick, R. M., and Phillips, I. T., "Global and Local document degradation models," *Proc. Second International Conference on Document Analysis and Recognition*, October 1993, Tsukuba City, Japan.

[17] Lam, L., S. -W. Lee, and C. Y. Suen, "Thinning Methodologies, a Comprehensive Study," *IEEE Transactions on Pattern Analysis and Machine Intelligence*, Vol. 14 No. 9, 1992, pp. 869–85.

[18] Lee, L. Lam and C. Y. Suen, "Performance Evaluation of Skeletonization Algorithms for Document Image Processing," *Proc. IAPR First Int'l Conf. on Document Analysis and Recognition*, Saint Malo, France, October 1991, Vol. 1, pp. 260–71.

[19] Lindman, Harold R., *Analysis of Variance in Experimental Design*, Springer-Verlag., 1992

[20] Naccache, N. J., and Shinghal, R., "SPTA: a proposed algorithm for thinning binary patterns," *IEEE Transactions of Systems Man and Cybernetics*, Vol. 14, No. 3, 1984, pp. 409-418.

[21] Plamondon, R., Bourdeau, M., Chouinard, C., and Suen, C. Y., "Validation of Preprocessing Algorithms: A Methodology and its Application to the Design of a Thinning Algorithm for Handwritten Characters," *Proc. Second International Conference on Document Analysis and Recognition*, October 1993, Tsukuba City, Japan.

[22] Ponce, J., On Characterizing Ribbons and Finding Skewed Symmetries, *Computer Vision, Graphics, and Image Processing*, Vol. 52. 1990, pp. 328–40.

[23] Rosenfeld, A., Axial Representations of Shape, *Computer Vision, Graphics, and Image Processing*, Vol. 33. 1986, pp. 156–73.

[24] Rutovitz, A., "Pattern Recognition," *Journal of Royal Statistical Society*, Vol. 129, Series A, 1966, pp. 504-530.

[25] Stefanelli, R., and Rosenfeld, A., "Some parallel thinning algorithms for digital pictures," *Journal of the ACM*, Vol. 18, No. 2, 1971, pp. 255-264.

[26] Suzuki, S., and K. Abe, "Binary Picture Thinning by an Iterative Parallel Two-subcycle Operation," *Pattern Recognition*, Vol. 20, 1987, pp. 297–307.

[27] Suzuki, S., and K. Abe, "Sequential Thinning of Binary Pictures using Distance Transformation," *Proceedings of the 8th International Conference on Pattern Recognition*, Paris, 1986, pp. 289-292

[28] Tamura, H., "A comparison of line thinning algorithms from digital geometry viewpoint," *Proceedings of the 8th International Conference on Pattern Recognition*, Paris, 1986, pp. 289-292.

[29] Zhang, T. Y. and Suen, C. Y., "A fast parallel algorithm for thinning digital patterns," *Communications of the ACM*, Vol. 27, No. 3, 1984, pp. 847-851.

# Tracking with Adaptive Adjacency Graphs

PIOTR JASIOBEDZKI

*Dept. of Computer Science, University of Toronto*
*Canada M5S 1A4*
*email: piotr@vis.toronto.edu*

## ABSTRACT

A new model of an Adaptive Adjacency Graph (AAG) for representing a 2D image or a 2D view of a 3D scene is introduced. The model makes use of an image representation similar in form to a Region Adjacency Graph. The Adaptive Adjacency Graph, as opposed to Region Adjacency Graph, is an active representation of the image. The AAG can adapt to the image or track features and maintain the topology of the graph. Adaptability of the AAG is achieved by incorporating active contours ("snakes") in the graph and linking them to form a network. Regions, defined by active contours, deform according to image data, internal energy of bounding contours and interactions with other connected contours. A separate process monitors changes in shape and size of regions and detects visual events. Such events can be used to trigger modification of the graph topology. Methods for creating the AAGs are discussed and results obtained for tracking with the AAG are presented.

## 1. Introduction

Segmented 2D images or 2D views of 3D scenes are represented in forms that contain detected features or objects, their properties, their locations in the image and some relationship (for example, adjacency) between them. Region Adjacency Graphs (RAG) have been used for this purpose [2]. The RAG is a rigid form of image representation, i.e., features in the image are detected once, their properties are measured and corresponding relationships are established. Further grouping or recognition involves operations on the RAG without referring to the original or new images.

The Adaptive Adjacency Graph (AAG) is an active representation of the image. The AAG combines the ability to represent features detected in an image, their properties and topology, with the ability of active contours to adapt to image data. Active contours ("snakes") [12] can adapt themselves to image features while maintaining their smoothness. Active contours, together with some high level user interface, have been used for finding salient contours in images, tracking moving contours and stereo matching. The AAGs can adapt to the image or track features and maintain the topology of the graph. Regions defined by the active contours can change their size, their shape and they can move in the image. If an Adaptive Adjacency Graph detected in one image is placed on another image that is slightly out of registration, then the graph will "pull" itself into place.

This paper presents results of tracking regions and their topology in sequences of images obtained from a mobile robot. The AAG tracks regions detected in the first image and maintains correspondence between the initial representation and new images. During this time recognition and / or close inspection of regions using other sensors is carried out.

## 2. Region Adjacency Graphs

Region Adjacency Graphs (RAG) are often used to represent an image during segmentation or recognition [2]. In the simplest case a RAG consists of vertices representing regions and links representing their adjacency. Region vertices are additionally described by vectors of properties derived from the original image (intensity, colour components, texture, etc.) and geometrical properties of regions (shape, size, geometrical moments). Regions in the graph contain some representation of their spatial extent in form of a bounding contour, a pixel mask or a blob (grouping of pixels obtained by filling in the bounding contour). An extension of the standard graph is a Dual Region Adjacency Graph (DRAG). The DRAG, in addition to regions, contains representations of boundaries between adjacent regions. The boundaries are stored as curves and the graph contains information on their connectivity at nodes. Each of the graph components (region, curve and node) may be assigned properties measured from the original image, geometrical properties and properties derived from the adjacent components. For example, curves may be described by a similarity measure of adjacent regions, nodes can be described by a collinearity measure of connected curves.

Standard operations on adjacency graphs include modifications of the graph topology and matching the graph with another graph representing a model of an object. Modifications of the graph include region merging by removing the redundant boundaries and merging similar adjacent regions or splitting the region according to some homogeneity criterion.

## 3. Active Contour Models

### 3.1. Single active contours and shape models

Active contours ("snakes") proposed by Kass *et al.* [12] possess the ability to adapt themselves to image features while maintaining their smoothness and rigidity. Different versions and implementations of active contours exist [1,6,19], and have been used for finding salient contours in images, tracking moving contours and stereo matching.

Snakes are attracted to contrasting features in images. Depending on the formulation of image forces, they can be attracted to dark (bright) lines or edges of high contrast. Essentially, any image preprocessing technique can be used to create a potential force image with lines that snakes can be attracted to. In this way, it is possible to generate active contours that are attracted to boundaries between regions of different texture, colour or combination of various image properties. Image forces are spatially limited and are active only in a local "zone of influence". The contour must be initially placed near an image feature of interest to avoid becoming locked in local minima, especially when operating on noisy images. The desired effects of snake dynamics are achieved by selecting the relative weights of physical parameters controlling the snake.

Terzopoulos [18] applied a Langrangian model to a snake with distributed mass. Such a snake would move until its kinetic energy was dissipated. A Kalman filter was used to maintain the initial shape and motion of the snake in the absence of reliable image data or in the presence of noise. Front propagation between solid/liquid interfaces has been used to reconstruct the shape of irregular objects with protrusions [15].

The interface was modelled as a closed, non−intersecting, surface flowing along its gradient field with speed depending on the curvature.

Etoh [8] used active contours on clustered multi−band images. The original colour image was clustered in a feature space and a new image representing clusters was created. The mixture density distributions in sub−regions on both sides of the contour were used to create new forces. The forces moved the contour to the position maximising a log−likelihood function. Parametrized templates of eye and mouth regions were proposed in [20]. The templates, which took the form of several second order polynomials, adapted to image data by changing their parameter values so as to minimise the total template energy (due to image and internal potentials). The distribution of labelled points along the object boundary was used to create Active Shape Models (ASM) [5]. The ASM captured the statistical variability of object shape present in a training data set. The deformation modes, automatically learned from the data, were used to guide adjustment (translation, rotation, scaling and deformation) of the model to a new image.

### 3.2. Multiple interacting active contours

Interactions between multiple active contours or changes of contour connectivity have received less attention so far. Distribution of strain energy along a contour placed around a cell undergoing mitosis (division) was used to detect breaking conditions [16]. The expansion forces of two separated cells increased the contour strain energy until the maximum elasticity of the contour was reached and the contour broke into two parts. The resulting open contours were rejoined into two separate closed curves outlining each of the new cells.

Zucker [21] proposed a description of an image in the form of a discrete tangent field. The tangent field was used to generate a covering of curves in the image by a set of snakes of unit length. The snakes moved according to image forces, their inner energy and attracting forces amongst nearby snakes. The attracting inter−spline forces operated at small distances and caused adjacent splines to overlap. The splines were allowed to grow and to link into larger snakes; eventually creating a full covering of global curves.

Multiple active contours were also used for finding skeletons (Medial Axis Transform) of binary objects [13]. First, a distance transform of a binary image was calculated. The snakes were initiated at object boundaries with their ends attached to high curvature points. The distance transform image provided forces that caused the snakes to migrate into the object while their end points remained attached. The snakes originating from adjacent or opposite sides eventually met along lines that corresponded to the skeleton. Jasiobedzki used connected networks of snakes to represent vascular trees in retinal images [9,10]. This deformable representation was used to register with other images of the same subject.

### 3.3. Adaptive meshes

Adaptive meshes have been used for image sampling and reconstruction [17]. Adaptive meshes are constructed of nodal masses connected by adjustable springs and consist of regular triangular or rectangular elements. Nodes observe interesting image properties and the stiffness of springs depend on observation function values. For example, in the case of grey level images, the observation function may assign high values to high contrast regions. As the stiffness of springs connected to a node increases for high function values, the nodes tend to group close to edges. This feature was used for irregular sampling and reconstructing grey level and 3D images. An adaptive mesh could be represented as a region adjacency graph: nodes correspond to regions and springs to symbolic links between adjacent regions. It is important to note that the position of nodes in the image is a combined effect of image data, observation function and stiffness of springs. The location of nodes does not directly correspond to any local features like curves or homogeneous regions.

## 4. Creating Adaptive Adjacency Graphs

Adaptive Adjacency Graph (AAG) is a representation of an image that consists of a network of active contours connected at their end points, nodes where contours are connected,regions outlined by the contours and their full adjacency information. The Adaptive Adjacency Graph is created from a Dual Region Adjacency Graph representing a segmented image or by a higher level. The rigid objects in the graph (curves between adjacent regions and region representations) are converted into flexible active contours. The nodes where rigid curves are connected are represented as a set of constraints applied to active contours.

### 4.1. Creating a Region Adjacency Graph

Initial segmentation of an image regions can be performed using a variety of methods using, for example, the region homogeneity criterion. The segmented image is represented either as a labelled image where each region is marked with a unique label or as a network of curves dividing the image into disconnected regions. Creation of a DRAG usually starts by detecting nodes in the network image and following the curves between the nodes. Regions are detected as shapes fully outlined by a group of curves. Adjacency relationships between regions, curves and nodes are built at the same time. Objects represented in the graph are assigned parameters measured in the original image (see section 2). The objects in the graph can be assigned into separate classes depending on their parameters. Alternatively the graph can be created by generating an expected view of a scene by a higher level.

### 4.2. Converting into Adaptive Adjacency Graph

The rigid curves represented in the initial graph are converted into flexible active contours to make the graph adapt to the image data. A chain of connected pixels is converted into an active contour by resampling. Active contours are controlled by internal and external forces and change their shape and location so as to minimize their total energy [12]:

$$E_{contour} = \int_0^1 (E_{int}\ (v(s)) + E_{image}(v(s)) + E_{con}\ (v(s)))\ ds \qquad (1)$$

$v(s)$ is a parametric representation of the contour.

The internal energy $E_{int}$ corresponds to the effects of contour bending or spanning discontinuities. This energy represents membrane and thin plate behaviours of the contour. The external energy consists of two terms $E_{image}$ representing forces exerted by the image and $E_{con}$ – external constraints.

The main feature of Adaptive Adjacency Graphs is their adaptability to external and internal forces while retaining their topology. We achieve such a behaviour by specifying a set of constraints that preserves the connectivity of the contours at their nodes. These constraints are included in the $E_{con}$ term in the form of linear and circular springs. The linear spring exerts a force proportional to the change in its length. For the circular spring, the force depends on the change in the angle between two points on the connected contours and the node:

$$\text{linear spring} \qquad F_l = -k_1 \Delta s \qquad (2)$$

$$\text{circular spring} \qquad F_c = -k_2 \Delta a \qquad (3)$$

Figure 1 illustrates some of the possibilities for linking four contours at a central node (the contours are shown as thick lines, nodes as squares). Such a node can be con-

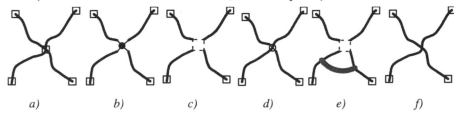

Figure 1. Different types of nodes: a) original representation, b) anchored node,
c) floating node, d) connected node, e) constrained node, f) unconnected node

verted into an *anchored* node (figure 1b), a *floating* node (figure 1c), a *connected* node (figure 1d), a *constrained* node (figure 1e) or an *unconnected* node (figure 1f). An *anchored* node represents a connection where each of the connected active contours is attached to a particular image location (figure 1b). Such a node cannot change its location. A *floating* node is a connection where all of the connected contours are linked together using springs (figure 1c). Such a node can move freely in the image under combined effect of forces acting on each of the contours. A *connected* node is a connection similar to the *floating* node (figure 1d). The difference is that two of the connected contours are represented as a single active contour. A *constrained* node is a variation of the *floating* node with a constraint between two (or more) contours in form of a circular spring (figure 1e). The *unconnected* node is a trivial case, where there is no connection between two crossing contours (figure 1f).

Figure 2 shows possible deformations of different node types. In the case of the *anchored* node only the contour that experiences the force changes, other contours do not change as their ends remain constrained. The *floating* node transmits the forces to connected contours causing their deformation and moving the node position. There is a discontinuity in orientation between two initially collinear contours. Deformation of the *connected* node is shown in the figure 2d. All of the connected contours deform, the node moves but the continuity in orientation of contours at the node is retained. The *constrained* node deforms in such a way that both contours linked by the circular spring maintain their relative orientation (figure 2e). In the case of *unconnected* node deformations of one of the contours are not transferred to the other one.

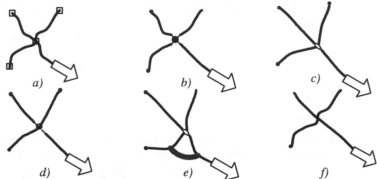

Figure 2. Deformation for different types of nodes: a) original representation, b) anchored node, c) floating node, d) connected node, e) constrained node f) unconnected node

### 4.3. Selection of parameters for contours and node types

The objects represented in the adjacency graph are described by a set of parameters and can be assigned to different classes according to a domain specific model. Parameters of the newly created active contours (stiffness, elasticity, damping) may depend on the interpretation assigned to them during the image segmentation process. For example, in the case of the sequence discussed in section 6 strong vertical contours can be assigned much higher stiffness than other contours.

Selection of which node model to use depends on an application and may depend on results of segmentation. To continue with the above example, nodes detected along a strong vertical contour should be of the *connected* type. If parts of the graph are known not to change their position corresponding nodes should be *anchored* to the image.

### 5. Operations on Adaptive Adjacency Graphs

Modifications of the graph are used to maintain correspondence between the image representation and new images. The graph modifications include deformations of contours and regions, and modifications of the graph topology. As the images change and the graph deforms it is necessary to update image and shape parameters of regions and curves represented in the graph.

### 5.1. Tracking and monitoring contours and regions

The basic behaviour of the AAG is to track the image features while maintaining connectivity of contours and preserving the topology of the graph. This behaviour will be maintained as long as the positions of active contours in consecutive images remain close to corresponding image features.

While tracking the properties of the objects in the graph are monitored. In the case of individual contours their length and curvature is easily obtained from their representations. The image intensity of the underlying grey level image or it's gradient is measured by interpolating between the contour points and sampling the image. For regions, measuring their shape, size and image properties is more complex as their previous representations as masks or blobs are no longer valid. The updated representation is created by concatenating contours outlining each region (the topology does not change) and building the required region representation. The bounding contour itself is sufficient to calculate the shape descriptions in the form of geometric moments.

Two dimensional moments $m_{pq}$ of an area $A$, and a continuous image function $f(x,y)$, can be calculated from the following integral:

$$geometrical \quad moments \quad m_{pq} = \int\int_A x^p y^q f(x, y) dx dy$$

Function $f(x, y)$ is set to 1 as usually the shape of the region and not the grey level content are important. Central moments $\mu_{pq}$ are translation invariant and are calculated by moving the coordinate frame to the centre of gravity $(\bar{x}, \bar{y})$ of the area $A$:

$$central \quad moments \quad \mu_{pq} = \int\int_A (x - \bar{x})^p (y - \bar{x})^q dx dy$$

$\bar{x} = m_{10}/m_{00}$ and $\bar{y} = m_{01}/m_{00}$ are the coordinates of the centre of gravity

Various shape descriptors can be derived from the central moments: length and orientation of major axes, eccentricity, spread (see [13]). By applying Green's theorem, the moment calculations can be reduced to integrating along the bounding contour. Several efficient algorithms exist that implement the following equations [3,4,11]:

$$m_{pq} = \frac{1}{p + 1} \int_C x^{p+1} y^q dy = \frac{-1}{q + 1} \int_C y^{q+1} x^p dx$$

the closed curve C bounds the region A

Cipolla *et al.* [4] used the the relative change of an area enclosed by an active contour to estimate the time to contact. Region size change was also used to trigger the change in the adaptive adjacency graph topology by using a higher level model in form of an aspect graph model [7].

Measuring image properties of a deformed region requires accessing pixels inside it, so it is necessary to obtain a representation in the form of a pixel mask or a blob. We create the blob by filling in the closed contour, then use this description to sample the new image and update image properties of the region.

### 5.2. Modification of the topology

All standard operations performed on Region Adjacency Graphs such as region merging or splitting based on some region homogeneity criteria can be performed on Adaptive Adjacency Graphs as well. Pruning of the graph is performed by identifying weak boundaries between similar regions and deleting them. Splitting of non–homogeneous regions along a new boundary is performed by adding a curve located close to the boundary, creating new nodes and connecting them with a new contour.

Various visual events can trigger a modification of the graph topology. For example, a significant deformation (or disappearance) of a region or a curve may signal that the graph does not track the new image. Such events can be detected by continuously monitoring the shape and size of the objects in the graph. The actual modification of the topology requires information from a higher level. In extreme cases, the new image has to be segmented and a new graph created.

## 6. Results

The concept of adaptive adjacency graphs is now used for segmentation and maintaining correspondence during translation of a camera mounted on a mobile robot. Selective measurements using other sensors on the vehicle (for example, a rangefinder) and recognition of objects require an ability to maintain correspondence between the initial representation and new images. The AAG uses the initial segmentation and by applying the rule of "least commitment" tracks regions and their topology in the sequence. The fist image of a sequence is shown in figure 3. This image is segmented into

 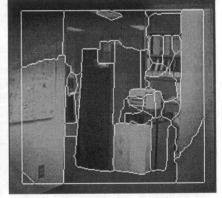

Figure 3. First image in the sequence    Figure 4. Segmented image from figure 3

closed regions of uniform intensity. The resulting regions, overlaid on the original image, are shown in figure 4 and the corresponding AAG is depicted in figure 5. Continuous lines correspond to active contours, dotted lines to connecting springs. All nodes have been converted to *floating* nodes. The graph was applied to the sequence of 15 images. Figures 6, 7 and 8 show the graph tracking features in the sequence.

## 7. Conclusions

We have presented a representation of segmented images in form of Adaptive Adjacency Graphs. The AAGs can be used for representing 2D images or 2D views of 3D scenes. The AAGs maintain correspondence between the image representation as the graph and features in new images. Active contours incorporated in the graph align

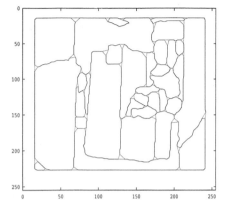

Figure 5. AAG representation for the image in figure 4

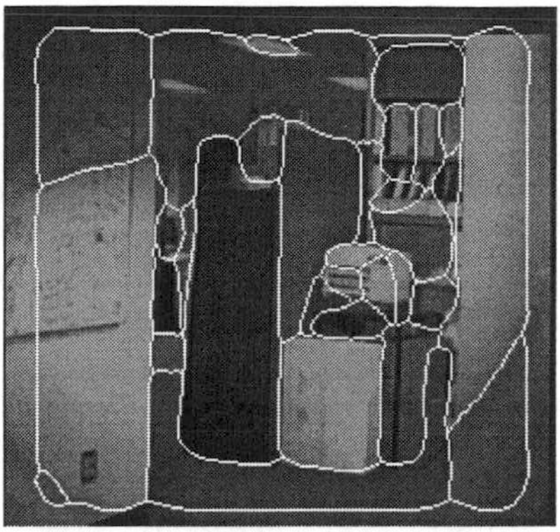

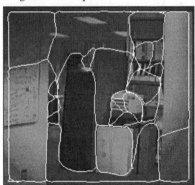

Figure 6. AAG adapting to one of the images in the sequence

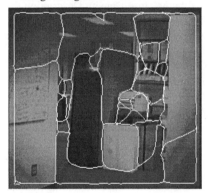

Figure 7. Tracking images with the AAG

Figure 8. AAG overlaid on the last image in the sequence

themselves with features in new images. Constraints imposed on contours maintain their connectivity at nodes and topology of the graph. Algorithms for creating AAGs have been discussed. The results of using AAGs have been demonstrated for a sequence of images of a 3D scene. We have applied AAGs for registration of retinal images as well [9]. We are working now on incorporating region based image forces into the AAG model.

## 8. Acknowledgements

Funding for this work was provided, in part, by the ARK (Autonomous Robot for a Known environment) Project, which receives its funding from PRECARN Associates

Inc., Industry Canada, the National Research Council of Canada, Technology Ontario, Ontario Hydro Technologies, and Atomic Energy of Canada Limited.

## 8. References

1.Amini A., Weymouth T., Jain R.: Using Dynamic Programming for Solving Variational Problems in Vision. *PAMI–12* (3), 1990, p. 855–867.

2.Ballard D., Brown C..: Computer Vision. Prentice Hall, 1982.

3.Bing–Cheng L., Shen J.: Fast Computations of Moment Invariants. *Pattern Recognition.* v. 24, no.8, 1991, pp. 807 –812.

4.Cipolla R., Blake A.: Motion Planning Using Image Divergence and Deformation. Active Vision, eds. Blake A. and Yuille A., MIT 1992, pp. 189 – 201.

5.Cootes T.F., Taylor C.J.: Active Shape Models – "Smart Snakes". *BMVC.* 92, p. 266–275.

6.Curwen R., Blake A., Cipolla R..: Parallel Implementation of Lagrangian Dynamics for real–time snakes. *BMVC '91*,pp. 27 – 35.

7.Dickinson S., Jasiobedzki P., Olofson G., Christensen H.: Qualitative Tracking of 3–D Objects using Active Contour Networks, *CVPR 94*, 6 pages (in print).

8.Etoh M., Shirai Y., Asada M.: Contour Extraction by Mixture Density Description Obtained from Region Clustering. *ECCV–92*, p. 24–32.

9.Jasiobedzki P.: Registration of Retinal Images Using Adaptive Adjacency Graphs. Proc of IEEE Symposium on Computer Based Medical Systems, *CBMS 93*, June 1993.

10.Jasiobedzki P .: Adaptive Adjacency Graphs. *GMCV II*, SPIE–2031, 1993, p. 294–303.

11.Jiang X.Y., Bunke H.: Simple and Fast Computation of Moments. *Pattern Recognition,* v. 24 no. 8, 1991, pp. 801 – 806.

12.Kass M., Witkin A., Terzopolous D.: Snakes: Active Contour Models. *IJCV* 1(4), 1988, pp.321–331.

13.Levine M.D.: Vision in Man and Machine. McGraw Hill 1985.

14.Leymarie F., Levine M.D.: Simulating the Grassfire Transform Using an Active Contour Model. *PAMI–14*, no. 1, Jan 1992, pp. 56 – 75.

15.Malladi R, Sethian JA, Vemuri BC: A Topology Independent Shape Modelling Scheme. *GMCV II*, SPIE–2031, 1993, p. 246–258.

16.Samadani R.: Changes in Connectivity in Active Contour Models. *Proc. of IEEE Workshop on Visual Motion,* Irvine CA, March 1988, pp. 337–343.

17.Terzopoulos D., Vasilescu M.: Sampling and Reconstruction with Adaptive Meshes. *CVPR 91*, p. 70–75.

18.Terzopoluos D., Szeliski R.: Tracking with Kalman Snakes. Active Vision, MIT 1992, p. 3–21.

19.Wiliams D., Shah M.: A Fast Algorithm for Active Contours and Curvature Estimation. *CVGIP* vol.55, no. 1, January 1992, pp.14–26.

20.Yuille AL, Hallinan P, Cohen D: Feature Extraction from Faces Using Deformable Templates. *IJCV* 8(2), 1992, p. 99–111.

21.Zucker S., David C., Dobbins A., Iverson L.: The Organization of Curve Detection: Coarse tangent fields and fine spline coverings. 2 *ICCV*, 1988, pp. 568 – 577.

# DIGITAL REPRESENTATION OF 3-D CURVES:
# SURVEY AND ANALYSIS

AMNON JONAS[1]

*Department of Electrical Engineering, Technion*
*Haifa 32000, Israel*

and

NAHUM KIRYATI

*Department of Electrical Engineering, Technion*
*Haifa 32000, Israel*

## ABSTRACT

Digitization and chain encoding of three dimensional curves are considered. Existing two dimensional discretization methods are first reviewed, then methods applicable to curves in three and higher dimensional spaces are described. Desirable properties of curve representation schemes are identified and quantitative comparison of the various methods is carried out. Conclusions concerning the optimal selection of 3-D discretization methods for shape analysis and coding are drawn. It is shown that grid intersect quantization is a poor method for curve quantization in 3-D space and that cube quantization, leading to 6-connected chain codes, meets all the identified requirements and has the best coding efficiency.

## 1. Introduction

Digital representation of curves is important in the field of shape analysis. Many algorithms are based on chain code representation of curves. This requires a definition of the digitization process used for converting the continuous curve to the discrete representation.

Many two dimensional methods were suggested [16, 13, 14, 18, 15, 17, 29, 23, 44, 41] and their quality has been analysed and compared by various quantitative measures [16, 35, 29, 40, 41, 34]. Special emphasis was put on digitized straight lines segments as a basic element in common shapes and as a limiting case for fine sampling of smooth curves. The properties of two dimensional digital straight lines are thoroughly discussed in [13, 37, 23, 45, 10, 11, 32, 20, 19, 2, 5, 30, 7, 12, 46, 33].

The increasing importance of three dimensional shape analysis in medical imaging, range image processing, image sequence analysis and other domains necessitates the definition, evaluation and selection of curve discretization methods in three (or higher)

---

[1]Currently with Quasar Communication Systems, POB 3803, Jerusalem, Israel.

dimensional spaces. The three dimensional chain code was already defined by Freeman in 1974 [14], but a precise quantization method was not defined. In the last decade a few quantization methods were suggested. One of them is a generalization of the 2-D Grid Intersect Quantization (GIQ) scheme [24, 27, 2]. As pointed out in [42], certain properties which have been indicated in those papers are incorrect. Another method was suggested (with certain variations) in references [1, 42, 4, 8], but is limited to the special case of straight lines. Other techniques were presented in [27, 26]. These and other techniques are discussed in the sequel.

The paper is organized as follows: basic definitions and notation are introduced in the next section. Desirable properties of discretization methods are identified in section 3. 2-D discretization methods are briefly reviewed in section 4. In section 5, several methods are generalized to higher dimensions and other methods, applicable to two and higher dimensions, are discussed. Quantitative comparison of the various methods is carried out in section 6, and the main conclusions are summarized in section 7.

## 2. Notation and Basic Definitions

Basic terms concerning two-dimensional digital lines are explained in [13, 36]. Some of the concepts are extended to 3-D in [14, 38] and general formulations for multidimensions are described in [43, 9]. In this section the basic definitions and notation used in this paper are presented.

The term *(n-dimensional) lattice* in this paper refers to the set of all points in $R^n$ with integral coordinates. An *n-dimensional centered hypervoxel* is an n-dimensional cube of unit length edge, with its center on a lattice point and its edges parallel to the axes. An *n-dimensional shifted hypervoxel* is an n-dimensional unit length cube, with all of its corners on lattice points. A two dimensional hypervoxel (centered or shifted) is a *pixel*. A three dimensional hypervoxel is a *voxel*. In [6] the term *rexel* is suggested for a four dimensional hypervoxel.

Two distinct points on an n-dimensional lattice are *O(r)-adjacent* if each coordinate of one of them differs from the corresponding coordinate of the other by at most 1, and at least n-r coordinates are equal. The points that are O(r)-adjacent to a specific point are called its *O(r)-adjacent neighbors*. In two or three dimensions it is common to use the term *L-adjacent* instead of O(r)-adjacent, where L is the total number of O(r)-adjacent points. Hence in 2-D "4-adjacent" and "8-adjacent" mean "O(1)-adjacent" and "O(2)-adjacent", and in 3-D, "6,18, or 26-adjacent" mean "O(1),O(2), or O(3)-adjacent", respectively. The term adjacency can also be used for hypervoxels. An *O(r)-chain* is a sequence (finite or infinite) of lattice points, with every two subsequent points O(r)-adjacent. A subset S of a Lattice L is *O(r)-connected* if for any two points in S, there is an O(r)-chain in S with the two points at its ends. An O(r)-chain in which each point (except the first and the last) has exactly two O(r)-adjacent neighbors, and the two end points have one O(r)-adjacent neighbor, is a *digital arc* (in the O(r)-connectivity sense).

## 3. Desirable Properties of Curve Representation

Let $\bar{l}(t)$ be a (continuous) curve. The goal is to represent it by an O(r)-chain $\overline{L}_n$ in n-dimensional lattice. Let us write $\overline{L}_n = Q\bar{l}(t)$. Since Q transforms from a continuous space to a discrete one, it is a noninvertible operator, that is, an infinite number of continuous curves generally correspond to a given chain. Hence, $\overline{L}_n$ may be only an approximation for $\bar{l}(t)$. This approximation should have the following properties:

The discretization process should conserve basic symmetry properties of the lattice and the curve. Specifically,

(a) Axial symmetry - The order of the axes and their directions should not affect the result.

(b) Direction symmetry - Discretization of the continuous curve in the opposite direction should lead to the same chain in reversed order, i.e.,

$$Q\bar{l}(T - t) = \overline{L}_{N-n} \tag{1}$$

This is a special case of axial symmetry, with all the axes reversed.

(c) Invariance to integral shifts - Shifting the continuous curve by an integer value at each axis should lead to the same chain shifted.

Other desirable properties are:

(d) The process should have a finite memory, that is, identical segments should be encoded similarly, and not be affected by remote segments, except for bounded length subsegments at the segment ends.

(e) The discretization should be a good model for the physical process that is involved in the data acquisition. This requirement is application dependent, and might conflict with the symmetry requirements.

(f) The process should minimize, in some sense, the distance between the chain and the original continuous curve.

(g) The chain should consist of as few elements as possible, subject to the other requirements.

(h) The projection property - Let $R_{ij}x$ be the projection of a 3-D curve or chain on the ij plane. Then $QR_{ij}l = R_{ij}Ql$. (If $QR_{ij}l \subset R_{ij}Ql$, with equality when $l$ is parallel to the ij plane, then the *weak* projection property is satisfied).

Additionally, for the special case of straight segments,

(i) The discrete curve representing a straight line should be a digital arc. This criterion is a consequence of the connectivity of a discrete curve and of the minimum number of elements requirement. Since the shortest chain between two lattice points is always a digital arc, it is reasonable to require that a digital straight line should be a digital arc. It can be shown that an n-D digital arc consists of at most n different vectors between succesive points in the chain. This property is widely used in 2-D straight line analysis.

## 4. Brief Review of Two Dimensional Discretization Methods

There are several known two dimensional curve discretization schemes. Consider first *Square Quantization* [13, 14, 23], in which the curve is implicitly segmented according to its intersections with centered pixels. The chain is taken to be the sequence of points at the centers of these pixels, following the order of the segments on the curve. For a random curve, the probability of crossing the pixel edge at the corner is zero and can be ignored, so a 4-chain is obtained.

Other schemes can be used to get 8-chains. Three of these are based on the intersection points between the curve and the edges (between two lattice points at the corners) of shifted pixels. In *Grid Intersection Quantization (GIQ)* [16, 13, 14] the curve is represented by taking, at each intersection, the closest of the pair of lattice points connected by the intersected edge. The order of points follows the order of intersections along the curve. Other approaches regard the curve as the boundary of an object. Then one of the pair of lattice points is in the object while the other is outside, i.e., in the background. *Object Boundary Quantization* [18] takes from each pair the point in the object and *Background Boundary Quantization* [18] takes the background point. The points are ordered as in Grid Intersect Quantization (GIQ).

In *Convex Quantization* [29] a convex domain is placed around each lattice point. If the curve passes through the domain, the lattice point is included in the chain. The order of points follows the curve, so if it passes through a domain twice, the corresponding point is included twice in the chain. In the special case of the domains being the centered pixels around each lattice point, square quantization is obtained. *Circle Convex Quantization*, in which the domain is a circle of unit diameter centered at the lattice point has also been suggested, and yields 8-chains.

Methods to obtain generalized chain codes (consisting of longer steps between successive elements) [15, 17, 35] and hexagonal grid quantization schemes [44, 41] have also been suggested.

## 5. Three Dimensional and N-dimensional Methods

Most of the two dimensional curve discretization methods do not lend themselves easily to generalization to higher dimensions. For example, Object Boundary Quantization and Background Boundary Quantization cannot be used in more than two dimensions since an object side and a boundary side of a curve do not exist. In Convex Quantization, connectivity is not always maintained, because the curve may pass between domains without crossing any one of them. For example, if one uses spherical domains as a generalization of Circle Convex Quantization to three dimensions, then even an infinite line can pass between the spheres without crossing any of them.

In two dimensional quantization schemes the properties specified in section 3 usually hold (except the projection property which does not apply to 2-D). In three dimensions most of the methods do not satisfy at least one of the requirements. A significant difficulty arises with property (i): in most 3-D schemes the digital representation of straight lines does not yield digital arcs, implying inefficient quantization. Most methods also do not satisfy the projection property (h). Without these two properties the extension of the available knowledge concerning the digital geometry of straight lines [13, 37, 23, 45, 19, 46] and other features from two to higher dimensions is difficult.

In the rest of this section several three dimensional discretization schemes are considered. A few of them are direct extensions of two dimensional techniques. Although the emphasis here is on three dimensional methods, the general approach is applicable to higher dimensions as well.

To obtain O(1)-chains, Square Quantization can simply be generalized to *Cube Quantization (CQ)* [27, 26] by substituting "centered voxels" for "centered pixels" in the definition of Square Quantization.

To obtain O(3)-chains[2], only Grid Intersect Quantization (GIQ) can be readily generalized to 3-D. In 3-D GIQ [24, 27, 8], one takes the closest of the four lattice points to each intersection of the curve with the face of the shifted voxel. This method does not satisfy properties (g),(h) and (i). In [42] it was shown that the statement made in [24] that requirements (h) and (i) are satisfied is incorrect. Later papers [27, 2, 8] unfortunately rely on that erroneous claim. GIQ was also extended by [25, 31] to allow 3-D surface quantization. This seems to be the natural extension of 2-D GIQ to 3-D. Using 3-D GIQ of a continuous curve, one can remove excess elements from the chain to get a digital arc. By averaging on random straight lines [3, 22] it can be shown that the mean number of excess elements with respect to a digital arc is 8.3%. The percentage of excess elements is smaller in the Maximum Length Quantization (MLQ) method.

In *Maximum Length Quantization (MLQ)*, the curve is divided into segments by its intersections with the integral coordinate planes perpendicular to one of the coordinate axes. For each segment, the lattice point with the longest subsegment in its centered voxel is picked. This process is repeated for each of the axes. The points are then ordered following the order of the corresponding subsegments on the curve. The resulting chain for a straight line has on average just 0.45% of excess elements with respect to a digital arc. This method is based on the fact that for a chain code to be connected, it must contain at least one element in each coordinate plane it passes

---

[2]Generally O(N), where N is the dimensionality of the space.

through. Here, for any such plane, one element is chosen according to the maximum length criterion. Unlike GIQ, in MLQ the quantization depends on the whole curve, not just on selected points of it. In 2-D, for a straight line, MLQ is equivalent to GIQ. Hence, it can be considered as another extension of GIQ to higher dimensions.

A method used in [26] is referred to here as *Thinned Cube Quantization (TCQ)*. One first gets the Cube Quantization chain. Then, each element along the chain is checked in order and, if it can be deleted while retaining the chain connectivity (in $O(N)$ adjacency), taking previous omissions into account, it is deleted. This method minimizes the number of elements and, for a straight line, always gives a digital arc. Its disadvantage is that it does not have properties (b) and (d).

Klette [27] develops a generalization of Convex Quantization that includes multi-dimensional Cube Quantization and Grid Intersect Quantization (GIQ). In addition, he suggests a generalization to Diamond Convex Quantization.

In [1, 42, 8, 4] quantization of straight lines is considered. The axis with the smallest angle to the line, called the main axis, is chosen, and the line is sampled at each integer value along this axis. The other coordinate values of the points are rounded [1, 42] or truncated [8, 4]. This method is only applicable to straight lines. In [42] two extensions of these techniques to general curves are suggested. One is based on approximation of the curve by straight line segments, in which large deviations from the original curve are introduced. The other considers the tangent to the curve at each coordinate crossing to locally define a main axis. It does not assure chain connectivity in the general case.

In certain applications, the quantization method should simulate the physical process involved in the acquisition of the data. For example, in range imaging one may sample a curve on a $2\frac{1}{2}$-D surface by first using one of the 2-D methods in the X-Y plane, then quantizing the corresponding Z value. Interpolation may be needed to ensure chain connectivity. In tomographic applications one can sample the curve on the Z axis, quantize the corresponding X,Y values, then interpolate if necessary to retain connectivity. These application specific methods are not further discussed here.

## 6. Quantitative Comparison of 3-D Quantization Schemes

2-D quantization methods have been widely analysed and compared. In [16] the resolution needed for GIQ is examined in relation to a "minimum energy" criterion. In [35] the bit rate per unit length in a number of schemes is compared. The accuracy of the generalized chain code of [15, 17] is tested in [40]. A comprehensive comparison between the main techniques is given in [29] and a rate-distortion analysis is given in [34].

In this section various 3-D discretization methods are compared. This require us to first define quantitative measures of quantization quality.

- *Number of elements per unit length segment:* The mean value of the number of

Table 1: Performance measures of several 3-D discretization methods. *A:* Number of elements per unit length segment. *B:* Number of bits per unit length segment. *C:* Maximum euclidean distance between any chain lattice point and the curve. *D:* Maximum chessboard distance between any chain lattice point and the curve. *E:* Maximum euclidean distance between any curve point and the nearest chain lattice point. *F:* Maximum chessboard distance between any curve point and the nearest chain lattice point.

| *measure* | CQ | GIQ | MLQ | TCQ |
|---|---|---|---|---|
| A | 1.5 | 0.900 | 0.835 | 0.831 |
| B | 3.88 | 4.23 | 3.92 | 3.91 |
| C | $\sqrt{3}/2$ | $\sqrt{2}/2$ | $\sqrt{3}/2$ | $\sqrt{3}/2$ |
| D | 1/2 | 1/2 | 1/2 | 1/2 |
| E | $\sqrt{3}/2$ | $\sqrt{3}$ | $\sqrt{11}/2$ | $\sqrt{11}/2$ |
| F | 1/2 | 1 | 3/2 | 3/2 |

points in the chain, divided by the length of the corresponding curve segment. This measure is useful for coding purposes, where one wishes to minimize the volume of the representation. It quantifies the minimum elements requirement (g).

- *Number of bits per unit length segment:* This is a related measure that takes into account the smaller number of bits needed for coding a 6-chain element than for coding a 26-chain element. It measures the mean number of bits required for coding a unit length curve.

- *Maximum distance between any chain lattice point and the curve:* This is a measure of the representation accuracy of the curve by the chain. The distance is measured using the euclidean distance or the chessboard distance [39].

- *Maximum distance between any curve point and the nearest chain lattice point:* This is another measure for the representation accuracy. Again, one can use the euclidean distance or the chessboard distance. This measure and the previous one quantify requirement (f).

Table 1 shows the performance of several 3-D discretization methods in terms of these quality measures.

## 7. Conclusions

Several quantization schemes for curves in three dimensional space have been compared. It seems that Grid Intersect Quantization (GIQ) is a poor choice in 3-D due to lack of several important desirable features and inefficient coding. Maximum Length

Quantization (MLQ) is an alternative 26-chain technique that offers higher coding efficiency. The main conclusion of this paper is however that Cube Quantization (CQ), leading to 6-chains is the method of choice for 3-D curve representation. It gives the best bits/length rate and satisfies all of the desirable features identified in this research.

A full length version of this paper can be found in [21], together with a study on highly accurate 3-D length estimators that are based on cube quantization.

## 8. Acknowledgements

This research was supported in part by the Israeli Ministry of Science and Arts and by the Ollendorf Center of the Electrical Engineering Department, Technion.

## 9. References

[1] T.M. Amarunnishad and P.P. Das, "Estimation of Length for Digitized Straight Lines in Three Dimensions", *Pattern Recognition Letters*, vol. 11, pp. 207-213, 1990.

[2] T.A. Anderson and C.E. Kim, "Representation of Digital Line Segments and Their Preimages", *Comput. Vision Graphics Image Process.*, vol. 30, pp. 279-288, 1985.

[3] A.L.D. Beckers and A.W.M. Smeulders, "The Probability of a Random Straight Line in Two and Three Dimensions", *Pattern Recog. Letters*, vol. 11, pp. 233-240, 1990.

[4] A.L.D. Beckers and A.W.M. Smeulders, "Optimization of Length Measurements for Isotropic Distance Transformations in Three Dimensions", *CVGIP: Image Understanding*, vol. 55, pp. 296-306, 1992.

[5] C.A. Berenstein and D. Lavine, "On the Number of Digital Straight Line Segments", *IEEE Trans. Pattern Anal. Machine Intell.*, vol. PAMI-10, pp. 880-887, Nov. 1988.

[6] G. Borgefors, "Distance Transformations in Arbitrary Dimensions", *Comput. Vision Graphics Image Process.*, vol. 27, pp. 321-345, 1984.

[7] A. M. Bruckstein, "Self-Similarity Properties of Digitized Straight Lines", *Contemporary Mathematics*, vol. 119, pp. 1-20, 1991.

[8] S. Chattopadhyay and P.P. Das, "Estimation of the Original Length of a Straight Line Segment from its Digitization in Three Dimensions", *Pattern Recognition*, vol. 25, pp. 787-798, 1992.

[9] P.P. Das, P.P. Chakrabarti and B.N. Chatterji, "Generalized Distances in Digital Geometry", *Inform. Sci.*, vol. 42, pp. 51-67, 1987.

[10] L. Dorst and R.P.W Duin, "Spirograph Theory: A Framework for Calculations on Digitized Straight lines", *IEEE Trans. Pattern Anal. Machine Intell.*, vol. PAMI-6, pp. 632-639, Sep. 1984.

[11] L. Dorst and A.W.M. Smeulders, "Discrete Representation of Straight Lines", *IEEE Trans. Pattern Anal. Machine Intell.*, vol. PAMI-6, pp. 450-463, Jul. 1984.

[12] L. Dorst and A.W.M. Smeulders, "Discrete Straight Line Segments: Parameters, Primitives, and Properties", *Comtemporary Mathematics*, vol. 119, pp. 45-62, 1991.

[13] H. Freeman, "Boundary Encoding and Processing", in B.S. Lipkin and A. Rosenfeld (eds), *Picture Processing and Psychopictorics*, Academic Press, New York, pp. 241-266, 1970.

[14] H. Freeman, "Computer Processing of Line-Drawing Images", *Comput. Surveys*, vol. 6, pp. 57-97, 1974.

[15] H. Freeman, "Application of the Generalized Chain Coding Scheme to Map Data Processing", in *Proc. IEEE Comput. Soc. Conf. Pattern Recognition and Image Process.*, Chicago, pp. 220-226, 1978.

[16] H. Freeman and J.M. Glass, "On the Quantization of Line-Drawing Data", *IEEE Trans. Sys. Sci. Cyber.*, vol. SSC-5, pp. 70-79, 1969.

[17] H. Freeman and J.A. Saghri, "Comparative Analysis of Line-Drawing Modeling Schemes", *Computer Graphics Image Processing*, vol. 12, pp. 203-223, 1980.

[18] F.C.A. Groen and P.W. Verbeek, "Freeman-Code Probabilities of Object Boundary Quantized Contours", *Computer Graphics Image Processing*, vol. 7, pp. 391-402, 1978.

[19] S.H.Y. Hung, "On the Straightness of Digital Arcs", *IEEE Trans. Pattern Anal. Machine Intell.*, vol. PAMI-7, pp. 203-215, 1985.

[20] S.H.Y. Hung and T. Kasvand, "On the Chord Property and its Equivalences", in *Proc. 7th ICPR*, pp. 116-119, 1984.

[21] A. Jonas and N. Kiryati, Department of Electrical Engineering, Technion, Technical Report, in preparation. Also in A. Jonas, M.Sc. Thesis, Department of Electrical Engineering, Technion, in preparation.

[22] M.G. Kendall and P.A.P. Moran, *Geometrical Probability*, C. Griffin and Co., London, 1963.

[23] C.E. Kim, "On Cellular Straight Line Segments", *Computer Graphics Image Processing*, vol. 18, pp. 369-381, 1982.

[24] C.E. Kim, "Three-Dimensional Digital Line Segments", *IEEE Trans. Pattern Anal. Machine Intell.*, vol. PAMI-5, pp. 231-234, 1983.

[25] C.E. Kim, "Three-Dimensional Digital Planes", *IEEE Trans. Pattern Anal. Machine Intell.*, vol. PAMI-6, pp. 639-645, 1984.

[26] N. Kiryati and O. Kübler, "On Chain Code Probabilities and Length Estimators for Digitized Three Dimensional Curves", Tech. Rep. BIWI-TR-125, Institute for Communication Technology, ETH Zurich, Sep. 1991. Also in *Proc. 11th Int. Conf. on Pattern Recognition*, vol. A, pp. 259-262, The Hague, 1992.

[27] R. Klette, "The m-Dimensional Grid Point Space", *Computer Vision Graphics Image Processing*, vol. 30, pp. 1-12, 1985.

[28] T.Y. Kong and A. Rosenfeld, "Digital Topology: Introduction and Survey", *Comput. Vision Graphics Image Process.*, vol. 48, pp. 357-393, 1989.

306

[29] J. Koplowitz, "On the Performance of Chain Codes for Quantization of Line Drawings", *IEEE Trans. Pattern Anal. Machine Intell.*, vol. PAMI-3, pp. 180-185, 1981.

[30] J. Koplowitz and A.M. Bruckstein, "Design of Perimeter Estimators for Digitized Planar Shapes", *IEEE Trans. Pattern Anal. Machine Intell.*, vol. PAMI-11, pp. 611-622, 1989.

[31] X. Luo and L. Wu, "The Generalized Chord Property of Digital Plane Element", in *Proc. 8th Int. Conf. on Pattern Recognition*, Paris, 1986, pp. 1159-1161.

[32] M.D. McIlroy, "A Note on Discrete Representation of Lines", *AT&T Tech. J.*, vol. 64, pp. 481-490 1984.

[33] R.A. Melter, I. Stojmenovic and J. Zunic, "A New Characterization of Digital Lines by Least Square Fits", *Pattern Recognition Letters*, vol. 14, pp. 83-88, 1993.

[34] D.L. Neuhoff and K.G. Castor, "A Rate and Distortion Analysis of Chain Codes for Line Drawings", *IEEE Trans. Info. Th.*, vol. IT-31, pp. 53-68, 1985.

[35] D. Proffitt and D. Rosen, "Metrication Errors and Coding Efficiency of Chain-Encoding Schemes for the Representation of Lines and Edges", *Computer Graphics Image Processing*, vol. 10, pp. 318-332, 1979.

[36] A. Rosenfeld, "Adjacency in Digital Pictures", *Inform. and Control*, vol. 26, pp. 24-33, 1974.

[37] A. Rosenfeld, "Digital Straight Line Segments", *IEEE Trans. Comput.*, vol. C-23, pp. 1264-1269, 1974.

[38] A. Rosenfeld, "Three-Dimensional Digital Topology", *Inform. and Control*, vol. 50, pp. 119-127, 1981.

[39] A. Rosenfeld and A.C. Kak, *Digital Picture Processing*, Academic Press, New York, 1982.

[40] J.A. Saghri and H. Freeman, "Analysis of the Precision of Generalized Chain Codes for the Representation of Planar Curves", *IEEE Trans. Pattern Anal. Machine Intell.*, vol. PAMI-3, pp. 533-539, 1981.

[41] D.K. Scholten and S.G. Wilson, "Chain Coding with a Hexagonal Lattice", *IEEE Trans. Pattern Anal. Machine Intell.*, vol. PAMI-5, pp. 526-533, 1983.

[42] I. Stojmenovic and R. Tosic, "Digitization Schemes and the Recognition of Digital Straight Lines, Hyperplanes, and Flats in Arbitrary Dimensions", *Contemporary Mathematics*, vol. 119, pp. 197-212, 1991.

[43] J.K. Udupa, S.N. Srihari and G.T. Herman, "Boundary Detection in Multidimensions", *IEEE Trans. Pattern Anal. Machine Intell.*, vol. PAMI-4, pp. 41-50, 1982.

[44] A.M. Vossepoel and A.W.M. Smeulders, "Vector Code Probability and Metrication Error in the Representation of Straight Lines of Finite Length", *Computer Graphics Image Processing*, vol. 20, pp. 347-364, 1982.

[45] L.D. Wu, "On the Chain Code of a Line", *IEEE Trans. Pattern Anal. Machine Intell.*, vol. PAMI-4, pp. 347-353, 1982.

[46] J. Yuan and C.Y. Suen, "An Optimal Algorithm for Detecting Straight Lines in Chain Codes", in *Proc. 11th Int. Conf. on Pattern Recognition*, vol. C, pp. 692-695, The Hague, 1992.

# On The Shape Triangle

**Benjamin B. Kimia**
Brown University
Providence, Rhode Island 02912

**Allen Tannenbaum**
University of Minnesota
Minneapolis, MN 55455

**Steven W. Zucker**
McGill University
Montreal, Quebec

### Abstract

We are developing a theory for the generic representation of two-dimensional shape. We show that it is categorical in nature, and derive the categorical structure from the shocks (singularities) of a curve evolution process. We relate these shock categories to functional descriptions via three processes, and propose a representation called the shape triangle. Psychophysical evidence supports such a model.

## 1 Introduction

Whether one views a colleague at a distance, a Dürer woodcut in a museum, or a *Koren* cartoon in a magazine, the human form is immediately recognizable. This is despite the immense differences in geometric and photometric detail, and it exemplifies our spectacular ability to infer the generic structure of categories of objects and to place particular instances within them. Such an ability obviously supports the consistency of object identity across deformations, whether they derive from movement, perspective change, growth, or small mechanical changes. It also structures the organization of knowledge into abstraction hierarchies, as is required for efficent computational access to memory.

Although we clearly show evidence of generic object structure, attempts to model it have been difficult. While there is undoubtedly a semantic dimension to defining generic object categories (e.g., biological vs. man-made objects), we are here concerned with the visual component to them. Intuitively, then, we seek a theory of

---

*This work was supported by grants from the National Science Foundation, by the Air Force Office of Scientific Research, by the Army Research Office, and by the Natural Sciences and Engineering Research Council of Canada. S.W.Z. is a Fellow of the Canadian Institute for Advanced Research.

shape that is sufficently generic to underlie the above categorization and recognition abilities, but is sufficently well-formed scientifically to lead to testable predictions and computable implementations.

Therein lies the dilemma of generic shape: theories sufficently general to capture it tend to be non-applicable to real images. Thus conflicting requirements arise: generic notions of shape are inherently qualitative: they depend on the general structure of objects and not the particular details of their geometry. For example, a person's head is separated from her body by a neck, and this holds generically regardless of the details by which the bounding contour of her figure is defined. That is, "necks" define the categorical notion of parts. However, computational algorithms tend to focus on details. They are applicable to the details, say, of bounding contours.

The famous "Attneave cat" (Attneave, 1954) illustrates the problem. Points of high curvature are generic features of the shape. But how can such points of high curvature be detected, especially in the presence of noise (e.g., Hoffman and Richards' (1985) "electric" pear). They are not simply related to locally-estimated points of high-curvature along the boundary, but also reflect global properties of the shape.

We here report on the development of one such theory, which is based on the mathematics of curve deformation (Gage, 1986, Gage and Hamilton, 1986, Grayson, 1987, 1989; Osher and Sethian, 1988; Sethian, 1985) and the mathematical physics of interface configurations (e.g., Langer, 1980). It leads to two key aspects of shape: that such descriptions consist of (i) parts, protrusions, and bends arranged according to (ii) a hierarchy of significance. These notions are illustrated in Fig. 1, which shows the heirarchical structure of a "doll" derived by our system. As background, the system is overviewed in Sec. 2. The full paper is Kimia, Tannenbaum, and Zucker (in press); see also Kimia, Tannenbaum and Zucker (1990, 1992a, 1992b, 1992c).

## 1.1 Shape is Cognitively Categorical

The categorical nature of cognitive psychology is put most clearly by Eleanor Rosch (1978):

> ...the world consists of a virtually infinite number of discriminably differ-ent stimuli. Since no organism can cope with infinite diversity, one of the most basic functions of all organisms is the cutting up of the environment into classifications by which nonidentical stimuli can be treated as equiv-alent...by what principals do humans divide up the world in the way that they do?

Previous attempts to define the categories of shape are based on *a priori* classes of primitives (e.g., Biederman) for which no formal justification has been given. Our mathatical theory suggests the basis for defining the categories of shape: for a single level of the hierarchy, that is, for objects consisting of components at a single level of significance, the categories correspond to (1) part boundaries (i.e., necks), (2)

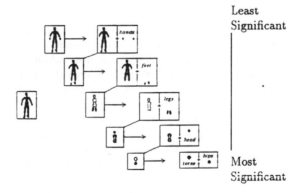

Figure 1: Illustration of the curve evolution paradigm on an outline figure of a doll. Various shocks form, in a way to be described in the paper, and these define the natural components of this shape. Note how the "feet" partition from the "legs" via second-order shocks (defined in Sec. 2) between frames 3 and 4, and how the legs are "absorbed" by migrating first-order shocks as time proceeds. The hierarchy of significance is shown on the right. In this paper we concentrate on a single level in the hierarchy.

protrusions (or intrusions), and (3) bends. We submit that, at a single level of the hierarcy, these are the generic categories for 2-dimensional shapes without holes.

## 1.2  Categorical Ambiguity and Stability

The categorical nature of shape introduces a problem for recognition, however. Any recognition strategy requires a notion of similarity, or a measure of distance, between items. When shapes are categorized, however, it must be done in a manner that does not introduce artificial "distances" between shapes that fall across category boundaries rather than just inside the same one. This is actually a stability criterion, since small distortions to a shape should not induce big changes in its description. It derives form the manner in which shapes are created. As D'Arcy Thompson (p. 11) put it:

> the form of an object is a 'diagram of forces'...in the case of a solid, of the forces which *have* been impressed upon it when its conformation was produced, together with those which enable it to retain its conformation;

This same philosophy has been formulated in modern terms by Leyton, who argued on semantic grounds that the interpretation of such a diagram is not unique. We illustrate a different side of this point in a purely structural fashion with the families of shapes introduced in Fig. 2. The "bowtie" shape is clear, although its morphogenesis is ambiguous. It could have been formed by composing two balls together (or pulling them apart), thus creating the negative extrema delimiting the join (Hoffman and Richards). The final shape in the sequence, "lasagna", looks mainly as if it were formed by indentations (or protrusions) onto a lump of pasta. But it could also have been formed by joining two large lumps together, and the bowtie could have been sculpted from a single lump of material by squeezing the central portion together (Leyton). Thus even very simple shapes can be perceived in different ways. Even though our recognition of the shape never changes, the interpretation can flip back and forth like a Necker cube. These observations point to a curious dilemma surrounding shape: the unique description required to support our recognition facility seems at odds with the different possible explanations. Our goal in this paper is to show how it is possible to reconcile this dilemma within an existing theory of shape, by articulating the morphogenetic equivalence classes behind a generic structural description in terms of three basis components, and to illustrate how our perception of simple shapes is consistent with this theory.

## 2  Shapes, Shocks, and Deformations

Our framework for representing shape derives from the axiom that slightly deformed shapes appear similar. Thus we studied the deformation of closed curves under de-

Figure 2: Three families of shapes that illustrate both the categorical nature of shape descriptions, and the delicate crossover between categories. (left) The "bowtie" shape at top is naturally perceived as two "parts" connected by a "neck", while the bottom shape appears as a "blob" with two indentations (or 4 protrusions). The intermediate shapes in this sequence can be seen either way. (middle) Sequence from a "snake" to a "lasagna". (right) Sequence from "sausages" to "snake". The left and middle sequences were made by adding material vertically, while the right sequence was made by shearing the bottom with respect to the top.

formations (see e.g. the references listed in the Introduction)

$$\mathcal{C}_t = \beta(s,t)\vec{N}, \tag{1}$$

where $\mathcal{C}$ is the curve, $t$ is time (or the amount of deformation), $s$ is the parameter along the curve (not necessarily the arclength), $\vec{N}$ is the normal. Intriguingly, arbitrary intrinsic deformations can be classified into constant motion along the normal to the boundary of the curve, and motion along the boundary with magnitude proportional to the curvature of the curve at that point. These two basic deformations have complementary properties and capture various properties of shape along the axes of linear/nonlinear, local/global and boundary/region. Formally,

$$\mathcal{C}_t = (\beta_0 - \beta_1\kappa)\vec{N}, \tag{2}$$

where $\kappa$ is curvature, and $\beta_0, \beta_1$ determine the combination of constant and curvature motions.

There is a fundamental connection between pure curvature motion and Gaussian smoothing:

**Theorem 1** *Consider the family of curves* $\mathcal{C}(s,t)=(x(s,t), y(s,t))$ *satisfying*

$$\begin{cases} \frac{\partial \mathcal{C}}{\partial t} & = -\kappa(s,t)\vec{N} \\ \mathcal{C}(s,0) & = \mathcal{C}_0(s), \end{cases} \tag{3}$$

*where* $\mathcal{C}_0(s) = (x_0(s), y_0(s)$ *is the initial curve,* $s$ *is some arbitrary parameter along the curve,* $t$ *is time,* $\kappa$ *is curvature, and* $\vec{N}$ *is the normal. Then the coordinates satisfy the diffusion equation*

$$\begin{cases} \frac{\partial x}{\partial t} & = \frac{\partial^2 x}{\partial \tilde{s}^2} \quad x(\tilde{s},0) = x_0(\tilde{s}) \\ \frac{\partial y}{\partial t} & = \frac{\partial^2 y}{\partial \tilde{s}^2} \quad y(\tilde{s},0) = y_0(\tilde{s}), \end{cases} \tag{4}$$

*where* $\tilde{s}$ *is the arclength parameter along the curve.*

In other words, locally, curvature motion smooths the boundary coordinates by the diffusion (heat) equation whose kernel is the Gaussian. Note that since arclength parameterization is not preserved in the smoothing process, smoothing by curvature motion is a nonlinear analogue of Gaussian smoothing.

Similarly, pure reaction enjoys a relationship to mathematical morphology.

For mathematical and numerical reasons the problem of curve evolution is cast as a higher-dimensional, surface evolution problem with the property that the zero-level set evolves according to equation(Osher, Sethian). Let the surface be defined by $z = \phi(x, y, t)$ such that its zero levet set $\phi(x, y, t) = 0$ is exactly the trace of the curve $\mathcal{C}(s,t) = (x(s,t), y(s,t))$. Thus, we have $\phi_t + \beta(\kappa)|\nabla\phi| = 0$, or when $\beta(\kappa) = \beta_0 - \beta_1\kappa$,

$$\phi_t + \beta_0|\nabla\phi| = \beta_1[-\frac{(\phi_{xx}\phi_y^2 - 2\phi_{xy}\phi_x\phi_y + \phi_{yy}\phi_x^2)}{(\phi_x^2 + \phi_y^2)^{3/2}}]. \tag{5}$$

## 2.1 The Role of Conservation Laws

It is interesting that constant motion leads to a hyperbolic conservation law (Lax) for the orientation of the curve:

**Theorem 2** *Orientation of a curve deformed by constant motion satisfies*

$$\frac{\partial \theta}{\partial t} + \mathcal{H}_\theta(\theta)_x = 0, \tag{6}$$

*where* $\mathcal{H}_\theta(\theta) = \cos(\theta)$, $-\pi/2 < \theta \le \pi/2$; *clearly a hyperbolic conservation law for orientation* $\theta$.

Curvature motion, on the other hand, adds viscosity to the system:

**Theorem 3** *Orientation of a curve deformed by a combination of constant motion and curvature motion satisfies*

$$\theta_t + \beta_0 [\mathcal{H}(\theta)]_x = \beta_1 \cos^2(\theta) \theta_{xx}, \tag{7}$$

*where* $\mathcal{H}_\theta(\theta) = \cos(\theta)$, *namely a viscous hyperbolic conservation law for orientation* $\theta$.

Since conservation laws are nonlinear, initially smooth functions often lead to singularities, or *shocks*. The formation and classification of these shocks is governed by a notion of *entropy* which is analagous to Sethian's formulation for flame propagation.

We define the space of all combinations of constant and curvature deformations for all times as the *reaction-diffusion* space. Formally, the reaction-diffusion space for a shape $S$ is the set of all shapes $S'$ generates by

$$\mathcal{RD}_{(\alpha,t)} : S \longrightarrow S', \tag{8}$$

where $\mathcal{RD}$ is the deformation with $\alpha$ as the ratio of constant motion to curvature motion magnitudes and $t$ is time; for examples, see Kimia, Tannenbaum, and Zucker.

## 2.2 Shocks as Generic Category Descriptors

Shocks are the discrete singularities that form during the continuous curve evolution process, and provide the basis for shape categories. Thus we must classify them (Fig. 3).

### 2.2.1 First-Order Shocks

First order shocks are associated with protrusions (indentations) in absence of other shocks. They arise because curvature accumulates most rapidly at extrema.

**Definition 1** *A* FIRST-ORDER SHOCK *is a discontinuity in orientation of the boundary of a shape.*

In the process of evolution by constant motion, each local curvature extremum leads to a first order shock, provided that only this local portion of the curve evolves.

314

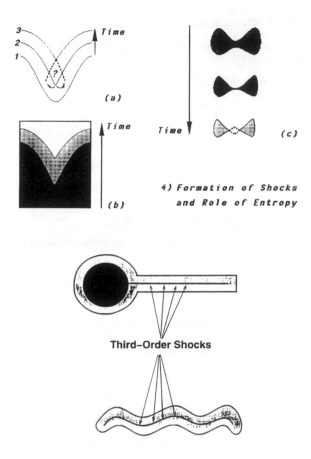

Figure 3: Illustration of the different shocks that can form during the contour evolution process. (top) (a) shows how curvature concentrates to form a first-order shock, and (c) shows how different portions of a boundary can meet to define a second-order shock. The entropy condition dictates how the dotted portions of the curves should be eliminated. (bottom) Third-order shocks are obtained from perfectly elongated structures.

### 2.2.2 Second-Order Shocks

A second kind of shock forms due to a collision of boundaries. In the peanut shape (Fig. 3c) evolving under a constant deformation, portions of the boundary collide and give rise to two cusps. These cusps are discontinuities, not in tangent, but in curvature. We call these *second-order shocks*. Note the change of connectivity at the instant it forms. Beyond this instant, portions of the boundaries cross each other (the dashed lines). The role of entropy in this case is to remove portions of the boundary that have reached a previously visited point. Formally,

**Definition 2** *When in the process of deformation two distinct non-neighboring boundary points join and not all the other neighboring boundary points have collapsed together, a* SECOND-ORDER SHOCK *is formed.*

The second-order shocks define *parts* of a shape. This notion of parts is different from that proposed by Hoffman and Richards, where parts were defined by negative minima of curvature.

Shocks of the first and second orders are generic, in the sense that such singularities cannot be removed by a small perturbation; see Arnold.

### 2.2.3 Third-Order Shocks

A third type of shock is generated when distinct boundary points are brought together as in second-order shocks, but the neighboring boundary points on each side have also joined with other distant boundary points. Formally,

**Definition 3** *When in the process of deformation two distinct non-neighboring boundary points join in a manner such that neighboring boundaries of each point also collapse together, a* THIRD-ORDER SHOCK *is formed.*

As defined above, third-order shocks cannot possibly change the topological connectivity of the shape. Rather, they indicate a symmetric axis (Blum; Pizer et al.), as in the case of an ellipse. However, this axis is not composed of first-order shocks where portions of the boundary collapse into a single point. Rather, this axis is the result of a region collapsing into points, Fig. 3(bottom). They indicate a *bending* of an extended region, rather than a protrusion of the boundary.

Although third-order shocks are not generic, the symmetric axis is. We conjecture that it is the locus of points swept out by first-order shocks that form a $C^1$ curve almost everywhere (i.e., except at those isolated points due to second-order shocks), and indicate both the third-order shock and the generic symmetric axis by this corner of the shape triangle.

### 2.2.4 Fourth-Order Shocks

In the process of inward evolution of a shape, regions shrink and form shocks. In time, remaining regions finally shrink to a point and disappear due to the entropy condition. All parts of a shape must eventually annihilate to a point (Grayson). These are the fourth-order shocks and are the *seeds* for shape.

**Definition 4** *When in the process of deformation a closed boundary collapses to a single point, a* FOURTH-ORDER SHOCK *is formed.*

# 3 The Shape Triangle Reveals Competing Descriptions

*Parts, protrusions*, and *bends* have been shown to be our computational elements of shape. (Since fourth-order shocks ground the hierarchical description of shape, we shall not consider them further in this paper.) Parts are components of *composition*, protrusions are *boundary deformations*, and bends are *region deformations*.

We now consider families of shapes, such as those in Fig. 1, and how stable their percept appears with respect to the above categories. E.g., when does the "worm" appear as a "lasagna"? As discussed in the Introduction, if stability is interpreted in D'Arcy Thompson's "force" terms, then the intermediate shapes in these sequences are highly ambiguous; were they formed by *bending* a long, thin object, or by forcing it indentations and *protrusions* onto a larger blob?

We capture this ambiguity by assigning a different process to compute each of these elements of shape and focus on effects at a single scale. Each process defines a corner in the *shape triangle* (Fig. 4).

We now illustrate how these different shapes are placed in the shape triangle (Fig. 5). First consider the bowtie, which is often perceived as having two parts. Thus is falls close to the upper left corner of the shape triangle, although there is a weak connection to the lower corner because it could be the result of indentations. The snake shape is close to the upper right in its triangle, while the lasagna is closest to the bottom.

Shapes are placed this way because, in the analysis of the sausages (bowtie) versus the lasagna, the bowtie has a strong part component and the boundary deformation process is giving a weak interpretation. In contrast, the boundary process gives a strong interpretation of the lasagna; the part process gives a weak interpretation of the lasagna. These interpretations are derived from the reaction-diffusion space for shapes as follows. For the bowtie, the reaction process gives parts due to a topological split and formation of a second order shock. Increasing the diffusion ratio only delays the time of shock (second order) formation. It is only for large diffusion values that this shock does not form. The lasagna has a different representation in the reaction-diffusion space, since second order shocks do not form, or at best form for only very small diffusion values. For the snake, the bend process claims a strong interpretation, while the boundary process gives a weak one (Figs. 5-7). In contrast, for the lasagna, the bend process gives a weak interpretation, while the boundary process asserts a

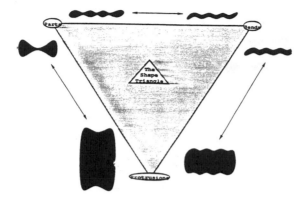

Figure 4: The Shape Triangle consists of three "process representations" for forming a shape, one at each corner. The shape families from Fig. 1 are shown. Observe how the bowtie or sausages at upper left appear to consist mainly of parts, while the lasagna's at bottom appear to have been formed by protrusions into a lump of pasta. Bends are at upper right.

strong interpretation. To relate this to shocks, for the snake third order shocks form quickly, while for the lasagna first-order shocks form.

# 4  Psychophysical Experiments

To test the categorical structure of shapes, and their representation in the shape triangle, we conducted a series of psychophysical search experiments. The task was to view a field of shapes, all of which were identical (the distractors) and to find the single different one (the target). For shapes that are very distant in the shape triangle search times should be short—the task should be easy—while for targets that are close to the distractors in the shape triangle the task should be more difficult. Examples of such stimuli are shown in Fig. 8. The subjects were graduate students in computer vision with normal or corrected vision, and the shapes were displayed on a Symbolics monitor in a dimly illuminated room. Times were indicated by clicking a mouse button. See also Elder and Zucker for procedural details.

The results of these experiments are shown in Fig. 9. When the target is far away from the distractors in the shape triangle, e.g., when it looks as if it were formed by different processes, then the search times are short. In Fig. 8 (top), for example, in a field of "bowties" (toward the right along the abscissa) with clear part structure it takes only very little time to locate a shape most likely formed by indenting the

318

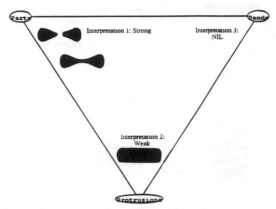

Figure 5: The representation of a specific shape via distance from the three corners of the shape triangle. The closer a shape is to the corner, the stronger that interpretation. Thus the bowtie is placed closest to the *parts* corner, with a long distance from the *protrusions* corner, indicating a weak link. There is nil connection to the *bends* corner, as a third-order shock is impossible, but the length of the symmetric axis is still defined.

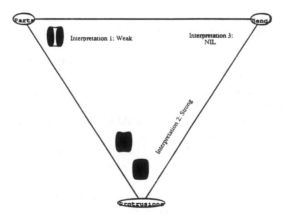

Figure 6: The representation of a "lasagna" shape. It is at the level of the shape triangle that the ambiguous functional interpretations of shapes can be compared, and that the categories can be stabilized.

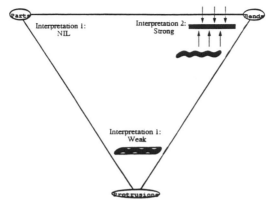

Figure 7: The representation of a worm shape is closest to the *bends* corner of the shape triangle.

sides (a lasagna), while another one with a similar description is more difficult to find. Thus the time curves are flat within a category, and rapidly climb at category boundaries.

# 5    Conclusions

We propose that shape is explained as the interaction of three shape processes. One shape process (parts) in biased to "see" parts and composition. It very optimistically searches for possibilities of compositions and reports its parts. The second shape process (protrusions) concentrates on the boundary and is entirely biased to see shapes as simpler shapes whose boundary was deformed. The third shape process (bends), is region-oriented and reports of modifications of the shape through its axis. Through competition and cooperation these processes explain a shape as a series of operations on simple shapes.

It is at the level of the shape triangle that the ambiguous functional interpretations of shapes can be compared, and that the categories can be stabilized.

While we showed in this chapter how the shape triangle can support shape descriptions, and indicated intuitively how it can be derived from the reaction/diffusion space, it remains to study them with the same mathematical precision utilized in earlier parts of our shape theory. More complex shapes will have to involve the shape triange at different levels of scale as well.

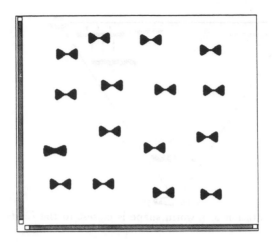

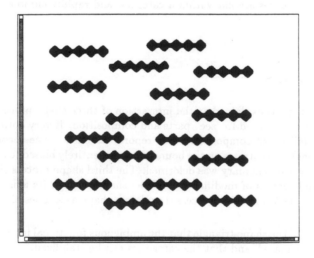

Figure 8: An illustration of the stimuli for the visual shape search task. (top) A field of "bowties" serves to distract from the single one with a thicker neck. Second-order shocks will form rapidly for the distractors, but much more slowly for the target (which may form first-order shocks first). (bottom) An illustration of the shape search task for sausages (distractors) and a worm—can you locate the target?

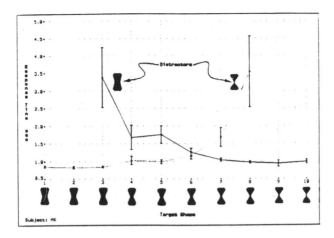

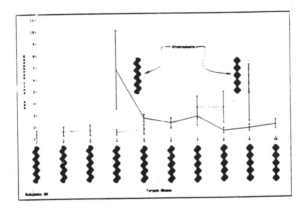

Figure 9: The results of the visual search experiments. (top) Data for locating a "bowtie" in a field of shapes ranging from short lasagna's to bowties. The abscissa shows the target shape, and the ordinate is search time in seconds. Data for two different distractor types are shown. Note how the curve for the "bowtie" distractors is flat within the "lasagna" category, but then rises sharply as the bowtie category is entered. The other curve is complementary. (bottom) Data for the "sausage" and "worm" task.

# 6 References

F. Attneave. Some informational aspects of visual perception. *Psych. Review*, 61:183–193, 1954.

I. Biederman. Recognition by components. *Psych. Review*, 94:115–147, 1987.

H. Blum. Biological shape and visual science. *J. Theor. Biol.*, 38:205–287, 1973.

D'Arcy Thompson, *On Growth and Form*, J. T. Bonner (ed) Cambridge University Press, Cambridge, 1961.

J. Elder, and S. W. Zucker. Contour closure and the perception of shape, *Vision Research*, 1993, **33**(7), 981 - 991.

M. Gage, On an area-preserving evolution equation for plane curves, *Contemp. Math.*, vol. 51, pp. 51–62, 1986.

M. A. Grayson, The heat equation shrinks embedded plane curves to round points, *J. Differential Geometry*, vol. 26, pp. 285–314, 1987.

M. Gage and R. S. Hamilton, "The heat equation shrinking convex plane curves," *J. Differential Geometry*, vol. 23, pp. 69–96, 1986.

M. A. Grayson. Shortening embedded curves. *Annals of Mathematics*, 129:71–111, 1989.

D. D. Hoffman and W. A. Richards. Parts of recognition. *Cognition*, 18:65–96, 1985.

B. Kimia, A. Tannenbaum, and S. W. Zucker. On the evolution of curves via a function of curvature, 1: The classical case, *J. Mathematical Analysis and Application*, 1992a, **163**(2), 438 - 458.

Kimia, B., Tannenbaum, A., and Zucker, S.W., Toward a computational theory of shape: An overview, *Proc. 1$^{st}$ European Conf. on Computer Vision*, Antibes, France, April, 1990. O. Faugeras (ed.), Lecture Notes in Computer Science, 427, Springer Verlag, New York.

Kimia, B., Tannenbaum, A., and Zucker, S.W., Entropy scale space, in C. Arcelli et al. (eds), **Visual Form**, 1992b. Plenum Press, New York, 333 - 344.

Kimia, B., Tannenbaum, A., and Zucker, S.W., On the evolution of curves via a function of curvature, 1: The classical case, *J. Mathematical Analysis and Application*, 1992c, **163**(2), 438 - 458.

B. Kimia, A. Tannenbaum, and S. W. Zucker. Shapes, shocks, and deformations, I, *Int. J. Computer Vision*, in press, 1994.

J. J. Koenderink and A. J. van Doorn. Dynamic shape. *Biol. Cyber.*, 53:383–396, 1986.

J. S. Langer, Instabilities and pattern formation in crystal growth, *Reviews of Modern*

*Physics*, vol. 52, no. 1, pp. 1–28, 1980.

P. D. Lax. *Hyperbolic Systems of Conservation Laws and the Mathematical Theory of Shock Waves*. SIAM Regional Conference series in Applied Mathematics, Philadelphia, 1973.

M. Leyton. *Symmetry, Causality, Mind.* MIT press, April 1992.

S. Osher and J. Sethian. Fronts propagating with curvature dependent speed: Algorithms based on hamilton-jacobi formulations. *Journal of Computational Physics*, 79:12–49, 1988.

S. M. Pizer, W. R. Oliver, and S. H. Bloomberg. Hierarchical shape description via the multiresolution symmetric axis transform. *PAMI*, 9(4):505–511, 1987.

E. Rosch. Principles of categorization, in E. Rosch and B. Lloyd (eds.) **Cognition and Categorization**, L. Erlbaum, Hilladale, N.J., 1978.

J. A. Sethian. Curvature and the evolution of fronts. *Comm. Math. Physics*, 101:487–499, 1985.

# The estimation of curves to subpixel accuracy

P C K Kwok and C Dong
Department of Computer Science
The University of Calgary, Calgary, Alberta T2N 1N4, Canada.

## ABSTRACT

Subpixel estimation is the reconstruction of edges of lines and curves from a digitized grayscale image to better than pixel accuracy.

The mathematical foundation for straight line estimation have been established by Kiryati/Bruckstein. The current work is on an iterative method for Kiryati/Bruckstein's solution and the emphasis here is on curved edges. A similar method has been used by Hyde/Davis for stright edges under a slightly different formulation. The new method is compared with Hyde/Davis's method using artificial images.

Before the implementation can be tested on real images, it is necessary to model the behaviour of the digitizer and to simulate the effects of quantization errors, misalignment, mismatch and rotational variancy of the digitizer. Quantization error is considered in this paper and the performance of the new method is estimated. The method outperformed Hyde/Davis's method in terms of accuracy with and without quantization errors.

## 1. Introduction

Subpixel estimation is the reconstruction of edges of lines and curves from digitized grayscale images to a better accuracy than is allowed by the digitizing grid. It is aimed at the improvement of resolution of a digitized image by analysing the grayscale information of pixels. It is a trade-off between grayscale information and resolution and relies on *a priori* knowledge of the relationship between the position of the edge with respect to a pixel and the grayscale value obtained by the digitizer.

A possible application area is in the use of a low cost television quality camera for measuring the thickness of a line in a remote scene. There are a number of aspects which has to be explored before a practical system can be developed: (1) Mathematical foundation; (2) Method of implementation; (3) Calibration of camera and digitizer to establish the relationship between the edge position and the grayscale value.

The mathematical foundation for subpixel estimation has been studied by Kiryati and Bruckstein. This work is an implementation of Kiryati/Bruckstein's formulation. Artificial images of curved edges are used to evaluate the method. Since Kiryati/Bruckstein's work was a formulation of the solution, and our work is a method to attain the solution, there is no attempt to make comparisons with

Kiryati/Bruckstein's work. The performance of our method can be evaluated by how close our results are from the solution. We also compare our results with Hyde/Davis's method, which was based on a slightly different formulation.

The next step of camera calibration is a non-trivial engineering process, involving many practical considerations. Before calibration is attempted it is worthwhile to model the digitization process and perform simulations to make sure that the method is feasible. In a practical situation, there are many factors which will limit the performance of the system: quantization error; rotational variancy; uneven lighting conditions; misalignment and mismatch of sensors, etc. These artifacts can be modelled as a random process. In the second part of the evaluation, quantization error is considered and the results are compared with the solution as well as those from Hyde/Davis's method.

## 2. Subpixel edge estimation methods

### 2.1. Derivative Methods

Edges are boundaries between two regions with relatively distinct grayscale values. They correspond to the places in the image where there appear to be sudden changes in greyscale values. In a digital image represented by a discrete rectangular array of grayscale values, one way to interpret *sudden changes* in value is to assume that the discrete array of values are results of sampling a real-valued function $f$ defined on the domain of the image. The change refers to the points of high first derivatives of $f$ or relative extrema in the first derivative of $f$, i.e., the zero crossings of the second derivative.

Fang and Huang [2] described an edge positioning method based on first derivative information. First, a gradient image $I'$ was derived from the original image $I$.[1] Then a second-order polynomial function is used to approximate the first derivative near the edge by fitting through three pixels of the gradient image either in the x-direction or in the y-direction. It is assumed that the exact edge position is at the maximum of the gradient magnitude. Such a position is given by calculating the location where the fitted quadratic-curve has its maximum.

Nomura *et al* [3] introduced a normal-distribution curve to fit the gradient magnitudes. Their methods is more suitable for a sharper edge than Fang and Huang's.

MacVicar-Whelan and Binford [4] developed a method using zero-crossings of the second derivative as references to the edge locations. They introduced a lateral inhibition operator to generate $I''$. When the second derivatives of two successive pixels have opposite signs, a linear function is mapped by connecting them in a straight line. The zero-crossing of this line is considered to be the position of an edge.

In general, a derivative method fits a regression function (a continuous function) to a discrete series of values. Thus, it makes the assumption that the image has

---

[1]In the following description, we use $I$ for the original digital image, $I'$ and $I''$ for the first and second derivatives of $I$ respectively.

spatially continuous differentiable intensities. It is applicable to any black-and-white images where the grayscale values change continuously, regardless of the shapes of the original objects or the forms of the edges. However, the assumption does not always hold.

The result of a derivative method provides a set of subpixel accurate locations through which the edge passes. Further processing is required to construct the edge fitting these locations. Moreover, the regression function is just an approximation of the original intensity function. It is impossible to find the edge exactly the same as the original, even under ideal conditions.

## 2.2. Structural Method

A structural method begins with an equation of a line and results in a line that best fits the grayscale values of the image. There is no extra effort required to construct the lines. It does not require the continuity of the intensity values. For example, an image digitized from a scene with the object against a high contrast background would have discontinuous intensities near the boundary of the object. A derivative method is not applicable in this case but a structural method is applicable. If the objects are of straight-edged silhouettes and are digitized into a continuous range of grayscale values, error-free reconstruction of the original object is possible.

The simple least-square SLS method is the most simple structural method. When the locations of the pixels along an edge are known, a straight line is fitted to these pixels. The best estimation of the parameters $\theta$ and $\rho$ (Figure 1) for that line is taken in least-square sense: minimizing the sum of squared distance from the centre of each pixel to the line. In this method, only the positions of the pixels affect the result. The grayscale values of the pixel are not taken into account.

A better estimation can be achieved by making use of the grayscale values of the pixels along the edge. This approach was first described by Hyde and Davis [5] and later formulated by Kiryati and Bruckstein [6]. Hyde and Davis improved the simple least-square method by choosing $\theta$ and $\rho$ to predict the greyscale values of the pixels where the edge $l(\theta, \rho)$ passes in the sense of least-squares. The predicted greyscale value of a pixel is calculated with respect to the edge $l(\theta, \rho)$. An iterative algorithm was proposed to solve the least-squares problem. They conducted experiments using a large number of pixels (5 or more) and concluded that grayscale does not offer any significant improvement over a simple least-square method. Contrary to the findings of Hyde/Davis, Dong and Kwok [1] discovered that when the number of pixels used in the estimation is small, or when there are noise in the data, the improvements can be significant.

Kiryati and Bruckstein derived a set of simultaneous equations for a straight line. Each equation corresponds to a pixel in terms of its coordinates and the amount of overlap with the line $l(\theta, \rho)$ in the $\theta/\rho$ space. The intersection point of the equations identifies the parameters for the straight line. However no methods were offered to solve the simultaneous equations.

## 3. Kiryati/Bruckstein's formulation of the solution

The following formulation is based on Kiryati/Bruckstein's work [6]. In the formulation, a pixel is represented by a circular disk (Figure 1). The disks for a pair of adjacent pixels in the $x$ or $y$ directions touch each other. In the digitizer, there is a sensor corresponding to each pixel. For the purpose of the present discussion, it is assumed that the grayscale value $g(i,j)$ of a pixel $(i,j)$ is equal to the distance $r_{ij}$ between the edge and the centre of the disk. In practice, in most types of digitizers, the response of an individual sensor is isotropic. There is a one-to-one mapping between $r_{ij}$ and $g(i,j)$. The exact relationship can be established by calibration. Given a grayscale value, the distance can be determined. The same principle can then be applied.

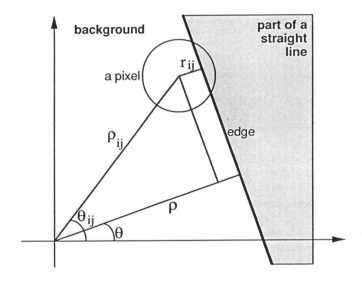

Figure 1. The edge of a straight line $l(\theta, \rho)$ overlapping with a pixel.

During reconstruction, the values of $\rho_{ij}$, $\theta_{ij}$ and the grayscale value $g(i,j) = r_{ij}$ (denoted by the term "actual greyscale value") are given for every pixel $(i,j)$ partially covered by the line along the edge. We place a test line with parameters $\theta$ and $\rho$. The grayscale value at pixel $(i,j)$ (denoted by the term "predicted grayscale value", to distinguish it from the actual grayscale value defined above) given by the test line is

$$G(\rho, \theta, i, j) = \rho - \rho_{ij} \times \cos(\theta - \theta_{ij}) \tag{1}$$

This is an equation with two unknowns $\rho$ and $\theta$. A set of simultaneous equations in terms of $\rho$ and $\theta$ can be obtained by considering a number of edge pixels. Two pixels will be sufficient to determine a unique solution. In general, more than two pixels may be used. In the absence of errors, a unique solution is possible. It corresponds to the intersection of a number of Cosine curves in the $\rho/\theta$ plane. This is the solution as formulated by Kiryati and Bruckstein.

## 4. An iterative method for Kiryati/Bruckstein's solution

The following is based on Dong/Kwok's work in [1] for the recovery of straight lines.

In Equation (1), if the test line is the same as the original line, there will be zero error between the actual value $g$ and the predicted value $G$, for all pixels along the edge. This is equivalent to the minimization of the sum of squared errors:

$$S(\theta, \rho) = \sum_{k=1}^{N} (g(i_k, j_k) - (\rho - \rho_{i_k j_k} \times \cos(\theta - \theta_{i_k j_k})))^2 \tag{2}$$

The minimization of $S(\theta, \rho)$ can be obtained by Newton Iteration.

When the initial values for $\theta$ and $\rho$ are very different from the actual values, it is possible that the algorithm will converge to the wrong minimum. This is the case with Hyde and Davis's method.

We have established that the values of $\theta$ and $\rho$ are bounded. Furthermore, we found that the above equation is very sensitive to $\theta$ but not to $\rho$. When the initial value $\theta_0$ is sufficiently close to the correct value, both $\theta$ and $\rho$ always converge to the correct value regardless of the initial value $\rho_0$. Otherwise, convergence to the correct result is not guaranteed. If an incorrect minimum is reached, the residual error is non-zero. The estimated error is compared to a threshold (which is determined during a training phase). If it is above the threshold, a new $\theta_0$ will be used and the iterative process is repeated. The method was tested on 50,000 set of randomly generated straight lines. It was found that in all cases, the correct minimum is attained within a small number of retries.

## 5. Piecewise recovery of curves

In this paper, we are presenting the results of piecewise reconstruction of curves. The difficulty here is that the distance between the centre of the pixel and the curve may not have a one-to-one relationship with the grayscale value. If the curve section is approximated and modelled by a straight line, the above method can be used, but there will be a error in our estimation due to the error introduced in the model. This error can be considered as noise and the best line will give rise to a non-zero $S(\theta, \rho)$ in equation (2).

A straight line section is reconstructed for every pixel partially covered by the edge. The straight line extends in opposite directions until it intersects with the straight line corresponding to its neighbour.

Let $p(i,j)$ be a pixel partially covered by the curved edge. A $3 \times 3$ window centred at $p(i,j)$ is considered. There are between 3 to 5 pixels partially covered by the curved edge. These pixels are used in the fitting of a straight line segment. The objective function $S(\theta, \rho)$ is defined in the same form as equation(2) over the edge pixels in that window. The minimization of $S(\theta, \rho)$ is obtained by the same iterative method for straight line, but $S(\theta, \rho)$ will not be zero even for the best fitting.

From experiments with curves, it is once again established that $S(\theta, \rho)$ is very sensitive to $\theta$ but not to $\rho$. When $\theta_0$ is close to the correct value, both $\theta$ and $\rho$ always converge to the correct values regardless of $\rho_0$. Since $\theta \in [-\pi, \pi]$, a search is performed for an appropriate $\theta_0$ from $-\pi$ to $\pi$ within the range. An arbitrary value for $\rho_0$ is used. The minimum of the minimum $S(\theta, \rho)$ gives the best fitting line.

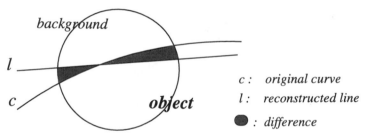

$c$ : original curve
$l$ : reconstructed line
● : difference

Figure 2. The error between the reconstucted straight line segment and the original curve.

## 6. Evaluation

### 6.1. Performance Measure

The derivation of the performance measures for curves are more complex than for straight lines because as indicated in the previous section, the distance between a curve and the centre point of a pixel may not be meaningful. One way is to compare the reconstructed straight line section and the original curve. The difference between the areas covered by the two lines is a measure of the error resulted in the reconstruction (Figure 2). For a closed curve, the total error is weighted by the area covered by the object. A second method is to estimate the squared difference between the predicted grayscale value and the actual grayscale value.

### 6.2. Test Images

Experiments were conducted on artificially generated circles and parabolae. In all cases, convergence to the correct line is achieved. Circles of different radii were considered. Different circles of the same radius were generated. For each circle all the straight line sections were recovered.

### 6.3. An Example

Figure 3 shows an example of an arc of a circle with radius 10. Two $3 \times 3$ windows are shown with a straight line segment (solid line) reconstructed against the centre pixel of each $3 \times 3$ window. The reconstruction is very close to the original arc.

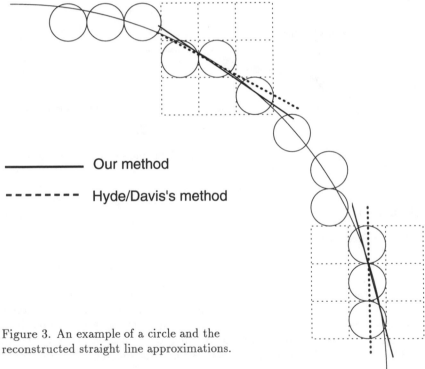

Figure 3. An example of a circle and the reconstructed straight line approximations.

Also shown are the results from Hyde/Davis's method, adapted to this framework. In Hyde/Davis's method, the initial value is given by the result of the method of simple least squares (SLS). In the two windows shown, the final results (dotted lines) are very close to the least squares straight line, constructed against the three edge pixels in each of the two windows. It is clear that the grayscale information did not have much influence on the reconstruction. The difference between the proposed method and Hyde/Davis's method is evident.

### 6.4. Empirical Results

Figure 4 shows a summary of the results of experiments on artificially generated circles. The $x$-axis is the radius of the circle (in units of the number of pixels) and the $y$-axis is the sum of the square error between the actual and predicted grayscale values, normalized to a per pixel basis. Both average and maximum errors are shown. It is obvious that when the radius is small, the curvature is large. The error in the model will be very large and the piecewise approximation is not meaningful. When the radius is large, piecewise fitting is a good approximation to the circle.

Similar experiments were also conducted on the fitting of straight line sections using the method of least squares and the method of Hyde and Davis. In Hyde/Davis's method, convergence to the correct line depends on the correct choice of the initial values. The situation is worse than in the case of straight lines because a small number (usually 3, as illustrated in Figure 3) of pixels are involved in the reconstruction of a segment. Figure 5 shows the results on a circle with curvature of 0.05. The vertical axis is the difference between the recovered and the original circle weighted by the area of the circle. The effect of quantization (3 to 7 bits) is also shown along with the unquantized case (on the extreme right). In this experiment, the initial values were chosen for Hyde and Davis's method so that it converges to the correct minimum. Notice that there is a significant improvement of Hyde and Davis's method over the method of least squares. This is because typically 3 pixels are involved in the estimation and the method of least squares gives very poor results. In all cases, the new method is superior to the other two methods.

## 7. Conclusion

A method for the subpixel estimation of edges have been presented. vAn objective function was defined, the minimum of which can be found by a Newton Iteration. In the case of straight lines, the method always finds the correct minimum and error free reconstruction is achieved.

The method is applied to the piecewise recovery of curves. Again, experiments have shown that the correct minimum can always be found. Evaluation shows that it provides a better estimation than is possible with existing methods.

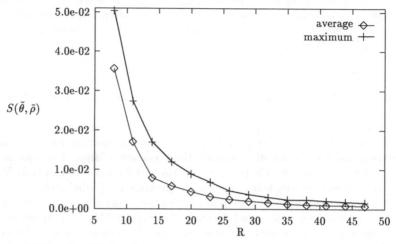

Figure 4. Result of fitting lines to circles: relationship between error and radius.

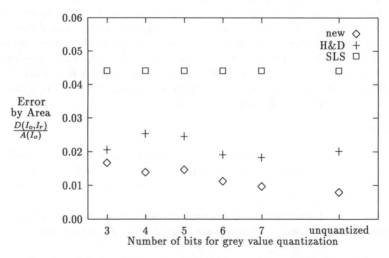

Figure 5. Results of fitting lines to a circle with curvature 0.05: Comparison of the three methods with and without quantization.

## 8. Acknowledgement

This work is supported by the Natural Sciences and Engineering Research Council of Canada.

## 9. References

[1] C. Dong and P.C.K. Kwok. "An iterative algorithm for the subpixel estimation of straight lines", *Proceedings of the Asian Conference on Computer Vision*, Osaka, November 1993, pp. 554 - 557.

[2] J. Fang and T.S. Huang. "Some experiments on estimating the 3-D motion parameters of a rigid body from two consecutive image frames", *IEEE Trans PAMI, 6*, 545 - 554, May 1984.

[3] Y. Nomura, M. Sagara, H. Naruse and A. Ide. "Edge location to subpixel precision and analysis", *Systems and Computers in Japan* **22**(9), 70-80, 1991.

[4] P.J. MacVicar-Whelan and T.O. Binford. "Line finding with subpixel precision", *Proceedings: Image understanding workshop*, L. Baumann, ed., 26 - 31, 1981.

[5] P.D. Hyde and L.S. Davis. "Subpixel edge estimation", *Pattern Recognition* **16**(4), 413 - 420, 1983.

[6] N. Kiryati and A. Bruckstein. "Grey levels can improve the performance of binary image digitizers", *CVGIP: Graphical models and image processing* **51**(1), 31 - 39, 1991.

# SHAPE–FROM–SILHOUETTES: A NEW ACTIVE APPROACH

Aldo Laurentini

*Dipartimento di Automatica ed Informatica, Politecnico di Torino, Corso Duca degli Abruzzi 24*

*10129 Torino, Italy*

ABSTRACT

The 2D silhouettes of a 3D object $O$ are important clues for understanding its shape. Each silhouette constrains $O$ inside the volume obtained by back–projecting the silhouette from the viewpoint. A set of silhouettes specifies a boundary volume $R$, obtained by intersecting the volumes due to each silhouette. This approach to the reconstruction of 3D objects is usually referred to as *volume intersection*. $R$ more or less closely approximates $O$, depending on the viewpoints and the object itself. It is clear that the reconstruction accuracy is affected by the viewpoints: to choose them efficiently is a basic problem for this technique. This paper shows that recent developments in shape–from–silhouette theory make it possible to define a *surface reconstruction accuracy*, which is suitable for implementing active, object specific volume intersection algorithms.

## 1. Introduction

Reconstructing 3D shapes from 2D images is an important area of research in computer vision. The silhouettes of a 3D object are sources of shape information which can usually be obtained with simple and robust algorithms from intensity images. With the word silhouette we indicate the region of a 2D image of an object $O$ which contains the projections of the visible points of $O$.

If no *a priori* information about $O$ is available, the information provided by a silhouette $S_i$ is that $O$ must lie in the solid region of space $C_i$ obtained by back–projecting $S_i$ from the corresponding viewpoint $V_i$. If $n$ silhouettes are available, they constrain $O$ within the volume $R$, which is the intersection of the regions $C_i$ :

$$R = \bigcap_{i=1}^{n} C_i$$

Many object reconstruction algorithms based on this idea have been presented[1–16]. They are usually referred to as *volume intersection* (V.I.) algorithms(Fig.1), and recover from a set of silhouettes a more or less precise approximation of $R$. The main feature of this approach to object reconstruction is that it does not requires to find correspondences between multiple images. Several V.I. algorithms specify $R$ with as an octree representation([3],[7],[13]). Other representations have also been used([2],[10]).

In this paper we consider V.I. as an ideal operation, able to exactly produce the bounding volume $R$. For perspective projection the regions $C_i$ are solid cones, for orthographic projections they are cylinders obtained by sweeping the silhouettes along the viewing di-

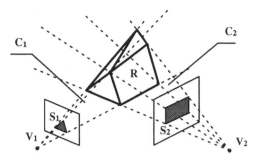

Fig.1–The volume intersection approach.

rections. In both cases the regions are bounded by ruled surfaces, generated by the lines tangent to $O$ and passing through the viewpoint $V$, or parallel to the viewing direction. We refer to these surfaces as to the *circumscribed cones* or *cylinders* of $O$. In the following, for simplicity we will speak of cones, conical surfaces and viewpoints referring both to perspective and parallel projections.

The V.I. approach raises the problem, which we address in this paper, of efficiently choosing the viewpoints. Each new silhouette and the related intersection operation can refine the reconstruction up to different degrees. The size of the volume deleted at each step, and therefore the accuracy and velocity of reconstruction, depend on the choice of the viewpoints. This choice is crucial for implementing effective volume intersection algorithms.

The purpose of this paper is to show that recent theoretical results in the shape–from silhouette area allow to define a *surface reconstruction accuracy(SAR)*, which can be computed from the reconstructed object $R$ at each step of the reconstruction process, *without any knowledge about the real object $O$*. This allows to understand if a sufficiently precise reconstruction of $O$ has been obtained. In addition, it will be shown that effective rules for choosing the next viewpoints can be constructed.

The content of the paper is as follows. In Section 2 we summarize some recent relevant theoretical results. In Section 3 we discuss, in the light of these results, the choices of viewpoints and the definition of reconstruction accuracy made in literature, and introduce the concept of surface reconstruction accuracy. In section IV we discuss the main lines of object–specific volume intersection algorithms for polyhedra and for smooth–surface objects. Section V contains concluding remarks.

## 2. Visual Hull and Inference of the Shape of the Unknown Object

### 2.1. The visual hull

The *visual hull* is a tool recently introduced for dealing with silhouette–based image understanding[17],[18], [19]. Here we resume the relevant material contained in [19], to which the reader is referred for formal definitions and proofs.The visual hull $VH(O,V)$ of a 3D object $O$ relative to a viewing region $V$ can be informally described as the volume enveloped by all the possible circumscribed cones of $O$ relative to viewpoints $\in V$.

336

It follows from the definition that $VH(O,V)$ is the closest approximation of $O$ that can be obtained using V.I. techniques with viewpoints $\in V$. A consequence is that an object $O$ can be exactly reconstructed by V.I. with viewpoints $\in V$ if and only if it is $O=VH(O,V)$

An object has infinite visual hulls, one for each viewing region. However, it can be shown that there is a unique visual hull, the *external* visual hull, or simply the visual hull **VH(O)**, for all the viewing region which completely enclose O without entering its convex hull. This is the case of main practical interest, since usually the object to be recognized or reconstructed lies at some distance and can assume any orientation with respect to the viewpoints. Examples of visual hulls of simple polyhedra are shown in Fig. 2. The visual hull relative to the unrestricted viewing region $V=E^3-O$ is defined to be the *internal* visual hull, and denoted **IVH(O)**.

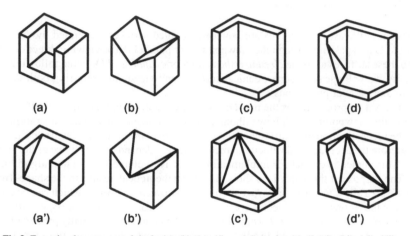

Fig.2–Four simple concave polyhedra(a), (b), (c), (d), and their visual hulls(a'), (b'), (c'), (d').

Algorithms for computing **VH(O)** and **IVH(O)** have been given for polygonal sets[17], polyhedra[19] and solids of revolution[18].

### 2.2. Inferring the shape of an object from its silhouettes

The problem of inferring the shape of the unknown object O from the object **R** reconstructed from the silhouettes has been discussed in [20]and [21]. The main results are summarized in the following. The bounding volume **R** supplies no precise information about the volume of O. However, the points of the *surface* of **R** can be divided into:
– *hard points,* which also belong to the surface of any possible object O originating **R**,
– *soft points,* otherwise.

Finding hard and soft points allows to divide the surface of **R** into a *hard part*, which is coincident with the surface of the original object, and a *soft part*, which is only an outer bound for O. The problem of finding the hard points has been considered in two cases: i) the ideal case of optimal reconstruction (when the visual hull is available); ii) the case of a generic reconstructed object.

Necessary and sufficient conditions for a point to be hard have been found in both cases. They allow to derive the hard points from the geometry of the reconstructed object. In particular, for polyhedral visual hulls an algorithm ALG1 has been given for finding the *hard edges* or parts of edges (the internal points of the planar faces are always soft)[21].

For the case of a generic reconstructed object **R**(i.e., when **R** is not the visual hull, or we do not know whether it is the visual hull or not), the following results hold. The surface of **R** consists of a number of strips ST(V), one for each viewpoint V. Each strip is what is left after the V.I. operations of the surface of the circumscribed cone having V as vertex. On each strip ST(V) there is a curve Cv consisting of points of the unknown object **O**, but if the strip has a certain width, we are not able to locate Cv on the strip and therefore all the points of the strip are soft. The only case in which we are able to locate hard points of the surface of **R** is when the course of the curve Cv is constrained by a strip of zero width.

As a consequence we have that, in the practical case of an object **R** reconstructed with a finite number of intersections, and thus with a finite number of strips, it is not possible to find hard surfaces for **R**, but only hard points or, at most, hard lines. Hard points are generated by the intersection of two strips, and can also be obtained for a smooth surface; hard lines requires creases(discontinuities of the surface normal) of the surface.

Hard points and lines can be obtained as side–products of a V.I. algorithm which updates, at each step, the description of the strips which form the surface of **R**. Let us call ALG2 such an algorithm.

## 3. Volume and Surface Reconstruction Accuracy

### 3.1. Volumetric accuracy

For evaluating the quality of the reconstruction obtained by V.I., it is necessary to define some accuracy index, that is some measure of the similarity between the original object **O** and the reconstructed object **R**. Since V.I. supplies volumes, usually([7], [9], [12], [13])the accuracy of reconstruction $Av$ is defined to be the ratio between the volume $Vol(O)$ of the original object and the volume $Vol(R)$ of the reconstructed object:

$Av=Vol(O) /Vol(R)$

This volumetric accuracy is not without shortcomings. One problem is that it mixes together two different kinds of reconstruction errors: those depending only on the intrinsic features of the object, and those related to the choice of the silhouettes. The visual hull concept allows us to overcome this problem(which was noted also by Ahuja and Veenstra[7]), by defining an accuracy $Av_H$ which makes reference to the volume $Vol(VH(O))$ of the visual hull:

$Av_H= Vol(VH(O)) / Vol(R)$

Let

$A_I=Vol(O) / Vol(VH(O))$

Then

$Av=Av_H \times A_I$

where the accuracy $A_I$ due to the intrinsic properties of **O** is separated from the accuracy $Av_H$ related to the choice of the viewpoints. Assuming for the moment $Av_H$ as accuracy, let us discuss the choices of the viewpoints presented in literature.

In some papers, orthographic projections along three mutually normal directions have been chosen([4], [14]). When this provides certain advantages for algorithms which compute the octree of the reconstructed object, crude approximations of the unknown object may result, for instance when its principal faces are not parallel to the viewing directions. Also in this more favorable situation, it is not possible to obtain the closest approximation, the visual hull, even of very simple objects. For instance, for the objects in Fig.2, obtained by deleting some volumes from a cube, the three silhouettes obtained with viewing directions parallel to the principal directions of the objects are squares and the volume obtained is a cube.

Ahuja and Veenstra[7] describe a volume intersection algorithm which uses thirteen orthographic views in fixed directions. Also in this case the viewing directions provide certain advantages for generating octrees. Using $Av$ as accuracy measure they verified the performance of the algorithm for a dozen of elementary objects in a large number of random orientations. Actually, since these objects were coincident with their visual hulls, the accuracy computed by Ahuja and Veenstra also was $A_{VH}$. Very good accuracy was obtained for the reconstruction of the test objects, and a good accuracy is likely to be obtained with many other objects. For instance, it can be verified that the visual hulls of objects (a) and (c) of Fig.2 can be exactly reconstructed by the algorithm, and good approximations can be obtained for objects (b) and (d). However, in spite of the satisfactory average behavior, significant details of the visual hull may be missed by the algorithm, and no bound to the worst case volumetric accuracy can be stated. It is not difficult to find objects such that $A_{VH}$ is arbitrarily small. For instance, we can imagine an object consisting of a convex polyhedron with a number of holes whose axes are all parallel to a direction $D$. This object is coincident with its visual hull and therefore perfectly reconstructable. It is clear that, if $D$ is not coincident with one of the thirteen directions of Ahuja and Veenestra, sufficiently small holes cannot be reconstructed. A vanishing thickness of the walls between the holes makes $A_{VH}$ arbitrarily small. The same solid can be used to show that the $A_{VH}$ can be made arbitrarily small for *any* set of fixed viewing directions. Similar arguments, that we omit, lead to examples of reconstruction with vanishing $A_{VH}$ for any set of fixed viewpoints.

In other papers on volume intersection ([11], [12], [13])there are no restriction on the viewpoints or viewing directions, but the focus is on the intersection algorithm and not on the choice of the silhouettes.

### 3.2. The idea of surface reconstruction accuracy

Without paying undue attention to extreme cases of objects with vanishing details, it is clear that for the effective use of the V.I. technique we must face the problem of obtaining sufficient accuracy(whatever its definition be) and at the same time limiting the number of silhouettes and thus the amount of computation.

For this purpose, an *object–specific, active* approach to the choice of the silhouettes could be effective. Following this idea, Shanmukh and Pujari [9]proposed a heuristic approach for finding the next viewing direction on the basis of the previous silhouettes. Some heuristics for the same purpose have also been proposed by Lavakusha et al., with viewing directions restricted to lie in one of the three principal planes[16].

The active approach proposed in this paper requires to reconsider the definition of reconstruction accuracy. It is clear in fact that the volumetric accuracy $A_{VH}$ is only suited for evaluating the performances of reconstruction algorithms for *known* objects. When we face the problem of constructing an active, object–specific algorithm, we need at each step of the reconstruction process a measure of accuracy capable of indicating if a sufficiently precise reconstruction of an *unknown* object has already been obtained

The volumetric accuracy measure $A_{VH}$ is obviously unable to support this process, since it cannot be computed for the current object. The results outlined in the previous section suggest an approach able to overcome this problem. We have seen that V.I. supplies precise information only about the surface of an unknown object: this suggests to introduce a *surface reconstruction accuracy(SAR)*, which can be computed at each step of the reconstruction process. The general idea is to compute at each step the hard surface of the current **R** and compare it in some way with the shape of whole surface of **R**. With this comparison we should be able to evaluate to what extent the surface of the current **R** can be explained by its hard part.

In practice, a definition of surface accuracy is not as simple and immediate as that of volumetric accuracy. Recall that a generic reconstructed volume **R** can only supply points or lines of the surface of the unknown object. It is not trivial to compare in a meaningful way these hard points and lines with the entire surface. In addition, the rules for efficiently choosing the next silhouette are related to this definition, and should be considered and specified jointly. A possible approach is to construct different definitions of SAR for different categories of objects. For showing that this approach is effective, in the next section we will discuss the guidelines for constructing active V.I. algorithms for polyhedra and smooth–surface objects.

## 4. Active V.I. Algorithms

### 4.1. Reconstruction of polyhedra

An idea suitable for polyhedra is to compare the set of hard edges $E_R$ of the current object **R**, determined according to algorithm ALG2 , with the set of hard edges $E_{VH}$ of the same object determined according to algorithm ALG1. In other words, $E_{VH}$ is computed *as if* **R** were the visual hull of the unknown object. At each step, the surface accuracy is defined as follows:

$SAR_P = F(E_R)/F(E_{VH})$

where $F$ is a suitable function of the hard edges, for instance the sum of their lengths. The rationale of this approach is that $SAR_P$ becomes unitary only when all the edges of **R** which *may* be hard have been actually found to be hard. This is a *necessary condition* for the reconstruction to be successfully terminated.

This definition of accuracy also suggests how to improve the reconstruction. At each step we have a set of edges, i.e. $E_{VH}-E_R$, which are candidates to become hard edges or be deleted in the subsequent steps. Therefore, the basic idea for improving the reconstruction is the following. *At each step consider one edge E of $E_{VH}-E_R$. Choose a new viewpoint such that its circumscribed cone is tangent at E to R.*

Actually, several edges can be tested at a time. For selecting in $E_{VH}-E_R$ the next edges to be tested, we can also consider features like their length and the type of the vertices(hard or soft). Since each new intersection might produce many new edges, we also need rules able to simplify the reconstructed object. For this purpose we can make hypotheses about the existence of undetected faces on the basis of known hard edges, and test these hypotheses by choosing viewpoints in the plane of these possible faces. Although to construct a detailed algorithm is beyond the scope of this paper, an example will be useful for illustrating these ideas. Let us consider some steps of an active V.I. process in the following case:

i)the unknown object is a cube centered on the origin and its principal directions are parallel to the axes;

ii) the active process starts from a reconstructed object $R_6$ which is obtained from six equal square silhouettes relative to six viewpoints $V_1$–$V_6$, lying on the coordinates axes at the same distance from the origin(see Fig 3(a)).

The hard points of $R_6$ computed according to ALG2 are highlighted in the figure. All the edges of $R_6$ are hard if they are computed according to ALG1( this can be immediately seen since a sufficient condition for an edge of a visual hull to be hard is that it is also an edge of the convex hull of the visual hull–see[20]). Thus $SARP$ is zero and we must continue the V.I. process. The edges to be checked at the next step are selected among those whose endpoints are hard. Four (or even six ) of them can be tested together. By choosing, another viewpoint $V_7$ on the y axis at a distance from the origin greater than that of the previous viewpoint, we obtain $R_7$ (Fig.3(b)) and four hard edges. $SARP$ has been increased, but four new edges have been introduced. Now we check the hypothesis that the hard edges found, which lie all on a plane, are the boundaries of one face. To do this, we select a viewpoint $V_8$ lying in the plane $p$ supporting the hard edges, as shown in Fig. 3(c)). The new V.I. operation supplies $R_8$, where four edges have been deleted and three new hard edges have been found. We omit the description of the following steps, which allow to quickly reach a unitary $SARP$.

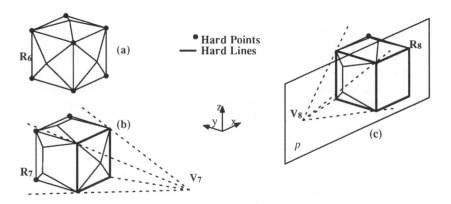

Fig.3–Object $R_6$ has been obtained from six square silhouettes relative to six viewpoints lying on the coordinates axes at the same distance from the origin; it has eight hard points(a). The viewpoint $V_7$ allows to obtain four hard edges(b). A substantial improvement of the reconstruction accuracy is obtained with $V_8$, which lies on the plane $p$ supporting these hard edges.

The example shows how an active approach could work: obviously, further developments are needed for actually implementing the algorithm.

As already observed, obtaining a unitary *SARP* is only a necessary condition for an exact reconstruction, since it does not guarantee that all the edges of **O** have been found. The theoretical worst case behavior of any active algorithm is no better than that of fixed viewpoints algorithms. This can be seen considering a cube cut through by one hole obtained by sweeping a polygon along a direction D. In theory, this object can be reconstructed with only three parallel views, one along D and two along any pair of the principal axes. Whatever be the algorithm for choosing the next silhouette, if none of the previous viewpoints is sufficiently near to the axis of the hole, no clue about the very existence of the hole is available. Even if we know *a priori* that the hole exists, but not its orientation, no algorithm for sampling the viewspace is guaranteed to find holes of vanishing dimension in a bounded number of steps.

In practice however we are neither interested in nor able to observe vanishing details. Therefore we think that effective V.I. algorithms can be constructed according to the active approach outlined.

### 4.2. Reconstruction of curved objects

Let us consider the reconstruction of smooth surfaces. In this case, the reconstructed object **R** supplies only hard points and not hard lines(see Section 2). The idea, used for reconstructing polyhedra, of comparing the hard points of **R** with those computed as if **R** were a visual hull cannot be applied. In fact, if **R** is considered as a visual hull, it is easy to understand that all the boundary lines of each strip are hard. However, they supply no useful information, since we know *a priori* that these lines do not belong to the surface of **O** (except for their intersections).

Two different approaches can be used for constructing definitions of surface accuracy suitable for driving active algorithms .

One idea is to use the hard points known at each step for constructing an approximate boundary $S_a$ of the objects( several algorithms for doing this are available). Let us define a *local weighted accuracy $A_h(P)$* as the number of hard points per unitary surface, weighted according to the local curvature. This takes into account that a zone with higher curvature needs more hard points than a zone with lesser curvature. The overall surface accuracy can be defined as the average value of this local accuracy:

$$A = 1/S \int_{S_a} A_h(P) dS$$

where S is the surface of $S_a$. Using the approximate boundary $S_a$ as a model of the object, we can choose viewpoints such that the circumscribed cone is tangent to $S_a$ at zones with lower weighted density: this will produce new hard points in these zones, thus improving the accuracy of the reconstruction.

Another possible approach is based on the observation that a close reconstruction of the unknown object can also be obtained with few hard points. A limit case can be seen in Fig.4, where we show the reconstruction of a sphere obtained from five viewpoints lying on a line D passing through the center of the sphere. By increasing the number of viewpoints on

342

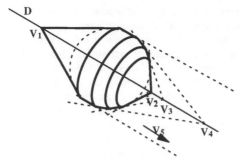

Fig.4– A sphere can be reconstructed with arbitrarily high precision adding viewpoints on D even if no hard points are constructed.

D, we can reconstruct the sphere with arbitrarily high precision, even if no hard point at all are constructed. This suggests to define a *strip accuracy* $A_{ST}(P)$, which for each point P depends on: i)the local width of the strip to which P belongs; ii) the local curvature, whose approximate value can be computed from the current reconstructed object. An overall accuracy can be obtained, as before, by averaging $A_{ST}(P)$ over all the surface. A definition along this line appears more versatile than the previous one, which only depends on hard points.

As before, a suitable heuristic for improving this accuracy consists of using the current reconstructed object as a model for finding viewpoints such that the circumscribed cones are tangent to this model at zones with lower $A_{ST}(P)$.

## 5. Summary

Object–specific V.I. algorithms require the capability of evaluating the reconstruction quality for unknown objects, as well as rules for choosing other viewpoints when the quality is not satisfactory. We have shown that a reconstruction accuracy can be defined for the surface of the objects reconstructed, which, unlike the volumetric accuracy, can be computed at each step of the reconstruction process. In addition, rules for choosing the next viewpoint able to improve the surface reconstruction accuracy have been presented.

Although the ideas outlined appear promising, further theoretical and experimental work is needed. The author is currently involved in implementing an active polyhedra reconstruction algorithm based on surface reconstruction accuracy. Future development will focus on the active reconstruction of general objects.

## 6. References

[1] S.N. Srihari,"Representation of three–dimensional digital images," *ACM Comput. Surveys,* Vol. 13, No.4, pp. 399–424, 1981
[2] Y.C. Kim and J.K. Aggarwal,"Rectangular parallelepiped coding for solid modeling," *Int. J. Robotics. Automat.*Vol. 1, pp.77–85, 1986
[3] C.Chien and J.K.Aggarwal,"Model reconstruction and shape recognition from occluding contours," *IEEE Trans.Pattern Anal. Machine Intell.*, Vol.11, pp.372–389,1989

[4] Lavakusa et al.,"Linear octrees by Volume Intersection," *Comput.Vision Graphics Image Process.*,Vol.45,pp.371–379,1989

[5] S. Srivastava and N. Ahuia,"An algorithm for generating octrees from object silhouettes in perspective views," in *Proc. IEEE Workshop Computer Vision, Miami Beach, Fl,* pp.363–365, Nov. 1987

[6] H.L.Tan et al.,"Inspection of machine parts by back–projection reconstruction," in *Proc. IEEE Conf. Robotics and Automat.,* North Carolina, pp. 503–508, April 1987

[7] N.Ahuja and J.Veenstra,"Generating Octrees from Object Silhouettes in orthographic views," *IEEE Trans.Pattern Anal. Machine Intell.,*Vol.11,pp.137–149,1989

[8] T.H.Hong and M.Schneier,"Describing a robot's workspace using a sequence of views from a moving camera," *IEEE Trans.Pattern Anal. Machine Intell.,*Vol.7,pp721–726,1985

[9] K. Shanmukh and A.K. Pujari,"Volume intersection with optimal set of directions," *Pattern Reco. Letters,* Vol.12, pp.165–170, 1991

[10] W.N.Martin and J.K.Aggarwal,"Volumetric description of objects from multiple views," *IEEE Trans.Pattern Anal. Machine Intell.,*Vol.5, pp.150–158,1983

[11] P.Srinivasan et al.,"Computational geometric methods in volumetric intersection for 3D reconstruction,"*Pattern Recognition,*Vol.23,pp.843–857,1990

[12] M.Potemesil,"Generating octree models of 3D objects from their silhouettes in a sequence of images,"*Comput.Vision Graphics Image Process.,*Vol.40,pp.1–29,1987

[13] H.Noborio et al."Construction of the octree approximating three–dimensional objects by using multiple views," *IEEE Trans.Pattern Anal. Machine Intell.,*Vol.10,pp.769–782,1988

[14] C.H.Chien and J.K.Aggarwal,"Volume/surface octrees for the representation of three–dimensional objects,"*Comput.Vision,Graphics and Image Processing,*Vol.36,pp100–113,1986

[15] V.Cappellini et al.,"From multiple views to object recognition,"*IEEE Trans.Circuits Syst.,*Vol.34,pp.1344–1350,1987

[16] Lavakusha et al.,"Volume intersection algorithms with changing directions of views,"in *Proc. MIV–89, Tokyo,* pp.309–314, 1989

[17] A. Laurentini,"The visual hull: a new tool for contour–based image understanding," *Proc. 7th. Scandinavian Conf. on Image Analysis,* pp. 993–1002, 1991

[18] A. Laurentini,"The visual hull of solids of revolution," in *Proc.11th IAPR Int.Conf.on Pattern Reco.,* The Hague, pp.720–724, 1992

[19] A. Laurentini,"The visual hull concept for silhouette–based image understanding," *IEEE Trans.Pattern Anal. Machine Intell.*Vol.16, February 1994

[20] A. Laurentini,"Inferring the shape of the real object from the object reconstructed by volume intersection," *IEEE Proc. Computer Vision and Pattern Reco. 1993, New York,* pp.280–285

[21] A. Laurentini,"How far 3D shapes can be understood from 2D silhouettes," to appear in *IEEE Trans.Pattern Anal. Machine Intell.*

# AN ITERATIVE ALGORITHM FOR SHAPE REGISTRATION

FENG LU

Department of Computer Science, University of Toronto,
Toronto, Canada M5S 1A4, lufeng@vis.toronto.edu

EVANGELOS MILIOS

Department of Computer Science, York University,
North York, Canada M3J 1P3, eem@cs.yorku.ca

### Abstract

We propose a new method called the iterative dual correspondence (IDC) algorithm for registering a data shape to a model shape without using features. The algorithm is iterative, and each iteration consists of the establishment of point correspondences and the estimation of the transformation between the two shapes. We use two correspondences for each data point which are the closest point on the model and the model point which has the same range as the data point. Experiments show that our correspondence rule results in very accurate estimation of the transformation and our algorithm converges much faster than the ICP algorithm.

## 1. Introduction

Shape registration is an important problem in pattern recognition and computer vision. The problem can be defined as follows: Given sensor data in a sensor coordinate system, which describes a shape that may correspond to a model shape, and given a model shape in a model coordinate system, estimate the optimal rotation, translation, and possibly scaling that aligns the model shape and the data shape by minimizing the distance between the shapes. In general, both the model and the data are noisy, and it is possible for parts of both the data and the model to be missing (for example due to occlusion). This extremely hard problem can be made tractable when an approximate registration between the model and the data is known a priori, and this is the focus of this paper. Important applications of this problem are: parts inspection by matching a range image to a CAD surface model, planar shape recognition from images, mobile robot pose estimation by matching range scans to a world model and map building by matching range scans with each other.

Most existing methods use distinguishable points or line segments as features and determine feature correspondence using some search technique [4]. This approach allows aligning shapes with arbitrarily large displacements and can tolerate certain amount of occlusion. But its effectiveness depends on the reliability of the feature extraction procedures. Also the search for feature correspondence is usually computationally expensive. Rotation and translation invariant shape descriptions, such as scale space images [11] and extended Gaussian images [10], have also been used for matching.

These descriptions often require the second derivatives of the shape and therefore they are unreliable in the presence of noise. Some methods use arc-length sampling of curves to establish correspondences [12]. They have difficulty in the presence of occlusion.

There is another class of methods which avoid the use of localized high level features. Typically, these methods iteratively establish correspondences of low level primitives (usually raw data points) to targets on the model and then solve a least-squares problem to minimize the distance between the data shape and the model. The target on the model corresponding to a data point can be the closest point on the model [1], the closest line segment of a polygonal model [3], the tangent line or plane of the model at a point close to the data point [2, 8]. Usually these approaches only converge to a local optimum. Therefore, a good initial estimate of the registration transformation is needed.

We present a new algorithm called the iterative dual correspondence (IDC) algorithm for shape registration. It is based on iterative least-squares solutions using point to point correspondences, similar to the iterative closest-point (ICP) algorithm [1]. But in addition to choosing the closest point on the model as the correspondence for a data point, we also choose the model point which has the same range as the data point as a correspondence. Our correspondence rule reveals substantial information about the rotation component. By using two correspondence sets, we can estimate the transformation very accurately and our method converges significantly faster than the ICP algorithm.

In this paper we first present the 2D case of the algorithm and some of its applications. Then we briefly describe the extension of the algorithm to the 3D case.

## 2. Registration of 2D Shapes

### 2.1 Iterative Algorithm

We consider the problem of matching 2D points to a curve model where the data shape and the model shape differ by a 2D similarity transformation. The transformation consists of a rotation angle $\omega$, a scaling factor $s$, and a translation vector $T = (T_x, T_y)^t$.

The algorithm is based on iteratively minimizing the distance from the data points to their corresponding points on the model. Upon convergence, the final solution is obtained via the composition of the transformations found at each step. Each iteration of the algorithm consists of the following operations: (1) For each point $P_i$ in the data set, use a simple rule (independent of the unknown transformation) to determine a corresponding point $P_i'$ on the model; (2) compute a least-squared solution of the relative transformation based on all the correspondence pairs of points; (3) apply the least-squared solution to transform the data set with respect to the model.

Based on $n$ pairs of corresponding points $(P_i(x_i, y_i), P_i'(x_i', y_i')), i = 1, \ldots, n$, the least-

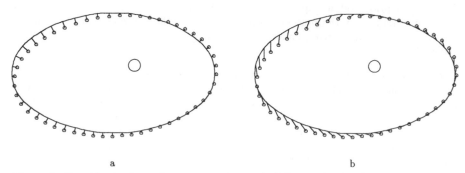

a                                                      b

Figure 1: Use rules to determine correspondences (which are joined by line segments in the figure). (a) Use the closest-point rule; (b) use the matching-range rule. The model is the ellipse. The data points are labeled by small circles. The big circle is the origin.

squared solution for the transformation variables $(\omega, s, T_x, T_y)$ can be derived by minimizing the following distance function:

$$E_2(\omega, s, T) = \sum_{i=1}^{n} |sR(\omega)P_i + T - P_i'|^2, \tag{1}$$

where $R(\omega)$ is the 2x2 rotation matrix. Closed-form solutions for $\omega$, $s$, and $T$ can be derived [6]. The central issue of the algorithm is to design the rules for finding correspondences, which we will discuss in the next section.

## 2.2 Rules for Correspondence

**Closest-Point Rule:** A commonly used rule is to choose the closest point on the model as the correspondence for a data point. Fig. 1(a) shows an example of finding the closest points in an elliptic model. Besl and McKay described a general-purpose iterative closest point (ICP) algorithm for shape registration based on this rule and they proved that the ICP algorithm always converges monotonically to a local minimum with respect to the least-square distance function [1].

One disadvantage of the ICP algorithm is that it converges very slowly. When the model is curved, the closest-point correspondences contain little information about the rotation. In fact, the vectors joining the correspondence pairs have very inconsistent directions and they tend to cancel out each other when used altogether to solve for the rotation. Moreover, the convergence speed of the algorithm is always very slow when the distance function approachs a local minimum. To accelerate the ICP algorithm, Besl and McKay used a line search method to heuristically determine the transformation variables based on their values in two or three recent iterations. Although this improves the convergence speed near a local minimum, the problem of slow convergence in solving the rotation still exists. Moreover, the acceleration method does not work when outliers should be rejected during the iterations.

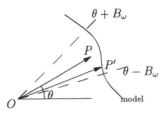

Figure 2: Matching-range rule: For a point $P$ of the data, the corresponding point $P'$ on the model shown lies within the sector centered at $O$ and bound by half-lines at angles $\theta - B_\omega$ and $\theta + B_\omega$ and its range $|OP'|$ is the closest to $|OP|$.

**Matching-Range Rule:** We propose a different rule which finds the correspondences in such a way that they significantly reveal the rotation component. We observe that, when translation and scaling are neglectable, the correspondence of a point $P$ under a rotation is a point which has the same polar range as that of $P$, and the polar angles of the corresponding points differ by the rotation angle $\omega$. This suggests that a good candidate for the correspondence point of $P$ is a point $P'$ where $|P'| = |P|$. To ensure a unique and reliable correspondence point, we only search within a local region of the model near $P$. Suppose that we can estimate a bound $B_\omega$ for the rotation $\omega$, i.e. $|\omega| \leq B_\omega$. We formulate the correspondence rule (called it *matching-range rule*) as the following: The correspondence for a data point $P$ is the point $P'$ on the model such that $|\arg P' - \arg P| \leq B_\omega$ and $|P'|$ is closest to $|P|$. The rule is illustrated in Fig. 2.

Fig. 1(b) shows an example of using the matching-range rule to find correspondences in the elliptic model. We can clearly see that the vectors joining the correspondence pairs consistently indicate the rotation direction. Therefore, the least-squared solution should be a good approximation to the true transformation, especially in the rotation component.

Based on this new rule, we design the iterative matching-range point (IMRP) algorithm. In this algorithm, the parameter $B_\omega$ controls the size of the neighborhood to be searched for a correspondence and also the maximum rotation possibly solved in one iteration. We generate the values for $B_\omega$ using an exponentially decreasing function of the form: $B_\omega(t) = B_\omega(0)e^{-\alpha t}$.

A comparison of the ICP algorithm and the IMRP algorithm is illustrated in Fig. 3. We notice that the IMRP algorithm converges faster than the ICP algorithm in estimating the rotation. As to the translation part, the IMRP algorithm is initially slower but it soon catches up after some iterations and converges faster than the ICP algorithm. The reason for this phenomenon is that the matching-range rule only tends to influence the translation component when the sector width $B_\omega$ becomes small enough. The scaling errors are reduced quickly by both algorithms.

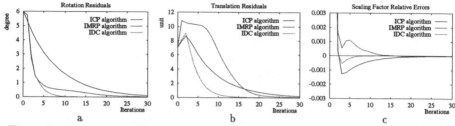

Figure 3: Comparison of iterative algorithms. (a) Rotation residuals from the three algorithms over 30 iterations. The initial rotation angle is 6 degrees. (b) Magnitudes of translation residuals. The magnitude of initial translation is 7.07 units. (c) Scaling factor residuals (relative errors of the derived scaling factors). The initial scaling factor is 0.8. The model and data set are given in Figure 1.

The cost of applying the matching-range rule to find a correspondence point is approximately the same as the cost of finding a closest point, as both require a search to minimize a distance function. The distance function for the closest-point rule is $|P' - P|^2$, while the distance function for the matching-range rule is $(|P'| - |P|)^2$.

**Combining the Two Correspondence Rules:** It is desirable to combine the two rules in order to achieve both the convergence speed of the IMRP algorithm and the stability of the ICP algorithm. We propose the *iterative dual correspondence* (IDC) algorithm which uses both rules, as the following:

1. For each data point $P_i$,

   (a) apply the closest-point rule to find a correspondence point $P_i'$ for $P_i$.

   (b) apply the matching-range rule to find a correspondence point $P_i''$ for $P_i$.

2. Compute the least-squared solution $(\omega_1, s_1, T_1)$ from the set of correspondence pairs $(P_i, P_i'), i = 1, \ldots, n$ (which are obtained using the closest-point rule).

3. Compute the least-squared solution $(\omega_2, s_2, T_2)$ from the set of correspondence pairs $(P_i, P_i''), i = 1, \ldots, n$ (which are obtained using the matching-range rule).

4. Form $(\omega_2, s_1, T_1)$ as the solution for the transformation in the current iteration.

5. Repeat all the steps until the process converges.

The basic idea of the above algorithm is to take the translation and scaling components from the closest-point rule solution and the rotation component from the matching-range rule solution to form the current solution for the transformation.

The combination of the two rules appears to achieve significantly better results than each of the individual rules. Not only is the stability of the iterations retained, but the convergence speed is also increased dramaticly. In fact, the two rules reinforce each other by reducing different components of the transformation, so that each of them can be more effective in the following iteration. We notice that the IDC algorithm is insensitive to the choices of parameter $B_\omega$.

Fig. 3 illustrates the residuals of the transformation components during the iterations of the three algorithms. The model and the data points in this example are the ones given in Fig. 1. The initial transformation consists of a rotation of -6 degrees, a scaling factor of 0.8, and a translation of (-5, 5) units (the width of the elliptic model is 1000 units). The comparison of the residuals clearly show that the IDC algorithm converges much more quickly than the other two single-rule algorithms.

### 2.3 Detecting Outliers

The above algorithms only consider the ideal situation when every point has a correspondence on the model. In the presence of occlusion, however, we need to identify the outlier points which do not correspond to any points on the model and exclude them from the mean-square distance function.

Assume that we also have a bound $B_r$ for the maximum displacement of a data point caused by translation and scaling, i.e. $||P'| - |P|| \leq B_r$ for a correct correspondence pair $P$ and $P'$. We can use this condition to test for outliers. For a pair of points found by one of the rules, we accept them as a correspondence pair only if the above condition is met. One way of setting the threshold is to discard a certain fraction $p$ of the data points which have the largest distances from their correspondence points and only use the remaining points to estimate the transformation. In this case, the threshold $B_r$ is the $k$th largest distance among all the correspondence pairs, where $k = np$ with $n$ being the number of data points.

For the thresholding technique to successfully recognize outliers, we require that the initial registration is accurate enough for the displacement of data points caused by the transformation to be small compared with the distance from the outlier points to the true shape. If the displacements are relatively large, we can run our matching procedure two or more times with gradually tighter values in the thresholds $B_r$ or $p$.

If the tangent information from both the data set and the model are available, we can use them to more robustly detect outliers. This idea is used by the "tangent-based matching algorithm" [8]. Another robust method of handling outliers is to statistically sample the data points and repeat the matching process with different sets of data points [9].

## 3. Applications of 2D Shape Registration

### 3.1 Registration of Planer Shapes from Image

In this section, we apply the IDC algorithm to register the contour of a planar shape

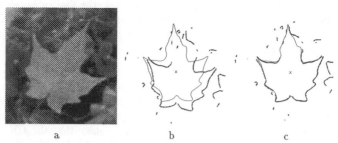

a          b          c

Figure 4: Registration of the shape of a maple leaf. (a) Image containing the leaf shape. (b) Initial registration of the leaf shape to the curve model. (c) Final result of registration.

to a given model. It is assumed that the contour pixels can be extracted from the image using an edge detector. The model for the shape contour is a closed curve represented in piecewise splines. We derive the curve model from a complete set of contour pixels of the shape (extracted from another clean image), using an optimal, adaptive fitting procedure [7].

In the example shown in Fig. 4, we register the shape of a maple leaf. The original image containing the leaf is shown in Fig. 4(a). Part (b) shows the a priori known registration of the leaf shape in the image to a curve model. Part (c) shows the final result after registration. The recovered transformation variables are: rotation angle 9.0°, scaling factor 0.96, translation (-12.5, 15.6) pixels. We applied the registration process twice with two different outlier thresholds. In the example, we used a low threshold (5%) to derive an approximate registration. Then we used a higher threshold (20%) to exclude more outliers and derive a more accurate final registration.

### 3.2 Matching Range Scans for Pose Estimation

Another application of shape registration is to match a range scan to a world model (or a previous "reference" scan) so as to estimate the pose of the robot (position and heading) from which the scan is taken. A range scan is a list of points corresponding to the intersection points of a laser beam with objects in the robot's environment.

The pose error of a robot is the difference of the pose where the robot "thinks" it is and the pose where it actually is. If the pose error is non-zero, the scan will be misaligned with the model by a rotation and a translation. By properly aligning the scan with the model, we can derive the relative rotation and translation and correct the pose error.

Considering that the reference scan is discrete, we need to interpolate the scan points in order to determine the correspondence points. More details about the method and experiments with real or simulated data can be found in [8].

We present an example of matching simulated range scans as shown in Fig. 5. Part

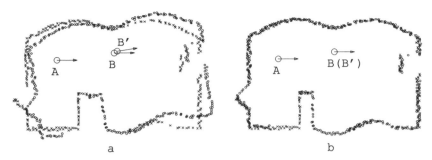

Figure 5: Aligning two simulated range scans. The robot went from pose A to pose B in reality, but due to odometry errors, it thinks it went to pose B'. Points on scans from pose A and B are labelled as x's and small circles respectively. Part (a) shows the alignment error due to the difference between pose B' and true pose B. Part (b) shows the result of aligning the two scans. The pose B' is corrected to the true pose B by the same transformation.

(a) shows two range scans which are misaligned with each other by a pose error (rotation $\omega = 7.5°$, translation $T = (20, 10)$ cm). The width of the environment is 10 meters. The range data contain sensing noises which are uniformly distributed with a maximum error of $\pm 10$cm. Part (b) shows the result of correcting the pose error and aligning the two scans using the IDC algorithm. The initial pose and the corrected pose are indicated by circles with arrows. Notice that the matching is accurate despite of the occlusion parts in the scans. To further test the robustness of the algorithm, we repeat the experiment 1000 times with randomly selected initial pose errors ($|\omega| \leq 7.5°$, $|T| \leq 25$cm). The standard deviations of the residual rotation and translation are less than $0.5°$ and less than $2cm$ respectively. Note that these error residuals are quite small compared with the magnitude of the sensing noise.

## 4. Registration of 3D Shapes

In this section, we extend the IDC algorithm to register 3D shapes. Assuming that we have a 3D surface model, the problem is to solve a rigid motion (3D rotation and translation) which registers a set of data points to the model.

The 3D rotation and translation can be solved in closed-form from a set of point-to-point correspondences, using a quaternion approach [1] or SVD method [5]. We have an alternative method which solves the rotation by factorizing the cross-covariance matrix into the rotation matrix and a symmetric matrix [6].

We extend the correspondence rules to the 3D case. The closest-point rule now chooses the closest point on the model surface as the correspondence of a data point, similar to the 2D case. A straightforward extension of the matching-range point rule to 3D is the following: For a data point $P$, its corresponding point is $P'$ on the model such that the angle between vectors $P$ and $P'$ is within a threshold $B_R$ and $|P'|$ is closest to $|P|$.

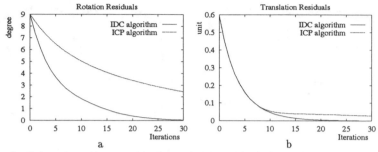

Figure 6: Comparison of rotation and translation residuals from ICP and IDC algorithms in the above example. (a) Rotation residuals; (b) translation residuals. Notice that the IDC algorithm converges much faster than the ICP algorithm in reducing the rotation.

But the disadvantage of this extension is that the correspondence given by the rule is usually not unique. We modify the rule to the following form: The correspondence $P'$ for a data point $P$ is the point on the model surface which minimizes the objective function $(|P'| - |P|)^2 + W(\theta, B_R)$. Here the penalty function $W$ is monotonical in the angle $\theta = \arccos \frac{P' \cdot P}{|P'||P|}$. Its value should be small when $\theta \leq B_R$ and becomes very large otherwise. A typical choice of $W$ is a power function. In implementation, we can use a standard optimization algorithm (such as the Newton's algorithm) to minimize the objective function and determine the correspondence point. If the the surface model is non-smooth or discrete, we can sample some directions within the cone and choose an appropriate intersection point with the model as the correspondence point.

We present an experiment to compare our 3D IDC algorithm with the ICP algorithm. The 3D surface model is an ellipsoid: $(x/a)^2 + (y/b)^2 + (z/c)^2 = 1$, where $a = 5, b = 4, c = 3$. We randomly choose 100 points on the surface as data points which are initially misaligned with the model by a rigid transformation. The rotation is 9° around axis $(\frac{2}{3}, -\frac{2}{3}, \frac{1}{3})$. Translation is $(0.5, -0.3, -0.1)$. No noise is assumed in this example. We use both the IDC algorithm and the ICP algorithm to correct the transformation. The magnitude of rotation and translation residuals from the two algorithms are plotted in Fig. 6. It can be seen that, with such a curved model, the ICP algorithm converges very slowly in solving the rotation. Our IDC algorithm significantly improves the convergence speed. The IDC algorithm also converges faster in solving the translation.

## 5. Conclusion

We have presented a new iterative dual correspondence (IDC) algorithm which uses both the closest-point rule and the matching-range point rule to associate correspondences for data points. The cost of applying the matching-range point rule is about the same as the cost of applying the closest-point rule. Therefore the complexity of one iteration of the IDC algorithm is about twice as that of one iteration of the ICP algorithm. However, the IDC algorithm converges much faster than the ICP algorithm, especially in solving the rotation component. The IDC algorithm can be used in general 2D or 3D free-form shape registration.

**Acknowledgement:** Funding for this work was provided by the Natural Sciences and Engineering Research Council of Canada and the ARK Project, which receives its funding from PRECARN Associates Inc., the Department of Industry, Science and Technology, the National Research Council of Canada, the Ontario Technology Fund. Ontario Hydro, and Atomic Energy of Canada Limited.

### References

[1] P. J. Besl and N. D. McKay. A method for registration of 3-D shapes. *IEEE Transactions on Pattern Analysis and Machine Intelligence*, 14(2):239–256, 1992.

[2] Y. Chen and G. Medioni. Object modelling by registration of multiple range images. *International Journal of Image and Vision Computing*, 10(3):145–155, 1992.

[3] I. J. Cox. Blanche: An experiment in guidance and navigation of an autonomous robot vehicle. *IEEE Transactions on Robotics and Automation*, 7(2):193–204, 1991.

[4] W. E. L. Grimson, T. Lozano-Pérez, and D. P. Huttenlocher. *Object Recognition by Computer: The Role of Geometric Constraints*. MIT Press, Cambridge, MA, 1990.

[5] K. Kanatani. *Geometric Computation for Machine Vision*. Oxford University Press, Oxford, 1993.

[6] F. Lu and E. Milios. An iterative method for shape registration. Technical Report (in preparation), Dept. of CS, University of Toronto, 1994.

[7] F. Lu and E. Milios. Optimal spline fitting to planar shape. *Signal Processing*, 37(1), 1994.

[8] F. Lu and E. Milios. Robot pose estimation in unknown environments by matching 2D range scans. In *IEEE Conference on Computer Vision and Pattern Recognition*, 1994 (to appear).

[9] T. Masuda and N. Yokoya. A robust method for registration and segmentation of multiple range images. In *Second IEEE CAD-based Vision Workshop*, pages 106–113, 1994.

[10] E. E. Milios. Shape matching using curvature processes. *Computer Vision, Graphics, and Image Processing*, 47:203–236, 1989.

[11] F. Mokhtarian and A. Mackworth. Scale-based description and recognition of planar curves and two-dimensional shapes. *IEEE Transactions on Pattern Analysis and Machine Intelligence*, 8(1):34–43, 1986.

[12] J.T. Schwartz and M. Sharir. Identification of partially obscured objects in two and three dimensions by matching noisy characteristic curves. *International Journal of Robotics Research*, 6(2):29–44, 1987.

# ON A ROTATIONAL SYMMETRY OF CONVEX SETS

G.L. MARGOLIN, A.V. TUZIKOV

*Institute of Engineering Cybernetics,*
*Academy of Sciences of Republic Belarus,*
*Surganova 6, 220012 Minsk, Belarus*
*mahaniok%bas10.basnet.belpak.minsk.by@demos.su*

### Abstract

We introduce and investigate a measure of a rotational symmetry of compact convex sets in Euclidean space. It is defined as the ratio of the volume (Lebesgue measure) of the given set to the volume of the generalized Minkowski symmetric set.

We describe the procedure of finding the measure of a rotational symmetry of compact convex sets for Euclidean plane based on the application of a perimetric measure. This procedure is much easier for polygons, since for them the perimetric measure is a discrete function being simply calculated.

We describe a decomposition of a compact convex set in Euclidean plane into the Minkowski sum of two sets. The first one is rotationally symmetrical with respect to the considered rotation group and the second one is completely asymmetrical in the sense that it doesn't allow such a decomposition.

## 1   Introduction

The aim of this note is the investigation of a rotational symmetry of compact convex sets in Euclidean space. We try to continue the approach suggested by G. Matheron and J. Serra [3] for the case of a central symmetry. We shall introduce a measure for a rotational symmetry on the compact convex sets. To do this we consider a generalization of the Minkowski symmetric set for the group of rotations. Then the ratio of the volume (Lebesgue measure) of the given set to the volume of the generalized Minkowski symmetric set defines the measure of a rotational symmetry of the original set.

We describe the procedure of finding the measure of a rotational symmetry for the case of $\mathbf{R}^2$. This procedure is based on the application of a perimetric measure (Matheron, 1975, p.93 or Serra, 1982, p.120). Given the perimetric measure of a compact convex set in a plane it is possible to find the measure of a rotational symmetry without finding explicitly the generalized Minkowski symmetric set. The volume of this symmetric is calculated using the perimetric measure of the initial set, since the perimetric measure is a linear function with respect to Minkowski addition. This procedure is much easier for polygons. In this case the perimetric measure is a discrete function being simply calculated for the polygon.

At the end of the paper we consider a decomposition of a compact convex set into the Minkowski sum of two sets. The first one is rotationally symmetrical with respect to the considered rotation group and the second one is completely asymmetrical in the sense that it doesn't allow such a decomposition.

# 2 Measure of a rotational symmetry

Let $\mathcal{K}$ be the set of non-empty compact sets in Euclidean space $\mathbf{R}^n$ and $\mathcal{G}(\mathcal{K})$ will denote the subfamily of $\mathcal{K}$ made up by its convex sets.

Denote by $G$ a group of rotations of $\mathbf{R}^n$ with respect to the origin $O$. We suppose that $G$ is a cyclic group of order $m$. Let $g$ be a generator of the group $G$, i.e., the rotation to the angle $2\pi/m$. Given set $M \in \mathbf{R}^n$, $g(M)$ denotes the results of the rotation of the set $M$, $g^i(M) = g(g^{i-1}(M))$, $g^m(M) = M$, $g^0(M) = M$.

For the sets $A, B \in \mathbf{R}^n$ denote by $\oplus$ the Minkowski sum, i.e.,

$$A \oplus B = \{a + b, \ a \in A, \ b \in B\},$$

where $a + b = ((a_1 + b_1), \ldots, (a_n + b_n))$, $a = (a_1, \ldots, a_n)$, $b = (b_1, \ldots, b_n)$.

Given $\lambda = (\lambda_0, \ldots, \lambda_{m-1}) \in \mathbf{R}^m$, $0 < \lambda_i < 1$, $\sum_{i=0}^{m-1} \lambda_i = 1$, define the set $S_m^\lambda(M)$ as follows

$$S_m^\lambda(M) = \oplus_{i=0}^{m-1} \lambda_i g^i(M).$$

If $\lambda = (1/m, \ldots, 1/m)$ we have a generalization of Minkowski symmetric set

$$S_m(M) = 1/m(\oplus_{i=0}^{m-1} g^i(M)).$$

**Definition 1** *The set $A$ is called rotationally symmetrical with respect to the rotation group $G$ of order $m$ if $g^i(A) = A$ up to translation for all $0 \leq i \leq m-1$ and $g \in G$.*

**Proposition 1** *The set $S_m(M)$ is a rotationally symmetrical set with respect to the group $G$.*

For $m = 2$ we have the set $S_2(M)$ which is centrally symmetrical.

Our aim is to define the measure of a rotational symmetry of the arbitrary set $M \in \mathcal{G}(\mathcal{K})$.

Denote first by $V(M)$ the volume of the set $M \in \mathcal{K}$ (or its Lebesgue measure). Given sets $M, N \in \mathcal{K}$, it is known from the Brunn-Minkowski inequality that

$$V^{1/n}(M \oplus N) \geq V^{1/n}(M) + V^{1/n}(N).$$

The equality holds iff $M, N$ are convex positively homotetic sets.

It is known (see, for example, Hadwiger, 1957, ch.4) that the following properties hold for compact convex sets

$$V(S_m^\lambda(A)) \geq V(A).$$

$$S_m^\lambda(\beta A) = \beta S_m^\lambda(A) \text{ for } \beta > 0,$$

$$S_m^\lambda(A \oplus B) = S_m^\lambda(A) \oplus S_m^\lambda(B).$$

$$\lim_{k\to\infty} A_k = A \text{ imply } S_m^\lambda(A_n) \to S_m^\lambda(A).$$

Let us now investigate the case when the equality holds

$$V(S_m^\lambda(M)) = V(M).$$

It is clear that if $M$ is a rotationally symmetrical convex set then all the sets $\lambda_i g^i(M)$ will be homotetic and due to Brunn-Minkowski theorem the above equality will hold. We will show that this condition is not only sufficient but also necessary. Thus the following theorem holds.

**Theorem 1** *Given a compact set $M \in \mathbf{R}^n$, a cyclic group $G$ of order $m$ and a vector $\lambda \in \mathbf{R}^m$, $0 < \lambda_i < 1$, $\sum_{i=0}^{m-1} \lambda_i = 1$, the following equality holds*

$$V(S_m^\lambda(M)) = V(M)$$

*iff $M$ is a convex and a rotationally symmetrical set with respect to the group $G$.*

Proof. We prove only the necessary condition. Suppose that the equality holds. Since $V(M) = V(g^i(M))$ and

$$V^{1/n}(S_m^\lambda(M)) = V^{1/n}(M) = \sum_{i=1}^{m-1} \lambda_i V^{1/n}(M) = \sum_{i=1}^{m-1} V^{1/n}(\lambda_i g^i(M)),$$

then it follows from Brunn-Minkowski theorem that all sets $\lambda_i g^i(M)$ are convex and positively homotetic, i.e., there exists $\rho_i > 0$ such that $g^i(M) = \rho_i M$ for every $1 \leq i \leq m - 1$. Since volumes of the sets $M$, $g(M),\ldots,$ $g^{m-1}(M)$ are equal then these sets coincide up to translation, i.e., the set $M$ is rotationally symmetrical with respect to the group $G$.

Q.E.D.

Let us consider the functional $\mu_m^\lambda : \mathcal{K} \longrightarrow \mathbf{R}^+$ defined as follows

$$\mu_m^\lambda(M) = V(M)/V(S_m^\lambda(M)).$$

The functional $\mu_m^\lambda$ takes values from the semi-interval $]0, 1]$ and $\mu_m^\lambda(M) = 1$ iff $M$ is a compact convex rotationally symmetrical set. So the functional $\mu_m^\lambda$ is a measure of the rotational symmetry for the compact convex sets.

Since the volume for convex sets, multiplying by a scalar and Minkowski sum are continuous in the Hausdorff metric (see Hadwiger, 1957) then $\mu_m^\lambda$ is a continuous function from $\mathcal{K}$ into $]0, 1]$.

# 3 Properties of the symmetry measure

Consider some properties of the set $S_m^\lambda(M)$ and of the functional $\mu_m^\lambda$.

1. Let $f$ be a rotation of $\mathbf{R}^n$ with respect to the origin $O$. Then holds

$$S_m^\lambda(f(M)) = f(S_m^\lambda(M));$$

$$\mu_m^\lambda(f(M)) = \mu_m^\lambda(M).$$

2. Let us consider a translation $M \oplus b$ of the set $M \in \mathcal{G}(\mathcal{K})$ to the vector $b \in \mathbf{R}^n$. Then

$$S_m^\lambda(M \oplus b) = S_m^\lambda(M) \oplus \sum_{i=0}^{m-1} \lambda_i g^i(b) \text{ and } \mu_m^\lambda(M \oplus b) = \mu_m^\lambda(M).$$

If $\lambda_i = 1/m$ for every $i$, then $\sum_{i=0}^{m-1} \lambda_i g^i(b) = 1/m(\sum_{i=0}^{m-1} g^i(b)) = 0$. So we have for Minkowski symmetric set $S_m$

$$S_m(M \oplus b) = S_m(M).$$

3. Given $\rho > 0$, holds $\mu_m^\lambda(\rho M) = \mu_m^\lambda(M)$.

4. Given two vectors $\lambda, \mu \in \mathbf{R}^m$ and a set $M \in \mathcal{K}$, it is true

$$S_m^\lambda(S_m^\mu(M)) = S_m^\mu(S_m^\lambda(M)).$$

5. Given vector $\lambda \in \mathbf{R}^m$ and a set $M \in \mathcal{K}$, it is true up to traslation.

$$S_m(S_m^\lambda(M)) = S_m(M).$$

6. Given two convex compact sets $A, B$, two positive numbers $\alpha, \beta \in \mathbf{R}^+$, then

$$S_m^\lambda(\alpha A \oplus \beta B) = \alpha S_m^\lambda(A) \oplus \beta S_m^\lambda(B).$$

7. We show that the infimum of values of the functional $\mu_m^\lambda(M)$ on the set of compact convex sets in $\mathbf{R}^2$ is equal zero. In fact this is true for the case of $\mathbf{R}^n$.

   **Proposition 2** *For the Euclidean plane $\mathbf{R}^2$ and $m > 2$ it is true*

   $$\inf\{\mu_n^\lambda(M), \ M \in \mathcal{G}(\mathcal{K})\} = 0.$$

8. Let us consider a composition of two generalized Minkowski symmetric sets. Denote by $[m, n]$ the largest common divisor of two integers $m$ and $n$.

**Proposition 3** *The following relation is true*

$$S_n(S_m(M)) = S_k(M), \quad \text{where } k = nm/[m,n].$$

*In particularly, if $[m,n] = 1$, i.e., $m$ and $n$ are mutually prime, we have*

$$S_n(S_m(M)) = S_{nm}(M).$$

Proof. We have

$$S_n(S_m(M)) = \frac{1}{nm} \oplus_{i=0}^{n-1} g_n^i(\oplus_{j=0}^{m-1} g_m^j(M)) = \frac{1}{nm} \oplus_{i=0}^{n-1} \oplus_{j=0}^{m-1} g_n^i g_m^j(M).$$

Here $g_n^i g_m^j$ is a rotation to the angle $2\pi(mi + nj)/nm$.

Let us consider three sets

$$Q = \{mi + nj, i = 0, \ldots, n-1, \ j = 0, \ldots, m-1\},$$
$$P = \{kd, k = 0, \ldots, (mn/d) - 1\}, \text{ where } d = [m,n],$$
$$R = \{sd, \ s \in \mathbb{Z}\}.$$

Let us show that $Q = P \pmod{nm}$. We have that $P = R \pmod{mn}$ and show also that $Q = R \pmod{mn}$.

Let us denote $Q' = \{(im + jn), \ i,j \in \mathbb{Z}\} = \{d(im' + jn'), \ i,j \in \mathbb{Z}\}$, where $n' = n/d$, $m' = m/d$. It is clear that $n'$ and $m'$ are mutually prime. It is known (Bezout's equality) that there exist $i,j \in \mathbb{Z}$ such that $im' + jn' = 1$. Thus $Q' = R$. We show also that $Q' = Q \pmod{mn}$. For every $i,j \in \mathbb{Z}$ we have $i = i' + np$, $j = j' + mq$, where $i' \in [0, n-1]$, $j' \in [0, m-1]$. Then $Q' = \{(mi' + nj' + mnl), \ i' = 0, \ldots, n-1, \ j' = 0, \ldots, m-1, \ l \in \mathbb{Z}\}$. It is easy to see now that $Q = Q' \pmod{mn}$ and consequently $Q = R \pmod{mn}$. We can conclude now that

$$S_n(S_m(M)) = S_k(M), \quad \text{where } k = nm/[m,n].$$

Q.E.D.

**Corollary 1** $\mu_m^\lambda$ *is a measure of a rotational symmetry which is invariant for the group of similitudes of $\mathbf{R}^n$.*

# 4  Euclidean plane

Since in $\mathbf{R}^2$ a compact convex set is characterized, up to translation, by its perimetric measure $s(d\alpha)$ we will apply the latter one for calculation of the measure of a rotational symmetry. The integral of a perimetric measure (see J. Serra, 1982) gives the arclength of the boundary of the set as a function of the direction $\alpha$ to the positive normal of the boundary. The measure $s(d\alpha)$ must be positive and satisfy the condition

$$\int_0^{2\pi} e^{i\alpha} s(d\alpha) = 0,$$

which denotes that the contour of the set is closed (Minkowski, 1903).

The correspondence between the set of compact convex sets of $\mathbf{R}^2$ and the set of positive measures $s(d\alpha)$ on the unit circle which satisfy the above condition is an isomorphism. Besides Minkowski addition and change of scale for sets correspond to the ordinary addition and multiplication of their measures.

Let us denote by $s_A$ the perimetric measure corresponding to the set $A \in \mathcal{G}(\mathcal{K})$. The volume $V(A)$ of the set $A$ (area in $\mathbf{R}^2$) could be expressed as a function of the measure $s_A$ as follows (G. Matheron and J. Serra, 1988, p. 367).

$$V(A) = \int_0^{2\pi} \sin\alpha \; s(d\alpha) \int_0^\alpha \cos\beta \; s(d\beta) = \int_0^{2\pi} \cos\alpha \; s(d\alpha) \int_0^\alpha \sin\beta \; s(d\beta).$$

The perimetric measure $g^i(s_A)$ corresponding to the set $g^i(A)$ is $s_A(d\alpha + 2\pi i/m)$. Here $g^i(A)$ is a rotation of $\mathbf{R}^2$ to the angle $2\pi/m$ with respect to the origin. The perimetric measure of the set $S_m^\lambda(A)$ is calculated as $\sum_{i=0}^{m-1} \lambda_i g^i(s_A)$ or $\sum_{i=0}^{m-1} \lambda_i s_A(d\alpha + 2\pi i/m)$. In particular, the perimetric measure of the generalized Minkowski symmetric set is given by

$$(1/m) \sum_{i=0}^{m-1} s_A(d\alpha + 2\pi i/m).$$

Thus given a perimetric measure $s_A$ of a set $A$, we can calculate the measure of a rotational symmetry $\mu_m$ by the definition

$$\mu_m(A) = V(A)/V(S_m(A)).$$

In this case it is not necessary to find directly the generalized Minkowski symmetric set $S_m(A)$.

If the set $A$ is a convex polygon with $k$ sides, then $s_A$ is a discrete measure concentrated in $k$ points of the unit circle. Directions of these points are orthogonal to the sides of the polygon and the value of $s_A$ in the direction $\alpha$ equals to the length of the side of the polygon which is orthogonal to this direction.

For the case of a convex polygon $A$ the volume $V(A)$ could be found as follows

$$V(A) = \sum_{j=1}^k m_j \sin\alpha_j \sum_{i=1}^j m_i \cos\alpha_i - 1/2 \sum_{j=1}^k m_j^2 \sin\alpha_j \cos\alpha_j,$$

where $\alpha_j$ is a normal direction to the side $j$ of the polygon and $m_j$ is the length of this side $j$.

The application of the perimetric measure allows us to perform the decomposition of the original compact convex set into Minkowski sum of two sets. One of these sets is rotationally symmetric and second one is totally rotationally asymmetric, i.e., it couldn't be decomposed in this way. This decomposition is made in the same way as by G. Matheron and J. Serra [3] for the case of a central symmetry.

Let $G$ be as before a rotation group of order $m$ and $g^i(s_A)$ be a perimetric measure of the set $g^i(A)$, $i = 0, 1, \ldots, m-1$, $g^0(s_A) = s_A$. The function

$$s_{A_0} = \inf_i \{g^i(s_A)\}$$

is positive and is a perimetric measure corresponding to a compact convex set $A_0$. It is clear that the set $A_0$ is rotationally symmetrical with respect to the group $G$. Besides this perimetric measure is smaller then $s_A$ and so

$$s_{A_1} = s_A - s_{A_0}$$

is a perimetric measure of a compact convex set $A_1$. This set is totally rotationally asymmetric in the sense that

$$\inf_i \{g^i(s_{A_1})\} = 0.$$

Thus any not totally rotationally asymmetric set compact convex set $A$ could be decomposed as follows

$$A = A_0 \oplus A_1,$$

where $A_0$ is rotationally symmetric and $A_1$ is totally rotationally asymmetrical.

## 5 Example

We would like to calculate the measure of a rotational symmetry of the polygon $M$ given at the figure 1 a) and show the decomposition of this polygon for the rotation group of order 4 into Minkowski sum of the rotationally symmetric set and totally rotationally asymmetric set. The side lenghts of the polygon are pointed at the figure in conditional units. The perimetric measure of the polygon $M$ is given at the figure 1 b). The Minkowski symmetric set $S_4(M)$ and its perimetric measure are represented at the figures 2 a) and 2 b), respectively.

Let us find the symmetry measure

$$\mu_4(M) = \frac{V(M)}{V(S_4(M))}$$

of the polygon $M$. The areas of the polygons $M$ and $S_4(M)$ equal 7/2 and 31/8, respectively. So $\mu_4(M) = 28/38$.

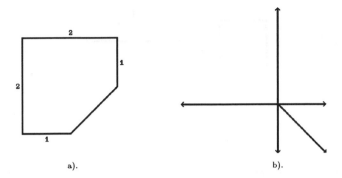

Figure 1: Original polygon $M$ a). and its perimetric measure b).

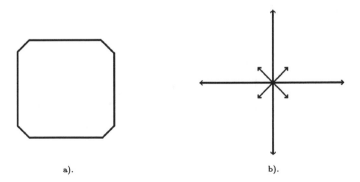

Figure 2: Minkowski symmetric set $S_4(M)$ a). and its perimetric measure b).

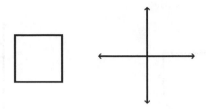

Figure 3: Rotationally symmetric set $M_0$ and its perimetric measure.

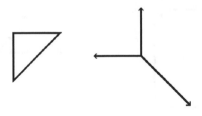

Figure 4: Totally rotationally asymmetric set $M_1$ and its perimetric measure.

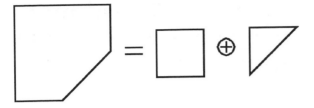

Figure 5: Decomposition of the original polygon $M$.

The rotationally symmetric set $M_0$ and its perimetric measure are represented at the figure 3. The totally asymmetric set $M_1$ and its perimetric measure are represented at the figure 4. So the original polygon $M$ is decomposed into Minkowski sum of two polygons $M_0$ and $M_1$ and this decomposition is represented at the figure 5.

# References

[1] H. Hadwiger. *Vorlesungen über Inhalt , Oberflache und Isoperimetrie.* Berlin, Springer, 1957.

[2] G. Matheron. *Random sets and integral geometry*, Wiley, New York, 1975.

[3] G. Matheron, J. Serra. Convexity and symmetry. In: Image analysis and mathematical morphology, vol. 2: Theoretical Advances, ch. 17, (J. Serra ed.), Academic Press, London, 1988.

[4] H. Minkowski. Volumen and Oberfläche. *Math. Ann.*, vol. 57, 1903, 447-495.

[5] J. Serra. *Image analysis and mathematical morphology,* Academic Press, London, 1982.

# Crest lines extraction in volumic 3D medical images : a multi-scale approach

Olivier Monga, Richard Lengagne, Rachid Deriche*

INRIA, Domaine de Voluceau - Rocquencourt
BP. 105, 78153 Le Chesnay Cedex, France
email: om@bora.inria.fr

### Abstract

Recently, we have shown that the differential properties of the surfaces represented by 3D volumic images can be recovered using their partial derivatives. For instance, the crest lines can be characterized by the first, second and third partial derivatives of the grey level function $I(x, y, z)$. In this paper, we show that :

- the computation of the partial derivatives of an image can be improved using recursive filters which approximate the Gaussian filter,

- a multi-scale approach solves many of the instability problems arising from the computation of the partial derivatives,

- we illustrate the previous point for the crest line extraction (a crest point is a zero-crossing of the derivative of the maximum curvature along the maximum curvature direction).

We present experimental results of crest point extraction on synthetic and 3-D medical data.

**keywords** : *volumic 3D medical images, surface modelling, curvatures, crest lines, multi-scale derivation, recursive filtering.*

## 1 Introduction

Volumic 3D images are now widely distributed in the medical field [8, 18, 7, 1]. They are produced from various modalities such as Magnetic Resonance Imagery

---

*At INRIA Sophia-Antipolis, 06565 Valbonne Cedex, France.

(MRI), Computed Tomography Imagery (CT), Nuclear Medicine Imagery (NMI) or Ultrasound Imagery (USI). Such data are represented by a discrete 3D grey level function $I(i, j, k)$ where the high-contrast points (3D edge points) correspond to the discrete trace of the surfaces of the geometrical structures [13, 12, 21]. A motivating issue is then to extract typical features of these surfaces. The most natural way is to look for differential Euclidean surface invariants such as : curvatures, crest lines, parabolic lines, umbilic points... [10, 16, 15], [17, 9, 11, 2, 19, 14]. Recently, we have shown that the differential properties of a surface defined by an iso-contour in a 3D image can be recovered from the partial derivatives of the corresponding grey level function [11]. In [11] crest lines are extracted using first, second and third order partial derivatives provided by 3D Deriche filters [12, 13]. The critical point of this approach also studied in [19] is the stability of expressions including second and third order partial derivatives such as the "extremality criterion" defined in [11, 19].

In this paper we propose recursive 3D filters to improve the computation of partial derivatives and also a multi-scale approach to extract the zero-crossings of the extremality criterion.

In Section II, we point out that derivative filters coming from isotropic (rotation invariant) smoothing filters should be used to ensure the Euclidean invariance of the curvatures. Then we derive an algorithm to compute first, second and third order partial derivatives of a 3D volumic image. These derivatives are used to obtain curvatures invariant by rigid motion (Euclidean invariant).

Section III deals with the computation of the curvatures of the surfaces traced by the iso-contours (3D edge points) from the partial derivatives of the image (for instance provided by the previous method). This section recalls the main results of the reference [11] and shows the problems induced by a single scale filtering.

In Section IV, we propose to use different widths of filters to compute the curvatures. This leads to a multi-scale curvature computation scheme where the scale is the width of the filters. We apply this principle to track the zero-crossings of the derivative of the maximum curvature points along the maximum curvature direction (extremality criterion) which correspond to the crest points. The zero-crossings coming from the different scales are merged using a valuated adjacency graph. We propose some simple and efficient strategies to extract stable zero-crossings from this graph.

In Section V we present experimental results obtained on synthetic and real data (CT and MR 3D images). We show that our approach combining a multi-scale scheme and also the use of better filters provides reliable crest lines even for noisy data.

# 2 Computation of the partial derivatives of a 3D image using linear filters : approximation of the Gaussian and of its derivatives using recursive separable filters

Recently R. Deriche has introduced recursive filters to approximate the Gaussian filter and its derivative [5]. First of all, we show the advantage of using such filters to compute differential Euclidean invariants. We recall the main results reported in [5]. Then, we extend Deriche's work to 3D and to the computation of third order derivatives. We also show how to normalize these filters in order to obtain coherent values for first, second and third order derivatives. Finally we develop an efficient algorithm to compute the partial derivatives of a 3D image.

Let $I(x, y, z)$ be a 3D image.

We are looking for the partial derivatives of $I(x, y, z)$ : $\dfrac{\partial^n(I(x, y, z))}{\partial x^m \partial y^p \partial z^q}$, $n = m + p + q$ that we represent using the subscript notation : $I_{x^m y^p z^q}$ (we will write only the variables, the power of which is not zero, for instance $I_{x^1 y^0 z^0}$ becomes $I_x$).

If $f(x, y, z)$ is the impulse response of a smoothing filter, the restored image $I_r$ is equal to $I * f$, where $*$ is the convolution product. Classically, using the properties of the convolution product we obtain

$$\frac{\partial^n I_r}{\partial x^m \partial y^p \partial z^q} = \frac{\partial^n (I * f)}{\partial x^m \partial y^p \partial z^q} = I * \left( \frac{\partial^n f}{\partial x^m \partial y^p \partial z^q} \right)$$

Then the impulse response of the filter which computes $I_{x^m y^p z^q}$ is $\dfrac{\partial^n f}{\partial x^m \partial y^p \partial z^q}$.

We develop a popular scheme which reduces the search of derivative filters of any order to the search of a smoothing filter [3, 5, 4, 6]. The question is now : what are the suitable properties for our smoothing impulse response if we are interested in the computation of Euclidean differential invariants ? The response is well-known and is that the impulse response of the smoothing filter should be isotropic.

Figure 1 shows the interest of using an isotropic filter when computing the partial derivatives; we compare the curvatures at the edges of a smoothed square and those of the image of this square when applying a 45 degree-rotation. The derivatives are successively computed with the (anisotropic) Deriche filter and with the approximation of the (isotropic) Gaussian filter.

The previous result clearly shows the great interest of computing the partial derivatives of an image using filters derived from an isotropic smoothing impulse response. Otherwise we can obtain gradient [12], Laplacian or curvatures [11] which are not invariant by a rigid motion. On the other hand, we also take interest in using separable recursive filters in order to obtain a reasonable computational cost. A way to join these two antagonist points is to use the recursive approximation of

Curvature values using

an anisotropic filter (Deriche filter)

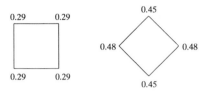

an isotropic filter (approximated Gaussian filter)

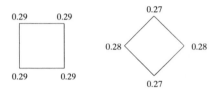

Figure 1: Comparison between curvatures from Gaussian and Deriche filters

the Gaussian filter (the only separable non trivial smoothing filter) introduced by R. Deriche in the recent reference [5].

We use the main result of the reference [5]. The 1D Gaussian smoothing filter is given by :

$$g(x) = e^{-\frac{x^2}{2\sigma^2}}$$

Using Prony's method, the positive and negative part of $g$ and of its normalized derivatives of first and second order can be approximated (with a normalized square error of about $\epsilon^2 = 10^{-6}$) by a 4th order Recursive operator (IIR)(see Appendix A) :

$$h(x) = (a_0 \cos(\frac{\omega_0}{\sigma}x) + a_1 \sin(\frac{\omega_0}{\sigma}x))e^{-\frac{b_0}{\sigma}x} + (c_0 \cos(\frac{\omega_1}{\sigma}x) + c_1 \sin(\frac{\omega_1}{\sigma}x))e^{-\frac{b_1}{\sigma}x} \quad (1)$$

Therefore, the 1D Gaussian filter and its first and second order derivatives can be recursively implemented. Using the separability property, we derive directly the recursive filters to compute the first and second order derivatives of a 2D image.

Using the separability of the filters we extend directly the previous scheme to the 3D case. Following the notations of Section II this amounts to setting :

$$f(x, y, z) = g(x)g(y)g(z)$$

We also extend this filtering scheme to the third order derivative case. We develop a set of recursive filters approximating the Gaussian and its derivatives which can be used to compute the first, second, and third order derivatives of a 3D image.

We stress that a very important point not carried out in [5] is the normalization of the filters which allows to obtain coherent values for the different derivatives. Here we use the scheme presented in [11].

# 3 Using the partial derivatives of a 3D volumic image to extract and to characterize 3D structures

The main stages of our algorithm allowing to extract crest lines in a 3D image are :

1. Computation of the first, second and third order partial derivatives of the image $I(x, y, z)$ ($\dfrac{\partial^n f}{\partial x^m \partial y^p \partial z^q}$, $m+p+q = 3$) using the recursive filters defined in Section 2 for a given value of $\sigma$ ;

2. Extraction of the 3D edge points using the first order partial derivatives (gradient) of $I$ (see section 3.2) ;

3. For each point of the 3D edge map, computation of :

   - the two principal curvatures and the corresponding principal curvature directions using the formulas of [11] ;

   - the extremality criterion (derivative of the maximum curvature along the corresponding principal direction) using the formulas of [11].

4. Building of a extremality criterion image $C_\sigma(x, y, z)$ such as at each edge point $(x, y, z)$, $C_\sigma(x, y, z)$ is set to the value of the extremality criterion and to 0 otherwise ;

5. Determination of an image $Z_\sigma(x, y, z)$ set to 1 at each edge point being a zero-crossing of the extremality criterion and to 0 otherwise.

The last stage of this algorithm consists of finding the zero-crossings of a function defined on the discrete trace of a surface (traced by the 3D edge points) which is a difficult task in itself. So far, we have only implemented simple strategies to extract these zero-crossings. But, in order to be solved properly, this delicate problem needs more attention. An interesting solution can be found in [19].

Therefore, the final output of our algorithm is an image $Z_\sigma$ representing the set of edge points which are zero-crossings of the extremality criterion. Each value of $\sigma$ defines an image $Z_\sigma$ representing the crest line for the scale defined by $\sigma$.

# 4 Multi-scale approach to extract crest lines in 3D volumic images

The use of the filters presented in section 2 yields to obtain curvatures invariant by a rigid motion which was not exactly the case with the filters presented in [11]. This improves the quality of the results, but it may not be enough to provide good results in noisy data. As we have seen in the previous section the result of our algorithms is an image $Z_\sigma$ where the zero-crossing of the extremality criterion are marked. $Z_\sigma$ defines the crest lines for the scale defined by $\sigma$ (see section 2). Generally, we see that :

- for simple data, we can obtain good results using a single value for $\sigma$ but we do not know how to find this value ;

- for more complex data the suitable value for $\sigma$ varies depending on the area of the 3D image ;

- for noisy data, only the crest lines that can be seen using different scales define reliable features.

Therefore, similar to the edge detection [20] and to the crest line extraction in depth maps [14], it is of great interest to use a multiscale approach. Moreover the recursive implementation of our filters makes it reasonable in terms of computational cost.

In order to merge the results obtained at different scales $\sigma_i, i = 1, n$ we propose a practical and efficient data structure that we will call the Multi-scale Adjacency Graph : $G_{\sigma_1,\sigma_2,...\sigma_n}$. $G_{\sigma_1,\sigma_2,...\sigma_n}$ is a valuated graph built as follows :

1. each node of $G_{\sigma_1,\sigma_2,...\sigma_n}$ is attached to a point $(i, j, k)$ such that for at least one scale $\sigma_m$ we have $Z_{\sigma_m}(i, j, k) = 1$ ;

2. the features attached to each node are :

   (a) the coordinates of the corresponding 3D point $((i, j, k))$ ;

   (b) the values of the scales for which this point is a crest point (all the $\sigma_p$ such that $Z_{\sigma_p}(i, j, k) = 1$) ;

   (c) the differential characteristics extracted for all the scales : principal curvatures and principal curvatures directions, value of the extremality criterion.

3. we define an edge joining two nodes of $G_{\sigma_1,\sigma_2,...\sigma_n}$ if and only if the two corresponding points are adjacent for the 26-connectivity ;

Therefore $G_{\sigma_1,\sigma_2,...\sigma_n}$ represents the results of the crest points extraction for the different scales and their spatial relationships. This data structure is particularly efficient when the stability of the crest point locations through different scales is a good selection criterion. Our experiments performed on real and synthetic data show that generally the position of the reliable crest points remain the same for different values of the scale $\sigma$ (i.e. the shifts of the crest points are less than one pixel).

For instance, the following simple pruning strategy for the graph $G_{\sigma_1,\sigma_2,...\sigma_n}$ can be used :

1. select all nodes corresponding to points which are crest points for at least a given number of scales ;

2. select the connected components having at least a given number of nodes (this threshold corresponds to the minimal number of points of a crest line).

We come up with the following algorithm :

1. Computation of the zero-crossings of the extremality criterion for a given set of scales : $\sigma_1, \sigma_2, ...\sigma_n$ ; the result is a set of images $Z_{\sigma_1}, Z_{\sigma_2}...Z_{\sigma_n}$ (see section 3.5) ;

2. building of the multi-scale graph $G_{\sigma_1,\sigma_2,...\sigma_n}$ (see section 4.2) ;

3. pruning of $G_{\sigma_1,\sigma_2,...\sigma_n}$ to select reliable crest points.

# 5   Experimental results

We present experimental results obtained on synthetic and real data from the implementation of the algorithms described in the previous section

We have tested our method on two 3D X-ray scanner images of the same skull taken at two different positions. In that case, we have chosen to extract only the extrema of the maximum curvature in the maximum curvature direction. The stability of the results we obtain for a single scale illustrates the rotation invariance of our computation of the curvatures and of the extremality criterion (see section 2). We also show that the multiscale scheme allows to remove many spurious crest points. We notice that the result obtained by thresholding the maximum curvature is acceptable for some scales but depends completely on the threshold. On the other hand the results provided by the zero-crossing of the extremality criterion may seem worse for some scales but do not depend on any threshold.

We point out that the size of the convolution mask for a direct implementation of a 3D Gaussian of variance $\sigma^2$ is $(8\sigma)^3$ (for $\sigma = 4$ we obtain 8192 !). The use of recursive filters of order 4 reduces this computational cost to about 100 operations per point for any value of $\sigma$. Of course, the previous remark applies also for the derivatives of the gaussian filter. Therefore, even for a single space scheme, the recursive filtering appears as a crucial tool.

Those results show that the multi-scale approach is much more efficient if we extract the zero-crossings of the extremality criterion instead of the high maximum curvature points. The smoothing removes many spurious points in the results coming from the high maximum curvature point extraction, but makes the crest lines thicker. On the contrary, the lines coming from the detection of the zero-crossings of the extremality criterion are still precise if $\sigma$ is set to a high value, even if some points are removed. We now show the images of the zero-crossings of the extremality criterion computed on the entire skull, for the positions A and B and for some values of $\sigma$.

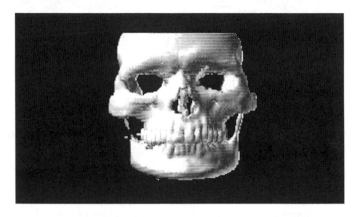

Figure 2: Perpective view of the 3D edge map for the position A

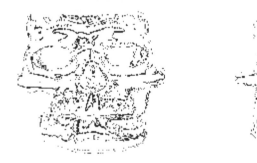

Figure 3: $\sigma$ is set to 3

# 6 Conclusion

We have presented a multi-scale approach to extract crest lines of the surfaces represented by 3D volumic images. Compared to the method described in [11] we have developed the following points :

Figure 4: $\sigma$ is set to 5

- we show the great theoretical interest in using filters derived from an isotropic smoothing filter to compute partial derivatives of an image ;

- we propose to use recursive filters approximating the Gaussian and its derivatives to obtain differential characteristics invariant by rigid motion ;

- in order to improve the stability of the computation of the differential characteristics (curvatures, derivative of the curvature) we use a multi-scale approach.

Moreover, we present experimental results on synthetic and real data. We stress that the same sketch could be used to extract other differential singularities such as : parabolic lines, umbilic points... Besides, this methodology could also be used in 2-D images like interior scenes, to extract corners for instance.

# References

[1] Nicholas Ayache. Computer vision applied to 3d medical images : Results, trends and future challenges. *INRIA Report research*, September 1993.

[2] J. Koenderink B. Romeny, L. Florack. Invariant third order properties of isophotes: T-junction detection. In *Proc. 7th Scandinavien Conference on Image Analysis, Aalborg*, August 1991.

[3] John Canny. A computational approach to edge detection. *IEEE Transactions on Pattern Analysis and Machine Intelligence*, PAMI-8(6):679–698, November 1986.

[4] R. Deriche. Fast algorithms for low level vision. *IEEE Transactions on Pattern Analysis and machine Intelligence*, 1989.

[5] R. Deriche. Recursively Implementing the Gaussian and Its Derivatives. In *Proc. Second International Conference On Image Processing*, pages 263–267, Singapore, September 7-11 1992. A longer version is INRIA Research Report RR-1893.

[6] Rachid Deriche. Using Canny's criteria to derive a recursively implemented optimal edge detector. *International Journal of Computer Vision*, pages 167–187, 1987.

[7] Richard Gordon, Gabor T. Herman, and Steven A. Johnson. Image reconstruction from projections. *Scientific American*, 233(4):56–68, October 1975.

[8] Gabor T. Herman and Hsun Kao Liu. Three-dimensional display of human organs from computed tomograms. *Computer Graphics and Image Processing*, 9:1–21, 1979.

[9] Jan J. Koenderink. *Solid Shape*. MIT Press, Boston, 1990.

[10] O. Monga, N. Ayache, and P. Sander. From voxel to intrinsic surface features. *Image and Vision Computing Volume 10, Number 6*, Aout 1992. a shortened version is in IPMI'91, Lecture Notes in Computer Science 511, Springer Verlag.

[11] Olivier Monga, Serge Benayoun, and Olivier D. Faugeras. Using third order derivatives to extract ridge lines in 3d images. In *IEEE Conference on Vision and Pattern Recognition*, Urbana Champaign, June 1992.

[12] Olivier Monga, Rachid Deriche, and Gregoire Malandain. Recursive filtering and edge closing: two primary tools for 3d edge detection. *Image and Vision Computing, Vol. 9, Number 4*, August 1991. A shortened version is in proc. of ECCV'90, Lecture notes in Computer Science 427.

[13] Olivier Monga, Rachid Deriche, and Jean-Marie Rocchisani. 3d edge detection using recursive filtering: Application to scanner images. *Computer Vision Graphic and Image Processing, Vol. 53, No 1, pp. 76-87*, January 1991.

[14] Jean Ponce and Michael Brady. Toward a surface primal sketch. In *Proceedings, IJCAI*, 1985.

[15] Peter T. Sander. Generic curvature features from 3-D images. *IEEE Transactions on Systems, Man, and Cybernetics*, 19(6):1623–1635, November 1989.

[16] Peter T. Sander and Steven W. Zucker. Singularities of principal direction fields from 3-D images. *IEEE Transactions on Pattern Analysis and Machine Intelligence*. To appear. Available as Technical Report CIM-88-7, McGill Research Center for Intelligent Machines, McGill University, Montréal.

[17] Peter T. Sander and Steven W. Zucker. Inferring surface trace and differential structure from 3-D images. *IEEE Transactions on Pattern Analysis and Machine Intelligence*, 12(9), September 1990.

[18] Micheal M. Ter-Pogossian, Marcus E. Raichle, and Burton E. Sobel. Positron-emmision tomography. *Scientific American*, 243(4):170–181, October 1980.

[19] J-P. Thirion and Gourdon A. The 3d marching lines algorithm and its application to crest lines extraction. Technical Report 1672, INRIA, May 1992.

[20] A. Witkin. A multi-scale approach to extract zero-crossings of the laplacian. In *Proceedings of International Joint Conference on Artificial Intelligence*, 1982.

[21] S.W. Zucker and R.M. Hummel. A three-dimensional edge operator. *IEEE Transactions on Pattern Analysis and Machine Intelligence*, PAMI-3(3):324–331, May 1981.

## GENERAL SHAPE AND SPECIFIC DETAIL: CONTEXT-DEPENDENT USE OF SCALE IN DETERMINING VISUAL FORM

BRYAN S. MORSE, STEPHEN M. PIZER, AND CHRISTINA A. BURBECK

*Department of Computer Science, University of North Carolina at Chapel Hill*
*CB #3175 Sitterson Hall, Chapel Hill, North Carolina 27599-3175, U.S.A.*

### ABSTRACT

This paper demonstrates how multiscale measurements using scales proportional to the size of the respective objects can separate larger-scale general shape properties of image objects from smaller-scale detail. Such separation allows for broader classification and matching of objects based on their shape while still retaining the essential differences. Computational methods are briefly presented that allow for the extraction of object representations from a transformation of multiscale measurements. The resulting representations describe objects not merely at a single scale (or at a single scale at a time), but simultaneously across a range of scales that vary with the local object width.

## 1. Introduction

Because of Nature's variations, noise, and the error introduced by such computational processes as discrete sampling and quantization, it is impractical to always make precise comparisons of shape. Instead, it is often useful to describe shape in a somewhat broader fashion. For example, in everyday speech we describe objects as being "like a square" or "circular." Quite often we simply leave out the qualifiers altogether and call an object a "square" or a "circle" even when we know full well that they are not precisely so. Yet, when called upon to do so, we can readily point out where the shape deviates from this general form. We distinguish between these two disparate notions of general form and specific detail, using either when appropriate for the task at hand. David Marr put this conflicting need well when he wrote

> To be useful for recognition, the degree of similarity between two shapes must be reflected in their descriptions, but at the same time even subtle differences must be expressible. These opposing conditions can be satisfied only if it is possible to decouple stable information, that captures the more general and less varying properties of a shape, from information that is sensitive to the finer distinctions between shapes. [1]

The shape in Fig. 1 may more readily be described as "a rectangle with a sawtoothed edge" than as "a figure with thirteen straight-edged segments." Somehow we are able to grasp both the general property (the rectangular shape) and the specific detail (the teeth). The teeth on the side of the figure do not reduce the overall rectangularity of the shape, nor do the general shape impair our ability to recognize the triangularity of the teeth.

Figure 1: General shape and specific detail: a rectangle with a sawtoothed edge.

What deviations are important? In practice, the answer to this question depends on the specific task at hand, but it is possible to address this question at a more general "front end" level. As one resizes an object, its representation should remain the same, only resized (a property called "zoom invariance"). This means that the importance of variations between shapes must be relative rather than absolute. Specifically, the importance of variations is based on the size of that variation *relative to the size of the object itself.*

Consider the shapes shown in Fig. 2. The variations in the boundaries on the left and right sides are identical across the shapes, having only been stretched horizontally with the rest of the object. In the first shape, the object appears to wiggle more from side to side while in the third the sides of an otherwise straight object wiggle from side to side. Although the objects have the same sides, they have different internal shapes because of the change in the relative importance of the edge variations as the width of the object changes.

Figure 2: Three different "wiggle" figures. The objects have similar edges but different perceptual form because of the diminishing relative importance of the detail of the edge as the width increases.

## 2. Suggestions from Psychophysical Studies

This principle of sensitivity to detail inversely proportional to width is suggested by psychophysical studies of the human visual system, specifically in studies regarding *Weber's Law for separation discrimination.*

When asked to judge the relative spatial separation of two bars, an observer's ability to detect changes in separation is proportional to the separation itself [2]. While the ratio of proportionality may change depending on experimental conditions (effective contrast, exposure duration, etc.), the proportional nature of this relationship holds over a wide range of separations, breaking down only at extremely small separations as the limits of the spatial resolution the eye are exceeded [3].

Burbeck [4] has shown that this behavior cannot be accounted for by spatial frequency decomposition alone. It appears that visual computation of separation is a two-stage process: the first stage localizing significant information in the image and the second computing the separation. This latter stage appears to perform spatial integration on the position information using integration areas proportional to the separation [5], thus producing behavior consistent with Weber's Law. This type of two-stage model will be used in the methods shown later in this paper.

## 3. Overview of the Proposed Methods

### 3.1 Multiscale Methods

One way to control how much weight is given to local variation is through the use of *multiscale image analysis*. These methods consider the *scale* (aperture or tolerance) of physical measurements such as those used to acquire images. By simulating image acquisition using larger (lower resolution) apertures, one may more readily identify larger-scale properties of the imaged scene. This is, for example, what low-pass filtering techniques for noise removal do—blur away the fine detail (in this case, noise) and leave the (blurred) remainder for analysis. This idea can be extended to acquiring the image over a wide range of scales with each scale capturing a different level of detail. Such information, when measured over a domain of different spatial positions and scales is referred to as a *scale space* [6,7].

### 3.2 Medial Methods

If we are to weight the effects of image detail by their size relative to the local width of the object, it is desirable that width be readily accessible from the object representation. Such width-based representation may be found within a class of computer vision techniques known as *medial* representations. Specifically, they capture both the position (middle) of the object and the associated width of the object at each point. The methods presented here are based on the *symmetric axis* proposed by Blum [8,9,10]: the locus of centers of circles that lie within the object and touch the object boundary in two or more places.

### 3.3 The Core

Taken together, these ideas of medial representations (which reflect the width of an object), multiscale analysis (which considers the scale of measurement) , and Weber's Law (which relates width and measurement scale) form the basis for an object representation that we call a *core*.[1] Specifically, a core is a locus of points where each point represents the spatial position (middle) and size (width) of an object *as measured at scales proportional to that width*.

Examples of such cores are shown in Fig. 3: the long, curving core represents the general shape of the object while the smaller cores represent smaller-scale deviations from that general shape.

---

[1]Known in previous work by these authors and colleagues as the "Multiscale Medial Axis" or MMA.

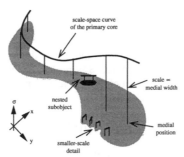

Figure 3: Cores as curves in scale space.

This definition of a core is obviously circular: one must measure properties of the object at scales proportional to its width, but in order to determine the width of the object one must first make a set of measurements at some scale. To avoid this circularity, cores are computed by [15]

1. considering the image at each of a range of scales (a scale space);
2. computing various properties of these images, specifically
   a. making local geometric measurements (differentiation) in that space to quantify each point as a potential boundary, and
   b. applying a transformation that establishes the relationship between potential boundary points and potential core points; and
3. geometrically identifying those positions *and* corresponding scales that best satisfy the definition of a core point.

This simultaneously extracts image objects and selects measurement scales appropriate to those objects.

This process need not, however, be a strictly feed-forward one but may include feedback between later stages of processing and earlier ones. For example, the transformation referred to in Step 2b is, as will be explained in more detail later, similar to the Hough transform [11]. In such a transformation, evidence of certain image features (boundaries) contributes to collective evidence for other, more complicated, features (cores). In this sense, the transformation determines a conditional probability of the existence of a core as a specific point in scale space. As certain hypotheses are shown to be less probable, one may reject them and use these rejected hypotheses to recompute the remaining conditional probabilities. This has the effect of sharpening the differences between the resulting possible solutions and making later decision steps simpler.

By computing shape representations for larger objects using larger, less sensitive, scales, these techniques should be able to capture larger, more general shape properties in a manner that is relatively insensitive to smaller-scale variation. Similarly, by computing shape representations for smaller objects using smaller, more accurate, scales, these methods should be able to accurately represent smaller objects and smaller-scale detail on larger ones.

## 4. Computational Methods

### 4.1 Measuring Boundaries

The first step in the computation is to apply scaled, directional, boundary-sensitive operators to the image. For example, a simple directional boundary function $B: \Re^n \times \Re^+ \times S^n$ (where $S^n$ is the set of all unit vectors in $\Re^n$) is the change in intensity $I(x)$ in direction $u$ as measured at scale $\sigma$:

$$B(x, \sigma, u) = \left| u \bullet \nabla \big( I(x) \otimes G(x, \sigma) \big) \right| \tag{1}$$

where $I(x) \otimes G(x, \sigma)$ is the convolution of the image intensity by a normalized Gaussian $G(x, \sigma)$ with standard deviation $\sigma$. This is not, of course, the only way to detect intensity boundaries, nor are all desired boundaries in images produced by simple changes in intensity. Any suitable boundary measure will do.

This operator can be used to measure the boundary-like properties at every position in the image and at each of a number of scales. Such a measure may be considered a characteristic function for a fuzzy set of edges and is called *boundariness*. Classical edge detection usually involves reducing this fuzzy set to a binary one through some optimization process, and the majority of algorithms for extracting object shape usually assume this form of binary classification of edges. This reduction of information at such an early stage causes loss of information that may be useful at later stages. Instead, we use this fuzzy information directly, retaining the fuzziness of the computation until the latest possible stages of processing.

### 4.2 Relating Boundary Properties to Medial Properties

Just as boundary positions measured by selected scale operators are determined only to within a fuzzy approximation, so too are any medial positions derived from these boundaries. This fuzzy medial property is called *medialness* and reflects the degree to which any spatial position and associated width is on the core of the object.

Medialness may be computed from boundariness measurements by considering the geometry of cores and letting each boundariness measurement vote for possible medialness values in a manner similar to the Hough transform. By Blum's definition of the symmetric axis, a point is medial with respect to a specified object half-width $r$ if a circle of radius $r$ centered at that point is tangent to two or more boundary points. (This uses a generalized definition, also proposed by Blum [9], where the disk is not restricted to being entirely within the object.) Using a fuzzy measure of medialness, this definition may be extended by considering not at how many points such a circle touches the object boundary, but by computing how much this circle appears to be tangent to boundaries.

Moreover, these boundaries should be, by Weber's Law, selected from measurements taken at scales proportional to the radius of that circle. This relationship between the measurement scale $\sigma$ and the radius $r$ may be written as

$$r = k\sigma \tag{2}$$

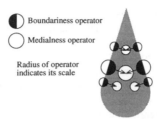

Figure 4: Boundariness contribution to object medialness. Each boundary measurement at each scale and direction contributes to medialness at a distance proportional to that scale. Only those operators producing significant boundariness are illustrated here, but all points cast votes in similar fashion.

Thus, the boundariness at every point and direction may then be used to accumulated evidence for other points lying on a core (Fig. 4):

$$M(x,r) = \int_S B(x - ur, \sigma, u)\, du$$

Because of discrete spatial sampling there may be few pixels that lie *exactly* at distance $r$ from a specific pixel. Boundariness must therefore be integrated over a fuzzy circle of approximate radius $r$:

$$M(\mathbf{x}_a, r) = \int B\left(\mathbf{x}_b, \sigma, (\mathbf{x}_b - \mathbf{x}_a)/\|\mathbf{x}_b - \mathbf{x}_a\|\right) W\left(\|\mathbf{x}_b - \mathbf{x}_a\|, r\right) d\mathbf{x}_b \qquad (3)$$

where $W\left(\|x_b - x_a\|, r\right)$ is a weighting function that controls the contribution from $x_B$ to $x_A$ for a given radius $r$.

Equation 3 is the basis for an algorithm, similar to the Hough transform, referred to as the Hough-like Medial Axis Transform (HMAT):

1. Apply boundary-sensitive operators at every position $x_B$ in the image at a number of scales $\sigma_i$;
2. For every position $x_A$ and every radius $r_i$,
   a) use the boundary measurements at $x_B$ and at scale $\sigma_i$ to compute the directional boundariness at $x_B$ in the direction from $x_B$ to $x_A$,
   b) multiply this by the weight $W\left(\|x_b - x_a\|, r\right)$ between the boundariness at $x_B$ and scale $\sigma_i$ to the medialness at $x_A$ and radius $r_i$, and
   c) Add this contribution to the accumulator for the medialness at $x_A$ and $r_i$.

The result of this algorithm is a transformation from an $(x; \sigma)$ scale space of boundariness to an $(x; r)$ scale space of medialness. Cores can then be determined as a ridge in the scale space of this medialness function.

## 4.3 Refining the Boundary-Medial Relationship

The results of the HMAT may be further refined by constraining the contribution of individual boundary points through a process we call *credit attribution*. This introduces additional voting phases where each point contributes to the accumulator in a more discriminating way by examining the accumulator produced by the previous voting phase and lessening its voting where there is lesser agreement with other voters. This technique has been called "backlinking" [12] or "feature binding" [13] by previous researchers.

Credit attribution refines medialness, disassociating object boundaries and causing each boundary to contribute more discriminately to the core for that object. As object representations (cores) form in the medial response space, they begin to claim their contributing boundaries and to exert an inhibitory influence on the contribution of those boundaries to other objects.

The credit attribution algorithm is as follows:

1. Generate the medialness accumulator using the HMAT.
2. For each boundary point examine the locus of points that it contributed to in the accumulator and compute the sum of these accumulator values weighted by
$$W\left(\left\|x_b - x_a\right\|, r\right).$$
3. Regenerate the accumulator, this time weighting each vote by the ratio between the previous value of that accumulator point and the sum of all accumulator values to which the boundary point contributed.
4. Repeat from Step 2 until the algorithm converges.[2]

The claiming influence of medial points may be extended across scales by computing the cross-scale sum in Step 2, thus forcing medial points to compete for ownership with other scales. By weighting the cross-scale interaction across a scale neighborhood, this competition can be constrained to similar scales only.

### 4.4 Finding Ridges

The next step in the computation is to find ridges in the medialness by examining the local geometry to find points that exhibit ridge (locally optimal) properties. Since the medialness space is three-dimensional (two spatial dimensions and the scale dimension), it is necessary to extend the landscape notion of a two-dimensional ridge to a third dimension. These ridges form a set of one-dimensional space curves through the three-dimensional scale space.

The ridge definition used here is similar to one used by Haralick [14] for two dimensions and extended by us to higher dimensions and to scale spaces [15–17]. The definition may be easily extended to any arbitrary dimensionality of space or ridge within that space. The general notion in two dimensions is that a ridge point in a function $f$ is a local maximum in $f$ along the direction of the greatest principal curvature of $f$. In other words, at a ridge point the direction of greatest curvature of $f$ is the cross-ridge (folding) direction and the value of $f$ at the ridge point is greater than the neighboring points on either side of the ridge. In higher (n) dimensions, this extends not to a single direction of greatest curvature, but to a set of $n - 1$ orthogonal directions of greatest curvature.

Additional care must be taken when the space involved is not a Euclidean space but a scale-space in which one of the dimensions is the scale of measurement. Eberly has shown that scale space is indeed non-Euclidean so the geometric measurements (differentiation) used to detect ridges must be made with a specific choice of metric [17].

---

[2]Strict convergence is not actually required—each iteration of the algorithm improves the overall result.

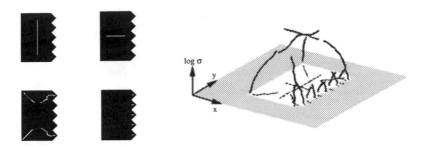

Figure 5: Core segments for the shape in Fig. 1 as projected onto the image (left) and in scale space (right). The first (largest scale) core represents the vertical orientation of the object and the symmetry of the longer sides. The second core represents the symmetry between the top and bottom of the object. The third set represents the four corners of the object. The fourth set represents the detail of the individual teeth.

## 5. Examples

The results of applying these method to the shape in Fig. 1 are shown in Fig. 5. The first and third sets of cores form the familiar symmetric axis for a rectangle (with the second appearing in the more general definition) and the fourth set represents the teeth of the sawtoothed edge. In this way, the cores capture the general-shape rectangularity of the figure in spite of the variations of the teeth on the left side. In this figures on the left the cores have been projected spatially onto the image, but in the actual representation each point on the core has an associated object width or scale (as shown in the right figure).

The vertical core is the dominant feature, representing elongation in the vertical direction and the symmetry between the left and right sides. This segment alone is enough to classify this shape with other elongated shapes such as ovals and rectangles. Four separate cores represent the four corners of the rectangular figure and these five segments together match the cores of a rectangle. At smaller scales, there are individual cores for each triangular tooth of the edge. These smaller-scale shape features can be used to differentiate between this and similar rectangular shapes.

It should be observed here that these segments need not be connected as are traditional medial representations. This separation of cores across scale makes the resulting representation robust—larger scale cores are extracted with relative insensitivity to smaller (or larger) scale features.

Though separated, these cores may be constructed into a hierarchy describing the entire object in increasing detail. Because each point on a core has an associated width, the related boundary regions can be identified and examined to find smaller-scale cores that further refine the object description near that boundary.

The results of applying these methods to the shapes in Fig. 2 are shown in Fig. 6. The core of the narrowest figure appears to wiggle from side to side with the edges. For the medium-width figure, these edge variations diminish in influence and the overall

382

Figure 6: Cores computed for the "wiggle" figures shown earlier in Fig. 2.

representation is of a generally straight figure with individual cores for the edge variations. The largest-width figure retains the straight general-shape representation of the medium-width figure, but the scale of the general shape has increased to where the overall anti-symmetry between the right and left sides causes the figure itself to lean slightly to the right. These are specific predictions that can be tested psychophysically [18].

## 6. Conclusion

What makes cores promising for computational tasks such as identification or registration is their ability to respond selectively to scales appropriate for the objects involved. By *automatically* selecting scales relative to the size of the objects involved, registration may be based on larger shape properties without concern for minor detail, including image noise. Smaller-scale shape properties are captured at their appropriate scales and may still be used where needed. Because this scale selection is based on local object properties, scale separation is relative—objects of various sizes may be registered simultaneously without sensitivity to their respective smaller-scale detail. This behavior is not found in purely global methods (which cannot treat different-sized objects accordingly) or purely local methods (which cannot consider the overall properties of those objects).

## 7. Acknowledgments

The authors would like to acknowledge the contributions of James Coggins and Daniel Fritsch in the development of the core model and algorithms; Jonathan Marshall for his help with the credit attribution algorithm; and David Eberly, Christine Scharlach, and Robert Gardner for their help with the formulation of the ridge definition used here.

This research was supported by a fellowship from the UNC Graduate School, by NIH grant #P01 CA47982, and by Air Force grant #FQ8671-92-J-0114.

## 8. References

[1]    D. Marr and H. Nishihara, "Representation and recognition of the spatial organization of three-dimensional shapes", *Proc. Royal Soc. of London, Series B*, vol. 200, 1978, pp. 269–294.

[2]    T. Wolfe, "On the estimation of the middle of lines", *Amer. J. Psych.*, vol. 34, pp. 313–358, 1923.

[3]     D. Levi and G. Westheimer, "Spatial-interval discrimination in the human fovea: What delimits the interval?", *J. Opt. Soc. of America A*, vol. 4, no. 7, pp. 1304–1313, 1987.

[4]     C. Burbeck, "Position and spatial frequency in large-scale localization judgments", *Vision Research*, vol. 27, no. 3, pp. 417–429, 1987.

[5]     C. Burbeck and S. Hadden, "Scaled position integration areas: Accounting for Weber's law for separation", *J. Opt. Soc. of America A*, vol. 10, no. 1, pp. 5–15, 1993.

[6]     A. Witkin, "Scale space filtering", *Proceedings IJCAI*, 1983, pp. 1019–1021.

[7]     B. ter Haar Romeny, L. Florack, J. Koenderink, and M. Viergever, "Scale-space: its natural operators and differential invariants", in A. Colchester and D. Hawkes, eds., *Information Processing in Medical Imaging (IPMI'91)*, 1991, vol. 511 in *Lecture Notes in Computer Science*, Springer-Verlag, pp. 239–255.

[8]     H. Blum, "A transformation for extracting new descriptors of shape", in W. Wathen-Dunn, ed., *Models for the perception of speech and visual form*, MIT Press, 1967.

[9]     H. Blum, "Biological shape and visual science, Part I", *J. Theoretical Biology*, vol. 38, pp. 205–287, 1973.

[10]    H. Blum and R. N. Nagel, "Shape description using weighted symmetric axis features", *Pattern Recognition*, no. 10, pp. 167-180, 1978.

[11]    P. Hough, "Method and means of recognizing complex patterns", U. S. Patent 3,069,654, 1962.

[12]    G. Gerig, "Linking image-space and accumulator-space: a new approach for object recognition", in *Proc. First International Conference on Computer Vision (ICCV'87)*, 1987, pp. 112–122.

[13]    T. Olsen, "An architectural model of visual motion understanding", Ph. D. thesis, Dept. of Computer Science, Univ. of Rochester, 1989.

[14]    R. Haralick, "Ridges and valleys in digital images", *Computer Vision, Graphics, and Image Processing*, vol. 22, pp. 28–38, 1983.

[15]    B. Morse, S. Pizer, and A. Liu, "Multiscale medial analysis of medical images", in H. H. Barrett and A. F. Gmitro, eds., *Information Processing in Medical Imaging (IPMI'93)*, vol. 687 in *Lecture Notes in Computer Science*, Springer-Verlag, 1993. To appear in *Image and Vision Computing*, 1994.

[16]    D. Eberly, R. Gardner, B. Morse, S. Pizer, and C. Scharlach, "Ridges for image analysis", Tech. Rep. TR93-055, Dept. of Computer Science, Univ. of North Carolina at Chapel Hill, 1993. To appear in *J. Mathematical Imaging and Vision*.

[17]    D. Eberly, R. Gardner, B. Morse, and S. Pizer, "The differential geometry of scale space". To appear as a chapter in *Geometry-Driven Diffusion*, Kluwer Publishers, Holland, 1994.

[18]    C. Burbeck and S. Pizer, "Object representation by cores". Tech. Rep. TR94-106, Dept. of Computer Science, Univ. of North Carolina at Chapel Hill, 1994.

# GENERALIZED CYLINDERS - WHAT ARE THEY ?

AMBJÖRN NAEVE and JAN-OLOF EKLUNDH

*Computational Vision and Active Perception Laboratory (CVAP)*
*Department of Numerical Analysis and Computing Science*
*Royal Institute of Technology (KTH), S-100 44 Stockholm, Sweden*

## ABSTRACT

In an influential paper Binford 1971 proposed generalized cylinders as a model for representing visual shape. Binford´s model, which has a great intuitive appeal, is however quite general, and only special cases of it, like the straight homogeneous generalized cylinders, have been discussed in detail in the literature. In this paper we propose a means of systematically taxonomizing the GCs from a suitable parametrization. In this way we obtain a rich set of geometric surface classes suitable for future studies with respect to invariants and visually observable properties.

## 1. Introduction

In an influential paper Binford 1971 [1] proposed generalized cylinders as a model for representing visual shape. With reference to Blum´s medial axis transform he argued that objects, or at least their parts, often can be considered as generated by sweeping a planar curve, the cross section, along an axis or a spine. For instance, both manufactured objects and objects that accrue from natural growth or wearing tend to have such shapes.

Extensive work on shape representation and shape understanding in computer vision has since been based on this notion, see e.g. Marr and Nishihara [2], Brooks [3], Nevatia and Binford [4], and Ulupinar and Nevatia [5], to take a few examples. Biederman has used generalized cylinders as shape primitives in his Recognition By Components theory for object recognition by humans [6], which also has attracted considerable interest in computer vision, see e.g. Dickinson et al [7], and Bergevin and Levine [8].

Despite these vast efforts on applying the generalized cylinders to problems on shape, the general representation that Binford suggested does not necessarily define non-singular surfaces, i.e. surfaces that are boundaries of physical objects. This problem has largely been addressed by only considering very special cases, the main one being that of straight homogeneous generalized cylinders. See Shafer and Kanade [9], Ponce et al [10] and Ponce [11] for such work.

In his brief "Intermezzo" on tubular surfaces Koenderink ([12], p. 593) makes the remark that "There exist several other less precisely defined and often very complicated notions of what are often called "generalized cylinders". In some cases the definitions are so broad that it is hard to see what surfaces do not belong to the intended class. In such cases the notion becomes obviously less natural, and usually other methods will serve the goal better." This quote stresses that the GC notion is so general that it contains almost everything. Later on the same page it is also noted that even the simple definition of a tubular surface can create the opposite problem, namely that the axis cannot be to sharply bent.

Of course, one can argue that it is more natural to consider volumetric representations than surface representations for physical objects. Nevertheless, it is undisputable that surfaces can be observed visually. It is also true that the intuition behind Binford´s suggested model is quite natural. The attempts to either restrict the model to oversimplified cases, or to only consider local properties is no doubt critical for solving certain recognition problems, but they neither fully exploit the global aspect, nor the intuitiveness of Binford´s definition. Therefore, it must be of interest to ask if there is any more precise definition of generalized cylinders that specifies the notion better.

In this paper we will consider this question from two different points of view. First, we will consider the general definition and from it derive conditions that guarantee a non-singular surface. Secondly, we will consider some classes of surfaces that obviously fall within the original definition, but are more general than the SHGC. Here we will not discuss the problem that presumably has caused the development into mainly studying SHGC:s namely that of what properties can be observed from an image, i.e. invariants in a general sense. In the end this is of course the underlying question that must guide the development towards a better taxonomy that we are attempting. There is a wealth of such results, in particular concerning SHGC:s, see e.g. [10] and [13] - [18] for a few recent contributions. However, we feel that the basic geometry of the situation is worth to analyze on its own account, and this is the topic of the present paper.

As is well known, the differential geometry of a surface contains two different "points of view", the *embedding invariant* aspects, which are determined by its *first* fundamental form, and the *embedding variant* aspects, which are determined (in addition) by its *second* fundamental form. The embedding invariant part of surface geometry is concerned with concepts such as e.g. the Gaussian curvature and the geodesics of the surface, while the embedding variant part deals with concepts relating to surface shape, i.e. to the surface normal and its various derivatives.

The study of machine perception of real world objects certainly invokes the notions of embedding variant representations. However, the success of the Gauss-Riemann approach to the theory of surfaces has led to an emphasis on embedding invariance in the entire field of differential geometry - most clearly manifested in the modern theory of differentiable manifolds. An unfortunate effect of this historical development has been a tendency to neglect the embedding variant aspects of surface differential geometry - especially during the modern abstract period of this century. In fact, there is a wealth of structurally rich and computationally powerful embedding variant results from the classical "concrete" period of the last century, expressed in the works of such magnificient geometers as Darboux, Bianchi, Salmon, Lie and many others. Unfortunately, this historic treasure seems to have been largely forgotten and remains untapped in the cellars of the academic libraries.

In this work we especially bring out the concept of the focal surface, as an example of such forgotten gemetric treasures, and use it as a help in classifying the geometric structure of some of the subtypes of generalized cylinders that we introduce, notably the Monge surfaces.

## 2. General Parametrization and Condition of Regularity

We will now give a general parametrization method for generalized cylinders that formalizes Binford´s intuitive idea. We will use this parametrization both to formulate a general regularity condition for generalized cylinders and (in the next paragraph) as the basis for a taxonomy of such surfaces.

A generalized cylinder $S$ (in the sense of Binford) is generated as a point-locus of a planar curve $C$ (the cross-section curve) that is subjected to some motion $M$ in space and allowed to change its shape during this motion. Let the plane of $C$ be called $\pi$ and let any one of the two unit normals of $\pi$ be denoted by $\mathbf{u}$. Consider a fixed point $O$ in $\pi$ and choose a 2-dimensional cartesian coordinate system in $\pi$ with the origin at $O$ and unit base vectors $\mathbf{i}$ and $\mathbf{j}$. By tracking $O$ during the motion $M$ of $\pi$ we associate with this motion a space-curve $\Gamma$ called a spine-curve of $S$. Using the arclength $s$ of $\Gamma$ as parameter, the motion $M(s)$ can be decomposed into a translation $T(s)$ of the point $O$ and a rotation $A(s)$ of the plane $\pi$ around the point $T(s)O = O(s) = (x_o(s), y_o(s), z_o(s))$. If $\xi$ and $\eta$ denote the internal coordinates of the cross-section curve $C$ in the system $\{\mathbf{i}, \mathbf{j}\}$ of $\pi$, the cross-section curve $C(s, t)$ is given relative to the point $O(s)$ by the expression

$$C(s, t) = \xi(s, t)\mathbf{i}(s) + \eta(s, t)\mathbf{j}(s) \tag{1}$$

In equation (1) $t$ represents the internal parameter of the cross-section curve $C$ while $s$ represents the external parameter of the motion $M$. The dependence of $\xi$ and $\eta$ on the parameter $s$ reflects the possibility of shape change of $C$ during the motion.

Making use of the above notation, we can therefore express the points on the generated surface $S$ relative to the surrounding space in the following way:

$$S(s, t) = T(s)O + A(s)(\xi(s, t), \eta(s, t)) \tag{2}$$

or in coordinate form

$$\begin{pmatrix} x(s, t) \\ y(s, t) \\ z(s, t) \end{pmatrix} = \begin{pmatrix} x_0(s) \\ y_0(s) \\ z_0(s) \end{pmatrix} + \begin{pmatrix} i_1(s) & j_1(s) & u_1(s) \\ i_2(s) & j_2(s) & u_2(s) \\ i_3(s) & j_3(s) & u_3(s) \end{pmatrix} \begin{pmatrix} \xi(s, t) \\ \eta(s, t) \\ 0 \end{pmatrix} \tag{3}$$

Here the columns of the 3x3-matrix are the "external" coordinates of the vectors $\mathbf{i}(s)$, $\mathbf{j}(s)$ and $\mathbf{u}(s)$ respectively. With $\mathbf{x} = (x, y, z)$, $\mathbf{r} = (x_0, y_0, x_0)$ and $\mathbf{c} = (\xi, \eta, 0)$ we can write (3) in the form

$$\mathbf{x}(s, t) = \mathbf{r}(s) + A(s)\mathbf{c}(s, t) \tag{4}$$

It is clear from its construction that (4) represents a way to parametrize any form of generalized cylinder. Of course, whithout some kind of constraints on the spine-curve $\Gamma = \mathbf{r}(s)$ and the cross-section $C = \mathbf{c}(s, t)$, this kind of parametrization of a given surface is by no means unique. In fact, for any given space-curve $\Gamma$, any surface $S$ can be regarded as a generalized cylinder with spine $\Gamma$ in an infinity of different ways. This is obvious, because any way we choose to "slice up" the surface $S$ in plane sections (with continuously varying directions) will clearly lead to a representation of type (4) relative to

$\Gamma$. Of course, in practice, the choice of spine-curve $\Gamma$ and cross section plane $\pi$ will be guided by the symmetry of the modelled object in such a way as to minimize the analytical complexity of the parametrization (4). For the most commonly studied generalized cylinders, such symmetry considerations lead to choosing the location of the spine-curve in the interior of the object, i.e. the point $O(s)$ of (2) will be chosen in the interior of the cross section curve $C(s, t)$. E.g. for rotationally symmetric surfaces, the spine-curve is always chosen to coincide with the axis of rotation, thus making the cross section circles $C(s, t)$ homogeneous (related by a simple scaling) in the internal cross section coordinate system $\{i, j\}$. However, it is important to observe that such a choice is guided by the underlying symmetry of the object that is being modeled, and not by logical necessity. There is nothing to prevent us from choosing the spine-curve in the exterior of the the object, in fact it is advantageous to do so if this can simplify the parametrization (4).

In view of its complete generality, it is evident that the usefulness of the parametrization (4) will depend on the various constraints that can be introduced on the spine-curve $\Gamma$, the orthogonal transformation $A$ and the cross section $C$ in order to capture the geometrical shape of a given surface $S$. Neverthless from the general form of parametrization given by (4) we can easily deduce a general condition of regularity for the corresponding surface.

As is well known, in differential geometry a surface $S$ is called *regular* if it has a tangent plane at every point [11]. Assuming the existence of a parametrization of type (4) for the surface, differentiating with respect to $s$ and $t$ gives

$$
\begin{cases}
\mathbf{x}_s(s, t) = \mathbf{r}'(s) + A'(s)\mathbf{c}(s, t) + A(s)\mathbf{c}_s(s, t) \\
\mathbf{x}_t(s, t) = A(s)\mathbf{c}_t(s, t)
\end{cases}
\tag{5}
$$

Now the standard regularity condition of surface theory can be expressed as

$$
\mathbf{x}_s \times \mathbf{x}_t \neq \mathbf{0}
\tag{6}
$$

which guarantees that $\mathbf{x}_s$ and $\mathbf{x}_t$ are linearly independent tangent-vectors to $S$ and hence that the normal to $S$ exists - and is parallel to $\mathbf{x}_s \times \mathbf{x}_t$ - for each point $(s, t)$ that satisfies (6). Hence (5) and (6) constitute a way to verify that a given generalized cylinder parametrization defines a regular surface. Of course, as is well known, the vanishing of $\mathbf{x}_s \times \mathbf{x}_t$ - does not necessarily imply the non-existence of the surface normal at the corresponding point.

We will not pursue this matter further here, but note that Ponce [11] in fact gives a necessary and sufficient condition for the regularity of a SHGC.

## 3. The Focal Surface

Before attempting to present a taxonomy of generalized cylinders based on the parametrization (4), we will take the time to introduce a concept from classical differential geometry known as the *focal surface*.This will be helpful in clarifying the geometric structure of some of the surface types that we will encounter below, especially the so called Monge surfaces.

The focal surface of a given surface $S$ can be regarded as the "tangential locus" of the normals $N$ to $S$, because it can be shown that the lines of $N$ are in general tangent to two other surfaces $(S_1, S_2)$ called the *focal sheets* of $S$. Of course, depending on the shape of $S$, the focal sheets $(S_1, S_2)$ can degenerate in various ways. Two well known examples are the case of a sphere $S$, where both focal sheets have degenerated into (the same) point, and the case of a rotational surface, where one focal sheet has degenerated into a straight line (the axis of rotation). Other possible degenerations of the focal sheets include various forms of curves and developables. A thorough discussion of the geometry of the focal surface is given in Naeve [19].

For our purposes here it will suffice to consider two different types of focal degeneration cases where (i) : one focal sheet has degenerated into a *curve*, and (ii) : one focal sheet has degenerated into a *developable*. The corresponding surface $S$ is called a *Canal surface* in case (i) and a *Monge surface* in case (ii). In passing we also remark that if both focal sheets have degenerated into curves, the surface $S$ is called a *Dupin cyclide* (a well known type of surface in classical differential geometry). Moreover, it is an interesting fact that a degeneration of both focal sheets into developables is impossible for any type of surface (see [19] for a proof).

Representing a surface $S$ by a parametrization of its focal surface $(S_1, S_2)$ is called *focal representation* of $S$. This is a special kind of *normal parametrisation*, i.e. representing a surface by its normals. Hence it can only be performed up to a 1-parameter family of so called *parallel surfaces*, since such surfaces share the same normals. It is demonstrated in [19] that focal representation is a powerful tool for geometric analysis of surface shape, because the shape of the focal surface turns out to reflect the most common symmetries of the original surface in a natural way.

## 4. Taxonomy

### 4.1. The Shape Graph

Having defined a general way to parametrize a generalized cylinder, and expressed the regularity condition of the surface relative to this parametrization, we will now use our parametrization to attempt a taxonomy of generalized cylinders. This will be done by introducing a hierarchy of constraints on this parametrization (4) that define parametric subclasses in the corresponding way. These constraints are chosen to include the traditional classification of generalized cylinders within the field of computer vision - such as e.g. SHGC, Piped surfaces and Rotational surfaces. However, our subdivision also suggests other geometrically natural classes, which have not received much attention in the modern literature. Among these we emphasize the Monge surfaces, the Molding surfaces and the Developables - surfaces that were well known in classical times, and which have interesting geometric properties that could be exploited in various forms of surface representation and approximation techniques. We also introduce two natural steps of generalization of Rotational surfaces - called Circular Sections Twist Compensated surfaces (CSTC) respectively Parallel Sections Twist Compensated surfaces (PSTC). The surfaces of type CSTC relax the constraint of straight spine (= axis of rotation), and the surfaces of type PSTC relax as well the constraint of circular section curves for a Rotational surface. What survives in both of these cases is the orthogonal net corresponding to the curves of section and their orthogonal trajectories, whence generalizing the net of meridians and parallel circles in the case of a Rotational surface.

The constraint hierarchy that we introduce can be seen as a process of shape evolution by successive specializations. The underlying analogy is the application of machine tools to an initital object of generic shape S. A collection of shape subtypes of S could be imagined as a set of machine made surfaces, where each machine takes a surface of generic type (S) as input and leaves its mark of symmetry on the produced "output surface". For example, a lathe turns out a rotational surface, and laminating rollers produce a developable surface.
The hierarchy of constraints is presented in the form of a so called *shape graph*, (Figure 1) where each shape type (box) is considered as a specialization of the types connected to it from above. Most of the specializations are simply expressed by multiple inheritance (i.e. several paths leading down into the same shape subtype box), but sometimes an additional constaint is needed in order to arrive at the corresponding subtype. In such cases this additional constraint is expressed by a number (e.g. **5.** in Figure 1) directly on top of the subtype to which the constraint applies. This number also appears in the text, together with an equation expressing the corresponding parametric constraint.

In this way a general parametrization of type (4) gives rize to a dynamic shape type system of subclasses of generalized cylinders, where each subtype is conceived as having evolved from a general prototype by a process of specialization (a "constructional history") - corresponding to a sequence of successive tightenings of parametric constraints. Naturally, any shape graph will always be incomplete - showing only the shape types and transitions that we want to consider for some reason or other. However, it is an important feature of the shape graph that it is open to expansion. *New shape types can always be added later and their corresponding type transitions incorporated into the graph.* A thorough discussion of this kind of dynamic shape type system is given in [19].

Referring to Figure 1 we now describe our shape graph of generalized cylinders. The completely unconstrained generalized cylinder parametrization is denoted by Generalized Cylinder (GC) and represented by the box at the top of the figure. As mentioned above, this corresponds to a completely general type of surface, since any surface can be given a parametrization of type (4).

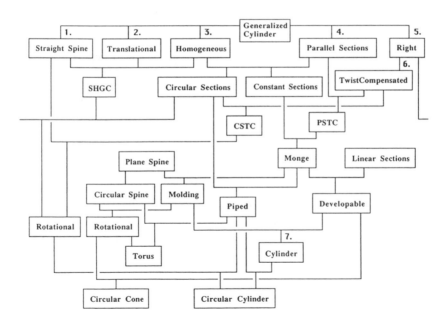

Figure 1.    The shape graph of generalized cylinders.

From the general GC box of Figure 1 we see five different parametric constraints:

**1.**  $\mathbf{r}'(s) = $ constant vector  (7)

**2.**  $A(s) = $ identity matrix  (8)

**3.**  $\mathbf{c}(s,t) = \begin{pmatrix} f(s)g_1(t) \\ f(s)g_2(t) \\ 0 \end{pmatrix}$  (9)

**4.**  $\mathbf{c}(s,t) = $ ParallelCurve(distance$(s)$, $\mathbf{c}(s_0,t)$)  (10)

**5.**  $\mathbf{u}(s) = k\,\mathbf{r}'(s)$,  $k = $ const.  (11)

leading downwards to five corresponding shape subtypes of GC. The numbers **1 - 5** correspond between the above formulas and Figure 1. The constraint **1** leads to the type *Straight Spine Generalized Cylinder* since this constraint obviously implies that the spine curve $\mathbf{r}(s)$ must be a straight line segment. If **2** is fulfilled, it is clear that the planes of cross section must all be parallel to each other, since in this case they are moved by a pure translation. Hence the corresponding shape subtype could be termed *Translational Generalized Cylinder*. The constraint **3** indicates that the cross section curves $\mathbf{c}(s, t)$ are related by a pure scaling function $f(s)$ relative to the origin $O$ of the cross section plane coordinate system (i.e. the point of intersection between the cross section plane and the spine curve). The corresponding shape subtype could therefore be termed *Homogeneous Generalized Cylinder*. The constraint **4** expresses the fact that the cross section curves are parallel curves of each other, i.e. they share the same normals. This shape subtype we have called *Parallel Sections Generalized Cylinder*. Finally, the constraint **5** implies that the normal $\mathbf{u}(s)$ to the cross section plane is parallel to the tangent of the spine curve at the point $O$ of intersection between this curve and the cross section plane. Hence the corresponding shape subtype could be naturally termed *Right Generalized Cylinder*.

Continuing downwards in Figure 1 and combining the constraints **1, 2** and **3** we arrive at the familiar SHGC (*Straight Homogeneous Generalized Cylinder*) which is the most commonly discussed subtype of generalized cylinder in the literature (see the references above). Combining constraints **3** and **4**, it is easy to see that the only type of cross section curve that is transformed into a parallel curve by homogeneous scaling is given by the circle. Hence the subtype *Circular Sections Generalized Cylinder* is the combination of the subtypes Homogeneous and Parallel Sections. However, if the cross section curve is constant, this curve can be considered as scaled by unity ( $f(s) = 1$ in condition **3** ) as well as parallel displaced by zero ( distance$(s) = 0$ in condition **4** ). Therefore we must also admit the *Constant Sections Generalized Cylinder* as a legitimate subtype of Homogeneous and Parallel sections.

## 4.2. Twist Compensated Generalized Cylinders

The underlying geometric meaning of the constraints **1** - **5** above is intuitively clear. We will now introduce a constraint that requires somewhat more of a geometric explanation. Consider the Right Generalized Cylinder subtype defined by constraint **5**, and let the Frenet-frame - i.e. the unit-tangent, principal normal and binormal - of the spine-curve $\Gamma$ be denoted by $\{\mathbf{t}(s), \mathbf{n}(s), \mathbf{b}(s)\}$. Since the plane of cross section in this case is perpendicular to the tangent **t** of the spine-curve, we are free to choose $\{\mathbf{i}, \mathbf{j}\} = \{\mathbf{n}, \mathbf{b}\}$ as the coordinate system for internal representation of the cross section curve $C$ in the plane of cross section $\pi$, and $\mathbf{u} = \mathbf{t}$ as the unit normal of this plane. Let us now consider how to express the most general orthogonal transformation $A(s)$ for the Right Generalized Cylinder subtype. Our choice of internal coordinate system in the cross section plane $\pi$ guarantees that this plane remains perpendicular to the spine-curve $\Gamma$ as the plane $\pi$ moves along this curve. In order to express a general orthogonal transformation $A(s)$ which is subject to this constraint, we must therefore transform the vectors $\{\mathbf{n}, \mathbf{b}\}$ by a general rotation in the cross section plane itself - i.e. by a rotation with axis **t**. Denoting the angle of this "internal rotation" by $\varphi(s)$, we can express the general orthogonal transformation $A(s)$ corresponding to the Right Generalized Cylinder subtype as :

$$A(s) = \begin{pmatrix} n_1(s) & b_1(s) & t_1(s) \\ n_2(s) & b_2(s) & t_2(s) \\ n_3(s) & b_3(s) & t_3(s) \end{pmatrix} \begin{pmatrix} \cos\varphi(s) & \sin\varphi(s) & 0 \\ -\sin\varphi(s) & \cos\varphi(s) & 0 \\ 0 & 0 & 1 \end{pmatrix} \qquad (12)$$

We empasize that the representation (12) is valid - with suitably chosen internal rotation angle $\varphi(s)$ - for any surface of type Right Generalized Cylinder. We will now restrict this type by introducing a constraint on the function $\varphi(s)$. For this purpose we note that the the torsion (= twist) of the spine-curve gives rise to a certain internal rotation of the cross section coordinate system $\{\mathbf{n}(s), \mathbf{b}(s)\}$ itself, as the cross section plane moves along the spine-curve. From the Frenet formulas for the spine-curve we have

$$\mathbf{b}'(s) \;=\; \tau \, \mathbf{n}(s) \tag{13}$$

where $\tau$ is the torsion of the spine-curve. Hence the internal twist-angle $\psi(s)$ of the $\{\mathbf{n}(s), \mathbf{b}(s)\}$ coordinate system is given by the integral of the torsion of the spine-curve with respect to its arc-length $s$:

$$\psi(s) \;=\; \int \tau(s)ds \tag{14}$$

Relative to some arbitrarily chosen initial position $s_o$ , the internal twist of the cross section coordinate system can therefore be expressed as

$$( \,\mathbf{n}(s) \quad \mathbf{b}(s) \,) \;=\; ( \,\mathbf{n}(s_0) \quad \mathbf{b}(s_0) \,) \begin{pmatrix} \cos\psi(s) & \sin\psi(s) \\ -\sin\psi(s) & \cos\psi(s) \end{pmatrix} \tag{15}$$

We are now in a position to introduce the promised constraint on the internal rotation angle $\varphi(s)$ of expression (12). The subtype of Right Generalized Cylinder that we have in mind corresponds to the following choice of $\varphi(s)$ :

**6.** $\quad \varphi (s) \;=\; -\psi(s) \;=\; -\int \tau(s)ds \tag{16}$

The geometric meaning of this constraint is to compensate the cross section curve $C$ for the internal twist of the coordinate system $\{\mathbf{n}(s), \mathbf{b}(s)\}$ and rotate the curve $C$ with the same amount in the opposite direction. Hence the corresponding subtype will be called *Twist Compensated Generalized Cylinder*. It turns out (see Naeve & Eklundh [20]) that if, in addition to the constraint **6**, the cross section curve remains constant, we will generate an interesting (and classically well-known) type of surfaces known as the surfaces of Monge, or the *Monge surfaces*[1].

### 4.3. Monge Surfaces

The Monge surfaces are discussed mathematically in [20], where it is shown that the following five definitions are equivalent :

---

[1]   The term *Monge surface* should not be confused with the term *Monge patch*, which is often used
in differential geometry to denote a surface coordinate patch of type $(x, y, f(x, y))$

(i)   A *Monge surface* is a surface which has a one parameter family of plane curves of curvature which are also geodesics on the surface.

(ii)  A *Monge surface* is a surface which is the locus of a simple infinity of orthogonal trajectories of a 1-parameter family of planes.

(iii) A *Monge surface* is a surface which has a developable focal sheet.

(iv)  A *Monge surface* is a surface that is generated by a plane (profile) curve whose plane rolls without slipping over a developable surface[2].

(v)   A *Monge surface* is a *Constant Section Twist Compensated Generalized Cylinder*.

Accepting these equivalences, and recalling that the curves of curvature form an orthogonal net on any (non-spherical) surface, it is clear that the orthogonal trajectories of (ii) and the plane curves of curvature of (i) taken together form the *principal net*[3] of a Monge surface. Hence, for any given constant cross section curve $C$, our parametrization (12) with the constraint (16) will describe the principal net of the corresponding Monge surface.

When a Monge surface is parametrized as a Generalized Cylinder it has an interesting type of ambiguity with respect to the spine-curve. Since the cross section curve $C$ is constant, it is clear that *any one of the orthogonal trajectories of the cross section planes will qualify as the spine-curve $\Gamma$ of the parametrization* (4). Moreover, for all points in the same cross section plane, these orthogonal trajectories have parallel Frenet-frames[4], and therefore the twist-angles (15) will be the same no matter which of the orthogonal trajectories we choose as the spine-curve.

## 4.4. Generalized Rotational Surfaces

We will now generalize the rolling profile construction (iv) for Monge surfaces to generate a subtype of Generalized Cylinder which we call *Parallel Sections Twist Compensated*

---

2   It is shown in [20] that this surface is identical to the developable focal sheet of (iii). It is called the *director-developable* of the Monge surface.

3   i.e. the net of curves of curvature.

4   In fact, the orthogonal trajectories of any one-parameter family of planes form a two-parameter family of curves, having the edge of the developable of the planes as a common curve of centers of their osculating spheres. At corresponding points of a twisted curve and the locus of the center of its osculating sphere the principal normals are parallel, and the tangent to one curve is parallel to the binormal of the other (see [21], p.51).

*Generalized Cylinder.* Moreover, we will show why it constitutes the natural generalization of rotational surfaces that was mentioned above. We begin by choosing a family of parallel curves $\{C_p : p \in \mathbf{R}\}$ in the plane of cross section $\pi$. Then, as the latter plane rolls over the developable surface, we let the cross section curve $C$ vary continously among this family according to some arbitrarily chosen law $p = p(s)$, where $s$ parametrizes the position of the cross section plane $\pi(s)$. Hence, in this case, the cross section curve is given by

$$C(s, t) = C_{p(s)}(t) . \tag{17}$$

For fixed $t = t_0$, consider the curve $C(s, t_0)$, which is traced out for varying $s$ by the point $Q(s_0, t_0)$ on the curve $C(s_0, t_0)$. Then, for a small increment $ds$, the corresponding displacement $dQ(s) = Q(s+ds, t_0) - Q(s, t_0)$ can be regarded as the result of two composant motions - one internal "parallel curve displacement" within the cross section plane, and one external rotating motion displacement around the corresponding generating line of the developable "contact surface" for the rolling motion of $\pi(s)$. Now, since parallel curves share the same normals, and since rotating motion of a plane traces out orthogonal trajectories of each of its points, it follows that each of these two composant motions of $Q(s, t_0)$ is perpendicular to the cross section curve $C(s, t_0)$. Therefore this orthogonality condition must also hold for their resulting sum. Hence the parametric net of (12) with the constraints of (16) and (17) will generate a family of plane parallel curves ($s = $ const) and their orthogonal trajectories ($t = $ const).

In order to explain the way in which the Parallel Sections Twist Compensated Generalized Cylinders constitute a generalization of the Rotational Surface type, we will reverse the process and specialize the former type of surface into the latter. First, by specializing the parallel curves of cross section into a family of concentric circles, and choosing the curve traced out by their common center point as the spine curve, we get the subtype (Homogeneous) *Circular Sections Twist Compensated Generalized Cylinder*[5] (CSTC in Figure 1). In this case, the parametrization (12) with the constraints (16) gives a curve net consisting of a family of circles and their orthogonal trajectories.

Secondly, we specialize the spine curve into a straight line. Then, since Twist Compensated is a subtype of Right, the corresponding type must be a subtype of

---

[5]  When we speak about the *Circular Sections* subtype of Generalized Cylinder, we will always assume that it is *Homogeneous*. Hence these two subtypes are correspondingly related in Figure 1.

Translational. Therefore, the result of this second specialization step can be expressed in two equivalent ways :

1)    *Straight Spine Circular Sections Twist Compensated GC.*

2)    *Circular Sections Right SHGC.*

The second expression is clearly just another way to express the subtype *Straight Spine Rotational Surface* - the straight spine corresponding to the axis of rotation and the circular sections to the latitude circles.

The two specializations 1) and 2) correspond in Figure 1 to the two different paths leading down into the subtype Rotational surface. Note the cylindrical connectivity of the shape graph. The path that leads downwards from the Right subtype, and which seems to leave the diagram to the right, is rejoining it again on the same level at the opposite side of the figure.

It is interesting to observe what happens to the parametrization (12) of the orthogonal matrix $A(s)$ when the spine-curve gets "straightened out" continously, i.e. when the latter curve approaches a straight line in such a way that both its curvature $\kappa$ and its torsion $\tau$ vary in a continous way. Since a straight line has no Frenet-frame, (12) is not valid in the limit. However, let us consider a sequence of spine-curves where the curvature $\kappa$ tends to zero. As $\kappa \to 0$, we must have $\tau \to 0$, and therefore the twist-angle $\varphi(s) \to 0$ in (16). Hence the second matrix of (12) approaches the unit matrix. Moreover, as $\kappa \to 0$, the Frenet frame of the spine curve decreases its variation and becomes "increasingly constant", i.e. $\{\mathbf{n}(s), \mathbf{b}(s), \mathbf{t}(s)\} \approx \{\mathbf{n}(s_0), \mathbf{b}(s_0), \mathbf{t}(s_0)\}$. Choosing the latter vector triple as basis, it is clear that the first matrix of (12) approaches the unit matrix as well. Hence we have found that as the spine-curve gets straightened out in a continous way, the parametrization $A(s)$ of (12) approaches the "translational constraint" of (8).

This expresses the fact that Straight Spine Rotational Surface is a subtype of Translational Generalized Cylinder, which means that such a rotational surface has parallel planes of cross section.

Finally, let us consider the parametric net of (12), (16) and (9) with the circular section constraint $g_1(t) = \cos t$, $g_2(t) = \sin t$. From the preceding limit discussion it follows immediately that as the spine-curve gets straightend out, this net turns into the net of parallel circles and meridians of the corresponding Straight Spine Rotational Surface. This is the reason for our claim that the CSTC and the PSTC subtypes constitute a natural two step generalization of a Straight Spine Rotational Surface. First we get rid of the straight spine and introduce a "curved axis"  -  while still keeping the circular perpendicular cross section curves (CSTC). Then we get rid of these circles as well, and introduce the parallel-curve perpendicular cross section curves (PSTC). In both cases the parametrization given by (12) and (16) delivers the generalized orthogonal net which corresponds to the orthogonal net of parallel circles and meridian curves in the case of a rotational surface.

### 4.5. Subtypes of Monge surfaces

Continuing our presentation of the shape graph of Figure 1 , we will now concentrate on some subtypes of the Monge surfaces. If the cross section curve is a straight line segment, we have termed the corresponding subtype Linear sections GC. Combining this constraint with the Monge surface we get a surface that can be generated by a fixed straight line segment whose plane rolls without sliding over a developable surface. Since the generated surface must have the same normal direction along the entire cross section curve, it follows that this surface will possess merely a 1-parameter family of normals, and therefore it must itself be developable. Conversely it is easy to see that every developable surface can be generated in this way. Hence we can conclude that the *Linear Sections Monge* surfaces consist precisely of the surfaces that are *Developable*.

Next, we have the Monge surfaces with plane spine-curves, i.e. with spine-curves that are located in a fixed plane. Since the cross section plane that generates the Monge surface is rolling on a developable surface (one of the focal sheets of the Monge surface), and at the same time the cross section plane is remaining perpendicular to the spine-curve, it follows that the developable focal sheet must in fact be a cylinder with its cylindrical direction perpendicular to the plane of the spine-curve. Hence the generated surface will be a so called *Molding surface*. A special form of parametrization for the Molding surfaces is given in [20].

Let us now consider a Molding surface with a circular spine-curve. In this case the trajectory of any fixed point of the cross section plane (under the rolling motion) must be circular. It follows that the envelope of these rolling planes - i.e. the developable focal sheet - must in fact coincide with a straight line. Hence the generated Molding surface must have rotational symmetry. Thus the Molding surfaces with circular spine-curves coincide with the rotational surfaces with circular spine-curves.

It is important to observe that in the shape graph of Figure 1 we have arrived at the Rotational surfaces in two different ways, corresponding to Rotational surfaces with straight spine-curve and Rotational surfaces with circular spine-curve. This corresponds to a significant difference of constructional histories for surfaces with rotational symmetry. A Rotational surface with a straight spine-curve can always be regarded as a Rotational surface with a circular spine-curve, simply by rotating a meridian curve of the surface around the axis of its rotational symmetry. However, a Rotational surface with a circular spine-curve - such as e.g. a torus - cannot in general be considered as a Rotational surface with a straight spine-curve, because the corresponding cross section curve will not be arcwise connected. For instance, in the case of the torus, the "straight spine cross section curve" would consist of a circle that splits up into two concentric circles that move apart and then gradually approach each other and finally merge back into one circle again. Such a cross section curve is incompatible with the general idea of a generalized cylinder as expressed by parametrization (4). Hence we must regard the two subtypes marked as Rotational in the shape graph of Figure 1 as being different from one another.

Moving on downwards in the shape graph, we next consider Monge surfaces with circular sections. Since the cross section curve of a Monge surface is constant, it follows that one of the curve families of the principal net of a Monge surface with circular sections will consist of circles with constant radius. Such a surface is sometimes called a *tubular surface*[6] and sometimes a *canal surface*[7] in the geometric literature. To avoid this unfortunate ambiguity we have introduced the term *Piped* for this kind of surface, since its shape can be compared to a curved pipe-line or a piece of piped plumbing. If a Piped surface also possesses a circular spine-curve, then the surface must be a Molding surface (since it is Monge with plane spine) and therefore it must be Rotational with circular spine. Such a surface can therefore be generated by a circle of fixed radius, whose plane rotates around a fixed axis not intersecting the circle. It follows that a Piped surface with a circular spine-curve is in fact a *Torus*.

Consider now a Molding surface that is also Developable. It follows from what has been said above that such a surface can be generated by a straight line segment, whose plane rolls without sliding on a cylinder. If, in addition, we introduce the following constraint:

7 .    The cross section line segment is perpendicular to the spine-curve.

It follows that the cross section line segment must be parallel to the direction of the cylinder. Therefore the generated surface must itself be of type *Cylinder*, and it is easy to

---

6    see e.g. Koenderink [12].

7    see e.g. Eisenhart [21].

see that each cylinder can be constructed in this way. Hence we can conclude that the Developable Molding surfaces that satisfy constraint **7** are precisely the Cylinders.

To conclude our discussion of the shape graph of Figure 1, it remains to make the following two observations: First, it is clear that a Developable Rotational surface with circular spine is a *Circular Cone* - unless it satisfies constraint **7**, in which case it is a Circular Cylinder. Second, it is obvious that a Piped Rotational surface with straight spine - as well as a Piped Cylindrical surface - is in fact a Circular Cylinder.

## 5. Examples

In order to illustrate the preceding discussion and demonstrate the descriptive power of our representation we will now present some pictorial examples generated by Mathematica (on a Macintosh Powerbook 170). The spine curves chosen are the circular helix and the twisted cubic. Since the circular helix has constant torsion, the calculation of the twist-angle (14) is trivial in this case. In order to speed up the twist-angle calculation in the second case, the coefficients of the twisted cubic were chosen to make the integral (14) analytically solvable. Of course this integral can be solved numerically for any kind of spine-curve.

Our first example is shown in Figure 2. It shows a piped surface with twisted cubic spine curve. From our taxonomic shape graph we see that a Piped surface is a Monge surface with circular cross section curves, and therefore it is a Right Constant Circular Section Generalized Cylinder. Observe that since the cross sections are circular, the twist compensation has no effect on the shape of the surface but only changes the parametric coordinate system. Figure 2.a shows the non twist compensated case, while Figure 2.b shows the effect of twist compensation. The shape of the surface is the same, but the parameteric coordinate system is now identical to the principal curves of the surface.

Figure 3 differs from Figure 2 only in the fact that the cross section curve is now elliptic instead of circular. In this case the twist compensation must change the shape of the surface and not just the parametric representation. Figure 3.a shows a Right Constant (elliptical) Sections GC, and Figure 3.b shows the effect of twist compensation: The surface turns into a Constant (elliptical) Sections Twist Compensated GC - i.e. a Monge surface with elliptical sections - and the parametric net becomes principal.

Figure 4 shows a Monge surface with elliptical sections and circular helix spine-curve. It is the result of changing the spine-curve of Figure 3.b from twisted cubic to circular helix.

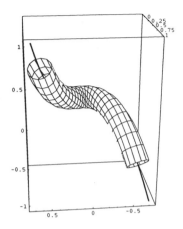

Figure 2.a.    Right Constant Circular
               Sections GC.

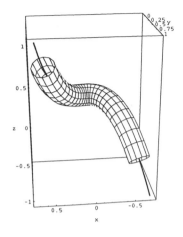

Figure 2.b.    Constant Circular Sections
               Twist Compensated GC.

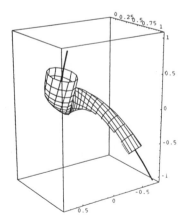

Figure 3.a.    Right Constant Sections GC.

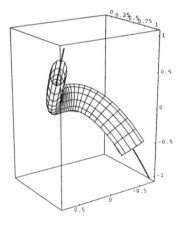

Figure 3.b.    Right Constant Sections
               Twist Compensated GC

402

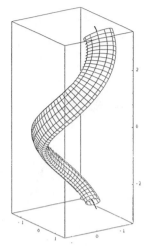

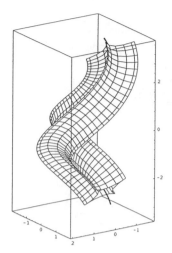

Figure 4.  Monge surface with circular
         helix spine-curve and elliptical
         cross section curve.

Figure 5.  Monge surface with circular
         helix spine-curve and cross
         section curve with four cusps.

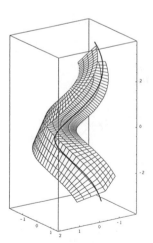

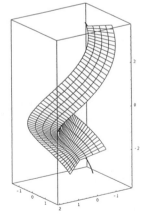

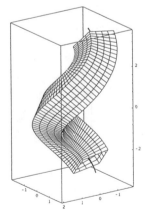

Figure 6.a.  Monge surface
          with half-square
          cross sections.

Figure 6.b.  Monge surface
          with half-square
          cross sections.

Figure 6.c.  Combination of
          figures 6.a. and 6.b.

Figure 5 illustrates a Monge surface with circular helix spine curve and four singular edge curves. The cross section curve is of type $|x|^{1/2} + |y|^{1/2} = 1$, and it has four singular points that trace out the singular curves of the surface.

In Figure 6 we see a "twisted square pipe" which is a Monge surface with circular helix spine-curve and cross section curve of type $|x| + |y| = 1$. Since this curve consists of four line segments, it follows that the surface can be assembled from four Monge surfaces with Linear sections, i.e. from four developable surfaces. Figure 6.a shows the two developable parts that are situated "behind" the spine curve (relative to the viewing direction), and Figure 6.b. shows the two developable parts in front of the spine-curve. Figure 6.c shows the assembly of 6.a and 6.b into a finished square pipe.

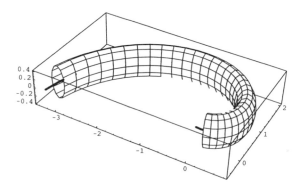

Figure 7.      Molding surface with elliptical cross section curve.

Figure 7 shows a Monge surface with elliptical sections and plane spine curve. From the taxonomic shape graph we see that this is a Molding surface. In fact this surface is the result of replacing the circular helix spine curve of the Monge surface in Figure 4 with a plane spine curve.

In Figure 8 we see a Circular Sections Twist Compensated GC with a cylindrical helix spine curve. Figures 8.a and 8.b show the same surface from two different viewpoints. This is the first step generalization of rotational surface that was mentioned above. Hence the parametric net is orthogonal but since the surface is not (in general) a Canal surface, the parametric net is not principal. Figures 9.a and 9.b show two different views of another surface of the same type (CSTC) which has a twisted cubic spine curve.

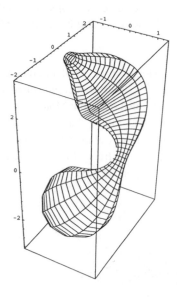

Figure 8.a.     Circular Sections
Twist Compensated GC
with circular helix spine-curve.

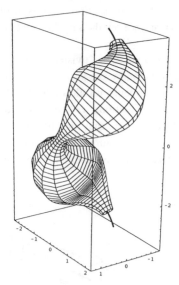

Figure 8.b.     Another view of the surface
from Figure 8.a.

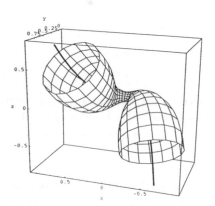

Figure 9.a.     Circular Sections
Twist Compensated GC
with twisted cubic spine-curve.

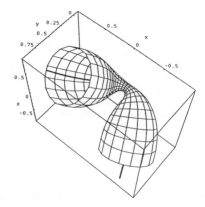

Figure 9.b.     Another view of the surface
from Figure 9.a.

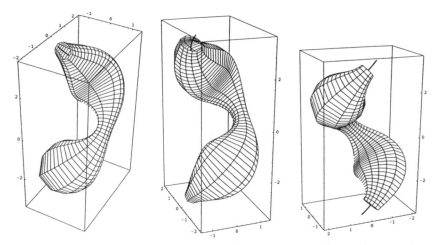

Figure 10.a. PSTC with circular     Figure 10.b. Another view of     Figure 10.c. A third view of
helix spine-curve.                          the surface of 10.a                    the surface of 10.a

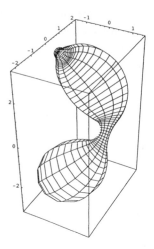

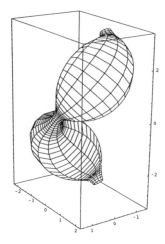

Figure 11.a. Canal surface with circular        Figure 11.b. Another view of
helix degenerated focal sheet.                        the surface of 11.a.

The second step generalization of rotational surface is illustrated in Figures 10.a, 10.b and 10.c, which show three different views of a surface of type Parallel Sections Twist Compensated GC (with circular helix spine curve). In fact this PSTC surface has been constructed from the CSTC surface of Figure 8 by changing the circular cross section curves into an ellipse and its parallel curves. Since the surface is of type PSTC, it follows that the parametric net is orthogonal.

## 6. Additional Remarks

The taxonomy of generalized cylinders that we have presented above is based on the parametrization (4) and the constraints given in the shape graph of Figure 1. Although the question of representation uniqueness is not the main topic of this paper, it is still appropriate to include a few remarks concerning this issue here.

First it is important to observe the structural difference between the GC-representation of a surface $S$ in terms of a spine-curve $\Gamma$ and a family of cross section curves $C$ on the one hand, and the focal surface $(S_1, S_2)$ of $S$ on the other. As we have seen, the GC-parametrization of $S$ has an inherent ambiguity, which necessitates a choice - guided by the symmetry of $S$ - in order to obtain analytical simplicity. On the other hand, the focal surface of $S$ is determined solely by the geometry of $S$ and is therefore unique. Hence a GC-parametrization of $S$ that is related to its focal surface will correspond more closely to the underlying geometry of the represented surface. As an example, consider the situation for a Monge surface $S$. Since the envelope of the cross section planes of the GC-parametrization of $S$ is identical to the developable focal sheet of $S$, it follows that the cross section curves $C$ must be principal curves and geodesics, and their orthogonal trajectories must form the other family of principal curves on the surface. On the other hand, the spine-curve of a Monge surface bears no relation to its focal surface, and therefore it has no direct geometric relation to the surface. As we have pointed out above, in the case of Monge surfaces, *any* orthogonal trajectory of the family of cross section planes will qualify as a spine-curve of the parametrization (4), since the cross section curves are constant no matter which point is chosen as the origin $O$ of the coordinate system of the cross section plane. Hence the symmetry of a general Monge surface gives no guidance as regards the choice of spine-curve, but no matter what choice is made, the resulting parametric net is the principal net, which is geometrically unique.

Let us review this situation in the special case that the Monge surface $S$ is Piped. In this case the cross section curves are circles with constant radius, and their centers form a curve

$K$ which is a (degenerated) focal sheet of $S$. The other focal sheet is still given by the envelope of the cross section planes. Now the symmetry of $S$ suggests the choice of $K$ as the spine-curve, which leads to a geometrically significant spine-curve as well as to a maximally simple analytical form of the GC-parametrization (4).

While discussing Monge surfaces, let us point out that the rolling profile construction mentioned above (p.9, (iv)) gives a method for varying the shape of a Monge surface $S$ dynamically. It is easily seen that the non-developable focal sheet of $S$ is generated by the evolute of the cross section curve $C$ as the plane of the latter rolls over the other (developable) focal sheet of $S$. Hence by independently varying the shape of the developable focal sheet as well as the cross section curve, we independently change the shape of the two focal sheets of a Monge surface without breaking the geometric constraints of this surface type. In this way the rolling profile construction leads to a robust way of controlling the shape of a Monge surface. A more thorough discussion of this matter can be found in [19].

A family of surfaces that is sometimes mentioned in connection with generalized cylinders are the envelopes of 1-parameter families of spheres. In the geometric literature such surfaces are often called *Canal surfaces* [8]. In terms of the focal surface, Canal surfaces are characterized by the fact that one of their focal sheets have degenerated into a curve,, whichn is identical to the locus of the centers of the generating spheres. This fact directly implies that one of the two families of principal curves of a Canal surface consists of circles, and the normals to the surface along one of these circular principal curves form a circular cone with its vertex on the degenerated (curve-like) focal sheet (see [19] for more details). An example of a Canal surface with a circular helix as its curve-like focal sheet is shown in Figure 11.

In view of the pictorial similarities betweeen the Canal surface of Figure 11 and the CSTC-surface of Figure 8 it might be surmised that a Canal surface $S$ would have a natural parametrization as a CSTC-type of generalized cylinder. This is however not the case.

---

[8] There is a most unfortunate divergence of terminology involved here. We follow the german tradition, which takes the term *Kanalfläche* to mean the envelope of a general 1-parameter family of spheres. When the radius is constant, the germans refer to a *Rohrenfläche*, which we have translated into *Piped surface*. Some English writers (notably Eisenhart) use the term *Canal surface* in this more restricted case of constant radius. To make matters worse, the term *Tubular surface* is also used in two ways by the geometric community ; sometimes referring to a general spherical envelope (e.g. by Eisenhart), and sometimes to a spherical envelope with constant radius (e.g. by Koenderink).

408

To see why, let $C$ denote a circular principal curve of $S$ and consider the two curves generated by the center of $C$ respectively by the vertex of the circular cone of surface normals corresponding to $C$. The latter curve is identical to the degenerated focal sheet of the surface $S$, while the former curve (in general) has no geometric relation to the surface $S$. Hence, for a generic Canal surface, the curve of centers of the circular principal curves is not perpendicular to the planes of the circular cross sections. Now, from the shape graph of Figure 1, it is seen that any type of Twist Compensated GC must be Right. Therefore a Canal surface has no representation as an SCTC type of generalized cylinder.


## 7. Summary

We have proposed an approach to systematically taxonomizing generalized cylinders by an appropriate parametrization. In this way we obtain a rich set of geometric surface classes suitable for future studies with respect to invariants and visually observable properties. By computer generated examples we have demonstrated the descriptive power of our taxonomy.


## 8. Acknowledgements

This work has been supported by a grant from the Swedish Research Council for Engineering Science, which is gratefully acknowledged.


## 9. References

[1]    T.O. Binford, "Visual perception by computer," *IEEE Conference on Systems and Controls*, December 1971, Miami.

[2]    D. Marr and K. Nishihara, "Representation and recognition of the spatial organization of three dimensional shapes", *Proc. Roy. Soc. London*, B-200, 269-294, 1978.

[3]    R.A. Brooks, "Model-based three dimensional interpretation of two dimensional images", *IEEE Transactions* PAMI, 5 pp.140-150, 1983.

[4]    R. Nevatia and T.O. Binford, "Description and recognition of complex curved objects", *Artificial Intelligence*, 8, pp.77-98, 1977.

[5]    F. Ulupinar and R. Nevatia, "Perception of 3-D surfaces from 2-D contours", *IEEE Transactions* PAMI, 15, pp.3-18, 1993.

[6] I. Biederman, "Recognition by components : A theory of human image understanding", *Psychological Review*, 94, pp.115-147, 1987.

[7] S. Dickinson, A.P. Pentland, and A. Rosenfeld, "3-D shape recovery using distributed aspect matching", *IEEE Transactions* PAMI, 15, pp.174-198, 1992

[8] R. Bergevin, and M.D. Levine, "Generic object recognition: Building and matching coarse descriptions from line drawings", *IEEE Trans.* PAMI, 15, pp.19-36, 1993.

[9] S.A. Shafer and T. Kanade, "The theory of straight homogeneous generalized cylinders", *Technical Report* CS-083-105, Carnegie Mellon University, 1983.

[10] J. Ponce, D. Chelberg and W.B. Mann, "Invariant properties of straight homogeneous generalized cylinders and their contours", *IEEE Transactions* PAMI, 11, pp.951-966, 1989.

[11] J. Ponce, "Straight homogeneous generalized cylinders: differential geometry and uniqueness results", *Internat. Journal of Computer Vision*, 4, pp.79-100, 1990.

[12] J.J. Koenderink, *Solid Shape*, MIT Press, Cambridge, Mass, 1990

[13] M. Richetin, M. Dhome, J.T. Lapreste and G. Rives, "Inverse perspective transform using zero-curvature contours points: Applications to the localization of some generalized cylinders from a single view", *IEEE Transactions* PAMI, 13, pp.185-192, 1991.

[14] M. Dhome, R. Glachet and J.T. Lapreste, "Recovering the scaling function of a SHGC from a single perspective view", *Proc. of IEEE* CVPR, pp.36-41, 1992.

[15] J. Liu, J. Mundy, D. Forsyth, A. Zisserman and C. Rothwell, "Efficient recognition of rotationally symmetric surfaces and straight homogeneous generalized cylinders", *Proceedings of IEEE* CVPR, pp.123-128, 1993.

[16] C.A. Rothwell, D.A. Forsyth, A. Zisserman and J.L. Mundy, "Extracting projective structure from single perspective views of 3D point sets", *ICCV*, pp.573-582, Berlin, Germany, 1993.

[17] H. Sato and T.O. Binford, "Finding and recovering SHGC objects in an edge image", *Computer Vision Graphics and Image Processing*, 57, pp.346-356, 1993.

[18] M. Zerroug and R. Nevatia, "Quasi-invariant properties and 3D shape recovery of non-straight, non-constant generalized cylinders", *Proceedings of IEEE* CVPR, pp.96-103, New York, 1993.

[19] A. Naeve, *Focal Shape Geometry of Surfaces in Euclidean Space*, Dissertation, TRITA-NA-P9319, KTH, Stockholm, 1993.

[20] A. Naeve, and J.O. Eklundh, "A taxonomy for generalized cylinders", in preparation, KTH, Stockholm, 1994.

[21] L. Eisenhart, *A Treatise on the Differential Geometry of Curves ans Surfaces*, Ginn and Company (The Athenæum Press), Boston, Ma, 1909.

# AN INDUCED TAXONOMY OF VISUAL FORM

GEORGE NAGY

Rensselaer Polytechnic Institute

Troy, NY, 12180 USA

## ABSTRACT

We attempt to classify the 59 research papers published in the Proceedings of the 1991 Capri Workshop on Visual Form from the point of view of our preconceived notion of shape based on equivalence classes induced by a shape-extraction operation. We observe that some of the papers present a hierarchy of shape transformations, while others select a single arbitrary level of operation, relatively distant from the ultimate application objectives. We also coarsely classify the types of data used in the various studies into four categories: "none," "simulated," "sensed-simplified," and "sensed-realistic."

## 1. Introduction

Driven by curiosity about the nature of shape, we read some of the extensive literature on the subject and prepared a short survey (with a long bibliography) for the first International Workshop on Visual Form. Endeavouring to capture some commonality among the many disparate views, we presented the following definition:

> SHAPE is a property of both *a set of objects* and *a particular method of observation or measurement.*

> The universe of objects may be finite (e.g., a set of printed characters on a page), or infinite (the set of all triangles). The objects are geometric figures or solids (or, more precisely, compact point-sets in $E^2$ or $E^3$).

> The observations are restricted to the *geometry* of the envelope (boundary) of the objects. Only measurements that are invariant to translation, scale, and rotation are considered (e.g., ratio of perimeter-length or surface-area to length or area of convex hull).

> Then all objects that cannot be distinguished by the given method of observation are said to have the same shape.

Thus we considered shape in terms of *equivalence classes* induced on a particular context or application (the universe of objects) by a particular system of features or measurements (*probes*). This point of view was possibly colored by our background in pattern recognition, but the notion of an "observer" (or "frame of reference") is well established in modern physics.

This definition does not reflect the idea that shape is a global property that is not affected by insignificant variations of the boundary. Indeed, the notion of *significant variation* is recognized to be thoroughly application-dependent. For instance, the glyph that dis-tinguishes the silhouette of a Q from that of an O has no effect when appended to an R.

Our objective here is to test this paradigm against the results of research on shape reported in the proceedings of the First Workshop on Visual Form, which was held in Capri in May 1991 [*Visual Form: Analysis and Recognition,* C. Arcelli, L.P. Cordella, G.Sanniti di Baja, editors, Plenum, 1992.]. Taking the attitude that shape is whatever shape researchers consider fit to present at a shape conference, we attempted to classify the objects and the methods of observation.

On examining the material presented at the Workshop, a significant defect in our definition quickly became evident. Our definition did not emphasize the *hierarchical* nature of many shape extraction schemes. For instance, from gray-level pixels one may extract edges (which are invariant under image-intensity transformations), and from the edges extract face structure (a projective invariant).

Our view is still that a shape *operator*, applied to some description or representation of an object, produces a new description or representation. The transformation is many-to-one because some primitives are grouped into equivalence classes: in general, the original description cannot be obtained from the new description. But further shape operators may be applied to the new description. Much of the richness of the field is a consequence of this hierarchical approach.

## 2. Methodology

The experimental paradigm consisted of clustering both the primitive objects for which the various shape features are intended, and the methods of observation or measurement (*probes* for short). The clustering was performed with an agglomerative bottom-up) multi-link gedanken algorithm with a subjective metric that took into account citations and keywords. No special weighting factor was applied to the twelve invited papers. Overlapping clusters were allowed. The classification attempted to take into account the dominant features of each approach rather than every feature considered. The lower bound on the residual error of classification is 10%.

The input consisted of the 59 papers in the Red Book (*op.cit.*) The output is a hierarchy of probes or shape operators, aggregated according to the representation and the nature of the input data. The Appendix provides a capsule summary of each paper from the point of view of the classification.

## 3. Results

The raw results are displayed in Table 1. The study attributed to each category is listed in the rightmost column according to its title-page number in the Book. Levels of the hierarchy are measured from the input: primitives are on the left, with shape features increasing in complexity to the right. About two-thirds of the papers (the top part of the

Table 1.  Hierarchy of shape extraction methods

| Input | Method | | | Output | No. |
|---|---|---|---|---|---|
| b/w pix | convex hull | | | | 57 |
| b/w pix | Hough transform | straight-line segments | | | 165 |
| b/w pix | line image | | | | 127 |
| b/w pix | morphological filter | | | noise-invariant object | 275 |
| b/w pix | morphological operations | | | | 293 |
| b/w pix | morphology | characteristic pattern | | object description | 633 |
| b/w pix | quad tree | | | object description | 451 |
| b/w pix | rectangle paramaters | | | | 47 |
| b/w pix | scale-space | smoothed contours | | | 333 |
| b/w pix | skeleton | | | | 345 |
| b/w pix | skeleton | object decomposition | | | 537 |
| b/w pix | skeleton | | | | 21 |
| b/w pix | skeleton | circular arcs | | object description | 155 |
| b/w pix | skeleton | vectorization | | | 249 |
| grey pix | 2-D silhouette | | | reconstructed object | 67 |
| grey pix | contours | splines | affine invariants | | 323 |
| grey pix | contours | | | | 137 |
| grey-pix | edge/line segments | | | | 479 |
| grey pix | edges | triple chains | view classes | object description | 99 |
| grey pix | edges | tetrahedralization | | | 231 |
| grey pix | edges | scale space | contour descriptions | | 197 |
| grey-pix | edges | junctions | | reconstructed object | 259 |
| grey pix | edges & regions | | object description | scene description | 593 |
| grey pix | edges and corners | | pose description | object description | 213 |
| grey pix | face graph | face groups | geons | | 527 |
| grey-pix | grey-level-difference stats | surface orientation | | object description | 603 |
| grey pix | interest points | generalized Hough | articulation-invariants | | 39 |
| grey pix | optical flow | planar surfaces | | | -"- |
| grey pix | optical flow | | egomotion parameters | | 1 |
| grey pix | skeleton | | | | 11 |
| grey pix | skeleton | quadratic patches | multiple views | scene description | 495 |
| grey-pix | stereo | image warping | | | 287 |
| grey pix | triangular patches | splines | motion parameters | | 29 |
| grey pix | vertical edges | wireframe | | | 205 |
| color pix | boundary | polygons | shape index | | |

(to be continued)

(continued from the previous page)

Table 1.   Hierarchy of shape extraction methods

| | | | | | |
|---|---|---|---|---|---|
| x-y coords | Kalman filter | noise-invariant curve | | | 469 |
| x-y coords | contour | k'th autocorrelation | shape index | | 109 |
| polygons | visual hull | | | | 355 |
| polygons | splines | circular arcs | | | 431 |
| polygons | rotational symmetry | | | | 507 |
| polygons | symmetric forms | | | | 517 |
| polygons | affine transformations | equivalence classes | | | 583 |
| polylines | form elements | affine transformation | | | 267 |
| contours | curvature & symmetry | formation-process | | | 379 |
| contours | perspective transformation | generalized cylinders | invariant contour | object description | 613 |
| curve eq'ns | invariant differentials | | | | 89 |
| edges | circle Hough transform | | | | 119 |
| range map | collinear triplets | optical flow | egomotion parameters | | 175 |
| range map | collinear triplets | optical flow | surface discontinuities | | -"- |
| range map | planar patches | face hierarchy | | | 313 |
| range map | edge-junction graph | | geons | object description | 363 |
| range map | superquadric ellipsoids | spline deformations | | object description | 389 |
| b/w vox | spherical harmonics | | | | 79 |
| grey voxels | edges | gaussian and mean | curvature gradients | | 399 |
| grey voxels | medial surface | wireframe skeleton | | | 443 |
| grey voxels | oct-tree | | | | -"- |
| grey voxels | distance transformation | alpha hull | | object description | 547 |
| grey voxels | quadratic surface patches | rotation invariants | pose description | object decomposition | 623 |
| x-y-z coords | rotational symmetry | | | | 303 |
| CAD model | adjacency topology | holes, bosses, slots | | | 187 |
| geometric model | encoded features | | | object description | 421 |
| arbitrary features | | | | | 565 |
| low-level description | | transformations | | high-level description | 565 |
| verbal flow | self-reference | | | | 409 |

Table) discussed methods based on two-dimensional inputs obtained from either conceptually "flat" entities or projections of three-dimensional objects.

Most of the 2-D methods presented started with a pixel-based image representation. Applications to gray-level images slightly outnumbered applications to black/white images, and there was only a single example exploiting colored pixels. Some of the 2-D methods were designed for essentially 2-D objects, such as alphabetic characters or silhouettes of leaves. Most, however, addressed pictures of 3-D objects, and attempted to recover 3-D properties.

In 3-D, only one paper discussed black/white voxel primitives, but several were based on gray voxels. An intermediate $2^1/2$-D representation, range maps, formed the starting point of several methods aimed at high-level descriptions.

Bottom-level primitives not based on array representations were point sets of x-y and x-y-z coordinates on the one hand, and ordered lists comprising polygons, polylines, and contours on the other.

Examples of local shape features extracted from primitives were edges, lines, splines, collinear triplets, and surface patches. At the next level of the hierarchy, medial transforms formed the single most popular grouping, with other global features represented by the convex hull, the visual hull, quad and oct trees, and various mathematical transformations. As expected, entities considered as primitives by some researchers, such as polygons or splines, were the results of several processing steps in other work.

At the top level, some of the systems produced an object or scene description, or a reconstructed object. In other instances, motion, pose, view-class, surface orientation, or surface discontinuities were extracted. At these higher levels, shape extraction blends smoothly into pattern recognition and computer vision.

Many of the studies confirm that the notion of equivalence classes is natural for features invariant under digitization noise, illumination, translation, rotation, affine and perspective transformations, and rigid motion.

Table 2 - Shape hierarchy for 2-D processing

| b/w pixels | edges | curve equations | skeletons | face groups |
|---|---|---|---|---|
| gray pixels | polylines | circular arcs | quad-trees | articulation invariants |
| color pixels | contours | splines | wireframes | shape index |
| x-y coordinates | curve equations | planar surfaces | affine invariants | warp invariants |
| | morphological operators | quadratic patches | pose | pose description |
| | Hough transforms | generalized cylinders | | |
| | | geons | | |

Table 3 - Shape hierarchy for 3-D processing

| range map | collinear triplets | holes, bosses, slots | skeletons | rotation invariants |
|---|---|---|---|---|
| b/w voxels | planar patches | gaussian and mean curvature | | face hierarchy |
| gray voxels | edge-junction graph | superquadric ellipsoids | | motion parameters |
| x-y-z coordinates | | geons | | spline-deformation invariants |

Tables 2 and 3 show most of the shape categories that we have found, arranged from left to right roughly according to how *local* or *global* are the corresponding invariant features are with respect to an entire visual scene. Not shown on the right are the ultimate results of the processes. As mentioned, these are descriptions or reconstructions of objects or scenes. Most of the reported research projects do not carry the processing to the final level: in fact, many are focused on a single operation.

Table 4 - Types of data used in the various projects

| Data | Number of articles |
|---|---|
| no data | 5 |
| simulated or artificial data | 30 |
| real data - simple sensed objects | 7 |
| real data - realistic objects | 17 |

We have also divided the projects according to the type of object that was processed. In Table 4, *no data* refers to a purely theoretical investigation without actual examples. *Simulated data* refers to manually or computer constructed objects that did not involve a sensor, such as freeform blobs. *Simple sensed object* refers to a laboratory construct (acquired with a sensor) with known properties that is used to perform experiments under controlled conditions. An example would be isothetic blocks. *Realistic object* refers to a scene that might actually represent an eventual application, such as a corridor view. There is no implication that the degree of realism bears in any way on the merits of the paper.

## 4. Conclusions

One possible use of this study is to determine where there are gaps in the hierarchy, and which shape extraction operations require additional attention. It is clear, for example, that much of the research is concentrated on extracting second-level representations from pixel arrays, and relatively few proceed up the hierarchy to object description, reconstruction, or classification. Yet it would seem desirable to study the effects of feedback on low-level shape extraction. Surely no shape primitive is so primitive that its detection would not be facilitated by determining whether its presence "makes sense" at a higher level.

The book contains several valuable reports on motion determination, but optical flow is often only tangentially related to shape except at the lowest levels. One wonders whether more complex shape features could ease the computational burden. Other areas of increasing emphasis include scale-space, mathematical morphology, swept volumes, pose determination, symmetries, quadratic shape descriptors, geons, and parallel algorithms (so far, primarily in 2-D).

Although skeletons remain a popular field of study, with novel extensions in many directions, there is a dearth of research on using them as input for symmetry detection, segmentation, viewpoint (pose) normalization, or motion determination. Furthermore, they are seldom applied to sensed 3-D objects. Established applications include thinning and vectorization.

There appears to be relatively little agreement so far on precise formulation of important unsolved problems. Furthermore, it seems very difficult to characterize and delimit the domain of input data where a given technique can be successfully applied. If theoretical characterization is, in fact, impossible, then experimental delineation of the boundaries of successful application takes on additional importance. We hope, in the future, to see equal emphasis on examples where a method *fails*.

We can expect that eventually the balance will shift from experiments on simulated data to sensed realistic data, which was used in fewer than a third of the projects reported here. There is, after all, an abundance of shapely objects in the physical world, and the conversion of visual data to digital form is now within everyone's reach. This will perhaps draw us closer to the paradigms of the longer-established sciences, where theoreticians formulate theories and experimentalists verify or disprove them.

A compendium of shape such as this can potentially help in choosing appropriate processing methods for various steps in a specific application, if only by providing a panoramic view of available techniques. Yet it appears that there are few satisfactory points for the synchronization of different approaches. The lack of reuse of programs, and even of algorithms, is striking. Most of the reports give little emphasis to implementation, but as far as one can tell existing image processing libraries seem seldom used even for primitive functions. Almost every group implements everything *ab ovo*. The shape-extraction community appears to communicate primarily through conferences and publications, and seldom through the exchange of working code or intermediate computed results such as feature-level characterization. In fact, even original synthetic or sensed data is seldom shared. Perhaps periodic opportunities for thorough discussion on some beautiful island will result in more pro-active collaboration, accelerated progress, and larger-scale endeavours.

The author still hopes that adopting the point of view that shape does not exist in the abstract, but is a function of the types of equivalances that one happens to be interested in, may increase the cross-pollination between shape researchers and the applied computer vision community. He hopes that researchers at the Second International Workshop on Visual Form will not hesitate to express their agreement or disagreement with the proposed paradigm. Regardless of the outcome, he found the materials examined intellectually immensely stimulating and looks forward to another four days of spirited discussion on the eclectic and elusive nature of shape and visual form.

## Acknowledgment

The author is grateful for thoughtful comments and suggestions provided by Dr. Carlo Arcelli and Professor Badri Roysam, and to the organizers of the Workshop for having put up with him for so many years.

## Appendix: capsule summaries

1. Improved gray-scale thinning: skeletons (gray pixels); *digitized terrain elevations.*
11. Decomposition into quadratic facets (stripe skeletons); *digitized cylinders and hands.*
21. Almost reversible skeletons (binary pixels); *simulated blobs.*
29. Wireframe from multiple stereo (vertical edges); *digitized complex parallelepipeds.*
39. Reconstruct planar surfaces and egomotion parameters from (optical flow); *simulated 2-D optical flow motion with white noise.*
47. Combinatorial parameter optimization for recognizing and reconstructing rectangles (binary pixels); *simulated isothetic silhouettes with white noise.*
57. Parallel raster convex hull and difference (binary pixels); *simulated blobs.*
67. Reconstruction from multiple views (2-D silhouettes); *digitized manufactured objects.*
79. Spherical harmonics for 3-D objects (binary voxels); *3-D geometric constructs.*
89. Invariant differentials of planar curves (analytical curve equations); *2-D geometric constructs.*
99. Delaunay tetrahedralization from triangulation (edges); *digitized blocks.*
109. Indexing by k-th order correlation (contour curves); *simulated leaf silhouettes.*
119. Circle Hough transform in gray-scale pics (edges); *digitized manufactured objects and satellite pics.*
127. Vector representation by zigzag (binary pixels); *digitized engineering drawings.*
137. Parallel contour (edge) following (gray pixels); *digitized aerial photos??*
155. OCR from circular arcs (skeletons); *digitized printed and handprinted characters.*
165. Straight line Hough transform (edges); *simulated binary blobs.*
175. Egomotion from range maps (collinear triplets); *digitized, partially-occluded cylindrical prisms with white noise.*
187. Local topology for CAD/CAM (faces and edges); *3-D isothetic planar-faced geometric constructs.*
197. Analytical model for perspective in 3-D planar-faced objects (edges); *digitized planar-faced block.*

# INTEGRATING STRUCTURAL DESCRIPTION AND GEOMETRICAL/STATISTICAL TRANSFORM

HIROBUMI NISHIDA

*School of Computer Science and Engineering*
*University of Aizu*
*Aizu Wakamatsu, Fukushima 965-80, Japan*

## ABSTRACT

The prime difficulty in research and development of handwritten character recognition systems is in the variety of shape deformations. The key to recognizing such complex objects as handwritten characters is in shape description which is robust against shape deformation and quantitative estimation of the amount of deformation. In this paper, on the basis of the structural description by Nishida (1992), we propose a shape matching algorithm and a method of analysis and description of shape transformation for handwritten characters. The object is described in terms of qualitative and global structure which is robust against deformation, and it is matched against the built-in models. On the basis of the correspondence of components between the object and the model, geometrical and statistical transformations are estimated, and the decision of recognition or rejection is made based on the estimations. Structural description and geometrical/statistical transform are integrated in a systematic way. Experimental results are shown for handwritten digit recognition and on-line handwriting recognition.

## 1. Introduction

Handwritten character recognition has found many applications in various fields. Therefore, character recognition has been a main subject in pattern recognition and has stimulated basic research and development of practical systems [2]. Compared with machine-printed character recognition, the prime difficulty in research and development of handwritten character recognition systems is in the variety of shape deformations. Human beings can recognize deformed characters easily, but the mechanism of pattern recognition of human beings is unknown. Furthermore, shapes of characters are defined artificially and have little logic. The key to recognizing such complex objects as handwritten characters is in shape description which is robust against shape deformation and quantitative estimation of the amount of deformation.

In quantitative analysis of deformation, it is natural to assume that a point $x'$ on the *object* is mapped to a point $x$ on the *model* by a transformation $T$: $x = Tx'$. In general, the analysis of pattern deformation is difficult, because deformation of such patterns as handwritten characters is non-rigid and elastic, and $T$ is non-linear. Furthermore, the point correspondence between the model and the object must be known in advance to obtain $T$, but it is also difficult for the similar reason. Therefore, instead of analyzing, describing, and estimating deformation, *normalization* procedures with respect to moments or line densities are applied to character images as a *preprocessing* to cope with deformation [2]. However, since information available in the preprocessing stage is limited, it is known that such normalization procedures have various side effects.

An idea for finding the point correspondence and coping with non-linearity of $T$ is as follows: (1) Describe the shape in terms of qualitative and global structure which is robust against deformation, and match the object against the built-in models. Then, the correspondence of components (units in the structural description) is found between the model and the object. The point correspondence can be found by choosing some reference points on the components. (2) Regard the transformation $T$ as a composition of a simple geometrical transformation (coordinate transformation) $T_g$ and a statistical transformation $T_s$ representing complex transformation which cannot be described by the geometrical transformation.

For exploring shape description in terms of qualitative and global structure which is robust against deformation, it is essential to study primary features of handwritten characters. In particular, throughout more than a quarter of a century of research, it is found that such *quantitative* shape description with straight lines, arcs, and corners is not appropriate for handwritten characters, but some *qualitative* features are powerful and flexible, such as (1) *quasi-topological* features (convexity, concavity, and loop), (2) directional features, (3) *Singularities* (branch points and crossings). On the basis of this observation, Nishida [4], [5] proposed a method for structural description of character shapes by few components with rich features. This method is clear and rigorous, can cope with various deformations, and has been shown to be powerful in practice, particularly when it is applied to strokes (thin-line) of characters. Furthermore, a remarkable point is that shape prototypes (structural models) can be constructed automatically from the training data [6].

In this paper, on the basis of the structural description by Nishida [4], [5], we propose a shape matching algorithm and a method for analysis and description of shape transformation for handwritten characters. We present a systematic approach to the problem of coping with pattern deformation of handwritten characters by integrating structural description and geometrical/statistical transform. The object is described in terms of qualitative and global structure which is robust against deformation, and it is matched against the built-in models. Then, the correspondence of components (units in the structural description) is found between the model and the object. The point correspondence can be found by choosing some reference points on the components. $T_g$ is obtained on the basis of the correspondence of components between the object and the model. By transforming each point on the object by $T_g$, the object is normalized with respect to the model. Then, $T_s$ is estimated on the normalized shape and the decision of recognition or rejection is made on the basis of $T_g$ and $T_s$.

This paper is organized as follows: In Section 2, quantitative analysis of pattern deformation is introduced on the basis of the point correspondence between the models and the object which has been determined by the structural matching. The handwritten character recognition system and performance statistics are described in Section 3. Section 4 is the conclusion. The reader is referred to Nishida and Mori [4], [5] for the structural analysis and description of curves, Nishida and Mori [6] for model construction, and Nishida and Mori [5], Nishida [3] for structural matching.

## 2. Analysis of Pattern Deformation

The shape description scheme [4], [5] gives a flexible and compact description by a few components with rich features and can cope with various deformation of shape. The structural matching [5], [3] can find the correspondence of components between a class and an object even for a heavily deformed object. However, the structural description is so flexible that sometimes an object is matched against two or more classes or too distorted an object can be matched against some classes. Therefore, it is also important to estimate the amount of deformation of the object from the model quantitatively in order to decide which class should be selected from the matched classes or whether the object should be recognized or rejected. For this purpose, we utilize parameters computed for each component of structural description [4], [3]. Since several parameters are computed for each component (primitive sequences and singular points[1]), some reference points can be chosen on the shape. The coordinates of the point on the model (class) is computed from the statistics (mean value) of the parameters. The point correspondence between the model (class) and the object can be found on the basis of the correspondences of the components. The mapping between a reference point on the model $x = (x, y)^t$ ($t$ is transpose of a matrix) and the corresponding point on the object $x' = (x', y')^t$ can be modeled with a geometrical transformation $T_g$ and a statistical transformation $T_s$:

$$x = T_s \ (T_g x'). \tag{1}$$

Now, we give explicitly $T_g$ as Affine transformation:

$$T_g : x \to Ax + b, \tag{2}$$

where $A = (a_{ij})$ as a $2 \times 2$ regular matrix whose determinant $\det A$ is positive, and $b = (b_x, b_y)^t$ as a translation vector. $T_s$ is defined as:

$$T_s : x \to x + e(x), \tag{3}$$

where $e_x(x)$ and $e_y(x)$ are random variables with the mean 0 and the standard deviation $\sigma_x(x)$ and $\sigma_y(x)$, and $e(x) = (e_x(x), e_y(x))^t$. Therefore, the relation between $x$ and $x'$ is expressed explicitly as $x = Ax' + b + e(Ax' + b)$.

### 2.1. Affine Transformation

Some points on primitive sequences and singular points are taken as reference points in the following way: (1) PS-label $\langle ps(\geq 2), * \rangle$– h-point, t-point, middle point of each side of the bounding box (6 points, in total). (2) PS-label $\langle 1, * \rangle$– h-point, t-point, the farthest point from the chord (3 points). (3) PS-label $\langle 0, 0 \rangle$– middle point of each side of the bounding box (4 points). The correspondence of reference

---

[1]Throughout this paper, terms introduced in [4] are used without definition.

points between the model and the object can be found from the correspondence of the primitive sequences and the singular points. Let $\left\{ \boldsymbol{x}_i = (x_i, y_i)^t \mid i = 1, 2, \ldots, N \right\}$ be the set of reference points of the model, and $\left\{ \boldsymbol{x}'_i = (x'_i, y'_i)^t \mid i = 1, 2, \ldots, N \right\}$ be of the object. Now, for simplicity, we assume that $\boldsymbol{x}_i$ $(i = 1, 2, \ldots, N)$ corresponds to $\boldsymbol{x}'_i$. We can easily obtain $A$ and $\boldsymbol{b}$ that minimize

$$D_N = \sum_{i=1}^{N} \left\{ \left( \frac{x_i - a_{11}x'_i - a_{12}y'_i - b_x}{\sigma_x(i)} \right)^2 + \left( \frac{y_i - a_{21}x'_i - a_{22}y'_i - b_y}{\sigma_y(i)} \right)^2 \right\}, \quad (4)$$

where $\sigma_x(i)$ and $\sigma_y(i)$ are the standard deviations of distribution of $(x_i, y_i)$, which are computed from the statistics for parameters in the model.

## 2.2. Analysis of Affine Transformation

We give an analysis of the matrix $A$ and the vector $\boldsymbol{b}$ to give a quantitative description and estimation of geometrical factors of pattern deformation. We will use the analysis in putting constraints on shape deformation in the decision making stage of the character recognition system. An Affine transformation can be decomposed into the eight elementary transformations:

$$T_1(\alpha) : \boldsymbol{x} \rightarrow \boldsymbol{x} + \begin{pmatrix} \alpha \\ 0 \end{pmatrix} \text{ (x-Translation)}, \quad T_2(\beta) : \boldsymbol{x} \rightarrow \boldsymbol{x} + \begin{pmatrix} 0 \\ \beta \end{pmatrix} \text{ (y-Translation)}$$

$$T_3(\lambda_x) : \boldsymbol{x} \rightarrow \begin{pmatrix} \lambda_x & 0 \\ 0 & 1 \end{pmatrix} \boldsymbol{x} \text{ (x-Dilatation)}, \quad T_4(\lambda_y) : \boldsymbol{x} \rightarrow \begin{pmatrix} 1 & 0 \\ 0 & \lambda_y \end{pmatrix} \boldsymbol{x} \text{ (y-Dilatation)}$$

$$T_5(\gamma_x) : \boldsymbol{x} \rightarrow \begin{pmatrix} 1 & \gamma_x \\ 0 & 1 \end{pmatrix} \boldsymbol{x} \text{ (x-Shearing)}, \quad T_6(\gamma_y) : \boldsymbol{x} \rightarrow \begin{pmatrix} 1 & 0 \\ \gamma_y & 1 \end{pmatrix} \boldsymbol{x} \text{ (y-Shearing)}$$

$$T_7(\mu) : \boldsymbol{x} \rightarrow \mu\boldsymbol{x} \text{ (Similarity)}, \quad T_8(\theta) : \boldsymbol{x} \rightarrow \begin{pmatrix} \cos\theta & -\sin\theta \\ \sin\theta & \cos\theta \end{pmatrix} \boldsymbol{x} \text{ (Rotation)}$$

Obviously, $\boldsymbol{b} = T_1(b_x) + T_2(b_y)$. In our case, since the position and size of the shape are not of interest, $T_1(b_x)$, $T_2(b_y)$, and $T_7(\mu)$ have no particular meaning. Therefore, assuming that $\mu = \sqrt{\det A}$ and $\lambda_x \cdot \lambda_y = 1$, we analyze the degree of deformation in terms of $T_3(\lambda_x)$, $T_5(\gamma_x)$, $T_6(\gamma_y)$, and $T_8(\theta)$. Since the parameter $\mu$ has no meaning, there are only three independent variables in the $2 \times 2$ matrix $A$, whereas we are interested in four parameters $\lambda_x$, $\gamma_x$, $\gamma_y$, and $\theta$. Therefore, we give some interpretations of the Affine transformation by posing some constraints on the variables.

When we assume $\gamma_x = \gamma_y$, a square matrix $A$ can be decomposed into a product of an orthonormal matrix $Q$, and a positive semi-definite and symmetric matrix $S$ [1]: $A = QS$. By this theorem along with LDU-decomposition applied to $S$, the transformation matrix $A$ is decomposed into the form:

$$\textbf{D1:} \quad A = \mu \begin{pmatrix} \cos\theta & -\sin\theta \\ \sin\theta & \cos\theta \end{pmatrix} \begin{pmatrix} 1 & 0 \\ \gamma & 1 \end{pmatrix} \begin{pmatrix} 1 & 0 \\ 0 & 1/\lambda_x \end{pmatrix} \begin{pmatrix} \lambda_x & 0 \\ 0 & 1 \end{pmatrix} \begin{pmatrix} 1 & \gamma \\ 0 & 1 \end{pmatrix}$$

$$= T_7(\mu) \cdot T_8(\theta) \cdot T_6(\gamma) \cdot T_4(1/\lambda_x) \cdot T_3(\lambda_x) \cdot T_5(\gamma) \quad (5)$$

The geometrical transformation can be described by a three tuple $(\theta, \gamma, \lambda_x)$.

When we assume $\gamma_y = 0$, a square matrix $A$ can be decomposed into a product of an orthonormal matrix $Q$ and an upper triangular matrix $R$ (QR-decomposition): $A = QR$.

$$\textbf{D2:} \quad \begin{aligned} A &= \mu \begin{pmatrix} \cos\theta & -\sin\theta \\ \sin\theta & \cos\theta \end{pmatrix} \begin{pmatrix} 1 & 0 \\ 0 & 1/\lambda_x \end{pmatrix} \begin{pmatrix} \lambda_x & 0 \\ 0 & 1 \end{pmatrix} \begin{pmatrix} 1 & \gamma_x \\ 0 & 1 \end{pmatrix} \\ &= T_7(\mu) \cdot T_8(\theta) \cdot T_4(1/\lambda_x) \cdot T_3(\lambda_x) \cdot T_5(\gamma_x) \end{aligned} \tag{6}$$

The geometrical transformation can be described by a three tuple $(\theta, \gamma_x, \lambda_x)$.

When we assume $\gamma_x = \gamma_y = 0$, a square matrix $A$ can be decomposed into a product of two orthonormal matrices $Q_1$ and $Q_2$, and a diagonal matrix $D$ (Singular Value Decomposition): $A = Q_1 D Q_2$ ($\det Q_1 > 0$, $\det Q_2 > 0$).

$$\textbf{D3:} \quad \begin{aligned} A &= \mu \begin{pmatrix} \cos\theta_1 & -\sin\theta_1 \\ \sin\theta_1 & \cos\theta_1 \end{pmatrix} \begin{pmatrix} 1 & 0 \\ 0 & 1/\lambda_x \end{pmatrix} \begin{pmatrix} \lambda_x & 0 \\ 0 & 1 \end{pmatrix} \begin{pmatrix} \cos\theta_2 & -\sin\theta_2 \\ \sin\theta_2 & \cos\theta_2 \end{pmatrix} \\ &= T_7(\mu) \cdot T_8(\theta_1) \cdot T_4(1/\lambda_x) \cdot T_3(\lambda_x) \cdot T_8(\theta_2) \end{aligned} \tag{7}$$

The geometrical transformation can be described by a three tuple $(\theta_1, \theta_2, \lambda_x)$.

When we assume $\theta = 0$, a square matrix $A$ can be decomposed into a product of a lower triangular matrix $L$, a diagonal matrix $D$, and a upper triangular matrix $U$ (LDU-decomposition): $A = LDU$.

$$\textbf{D4:} \quad \begin{aligned} A &= \mu \begin{pmatrix} 1 & 0 \\ \gamma_y & 1 \end{pmatrix} \begin{pmatrix} 1 & 0 \\ 0 & 1/\lambda_x \end{pmatrix} \begin{pmatrix} \lambda_x & 0 \\ 0 & 1 \end{pmatrix} \begin{pmatrix} 1 & \gamma_x \\ 0 & 1 \end{pmatrix} \\ &= T_7(\mu) \cdot T_6(\gamma_y) \cdot T_4(1/\lambda_x) \cdot T_3(\lambda_x) \cdot T_5(\gamma_x) \end{aligned} \tag{8}$$

The geometrical transformation can be described by a three tuple $(\gamma_x, \gamma_y, \lambda_x)$.

### 2.3. Normalization and Distance Calculation

In traditional pattern recognition techniques, particularly handwritten character recognition, normalization of patterns is performed as a *preprocessing* in the system. However, since information available in the preprocessing stage is limited, it is known that such normalization procedures have various side effects. In our approach, the object is normalized on the basis of results of structural matching in terms of global and qualitative features of the shape as follows: The object is described by the quasi-topological structure of each stroke and singular point structures, then the description is matched against the built-in models. On the basis of the correspondence of components between the object and the class in the model, the matrix $A$ and the vector $b$ in are obtained. By transforming each point $x'$ on the object to $Ax' + b$, the object is normalized with respect to the class in the model.

Since the minimum value of $D_N$ in Eq. 4 can be considered to be Mahalanobis distance between the object and the class, this distance can be used to estimate the probability that the object belongs to the class. If we assume that each variable obeys the normal distribution, then $D_N$ obeys the $\chi^2$ distribution of freedom $p = 2N$. Estimation of $D_N$ depends on the number of parameters $p$. $D_N$ can be transformed to $D$ independent of $N$ by the Fisher's approximation

$$D = \sqrt{2D_N} - \sqrt{2p-1} \tag{9}$$

or Wilson-Hilferty's approximation

$$D = \frac{\left(\frac{D^2}{p}\right)^{1/3} + \frac{2}{9p} - 1}{\sqrt{\frac{2}{9p}}}. \tag{10}$$

$D = d$ gives the probability of $D > d$ by

$$\frac{1}{\sqrt{2\pi}} \int_d^\infty \exp\left(-\frac{x^2}{2}\right) dx. \tag{11}$$

In some cases, there are two or more correspondences of primitive sequences and singular points between an object and a particular class, and the correspondence is not necessarily determined uniquely. In such a case, the matching that minimizes $D$ is chosen as the optimal matching between the object and the class.

### 2.4. Decision Making in Character Recognition Systems

When a structural matching is found between an object and a class in the model, the amount and factor of deformation can be estimated quantitatively by the three parameters representing the geometrical transformation and the statistical distance $D$. For the less deformed object, $\theta$ and $\gamma$ are near 0, $\lambda$ is near 1, and $D$ is a negative number with a large absolute value. On the other hand, for the more deformed object, $\theta$ and $\gamma$ are far from 0 (large absolute value), $\lambda$ is far from 1, and $D$ is a positive number with a large absolute value.

In the structural matching described in Nishida and Mori [5], Nishida [3], an object is often matched against two or more classes in the model. Therefore, it is necessary to assign the priority to the candidate classes on the basis of the four deformation parameters (three for geometrical transformation and one for statistical transformation). A criterion is: (1) Put constraints on the ranges of the three parameters for geometrical transformation (for instance, $\theta$, $\gamma$, and $\lambda_x$ for the decomposition Eq. 5). If some parameter is out of the range, then the class is removed from the candidate list. (2) Sort the candidates in the increasing order of $D$. (3) If $D$ of the first candidate is small and the difference of $D$ between the two top choices is large enough, output the first candidate as a recognition result. Otherwise, output "reject."

We describe the constraints explicitly in Section 3.

| "B" | "H" | "I" | "J" | "Ja" | "L" | "N" | "T" | "U" |

Figure 1: Examples of model shapes.

Table 1: Decomposition of the matrix $A$ for Fig. 2(a).

| | Class $B$ $(D = -1.57)$ | | | |
|---|---|---|---|---|
| | $\theta$ | $\gamma_x$ | $\gamma_y$ | $\lambda_x$ |
| D1 | 7° | −0.12 | −0.12 | 0.95 |
| D2 | 1° | −0.23 | 0 | 0.93 |
| D3 | −58°, 65° | 0 | 0 | 1.14 |
| D4 | 0° | −0.25 | 0.01 | 0.93 |

*2.5. Examples*

We give some examples of model shapes in Fig. 1 and some images along with normalized shapes in Fig. 2. For each object, decompositions of the matrix $A$ are shown in Tables 1–5.

## 3. Handwritten Character Recognition

In this section, we describe performance of the handwritten character recognition system. We assume that each character has been extracted from the document image, and thinning is used as a feature extraction technique from the character image.

All the algorithms were implemented using C Programming Language on Sun Sparc Station IPC. We use the thinning algorithm [7], the structural analysis and parameter computation [4], [5], and structural matching [5], normalization and distance calculation of Section 2. Prototypes (structural models) are created with the model construction program [6]. We use the decomposition D1 for describing geometrical transformation and the deformation is described by $(\theta, \gamma, \lambda_x, D)$. The constraints for deformation parameters are set as follows: $|\theta| < 30°$, $|\gamma| < 0.25$, $2/3 < \lambda_x < 1.5$, $D < 6.0$. If two or more classes are matched and the difference of $D$ between the top two choices is less than 3.0, then the image is rejected.

We show performance of handwritten digit recognition. The detailed descriptions of the data sets are given in [4] and [5]. The loosely constrained data set (see Section

Table 2: Decomposition of the matrix $A$ for Fig. 2(b).

|  | Class $I$ $(D = 2.57)$ | | | | Class $H$ $(D = 2.79)$ | | | |
|---|---|---|---|---|---|---|---|---|
|  | $\theta$ | $\gamma_x$ | $\gamma_y$ | $\lambda_x$ | $\theta$ | $\gamma_x$ | $\gamma_y$ | $\lambda_x$ |
| D1 | $3°$ | $-0.19$ | $-0.19$ | $0.90$ | $-65°$ | $0.11$ | $0.11$ | $1.73$ |
| D2 | $-7°$ | $-0.39$ | $0$ | $0.90$ | $-39°$ | $1.38$ | $0$ | $0.73$ |
| D3 | $-63°, 66°$ | $0$ | $0$ | $1.23$ | $80°, 15°$ | $0$ | $0$ | $0.57$ |
| D4 | $0°$ | $-0.24$ | $-0.12$ | $0.89$ | $0°$ | $2.93$ | $-0.82$ | $0.56$ |

Table 3: Decomposition of the matrix $A$ for Fig. 2(c).

|  | Class $N$ $(D = 4.72)$ | | | |
|---|---|---|---|---|
|  | $\theta$ | $\gamma_x$ | $\gamma_y$ | $\lambda_x$ |
| D1 | $6°$ | $-0.09$ | $-0.09$ | $0.68$ |
| D2 | $8°$ | $0.11$ | $0$ | $0.68$ |
| D3 | $-4°, 2°$ | $0$ | $0$ | $0.68$ |
| D4 | $0°$ | $-0.19$ | $0.14$ | $0.67$ |

V-D of [4]) was used as the training set, and the test was made on the unconstrained data set (see Section V-E of [4]). The nature of the test set is quite different from the training set and the size of the test set is about 10 times as large as the training set. The total number of classes (prototypes) is fifty. In this experiment, we also prepared some additional procedures for discriminating confusing pairs. These procedures were also tuned up only on the training set. Note that we neither added nor modified functionalities in the program or models/parameters to accommodate unconstrained data. The result is as follows: correct recognition 95.9%, rejection 2.8%. substitution error 1.3%, reliability 98.6%. When we do not employ the model-based normalization, i.e., assuming that $A$ is the unit matrix and $b$ is the zero vector, the result is as follows: correct recognition 95.4%, rejection 2.9%, substitution error 1.7%, reliability 98.2%. Therefore, both the recognition rate and reliability have been improved by the model-based normalization.

Furthermore, some experimental results of on-line handwriting recognition are described in Nishida [3] along with comparison with a pattern matching method. We mention here the results of alphanumerics recognition. For the proposed method, correct recognition rate is 99.11% and substitution error rate is 0.77%. On the other hand, for the stroke-based DP method, correct recognition rate is 97.89% and substitution error rate is 2.11%. Flexibility and reliability are incompatible with one another, but the result shows that the the proposed method has the both properties, and that it can cope with various deformations effectively.

Table 4: Decomposition of the matrix $A$ for Fig. 2(d).

|  | Class $Ja$ $(D = 3.49)$ | | | | Class $T$ $(D = -3.30)$ | | | |
|---|---|---|---|---|---|---|---|---|
|  | $\theta$ | $\gamma_x$ | $\gamma_y$ | $\lambda_x$ | $\theta$ | $\gamma_x$ | $\gamma_y$ | $\lambda_x$ |
| D1 | $-4°$ | $-0.06$ | $-0.06$ | $0.86$ | $5°$ | $-0.17$ | $-0.17$ | $0.88$ |
| D2 | $-9°$ | $-0.19$ | $0$ | $0.87$ | $-3°$ | $-0.35$ | $0$ | $0.87$ |
| D3 | $-81°, 77°$ | $0$ | $0$ | $1.18$ | $-66°, 71°$ | $0$ | $0$ | $1.23$ |
| D4 | $0°$ | $0.01$ | $-0.15$ | $0.86$ | $0°$ | $-0.26$ | $-0.06$ | $0.87$ |

Table 5: Decomposition of the matrix $A$ for Fig. 2(e).

|  | Class $J$ $(D = 17.52)$ | | | | Class $L$ $(D = 4.82)$ | | | | Class $U$ $(D = 7.18)$ | | | |
|---|---|---|---|---|---|---|---|---|---|---|---|---|
|  | $\theta$ | $\gamma_x$ | $\gamma_y$ | $\lambda_x$ | $\theta$ | $\gamma_x$ | $\gamma_y$ | $\lambda_x$ | $\theta$ | $\gamma_x$ | $\gamma_y$ | $\lambda_x$ |
| D1 | $10°$ | $0.03$ | $0.03$ | $0.46$ | $-3°$ | $-0.01$ | $-0.01$ | $0.63$ | $4°$ | $0.03$ | $0.03$ | $0.66$ |
| D2 | $40°$ | $2.19$ | $0$ | $0.60$ | $-8°$ | $-0.32$ | $0$ | $0.64$ | $11°$ | $0.37$ | $0$ | $0.68$ |
| D3 | $0°, 10°$ | $0$ | $0$ | $0.46$ | $-89°, 86°$ | $0$ | $0$ | $1.58$ | $1°, 5°$ | $0$ | $0$ | $0.66$ |
| D4 | $0°$ | $-0.15$ | $0.85$ | $0.46$ | $0°$ | $0.04$ | $-0.15$ | $0.63$ | $0°$ | $-0.04$ | $0.19$ | $0.66$ |

## 4. Conclusion

Handwritten character recognition has been a main research subject in pattern recognition. The prime difficulty in research and development of the technology lies in the variety of shape deformation. Various methods such as contour analysis and background analysis [2] have been proposed. Since most of the practical methods utilize some kinds of distance measures or matching methods on the feature space in which the features are position-dependent, the normalization on the image is indispensable for coordinate transformation. In other words, image normalization has been a main method to cope with shape deformation. However, it is difficult to know the extent of displacement of the image with respect to the standard coordinate system before recognizing it. It implies that malfunction of normalization distorts the shape and results in rejection or substitution error.

We have presented a systematic approach to this problem by integrating structural description and geometrical/statistical transform. We describe the shape of characters by two types of features, i.e., symbolic, qualitative, and discrete features (quasi-topological features and singular points), and numerical, quantitative and continuous features (geometrical parameters). The former is regarded as dominant information, while the latter is secondary information attached to structural components. Since the structural description is size and translation invariant, but depends only on the direction of coordinate axes, a heavily deformed object can be matched against some models. Then, model-based normalization is applied to the object, and the decision is made on the basis of deformation parameters $(\theta, \gamma, \lambda_x, D)$.

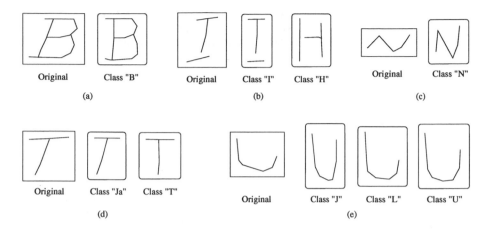

Figure 2: Examples of normalization.

## 5. References

[1] B. K. P. Horn, H. M. Hildin, and S. Negahdariour, "Closed-form solution of absolute orientation using orthonormal matrices," *J. Opt. Soc. America,* vol. A–5, no. 7, pp. 1127–1135, 1988.

[2] S. Mori, C. Y. Suen, and K. Yamamoto, "Historical review of OCR research and development," *Proc. IEEE,* vol. 80, no. 7, pp. 1029–1058, 1992.

[3] H. Nishida, "Model-based shape matching with structural feature grouping," Tech. Rep. 94–1–001, Dept. Comput. Software, Univ. Aizu, 1994.

[4] H. Nishida and S. Mori, "Algebraic description of curve structure," *IEEE Trans. Pattern Anal. Machine Intell.,* vol. 14, no. 5, pp. 516–533, 1992.

[5] H. Nishida and S. Mori, "Structural analysis and description of curves by quasi-topological features and singular points", in *Structured Document Image Analysis* (H. S. Baird, H. Bunke, and K. Yamamoto, Eds.), New York: Springer-Verlag, 1992, pp. 139–187.

[6] H. Nishida and S. Mori, "An algebraic approach to automatic construction of structural models," *IEEE Trans. Pattern Anal. Machine Intell.,* vol. 15, no. 12, pp. 1298–1311, 1993.

[7] T. Suzuki and S. Mori, "Structural description of line images by the cross section sequence graph," *Int. J. Pattern Recognition Artificial Intell.,* vol. 7, no. 5, 1993.

# A MULTISCALE MAT FROM VORONOI DIAGRAMS: THE SKELETON-SPACE AND ITS APPLICATION TO SHAPE DESCRIPTION AND DECOMPOSITION

## R. L. OGNIEWICZ

*Communication Technology Laboratory*
*Swiss Federal Institute of Technology ETH*
*CH-8092 Zurich, Switzerland, e-mail: rlo@vision.ee.ethz.ch*

## ABSTRACT

A multiscale extension to the *medial axis transform(MAT)* or *skeleton* can be obtained by combining information derived from a scale-space hierarchy of boundary representations with region information provided by the MAT. The *skeleton-space* is constructed by attributing each skeleton component with a hierarchically ordered sequence of residual values, each expressing the saliency of the component at a distinct resolution level. Our multiscale MAT is capable of describing complex shapes characterized by significantly jagged boundaries. Tracking the evolution of prominent loci of the MAT such as nodes across scales permits to assess the most significant skeleton constituents and to *automatically* determine pruning parameters. We demonstrate the capability of the skeleton-space to describe/decompose complex shapes characterized by significantly jagged boundaries.

## 1. Introduction

A frequently proposed technique to describe planar shapes is the *medial axis transform(MAT)* [1–5], also termed *skeletonization* or *thinning* [6], which reduces the shape to a one-dimensional graph-like structure, the *medial axis*. A multiresolution representation of the medial axis can be obtained by first smoothing the shape and then by computing the MAT for each shape instance [7]. Unfortunately, the MAT according to its original definition tends to overemphasize boundary details. In the sequel, the task to determine the correct correspondences between medial axis components at distinct levels of detail becomes a very difficult problem. The transition from one scale to the other may be accompanied by substantial changes of the medial axis structure. The problems are compounded in the case of 2-D operations such as blurring. Interference effects occurring during unsupervised blurring will typically lead to even more dramatic structural changes of the medial axis than does boundary smoothing. Similar problems are observed for gray-level MAT techniques [8–10].

In order to compute a multiscale MAT, this paper suggests a different technique which is characterized by the following properties:

- Our method always starts out from the MAT of the original, nonsmoothed object. The multiscale representation is obtained due to a *selection scheme* which allows to organize the components of the medial axis according to their structural importance. Our method is therefore rather a *symbolic* than an *iconic* approach.

- The multiscale MAT combines *boundary properties* derived at distinct scales with the *region information* of the medial axis. This contrasts with many shape simplification methods which are either solely boundary-based or region-based.
- Our technique introduces criteria to *judge the significance* of skeleton branches at each scale. In addition, a *hierarchic organization* of the medial axis constituents can be established *at each scale* independently.
- *No correspondence problem* between distinct scales must be solved.
- The proposed computation scheme is much less affected by interference between adjacent boundary sections.
- Coarse scale discontinuities along the boundary are largely retained.
- The analysis of structural changes of the skeleton occurring across scales permits to *automatically* select feasible scale and regularization parameters.

## 2. Medial Axis Approximation from Voronoi Diagram

An excellent intuitive perception of the MAT is afforded by the famous grassfire analogy [11]. Let us assume that shape $S$ is homogeneously covered with dry grass. Setting fire to the border of $S$ will result in its medial (= local symmetry) axis or skeleton, the locus where the fire fronts meet and quench. The discrete analogue of this process is to let each boundary point $p_i \in P$ initiate a concentric fire front. The locus where the fronts meet is then nothing but the Voronoi diagram (VD) of $P$, $\mathrm{Vor}(P)$. Henceforth, the Voronoi diagram of a (discrete) set of boundary points will be equivalently termed the *discrete Voronoi medial axis(DVMA)*.

It has been shown formally [12] that the DVMA will become an increasingly precise approximation of the continuous MAT as the density of boundary samples is increased. However, also the DVMA is characterized by the typical deficiencies of the medial axis transform such as sensitivity to noise effects upon the boundary and incapability of describing shapes with a significantly jagged boundary. In addition, the DVMA is cluttered with a large number of Voronoi edges which are not relevant for the basic form of the skeleton.

## 3. Regularizing the MAT

In order to prune the MAT to its stable inner branches (see e.g. [4, 13, 12, 5] for other pruning techniques), we have proposed so-called residual functions [14, 15]. The detailed justification of this approach has been outlined in other publications [15]. The technique bases itself on the following significance attribute. For each DVMA edge $e$, the two boundary points which have generated $e$, e.g. $p_i$ and $p_j$, are determined. Henceforth, $p_i$ and $p_j$ will be termed the *'anchor points'* of $e$. The *'anchor distance'* denotes the length $w_{ij} = \mathrm{dist}^B(p_i, p_j)$ (also termed $\mathrm{dist}^B(e)$) of the shortest path along boundary $B$ which connects $p_i$ and $p_j$.

The computation of the 'anchor distances' can be implemented in a particularly time-efficient manner if the boundary consists of simple (without branching points) closed or nonclosed chains. We introduce a boundary potential function $W(p_i)$ for every boundary point $p_i$. In order to create $W(p_i)$, it is necessary to track each boundary chain and assign to each point the current length of the path relative to an arbitrary origin. E.g., for a closed boundary, we obtain $w_{ij}$ from

$$\mathrm{dist}^B(p_i, p_j) = \min\{|W(p_i) - W(p_j)|, L_B - |W(p_i) - W(p_j)|\}, \tag{1}$$

where $L_B$ denotes the total length of the boundary. The prerequisite of the boundary consisting of a collection of simple chains is generally fulfilled in the case of segmented shapes. The extension to more complex descriptions (shapes with holes, graph-like structures) is given in [15].

**The Potential Residual.** The *potential residual* $\Delta R_P(e)$ for edge $e \in$ DVMA is obtained by attributing $e$ with the associated 'anchor distance':

**Definition 3.1 (Potential Residual)**

$$\Delta R_P(e) \stackrel{\text{def}}{=} w_{AB} \stackrel{\text{def}}{=} \text{dist}^B(e), \quad e \in \text{DVMA}(S). \tag{2}$$

The most straightforward pruning strategy amounts to the removal of all edges $e$ which have been assigned a residual value lower than a user-defined threshold $T$. The remaining subset of the DVMA, $\text{Ske}(S, T)$, is termed *discrete Voronoi skeleton (DVSK)*.

The properties of the potential residual, in particular the distribution of the potential residual values over the DVMA, have been discussed in detail in [15]. In particular, it can be shown that pruning by means of the potential residual will preserve the connectivity of the skeleton. The proof of this property does not require a *uniform* increase of the potential function along the boundary nor that the potential values have to correspond to 'real' distances. Consequently, it is possible to assign an arbitrary 'weight of prominence' to each boundary segment. The definition of the skeleton-space will base itself on this characteristic.

**The Chord Residual.** A regularization criterion can be derived from the straight line dual of the VD, the Delaunay triangulation [16]. In Fig. 1, the anchor points of edge $e$ are $p_A$ and $p_B$.

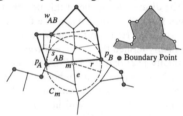

Fig. 1: Chord Residual.

The so-called chord residual $\Delta R_H(e)$ associated with Voronoi edge $e$ is obtained by comparing the 'anchor distance' from $p_A$ to $p_B$, $w_{AB}$, with the length $s_{AB}$ of chord $\overline{p_A p_B}$:

**Definition 3.2 (Chord Residual)**

$$\Delta R_H(e) \stackrel{\text{def}}{=} w_{AB} - s_{AB} = \Delta R_P(e) - s_{AB}, \quad e \in \text{DVMA}(S). \tag{3}$$

$\Delta R_H(e)$ is a measure of the degree of approximation between the original shape and a subset of its Delaunay triangulation. Pruning thus amounts to the peeling-off of peripheral Delaunay triangles (since every erased Voronoi edge corresponds to one side of a triangle being withdrawn from the initial triangulation) which are irrelevant for representing the object at coarser scales.

**Computing a Useful Regularization Threshold.** Analysis of typical boundary artifacts and their effects upon the medial axis allows us to predict the threshold necessary to separate spurious from significant medial axis constituents [14, 15]. An example is shown in Fig. 2(a).

## 4. Hierarchic Voronoi Skeletons: the Skeleton-Pyramid

Residual-based pruning will yield satisfying results in the case of simple shapes with a fairly smooth boundary. A characteristically jagged boundary, however, will induce an undue number of spurious skeleton branches. Increasing further the threshold will cause these branches

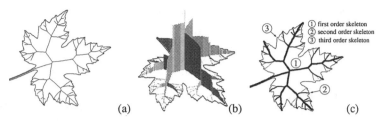

Fig. 2: The Hierarchic Skeleton. (a) The Voronoi skeleton computed for the interior of the maple leaf shape. Regularization with the chord residual, $T = 3.0$. (b) The values of the chord residual are rendered as the height of each Voronoi edge. The high ridges running along the object indicate skeleton components which belong to higher levels of the skeleton-pyramid (first order and second order skeleton). (c) The skeleton-pyramid extracted from (b), consisting of three levels, as denoted by the numbers (the hierarchy starts at level one) and the thickness of the skeleton branches. The thickest branches belong to the first order skeleton and indicate the most significant features such as the five 'fingers' of the leaf. The second order skeleton is obtained by adding all skeleton branches which are directly connected to the first order skeleton.

to be cut back and to disappear eventually, although at the cost of all other branches being trimmed as well. Unfortunately, *neither the distance of the skeleton points from the boundary nor branch length are reliable criteria to judge branch significance.* A solution to this problem is to extend the above basic regularization scheme by establishing a hierarchic organization of the skeleton, henceforth termed *Skeleton-Pyramid, Hierarchic Medial Axis Transform (HMAT)* or *Hierarchic Voronoi Skeleton.* An illustrative understanding of the skeleton-pyramid can be afforded if the prominence measure is interpreted as the 'height' of each skeleton component (Fig. 2(b)). The attributed skeleton represents a 'residual mountain' where the highest ridges correspond to the most salient local axes of symmetry. The generation of the hierarchy amounts to a downhill ridge-riding according to the strategy of least steep descent. The algorithmic details of this procedure are outlined in [15, 14]. The build-up of the hierarchy *does not require a threshold-operation.* The skeleton-pyramid algorithm allows for tracking the most prominent branches of each skeleton until the branch 'hits' the boundary.

## 5. The 'Skeleton-Space'

In order to provide a scale-space representation of the DVSK, we have to include a smoothing operation into the residual functions. However, instead of directly modifying the shape, the build-up of the scale-space hierarchy will be performed *indirectly by adapting the boundary potential function.*

**Smoothed Boundary Potential.** The generic smoothing operator will be denoted by $\mathcal{L}(\ldots, \sigma)$, where $\sigma$ selects the scale. $\mathcal{L}(p_i, \sigma)$ represents the transformed instance of boundary point $p_i$. With $u_{AB}$ denoting a boundary segment (here: also its length) that connects $p_A$ and $p_B$, $\mathcal{L}(u_{AB}, \sigma)$ represents its smoothed counterpart. Consequently, $\text{dist}^{\mathcal{L}(B,\sigma)}(p_i, p_j)$ denotes the length of the shortest path from $\mathcal{L}(p_i, \sigma)$ to $\mathcal{L}(p_j, \sigma)$, taken along the *smoothed* boundary. We define a 'scale-space' variant of the potential residual, the smoothed potential residual $\Delta R_{SP}$:

**Definition 5.1 (Smoothed Potential Residual)**

$$\Delta R_{SP}(e, \sigma) \overset{\text{def}}{=} \text{dist}^{\mathcal{L}(B,\sigma)}(e), \ e \in \text{DVMA}(S). \tag{4}$$

434

**Smoothed Chord Residual.**   We introduce the *smoothed chord residual* $\Delta R_{SH}$ by

**Definition 5.2 (Smoothed Chord Residual)**

$$\Delta R_{SH}(e,\sigma) \overset{\text{def}}{=} \mathcal{L}(w_{AB},\sigma) - \mathcal{L}(s_{AB},\sigma) = \Delta R_{SP}(e,\sigma) - \mathcal{L}(s_{AB},\sigma), e \in \text{DVMA}(S), \quad (5)$$

*where* $\mathcal{L}(s_{AB},\sigma) = d_e(\mathcal{L}(p_A,\sigma),\mathcal{L}(p_B,\sigma))$ $(d_e(..,..):$ *Euclidean distance).*

In the presented case, the smoothing operation $\mathcal{L}()$ is defined as a convolution with a 1-D Gaussian. In order to establish a 'skeleton-space', we first define a sequence of feasible scales $\{\sigma_1, \ldots, \sigma_n\}$. For each scale $\sigma_i$, the residual $\Delta R_{SH}(e_k,\sigma_i)$ is computed for each edge $e_k$ of the DVMA. Thereafter, the skeleton-pyramid algorithm traverses the attributed DVMA$(S,\sigma_i)$ of shape $S$ and assigns the corresponding hierarchy label hier$(e_k,\sigma_i)$ to every edge $e_k$.

## 6. Describing Shapes by the 'Skeleton-Space'

Fig. 3(a) depicts the 'skeleton-space' consisting of four resolution levels $\sigma_i = 2, 10, 50, 100$, computed for a 'semi-jagged' rectangle. In order to illustrate the separation into important skeleton branches and components associated with detail features at a particular scale, Row A shows the skeleton after pruning with a threshold of 1.0 within the original (unprocessed) object contour. The threshold value of 1.0 is based on the assumption that skeleton branches related to features (of the *smoothed* boundary) below pixel size can be removed. Row B contains the smoothed instances of the objects with the corresponding Voronoi skeletons after conventional threshold-based pruning with threshold $T = 3.0$ (obtained from the analysis of model artifacts [14, 15]). Row C depicts the 3-D plots of $\Delta R_{SH}(.,\sigma_i)$, and Row D comprises the shapes obtained by reconstruction from the DVSK in Row A (by drawing the corresponding largest inscribed disk at each Voronoi vertex).

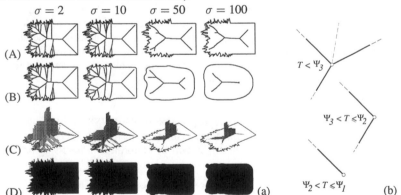

Fig. 3: (a) The Skeleton-Space: 'Jagged Rectangle'. (b) 'Birth'–Set.

We observe a drastic simplification of the Voronoi skeleton occurring from left to right during the transition from a fine-grain scale towards a coarse scale boundary representation. At $\sigma_i = 100$, the structure of the left-hand section of the DVSK shows large structural resemblance to the DVSK segment on the right side. This effect is also visible in the 3-D plots in Row C. The reduced jaggedness of the boundary induces shorter anchor distances and therefore a flatter and more symmetric 'residual mountain'. On the contrary, conventional pruning techniques would cut back all branches simultaneously. The necessary selection of a higher threshold to remove the spurious branches on the left side would eventually eliminate the right-hand bifurcation. The same problem would be observed when the 'conventional' DVSK of the smoothed shape would be computed instead: at coarse scales, the right-hand corners are not prominent enough to generate MAT branches (Row B). Consequently, a recognition process which bases itself on the particular symmetries of the MAT of a rectangle will not be able to perceive the rectangular characteristic. Shape reconstruction from the Voronoi skeleton at $\sigma = 50$ and $\sigma = 100$ returns a much better simplification of the original shape (e.g. consider the right-hand corners) than does plain Gaussian smoothing in Row B.

## 7. The 'Birth'–Set

The 'birth'–set represents a concise method to encode the topology at a vertex of the DVMA. A vertex of a Voronoi skeleton can appear in one of the three following configurations: It can be an 'ordinary' member of a skeleton branch (exactly two incident edges, Fig. 3(b):middle), a *node* (three or more incident edges, Fig. 3(b):top), or an 'endpoint' of the skeleton (Fig. 3(b):bottom). According to the above classification, the three incident edges with the highest residual values unambiguously determine the topology at a vertex.

**Definition 7.1 ('Birth'–Set)** *Let $E$ denote the set of all incident edges on vertex $v$, $E = \{e_1, \ldots, e_i, \ldots, e_n\}$. For each $e_i \in E$, a critical residual value $r_i$ is computed, which determines whether (1) $e_i$ or a portion of it belongs to the skeleton and (2) $v$ is member of this portion of $e_i$. The set of all $r_i$ is symbolized by $D_r$. Then, $v$ is attributed with a set (triplet) $\Psi(v) = \{\Psi_1(v), \Psi_2(v), \Psi_3(v)\}$ according to*

$$\Psi_1(v) \stackrel{\text{def}}{=} \max_{D_r} r_i, \quad \Psi_2(v) \stackrel{\text{def}}{=} \max_{D_r \setminus \{\Psi_1\}} r_i, \quad \Psi_3(v) \stackrel{\text{def}}{=} \max_{D_r \setminus \{\Psi_1, \Psi_2\}} r_i. \tag{6}$$

In the case of the smoothed chord residual, the obvious choice is $r_i \stackrel{\text{def}}{=} \Delta R_{SH}(e_i)$. The selection of $r_i$ for other residual functions is discussed in [15]. Now the three vertex types can be characterized by means of the components of ($S$: shape, $v$: vertex, $T$: threshold):

$$\begin{array}{llll} \Psi_1(v) & < & T & v \notin \text{Ske}(S,T) \\ \Psi_2(v) & < & T \leq \Psi_1(v) & v \text{ is endvertex} \\ \Psi_3(v) & < & T \leq \Psi_2(v) & v \text{ within branch} \\ & & T \leq \Psi_3(v) & v \text{ is node} \end{array} \tag{7}$$

Consequently, elements $\Psi_1$, $\Psi_2$, and $\Psi_3$ can be interpreted as specific threshold levels which trigger the 'birth' of an additional incident edge. If the 'birth'-set is computed for each scale $\sigma$ of the 'skeleton-space' (denoted by $\Psi(v, \sigma)$), the $\Psi(., \sigma)$ set can be employed to assess the structural importance of a $n$-furcation (node) of the skeleton across changing scales. Since a $n$-furcation of the skeleton consists of at least three joining edges, the prominence of node $v$ at scale $\sigma$ is reflected by the value of $\Psi_3(v, \sigma)$.

Consider Fig. 4(a–b). The illustrations show the distribution of the $\Psi_3(., \sigma_i)$ values over an interval of scales $\sigma_i = 2 \ldots 50$. For each vertex $v$ of the DVMA, the corresponding $\Psi_3(v, \sigma_i)$ values are plotted on the $y$-axis, as long as $\Psi_3(v, \sigma_i) > T := 1.0$. Fig. 4(a) contains the results for the 'jagged rectangle' of Fig. 3(a). The flattening of the 'residual mountains' in Fig. 3(a):Row C corresponds to the monotonic decrease of the $\Psi_3(v, \sigma_i)$ 'trace' of a node $v$. For most of the $n$-furcations, the significance measure $\Psi_3$ goes below the 1.0 threshold as $\sigma$ is increased. The most prominent 'survivors' correspond to the two characteristic bifurcations induced by the four 'coarse scale corners' of the rectangle. Similar observations (Fig. 4(b)) can be made for other shapes such as the 'maple leaf' in Fig. 5.

## 8. Automatic Selection of Scale and Pruning Parameters

The analysis of the $\Psi_3$ 'traces' allows to predict a feasible degree of smoothing $\sigma_x$ such that the extracted medial axis will only capture the most salient shape features. Thereafter, the skeleton-pyramid algorithm is employed to determine the corresponding first order skeleton. Consider Fig. 4(c) depicting a typical arrangement of $\Psi_3$ traces (comparable to the situation in

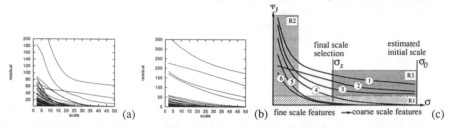

Fig. 4: $\Psi_3$ Traces: (a) 'jagged rectangle' (b) 'maple leaf'. (c) automatic selection of pruning parameters.

Fig. 4(a)). Three particular regions $R1$, $R2$, and $R3$ are indicated in the illustration. Region $R1$ comprises $\Psi_3$ values which are lower than threshold $T = 1.0$. Skeleton nodes associated with $\Psi_3$ values within $R1$ are considered *insignificant*, since they have been generated by boundary details (*after* smoothing) below pixel size. Region $R2$ contains *intersections* of $\Psi_3$ traces. Intersections indicate that even small variations of $\sigma$ can change the rank ordering of skeleton nodes according to their residual values. Since the rank ordering of skeleton nodes determines the structure of the skeleton-pyramid, selecting a scale associated with $R2$ would lead to a rather arbitrary construction of the hierarchy.

In order to find a feasible scale $\sigma_x$, an initial scale estimate $\sigma_0$ is determined by analyzing the length of the first order ellipse computed from the Fourier series expansion of the object contour. The value of $\sigma_0$ corresponds to the right-hand border of region $R3$. $R3$ is defined as the region which (a) lies to the left side of $\sigma_0$, (b) contains only the *significant* traces found at scale $\sigma_0$, and (c) does not contain intersections of $\Psi_3$ traces. Typically, the initial guess $\sigma_0$ is far too high. Pruning at $\sigma_0$ would result in unduly 'flat' 'residual mountains', which obstruct the detection of salient ridges. Skeleton-pyramid evaluation at scale $\sigma_0$ would generally lead to a rather arbitrary selection of first order components and potentially to missing branches. Consequently, the algorithm first analyzes the number and rank ordering (according to their residual values) of the $\Psi_3$ traces (outside region $R1$) at $\sigma_0$ (in Fig. 4(c), traces $1$, $2$, and $3$). Thereafter, the algorithm queries the $\Psi_3$ information in order to find the left-hand border ($\sigma_x$) of region $R3$; in the situation depicted, $\sigma_x$ would be selected in a manner that trace $4$ would still be contained in $R1$. The $\Psi_3$ values at $\sigma_x$ also control the generation of the skeleton-pyramid (clustering parameters), such that skeleton nodes associated with traces $1, 2$, and $3$ are guaranteed to become nodes of the first order skeleton. Fig. 5 depicts some sample objects together with the corresponding first order skeleton extracted by the above automatic pruning process (Rows A and C). The shapes reconstructed from the first order skeleton are shown in Rows B and D.

Row A illustrates the robustness of the proposed automatic pruning when confronted with a series of 'rectangular' shapes, the degree of boundary distortion increasing from left to right. Even in the case of significantly jagged boundaries (Fig. 5(d)) the algorithm correctly identifies a salient subset of the skeleton which is structurally equivalent to the MAT of an ideal rectangle (Fig. 5(a)). A limitation of automatic pruning is visible in Fig. 5(e): without additional criteria

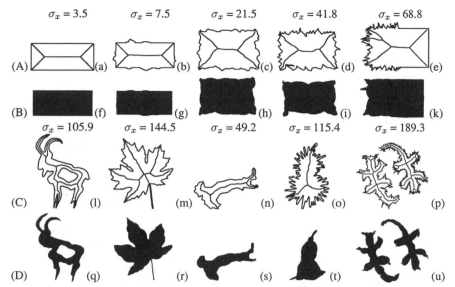

Fig. 5: Automatic Pruning: first order skeletons (Rows A and C) extracted by the skeleton pyramid algorithm at a resolution level $\sigma_x$ determined *automatically* according to the procedure outlined in Section 8. Rows B and D contain the shapes reconstructed from the first order skeleton. The skeleton-pyramid is capable of suppressing fine-scale boundary details, whereas coarse scale discontinuities are largely preserved.

such as 'good continuity', the algorithm is not able to decide which of the branches in the upper left section of the shape should become member of the first order skeleton ('undersegmentation'). On the contrary, the 'billy-goat' shape in Fig. 5(l) suffers from 'oversegmentation', as one of the rather salient forelegs is excluded from the main medial axis. Yet the hierarchical organization of skeleton branches guarantees that the missing branch will still be processed before spurious MAT components. In future applications, additional criteria such as collinearity or the characteristics of the local shape diameter could be incorporated into the skeleton-pyramid algorithm, such that the construction of the hierarchy would be even more in accordance with human perception.

## 9. Example: Shape Decomposition

The benefit of hierarchic organizations of the medial axis such as the skeleton-space and the skeleton-pyramid is the fact that both techniques permit to access and analyze the medial axis in a *systematic way, proceeding from coarse to finer levels of detail*. Since each segment of the medial axis is associated with a particular section of the outline, the skeleton-pyramid/skeleton-space also defines a *hierarchic organization of boundary segments*.

Branching points on the skeleton occurring both within the same level and between consecutive levels of the hierarchy flag *candidate locations for separation of the shape into subparts*. The inclusion or removal of branches and, consequently, of the associated outline features is selective, i.e., the shape is modified only locally. Therefore, *no correspondence problem* must be solved.

The combination of boundary and region information alleviates the analysis of shapes

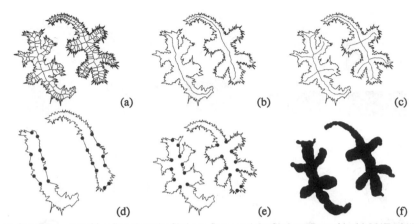

Fig. 6: Shape Decomposition Based on the Skeleton-Space and the Skeleton-Pyramid. (a) MAT of 'lizard' shapes characterized by a significantly jagged boundary. Conventional, threshold-based pruning strategies are not able to remove the undue fragmentation of the skeletons without accidental deletion of meaningful branches. (b) First order skeleton derived from the skeleton-space at level $\sigma = 100$ and subsequent processing by the skeleton-pyramid algorithm. The first order skeleton complies with the human perception of a 'spine'. (c) Corresponding second order skeleton. The second order skeleton is formed by including prominent branches which are attached to the first order skeleton. (d) The bifurcations occurring between first order and second order skeleton indicate candidate locations (drawn as black dots) for a decomposition of the shape, e.g. between 'body' and 'legs' of the 'lizards'. The illustration in (d) depicts the basic form (comparable to a 'first order outline') of the 'lizards' as indicated by the first order skeleton in (b). Gaps introduced by the separation has been simply bridged by straight line connections. (e) The corresponding outline derived from the second order skeleton. (f) Reconstruction of the shapes from the second order skeleton in (c) by drawing the corresponding largest inscribed disk at each (Voronoi) vertex of the DVSK.

characterized by extremely jagged boundaries. Consider, e.g., the 'spiny-lizard' shapes in Fig. 6. Local curvature extrema do not contribute much to the understanding of the shape, since they are distributed rather arbitrarily over the outline. We have developed a method [17] which allows to indicate candidate loci for the decomposition of a shape by mapping the information derived from the skeleton-space (residual values, level of hierarchy) onto the boundary. By analyzing the structural properties of the skeleton graph, each boundary point is assigned a tuple of values describing the prominence of the boundary point with respect to the shape's global characteristics. The attributes of the boundary points allow to extract the basic form of the object during a single scan of the outline and then gradually incorporate features at lower hierarchical levels. An example of applying this technique to the 'spiny-lizard' shapes is presented in Fig. 6(d)–(e).

## 10. Conclusions

This paper has introduced an alternative method of computing a *multiscale medial axis*. In contrast to common techniques which require the MAT to be evaluated for each smoothed instance of the original shape, our approach is based on a *scale-space-driven selection scheme* which is capable of identifying MAT components associated with coarse scale features (and thus effectively supporting hierarchic shape decomposition), even in the case of compound shapes with a significantly jagged boundary.

Notably, (a) *no correspondence problem* between distinct resolution levels must be solved and (b) our technique allows to *automatically* select pruning parameters by tracking the evolution of prominent skeleton nodes across scales.

## References

[1] F. Meyer, "Skeletons in digital spaces," in *Image Analysis and Mathematical Morphology* (J. Serra, ed.), vol. 2: Theoretical Advances, London: Academic Press, 1988.

[2] G. Matheron, "Examples of topological properties of skeletons," in *Image Analysis and Mathematical Morphology* (J. Serra, ed.), vol. 2: Theoretical Advances, London: Academic Press, 1988.

[3] D. Lee, "Medial axis transformation of a planar shape," *IEEE Transactions on Pattern Recognition and Machine Intelligence*, vol. 4, no. 4, pp. 363–369, 1982.

[4] D. Attali and A. Montanvert, "Squelettes et diagrammes de voronoi," Tech. Rep. RR 922 -I-, Laboratoire TIMC-IMAG,équipe INFODIS, CERMO BP 53, 38041 Grenoble Cedex 9, 1993.

[5] F. Leymarie and M. D. Levine, "Simulating the grassfire transform using an active contour model," *IEEE Transactions on Pattern Recognition and Machine Intelligence*, vol. 14, no. 1, pp. 56–75, 1992.

[6] C. Arcelli and G. Sanniti di Baja, "A width-independent fast thinning algorithm," *IEEE Transactions on Pattern Recognition and Machine Intelligence*, vol. 7, no. 4, pp. 463–474, 1985.

[7] A. R. Dill, M. D. Levine, and P. B. Noble, "Multiple resolution skeletons," *IEEE Transactions on Pattern Recognition and Machine Intelligence*, vol. 9, no. 4, pp. 495–504, 1987.

[8] S. M. Pizer, W. R. Oliver, and S. H. Bloomberg, "Hierarchical shape description via the multiresolution symmetric axis transform," *IEEE Transactions on Pattern Recognition and Machine Intelligence*, vol. 9, no. 4, pp. 505–511, 1987.

[9] S. M. Pizer, W. R. Oliver, J. M. Gauch, and S. H. Bloomberg, "Hierarchical figure-based shape description for medical imaging," in *Mathematics and Computer Science for Medical Imaging* (M. A. Viergever and A. E. Todd-Pokropek, eds.), pp. 365–387, Berlin Heidelberg: Springer-Verlag, 1988. NATO ASI Series, Vol. F39.

[10] J. M. Gauch and S. M. Pizer, "The intensity axis of symmetry and its application to image segmentation," *IEEE Transactions on Pattern Recognition and Machine Intelligence*, vol. 15, no. 8, pp. 753–770, 1993.

[11] H. Blum, "A transformation for extracting new descriptors of shape," in *Models for the Perception of Speech and Visual Form* (W. Wathen-Dunn, ed.), Cambridge MA: MIT Press, 1967.

[12] J. W. Brandt and V. R. Algazi, "Continuous skeleton computation by voronoi diagram," *Computer Vision, Graphics, and Image Processing*, vol. 55, no. 3, pp. 329–338, 1992.

[13] H. Talbot and L. Vincent, "Euclidean skeletons and conditional bisectors," in *SPIE Proc.: Visual Communication and Image Processing '92*, vol. 1818, pp. 862–876, SPIE – The International Society of Photo-optical Instrumentation Engineers, 1992.

[14] R. L. Ogniewicz and M. Ilg, "Voronoi skeletons: Theory and applications," in *Proc. Conf. on Computer Vision and Pattern Recognition, Champaign, Illinois*, pp. 63–69, June 1992.

[15] R. L. Ogniewicz, *Discrete Voronoi Skeletons*. Konstanz, Germany: Hartung-Gorre Verlag, 1993. Revised and extended version of Ph.D. thesis No 9876, ETH-Zurich, Switzerland.

[16] F. P. Preparata and M. I. Shamos, *Computational Geometry*. Texts and Monographs in Computer Science, New York: Springer-Verlag, second ed., 1990.

[17] R. L. Ogniewicz, G. Székely, and O. Kübler, "Detection of prominent boundary points based on structural characteristics of the hierarchic medial axis transform," in *Proceedings of the 10th Israeli Conference on Artificial Intelligence, Computer Vision and Neural Networks, Ramat Gan, Israel*, pp. 337–346, December 1993.

# CONTEXT DEPENDENT SHAPE PERCEPTION
## (OR: WHY MACHINES ARE POOR READERS)

T. PAVLIDIS

*Dept. of Computer Science*
*SUNY*
*Stony Brook, NY, 11794-4400*
*U.S.A.*

## ABSTRACT

Recent large scale tests of commercial OCR machines have demonstrated that slight distortions of the input, that hardly interfere with human readability, cause significant deterioration in OCR machine performance. One possible explanation is that human readers rely on visual context so that the same geometric shape will be perceived as a straight line or as a curved arc depending on the characters surrounding it. Such dependence requires postponements of decisions about features until the final classification stage. We will discuss the requirements for building such a system and describe some preliminary results which are encouraging in terms of recognition performance but discouraging in terms of computational resources required. One possible conclusion is that in order to build OCR machines that match human performance we may need far more resources than currently used.

## 1. Introduction

Machine vision has proven to be a very difficult problem as witnessed by the slow rate of progress over the last 40 years. I have discussed this issue elsewhere [1] in general terms and suggested three types of impediments to progress: lack of integration of methodologies, commitment to obsolete models, and the "layered approach." By the latter term I meant the bottom up or top down approaches where recognition proceeds only in one direction. I also suggested that this was the more serious impediment of the three because we did not know enough about integrating interpretation and analysis and how to provide our algorithms with the ability to change context.

When one is faced with a very difficult problem it is logical to look for special cases that might be more tractable and plane shape recognition is certainly a very special case. Given the great commercial interest in Optical Character Recognition (OCR) which is itself a special case of plane shape recognition we may try to solve that problem rather than the general machine vision problem.

The existence of many commercial OCR products suggests that this is an already solved problem and not worth our attention. But what does "solved" mean? From a scientific viewpoint we should define a machine vision problem "solved" only when a computer program replicates human visual performance. Replicating human performance is not only a scientific requirement, but also a practical one. Most users expect their OCR machine to read any document they can read.

While OCR is a problem that has been repeatedly declared as solved OCR machines still fail to read documents that human readers can read. The earliest optimistic citation dates from 1947 (in Norbert Wiener's book "Cybernetics") where it is claimed that a neural net handled both OCR and Speech Synthesis. On the other hand, the first commercial machine that performed these tasks in any credible way did not materialize until about 30 years later. There is a big gap between "encouraging results" and "practical solutions." Even today, after three decades of OCR technology development, only approximately half of the machine printed addresses (and none of the handwritten) can be read by the U.S. Postal Service OCR machines.

In this paper we will discuss why OCR machines fail to match human performance and what can be done to bring them closer to such performance.

## 2. Some Experimental Results

It is quite difficult to explain a phenomenon without adequate data. Fortunately, during the last few years, such data have become available. The major source is an evaluation of commercial OCR machines by the Information Science Research Institute of the University of Nevada at Las Vegas under a contract by the U.S. Department of Energy [2, 3, 4]. (It will be referred to throughout this paper as the "UNLV study".) More recently, results from another systematic study at the Matsushita Information Technology Laboratory at Princeton have become available [5]. (It will be referred to throughout this paper as the "MITL study".)

A major finding of all these studies is that machine recognition performance drops with the quality of input much faster than human recognition performance. In the UNLV study four of eight commercial machines exhibited character accuracy rates better than 99.8% for high quality documents. This is about two errors per page of printed text (2000-3000 characters), which competitive with that of human transcribers. The accuracy of the other four machines was lower but still above 99% (less than ten errors per page). However, for low quality documents the rates varied from 81.5% to 93.2%. The latter corresponds to about 140 errors per page, while the former to nearly 400 errors per printed page. Text with so many errors is unreadable. What is the most surprising result of these studies is that the original text is easily readable by humans.

Figures 1, 2, 3, and 4 show examples of "difficult" text in the UNLV study, while Figures 5, 6, and 7 show examples of "difficult" text in the MITL study. It may be possible to identify the reasons for failure of OCR in the above examples but certainly such performance does not match that of human readers. We may have to look hard at some of these examples to find what is wrong with them. What are the reasons behind the huge discrepancy between human recognition and mechanical recognition? We will try to answer this question in the next two sections.

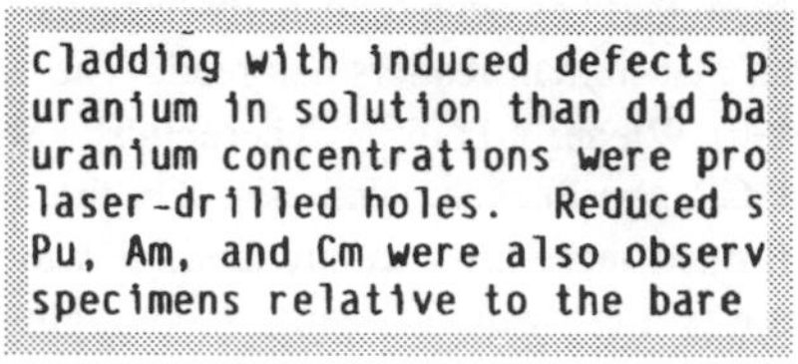
cladding with induced defects p
uranium in solution than did ba
uranium concentrations were pro
laser-drilled holes. Reduced s
Pu, Am, and Cm were also observ
specimens relative to the bare

**Figure 1:** Example of ''difficult'' text (fourth quality group) of the UNLV studies. (Figure 4a in [2].)

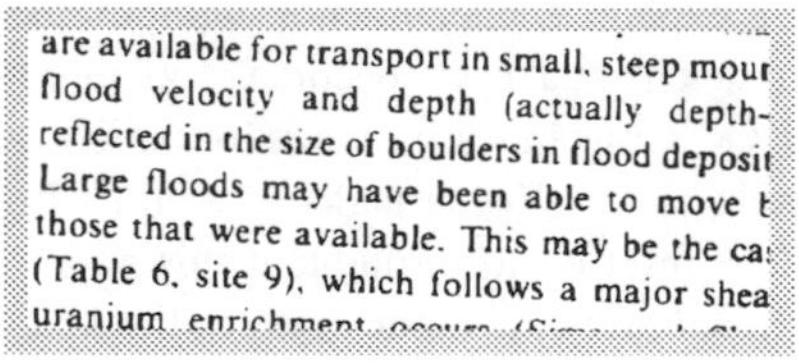
are available for transport in small, steep mour
flood velocity and depth (actually depth-
reflected in the size of boulders in flood deposit
Large floods may have been able to move t
those that were available. This may be the ca
(Table 6, site 9), which follows a major shea
uranium enrichment

**Figure 2:** Example of ''difficult'' text (fourth quality group) of the UNLV studies. (Figure 4b in [2].)

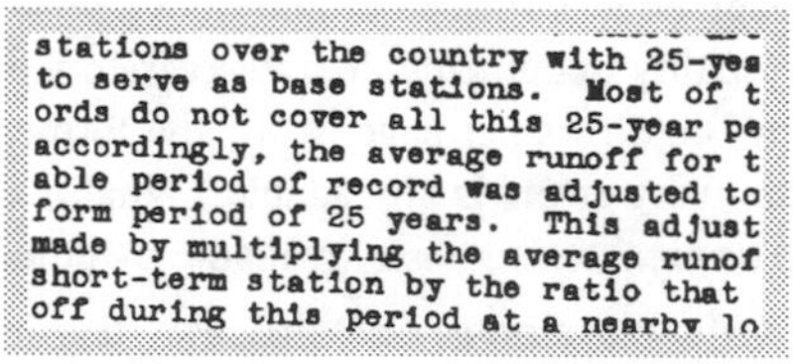
stations over the country with 25-yea
to serve as base stations. Most of t
ords do not cover all this 25-year pe
accordingly, the average runoff for t
able period of record was adjusted to
form period of 25 years. This adjust
made by multiplying the average runof
short-term station by the ratio that
off during this period at a nearby lo

**Figure 3:** Example of ''difficult'' text (fifth quality group) of the UNLV studies. (Figure 5a in [2].)

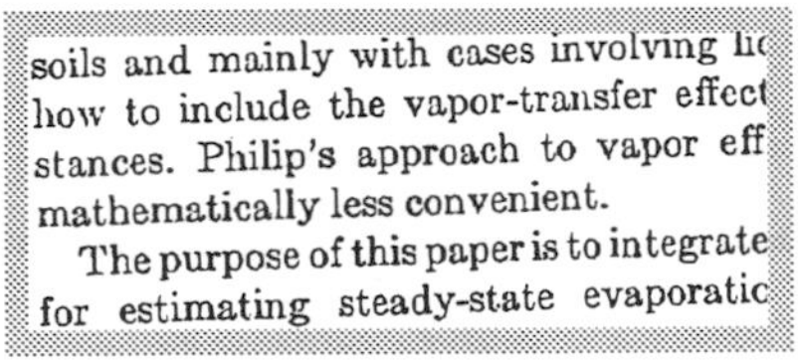

soils and mainly with cases involving he
how to include the vapor-transfer effect
stances. Philip's approach to vapor eff
mathematically less convenient.
    The purpose of this paper is to integrate
for estimating steady-state evaporatic

**Figure 4:** Example of "difficult" text (fifth quality group) of the UNLV studies. (Figure 5b in [2].)

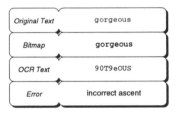

**Figure 5:** Example of text where an OCR system has made the wrong guess of the baseline. (From Appendix A of [5].)

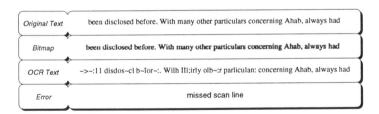

**Figure 6:** Numerous OCR errors have been caused by a missed scanline. (From Appendix A of [5].)

444

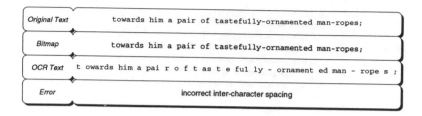

| Original Text | towards him a pair of tastefully-ornamented man-ropes; |
|---|---|
| Bitmap | towards him a pair of tastefully-ornamented man-ropes; |
| OCR Text | t owards him a pai r o f t as t e ful ly - ornament ed man - rope s ; |
| Error | incorrect inter-character spacing |

**Figure 7:** Failure of an OCR system to detect proper spacing. (From Appendix A of [5].)

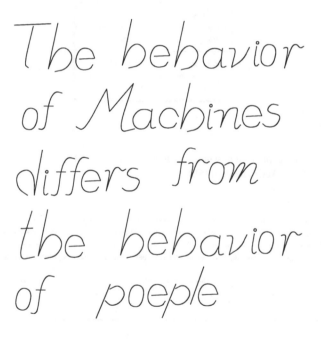

**Figure 8:** What is remarkable about this phrase?

## 3. Linguistic Context

### 3.1. Linguistic Context is Necessary but not Sufficient

Human readers rely heavily on linguistic context for enhancing recognition and this fact has been discussed widely in the literature. Indeed the most common explanation for the superiority of human over machine vision is the human reliance on high level linguistic context. This has led to the belief that if we could only build such a context into an OCR system, it would match human performance.

It is certainly true that *linguistic* context can overcome significant shape variations. Figure 8 shows some samples of text that are unremarkable until one looks carefully at the form of the characters. The same shape is used for different characters without apparently disturbing a human reader. Somehow word and character recognition proceed in parallel without us being conscious of the process.

The main challenge is how to use linguistic context in OCR. The typical use of context in OCR requires checking the recognized words against a dictionary and then attempting to correct those rejected by replacing the top choice of the character recognizer by another high choice. Another approach is to ask the shape recognizer to offers $k_i$ alternatives for the $i^{th}$ character rather than just one. Then $\prod_{1=1}^{n} k_i$ words are formed from such alternatives and then a dictionary entry is selected from them. (It is easy to modify this formalism to deal with cases of different groupings of connected components.) Unfortunately such methods have severe limitations.

Consider for example the word "date". If the tiny crossbar of the letter "t" is missed during thresholding, the word will be recognized as "dale". This is a correct English word and will not be rejected by a spelling checker. Of course human readers may not even notice the error in a sentence such as: *Please note that the dale of the meeting has been changed to June 1*.

This problem occurred because context was used only at one particular level of the recognition process. The "dale/date" problem could be resolved by looking at higher level context, for example by parsing the text and recognizing that "dale" does not make sense. This is a rather formidable task, so a more modest approach might be to recognize that the document is, for example, a business letter and therefore the word "date" is far more likely than "dale". Of course using word probabilities is much of an improvement over using a dictionary. The latter implies probabilities that are either 0 or 1. If we use a wider set of probability values, but accept always the more likely word, we will introduce other errors. For example, in a poem both "dale" and "date" may appear and accepting the most likely one may introduce more errors than if we did not use this strategy. Clearly, going to a higher context level will not solve the problem. We need to use additional evidence.

In this particular example such evidence would be available if, after thresholding the original scanned image, we kept some information about the original gray scale. Faced with the "dale" versus "date" question, we could go and examine the pixels near the upper half of the third character and finalize our decision on the basis of their values. Note that the recognition confidence level of the classifier is of no use here. Once the pixels of the crossbar of the "t" are dropped the resulting bitmap may look like a perfect "l" both to a human and a machine, so the confidence level will be high.

What this example shows is that a low level decision (whether a pixel is black or white) cannot be made until very high level context is available. Human readers use instinctively such a process, therefore they are bound to outperform machines that do not do so.

### 3.2. Linguistic Context may be Harmful (if Over-used)

Unfortunately, reliance on context may be counterproductive some times. Words that are not found in the dictionary are not necessarily wrong. During the 1993 SIG-GRAPH conference at Anaheim, California, *Apple Computers* demonstrated the machine *Newton*™ which came with handwriting recognition based on dictionary look-up. Many visitors asked the person in the *Apple* booth to write the word "SIGGRAPH". Since no one had thought to include that word in the *Newton*™ dictionary, the machine would always come back with an erroneous answer. Clearly, the company was wrong in not including "SIGGRAPH" in their dictionary and one expects such errors to be corrected with time. The Unix™ spelling checker provides means for dynamic updating of dictionaries by monitoring its own use. When a misspelled word is left repeatedly uncorrected in a document that word is is added to the dictionary. A similar strategy might be incorporated in an OCR environment.

But how about "IWVF2"? A person who has never seen the acronym "IWVF2" will accept it, if it is clearly printed. Only a very smudged printed or sloppily handwritten version of "IWVF2" might be read as "LOVES", a word found in a dictionary. The recognition process here is similar to the one outlined in the dale/date example, but applied in the opposite way. If a character is recognized with high confidence and its surrounding area does not contain pixels that are close to the threshold value, then it is accepted regardless of context.

## 4. Visual Context

While the use of linguistic context can explain certain cases where human readers outperform OCR machines, it does not cover all of them. Figures 2 to 4 show that a slight tilt confuses the current commercial OCR systems. There is no clear explanation why the text shown in Figure 1 is difficult for OCR, but it is easily readable by humans without relying on context. Certainly "Pu", "Am", and "Cm" are recognized event though they have no meaning to those unfamiliar with heavy element chemistry.

Apparently humans rely on a much richer model of shape than OCR machines. One possible explanation is that a very large number of features is used to define each character class. OCR machines may use a small subset of such features so that, if this particular subset cannot be extracted, mechanical recognition fails. Since there are many more features available to humans, their recognition is not affected. This point of view was discussed in [6].

Some of the UNLV results suggest that this may not be the case. If OCR systems use only a small subset of all available features, then it is reasonable to assume that each particular OCR system uses a subset that it is not identical with that of the other systems. In such a case we could use different OCR systems and apply a voting scheme to combine their results. Tables 17 and 18 of [7] report the effects of voting on different quality documents. For high quality documents there is significant improvement: the number of errors was reduced by 79% and 50% in two sets of documents. However for low quality documents the reduction was only 33% and 8%. Note that the total number of errors was very small in the high quality documents (129 and 244 initially) but quite large for the low quality documents (8,501 and 12,072 initially).

What do such results mean? For high quality documents the hypothesis of partly different feature sets seems to be confirmed. For low quality document which are the most puzzling (because "low" applies only to OCR readability rather then human) the hypothesis is not confirmed. It could still be true if all commercial systems used largely overlapping features sets and all of them ignored many others but that is a rather unlikely situation. These are not hard conclusions because, in the UNLV tests, OCR systems are used as "block boxes". However they suggest that we should consider other explanations besides the "small subset of features" explanation.

A look at the pages where machines fail provides some clues. Many are skewed by one to two degrees, a distortion that does not affect human readers at all. (One may have to increase the skew in excess of 20° before human readers have any difficulty.) Other pages are slightly faint and others slightly too dark. Others use an unusual (but clearly readable) font. For each of these conditions there is an appropriate filter that could be applied before OCR is attempted. Skew correction, morphological expansion (for faint pages), morphological shrinking (for dark pages), etc. The trouble is that OCR systems lack the global view that human readers have.

We shall use the term *visual context* to refer to the conditions that affect the decisions made during the recognition process, before any *semantic* or *linguistic context* enter the picture. Most people will probably agree on the desirability of using visual context. The question is how to do so. Preprocessing of a page or a zone of text is not enough because the visual context may change within such large areas. Besides the examples given above, other properties such as typeface style, font, size, etc., can also be included under visual context. G. Nagy [8] has advocated for a long time that dynamic estimations of font and other properties could be used to improve recognition.

We could describe the use of visual context as an *adaptive* mechanism but the word "adaptive" has a particular physiological meaning which makes it appropriate for compensating for too dark or too light text but not for the more complex adjustments caused by recognition of font type.

How can we take advantage of visual context? If a character is recognized reliably, then the system may attempt to extract information from it about the visual context. For example, thickness may be measured and used to construct a normalizing factor for the other characters. Similarly, serifs may be detected and the recognition process for the remaining characters adjusted. There is need for careful planning for such strategies which is beyond the scope of this paper. They may also not be sufficient.

## 5. Human versus Machine Vision

### 5.1. The Dot Matrix Puzzle

One place where visual context is strikingly apparent is in reading dot matrix text where white areas are ignored even though similar areas are observed when small point size text is read. To the best of my knowledge no commercial OCR system can read *both* dot matrix text and small point text at the same time. Even bar code readers have trouble in this area. They can read easily dot matrix symbols with a wide laser light beam which blurs the details of the printer but a much thinner beam must be used to read high density symbols. A blurring technique can also be used in OCR and some commercial systems include a dot matrix switch.

The experimental OCR system under development in the author's laboratory at Stony Brook is able to read both types of text by using the following strategy. Features are extracted directly from gray scale and represent the topology of the gray scale intensity when viewed as a 3D surface [9]. Narrow gaps result in *saddle points* so when a piece of text is read the number of saddle points is counted. If there many of them compared to the size of the text area, then it is assumed that dot matrix text has been read and the saddle point regions are added to the foreground. Otherwise it is assumed that high density (small print) text has been read and the saddle point regions are added to the background.

This strategy works quite well, provided that each form of printing occurs in a sufficiently large block to collect statistics. This is the case with postal addresses where some addresses are printed with dot matrix printers and others with laser printers but no address is printed by a mixture of the two. On the other such a method will have difficulty handling the example of Figure 9. Most likely, it will assume that everything is dot matrix and will treat the small print as noise. Or, if there is a lot of small print, it will treat each large dot as a character.

**Figure 9:** Mixture of dot matrix and small print text that is easily readable by human readers but not by OCR machines. Note the lack of any linguistic context.

## 5.2 A Word on Skew Correction

Many of the pages of the "difficult" text in the UNLV study were skewed during scan and the inclusion of skew correction in OCR systems should help improve the results. However skew correction can be applied only on large blocks of text because of the methods used (see for example [10]). In contrast human readers can easily read text with a mixture of skews. We are facing a similar problem as in the dot matrix versus high density print discrimination.

## 5.3. Psychobiological Explanations

Which are the factors that enable people to read much more easily than machines? We just described two examples where it is difficult to design a mechanical system that will match human performance. I believe the major difference is that people employ far more complex process than the simple perceptual models used to guide machine vision.

First we must admit that reading is *not* a simple visual task. It is simple only within a particular machine vision paradigm which apparently is wrong. Reading, or, more generally, subtle shape discrimination is an ability that occurred rather late in the history of evolution. In contrast stereopsis, motion and color detection have occurred much earlier. The work of Bela Julesz has established that early vision is strictly bottom-up (see for example [11]). While this is certainly true for depth perception, it need not be true for subtle shape discrimination. He also states that "in real-life situations, bottom-up and top-down processes are interwoven in intricate ways," and that "progress in psychobiology is ... hampered ... by our inability to find the proper levels of complexity for describing mental phenomena" (*ibid*).

The last two statements point out the same type difficulties for understanding *human* vision as the difficulties faced by machine vision stated in the introduction. The extreme complexity of human vision and its differences from machine vision has also being pointed out in an excellent article by V. S. Ramachandran [12]. The article includes examples (such as Figure 31) which clearly demonstrate that some of the popular machine early vision models are inadequate.

In spite of this discouraging start, there are some inferences that can be drawn from reading the psychobiological literature. Julesz has pointed out the importance of local nonlinear feature for the discrimination of texture [11]. He has called such features *textons*. Are textons important for character recognition? I believe that they offer a solution to the dot matrix puzzle. One of the textons is quasicollinearity and this suggests the following method for discriminating gaps in dot matrix text.

If a set of saddle points are mutually collinear and are uniformly arranged than the regions around them should be given the foreground color.

Note that this is a local measure, in contrast to the global one used in our OCR system. Therefore it could take care of the example of Figure 9. I should point out that *it is no coincidence* that the dot matrix letters of Figure 9 contain only vertical and horizontal strokes. Examples with diagonal dot lines are far more difficult to read without bringing in linguistic context. The preference to vertical and horizontal directions is also supported by psychobiological evidence [11].

The price we pay for local dot matrix detection is additional computation. While there exist well known algorithms for computing the collinearity of groups of points [13], they require far more time than the simple counting of points.

It is worth quoting one more piece of evidence in favor of the fundamental difference between human information processing and the dominant bottom up models used in OCR. Apparently, reaction times for certain tasks are not additive suggesting that in a multistage system information is passed from one stage to the next before completion of the task assigned to the stage [14]. Such early forwarding of information would offer ample opportunity for feedback from the later to the earlier stages.

## 6. Using Visual Context in an OCR System

The main feature of a system that uses context is the deferral of individual decisions as well as the modification of earlier decisions on the basis of later evidence. These principles form the basis of an OCR systems been built at Stony Brook. We already mentioned in Section 5.1 how the system deals currently with the dot matrix problem and in Section 5.3 how it could be modified to deal more effectively with that problem on the basis of psychobiological evidence. Here we will describe some other aspects of it. For a detailed description of its various components the reader is referred to [9, 15 - 16].

The system does not perform binarization, but extracts features directly from the gray scale image. In addition to features that are assigned immediately to foreground (black) there are others whose designation is left undetermined (saddle points and bridges). Segmentation is attempted only at the word level, or when a character is well separated from others. For large part of the text segmentation follows recognition.

Character shapes are defined through hand drawn prototypes (usually one to three per class) and the main recognition step deals with matching of the prototype graphs to the feature graph. This is equivalent to sub-graph homeomorphism which is a computationally expensive process but it is able to capture certain shapes in the presence of significant noise.

Features are labeled as strokes or arcs tentatively and the matching process during classification is allowed to map strokes into arcs. Other distortions are also allowed so that the matching is flexible. This enables the system to handle many distortions, even those that were anticipated during its design.

One of them is skewed input. Skew was absent in all the data we used during the development of the system but when we observed the results of the UNLV tests we decided to try it on a page tilted by 3°. The error rate went from about 0.3% to about 2.3%. This is a large drop in the recognition rate (2%) but it is smaller than that exhibited by commercial OCR systems in the UNLV tests (Graph 1a in [7]). For two products the error rate increased from about 4% for skew angle less than 0.5° to nearly 8% for skew angle greater than 1° but less than 2.4°. For others the respective rates dropped anywhere from 1 to 2 percentage points. Note that these drops are averages for the 1° to 2.4° range and the decrease at the high end of the range should be higher. Given the different conditions of the tests one should be careful about the interpretation of the results but it seems that a system based on flexible graph matching is more robust than current commercial OCR systems with respect to skew.

In retrospect this is not surprising because anywhere the system uses information about orientation, it assumes a tolerance of a few degrees. It does not classify features as vertical, or horizontal, etc. If a prototype has a vertical feature this can be matched to a feature with significant deviation from the vertical but with a penalty. If no other matching has a lower penalty, then the "tilted" matching is accepted.

Other examples where the system handles "difficult" input can be found in the papers cited [9, 15 - 16]. The major disadvantages of the system are its complexity and the use of time consuming procedures. The processing time can be reduced by using more powerful CPUs or even parallel processing. It is also possible that more efficient algorithms can be found. One such algorithm for the gray scale feature extraction has been described recently by Lee and Kim [17]. On the other hand the complexity is a problem that has delayed the development of the system. However the earlier discussions of this paper suggest that it is not complex enough! If the system is going to match human recognition, it needs certain extensions. We already pointed out one in Section 5. The main addition will be one of history to infer context. Here are some possible uses of such history.

Currently many classes have more than one prototype. If some decisions are made using only one prototype, this may be the only one tested in subsequent steps.

If bridges have not been used over certain strings of characters, they may be ignored later on.

When a character is rejected an attempt should be made to apply a transformation and reclassify it. If a particular transformation is found useful, then it should be applied to all subsequent characters.

## 7. Conclusions

Both the UNLV and the MITL studies suggest that current commercial OCR systems are far from matching human performance, especially because of the large number of errors on text which is easily read by people. We offer as an explanation the use of a strict bottom approach in such systems, at least until a dictionary is used. There is no evidence that any of them take advantage of visual context. Certainly all of them binarize the input before any feature extraction [18].

An effort to build a system that reads poorly printed text has been under way but that requires much larger computational resources than the current commercial OCR systems and it is likely that it may have to become even more complex before it can achieve its objectives.

The key question from a practical viewpoint is whether it is worthwhile to build a system with performance comparable to that of human readers, if that system is going to cost an order of magnitude more than current OCR systems. The main reason that OCR is desirable is that it will enable automatic information retrieval as well as economies in storage if the ASCII form rather than bitmaps of document pages are stored. If the cost of building a "super-reliable" system OCR is too high, then we may decide to limit OCR to the role of assisting information retrieval. This of course poses a new set of research topics which are beyond the scope of this paper.

From a scientific viewpoint (as well as long term practical) building such a system will have important implications both for machine vision and artificial intelligence in general.

## 8. Acknowledgments

I want to thank the following people for helping me with this paper. Professor Thomas A. Nartker and other members of the staff of UNLV-ISRI for providing the postscript files to produce Figures 1 to 4 as well as the permission to use them. Drs. D. P. Lopresti and J. S. Sandberg of the Matsushita Information Technology Laboratory at Princeton for providing the originals used for Figures 5 to 7 as well as the permission to use them. Professor Bela Julesz for discussing some of his work with me (but I take full responsibility for any errors of interpretation). Harry Pavlidis for pointing out the research on reaction times (ref. [14]).

Many of ideas in the paper developed over the years as a result of numerous discussions with (in alphabetical order) Dr. Henry S. Baird of AT&T Bell Labs, Professor Shunji Mori of Aizu University, Japan, and Professor George Nagy of RPI. I want to thank my current and former students, visitors, and associates at Stony Brook without whose hard work the development of our OCR system would have been impossible: Angelo Marcelli (Univ. of Naples), Bill Sakoda, Jairo Rocha, Li Wang, Sophie Zhou, and George Sazaklis. The latter conducted the experiment with the skewed text reported for the first time in this paper.

I am particularly greatful for the long standing support of the National Science Foundation (IRIS division) and the program directors: Dr. Howard Moraff and before him Dr. Y. T. Chien. The current grant is IRI-9209057.

## 9. References

[1]  T. Pavlidis "Why Progress in Machine Vision is so Slow," *Pattern Recognition Letters,* **13** (April 1992), pp. 221-225.

[2]  S.V. Rice, J. Kanai, and T.A. Nartker "An Evaluation of OCR Accuracy," *1993 Annual Report of UNLV Information Science Research Institute, pp. 9-33.*

[3]  T.A. Nartker "On the Need for Information Metrics", in *Proc. SPIE Symposium on Document Recognition,* San Jose, CA, Feb. 1994, Paper No. 2181-19 (in press).

[4]  F. Jenkins and J. Kanai "The Use of Synthesized Images to Evaluate the Performance of Optical Character Recognition Devices and Algorithms", *in Proc. SPIE Symposium on Document Recognition,* San Jose, CA, Feb. 1994, Paper No. 2181-20 (in press).

[5]  J. Esakov, D.P. Lopresti, and J.S. Sandberg "Classification and Distribution of Optical Character Recognition Errors", *in Proc. SPIE Symposium on Document Recognition,* San Jose, CA, Feb. 1994, Paper No. 2181-21 (in press).

[6]  T. Pavlidis "How to bring Computer Recognition to the Level of Human Recognition" *Proc. IPTP Symposium on Handwritten Character Recognition -Past, Present, Future -,* Tokyo, Japan, April 2, 1993, pp. 1-6.

[7]  S.V. Rice, J. Kanai, and T.A. Nartker "The Third Annual Test of OCR Accuracy," *1994 Annual Report of UNLV Information Science Research Institute, pp. 11-38.*

[8]  G. Nagy "What does a Machine Need to Know to Read a Document?" *Proc. Symp. on Document Analysis and Information Retrieval,* March 16-18, 1992, Las Vegas, Nevada, pp. 1-10.

[9]  L. Wang and T. Pavlidis "Direct Gray Scale Extraction of Features for Character Recognition" *IEEE Trans. on Pattern Analysis and Machine Intelligence,* vol. 15 (Oct. 1993), pp. 1053-1067.

[10] H. S. Baird "The Skew Angle of Printed Documents," *Proc., 1987 Conf. of the Society of Photographic Scientists and Engineers,* Rochester, New York, May 20-21, 1987.

[11] B. Julesz "Early vision and focal attention," *Reviews of Modern Physics,* vol. 63 (July 1991), pp. 735-772.

[12] V. S. Ramachandran "Visual Perception in People and Machines," in *AI and the Eye,* edited by A. Blake and T. Troscianko, J. Wiley, 1990.

[13] T. Pavlidis *Algorithms for Graphics and Image Processing,* Computer Science

454

Press, Rockville, Maryland, 1982.

[14] J. Miller "A Queue-Series Model for Reaction Time, With Discrete-Stage and Continuous-Flow Models as Special Cases," *Psychological Review,* vol. 100, No. 4 (1993), pp. 702-715.

[15] B. Sakoda, J. Zhou and T. Pavlidis "An Address Recognition System Based on Feature Extraction from Grayscale" *Proc. SPIE Conf. Character Recognition Technologies,* San Jose, CA, Feb. 1-2, 1993, pp. 21-29.

[19] B. Sakoda, J. Zhou, and T. Pavlidis "Refinement and Testing of a Character Recognition System based on Feature extraction in Grayscale Space," *Proc. Second Intern. Conf. on Document Analysis and Recognition* (ICDAR'93), Tsukuba, Japan, Oct. 20-22, 1993, pp. 464-469.

[20] J. Rocha and T. Pavlidis "A Solution to the Problem of Touching and Broken Characters," *Proc. Second Intern. Conf. on Document Analysis and Recognition* (ICDAR'93), Tsukuba, Japan, Oct. 20-22, 1993, pp. 602-605.

[21] A. Marcelli and T. Pavlidis "Using projections for pre-classification of character shape," *Proc. SPIE Symposium on Document Recognition,* San Jose, CA, Feb. 1994, Paper No. 2181-02 (in press).

[22] J. Rocha and T. Pavlidis "A Shape Analysis Model with Applications to a Character Recognition System," *IEEE Trans. on Pattern Analysis and Machine Intelligence,* vol. 16 (April 1994), (in press).

[16] G. Sazaklis and T. Pavlidis "Use of Constraints as a Second Stage Character Classification Technique," *Proc. Third Annual* Symp. on Document Analysis and Information Retrieval, April 11-13, 1994, Las Vegas, Nevada, pp. 289-298.

[17] S-W. Lee and Y. J. Kim "Direct Extraction of Topographic Features from Gray Scale Character Images," *Proc. Third Annual* Symp. on Document Analysis and Information Retrieval, April 11-13, 1994, Las Vegas, Nevada, pp. 253-261.

[18] T. Pavlidis and S. Mori, editors *Special Issue on Optical Character Recognition, IEEE Proceedings,* vol. 80 (July 1992).

# ROBUST SKELETONIZATION AND OBJECT RECOGNITION FROM GREY IMAGES

M. PETROU, P.L. PALMER, W.J. CHRISTMAS, J. KITTLER

*Department of Electronic and Electrical Engineering*
*University of Surrey, Guildford, Surrey, GU2 5XH, U.K.*

### ABSTRACT

We present an algorithm appropriate for the skeletonization and recognition of objects from their gray images. The skeletonization algorithm is based on the distance transform of the objects computed with the help of Hough line representation of the object boundary. The recognition algorithm is based on Bayesian reasoning taking into consideration the explicit inclusion of the binary relations between the object primitives as derived from the unary attributes of them. In the particular application as object primitives we use the straight line segments of the skeleton and as binary relations the relative orientations of the line segments. Our approach is both sensitive to shape variations and robust to imperfections. Further, it is amenable to parallel implementation.

## 1. Introduction

One of the reasons that the human visual system is so robust, is its reliance on co-operative processes. Examples of such processes are the identification of objects in context, the identification of straight lines by continuity arguments and the completion of contours according to the laws of continuity and "good shape" of Gestalt psychology [11, 4]. On the other hand, one of the weaknesses of machine vision is exactly the lack of cooperation between the various processes. A lot of work has been put into the horizontal cooperation of processes, ie contextual image analysis, and only now has some work started appearing concerning the vertical cooperation between processes, ie vision systems with feed-back loops between the various moduli.

We argue here, that in a recognition task, it is not necessary to make sure the output of each module is perfect, or even near perfect, but only within the tolerance of the module in the level above in the process of vision. Thus, imperfect edge maps may be used to recognize objects perfectly!

An example in hand is the skeletonization of grey objects for the purpose of recognition. Various methods have been proposed for the skeletonization of grey objects based mainly on morphological operators [6, 7, 10, 12]. In this paper, we advocate the skeletonization of objects from the distance map computed *after* the outline of the object has been fitted with a set of parametric curves. One can argue at this point that if the outline of an object is fitted with parametric curves, one does not need to involve the skeleton of the object; the object might as well be recognized directly from the shape of its outline. We believe that although this is possible, when one deals with large object databases which have to be stored and searched for the task of object recognition, skeletons offer a very compact and efficient way of representing an object. They may act like Chinese characters indexing an encyclopaedia, ie they can be used as indexing labels which may invoke further information for object identification.

To exemplify our ideas, we fit the object boundaries by line segments extracted with the help of Hough transform, but the method can be extended to incorporate any parametrically described set of curves. The use of the Hough lines has the following advantages:

- A Hough line is the continuous representation of a string of discrete points and as such it smoothes out any discontinuities, local deformations, breakages and discretization effects.

- The equation of the Hough line is known in such a way that in order to find the distance of a pixel from it one has only to plug into the formula the coordinates of the pixel. Thus, the distance transform of the image is computed by considering the distance of each pixel from a small number of line segments and choosing the smallest, as opposed to considering the distance from unreliable individual pixels or resolving to approximations.

The next stage in the process of vision is the identification of the object from its skeleton. The matching algorithm we present is based on the explicit use of binary relations between the line segments which make up the skeleton of the object. The object skeleton as well as the model skeletons in the database are represented by attributed relational graphs where each node is a segment and each arc expresses the relative orientation and position of the nodes it connects. The binary relations are used to express the contextual support when a part of a skeleton is matched against a part of one of the model skeletons. In effect, this algorithm imitates what a human would do if he was to match a noisy skeleton against a collection of "perfect" skeletons: the human would try to place one skeleton on the top of the other by making a certain segment of the skeleton coincide with a segment of the model and checking the relative orientations and positions of the remaining segments. We use the theory of Bayesian probability to derive a formula which expresses the probability of an object segment matched with a model segment. The explicit inclusion of the binary relations results in a very robust algorithm which can cope with the imperfections of the derived skeletons.

This paper is organized as follows: In section 2 we describe the algorithm for skeletonization and in section 3 we discuss the matching process. We apply our ideas to the problem of spanner identification from grey images, using a model database with their "perfect" (hand made) skeletons, and present our results in section 4. We conclude in section 5.

## 2. The skeletonization algorithm

We assume here that we are dealing with grey tone images each depicting a single object. The object and background are not necessarily of uniform brightness, but the object is either persistently brighter, or persistently darker than the background. The reason for the latter assumption is to enable the use of labelling edge detection, which assigns to the edge pixels an arrow with direction indicating the side on which the step edge is brighter. That way, we can avoid computing "skeleton lines" for the background. (Notice that this requirement is not necessary if the instantiation of an object is sought in a cluttered environment, but it is useful if an object is to be recognized from its skeleton. However, our matching algorithm is robust enough to be able to cope even if this requirement is not fulfilled.) Next we assume that we have performed edge detection and that the edge map of the image has been input to a Hough line detection algorithm, so that the edges of the object in the scene have been approximated by straight line segments.

Each line segment is characterised by four parameters: The usual Hough line parameters $\rho$ and $\theta$, which define the distance of the line on which the segment belongs from the origin (taken at the centre of the image) and the orientation of the segment relative to the sides of the image. The equation of the line can be written:

$$\rho - x \cos \theta - y \sin \theta = 0 \qquad (1)$$

The other two parameters are measured along the line from the foot of the normal which passes through the origin to the start and end of the line segment. These distances are given by the expression:

$$\ell = -x \sin \theta + y \cos \theta \qquad (2)$$

where $x$ and $y$ are the co-ordinates of the start or end of the line segment. We shall denote the values of $\ell$ corresponding to the start and end of the segment as $\ell_S$ and $\ell_E$ respectively.

Any pixel that belongs to the line satisfies equation 1. Pixels, however, which do not lie on the line are at a distance from it equal to the left-hand-side of the same equation. The quantities $\cos \theta$ and $\sin \theta$ of each line can be computed once, during the Hough stage, and stored alongside the segment parameters so that the calculation of the distance of a pixel from a line involves only two multiplications and one addition.

Although the above expression gives the distance of a pixel from a line, this distance may not necessarily be the distance of the pixel from the boundary which lies on this line. This is because boundaries are line segments and not lines, and a pixel may even lie on the line itself and still be very far from the boundary segment. To avoid this problem, we introduce the concept of the "shadow" of a line segment. The "shadow" of a line segment consists of all the pixels which project on the segment itself. A pixel with coordinates $(x_i, y_i)$ is in the shadow of a line segment with parameters $\theta$, $\ell_S$ and $\ell_E$ if the quantity $-x_i \sin \theta + y_i \cos \theta$ lies between $\ell_S$ and $\ell_E$.

We compute the distance of each object pixel from each boundary segment using equation 1. If the pixel is not in the "shadow" of the line segment, and its distance to the corresponding line is less than the distance of the pixel calculated from any other line segment so far, then we compute the Euclidean distance of the pixel to *the end of the line segment* which is closest to it. In other words, if the distance computed by expression $\rho - x_i \cos\theta - y_i \sin\theta$ is $d_P$ and $\ell < \ell_S$, say, then the distance of the pixel from this part of the boundary is given by:

$$D = \sqrt{d_P^2 + (\ell_S - \ell)^2} \qquad (3)$$

This procedure for computing the distance map contains three advantages. Firstly, local defects in the string of edge points around the object have been smoothed out by computing the straight line segments. Secondly, the actual Euclidean distance is only rarely computed and the vast majority of distances are computed by two multiplications and two additions. So the algorithm is fast and robust. Thirdly, the equations of the Hough lines can be computed to arbitrary accuracy (eg [9]), and so the distance map that is computed is not subject to discretization effects. Thus, the distance map computed can be very accurate.

We extract the skeleton from the distance map using a very simple algorithm, ie looking for local maxima in the distance map with symmetric profiles. Better results might be obtained if a more sophisticated skeletonization algorithm is used on the distance map (eg [1, 3, 2]). However, for the purpose of this work, the results of this algorithm seem adequate.

## 3.   The matching algorithm

To match the derived object skeletons to the model skeletons of an object database, we use the method of Maximum A Posteriori probability matching for attribute relational graphs. In effect, we represent each object to be matched by a graph, the nodes of which are straight line segments with which the skeleton of the object can be approximated and the arcs between any two nodes represent relationships between the corresponding nodes. Each node is characterised by its orientation and location of its end points in the coordinate system of the image in which it resides. The binary relations used between nodes represent the relative orientation and relative location of the two segments represented by the nodes, calculated from the unary attributes. The problem we have to solve is then to try to match the derived skeleton to each one of the object database skeletons. To achieve this, we examine the possible matches of each individual segment in turn, taking into consideration the binary measurements between the segments, ie in effect using contextual information expressed in terms of these binary relations. Each segment is matched to the segment for which the probability of matching is maximal, given the contextual information. That is, an object $a_i$ in the scene is matched with a node $\omega_\alpha$ in the model if $\omega_\alpha$ maximizes the quantity below:

$$\omega_\alpha = arg\left\{Max_{\omega_\beta}\frac{Q_i(\omega_\beta)}{\sum_{all\ model\ nodes\ \omega_\lambda} Q_i(\omega_\lambda)}\right\} \qquad (4)$$

where

$$Q_i(\omega_\beta) = \prod_{\substack{(all\ objects\ a_j \neq a_i)}} \sum_{\substack{(all\ nodes\ \omega_\gamma\ in\ model)}} p(\mathcal{A}_{ij}|a_j \rightarrow \omega_\gamma, a_i \rightarrow \omega_\beta) \qquad (5)$$

and $p(\mathcal{A}_{ij}|a_j \rightarrow \omega_\gamma, a_i \rightarrow \omega_\beta)$ is the probability density function of the binary measurement $\mathcal{A}_{ij}$ between objects $a_i$ and $a_j$, distributed about the "correct" value conveyed by the corresponding model nodes $\omega_\gamma$ and $\omega_\beta$. The above formulae hold under the assumptions that the unary measurements, from which the binary measurements were derived, were uniformly distributed within their range of possible values, and the prior probability of matching a given object with any model node is a constant. This is a one pass algorithm and is described in detail in [5]. The form of $p(\mathcal{A}_{ij}|a_j \rightarrow \omega_\gamma, a_i \rightarrow \omega_\beta)$ adopted in this application is a Gaussian with standard deviation reflecting the error in the binary measurement.

The overall quality of the match between the derived skeleton and a model skeleton can be assessed by either one of two numbers, one expressing the average probability of matching individual segments (ie the average value of the quantity on the right hand side of 4), and the other assessing the degree of average contextual support for each segment match (ie the average value of the quantity $Q_i(\omega_\alpha)$). The match with the model that gives the highest overall value is chosen as the correct match.

## 4. Experimental results

To demonstrate our ideas we consider the following problem: given the grey images of figure 1 and the database of skeleton models of figure 2, identify the objects.

Figure 3 shows the distance maps obtained with the help of the Hough transform. Notice that these maps are not perfect. The presence of gaps in the boundary create artificial ridges in the distance map as can be seen from figures 3a,b,c. Indeed, one of the main problems of finding line segments with the Hough transform algorithm is that the line segments stop short of junctions due to the poor edge orientation that is calculated from the local information used in the edge detector [8] This means that the boundary of the object contains gaps around the corners, and so extra ridges are produced in the distance map. We therefore expect to have extra features in the skeleton due to missing parts of the object boundary. This may be found even if the object boundary has no rounded corners, and is an artifact of the poor determination of the edge orientation at the edge detection stage. However, our purpose is the shape recognition, and a small number of extra skeleton artifacts is not going to obstruct the process of object recognition, as our matching algorithm has been shown to be robust enough to tolerate much worse distortions.

Figure 4 shows the results of our skeletonization algorithm run on the distance maps. As expected, the skeletons have several extraneous segments due to artifacts of the distance map. In particular, shadows and illumination artifacts have caused a strong linear feature in the skeleton of the third image, (marked with an arrow in figure 4c).

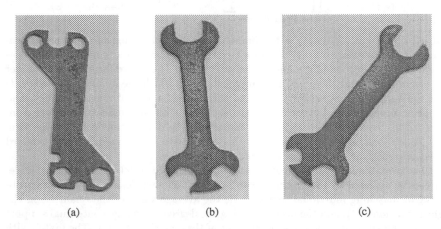

Fig. 1　Grey images of three spanners

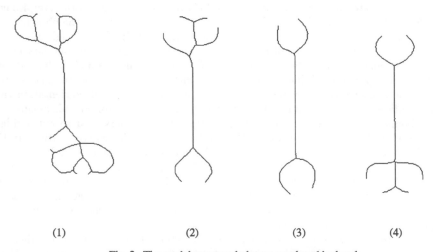

(1)　　　　　　　　　(2)　　　　　　　　　(3)　　　　　　　　　(4)

Fig. 2　The model spanner skeletons, produced by hand

| model | image a | image b | image c |
|:-----:|:-------:|:-------:|:-------:|
| 1 | 0.994/72.5/* | 0.970/11.1 | 0.981/18.0 |
| 2 | 0.985/0.2 | 0.957/9.1 | 0.986/25.1/* |
| 3 | 0.989/1.1 | 0.984/4.6 | 0.962/9.04 |
| 4 | 0.987/2.3 | 0.998/44.3/* | 0.974/13.4 |

Table 1: Results of the match algorithm. The first number indicates the average probability with which an individual object node is matched to a model node. The second number indicates the average value of the support function (equation 19) evaluated for each pair of matched nodes. The star indicates the correct match.

From the skeleton of each object we extract the following three unary measurements concerning each line segment, namely, the absolute orientation of each line segment and the absolute position in the x and y directions of the mid point of each line segment. We use four binary relations, namely the angle between two line segments, the minimum distance between the end-points of two line segments and the orientation and distance of the midpoint of a segment with respect to another segment.

Table 1 above shows the results of our matching algorithm when each of the objects is matched against each of the model skeletons. The same values of the various parameters were used throughout the runs. The first number of each entry represents the average probability with which a particular segment of the object skeleton matches a particular segment of the model skeleton, and the second number represents the average contextual support for each individual node match. (We actually use the average log of the support function to have a more reasonable range of numbers.) It is clear from these results that the correct match (indicated by a * in the table) is picked each time by either of the two numbers as a criterion for the best match. It is also clear that, although the average match probability (which could be expressed as the confidence in the match of individual nodes) is not very sensitive to the correct/incorrect match, the average support function is extremely sensitive, as can be seen from its relative values. Thus, the values of the support function are a better criterion for choosing the best match. In fact, if one deals with a very large object database, it may not be necessary to match each object against each model but instead to examine each model sequentially and stop when a match with support larger than a certain threshold is achieved.

It is worth noting that there was no confusion in picking the right model even between objects (b) and (c), the skeletons of which are only slightly different due to an asymmetry at one end. Indeed, if one was to identify the different spanners from the grey images directly, even with the human vision system, one would have difficulty due to the subtlety of the difference in shape and the different pose. This demonstrates the usefulness of the skeletonization process which is very sensitive even

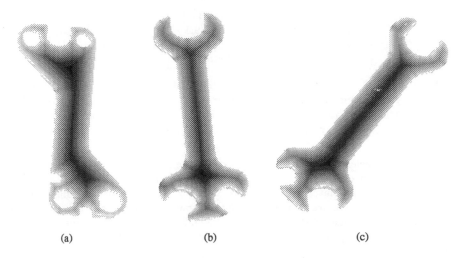

(a)                              (b)                              (c)

Fig. 3  The distance maps of the images in fig. 1 in the corresponding panels

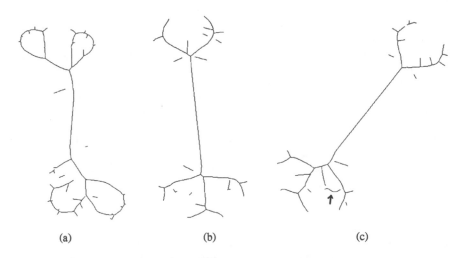

(a)                              (b)                              (c)

Fig. 4  The skeletons of the objects in fig. 1, computed from the
distance maps of fig. 3 in the corresponding panels

to minute shape differences. The skeletonization process has amplified this difference sufficiently to be picked up by the matching stage, which in its turn is sufficiently robust to extraneous/noisy data and sufficiently sensitive to context that did not have any problem in identifying clearly the two different objects. Finally, note that the matching algorithm did not have any problem in identifying the right spanner although the pose of the object spanner was very different from the pose of the model spanner. This is due to the fact that relative relations between the object primitives were used which were independent of the relative position and orientation of the reference frames of the model and the object with respect to which the unary measurements were calculated.

## 5. Conclusions

We have presented here a process for the identification of objects by their skeletons, computed from grey images. The skeletonization method we presented is based on the parametric fitting of the edge boundary of the object with the help of the Hough transform. We have demonstrated that this method preserves the sensitivity of the skeletonization process to subtle shape differences, while at the same time it irons out any minor artifacts and fluctuations caused by inadequate boundary detection either through thresholding or edge detection. The skeletons produced were not perfect, but good enough to be within the tolerance of the robust match algorithm used to identify and classify the objects involved. We argue that this is sufficient as the purpose of a Vision system is the object identification.

For the matching stage we used an algorithm which is based on contextual information expressed in terms of binary relations between the nodes of object primitives and computed from the unary attributes of these primitives. This is a non-iterative one pass algorithm which can be easily implemented in a parallel architecture. This is a major advantage if one is interested in real time implementations. Similarly, other modules of the algorithm are parallelizable to make their real time performance a true possibility. Further, there are other ways by which the algorithm can be extended and improved. For example, one could incorporate circular arcs in the parametric boundary fitting to avoid the sharp corners created by the straight line segments fitted to a curved part of the boundary. One also may use a more sophisticated skeletonization algorithm (eg [1, 3, 2]) to compute the skeleton from the distance map.

Finally, the algorithm can be turned around to be used for the identification of a given object in a cluttered environment. In this case it is not necessary to assume that the object is systematically brighter or darker than the background. The penalty for dropping this assumption will be a distance map which will be computed for all pixels in the image, either object or background pixels, and a cluttered skeleton line drawing, part of which will form the object skeleton to be identified by the matching algorithm.

## 6. References

[1] C Arcelli, L P Cordella and S Levialdi, 1981. From local maxima to connected skeletons. *IEEE Transactions on Pattern Analysis and Machine Intelligence*, 3, pp 134–143.

[2] C Arcelli and G Sanniti di Baja, 1988. Finding local maxima in a pseudo-euclidean distance transform. *Computer Vision, Graphics and Image Processing*, 43, pp 361–367.

[3] C Arcelli and G Sanniti di Baja, 1992. Ridge points in Euclidean distance maps. *Pattern Recognition Letters*, 13, pp 237–243.

[4] E B Goldstein, 1989. *Sensation and perception*, 3rd edition, Wadsworth Publishing Company.

[5] W J Christmas, J Kittler and M Petrou, 1994. Non-iterative contextual correspondance matching. *European Conference on Computer Vision, ECCV'94*.

[6] C R Dyer and A Rosenfeld, 1979. Thinning algorithms for grey scale pictures. PAMI, Vol 1, pp 88–89.

[7] L D Griffin, A C F Colchester and G P Robinson, 1992. Scale and segmentation of grey level images using maximum gradient paths. Image and Vision Computing, Vol 10, pp 389–402.

[8] P L Palmer, J Kittler and M Petrou, 1993. Using focus of attention with the Hough transform for accurate line parameter estimation. *Pattern Recognition*, to appear.

[9] P L Palmer, M Petrou and J Kittler, 1993. Accurate line parameters from an optimising Hough transform for vanishing point detection. *4th International Conference on Computer Vision*, pp 529–539.

[10] K Qian and P Bhattacharya, 1992. A template polynomial approach for image processing and visual recognition. *Pattern Recognition*, Vol 25, pp 1505–1515.

[11] Sha'ashua and Ullman, 1988. *Proceedings of the 2nd International Conference on Computer Vision*, pp 321–327.

[12] S-S Yu and W-H Tsai, 1990. A new thining algorithm for grey scale images by the relaxation technique. *Pattern Recognition*, Vol 23, pp 1067–1076.

# A HIERARCHY OF REPRESENTATIONS FOR CURVES

PAUL L. ROSIN

*Institute for Remote Sensing Applications, Joint Research Centre*
*I-21020 Ispra (VA), Italy*
`paul.rosin@jrc.it`

ABSTRACT

A variety of representations are available for describing the shapes of curves. This paper suggests combining a number of alternative curve representations (e.g. lines, superellipses, codons). These are arranged to form a hierarchy of increasing specificity, ranging from qualitative through to quantitative representations. Different levels provide different trade-offs between the various desirable but mutually incompatible properties of shape representations. Depending on the application, the model and image curves may be represented by the complete hierarchies or by the subset of the representations for each sub-sections that is most appropriate in terms of robustness, flexibility, etc. Each representation needs to be applied at the scales which isolate important structures, and so the curve's "natural" scales are selected by an automated process. This multi-scale analysis produces a hierarchy of parts, and thus a hierarchy of hierarchies is formed.

## 1. Introduction

Many different representations have been suggested or developed for describing the shapes of curves for use in computer vision systems. Examples include straight lines, circular and elliptical arcs, splines, Fourier descriptors, codons, the curvature primal sketch, and scale-space plots of zero-crossings. This paper suggests combining a number of such representations to form a hierarchy of representations.

Hierarchical representations have played an extensive role in Artificial Intelligence. Their advantage is that they provide a more powerful (in terms of flexibility, expressibility, etc.) representation than single flat representations. One of the most common applications of hierarchical representations is for decomposing a model into parts. However, decomposing a model is carried out top-down, with a priori knowledge about the identification and function of its various parts. Since this information is not directly available when analysing an image curve bottom-up it can only be inferred. This is usually performed by analysing the curve at multiple scales. The order of emergence of parts over scale determines their levels in the tree. Of course, this spatial organisation will not always correspond to a functional part decomposition.

Another popular model hierarchy is the specialisation tree. This enables a model to be identified by increasingly precise classifications. These classifications usually require top-down information about the model. It would be difficult to translate this hierarchy into a bottom-up version for describing image curves before they have been assembled into an object and identified from the model database. However, the hierarchy of curve representations proposed here provides a bottom-up equivalent. Whereas the specialisation hierarchy describes the classification of an object in increasing detail, the hierarchy of representations describes the shape of the curve in increasing detail. It should be noted that the increasing classification and shape detail referred to here differ from the increasing spatial detail provided by the decomposition hierarchy.

Despite the popularity of the decomposition (multi-scale) hierarchy for describing curves little attention has been paid to hierarchies of shape representations. Most computer vision systems use a single feature or class of features to represent curves. This paper describes how multiple shape representations can be combined into hierarchies. Since each representation will be applied over multiple scales to form a hierarchy this forms in effect a hierarchy of hierarchies. The benefits that follow from such a scheme are discussed, and its application to image curves is demonstrated.

## 2. Multiple Shape Representations

A number of important criteria exist for assessing curve representations [11]. These include: expressiveness; completeness; robustness under occlusion and noise; invariance under Euclidean transformations; invariance within a generic viewpoint; the number of parameters and the sensitivity to changes of their values; efficiency of computation; and ease of implementation. These criteria allow curve representations to be compared against each other. None will completely and perfectly satisfy all the criteria. In part, this is because some of the criteria are conflicting, and the various representations are compromises biased towards one set of criteria or another. For instance, it is difficult to be both expressive to subtle variations of shape but yet insensitive to noise. The first criterion is important so that specific shapes can be recognised. The second criterion is essential so that shapes of curves extracted from the real world can be matched reliably. Therefore, rather than search for some ideal, perfect shape representation it is more realistic to use a set of sub optimal representations. These can be combined so that the strengths of one can overcome the weaknesses of another.

Much of the variation between curve representations arises from their amount of reliance on metric descriptions. Some representations are extremely precise while others are relatively vague. Based on this observation we will order representations in terms of increasing specialisation or precision. This can also be considered as a progression from qualitative descriptions through to quantitative descriptions. In other contexts a similar range of shape representations have been recently proposed which are ordered in terms of their invariance to transformations [15] and their robustness to noise and poor resolution [3].

Three benefits of combining the various representations are:

• Robustness - The most appropriate curve representation obviously depends on the shape of the model. For example, for a restricted set of models such as geons, a curve representation consisting of just concave/convex/straight arcs would be entirely adequate [4]. However, the representation's appropriateness is also affected by the context of the scene in which the object is viewed. For instance, a circular boundary of an object may be detected by representing the image curve by ellipses. However, if there is inadequate data either due to noise, occlusion, or because the component appears too small, then ellipse fitting is likely to be unreliable and therefore unsuitable

• Flexibility - Combining different curve representations enables a model to be described by a mixture of feature types. This is particularly interesting if different parts of the model are described by representations at different levels of the qualitative/quantitative spectrum. Certain portions may then be described more rigidly than others. For instance, a section might be constrained to be precisely specified by straight lines and elliptical arcs. Conversely, another section could be allowed some variation of its shape parameters (e.g. size, skewness, compactness) by representing it by codons. This approach has some relation to work done to model industrial parts, allowing tolerances for various types of deviations (e.g. variations in translation, orientation, and area between lines and circles). But rather than a precise metric technique, our method is more qualitative.

• Comparability - An additional benefit of the multi-representation scheme is that it enables comparisons to be easily made between different representations. This will be useful if just a simplified description using a single representation is eventually preferred. Although the design criteria detailed above are one way to compare representations, viewing the results of the fitted representations provides a more experimental approach.

## 3. Combining Representations

In order to easily combine different curve representations the various feature primitives should share endpoints. Often the determination of breakpoints when segmenting a curve depends on the type of feature being fitted (e.g. straight lines versus circular arcs [16]) or the particular segmentation algorithm (e.g. recursive subdivision [16] versus seed growing [13]). One possibility would be to use one representation to determine the potential breakpoints for other representations. For instance, this is the case when circular arcs are fitted to curves which have already been segmented into straight lines, and subdivision is only considered at line endpoints [16].

However, rather than preselecting some privileged representation, a more general approach will be taken. Segmentation will be based on the singular points of curvature. These have the advantage that they are intrinsic, local properties, and so are invariant under occlusion and Euclidean transformations of the curve within the plane. Under 3D transformations only the zeros of curvature (and not curvature extrema) are invariant [14]. In addition, curvature has been shown to be a perceptually significant feature for human perception of shape [2]. Because of these properties, and because they contain much information about the curve, the singular points of curvature have been a popular tool for analysing curves [5]. Therefore, an important benefit of using singular points is that it enables some of these representations (e.g. codons) to be incorporated.

One of the problems of analysing the curve based on its singularities of curvature is that curvature measurements are extremely prone to noise. However, this can be overcome if the curve is smoothed as part of the multi-scale processing. Since most curve representations operate at a single scale they can then be applied to the curve at each scale.

## 4. Multiple Model Representations

In addition to representing the image curves in different ways the hierarchical representation approach can be applied to the model boundaries. This would enable a hierarchical matching scheme to be applied to the representation type as well as hierarchical matching of parts (i.e. the multi-scale analysis). Matching between image and model curves would be performed first between the most qualitative representation. The initial potential matches would then be refined and verified by progressing down the tree to more quantitative representations until reliable image feature extraction or adequate image to model feature matching can no longer be performed.

Alternatively, each model part could be described by only a single or a few of the representations from the hierarchy. Several approaches are possible to decide which representation is the most appropriate. First, as mentioned above, is robustness. This suggests that certain representations should be eliminated as unsuitable. For instance, small, short, curved sections of a model will generally not be adequately imaged to provide good ellipse fits. Knowledge of the expected nature of the scene can also be used to influence this decision. Noisy, cluttered outdoor scenes will require more robust representations than well controlled indoor ones. For instance, if occlusion is likely then global features such as Fourier descriptors and moments will perform poorly.

Second, the range of shapes within the object models may eliminate certain representations. This can arise either because the representations are not complete and cannot represent some of the shapes, or because the representation would be unnecessarily cumbersome. For instance, the set of codons defined by Hoffman and Richards [5] are restricted to continuously varying, smooth, closed curves. Curves with straight sections, cusps, or open ends cannot be represented by such codons, and so an alternative representation is required. Another example of an unsuitable representation is the use of straight lines for a model consisting of curved surfaces. Individual curves might have to be represented by many lines, complicating subsequent matching.

The range and similarity of the models to be recognised is also important. If all the models are relatively distinctive then an imprecise, qualitative representation may be sufficient. Otherwise more quantitative representations are necessary to discriminate between more subtle differences in shape. However, only the distinguishing features may need to be represented in this manner. Also discussed above was the issue of flexibility. If some parts of the model are allowed greater variation than others, they can be defined by a qualitative representation rather than a more precise, quantitative representation.

Finally, the requirements of the task of the vision system will indicate the appropriate representations. Certain features can provide more suitable information than others. For instance, concave and convex sections of curves determine the type of adjoining surface curvature (hyperbolic or elliptical), and can be used for reconstructing the 3D shape of the object. Another example is the ellipse which, if it is the projection of a circular feature in the object, determines the pose of the object (with two fold ambiguity).

## 5. Additional Hierarchies and Axes

There are several other hierarchies and ranges or axes related to the representations. Associated with each curve representation will be a suitable method for assessing correspondences between model and image features. Just as the representations range from qualitative to quantitative, the methods for matching will range from high level symbolic ones to more numeric ones. The more qualitative representations will only be described by labels (e.g. concave/convex/straight) and so matching could simply be a test for identical labels or application of a shape deformation grammar [11]. More quantitative representations provide more information, and comparisons will have to be made between their parameters, resulting in a similarity measure (or equivalently a distance in feature space).

We stated that the curve would be analysed at multiple scales, and the various representations independently applied to the curve at each of these scales. However, there are a range of approaches between standard single and multi-scale techniques, such as determining the natural scales [10]. These methods provide a trade-off between compactness and expressiveness of the representation.

Another issue is the manner in which the multiple scales are generated. The most common technique is to smooth the curve, although alternatives include grouping and pyramids. Smoothing can be performed so that the topology of the curve is preserved (e.g. by smoothing along the curve) or is not preserved (e.g. by smoothing the region the curve encloses). Again there is a range of intermediate approaches [6].

## 6. An Example Hierarchy

Figure 1 shows an example of a hierarchy of representations. The two most qualitative representations are formed by segmenting at either the zero crossings of curvature to form

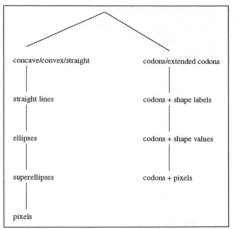

figure 1 - an example of a hierarchy of representations

concave/convex/straight sections, or at the minima of curvature to form codons. Either the restricted set [5] or the extended set [11] of codons can be used. The latter is more complete, and can cope with straight lines, open curves, and cusps, but has the disadvantage that many more codon labels are required. Therefore, whichever is most appropriate to the model data is selected. The concave/convex/straight sections can be described with increasing fidelity by straight lines, ellipses, superellipses, or ultimately, the raw pixel data. Codons can also be described with increasing amounts of detail by incorporating shape labels (e.g. left-skew, very-compact), which can then be quantified (e.g. compactness = 0.68) and augmented by additional metric techniques such as Fourier descriptors and moments. Methods for calculating the codon shape measures of skew, roundness, compactness, length, and orientation are given in [11].

Matching the concave/convex/straight sections or the basic codons would only require checking that they have identical type and shape labels. The codon shape values, and also the lines and ellipses would be compared by calculating the difference in feature space (e.g. the similarity of two straight lines would be some function of their difference in length, orientation, and position). And finally, pixel lists could be compared by correlation techniques.

In this example the curves are only represented at their natural scales [10]. Gaussian smoothing along the curve is performed using Lowe's correction technique [7] to prevent the curve shrinking towards the centre of curvature.

The concave/convex/straight sections are determined as the portions of the curve bounded by the zero crossings of curvature. The codons are terminated by curvature minima, and their labels are identified by examining triples of signed curvature extrema and/or the curvature signs at the ends of the curve [11]. Straight lines are fitted by connecting their

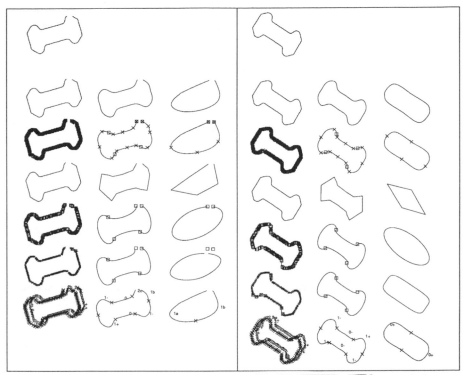

figures 2 & 3 - two views of the gizmo at their natural scales and their segmentation into various features bounding extremal points.

Ellipses are found by performing a least squares fit of the algebraic distance [1] constrained using Lagrange multipliers to go through the bounding extremal points. The above procedure provides a closed form solution, but has the disadvantage that non-elliptical conics (i.e. hyperbolae and parabolae) may also be fitted. In such situations the conic is discarded and a circular arc is fitted instead.

An iterative technique is necessary to fit the superellipses [12]. This involves minimising the sum of the distances between each data point and the superellipse along the ray from the point to the centre of the superellipse. The procedure is initialised using an ellipse if this can be obtained by fitting a conic, or a circle otherwise. In the latter case the initial orientation is determined using central moments.

In the following figures part (a) shows the original curve, (b) the set of automatically determined natural scales at which to describe the curve, (c) the curve at its natural scales marked with the zero crossings (plotted as boxes) and extrema (crosses) of curvature, (d) straight lines drawn through the singularities of curvature, (e) ellipses fitted to the concave/convex sections, (f) superellipses fitted to the concave/convex sections, and (g) the sections between minima labelled as the extended set of codons.

Figures 2 and 3 show two views of the gizmo - a simple manufactured object. The natural scales capture: (i) the fine noise and quantisation effects, (ii) the basic shape without the noise, and (iii) an overall blob. The open curve is slightly distorted as the highest scale. This is due to difficulties in estimating extensions of the curve which are necessary for the convolution process of Gaussian smoothing. At the finest scales the noise creates numerous spurious singularities of curvature, causing the curve to be segmented into many tiny sections which are of little use when performing object recognition. The coarser scales provide more useful descriptions. Since the descriptions are local they are insensitive to the transformation and occlusion of the gizmo. Comparing the representations at the middle scale the lines are less appropriate since the bulges of the gizmo are fragmented. In contrast, each bulge can be represented by a single convex section. In this example, the superelliptic arcs are only slightly more accurate than the ellipses. The codon representation is similar to the arcs although each bulge is broken into its two halves. This is because even though the ends may appear straight there is a slight curvature. Reliably determining straight sections based on curvature is problematic [11]. At the coarsest scale the two sets of descriptions obtained in figures 2 and 3 are very similar with the exception of the codons. This arises because specific labels are generated for curve sections adjoining open boundaries. While this also occurs at the previous scale the curve sections are relatively short with respect to the complete curve. At the coarsest scale *all* the curve sections terminate at an open end of the curve. The improvement of the superelliptical arcs over the elliptical ones is more evident at the coarsest scale. If each section of curve were to be described by a single representation then at the medium scale the ellipses or codons are most suitable. The superellipses do not provide enough improvement in shape fidelity over the ellipses to be worth the additional processing and potential instabilities of the fitting process. However, at the coarsest scale both codons and lines are unsuitable since the former are sensitive to occlusion and the latter do not describe the shape accurately. The ellipses or superellipses are more appropriate.

## 7. Conclusions

We have described how various curve representations can be combined to form a hierarchy of representations. This allows the strengths of one representation to be played off against the weaknesses of another. In addition it facilitates the comparison of different representations which is especially useful for complex shapes where the most appropriate representation is not otherwise immediately obvious. The multi-scale analysis (coarse → fine spatial scale) and multiple representations (qualitative → quantitative shape descriptors) can be thought of as two axes of a two dimensional feature space. The complete feature space is useful for describing shapes rather than just representations at points or lines within the space as is the more common practice.

A feature of the techniques involved in the processing (including the smoothing, scale selection, segmentation, and fitting) is that they are all non-parametric. This is essential if a general purpose, robust system is required that can cope with a variety of data without requiring user intervention for the tweaking of parameters.

The example hierarchy presented here can be extended in many ways. Additional representations could be included, and more degrees of freedom given to the existing representations (e.g. tapering and bending of superellipses). Another approach would be to add representational layers to support higher level groupings of consecutive features. For instance, sequences of straight lines can be combined into corners and arcs [8] and codons can be combined to form various bumps [11]. The current selection mechanism for breakpoints could also be extended to provide greater sensitivity to subtle variations in shape. One approach would be to use singularities of higher order derivatives of curvature.

Finally, it would be of interest to investigate the performance of human visual perception in more detail. Earlier an analogy was made between the top-down specialisation hierarchy and the shape representation hierarchy. Rosch [9] has shown that humans first recognise objects at a specific "basic level" in the specialisation hierarchy, and then continue to categorise them in more detail. Likewise, there may be some support for the hypothesis that object shapes are best initially described at some particular level in the representation hierarchy. Currently we have only informally discussed the suitability of particular curve representations for each model curve section in terms of robustness, discriminability, flexibility, etc. Future work will concentrate on methods for automatically selecting appropriate representations by assessing their suitability.

## 8. References

[1] A. Albano, "Representation of digitized contours in terms of conic arcs and straight-line segments", *CGIP*, Vol 3, pp. 23-33, 1974.

[2] F. Attneave, "Some informational aspects of visual perception", *Psychological Review*, Vol. 61, pp. 183-193, 1954.

[3] A.F. Bobick and R.C. Bolles, "The representation space paradigm of concurrent evolving object descriptions", *Trans. IEEE PAMI*, Vol. 14, pp. 146-156, 1992.

[4] S.J. Dickinson, A.P. Pentland, and A. Rosenfeld, "3-D shape recovery using distributed aspect matching", *Trans. IEEE PAMI*, Vol. 14, pp. 174-198, 1992.

[5] D.D. Hoffman and W.A. Richards, "Representing smooth plane curves for recognition", in *Proc. AAAI*, pp. 5-8, 1982.

[6] B.B. Kimia, A. Tannenbaum and S.W. Zucker, "Entropy scale-space", *Visual Form*,

pp. 333-344, 1992.

[7]    D.G. Lowe, "Organization of smooth image curves at multiple scales" in *Proc. 2nd ICCV*, pp. 558-567, 1988.

[8]    T. Pavlidis and F. Ali, "A hierarchical syntactic shape analyzer", *IEEE Trans. PAMI*, Vol. 1, pp. 2-19, 1979.

[9]    E. Rosch., C.B. Mervis, W.D. Gray, Johnson D.M., and Boyes-Braem P., "Basic objects in natural categories", *Cognitive Psychology*, Vol 8, pp. 382-439, 1976.

[10]   P.L. Rosin, "Representing curves at their natural scales", *Pattern Recognition,* Vol. 25, pp. 1315-1325, 1992.

[11]   P.L. Rosin, "Multi-scale representation and matching of curves using codons", *CVGIP: Graphical Models and Image Processing*, Vol. 55, pp. 286-310, 1993.

[12]   P.L. Rosin and G.A.W. West, "Curve segmentation and representation by superellipses", *Proc. Australian and New Zealand Conference on Intelligent Information Systems*, Perth, Australia, 1993.

[13]   G. Taubin, "Estimation of planar curves, surfaces, and nonplanar space curves defined by implicit equations with applications to edge and range image segmentation", *Trans. IEEE PAMI*, Vol. 13, pp. 1115-1138, 1991.

[14]   A. Verri and A. Yuille, "Some perspective projection invariants", *J. Opt. Soc. Am.*, Vol. 5, pp. 426-431, 1988.

[15]   D. Weinshall, "A hierarchy of invariant representations of 3D shape", in *Proc. Workshop on Qualitative Vision*, 97-106, 1993.

[16]   G.A.W. West and P.L. Rosin, "Techniques for segmenting image curves into meaningful descriptions", *Pattern Recognition*, Vol. 24, pp. 643-652, 1991.

# COMPUTING AND COMPARING DISTANCE-DRIVEN SKELETONS

GABRIELLA SANNITI DI BAJA

*Istituto di Cibernetica, CNR,*
*80072 Arco Felice, Naples, Italy*

and

EDOUARD THIEL

*Equipe TIMC-IMAG, CERMO BP 53*
*38041 Grenoble Cedex 9, France*

## ABSTRACT

A unified distance-driven algorithm is presented to extract the skeleton of a digital pattern from its distance map. The algorithm equally runs whichever distance is selected to compute the distance map, among four commonly used path-based distance functions. The resulting skeletons are compared on a large set of $512 \times 512$ input pictures, in terms of reversibility and computation time.

## 1. Introduction

Distance maps, computed according to different distance functions, can be adopted to guide pattern skeletonization. On the discrete plane, path-based distances are commonly used, where the distance between two pixels is defined as the length of a shortest path linking them. The degree of approximation to the Euclidean distance depends on the number of different unit moves permitted along the path, and on the weights used to measure them. City-block distance (one unit move, unitary weight) and chessboard distance (two unit moves, both with unitary weight)) [1] are a natural choice on the square grid, but roughly approximate the Euclidean distance. Better approximations are obtained by using weighted distance functions allowing two (or three) differently weighted unit moves [2-5].

Skeletonization algorithms driven by the city-block distance $d_1$, the chessboard distance $d_{1,1}$, the two-weight distance $d_{3,4}$ and the three-weight distance $d_{5,7,11}$ can be respectively found in [6-9].

In this paper we provide a unique skeletonization algorithm equally running, whichever among the previous four distance functions is used to build the distance map DM of the pattern to be skeletonized. After computing the DM, the skeletal pixels (i.e. the centres of the maximal discs, the saddle points and the linking pixels) are identified and marked on it, during one sequential raster scan inspection of the DM. An unmarking process is then accomplished on the DM, so as to reduce to unit width the set of the skeletal pixels; finally, an unmarking-and-shifting process is done to prune the skeleton and to improve its aesthetics, during which the marker is removed from a skeletal pixel or is shifted to some of its non marked neighbors. Unmarking and unmarking-and-shifting can be accomplished by directly accessing on the DM the skeletal pixels, whose coordinates can be recorded at a limited memory expense. The performance of the algorithm when using each of the four distances is evaluated by comparing the results obtained on a large set of 512×512 input pictures, in terms of reversibility and computation time.

## 2. The distance driven skeletonization algorithm

Let $F=\{1\}$ and $B=\{0\}$ be the two sets constituting a binary picture digitized on the square grid. We select the 8-metric for F and the 4-metric for B. We suppose F constituted by a single 8-connected component, while no assumption is done on the number of 4-connected components of B.

The distance map DM of F with respect to B is a replica of F, where the pixels are labeled with their distance from B. Each pixel of DM can be interpreted as the centre of a disc fitting F, the label of the pixel being related to the radius length. A pixel is centre of a maximal disc if the associated disc is maximal, i.e. is not included by any other single disc of F.

The skeleton S of F is a subset of F characterized by the following properties: 1) S has the same number of 8-connected components as F, and each component of S has the same number of 4-connected holes as the corresponding component of F. 2) S is centred within F. 3) S is the unit-wide union of simple 8-arcs and 8-curves. 4) The pixels of S are labeled with their distance from B. 5) S includes almost all the centres of the maximal discs of F (complete inclusion is not compatible with fulfilment of property 3).

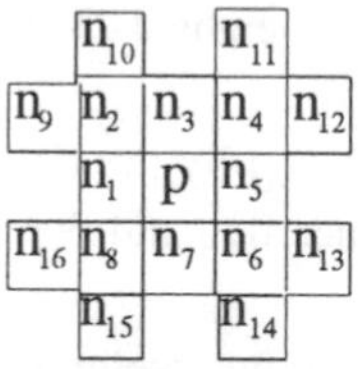

Figure 1. The set N(p).

Generally, the neighborhood $N(p)$ of a pixel p includes the neighbors $n_i(p)$ of p, i.e. the pixels that can be reached with a unit move from p. Accordingly, $N(p)$ should include from a minimum of 4 pixels, when $d_1$ is used, up to 16 pixels, when $d_{5,7,11}$ is used. In this paper, N(p) includes all the 16 pixels surrounding p, as shown in Figure 1. The $n_i(p)$ are also called horizontal/vertical neighbors, for i={1, 3, 5, 7}; diagonal neighbors, for i={2, 4, 6, 8}; and knight neighbors, for i={9, 10,..., 16}. The neighbors of $n_i(p)$ are indicated as $n_k(n_i)$ (k=1, 2,...,16). In the following, p will be used to indicate both the pixel and its associated label.

## 2.1 Distance map computation

To compute the DM, the sequential local operations $f_1(p)$ and $f_2(p)$ are respectively applied to every p in F, during a forward and a backward raster inspection of the picture.

$$f_1(p)= \min\{\min_{i=\{1,3\}} [n_i(p)+w_1], \min_{i=\{2,4\}} [n_i(p)+w_2], \min_{i=\{9,10,11,12\}} [n_i(p)+w_3]\}$$

$$f_2(p)= \min\{p, \min_{i=\{5,7\}} [n_i(p)+w_1], \min_{i=\{6,8\}} [n_i(p)+w_2], \min_{i=\{13,14,15,16\}} [n_i(p)+w_3]\}$$

The values to be used for $w_1$, $w_2$, and $w_3$, so as to cause correct propagation from p to the pixels $n_i(p)$ which are neighbors of p according to the selected distance function, are given in Table 1, where ∞ stands for a sufficiently high value.

Table 1

|            | $w_1$ | $w_2$ | $w_3$ |
|------------|-------|-------|-------|
| $d_1$-DM   | 1     | ∞     | ∞     |
| $d_{1,1}$-DM | 1   | 1     | ∞     |
| $d_{3,4}$-DM | 3   | 4     | ∞     |
| $d_{5,7,11}$-DM | 5 | 7   | 11    |

Table 2

| label | h/v     | d       | k       |
|-------|---------|---------|---------|
| p     | $p+w_1$ | $p+w_2$ | $p+w_3$ |

Table 3 ($d_{3,4}$-DM case)

| label | h/v | d | k |
|-------|-----|---|---|
| 3     | 4   | 6 |   |
| 6     | 8   | 9 |   |

Table 5

|            | $v_1$ | $v_2$ | $v_3$ |
|------------|-------|-------|-------|
| $d_1$-DM   | 2     | 3     | -1    |
| $d_{1,1}$-DM | 2   | 3     | -1    |
| $d_{3,4}$-DM | 3   | 4     | -1    |
| $d_{5,7,11}$-DM | 5 | 7   | 11    |

Table 4 ($d_{5,7,11}$-DM case)

| label | h/v | d  | k  |
|-------|-----|----|----|
| 5     | 7   | 10 | 14 |
| 7     | 11  |    |    |
| 10    | 14  | 15 | 20 |
| 14    | 18  | 20 |    |
| 16    |     | 22 |    |
| 18    | 22  |    | 28 |
| 20    |     | 26 | 30 |
| 21    |     | 27 |    |
| 25    | 28  | 30 | 35 |
| 27    |     | 33 |    |
| 29    | 33  |    |    |
| 31    |     | 37 |    |
| 32    |     | 38 |    |
| 35    | 39  | 41 | 45 |
| 38    |     | 44 |    |
| 39    |     | 45 |    |
| 40    | 44  |    |    |
| 42    |     | 48 |    |
| 46    |     | 52 |    |
| 49    |     | 55 |    |
| 53    |     | 59 |    |
| 60    |     | 66 |    |

## 2.2 Centre of maximal disc detection

With reference to the four distance functions adopted in this paper, centres of maximal discs can be detected by using local criteria involving suitable label comparisons [9,10], or by resorting to the use of look-up tables [11]. We prefer the second possibility, which makes the algorithm more homogeneous. Given a distance function, the corresponding look-up table has a number of entries, representing the labels occurring in the selected DM. Each entry p is associated a record containing as many fields as many are the different unit moves, which orderly identify the minimal label that the neighbors of p should have to prevent p to be centre of a maximal disc. A pixel p of the DM is marked as a centre of a maximal disc if its neighbors are labeled less than the values stored in the corresponding fields of the record associated to p.

The look-up table for the selected DM is built in during the distance map computation. Generally, the fields of a record are filled in by following the rule shown in Table 2, where h/v, d and k respectively refer to the horizontal/vertical, diagonal and knight neighbors of p. A few exceptions occur in the $d_{3,4}$-DM and $d_{5,7,11}$-DM case, and the records for which the filling rule of Table 2 does not apply have to be memorized . They are given in Table 3 and Table 4, respectively. Blank cells in these Tables correspond to fields where the filling rule correctly applies.

## 2.3 Saddle point detection

Saddle points constitute a ridge between two subsets of the DM, including pixels with higher label. Most of the saddle points are centres of maximal discs; the remaining ones are the pixels p for which at least one of the following conditions is satisfied:

(1) The set $\{n_1(p), n_2(p), ..., n_8(p)\}$ includes two (4-connected) components of pixels having label smaller than p;

(2) The set $\{n_1(p), n_2(p), ..., n_8(p)\}$ includes two (8-connected) components of pixels having label larger than p;

(3) The pixels of one of the triples $(n_1(p), n_2(p), n_3(p))$, $(n_3(p), n_4(p), n_5(p))$, $(n_5(p), n_6(p), n_7(p))$, $(n_7(p), n_8(p), n_1(p))$ are all labeled as p;

To count the 4-connected and the 8-connected components in Conditions (1) and (2), the crossing number [12] and connectivity number [13] are respectively used. Condition (3) is checked for all the pixels of the DM when $w_1=1$, only for the pixels labeled $w_1$, otherwise.

## 2.4 Linking pixel detection

Generally, the set including the centres of the maximal discs and the saddle points is not connected. The linking pixels, necessary to gain skeleton connectedness, are identified by growing paths through the ascending gradient in the DM. Path growing is attempted in correspondence of every marked pixel p of the DM (centre of maximal disc or saddle point). $N(p)$ includes at most two 8-connected components of pixels labeled more than $p$, from which an ascending path can be started. For each component, the neighbor $n_i(p)$ in correspondence of which the gradient assumes the maximal value is marked as the first linking pixel in the path. Then, the $n_k(n_i)$ are inspected to recursively identify the next linking pixel. (Note that only one component of pixels labeled more than $n_i(p)$ is likely to exist.) Path growing proceeds, through the ascending gradient, as far as pixels providing a positive gradient are found. For any $n_i(p)$ labeled more than $p$, the gradient is: $grad_i = [n_i(p) - p]/v_k$, where the $v_k$ assume the values indicated in Table 5.

Negative values are assigned to the $v_k$ corresponding to the unit moves which are not permitted in the selected DM. In the $d_1$-DM and $d_{1,1}$-DM cases, the values of the positive $v_k$ are different from the values of the $w_k$ used to compute the DM; this is done both to force the creation of 8-connected paths, and to avoid path thickening and fan creation. In the $d_{3,4}$-DM, at most a pair of neighbors $n_i(p)$ (for i=1, 2,..., 8), 4-adjacent to each other, equally maximize the gradient. When this is the case, only the $n_i(p)$ with i odd is accepted in the path, to avoid path thickening. In the $d_{5,7,11}$-DM case, three pixels could equally maximize the gradient: a horizontal/vertical neighbor, its 4-adjacent diagonal neighbor, and the intermediate knight neighbor (e.g., $n_1$, $n_2$ and $n_9$). To have an 8-connected path and to avoid path thickening, we accept as linking pixels both the knight neighbor and the horizontal/vertical neighbor. If only the knight neighbor maximizes the gradient, the horizontal/vertical neighbor and diagonal neighbor on its sides are checked, and the pixel, out of these two, providing the largest gradient is also accepted in the path. Whenever the knight neighbor is accepted as a linking pixel, path growing continues only from it.

## 2.5 Spurious hole filling

Spurious loops are created in the set of the skeletal pixels when two paths, aligned along parallel directions, are so close to each other that pixels in a path are diagonal neighbors of pixels in the other path. In the $d_1$-DM, $d_{1,1}$-DM and $d_{3,4}$-DM, the only possibility to create spurious loops occurs in presence of pairs of diagonally oriented paths. The enclosed spurious holes are one-pixel in size. In the $d_{5,7,11}$-DM, directions constituted by runs of two horizontal/vertical pixels are created during path growing, when the knight neighbor is accepted as a linking pixel. If two paths of this type are very close to each other, one more possibility exists to create spurious loops. The enclosed spurious holes are two-pixel in size.

Spurious holes have to be identified and filled, i.e., their pixels have to be marked as skeletal pixels. Hole filling does not create excessive thickening of the set of the skeletal pixels, since only a few sparse spurious holes generally exist. An unmarked pixel $p$ belongs to a spurious hole and is marked as skeletal pixel, if any of the following conditions is satisfied during a forward raster scan inspection of the DM:

(1) all the horizontal/vertical $n_i(p)$ are marked as skeletal pixels;

(2) $n_5(p)$ is not marked, while $n_1(p)$, $n_3(p)$, $n_4(p)$, $n_6(p)$, $n_7(p)$ and $n_5(n_5)$ are marked;

(3) $n_7(p)$ is not marked, while $n_1(p)$, $n_3(p)$, $n_5(p)$, $n_6(p)$, $n_8(p)$ and $n_7(n_7)$ are marked;

## 2.6 Reduction to unit width

Reduction to unit width of the set of the skeletal pixels can be obtained by applying topology preserving removal operations, designed in such a way to avoid excessive shortening of the skeleton branches. Reduction to unit width is here referred to as an "unmarking" process since we remove from any deletable pixel the marker, previously ascribed to distinguish it from the non-skeletal pixels of the DM.

To favor skeleton centrality within the figure, unmarking is accomplished within two inspections of the set of the skeletal pixels. The pixels which are 4-internal in the set of the skeletal pixels are preliminarily identified. They are prevented from unmarking during the first inspection. All the marked pixels undergo the unmarking process, during the second inspection.

A marked pixel p is unmarked during the first (the second) inspection of the set of the skeletal pixels, if it satisfies the following Condition (1) (Conditions (1) and (2)):

(1)    At least a triple of neighbors $n_i(p)$, $n_{i+2}(p)$, $n_{i+5}(p)$ exists (i=1, 3, 5, 7, addition modulo 8), such that $n_i(p)$ and $n_{i+2}(p)$ are marked, while $n_{i+5}(p)$ is not marked;

(2)    At least one horizontal/vertical neighbor of p is not marked;

Condition (1) prevents both altering the connectedness, and shortening skeleton branches, while Condition (2) prevents creation of holes in the set of the skeletal pixels.

## 2 .7 Pruning

Pruning is accomplished to simplify the skeleton structure by deleting peripheral branches (i.e. branches delimited by end points) that do not correspond to figure protrusions, significant in the problem domain.

To keep under control the loss of information caused by branch deletion, a criterion based on the relevance of the protrusion associated with the skeleton branch is used. A branch can be safely pruned if a negligible difference exists between the two sets recovered by applying the reverse distance transformation to the skeleton and to the pruned skeleton, respectively. Such a difference can be evaluated in terms of labels and relative distance of the extremes of the (portion of) skeleton branch to be pruned. The difference can then be compared with a suitable threshold to decide about pruning [8]. We generalize the expression used in [8], in such a way that it can be used whichever of the four distance functions is considered. Moreover, we do not limit pruning only to the branches which are peripheral in the initial skeleton.

Let H and D be the horizontal/vertical and diagonal unit moves, along a minimal length 8-connected path linking two pixels p and q. It is $H=(2d_{1,1}-d_1)$ and $D=(d_1-d_{1,1})$.

By taking into account that when $d_{5,7,11}$ is used any pair of (horizontal/vertical, diagonal) moves is substituted by a knight move, it is immediate to verify that the distance between p and q can be computed as follows:

$d_1 = H + 2D$ $\qquad\qquad\qquad$ $d_{1,1} = H + D$

$d_{3,4} = 3H + 4D$ $\qquad\qquad$ $d_{5,7,11} = 5H + 7D + (11\text{-}7\text{-}5) \times \min(H,D)$

A unique expression can be used to compute any of the four above distances:

$$d = w_1 H + w_2 D + \text{Flag} \times \min(H,D)$$

where Flag= 0 in the $d_1$-DM, $d_{1,1}$-DM, and $d_{3,4}$-DM cases, while Flag= -1 in the $d_{5,7,11}$-DM case.

Let K be the maximum number of peripheral rows and/or columns one accepts to lose in recovery due to branch deletion. Let p be the end point of a peripheral skeleton branch, and q and any other pixel on that skeleton branch. Pruning from p to q, q excluded, can be safely accomplished in the limits of the adopted tolerance if:

$$p - q + d \le K \times w_1$$

The most internal pixel up to which pruning can be accomplished is identified by checking the above condition on every pixel q, found while tracing the peripheral skeleton branch originating from p.

When a branch point is transformed into an end point, due to deletion of all the peripheral branches sharing it, a new peripheral branch is originated. This branch can be pruned without causing a summation effect in the loss of figure recovery. To this purpose, the information relative to the starting point(s) of the branch(es) is propagated through the branch(es) while performing pruning. In this way, the relevance of the entire protrusion mapped in the union of the current peripheral skeleton branch with the neighboring, already pruned, skeleton branches can be evaluated.

## 2.8 Beautifying

To have a skeleton whose shape is more appealing, the zigzags due to noise on the contour of F and/or to the process done to obtain a unit wide skeleton should be straightened. The beautifying process is accomplished by shifting the marker from a pixel p having just two marked neighbors $n_i(p)$ and $n_{i+2}(p)$ (i=2, 4, 6, 8; addition modulo 8) to its neighbor $n_{i+1}(p)$. Shifting the marker from p to $n_{i+1}(p)$ may cause either of $n_i(p)$ and $n_{i+2}(p)$ to become deletable. These neighbors of p are checked and possibly removed.

## 3. Discussion and Conclusion

In this paper, we have introduced a unified scheme to extract the labeled skeleton from the distance map, computed according to four commonly used path-based distance functions. The algorithm can be extended to treat DM computed by using other path-based distance functions, where the weights are different from the ones we have selected. Using different distance functions provides differently structured distance maps and, accordingly, different skeletons. Thus, one can select the distance function more suited to the specific needs. Moreover, the comparison among the different skeletons associated to the same figure by different distance functions is facilitated.

The skeletonization algorithm can be summarized as follows:

Step 1. Compute the distance map DM, and build the look-up table. (Two raster scans)

Step 2. Mark on the DM the skeletal pixels, i.e., the centres of the maximal discs, the saddle points and the linking pixels. (One raster scan interleaved with a path growing process)

Step 3. Mark on the DM the pixels inside the spurious loops of the set of the skeletal pixels and record the coordinates of all the marked pixels. (One raster scan)

Step 4. Unmark on the DM suitable skeletal pixels, so as to obtain the unit wide skeleton (The skeletal pixels are directly accessed)

Step 5. Unmark on the DM suitable skeletal pixels, so as to perform pruning and beautifying (The skeleton is traced starting from the end points)

At the end of the process, the skeleton is the set of pixels marked on the DM.

The computational cost of the algorithm is modest since only four raster scan inspections are necessary whichever is the thickness of the pattern to be skeletonized. However, the computation time depends on the ratio between the pixels of F and B, and on the adopted distance function.

The algorithm has been checked on a large number of patterns in $512 \times 512$ binary pictures. A set of 20 differently structured sample patterns is shown in Figure 2. From top left to bottom right the set includes: elongated rubber joints for car windows, rather free from digitization noise (p01-p07); complex clusters of differently sized blobs mutually overlapping (p08-p11); artificially drawn patterns characterized by remarkable thickness and significant contour curvature variations (p12-p15); and thin, but intertwined in a rather complex way, wood fibres in paper pulp (p16-p20).

Some results, pertaining the previous sample patterns are shown in Table 6. The last row refers to the mean value computed on the sample set. The second column (F/B) gives the percentage ratio between the number of pixels in the foreground F and in the background B. The successive 16 columns are grouped in quadruplets, respectively pertaining the $d_1$-DM, $d_{1,1}$-DM, $d_{3,4}$-DM, and $d_{5,7,11}$-DM cases. For each quadruplet, the first column (F/S) gives the ratio between the pixels of the foreground to the pixels of the skeleton and indicates the compression ratio measured in number of pixels; the second column (t) shows the computation time measured in seconds on a SUN Sparcstation 2; the third column (bp) and the fourth column (ap) indicate the percentage ratio to the pixels of F of the pixels which are not recovered starting from the skeleton before and after the

Table 6

| | F/B | d₁ | | | | d₁,₁ | | | | d₃,₄ | | | | d₅,₇,₁₁ | | | |
|---|---|---|---|---|---|---|---|---|---|---|---|---|---|---|---|---|---|
| | | F/S | t | bp | ap | F/S | t | bp | ap | F/S | t | bp | ap | F/S | t | bp | ap |
| p01 | 12.13 | 41.72 | 6.46 | 0.52 | 1.09 | 41.34 | 6.28 | 1.31 | 2.30 | 45.35 | 6.17 | 0.24 | 1.44 | 45.35 | 6.92 | 0.15 | 1.13 |
| p02 | 9.70 | 39.14 | 7.17 | 0.50 | 1.35 | 39.20 | 5.71 | 1.06 | 2.85 | 40.57 | 5.81 | 0.26 | 1.20 | 41.43 | 6.38 | 0.12 | 1.38 |
| p03 | 8.90 | 28.12 | 6.17 | 0.86 | 1.85 | 27.46 | 5.55 | 1.26 | 2.71 | 28.68 | 5.65 | 0.45 | 1.43 | 29.00 | 6.25 | 0.18 | 1.36 |
| p04 | 7.46 | 35.35 | 5.05 | 0.60 | 1.74 | 34.24 | 5.33 | 1.24 | 3.42 | 35.48 | 5.40 | 0.21 | 1.95 | 35.74 | 5.94 | 0.10 | 1.64 |
| p05 | 20.54 | 43.18 | 8.36 | 0.61 | 1.06 | 44.32 | 8.14 | 0.85 | 2.16 | 44.43 | 7.54 | 0.33 | 1.15 | 44.32 | 8.69 | 0.25 | 0.82 |
| p06 | 16.42 | 45.41 | 8.14 | 0.72 | 1.36 | 46.49 | 7.17 | 0.86 | 2.03 | 47.88 | 6.97 | 0.44 | 1.10 | 47.99 | 7.90 | 0.27 | 0.81 |
| p07 | 11.65 | 43.37 | 6.15 | 0.53 | 1.42 | 43.37 | 6.17 | 1.07 | 2.82 | 45.03 | 6.07 | 0.41 | 1.48 | 45.85 | 6.84 | 0.21 | 1.38 |
| p08 | 55.95 | 18.18 | 15.28 | 0.57 | 11.33 | 20.98 | 17.12 | 1.94 | 18.09 | 22.58 | 15.31 | 0.73 | 12.72 | 22.79 | 17.73 | 1.06 | 11.91 |
| p09 | 58.89 | 16.05 | 15.84 | 0.58 | 10.25 | 17.84 | 17.69 | 1.85 | 15.11 | 18.71 | 15.73 | 0.68 | 10.34 | 18.79 | 18.58 | 0.97 | 9.78 |
| p10 | 56.37 | 16.18 | 15.40 | 0.65 | 11.72 | 18.14 | 17.23 | 2.07 | 17.12 | 19.13 | 15.30 | 0.77 | 11.66 | 19.33 | 18.07 | 1.04 | 11.03 |
| p11 | 59.25 | 13.24 | 17.69 | 0.91 | 10.76 | 14.36 | 21.08 | 2.37 | 14.93 | 14.56 | 16.01 | 1.04 | 10.33 | 14.73 | 19.13 | 1.25 | 10.08 |
| p12 | 59.92 | 76.65 | 16.91 | 0.07 | 0.20 | 75.80 | 16.54 | 0.22 | 0.65 | 74.05 | 14.08 | 0.05 | 0.35 | 76.13 | 19.82 | 0.03 | 0.30 |
| p13 | 63.86 | 73.58 | 17.50 | 0.00 | 0.67 | 73.90 | 17.57 | 0.06 | 0.96 | 78.04 | 14.71 | 0.00 | 1.21 | 105.54 | 18.30 | 0.00 | 1.40 |
| p14 | 48.05 | 72.60 | 12.40 | 0.19 | 0.34 | 80.23 | 13.99 | 0.48 | 0.65 | 77.08 | 12.04 | 0.14 | 0.40 | 78.23 | 16.58 | 0.08 | 0.28 |
| p15 | 30.24 | 47.67 | 11.86 | 0.33 | 0.77 | 42.32 | 10.23 | 0.76 | 1.31 | 43.65 | 9.22 | 0.27 | 0.70 | 43.65 | 11.04 | 0.12 | 0.49 |
| p16 | 10.36 | 5.18 | 10.66 | 7.34 | 13.34 | 5.30 | 7.24 | 12.81 | 20.12 | 5.21 | 8.27 | 6.53 | 11.58 | 5.22 | 7.29 | 6.59 | 11.62 |
| p17 | 10.21 | 4.29 | 6.45 | 8.93 | 15.21 | 4.41 | 6.44 | 16.27 | 25.33 | 4.30 | 6.99 | 7.48 | 13.17 | 4.31 | 7.45 | 7.58 | 13.22 |
| p18 | 9.23 | 3.83 | 6.77 | 10.65 | 19.73 | 3.97 | 6.28 | 17.16 | 28.75 | 3.85 | 6.62 | 8.99 | 17.54 | 3.85 | 7.33 | 9.05 | 17.57 |
| p19 | 10.32 | 9.58 | 5.81 | 3.57 | 6.38 | 9.78 | 6.08 | 5.58 | 10.48 | 9.65 | 6.29 | 2.42 | 5.60 | 9.69 | 7.01 | 2.59 | 5.37 |
| p20 | 9.48 | 4.04 | 5.78 | 9.02 | 11.67 | 4.08 | 6.16 | 15.24 | 19.72 | 4.04 | 6.47 | 7.43 | 9.84 | 4.05 | 7.17 | 7.48 | 9.89 |
| avg. | 28.45 | 31.86 | 10.29 | 2.36 | 6.11 | 32.37 | 10.40 | 4.22 | 9.58 | 33.11 | 9.53 | 1.94 | 5.76 | 34.79 | 11.22 | 1.96 | 5.57 |

pruning step, respectively. The values in (bp) and (ap) give a measure of skeleton reversibility.

By looking at the mean values, we note that the computation time is a bit larger in the $d_{5,7,11}$-DM case, as expected due to the need of performing operations on a larger number of arguments. The larger time required in the $d_{1,1}$-DM case with respect to the remaining two cases, is mostly due to the generally larger thickness of the set of the skeletal pixels. (This can be appreciated by noting that the ratio bp is higher in the $d_{1,1}$-DM case, where a remarkable number of centres of maximal discs have to be canceled to reduce to unit width the set of the skeletal pixels.)

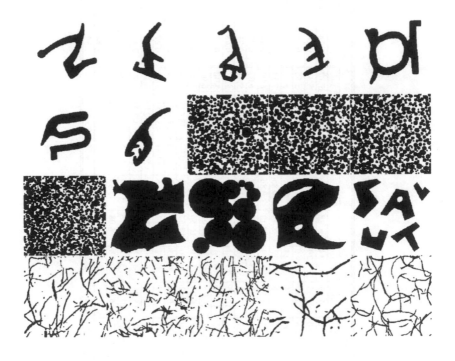

Figure 2. The set of sample patterns in $512 \times 512$ binary pictures.

A reasonable compromise between computation time and skeleton reversibility is obtained in the $d_{3,4}$-DM case. This skeleton also shows a good stability under pattern rotation, translation or scaling. Thus, the $d_{3,4}$-skeleton can be generally employed for applications. The $d_{5,7,11}$-skeleton has to be preferred when a considerable accuracy is required, since its geometrical features very closely reflect pattern features; the slightly

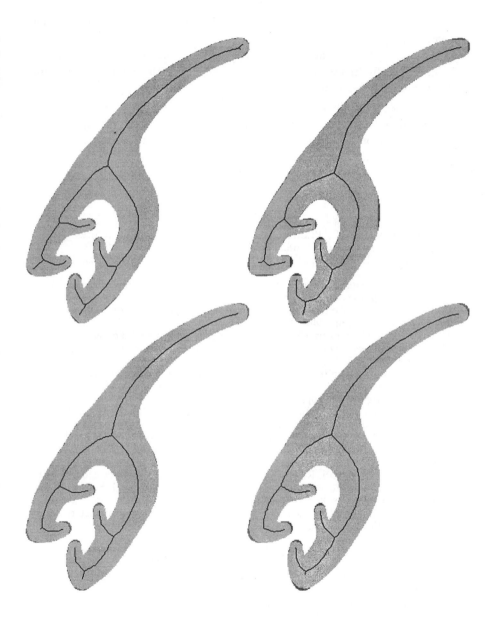

Figure 3. Skeletons driven by $d_1$, $d_{1,1}$, $d_{3,4}$, and $d_{5,7,11}$ (from top left to bottom right).

higher cost necessary for its computation is repaid by the higher stability degree under isometric transformations of the pattern.

In Figure 3, the performance of the skeletonization algorithm driven by the four different distance functions is shown on the test pattern p07. The four frames refer, from top left to bottom right, respectively to the $d_1$, $d_{1,1}$, $d_{3,4}$ and $d_{5,7,11}$ case. The threshold adopted during the pruning step is $2 \times w_1$. The skeleton (black pixels) is shown superimposed on the input pattern (grey pixels). To point out that the representative power of the skeleton is not remarkably biased by the unmarking process, the pixels of the input pattern which are not recovered starting from the pruned skeleton are shown in dark grey.

## References

1   A. Rosenfeld and J.L. Pfaltz, Distance funcions on digital pictures, *Pattern Recognition*, 1, pp. 33-61, 1968.

2   J. Hilditch and D. Rutovitz, Chromosome recognition, *Ann. New York Acad. Sci.*, 157, pp. 339-364, 1969.

3   G. Borgefors, Distance transformations in arbitrary dimensions, *Comput. Vision Graphics Image Process.*, 27, pp. 321-345, 1984.

4   G. Borgefors, Distance transformation in digital images, *Comput. Vision Graphics Image Process.*, 34, pp. 344-371, 1986.

5   E. Thiel and A.Montanvert, Chamfer masks: discrete distance functions, geometrical properties and optimization, *Proc. 11th Int. Conf. on Pattern Recognition*, The Hague, pp. 244-247, 1992.

6   C. Arcelli and G. Sanniti di Baja, A one-pass two-operations process to detect the skeletal pixels on the 4-distance transform, *IEEE Trans. on Pattern Analysis and Machine Intelligence*, 11, pp. 411-414, 1989.

7   C. Arcelli and G. Sanniti di Baja, A width-independent fast thinning algorithm, *IEEE Trans. on Pattern Analysis and Machine Intelligence*, 7, pp. 463-474, 1985.

8   G. Sanniti di Baja, Well-shaped, stable and reversible skeletons from the (3,4)-distance transform, *Journal of Visual Communication and Image Representation*, in press (1994).

9   C. Arcelli and M. Frucci, Reversible skeletonization by (5,7,11)-erosion, in *Visual Form Analysis and Recognition*, C.Arcelli, L.P.Cordella and G. Sanniti di Baja, Eds., Plenum, New York, pp. 21-28, 1992.

10  C. Arcelli and G. Sanniti di Baja, Weighted distance transforms: a characterization, in *Image Analysis and Processing II*, V. Cantoni et al. Eds., Plenum Press, pp. 205-211, 1988.

11  G. Borgefors, Centres of maximal discs in the 5-7-11 distance transform, *Proc. 8th Scandinavian Conf. on Image Analysis*, pp. 105-111, 1993.

12  D. Rutovitz, "Pattern recognition", *Journal of Royal Statist. Soc.*, 129, Series A, pp. 504-530, 1966.

13  S.Yokoi, J.l. Toriwaki, T. Fukumura, An analysis of topological properties of digitized binary pictures using local features, *Comput. Graph. Image Processing*, 4, pp. 63-73, 1975.

# MODAL SHAPE COMPARISON

STAN SCLAROFF and ALEX P. PENTLAND

*Perceptual Computing Section, The Media Laboratory*
*Massachusetts Institute of Technology*
*20 Ames St., Cambridge MA 02139, USA*

## ABSTRACT

Recently we proposed a new method for establishing correspondences and computing canonical descriptions, based on the idea of describing objects by their generalized symmetries, as defined by the object's vibration or deformation modes. In this paper we extend this method to the problems of shape alignment, description, and comparison. Object similarities are computed in terms of the amounts of modal deformation energy needed to align the objects. We also introduce a physically-motivated linear-combinations-of-models paradigm, where the computer synthesizes an image of the object in terms of a weighted combination of modally deformed prototype images. Examples of recognizing hand tools and airplanes are shown.

## 1. Introduction

Correspondence is often defined as the problem of matching points on two objects (or two views of one object) and has proven to be a very difficult problem. If, however, the points were given in body-centered coordinates rather than Cartesian coordinates, the problem would be nearly trivial. That is, it is easy to match up the bottom-left points on two objects once given the up-down and left-right axes of the two objects. This suggests that the best way to match two sets of feature points is to first compute a robust body-centered coordinate frame for each object.

An object's modes form such a coordinate frame. Modes are the eigenvectors for a shape's finite element model, and form an orthogonal object-centered coordinate system for describing feature locations in terms of a shape's natural deformations. In [4] we introduced *modal matching*, a correspondence technique that is based on matching a shape's low-order vibration modes. The resulting correspondence algorithm is relatively robust even in the presence of affine deformation, nonrigid deformation, local shape perturbation, or noise.

In this paper we extend our method to the problems of shape alignment, description, and comparison. Given correspondences between many of the feature points on two objects, we would like to measure their difference in shape in terms of modal deformations. Because the modal framework decomposes deformations into an orthogonal set, we can selectively measure rigid-body differences, or low-order projective-like deformations, or deformations that are primarily local. Consequently, we will be able to compare objects in a very flexible and general manner. We will demonstrate this method on examples of recognizing and categorizing images of airplanes and hand tools.

## 2. Background

Shape correspondence has previously been formulated as an equilibrium problem, which has the attractive feature of allowing integration of physical constraints [1, 3, 5, 6, 9]. To find correspondences, we first imagine that the collection of feature points in one image is attached by springs to an elastic body. Under the load exerted by these springs, the elastic body will deform to match the shape outlined by the set of feature points. If we repeat this procedure in each image, we can obtain a feature-to-feature correspondence by noting which points project to corresponding locations on the two elastic bodies.

### 2.1. Finite Element Method and Mode Superposition Analysis

A common numerical approach for solving equilibrium problems of this sort is the *finite element method* (FEM). The major advantage of the FEM is that it uses the Galerkin method of surface interpolation. In Galerkin's method, we set up a system of polynomial shape functions that relate the displacement of a single point to the relative displacements of the finite element nodes:

$$\mathbf{u}(\mathbf{x}) = \mathbf{H}(\mathbf{x})\mathbf{U}, \tag{1}$$

where $\mathbf{H}$ is the interpolation matrix, $\mathbf{x}$ is the local coordinate of a point in the element where we want to know the displacement, and $\mathbf{U}$ denotes a vector of displacement components at each element node. By using these functions, we can calculate the deformations which spread uniformly over the body as a function of its constitutive parameters.

In the FEM, energy functionals are formulated in terms of nodal displacements and iterated to solve for the nodal displacements as a function of impinging loads $\mathbf{R}$:

$$\mathbf{M\ddot{U}} + \mathbf{KU} = \mathbf{R}, \tag{2}$$

This equation is known as the FEM *governing equation*, where $\mathbf{M}$ and $\mathbf{K}$ are matrices describing the mass and material stiffness between each point within the body.

Unfortunately, deformable models do not by themselves provide a method of computing canonical descriptions, and are therefore difficult to use for shape comparison. To address this problem, we proposed a method in which shapes are represented as modal deformations from some prototype object [3]. By describing deformation in terms of the eigenvectors of the prototype object's finite element stiffness matrix, we were able to obtain a robust, frequency-ordered shape description. In addition, high-frequency eigenvectors can be discarded to obtain overconstrained, canonical descriptions of the equilibrium solution.

The FEM governing equations can be decoupled by posing the equations in a basis defined by the $\mathbf{M}$-orthogonalized eigenvectors of $\mathbf{K}$. These eigenvectors and values are the solution $(\phi_i, \omega_i^2)$ to the following generalized eigenvalue problem:

$$\mathbf{K}\phi_i = \omega_i^2 \mathbf{M}\phi_i. \tag{3}$$

The vector $\phi_i$ is called the $i$th *mode shape vector* and $\omega_i$ is the corresponding frequency of vibration. Each mode shape vector describes how each node is displaced by the $i^{th}$ vibration mode. The mode shape vectors are **M**-orthonormal; this means that $\Phi^T K \Phi = \Omega^2$ and $\Phi^T M \Phi = I$. The $\phi_i$ form columns in the transform $\Phi$ and $\omega_i^2$ are elements of the diagonal matrix $\Omega^2$.

This generalized coordinate transform $\Phi$ is then used to transform between nodal point displacements $U$ and decoupled modal displacements $\tilde{U}$, where $U = \Phi \tilde{U}$. We can now rewrite Eq. 2 in terms of these generalized or modal displacements, obtaining a decoupled system of equations:

$$\ddot{\tilde{U}} + \Omega^2 \tilde{U} = \Phi^T R, \tag{4}$$

allowing for closed-form solution to the equilibrium problem. By discarding high frequency modes the amount of computation required can be minimized without significantly altering correspondence accuracy. Moreover, such a set of modal amplitudes provide a robust, canonical description of shape in terms of deformations applied to the original elastic body. This allows them to be used directly for object recognition [3].

Cootes, *et al.* have also proposed method for obtaining canonical descriptions. They parameterize a deformable model based on a snake's principal variations over a given training set [2]. In the Cootes method, we are limited to measuring only the principal deformations revealed in the training phase, and therefore cannot easily build general models for recognition.

### 2.2. A New Formulation

Perhaps the major limitation of previous methods is is the requirement that every object be described as the deformations of a *single* prototype object. This implicitly imposes an *a priori* parameterization upon the sensor data, and therefore implicitly determines the correspondences between data and prototype. We would like to avoid this as much as possible, by letting the data determine the parameterization in a natural manner.

To accomplish this we use the data itself to define the deformable object, by building stiffness and mass matrices that use the positions of image feature points as the finite element nodes. In [4] we introduced a new finite element formulation which uses Gaussian basis functions as Galerkin interpolants; these interpolants are used to obtain generalized FEM mass and stiffness matrices. Because of space limitations, we will forego a review of this mathematical formulation; readers are referred to [4]. We will, however, briefly review our correspondence algorithm.

A flow-chart of our algorithm is shown in Fig. 1. For each image we start with feature point locations, which are used as nodes in building a finite element model of the shape. The algorithm assumes that features have already been detected and segmented from the images. Though the examples shown here use contour points, the features used to build a model can be any combination of junctions, corners, high-curvature points, etc.

We then compute the *modes of free vibration* $\Phi$ of this model using Eq. 3. For a 2D problem, the first three modes are the rigid body modes of translation and rotation, and the rest are nonrigid modes ordered by frequency. In general, low-frequency modes describe

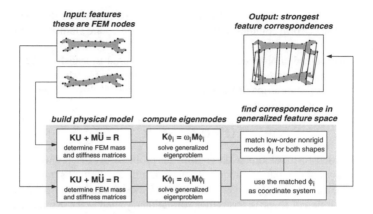

Figure 1: Modal matching system diagram.

global deformations, while higher-frequency modes do not. This frequency ordering of shape deformation will prove very useful for shape matching and comparison.

The modes of an object form an orthogonal *object-centered* coordinate system for describing feature locations. That is, each feature point location can be uniquely described in terms of *how it projects onto each eigenvector*, i.e., how it participates in each deformation mode. The transform between Cartesian feature locations $(x, y)$ and modal feature locations $(u, v)$ is accomplished by using the eigenvectors $\Phi$ as a coordinate basis, i.e.,

$$
\Phi = [\phi_1 \mid \ldots \mid \phi_{2m}] = \begin{bmatrix} \mathbf{u}_1 \\ \mathbf{v}_1 \\ \vdots \\ \mathbf{u}_m \\ \mathbf{v}_m \end{bmatrix} \tag{5}
$$

where $m$ is the number of nodes used to build the finite element model. The column vector $\phi_i$ is the $i^{th}$ *mode shape*, and describes the modal displacement $(u, v)$ at each feature point due to the $i^{th}$ mode, while the row vector $\mathbf{u}_i$ and $\mathbf{v}_i$ are the $i^{th}$ *generalized feature vectors*, which together describe the feature's location in the modal coordinate system.

Normally only the $n$ lowest-order modes are used in forming this coordinate system, so that (1) we can compare objects with differing numbers of feature points, and (2) the feature point descriptions are insensitive to noise. Depending upon the demands of the application, we can also selectively ignore rigid-body modes, or low-order projective-like modes, or modes that are primarily local. Consequently, we can describe, track, and compare nonrigid objects in a very flexible and general manner.

Given a body-centered coordinate frame for each of two objects, $\Phi_1$, $\Phi_2$, we now establish point correspondences between the two objects. The first step is to match the two sets of eigenmodes, thus establishing an equivalence between the coordinate frames for each object. This is accomplished by determining, for each eigenvector $\phi_{1,i}$ of object one, the eigenvector $\phi_{2,j}$ of object two that has the most similar direction [4]. The important idea here is that the low-order vibration modes computed for two similar objects will be very similar — even in the presence of affine deformation, nonrigid deformation, local shape perturbation, noise, or small occlusions. Point correspondences are then determined by comparing the two groups of generalized feature vectors $(\mathbf{u}_i, \mathbf{v}_i)$. The points that have the most similar and unambiguous coordinates are then matched, with the remaining correspondences determined by using the physical model as a smoothness constraint [4]. Currently, the algorithm has the limitation that it cannot reliably match largely occluded or partial objects.

## 3. Alignment, Description, and Comparison

An important benefit of our technique is that the modal vibrations computed for the correspondence algorithm can also be used to describe the rigid and non-rigid deformation needed to align one object with another. Once this *modal description* has been computed, we can compare shapes simply by looking at their mode amplitudes or — since the underlying model is a physical one — we can compute and compare the amount of deformation energy needed to align an object, and use this as a similarity measure. If the strain energy required to align two feature sets is relatively small, then the objects are very similar.

Before we can actually compare two shapes, we first need to recover the modal displacements which deform the matched points on one object to their corresponding positions on another. Given that modal transforms $\Phi_1$ and $\Phi_2$ have been computed, and that correspondences have been established, then we can solve for the aligning modal displacements directly. This is done by noting that the nodal displacements $\mathbf{U}$ which align corresponding features on both shapes can be written:

$$\mathbf{u}_i = \mathbf{x}_{1,i} - \mathbf{x}_{2,i}. \tag{6}$$

where corresponding nodes are stored in vectors $\mathbf{x}_1$ and $\mathbf{x}_2$. Recalling that $\mathbf{U} = \Phi\tilde{\mathbf{U}}$, and using the identity $\Phi^T\mathbf{M}\Phi = \mathbf{I}$ we recover modal displacements:

$$\tilde{\mathbf{U}} = \Phi^T\mathbf{M}\mathbf{U}. \tag{7}$$

Normally there is not one-to-one correspondence between the features. In cases where the recovery is overconstrained, we can solve via least squares. In cases where the recovery is underconstrained, we would like unmatched nodes to move in a manner consistent with the material properties and the forces at the matched nodes. This type of solution can be obtained by setting the spring forces $\mathbf{r}_i$ pulling on unmatched nodes to zero, and solving for unknown displacements via the FEM governing equation (Eq. 2).

Alternatively, we can solve for the modal displacements by using a mode-truncated version of Eq. 7. If correspondences were found for $p$ of the $m$ nodes, then we reduce the degrees of freedom by discarding $m - p$ of the high-frequency eigenvectors (columns $\phi_i$). We can again obtain a solution in closed-form, but we have assumed that modal displacements $\tilde{u}_i = 0$, for $i > p$. By requiring that strain-energy be minimized, we can use an iterative technique for obtaining non-zero $\tilde{u}_i$, for $i > p$. This strain energy can be measured directly in terms of modal displacements, *i.e.*:

$$E_I = \frac{1}{2}\tilde{U}^T\Omega^2\tilde{U} = \frac{1}{2}\sum_{i=0}^{m}\tilde{u}_i^2\omega_i^2, \tag{8}$$

where $\frac{1}{2}\tilde{u}_i^2\omega_i^2$ is the strain associated with the $i^{th}$ mode.

Once the mode amplitudes have been recovered, we can compute the strain energy incurred by these deformations by plugging into Eq. 8. This strain energy can then be used as a similarity metric. As will be seen in the examples, we may also want to compare the strain in a subset of modes which are deemed important in measuring object similarity.

Since each mode's strain energy is scaled by its frequency of vibration, there is an inherent penalty for deformations which occur in the higher-frequency modes. In our experiments, we have used strain energy for most of our object comparisons, since it has a convenient physical meaning; however, we suspect that (in general) it will be necessary to weigh higher-frequency modes less heavily, since these modes typically only describe high-frequency shape variations and are more susceptible to noise.

### 3.1. Alignment and Description

Fig. 2 demonstrates how we can align a prototype shape with other shapes and then use the resulting strain energy as a similarity metric. As input, we are given the feature correspondences computed for the various airplane silhouettes using modal matching[4]. Our task is to align and describe three target airplanes in terms of modal deformations of a prototype airplane. In each case, approximately 150 contour points were used, and correspondences were computed using the first 36 modes. On the order of 50 strongest corresponding features were used as input to the strain-minimizing version of Eq. 7.

The graphs in Fig. 2 show the 36 recovered modal amplitudes needed to align the prototype airplane with each target airplane. Mode amplitudes are a recipe for how to build each target airplane in terms of deformations from the prototype. The distribution of deformation energy in the various modes can be used judge the similarity of different shapes, and to determine if differences are likely due primarily to changes in viewpoint.

Fig. 2(a) shows an airplane that is similar to the prototype, and which is seen from a viewpoint that results in a similar image geometry. As a consequence, the two planes can be accurately aligned with little deformation, as indicated by the graph of mode amplitudes.

Fig. 2(b) depicts an airplane which is from the same class of airplanes as the prototype, but viewed from a very different angle. In this case, the graph of deformation mode amplitudes shows a sizable strain in the first few modes. This makes sense, since generally the first six to nine deformation modes account for affine-like deformations which are similar to the deformations produced by changes in viewpoint.

The final example, Fig. 2(c), is very different from the prototype airplane, and is viewed from a different viewpoint. In this case, the recovered mode deformations are large in both the low and higher-frequency modes.

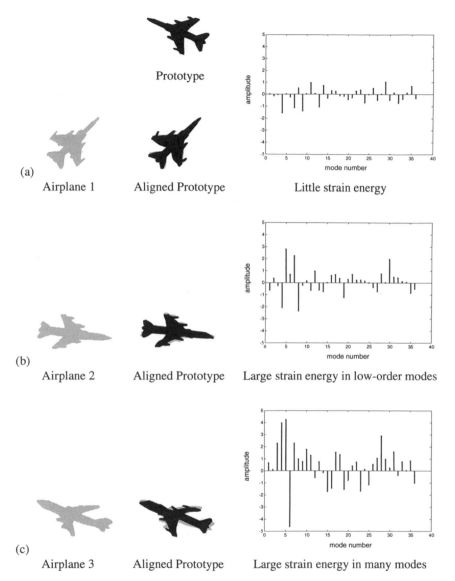

Figure 2: Describing planes in terms of a prototype. The graphs show the 36 mode amplitudes used to align the prototype with each target shape. (a) shows that similar shapes can be aligned with little deformation; (b) shows that viewpoint changes produce mostly low-frequency deformations, and (c) shows that to align different shapes requires both low and high frequency deformations.

494

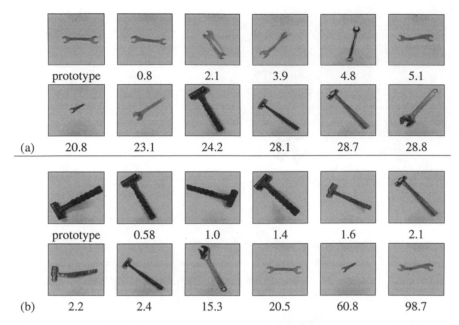

| prototype | 0.8 | 2.1 | 3.9 | 4.8 | 5.1 |

(a) 20.8     23.1     24.2     28.1     28.7     28.8

| prototype | 0.58 | 1.0 | 1.4 | 1.6 | 2.1 |

(b) 2.2     2.4     15.3     20.5     60.8     98.7

Figure 3: Using modal strain energy to compare wrench and hammer prototypes with different hand tools. The resulting modal strain energy is shown below each image.

### 3.2. Shape Comparison and Similarity

In the next example (Fig. 3) modal strain energy is used to compare two different prototype tools: a wrench and a hammer. Silhouettes were first extracted and thinned to appoximately 80 contour points from each tool image, and then the strongest corresponding points were found. Mode amplitudes for the first 22 modes were recovered and used to warp each prototype onto the other tools. The modal strain energy which results from deforming the prototype to each tool is shown below each image. A rotation, translation, and scale invariant alignment stage was employed as detailed in [4]. Total CPU time per trial (match, align, and compare) averaged 11 seconds on an HP 735 workstation.

Fig. 3(a) depicts the use of modal strain energy in comparing a prototype wrench with other hand tools. The shapes most similar to the wrench prototype are those other two-ended wrenches with approximately straight handles. Next most similar are closed-ended and bent wrenches, and most dissimilar are hammers and single-ended wrenches. Note that the matching is orientation and scale invariant (modulo limits imposed by pixel resolution).

Fig. 3(b) continues this example using a hammer prototype. The most similar shapes are three other images of the same hammer, taken with different viewpoints and illumination; the next most similar shapes are a variety of other hammers. As can be seen, strain energy provides a good measure for similarity.

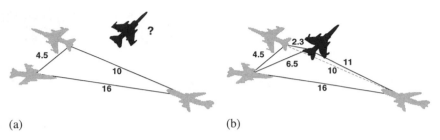

(a)  (b)

Figure 4: Physically-based linear-combinations-of-views. Three gray models define a triangle (a) with edge lengths proportional to the amount of strain needed to align each model. A pyramid (b) results when a fourth model cannot be completely explained by the three known models.

## 4. Modal Shape Analysis/Synthesis

Using methods similar to those employed by Ullman and Basri [8] we can describe objects as linear combinations of some collection of base models. The difference here is that we have a frequency-ordered description of shape; as a result we can analyze and decompose nonrigid shape deformation (and then synthesize shapes) in a principled way.

Fig. 4(a) shows a *shape space* defined by three prototype models. Using the algorithm described above, correspondences were determined and similarity (strain energy) was computed using the rotation and translation invariant version of Eq. 8. Each edge is labelled with its associated strain. Traveling along an edge in this triangle performs a linear blend, using the modal deformations, from one prototype model to another. Thus, each edge of the triangle describes a family of models which can be represented as linear combinations of the two prototypes. Similarly, we can describe an entire family of shapes by moving around inside the triangle defined by three models.

Adding a fourth model to the triangle creates a pyramid, unless the new model can be exactly described as a linear combination of the prototype models. Fig. 4(b) shows how the fourth plane model was synthesized from a combination of the three base models. The three base models cannot completely account for all of the new plane's shape (there are are missing nacelles, for instance). The distance between the new plane and the triangle of base shapes is the similarity between the new plane and the *class* of shapes defined by linear combinations of the prototype models. Using this similarity measure, we can decide whether or not the new shape is a member of the class defined by the prototype models.

The same methods can also be extended to model grayscale images. Fig. 5 shows the modal blending of two hand images as we move along the edge between the two base images 5(a) and 5(c). This image warping is accomplished by describing the deformation of the whole image in terms of the displacements calculated at feature points (typically edge points) for which correspondences have been determined. Image displacements are calculated by generating flow fields using the FEM interpolation functions [4].

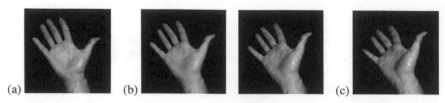

Figure 5: Given two images (a,c) and their corresponding features, we can use modal flow fields to synthesize intermediate images (b) as linear combinations of modal-deformed versions of (a,c).

## 5. Summary

The transformation to modal space not only allows for automatically establishing correspondence between clouds of feature points; the same modes (and the underlying FEM model) can be used to describe the deformations which take the features from one position to the other. The amount of deformation required to align the two feature clouds can be used for shape comparison and description.The descriptions computed are canonical, and vary smoothly even for very large deformations. This allows them to be used directly for object recognition as illustrated by the airplane and hand-tool examples in the previous section. Finally, because the deformation comparisons are physically-based, we can determine whether or not two shapes are related by a simple physical deformation. This has allowed us to identify shapes that appear to be members of the same category.

## References

[1] I. Cohen, N. Ayache, and P. Sulger. Tracking points on deformable objects. In *Proc. ECCV*, May, 1992.

[2] T. Cootes, D. Cooper, C. Taylor, and J. Graham. Trainable method of parametric shape description. *Image and Vision Computing*, 10(5):289–294, 1992.

[3] A. Pentland and S. Sclaroff. Closed-form solutions for physically-based shape modeling and recognition. *IEEE PAMI*, 13(7):715–729, 1991.

[4] S. Sclaroff and A. Pentland. A modal framework for correspondence and recognition. In *Proc. ICCV*, pp. 308–313, 1993. See also Vision and Modeling TR-201, MIT Media Lab.

[5] L. Staib and J. Duncan. Parametrically deformable contour models. In *Proc. CVPR*, pp. 98–103, 1989.

[6] D. Terzopoulos and D. Metaxas. Dynamic 3D models with local and global deformations: Deformable superquadrics. *IEEE PAMI*, 13(7):703–714, 1991.

[7] D. Terzopoulos, A. Witkin, and M. Kass. Constraints on deformable models: Recovering 3D shape and nonrigid motion. *Artificial Intelligence*, 36:91–123, 1988.

[8] S. Ullman and R. Basri. Recognition by linear combinations of models. *IEEE PAMI*, 13(10):992–1006, 1991.

[9] A. Yuille, D. Cohen, and P. Hallinan. Feature extraction from faces using deformable templates. In *Proc. CVPR*, pp. 104–109, 1989.

# ON SYMMETRY AXES AND BOUNDARY CURVES

DORON SHAKED

*Department of Electrical Engineering*
*Technion-I.I.T., Haifa 32000, Israel.*

and

ALFRED M. BRUCKSTEIN

*Department of Computer Science*
*Technion-I.I.T., Haifa 32000, Israel.*

## ABSTRACT

The paper deals with a representation of planar shape boundaries, based on the medial axis of the shape. This representation is shown to be efficient in calculating local boundary features. The problem of deciding whether an "axis-like" function is indeed an axis of a shape is addressed. The proposed representation scheme provides a basis for two local restrictions on axis functions. A theorem is stated, asserting these restrictions are both necessary and locally sufficient for an axis function. Finally a new skeletonization approach is proposed, determining the medial axis as the solution of a first order system of ordinary differential equations driven by the boundaries. Skeletonization examples using the proposed algorithm are presented.

## 1. Introduction

The medial axis of a planar shape consists of the locus of centers of maximal discs in the shape, and of their corresponding radii. A maximal disc in the shape, is a disc contained in the shape such that no other disc in the shape contains it [1]. The medial axis is considered an attractive representation of the shape. In addition to it being a lossless representation, it often provides an intuitively appealing thin version of the shape.

This paper addresses three questions. The first is: Can we go directly from the axis representation of the shape to its boundary representation? Due to the ease of the transformation from the axis to a direct representation of the spatial contents of the shape, this question has not gained a lot of interest, since the initial work of Blum and Nagel [2]. Blum and Nagel where mainly interested in extracting boundary features from the axis, rather then a full boundary representation. While the feature extraction in [2] is based on geometric considerations, the algebraic boundary representation proposed herein enables the extraction of the basic features as well as more complex features having less obvious geometric meaning. In [5] Bruce and Giblin use similar algebraic representations to derive the generic forms of continuously deforming symmetry sets.

The second question we address is: Can we go directly from a boundary representation to an axis representation of the shape? This is the problem of skeletonization. Skeletonization is a complex process with many implementation problems. Hence it has been approached from many different directions. Skeletonization from boundary descriptions has been addressed by Montanari [8] and by Lee [7] who suggested exact solutions for polygonal shapes. Some good algorithms approximating the above exact solutions where suggested by Bookstein [3] and by Brandt et al. [4] respectively. We show that the medial axis is the solution to a system of first order ordinary differential equations driven by the boundaries. The proposed system is highly unstable, therefore it is difficult to solve it directly. We incorporate the equations in a skeletonization algorithm together with equations suggested by Giblin and Brassett [6].

The third question addressed here is: Is there an easy way to tell whether a given axis representation is legal? By a legal axis function we mean a function that is indeed the axis of some real shape, and by an "easy way" we mean avoiding an attempt to reconstruct the corresponding shape. This problem has been previously addressed by Rosenfeld [9]. Rosenfeld argued that ultimately some reconstruction process has to be carried out, in order to approve a proposed axis function. He also indicated that in some cases it is possible to detect an illegal axis function by local inspection of the axis. We present two local conditions for an axis function to be legal, and prove that they are the only necessary local conditions. All further investigations would have to be of a global nature, involving some kind of shape or boundary reconstruction.

The next three sections address the three questions raised above, though in a different order. In section 2 we address the problem of boundary reconstruction, and show how we can use the new boundary representation to extract boundary features from the axis function. In Section 3 we present the local restrictions on the axis function. A theorem stating the main result of the section is cited, its proof being referred to [10]. In section 4 we address the problem of axis generation or skeletonization. We suggest a novel skeletonization approach, and present a new highly accurate and quick skeletonization algorithm incorporating it. Skeletonization examples are presented. We conclude with a summary in section 5. The rest of the introduction is devoted to the notation and terminology that we use.

A medial axis of a simple planar shape is a collection of axis segments, each being a continuous three dimensional parametric function $\mathcal{M}(a) = (X(a), Y(a), R(a))^T$. The first two coordinates of the medial axis function $X(a)$ and $Y(a)$, are the parametric description of a planar curve, the third coordinate $R(a)$, being the radius or so called "quenching function". In the following we sometimes refer separately to the medial axis curve as $\mathcal{A}(a) = (X(a), Y(a))^T$. The parameter $a$ that we normally use, is the standard arc-length parameter of the curve $\mathcal{A}$. If $p$ is an arbitrary parameterization of $\mathcal{A}$, then

$$a(p) = \int_0^p \sqrt{X'^2(\tau) + Y'^2(\tau)} d\tau$$

From now on we shall, use subscripts to indicate derivatives, thus $R_a = \frac{\partial}{\partial a}R$ and $\mathcal{A}_a = \frac{\partial}{\partial a}\mathcal{A}$.

The trivial way to define the shape $S$ of a given axis function $\mathcal{M}$ is through the union of axis disks.

$$S = \bigcup_{a \in \text{Domain}(\mathcal{M})} B_{\mathcal{M}}(a) \tag{1}$$

An axis disk $B_{\mathcal{M}}(a)$ is a disk of radius $R(a)$ centered on $(X(a), Y(a))^T$. Of course, not every three dimensional parametric function is a legal axis function. In order for it to be one, it must be the axis of some shape. Since a union shape Eq. 1 is defined for every axis like function, we may say that to be a legal axis function, an axis like function must be the axis of its union shape.

## 2. Reconstruction

Suppose we have a medial axis of a certain shape and we want to reconstruct the shape. We can obtain the shape using Eq. 1. This would give us an area description of the shape, whose boundary we seek. We can, however, reconstruct a boundary description of the shape directly from the axis description. This is made possible using a result by Blum.

In [1], [2], Blum asserted that each boundary point has at least one medial axis disk tangent to it, and that generically, each medial axis disk is tangent to the shape boundary at two points. Of the two points, one is located on the left of the medial axis and the other on its right. Blum also indicated that each of the two points is located at an angle $(180° − \theta)$ from the tangent to the axis so that

$$R_a(a) = \cos\theta \tag{2}$$

### 2.1. Boundary from Medial Axis Description

An axis point usually corresponds to two boundary points. Hence, an axis segment generically corresponds to two boundary segments, $\mathcal{L}(a)$ and $\mathcal{R}(a)$ located on the left side and on the right side of the medial axis respectively. A boundary point corresponding to the medial axis point with parameter $a$ of the axis, is located at a distance $R(a)$ from the axis curve point $\mathcal{A}(a)$. The azimuth of the boundary point is $\theta$ degrees from the direction of the tangent $-\mathcal{A}_a(a)$ to the axis curve at $a$. Here $\theta$ is determined by Eq. 2. Hence, we have the following reconstruction formula

$$\mathcal{L} = \mathcal{A} - R \begin{pmatrix} R_a & \sqrt{1-R_a^2} \\ -\sqrt{1-R_a^2} & R_a \end{pmatrix} \mathcal{A}_a$$

$$\mathcal{R} = \mathcal{A} - R \begin{pmatrix} R_a & -\sqrt{1-R_a^2} \\ \sqrt{1-R_a^2} & R_a \end{pmatrix} \mathcal{A}_a$$

(3)

Note that $\mathcal{A}_a$ is a unit vector indicating a direction tangent to $\mathcal{A}$. The matrix multiplying it from the left is a unit size rotation matrix, rotating $\mathcal{A}_a$ by $\theta = \arccos R_a$ degrees in the clockwise direction for $\mathcal{L}$ (or counter clockwise for $\mathcal{R}$). The directions obtained are the directions of $\mathcal{L}(a)$ and $\mathcal{R}(a)$ from the axis point $\mathcal{A}$. The distance to the boundary is the radius value $R(a)$.

The reconstruction formula Eq. 3 is formalized in the following lemma.

**Lemma 1** *If a segment of a* $\mathbf{C}^1$ *three dimensional parametric function is an axis segment, then the curves* $\mathcal{L}$ *and* $\mathcal{R}$ *of Eq. 3 are on the boundary of the shape the axis describes.*

The lemma is proved in [10]. Relying on the above explanation of Eq. 3 the proof concentrates on proving Eq. 2.

The only exception to this reconstruction rule is the case when either of the derivatives $R_a(a)$ or $\mathcal{A}_a(a)$ is not continuous. While the axis derivatives are not always continuous, the axis functions $R(a)$ and $\mathcal{A}(a)$ always are. Approaching a discontinuity at $a_0$ from one side of the axis, the boundary reaches a certain point in a direction corresponding to the limit value $(a \to a_0)$ of $R_a(a)$ and $\mathcal{A}_a(a)$ from that side. While approaching from the other side, the boundary similarly reaches a different point. Both points are, however, on the same circle of radius $R(a_0)$ centered on $\mathcal{A}(a_0)$. The gap between the two points is completed by a circular arc segment of this circle.

### 2.2. Boundary Features from Medial Axis Description

From the boundary description, boundary features are easily derived. The derivatives of Eq. 3 with respect to $a$, are

$$\mathcal{L}_a = \left( \frac{1-R_a^2 - RR_{aa}}{\sqrt{1-R_a^2}} + K_A R \right) \begin{pmatrix} \sqrt{1-R_a^2} & -R_a \\ R_a & \sqrt{1-R_a^2} \end{pmatrix} \mathcal{A}_a$$

$$\mathcal{R}_a = \left( \frac{1-R_a^2 - RR_{aa}}{\sqrt{1-R_a^2}} - K_A R \right) \begin{pmatrix} \sqrt{1-R_a^2} & R_a \\ -R_a & \sqrt{1-R_a^2} \end{pmatrix} \mathcal{A}_a$$

(4)

Where $K_A$ is the curvature of the axis curve $\mathcal{A}$. The unit tangent vectors to $\mathcal{L}$ and $\mathcal{R}$ are the derivatives of each curve segment with respect to it own arc-length, ($l$ and $r$ respectively). From Eq. 4 it is easy to derive the left and right arc-length information. Note that by the chain rule: $\mathcal{L}_a = \mathcal{L}_l \cdot l_a$ and $\mathcal{R}_a = \mathcal{R}_r \cdot r_a$. $\mathcal{L}_l$ and $\mathcal{R}_r$ are both unit vectors, and $l_a$ and $r_a$ are the scalar length coefficients of $\mathcal{L}_a$ and $\mathcal{R}_a$ respectively. In Eq. 4, the vector part and the magnitude part are apparently easy to separate. Note that $\mathcal{A}_a$ multiplied by a rotation matrix is of unit length, and therefore:

$$\mathcal{L}_l = \begin{pmatrix} \sqrt{1-R_a^2} & -R_a \\ R_a & sqrt1-R_a^2 \end{pmatrix} \mathcal{A}_a \qquad \mathcal{R}_r = \begin{pmatrix} \sqrt{1-R_a^2} & R_a \\ -R_a & \sqrt{1-R_a^2} \end{pmatrix} \mathcal{A}_a \qquad (5)$$

The derivatives of the mappings of axis arc-length into boundary arc-lengths, are the scalar magnitude parts of Eq. 4.

$$l_a = \left( \frac{1 - R_a^2 - RR_{aa}}{\sqrt{1-R_a^2}} + K_A R \right) \qquad r_a = \left( \frac{1 - R_a^2 - RR_{aa}}{\sqrt{1-R_a^2}} - K_A R \right) \qquad (6)$$

If we differentiate Eq. 5 with respect to $a$, and divide the result by Eq. 6, we get the second derivatives of the boundary with respect to its arc-length, the length of which is the boundary curvature.

$$K_L = \frac{K_A \sqrt{1-R_a^2} - R_{aa}}{1 - R_a^2 - RR_{aa} + K_A R \sqrt{1-R_a^2}} \qquad K_R = - \frac{K_A \sqrt{1-R_a^2} + R_{aa}}{1 - R_a^2 - RR_{aa} - K_A R \sqrt{1-R_a^2}} \qquad (7)$$

The radius of curvature of a boundary, is the inverse of its curvature hence

$$\rho_L = R + \frac{1 - R_a^2}{K_A \sqrt{1-R_a^2} - R_{aa}} \qquad \rho_R = R - \frac{1 - R_a^2}{K_A \sqrt{1-R_a^2} + R_{aa}} \qquad (8)$$

The above results are not new. They correspond to results obtained by Blum and Nagel [2] who derived them geometrically. Nevertheless, the technique presented here enables the derivation of other (more complex) boundary features that do not have a simple geometric meaning, such as derivatives of the curvature or higher order derivatives of the boundary.

## 3. Local Restrictions on the Medial Axis

As mentioned in the introduction, the way to verify that an axis-like function is indeed an axis of a shape, is a global problem involving a reconstruction of the shape via either Eq. 1 or Eq. 3. The question raised in this section is to what extent can local restrictions on the axis function help us reject candidate axes. Two such local restrictions are intuitively apparent:

- The cosine in Eq. 2 is bounded to $[-1, 1]$. Hence the first restriction is

$$|R_a| \leq 1 \tag{9}$$

- The arc-length sign in Eq. 6 should always be positive (or more accurately, the tangent of the boundary can not flip its direction), hence the second restriction.

$$(1 - R_a^2) - RR_{aa} \geq |K_A| R \sqrt{1 - R_a^2} \tag{10}$$

Indeed the following lemmas are proven in [10].

**Lemma 2** *If in a parameter $a_0$ of the parametric function, $|R_a| > 1$, then the parametric function is not an axis function.*

**Lemma 3** *If in a parameter $a_0$ of the parametric function, $(1 - R_a^2) - RR_{aa} < |K_A| R \sqrt{1 - R_a^2}$, then the parametric function is not an axis function.*

The next theorem formalizes the above two intuitive restrictions. The theorem is formally proven in [10].

**Theorem** *Every medial axis obeys the above two restrictions Eq. 9 and Eq. 10. Consider an infinitesimally short 3D parametric $\mathbf{C}^1$ function $(X(a), Y(a), R(a))$, with $a$ the arc-length of $(X(a), Y(a))$. If that segment obeys Eq. 9 and Eq. 10 with a strict inequality, it is a legal medial axis segment.*

The proof of the theorem is based on Lemmas 2, 3, and 4:

**Lemma 4** *If a parametric function obeys restrictions Eq. 9 and Eq. 10 with a strict inequality, then any axis disk is tangent to a boundary reconstruction as in Eq. 3 at two points. Also, the disk's curvature is larger then the reconstructed boundary's curvature at those points.*

## 4. Skeletonization

Skeletonization is a procedure that finds the medial axis of a given shape. It is also sometimes referred to as "The medial axis transformation". We show that the axis function $\mathcal{M}$ of a shape is a solution of a system of ordinary differential equations. Note that the reconstruction formulae Eq. 3 constitute a system of four first order equations having the left and right boundary segment coordinates as driving functions. This system should be enough to solve for the three unknown functions $X(a)$, $Y(a)$, and $R(a)$.

*4.1. Axis Representation*

Taking the difference of the equations in Eq. 3 we get

$$\mathcal{L} - \mathcal{R} = 2R\sqrt{1 - R_a^2} \begin{pmatrix} 0 & -1 \\ 1 & 0 \end{pmatrix} \mathcal{A}_a$$

Since $\mathcal{A}_a$ is a unit vector, we are interested only in the angle implied by the above equation, i.e.

$$\mathcal{A}_a \perp \mathcal{L} - \mathcal{R} \tag{11}$$

Summing $\mathcal{L}$ and $\mathcal{R}$ from Eq. 3 we get

$$\frac{2\mathcal{A} - (\mathcal{L} + \mathcal{R})}{2R} = R_a \mathcal{A}_a$$

Considering the norm of the above vector equation we get

$$R_a = \frac{\|2\mathcal{A} - (\mathcal{L} + \mathcal{R})\|}{2R} \tag{12}$$

By now we have obtained equations describing the axis from corresponding boundary information. All that is left to do is to make sure that the correspondence between the boundary segments, and the axis segment, is maintained through all the way. The information about the changes in the correspondence may be extracted from Eq. 6. We substitute the axis terminology of Eq. 6, to boundary terminology using Eq. 7, thereby obtaining

$$l_a = \sqrt{1 - R_a} \frac{1}{1 - K_L R} \qquad r_a = \sqrt{1 - R_a} \frac{1}{1 - K_R R} \tag{13}$$

The initial condition for the axis is naturally located normal to the boundary's curvature maximum, at a distance of $\frac{1}{K_M}$, where $K_M$ is the corresponding maximal curvature, see Figure 1a. The initial condition for the radius parameter is the local radius of curvature, $R(0) = \frac{1}{K_M}$. The same point of maximal curvature on the boundary, is the point where we "cut" the boundary, defining the two curves: $\mathcal{L}$ to the left of the axis and $\mathcal{R}$ to its right.

The system of equations Eq. 11, 12 and 13 serves as the engine of the proposed skeletonization algorithm. The engine must be applied to the boundary under the supervision of a control process. This process should determine initialization points for the axis, and handle junctions. Handling a junction involves: Locating the junction point, stopping the axis segments at their junction, checking what pair of boundary segments merged, and initiating a new axis segment driven by the remaining two boundary segments, see Figure 1b.

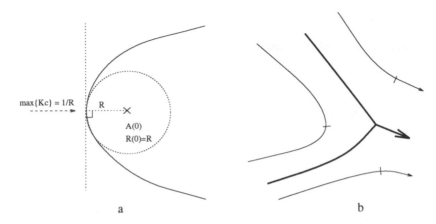

Figure 1: Initial condition and junction control in skeletonization.

## 4.2. Simulation Results

Since equations Eq. 11, 12 and 13 constitute a highly unstable differential equation system, it is impossible to implement the suggested approach directly. Hence, to make it implementable, we must use some stabilizing scheme. The engine of the proposed skeletonization approach has to be split into two stages. An estimation stage that relies on the differential equations, and a stabilizing stage that ensures, that the axis location and the corresponding boundary parameters are accurate enough.

In the stabilizing stage we use a description of the symmetry set of planar shapes, proposed by Giblin and Brassett. A symmetry set is a thin set that contains the medial axis. Giblin and Brassett argued that the symmetry set of a planar shape may be located from the zero set of

$$(\mathcal{L}(l) - \mathcal{R}(r)) \cdot (\mathcal{L}_l(l) - \mathcal{R}_r(r)) \tag{14}$$

After determining a couple of parameters $l$ and $r$ in the zero set of Eq. 14, the corresponding symmetry point is the intersection of the normals to the boundaries $\mathcal{L}$ and $\mathcal{R}$ at $l$ and $r$ respectively.

Since Eq. 14 uses only the $l$ and $r$, we rely only on Eq. 13 in the estimation stage. The estimated parameters initiate a simple search algorithm for the zeros of Eq. 14. Since the estimation stage is accurate enough, the zero search is very quick, and the accurate pair of parameters is very close to the estimated parameters. The location of the corresponding axis point is the intersection of normals to the boundary curves at the parameters. The radius function is the distance between the axis point and each of the corresponding boundary points.

It has to be noted that the estimation stage in the above scheme is important. If we substitute it by a simple procedure for the incrementation of the parameters, we generally obtain a description of the axis which is not evenly spaced. Occasionally, a simple incrementation procedurs may even lead to convergence problems in the stabilization stage. Zero searching on Eq. 14 stabilizes the method only when the search is initiated close enough to the accurate value of the parameters. Sometimes the accurate incrementation of the left side parameter will be very different from the corresponding incrementation of the right side parameter. In those cases the stabilization stage may converge to different parameters corresponding to a different axis segment.

In Figure 2 we present two examples of medial axes produced by the algorithm described above. The shapes in the figure are defined by spline boundaries.

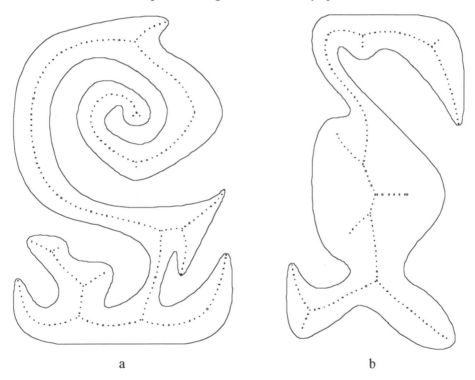

a                                    b

Figure 2: Skeletonization results.

## 5. Summary

In this paper, we advocated a representation of the shape boundary, based on the curve representation of the medial axis of the shape. This representation has been shown efficient in calculating boundary features. The proposed scheme has also led to two local restrictions on axis functions. We have stated a theorem, asserting conditions that are necessary and locally sufficient for an axis function. Finally we have proposed a new skeletonization approach determining the medial axis as a solution of a first order system of ordinary differential equation.

# References

[1] H. Blum, "Biological Shape and Visual Science (Part I)", *J. of Theor. Biology*, Vol. 38, PP. 205–287, 1973.

[2] H. Blum, and R. N. Nagel, "Shape Description Using Weighted Symmetric Axis Features", *Pattern Recognition*, Vol. 10, PP. 167–180, 1978.

[3] F. L. Bookstein, "The Line Skeleton", *CGIP*, Vol. 11, PP. 123–137, 1979.

[4] J. W. Brandt, and V. R. Algazi "Continuous Skeleton Computation by Voronoi Diagram", *CVGIP Image Understanding*, Vol. 55, PP. 329–338, 1992.

[5] J. W. Bruce, and P. J. Giblin, "Growth, Motion and 1-Parameter Families of Symmetry Sets", *Proceedings of the Royal Society Edinburgh*, Vol. 104A, PP. 179–204, 1986.

[6] P. J. Giblin, and S. A. Brassett, "Local Symmetry of Plane Curves", *American Mathematical Monthly*, Vol. 92, PP. 689–707, 1985.

[7] D. T. Lee "Medial Axis Transformation of a Planar shape", *IEEE Trans. on PAMI*, Vol 4, PP. 363–369, 1982.

[8] U. Montanari, "Continuous Skeletons from Digitized Images", *Journal of the ACM*, Vol. 16, PP. 534–549, 1969.

[9] A. Rosenfeld, "Axial Representations of Shape", *CVGIP*, Vol. 33, PP. 156–173, 1986.

[10] D. Shaked, and A. M. Bruckstein, "On Symmetry Axes and Boundary Curves", *Internal Report*, November 1992.

# ON THE ANATOMY OF VISUAL FORM

Kaleem Siddiqi
Kathryn J. Tresness
Benjamin B. Kimia

Brown University
Laboratory for Engineering Man-Machine Systems
Providence, RI, USA 02912

### ABSTRACT

Part based representations allow for recognition that is robust in the presence of occlusion, movement, growth, and deletion of portions of an object. We propose a general "form from function" principle arising from the interactions of objects in their environment, which, together with properties of visual projection, gives rise to two kinds of parts: LIMB-BASED parts arise from a pair of negative curvature minima with evidence for "good continuation" of boundaries on one side; NECK-BASED parts arise from narrowings in shape. We then test this hypothesis by requiring subjects to partition a variety of biological and nonsense 2D shapes into perceived components. We examine: 1) whether a subject determines components consistently across different trials of the same partitioning task, 2) whether there is evidence for consistency between subjects for the same partitioning task, and 3) how the perceived parts compare with the parts proposed by the "form from function" principle. The results are interpreted as suggesting that there are high levels of both intra-subject as well as inter-subject consistency and that a large majority of the perceived parts do in fact correspond to the proposed limbs and necks. Our proposal for parts envisions a role for them as an intermediate representation between local image features, *e.g.*, edges, and global object models; the implications are discussed in relation to figure/ground segmentation, and certain visual illusions.

# 1 Introduction

Part-based representations allow for recognition that is robust in the presence of occlusion, movement, deletion, or growth of portions of an object. In the task of forming high-level object-centered models from low-level image-based features, parts can serve as an intermediate representation. Evidence for part-based representations in human vision is strong [1, 11]. The computer vision literature is also rich with approaches to partitioning shape, see [14, 13] for a review. For example, Koenderink and van Doorn observe that as evidenced in works of art, elliptic (concave or convex) regions in three-dimensional (3D) objects have a 'thing-like' character whereas hyperbolic (saddle-shaped) regions act only as the glue that holds them together [9]. The dividing lines between these two types of regions are called parabolic lines, the projection

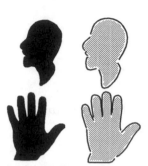

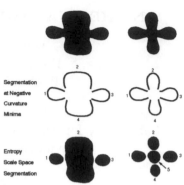

Figure 1: Hoffman and Richards' theory of curve partitioning segments a contour at negative curvature minima. The figure on the right of each pair depicts the parts as solid lines, with the shape shown in gray.

Figure 2: The shape on the top right is stretched through its region to create the shape on the top left. The minima rule does not reflect the change in percept to a shape with 3 parts (middle), whereas Kimia et al.'s proposal for parts at "necks" [7] does (bottom).

of which leads to inflection points on the shape's contour [8]. Hence, they suggest that 3D objects should be segmented along parabolic lines, and two-dimensional (2D) shapes at inflection points of the contour. Hoffman and Richards have pointed out that this proposal does not explain the reversal of perceived parts in a reversed 2D shape, or the perception of parts for everywhere parabolic surfaces [3]. Alternatively, they propose a theory of parts that relies on two "regularities of nature", in contrast to relying on the shapes of parts as described by primitives, leading to the following partitioning rule for plane curves: "divide a plane curve into parts at negative minima of curvature," i.e., at points where the curve is concave and the amount of bending is a local maximum. This rule successfully explains several figure-ground reversal illusions [3] and can lead to intuitive part decompositions, Figure 1. Braunstein et al. have carried out a psychophysical test of this rule [2].

Whereas the minima rule provides intuitive parts for the above cases, for others it leads to unintuitive parts: we present three classes of examples. First, observe that the perceived parts may change when a portion of the contour of a shape is stretched, while the remaining contours are left intact [7], Figure 2. Second, observe that when a portion of the boundary of a shape is shifted with respect to another portion, Figure 3 (bottom), narrow regions that are no longer bound by negative curvature minima may be perceived as part boundaries [6]. This partitioning at "necks" was suggested by the computational framework of Kimia et al. [7] where necks correspond to "second order shocks" that arise in the course of deforming shape. Note that this argues for a role for interaction of a shape's boundary points through its region. Third, observe that when the boundaries associated with a negative curvature minima pair do not show evidence for "continuation", Figure 3 (top), the decomposition suggested by the minima rule is not intuitive [13]. Again, note the necessary role for regional

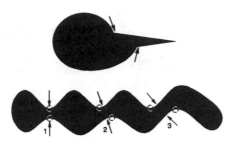

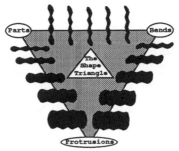

Figure 3: TOP: In the absence of "good continuation", a decomposition based on a pair of negative curvature minima may not be intuitive. BOTTOM: When a portion of the boundary of a shape is shifted with respect to another portion, narrow regions that are no longer bound by negative curvature minima may be perceived as part boundaries [6]. The negative curvature minima are marked by circles.

Figure 4: The nodes of the *shape triangle* represent three cooperative/competitive processes acting on shape, namely, *parts*, *protrusions*, and *bends* [6]. The sides of the triangle represent continua of shapes whose extremes correspond to the node and whose perception varies from one description to another.

interaction of boundary features.

Leyton [10, 11] contrasts approaches such as Hoffman and Richards' minima rule, where parts are viewed as rigid segments to be broken off, with a *process-based* view of parts. This view provides a causal explanation of a part as the outcome of a historical "protrusion" process acting on the shape's boundary, based on a biologically relevant Symmetry-Curvature duality principle [11]. Kimia *et al.* [6] propose a continuum connecting these two extreme views, and capturing the distinction between the *parts* extreme and the *protrusions* extreme. This continuum is one of three separate continua that reflect the cooperation and competition between three processes, *parts*, *protrusions*, and *bends*, to describe shape, Figure 4.

The focus of this paper is on the parts node of the shape triangle. Specifically, we address the question "How can parts of 2D shapes be reliably obtained?" Three approaches are possible. First, the question may be addressed in light of constraints imposed by object recognition, such as occlusion, movement of parts, and stability under changes in viewing conditions and object deformation [13]. Second, the question may be addressed in the context of how the human visual system may have acquired a notion of parts. What properties of objects and their projections as manifested in the retinal image, if any, may be used to robustly determine parts, even in the absence of such visual cues as color, texture, shading *etc.*? This may be viewed as addressing an "ecological aspect" of the question. Third, the question may be posed in the context of whether there is any evidence for a perceptual notion of parts in the human visual system. In particular, does a human subject determine components of known and unknown shapes in a consistent manner, over different trials? If so, is there consistency in the manner in which different subjects determine components of the same shapes? Finally, if there is evidence for an intra-subject as well as inter-subject

Figure 5: LEFT: Limb-based parts result from part-lines whose end-points are negative curvature minima, *and* whose boundaries boundaries continue smoothly from one end-point to the other. RIGHT: Examples of limb-based parts.

consistent partitioning mechanism, what relation does it bear to our computational proposal and algorithm [13]?

## 2   Form From Function

How might the human visual system have acquired a notion of parts? Hoffman and Richards have sought to explain a notion of parts based on regularities of nature. In their proposal, the defining regularity is found not in the shape of a part, *e.g.*, as defined by primitives, but in properties of part intersection: *transversality regularity* states that "when two arbitrarily shaped surfaces are made to interpenetrate they always meet in a contour of concave discontinuity of their tangent planes", *e.g.*, a straw in a glass of water. This provides a definition of parts in the 3D world. On the other hand, a different kind of regularity, *singularity regularity*, or "lawful properties of the singularities of the retinal projection", allows for the inference of parts from a 2D retinal projection, at negative curvature minima of the shape's contour.

Whereas we are in general agreement with Hoffman and Richards that a notion of parts should be motivated by a uniformity of nature, and not on the shapes of parts as defined by primitives, we suggest that a different type of regularity plays an important role. Observe that objects do not exist in isolation, rather, they must interact with their environment and with other objects in it. An object's two-dimensional form is influenced by both the nature of its *interaction* with other objects in a three-dimensional world, and the nature of its *projection* onto the retinal image. First, the interaction of objects has an influence on their form:

> **Principle 1** *Objects in their interaction with other objects in the environment specialize function differently across their volumes, either by evolution or by design.*

The *independent* specialization of function in two different, but connected regions is accompanied by sharp changes in a number of material and shape properties, *e.g.*, the beak of a bird is often hard, pointed, and distinct in color and texture from its head which is round and soft. Focusing on the shape properties alone, we can expect a sharp change in the surface of the object at the interface between the two connected regions, *e.g.*, the join between a bird's beak and its head, the shape of each region being *independently* suited to its particular function. The projection of these sharp

Figure 6: LEFT: Neck-based parts are the result of partitioning at the narrowest regions, namely, at part-lines whose lengths are a local minimum, *and* which are the diameter of an inscribed circle. These necks correspond to the second-order shocks of [7]. RIGHT: Examples of neck-based parts.

changes yields a pair of high curvature points. Moreover, when the constraint of the join is removed, in the vicinity of the interface the surface should have smooth continuations on (at least) one side. In the retinal image, the boundary at one high curvature point should smoothly continue to the boundary at the other one. This is a restatement of the Gestalt principle of "good continuation" for parts, and provides the first type of parts, the *limb-based parts*, Figure 5 (left). Examples of limb-based parts are shown in Figure 5 (right).

Second, Principle 1 is complemented by an assumption about the nature of *projection* of objects, which also leads to limb-based parts. Consider that when one portion of an object occludes another, *e.g.*, the cylindrical container of a mug occluding its handle, Figure 8, the projection of the occluding contour leads to a pair of concave discontinuities with evidence for good continuation:

**Principle 2** *The projection of a portion of an object, partially occluding another, gives rise to a pair of concave discontinuities where the boundary at one discontinuity "smoothly" continues to the boundary at the other discontinuity.*

Thus, projection may also lead to limb-based parts, but where the pairs of negative curvature minima are in fact concave discontinuities. To formalize these ideas: *a* PART-LINE *is a curve whose end-points rest on the boundary of the shape, which is entirely embedded in it, and which divides it into two connected components; a* PARTITIONING SCHEME *is a mapping of a connected region in the image to a finite set of connected regions separated by part-lines.* In the case of limb-based parts, the strongest form of smooth continuation is co-circularity [12]. Formally:

**Definition 1 (Limb)** *A* LIMB *is a part-line going through a pair of negative curvature minima with co-circular boundary tangents on (at least) one side of the part-line, Figure 5 (left).*

While for limb-based parts a distinction in function between two connected regions leads to a distinction in their shapes, when such a distinction is also accompanied by a need for *articulation* between the two regions, the space necessary for movement leads to a narrowing of the connecting region. This resulting "neck" can be a determinant of parts, *e.g.*, a human neck or wrist, or a tail of a fish, Figure 6 (right). This leads to our second type of parts, the *neck-based parts*. Formally:

> **Definition 2 (Neck)** *A* NECK *is a part-line which is also a local minimum of the diameter of an inscribed circle, Figure 6 (left).*

Articulation, however, is not the only cause of such narrowing. An emphasis on economy of mass in conjunction with the specialization of each region's shape to its particular function can also lead to a neck, *e.g.*, the neck of a spoon, Figure 6 (right). It is only natural that such narrowings be interpreted as the join between two parts, after all, a very narrow neck is the first place to break when an object falls or undergoes a collision. In addition, necks are often stable grasping sites. Of course, there are cases where a narrowing does not suggest functionally separate regions, *e.g.*, the neck of a vase, Figure 6 (right). However, it appears that the connection between distinction in function and necks is strong enough, and occurs frequently enough, that "partition at a neck" becomes the dominant rule; the neck of a vase is perceived as an equally good partitioning place as the neck of a person or the tail of a fish.

The above arguments in support of limb-based and neck-based parts together constitute the **"form-from-function"** principle which maintains that:

> **Principle 3** *Form is influenced by an* interaction *among objects and between objects and their environment.*

It is our contention that such interaction leads to the specialization of function across regions. This specialization of function results in distinctions in visual properties such as color, texture, *etc.*, and shape. Conversely, distinctions in these visual properties can lead to the recovery of the specialization in function, governed by general principles. Our visual system uses such principles to recover parts, as suggested by our limb-based/neck-based proposal. This proposal, motivated by a "form-from-function" regularity, differs in a number of properties from parts motivated by transversality, including the provision of roles for the regional interaction of boundary features, for "good continuation" and for occlusion junctions, Figures 7 and 8.

# 3 Experiments

We carried out a set of experiments to examine "psychophysical" aspects of how parts of 2D shapes may be obtained. Specifically, we addressed three questions. First, do human subjects determine components of 2D shapes consistently across different trials of the same partitioning task? Second, is there evidence for consistency between subjects for the same partitioning task? Third, if there is evidence for an intra-subject and inter-subject consistent partitioning mechanism, how do the perceived parts compare to our proposed limbs and necks? In these experiments, subjects were required to partition a variety of biological and nonsense 2D shapes into perceived components by drawing part-lines across them.

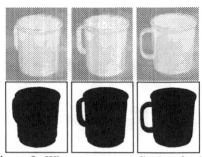

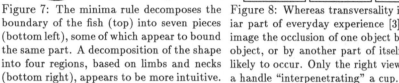

Figure 7: The minima rule decomposes the boundary of the fish (top) into seven pieces (bottom left), some of which appear to bound the same part. A decomposition of the shape into four regions, based on limbs and necks (bottom right), appears to be more intuitive.

Figure 8: Whereas transversality is a familiar part of everyday experience [3], in a 2D image the occlusion of one object by another object, or by another part of itself, is more likely to occur. Only the right view is one of a handle "interpenetrating" a cup.

**Subjects.** The 14 subjects (6 male, 8 female) were students and staff members at Brown University, or friends of the authors. Each subject participated voluntarily and had no prior knowledge of the purpose of the experiment, or of theories of visual perception of parts.

**Shapes.** 15 nonsense shapes, Figure 9, and 7 biological shapes, Figure 10, were used. The nonsense shapes and the *fish* and *leaf* shapes were hand drawn using the *idraw* program on a SUN workstation. The remaining shapes were obtained from a public domain database for Macintosh computers. Each image was black on white, with a resolution of $512 \times 512$. While the biological shapes represented familiar objects whose components had names and associated functions, the nonsense shapes represented the opposite extreme.

**Procedure.** The subject was seated in a dimly lit room in front of a SUN workstation with an 8 bit color monitor (16" or 19") with a resolution of $1152 \times 900$. The subject faced an interactive program that displayed the shapes in a random sequence in a display window located at the center of the screen. The subject was required to break off perceived components for each shape by drawing part-lines across them with the aid of a mouse. For every part-line drawn, the program stored its intersection points with the shape.

**Experiment One: Intra-Subject Consistency.** The goal of the first experiment was to measure a subject's consistency across different trials of the same partitioning task. Five subjects performed the same experiment twice, with an interval of roughly six months between the two trials, as described by the procedure above. The results are presented in Figure 11. It is evident that a subject's partitioning strategy does not vary much across time; 87% of the part-lines for the nonsense shapes and 72% of the part-lines for the biological shapes were drawn for both trials. Apparently a consistent mechanism might underlie the partitioning of biological as well as nonsense shapes. The next experiment examines the degree of similarity of this mechanism

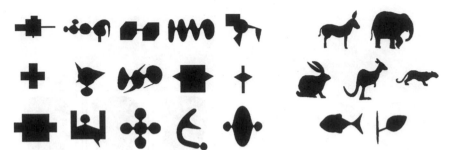

Figure 9: The 15 nonsense shapes.          Figure 10: The 7 biological shapes.

across subjects.

**Experiment Two: Inter-Subject Consistency.** The goal of the second experiment was to measure consistency across subjects. The results from the first trial of the five subjects in experiment one were pooled with those from nine additional subjects who performed the experiment once, as described by the procedure above. The results are presented in Figure 12. There is a high degree of consistency for the nonsense shapes; 81% of all the perceived part-lines were agreed upon by at least 11 out of 14 subjects. Evidence for inter-subject consistency for the biological shapes is strong as well; 60% of all the perceived part-lines were agreed upon by at least 11 out of 14 subjects. It appears that the partitioning strategies used by different subjects are indeed similar. The results of this experiment, coupled with the high level of intra-subject consistency, shown in experiment one, provide evidence for a perceptual notion of parts in the human visual system. The next experiment compares parts perceived by our subjects with parts computed by our algorithm.

**Experiment Three: A Comparison of Perceived and Computed Parts.** The goal of the third experiment was to determine the degree of similarity between perceived and computed (or proposed) part-lines. We first examined the percentage of perceived part-lines that were also proposed as necks or limbs, Figure 13. It is apparent that a high percentage of perceived part-lines were in fact proposed; 90% for the nonsense shapes and 67% for the biological shapes. This provides strong evidence in favor of our two proposed parts types. We then examined the percentage of part-lines proposed as necks or limbs that were also perceived, Figure 14. For the nonsense shapes 58% of the proposed part-lines were perceived, for the biological shapes the percentage was 49%. It is evident that whereas a significant proportion of proposed part-lines were also perceived, an appreciable proportion were not; we address this in the discussion. Finally, we examined the position and orientation errors between proposed and perceived part-lines that coincided, Figures 15 and 16. 87% of the position errors for the nonsense shapes and 76% for the biological shapes were less than 5 pixels (1% of the image size); 96% of the orientation errors for the nonsense shapes and 83% for the biological shapes were less than 10 degrees. There is striking evidence that the part-lines were placed precisely at proposed necks and limbs, not merely in their vicinity. Figure 17 is a powerful illustration of the high degree of

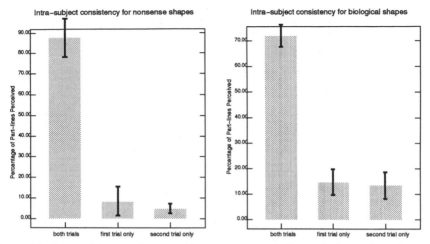

Figure 11: Intra-subject consistency: The percentages of all perceived part-lines that are drawn for both trials, or drawn for one trial only are plotted, averaging over five subjects, for the nonsense shapes (left) and the biological shapes (right).

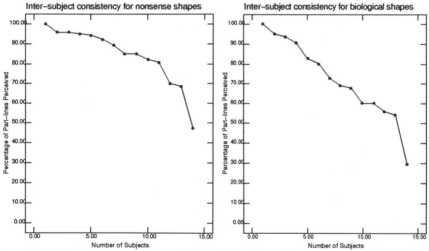

Figure 12: Inter-subject consistency: The part-lines drawn for a shape are divided into 14 (possibly overlapping) groups, the first containing those drawn by *at least* one subject, the second those drawn by at least two subjects, and so on. The number of part-lines in each group is stored as a percentage of the total number of part-lines drawn for the shape; the results are averaged over the nonsense shapes (left) and the biological shapes (right).

516

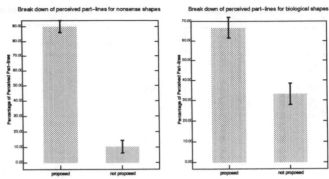

Figure 13: Proportions of perceived part-lines that were proposed, or were not proposed, averaged across all subjects for the nonsense shapes (left) and the biological shapes (right).

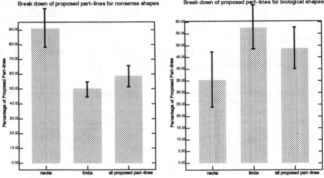

Figure 14: Proportions of proposed necks, proposed limbs and proposed part-lines (necks and limbs) that were perceived, averaged across all subjects for the nonsense shapes (left) and the biological shapes (right).

overlap between perceived and proposed part-lines. Each box depicts the original shape (left), the parts computed by applying our algorithm (middle), and the parts perceived by a majority of the 14 subjects (right).

**Discussion** We address three questions: (1) Why is the percentage of perceived part-lines that are also proposed lower for the biological shapes than for the nonsense shapes? First, cognitive knowledge may override perceptual evidence, *e.g.*, it is observed that some subjects break off components such as the feet of the animal shapes, even when perceptual evidence is weak or absent, leading to an "over-segmentation" of these in comparison to the nonsense shapes. Second, for some limbs perceptual evidence has been partially removed by the process of bending, leading to "trunks" or "tails", Figure 17 (E, F, G). In such situations, whereas one end-point is clearly defined, the placement of the second one is rather arbitrary. (2) Why is the percentage of proposed part-lines that are perceived lower than the percentage of perceived

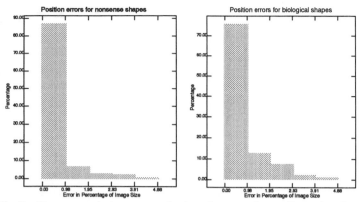

Figure 15: Position errors between perceived and proposed part-lines, for the nonsense shapes (left), and the biological shapes (right). The errors were extremely small, 87% of the position errors for the nonsense shapes and 76% of the position errors for the biological shapes were less than 5 pixels (1% of the image size).

part-lines that are proposed? Recall that no restriction was placed on the number of components to be broken off; each subject was required to use his/her best judgment. Whereas a large majority of the part-lines drawn do in fact correspond to proposed part-lines, subjects differ in their choice of which components to break off, in most cases *selecting only a subset* of all the necks and limbs. (3) What factors account for perceived part-lines that are not proposed? First, on occasion, subjects expressed their frustration at being limited to the use of a single straight line, their percept being that of a curve. Second, several subjects remarked that some shapes were more readily perceived in 3D, *e.g.*, as "two cubes connected by a bar", Figure 9 (top middle). Third, symmetry and regularity tend to influence a subject's behavior, *e.g.*, a subject who broke off one foot of the elephant often broke off the other two as well, despite the lack of perceptual evidence for parts. Lastly, the outliers, *e.g.*, part-lines perceived by only one subject, have not been excluded from the analysis.

# 4   Figure/Ground Segregation: The Role of Parts

In discussing the relationship between parts and figure/ground segregation, we are faced with somewhat of a chicken-and-egg problem. Whereas thus far we have assumed the availability of a 2D form, because intensity, color, and texture are usually not uniform across an object, segregating it from its background and from other objects in its vicinity is not an easy task. How can partitioning proceed when figure/ground separation has not taken place? We suggest a view of parts as an *intermediate representation* that allows for the flow of bottom-up as well as top-down information. Since part computations are local, edges of the appropriate polarity can interact to form necks and limbs *prior* to obtaining a separation of the object, *e.g.*, the arrows in Figure 18 (right) indicate a pairing of edges of the appropriate

518

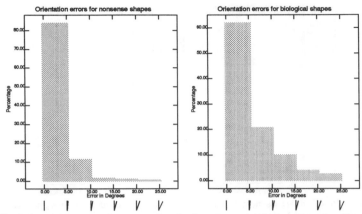

Figure 16: Orientation errors between perceived and proposed part-lines, for the nonsense shapes (left), and the biological shapes (right). The errors were small, 96% of the orientation errors for the nonsense shapes and 83% of the orientation errors for the biological shapes were less than 10 degrees.

polarity that provide evidence for the existence of a limb. This leads to the notion of a "PARTS RECEPTIVE FIELD", *i.e.*, a local operator that looks for pairs of edges of the appropriate polarity that provide evidence for the existence of limbs or necks, Figure 18 (left). This constitutes the bottom-up flow of information, *i.e.*, from local edge hypotheses to more global part hypotheses. Now part hypotheses can in turn play an integral role in the figure/ground segregation process through the top-down flow of information. A combination of likely parts can trigger an object hypothesis, followed by a figure/ground separation hypothesis for the image. During this stage, pairs of limbs that correspond to occluded contours ("hidden limbs" [13, 14]) can be used to group together portions of the scene which they connect, *e.g.*, two sides of an occluded branch, Figure 18 (right). Such a notion of parts may be key in resolving the bottom-up/top-down bottleneck of recognition.

## 5  Parts and Subjective Contours

There is an interesting, speculative connection between our partitioning proposal and the perception of certain subjective contours. Observe the Kanizsa illustrations in Figure 19 (top), each of which is perceived as a white object resting against the background. The edges, however, do not correspond to actual changes in intensity and hence are subjective or "filled in" by our visual system. One explanation lies in interpreting each illustration as the outcome of occlusion, where the occluding object happens to share the color of part of its background (white), although it appears to be brighter. It is then possible to *recover the subjective contours as limbs* arising from occlusion. To illustrate, the parts receptive fields depicted on the contrast reversed versions of the original illustrations, Figure 19 (middle), recover limbs which do indeed

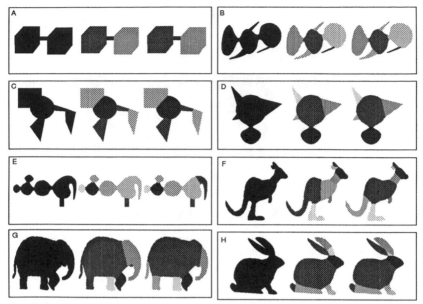

Figure 17: This Figure compares computed parts and perceived parts for a subset of the shapes used in our experiments. Each box depicts the original shape (left), the parts computed by applying our algorithm (middle), and the parts perceived by a majority of the 14 subjects (right). Note that for shapes (A) through (D), the computed and perceived parts are in exact agreement. Shapes (E), (F), and (G) illustrate discrepancies that occur due to the existence of bent limbs, *e.g.*, those manifested as the kangaroo's tail and the elephant's trunk.

Figure 18: This Figure depicts the application of a *"parts receptive field"* (LEFT) to a natural scene (RIGHT). It is clear that the separation of the rabbit's shape (figure) from those of other objects (ground) is not an easy task, especially when no color, texture or additional visual information is available. Nevertheless, local edge hypotheses can interact to form more global part hypotheses *prior* to obtaining an actual figure/ground segregation. The arrows indicate a pairing of edges of the appropriate polarity that provide evidence for the existence of a limb. In addition, pairs of "hidden limbs" [13, 14] (dashed lines) signal single objects under occlusion; these limbs can be used to group the corresponding parts on either side.

520

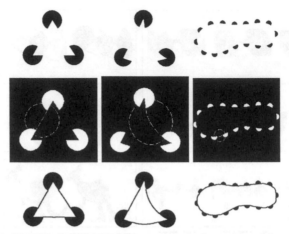

Figure 19: Top: The Kanizsa illustrations are perceived as white objects resting on top of the background. MIDDLE: The limbs are computed by a parts receptive field. BOTTOM: Superimposition of the results on the original illustrations. The limbs coincide with the subjective contours!

correspond to the subjective contours, Figure 19 (bottom). Edges alone, however, are not sufficient to explain such illusions, Figure 20. We have recently learned of similar ideas [5].

**Acknowledgements** The authors thank David Cooper, Allan Dobbins, James Elder, Danny Keren, Frédéric Leymarie, Francene Reichel, Jayashree Subrahmonia, Bill Warren and Steve Zucker for discussions and comments. We thank our subjects for participating in the experiments. The animal shapes were kindly provided by Fridtjof Stein of the University of Southern California. This research was supported by NSF grant CDA-9305630.

Figure 20: Edges alone cannot explain the illusory contours in this Kanizsa Figure [4]. LEFT: The figure on the right was created by reversing the polarity of each alternate edge of the figure on the left, while maintaining its location. The illusion is severely weakened. RIGHT: Computed limbs correspond to the illusory contours (LEFT). For the reversed polarity figure, whereas the boundary pieces continue to show "good continuation", the corresponding regions do not lie on the same side of the part-line, therefore no limbs result (RIGHT).

# References

[1] I. Biederman. Recognition by components. *Psych. Review,* 94:115–147, 1987.

[2] M. L. Braunstein, D. D. Hoffman, and A. Saidpour. Parts of visual objects: an experimental test of the minima rule. *Perception,* 18:817–826, 1989.

[3] D. D. Hoffman and W. A. Richards. Parts of recognition. *Cognition,* 18:65–96, 1985.

[4] G. Kanizsa. *Organization in Vision: essays on Gestalt perception.* Praeger, 1979.

[5] P. J. Kellman and T. F. Shipley. A theory of visual interpolation in object perception. *Cognitive Psychology,* 23:141–221, 1991.

[6] B. B. Kimia, A. R. Tannenbaum, and S. W. Zucker. The shape triangle: Parts, protrusions, and bends. Technical Report TR-92-15, McGill University Research Center for Intelligent Machines, 1992.

[7] B. B. Kimia, A. R. Tannenbaum, and S. W. Zucker. Shapes, shocks, and deformations, I: The components of shape and the reaction-diffusion space. *International Journal of Computer Vision,* To Appear, 1992.

[8] J. J. Koenderink. What does the occluding contour tell us about solid shape? *Perception,* 13:321–330, 1984.

[9] J. J. Koenderink and A. J. van Doorn. The shape of smooth objects and the way contours end. *Perception,* 11:129–137, 1982.

[10] M. Leyton. Inferring causal history from shape. *Cognitive Science,* 13:357–387, 1989.

[11] M. Leyton. *Symmetry, Causality, Mind.* MIT press, April 1992.

[12] P. Parent and S. W. Zucker. Trace inference, curvature consistency and curve detection. *IEEE Trans. Pattern Analysis and Machine Intelligence,* 11(8):823–839, August 1989.

[13] K. Siddiqi and B. B. Kimia. Parts of visual form: Computational aspects. *IEEE Trans. Pattern Analysis and Machine Intelligence,* To Appear, 1994.

[14] K. Siddiqi, K. J. Tresness, and B. B. Kimia. Parts of visual form: Ecological and psychophysical aspects. Technical Report LEMS 104, LEMS, Brown University, June 1992.

# SHAPE DECOMPOSITION
# USING PART-MODELS OF DIFFERENT GRANULARITY

FRANC SOLINA and ALEŠ LEONARDIS

*Computer Vision Laboratory, University of Ljubljana*
*Faculty of Electrical Engineering and Computer Science,*
*Tržaška 25, 61001 Ljubljana, Slovenia*

## ABSTRACT

In this paper we study the possibilities of recovering object structure from range images using part-level models of variable granularity. The approach is based on a new method of reliable and efficient recovery of part-descriptions in terms of superquadric models. Instead of pre-segmenting range images and then recovering volumetric part models from isolated regions, a direct and *simultaneous* recovery of part models from the whole unsegmented range image is achieved. This is possible by integrating a *superquadric* model fitting technique into the *recover-and-select* paradigm. By changing the compatibility constraints in this segmentation/part recovery scheme, models of different granularity can be recovered. In this way, the system can be adapted to different tasks which require different levels of description.

## 1. Introduction

The significance of detecting geometric structures in images has long been realized in the vision community. One of the primary intentions has been to build primitives that would bridge the gap between low-level features and high-level symbolic structures useful for further processing. To represent the "natural" structuring of the world and support recognition and learning of such "natural" structures from images people employ a part structure. Perceptually, the world can be broken down into parts, and the goal of computer vision is to recover from images this part structure (segmentation) and the metric properties of individual parts (shape recovery). This structure normally exhibits a hierarchy of parts. Larger parts are made up of smaller ones which are again made up of even smaller ones. There can be several such levels of details that are visible even to the unaided human eye. This part hierarchy is also reflected in the language since parts at different hierarchical levels have distinct names. Marr already envisioned such a part hierarchy for description (i.e., see the human body constructed of generalized cylinders in Fig. 1 after [17]).

For efficient communication people normally use words that refer to the highest level of this part hierarchy which makes sense in a given situation. Computer vision systems must therefore also provide descriptions at the appropriate level of details. The purpose of machine vision is not to reconstruct the scene in its entirety, but rather to search for specific features that enter, via data aggregation (i.e., model recovery), into a symbolic description of the scene at a level necessary to achieve a specific task.

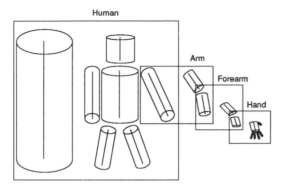

Figure 1: A hierarchy of different levels of part descriptions. Each model is a self-contained unit of shape information and has a limited complexity. (After [17].)

Many theories have emerged which emphasize the importance of extracting perceptually relevant image structures [17,5,18] indicating that a model-free interpretation is doomed to fail due to the underconstrained nature of the problem. Relevant models essentially encode the knowledge or expectations of how the data is structured and help augmenting imperfect visual data with intrinsic information, thus making the recovery process more robust.

Two types of volumetric models, generalized cylinders [6] and superquadrics [18] have emerged for such part-level modeling. Lately, superquadric models are gaining popularity in the vision [2,7,8,10,11,16,19,20,21,22,23,25] and robotics community (i.e., grasping [1], modeling kinematic chains [26]) because of their compact representation and robust recovery methods of individual models.

Although rigorous schemes for recovery of volumetric models have been developed, most of them make the assumption that the segmentation problem has been solved by some other means [12,22,21,25]. By trying to avoid, explicitly or implicitly, the phase of classifying and grouping together the image features that form individual volumetric models, the real complexity of the task is obscured. This is due to the difficulty of simultaneous classification (grouping) of image elements and model parameter estimation which has been a major obstacle to successful applications that require reliable extraction of volumetric models from the data. Only recently a method for direct and simultaneous recovery of superquadric models from unsegmented range images has been proposed [16]. Using this part segmentation/recovery method we study in this paper how a hierarchy of part representations can be constructed, much like the part hierarchy proposed by Marr [17].

The paper is organized as follows: in section 2 we discuss the related work. In section 3 we give a brief outline of part model segmentation using *superquadric recovery* in the *recover-and-select* paradigm. In section 4 we describe how different levels of part-hierarchy can be recovered in this segmentation/recovery approach and show some preliminary results. We conclude the paper with a summary and outline the work in progress.

## 2. Background and Related Work

Most approaches to segmentation in computer vision try to find part boundaries using local image information, such as edges, surface patches and surface normals. Such segmentation methods are inherently sensitive, they are susceptible to noise and details not relevant for the targeted level of representation. Sometimes, the local information for part boundary is entirely absent in the data. The segmentation using such local features is therefore often arbitrary. Essentially, local information cannot decide on the shape of the whole part if the concept of the whole part is not well defined as such. The problem of using part boundaries to define the shape of parts can be circumvented by defining the whole part shape directly. Biederman [5] proposed a set of 35 volumetric primitives, called *geons,* which he obtained by analyzing non-accidental changes on a generalized cylinder. These models could be used like phonemes in a language for describing all possible shapes.

Generalized cylinders are difficult to recover from images, at least in their general form. To make the recovery tractable, Pentland [18] introduced superquadric models which have an explicit and implicit equation of their surfaces. Pentland [19] proposed to recover superquadric models through a coarse search of the entire superquadric parameter space that combined model recovery with segmentation. This method, however, is computationally very expensive.

A much faster method for recovery of deformed superquadric models from range data, formulated as a least-squares minimization of a fitting function, was proposed by Solina and Bajcsy [2,22]. They approached also the problem of segmentation by describing the entire object with a single superquadric and then recursively splitting the models until an adequate description was achieved [2]. The implementation of this segmentation method, however, was not stable. A similar recursive formulation of segmentation using superquadric models was recently proposed by Horikoshi and Suzuki [10].

Pentland [20] later proposed a different segmentation method based on matching 2-D silhouettes (projections of 3-D superquadrics of different shapes, orientations, and scales) to the image. After such segmentation, 3-D superquadric models are fitted to range points of individual part regions. In a related work on recovery of superquadric-like physically based models Pentland pre-segmented range images using simple polynomial shape models [21].

This research on superquadrics was followed by other works using and extending the above superquadric recovery methods (Ferrie *et al.* [7], Gupta and Bajcsy [8]). However, segmentation in those systems still relies on surface [8] and/or contour fitting [7]. Since data points are grouped together on the basis of some other model types and not on the basis of the final superquadric models, this essentially decouples the classification and representation phases, so that the resulting segments do not always correspond well to the final superquadric primitives. When higher-level models are well defined, as is the case with superquadrics, one can attempt to find them directly and simultaneously as shown in [16,23] which successfully employs the representation to guide detection and grouping processes [4,3].

All of the above approaches are geared to recover the part structure only at a single description level. As we argued in the introduction a whole hierarchy of part descriptions is necessary to adequately represent the world for intelligent interaction (scale of representation with respect to the manipulating tools). In this paper we try to extend our previous work on part-level segmentation to incorporate this important feature.

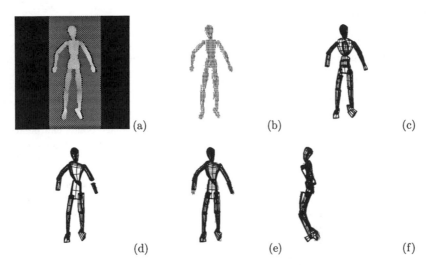

(a)          (b)          (c)

(d)          (e)          (f)

Figure 2: Part-level segmentation of a doll.

## 3. Part-Level Segmentation

To make the paper self-contained we give in this section a brief summary of the segmentation/recovery method which is described in [16,23]. The part-level segmentation method is a successful combination of a superquadric recovery method [22] and the recover-and-select paradigm [14,15]. The result of this method using deformed superquadrics is shown in Fig. 2. In the range image of a doll[1] (a), (b), a set of seed superquadrics are initiated. Models after first model selection are shown in (c), and in the middle of recovery in (d). The final result is shown in (e), (f), displayed against the input range points.

We will first describe the recover-and-select paradigm and then the integration of superquadrics into the paradigm. The extension of this method for construction of a part-level hierarchy is the topic of section 4.

### 3.1. Recover-and-Select Paradigm

The recover-and-select paradigm consists of two intertwined stages: model-recovery and model-selection. At the model-recovery stage a redundant set of models (in this particular case, superquadrics) is initiated in the image and allowed to grow, which involves an iterative procedure combining data classification and parameter estimation. All recovered models are passed to the model-selection procedure where only the models resulting in the simplest overall description are selected. By combining model-recovery and model-selection in an iterative scheme a computationally efficient procedure is achieved.

---

[1]We thank Frank P. Ferrie from McGill University, Montreal, Canada for providing the image of the doll.

### 3.1.1. Model Recovery

Recovery of parametric models is difficult because one has to solve **two** problems:

1. find image elements that belong to a single parametric model, **and**

2. determine the values of the parameters of the model.

For image elements that have already been classified (segmented) one can determine the parameters of a model by applying standard statistical estimation techniques. Conversely, knowing the parameters of the model, a search for compatible image points can be accomplished by pattern classification methods. In the recover-and-select paradigm these **two** problems are solved simultaneously by an iterative method, conceptually similar to the one described by Besl [4], which combines data classification and model fitting. One of the crucial dilemmas is where to find the initial estimates (seeds) in an image since their selection has a major effect on the success or failure of the overall procedure. To solve this problem we propose to *independently* build *all possible* models from *all* statistically consistent seeds and to use them as hypotheses for the final description. The result of such model-recovery procedure consists for each particular model $M_i$ of a triple (1. the set of data elements $n_i$ that belong to the model $M_i$, 2. the type of the parametric model and the corresponding set of parameters of the model, 3. the goodness-of-fit value $\xi_i$ to describe the conformity between the data and the model) which are subsequently passed to the model-selection procedure.

### 3.1.2. Model Selection

The model-recovery procedure provides a redundant representation where several of the models are completely or partially overlapped. Now only those models that produce the simplest description are selected. Intuitively, this reduction in complexity coincides with a general notion of simplicity which has a long history in psychology (Gestalt principles). The formalization of this principle led in information theory to the method of *Minimum Description Length* MDL, which has recently found its way to computer science, including computer vision [13,20].

The task of model selection is thus posed as an optimization problem. The objective function, which is to be maximized in order to produce the "best" description in terms of models, encompasses the information about the individual models and the overlap between them. Maximizing the objective function belongs to the class of problems known as combinatorial optimization (Quadratic Boolean problem). Since the number of possible solutions increases exponentially with the size of the problem, it is usually not tractable to explore them exhaustively. Due to the specific nature of the problem, a reasonable solution can be obtained by a direct application of the *greedy algorithm* which at any individual stage selects the option which is locally optimal. In other words, the models are selected in the sequence that corresponds to the size of their contributions to the objective function, which is equivalent to applying at each stage of the algorithm the *winner takes all* principle.

### 3.1.3. Model-Recovery and Model-Selection

In order to achieve a computationally efficient procedure the model-recovery and model-selection procedures are combined in an iterative fashion. The recovery of currently active models is interrupted by the model-selection procedure which selects a set of currently optimal models which are then passed back to the model-recovery procedure. This process is repeated until the remaining models are completely recovered. Several trade-offs can be selected in the dynamic combination of these two procedures. For details on the recover-and-select paradigm we refer the reader to [14].

## 3.2. Superquadric Models

Superquadrics are popular volumetric primitives in computer vision [2,7,8,10,11,16,19,20,21, 22,23,25] the reason being that they are convenient part-level models that can be further deformed and glued together to model articulated objects.

Superquadric surface is defined by the following equation

$$F(x, y, z) = \left( \left( \frac{x}{a_1} \right)^{\frac{2}{\epsilon_2}} + \left( \frac{y}{a_2} \right)^{\frac{2}{\epsilon_2}} \right)^{\frac{\epsilon_2}{\epsilon_1}} + \left( \frac{z}{a_3} \right)^{\frac{2}{\epsilon_1}}. \tag{1}$$

Changing shape parameters $\epsilon_1$ and $\epsilon_2$ provokes the change of the whole shape ranging from parallelepipeds to cylinders and ellipsoids. Modeling capabilities of superquadrics can be enhanced by deforming them in different ways, such as global tapering and bending, i.e. [22] or local deformations for detailed modeling, e.g. [25].

In our part-level segmentation method we used for recovery of superquadric methods the following fitting function:

$$f = \sqrt{a_1 a_2 a_3} \, (F^{\epsilon_1} - 1), \tag{2}$$

which is based on Eq. (1) for general position. This function has 11 parameters; accounting for size $(a_1, a_2, a_3)$, shape $(\epsilon_1, \epsilon_2)$, and position in space. For recovery an iterative least-squares method is used to compute the parameters of the model. Global deformations of superquadrics require some additional parameters that can be computed in the same way. The recovery method is described in detail in [22].

## 3.3. Superquadrics in the Recover-and-select Paradigm

Initial seeds are defined as squares in a grid-like pattern laid over the range image. We used small constant-size squares whose size could be adaptively changed depending on the task. A superquadric model is fitted to the data set in each seed. Seeds placed across part boundaries are eliminated because of a poor fit outright or later during model-selection. A decision whether a model should grow further or not, depends on the established similarity between the model and the data. If sufficient similarity is established, the currently estimated parameters, together with the current data set, are accepted and the search for more compatible points is started. While the actual fitting of superquadric models is based on Eq. 2, the comparison and selection of models is based on the approximation of the Euclidean distance[2].

In accordance with the paradigm, a search for more compatible points is performed in the vicinity of each model. This is achieved simply by enlarging the size of a particular model and testing range points included in such larger models. Initially, we enlarged the model

---

[2]The measure of goodness in Eq. 2 is efficient for fast and robust recovery but varies across the surface of the model and depends on the size of the model.

528

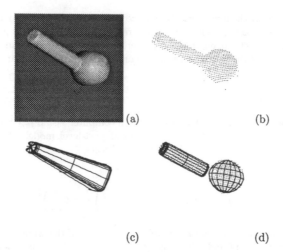

(a)                (b)

(c)                (d)

Figure 3: A sphere atop of a cylinder. Depending on the selected level of description, the system can recover from the scene (a-b): a tapered cylinder (c) or a cylinder and a sphere (d).

uniformly in all directions (multiplying all size parameters). Now, we enlarge the models only in those directions that corrupt the model in a lesser degree (if by enlargement points belonging to different part-models are included, those points provoke a very poor fit). On this enlarged set of points, a new superquadric model-recovery procedure is started.

We reported the preliminary results of this part segmentation method in [16,23]. The segmentation method is stable with respect to perturbations since we achieved stable part segmentation of objects even in range images taken from very different viewpoints [11]. Of course the part segmentation depends directly on the primitives chosen. This was even our primary motivation—*what is the best description of a scene given a particular shape language?* Since superquadrics seem to be a quite universal language for part-level shape description [18] which also closely corresponds to Hoffman's notion of parts [9] the obtained segmentation is in general perceptually acceptable. Those parts of the image that cannot be modeled with superquadrics (if the goodness of fit is not acceptable) remain un-modeled—an indication that another model type is required. We are still engaged in improving the described segmentation method and extending it in various directions. Merging of uncalibrated range images from several views, aided by such part-level segmentation, for reverse engineering purposes is one of the possible applications [11].

The segmentation method is being tested on a variety of real and synthetic range images. Processing of examples shown in this article took on the average less than 10 minutes (on a workstation HP-715/50). However, models could be recovered in parallel. The computation of the superquadric fitting function and its derivatives is independent for each range point and could be also done in parallel.

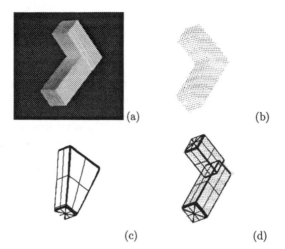

(a)                              (b)

(c)                              (d)

Figure 4: An L-shaped object: (a) intensity image, (b) range points, (c) coarse level description with a tapered superquadric, (d) finer description with two parallelepipeds.

## 4.  Building a Part Hierarchy

In this section we explain how the described part segmentation can be used to recover different levels of part description which was discussed in the introduction. If segmentation is separated from shape recovery of individual part models normally only one level of description in a part hierarchy can be recovered—we call it the basic part level. With a generalization or abstraction mechanism several adjoint parts could be merged into a single part on a coarser scale. Instead of joining smaller parts we propose to directly search for parts on any specific coarseness level. To enable the recovery of part models on a coarser level we are testing the following two techniques:

1. Increasing the threshold for model acceptance in the model-recovery procedure. This enables the superquadric models to grow over part boundaries on a lower level of the coarseness hierarchy.

2. Modifying the fitting function for superquadric recovery. The value of this function is zero for points on the model surface and increases with the square of distance for points away from the surface. The function can be modified so that all points inside a specified distance from the actual surface are also set to zero. By increasing this distance a coarser level of description should be achieved.

In the examples shown (Figs. 3, 4)[3] we obtained two levels in the part description hierarchy. We experiment with both techniques described above and would like to automatically determine the thresholds/distances for different model granularities. Finally, the necessary

---

[3]These two range images were kindly provided by Marjan Trobina from ETH, Zürich, Switzerland.

530

coarseness level for description should be determined by a task. We studied the problem of automatic determination of the appropriate scale of observation (for a particular task) in [24].

## 5. Conclusions

Since the combined recovery/segmentation method was made available only recently the experiments on recovering part hierarchies of different granularity are still under way. Some preliminary results are shown in this article. This approach to different coarseness levels of description is possible only because of a direct and simultaneous part-level segmentation where individual features (range points) are directly evaluated for the final description. We believe that recovering part hierarchies could be especially useful for object recognition and object manipulation since for these tasks only shape/structure recovery up to a discriminating level of detail is required.

There are still several open issues that we will address in our future work. Besides improving the basic part-level segmentation method, the central problem is how to determine different levels in the part description hierarchy and how to control the switching between these levels.

## 6. Acknowledgments

This research was supported in part by The Ministry for Science and Technology of The Republic of Slovenia (Project P2-1122). We thank Aleš Jaklič, Alenka Macerl, and Marko Rous for advice and help in programming.

## 7. References

[1] P. K. Allen and P. Michelman. Acquisition and interpretation of 3-D sensor data from touch. *IEEE Trans. on Robotics and Automation*, 6(4):397–404, 1990.

[2] R. Bajcsy and F. Solina. Three dimensional shape representation revisited. In *Proc. First Int. Computer Vision Conf.*, pp. 231–241, London, England, 1987.

[3] R. Bajcsy, F. Solina, and A. Gupta. Segmentation versus object representation – are they separable? In R. Jain and A. Jain, editors, *Analysis and Interpretation of Range Images*, Springer, New York, 1990.

[4] P. J. Besl. *Surfaces in Range Image Understanding*. Springer, 1988.

[5] I. Biederman. Human image understanding: recent research and theory. *Computer Vision, Graphics, and Image Processing*, 32:29–73, 1985.

[6] T. O. Binford. Visual perception by computer. *Proc. of the IEEE Conf. on Systems and Control*, Miami, 1971.

[7] F. P. Ferrie, J. Lagarde, and P. Whaite. Darboux Frames, Snakes, and Super-Quadrics: Geometry from the Bottom Up. *IEEE Trans. on Pattern Analysis and Machine Intelligence*, PAMI-15(8):771–784, 1993.

[8] A. Gupta and R. Bajcsy. Surface and volumetric segmentation of range images using biquadrics and superquadrics. In *Proc. Int. Conf. on Pattern Recognition*, The Hague, pp. 158–162, 1992.

[9] D. D. Hoffman and W. A. Richards. Parts of recognition. *Cognition*, 18:65–96, 1985.

[10] T. Horikoshi and S. Suzuki. 3D parts decomposition from sparse range data using information criterion. In *Proc. IEEE Computer Vision and Pattern Recognition Conf.*, pp. 168–173, 1993.

[11] A. Jaklič, A. Leonardis, and F. Solina. Iterative construction of CAD models from range images. *Proceedings Fourth COST #229 WG.1 and 2 Worskshops on Adaptive Methods and Emergent Techniques for Signal Processing and Communications.* Ljubljana, Slovenia, April 1994.

[12] D. J. Kriegman and J. Ponce. On recognizing and positioning curved 3D objects from image contours. *IEEE Trans. on Pattern Analysis and Machine Intelligence*, 1990.

[13] Y. G. Leclerc. Constructing simple stable descriptions for image partitioning. *Int. Journal of Computer Vision*, 3:73–102, 1989.

[14] A. Leonardis. *Image Analysis Using Parametric Models: Model-Recovery and Model-Selection Paradigm.* A Dissertation in Computer Science. University of Ljubljana, Faculty of Electrical Engineering and Computer Science. May 1993.

[15] A. Leonardis, A. Gupta, and R. Bajcsy. Segmentation of range images as the search for geometric parametric models. To appear in *Int. Journal on Computer Vision*, 1994.

[16] A. Leonardis, F. Solina, and A. Macerl. A Direct Recovery of Superquadric Models in Range Images Using Recover-and-Select Paradigm. *Proc. Third European Conf. on Computer Vision— ECCV'94.* Stockholm, Sweden, 1994.

[17] D. Marr. *Vision.* San Francisco, Freeman, 1982.

[18] A. P. Pentland. Perceptual organization and the representation of natural form. *Artificial Intelligence*, 28(2):293–331, 1986.

[19] A. P. Pentland. Recognition by parts. In *Proc. First Int. Conf. on Computer Vision*, London, pp. 612–620, 1987.

[20] A. P. Pentland. Automatic extraction of deformable part models. *Int. Journal of Computer Vision*, 4:107–126, 1990.

[21] A. P. Pentland and S. Sclaroff. Closed-form solutions for physically based shape modeling and recognition. *IEEE Trans. on Pattern Analysis and machine Intelligence*, PAMI 13(7):715–729, 1991.

[22] F. Solina and R. Bajcsy. Recovery of parametric models from range images: The case for superquadrics with global deformations. *IEEE Trans. on Pattern Analysis and Machine Intelligence*, 12(2):131–147, 1990.

[23] F. Solina, A. Leonardis, and A. Macerl. A direct part-level segmentation of range images using volumetric models. In *Proc. IEEE Int. Conf. on Robotics and Automation*, San Diego, CA, 1994.

[24] F. Solina and A. Leonardis. Selective scene modeling. In *Proc. 11th Int. Conf. on Pattern Recognition*, pp. A:87–90, The Hague, 1992. IAPR.

[25] D. Terzopoulos and D. Metaxas. Dynamic 3D models with local and global deformations: Deformable superquadrics. *IEEE Trans. on Pattern Analysis and Machine Intelligence*, PAMI 13(7):703–714, 1991.

[26] R. Volpe and P. Khosla. Manipulator control with superquadric artificial potential functions: Theory and experiments. *IEEE Trans. on Systems, Man, and Cybernetics*, 20(6):1423–1436, 1990.

# CALCULATING 3D VORONOI DIAGRAMS OF LARGE UNRESTRICTED POINT SETS FOR SKELETON GENERATION OF COMPLEX 3D SHAPES

G. SZÉKELY, CH. BRECHBÜHLER, M. NÄF, O. KÜBLER

Communications Technology Laboratory ETH-Zürich, CH-8092 Zürich, Switzerland

Tel: +411/632 52 88, FAX: +411/261 80 24, email: szekely@vision.ethz.ch

## ABSTRACT

Voronoi skeletons (= regularized Voronoi diagrams) have proved useful tools for describing and manipulating 2D shapes. The generalization of Voronoi skeleton generation to 3D would give us an appealing way to deal with the complex problems of handling 3D shapes. While algorithms for generating approximative 3D VD have been proposed previously, the 3D generalization of the regularization procedure is severely obstructed by the unavoidable errors of the approximation close to the object boundary.

In this paper we propose an algorithm which, through a divide and conquer approach, allows the generation of the exact VD of several 100.000 generating points on the discrete image raster. On segmented 3D brain data we show that, using vector label propagation methods, the generating points of the VD can be partitioned in very small clusters. The complete VD can then be trivially merged from the previously computed sub-VDs. The resulting 3D VD will allow to attack the regularization procedure leading to a practically useful skeletal description of 3D objects.

## 1 Introduction

The mathematical description and representation of 3D shape, capable of dealing with form of variable appearance, is one of the most challenging research topics in computer vision. Skeletonization based e.g. on the Medial Axis Transformation (MAT) proposed by Blum [1] is a widely used method to deal with variable shape and to represent its global characteristics in an intuitively appealing way.

The MAT is customarily defined in 2D although the concept generalizes to any number of dimensions in a natural way. Faithfully implementing the concept with all its facets in discrete 2D space has proved difficult since exact Euclidean metric has to be reconciled with raster-type connectivity [2]. Previous work [2, 3, 4] has shown that these difficulties can be solved in an elegant way, by generating and regularizing the Voronoi Diagram (VD) defined by the boundary points of the object to be analyzed. The regularized VD shall be called Voronoi skeketon.

In order to generalize the Voronoi Skeletons (VS) to 3D one has to cope with the problem of generating 3D Voronoi diagrams of extremely large numbers (up to $10^6$) of points. As presently known algorithms (e.g. [5, 6, 7]) can hardly cope with problems of this size, an approximation has been proposed [8], based on label propagation similar to that of the Danielsson distance transform algorithm [9]. Careful analysis of results on large medical objects (human brain segmented from Magnetic

Resonance images) has shown that while in most cases this approximation is very good, considerable deviations can be expected near to the object boundary. These effects proved to be especially disturbing during studies for the 3D generalization of 2D pruning algorithms, which start at the outmost branches of the VD, i.e. in the neighbourhood of the boundary and proceed inward in a recursive manner.

In order to open a way to study recursive pruning procedures in 3D, the approximative algorithm has to be replaced by methods generating exact 3D VDs within reasonable computing time. The present paper uses an approach based on the locality property of Voronoi Diagrams. Due to the fact that points far away do not change the local structure of the VD, a subdivision of the generating points into small local groups is proposed. Such a subdivision can be achieved by label propagation techniques, similar to those proposed for Euclidean distance transform algorithms [9, 10].

The organization of the paper is as follows: Section 2 summarizes the previous efforts for Voronoi Skeleton generation. Section 3 describes the proposed algorithm for nD Voronoi Diagrams. The implementation is discussed and illustrated by examples in Section 4. Section 5 contains the conclusions.

## 2  Voronoi Skeletons

An excellent intuitive perception of the MAT is afforded by Blum's famous prairie fire analogy. Setting fire to the border of a patch of dry grass will result in the medial (= local symmetry) axis or skeleton, the locus where the fire-fronts meet and quench. This intuitive picture generalizes directly to 3D. Propagating every point of the continuous bounding surface with spherical expansion characteristic into the object will result in a Medial Manifold now consisting of 2D and 1D constituents. A simple example is the MAT of an elongated cylinder, looking like two funnels joined by a rod.

Envisaging the MAT of a discrete 2D or 3D object becomes immediate by adopting a semi-continuous approach. We specify the object by the discrete set of points $S$ representing its border elements. Each point is allowed to expand continuously in circular or spherical manner until the wave-fronts meet. Each generating point thus creates its region of influence. The resulting regions partition continuous 2D-space or 3D-space into a cell complex of convex polygons or polyhedra which is nothing but the Voronoi Diagram (VD) generated by the set of border points $S$ [11].

The VD of $S$ shows a multitude of branches in 2D or laminae in 3D not normally associated with the concept of the MAT. This appearance is due to resolving the continuous macroscopic boundary into its atomic generators and their associated microscopic wave fronts. In order to develop the VD into a useful tool for the description and representation of variable shape according to the MAT concept, we must be able to distinguish between essential parts having their origin in macroscopic properties of the contour and irrelevant branches caused by the microscopic resolution. Regularization of the VD amounts to identifying a salient sparse subset (= *anchor points*) of the full discrete set of border points $S$. The concept of regularization and its implementation are most easily understood by referring to the straight line dual of the Voronoi-tesselation, the Delaunay triangulation.

The object as defined by the full set $S$ can be envisaged as being completely filled by (Delaunay) triangles which have the important special characteristic of being optimally space filling. The goal of regularization is to identify and remove all peripheral Delaunay triangles which are irrelevant for representing the object at coarser scales. By suppressing the corresponding parts of the VD we obtain the desired V-skeleton. Given an appropriate criterion for removal, the operation proceeds from the outside inwards in a recursive manner, eliminating twigs and reducing the VD to its stable inner branches. The pseudo-code of the regularization algorithm is shown on Figure 1.

---

1. $\forall T_j \in \{T_i\} \qquad \Delta R(S_a(T_i)) = \Delta R(S_b(T_i)) = \Delta R(S_c(T_i)) = 0$

2. Find the set

$$\Omega = \left\{ T_j \in \{T_i\} \,\middle|\, \sum_{x \in \{a,b,c\}} \mathcal{V}(S_x(T_j)) = 2 \right\}$$

   of all contour triangles, and re-index their sides, so that $\mathcal{V}(S_c(T_j)) = 0$

3. $\{T_i\}_{temp} = \{T_i\}$
   $\forall T_j \in \Omega$ **do**
     $\Delta R_{accum}(T_j) = \|S_a(T_j)\| + \Delta R(S_a(T_j)) + \|S_b(T_j)\| + \Delta R(S_b(T_j)) - \|S_c(T_j)\|$
     **if** $\Delta R_{accum}(T_j)) < \tau$ **then**     $\tau$: tolerance threshold
       $\Delta R(S_c(T_j)) = \Delta R_{accum}(T_j)$
       $\{T_i\}_{temp} = \{T_i\}_{temp} \setminus T_j$
     **endif**
   **enddo**

4. **if** $\{T_i\}_{temp} \neq \{T_i\}$ **then**
     $\{T_i\} = \{T_i\}_{temp}$
     **goto 2**
   **else TERMINATE**
   **endif**

---

where $\{T_i\}$ denotes the set of all Delaunay-triangles
$S_a(T_i), S_b(T_i)$ and $S_c(T_i)$ their three sides ($\|S_x\|$ denotes the side length).
$\Delta R(S_x(T_i))$ will denote the length error, assigned to side $x$ of $T_i$.

$$\mathcal{V}(S_x(T_i)) = \begin{cases} 1 & \text{if the side } x \text{ of the triangle } T_i \text{ is currently on the border of the object} \\ 0 & \text{otherwise} \end{cases}$$

**Figure 1**: Regularization algorithm for 2D Voronoi diagrams.

The extremely efficient algorithm and simple and powerful data structure for computing and representing the VD in 2D has no obvious generalization to 3D [11]. This has lead to the development of incremental procedures [5, 6]. One tries to reduce the expected complexity of the incremental algorithm by using special assumptions on the distribution of the generating points [5], or by randomizing the point insertion sequence [6]. However, application of an incremental algorithm still appears computationally prohibitive for our case of 3D MRI-data sets with a resolution of $256^3$ voxels and $0.25 - 0.5 \cdot 10^6$ surface elements.

In order to cope with problems of this size, the approximative generation of the VD can be considered. The approximation is based on label propagation, and was originally proposed for regular metrics [12]. In order to achieve reasonable transformation invariance, Euclidean metric has been used for 3D VD approximation [8]. The emerging problems due to conflicts between correct geometry and correct topology can be resolved by label propagation similar to the scanning algorithm of the Danielsson distance transform [9].

While the algorithms give reasonably good approximation of the real VD, in several cases deviations can be observed:

- The vertices of the approximative VD are forced to stay at the integer coordinates of the image grid. However this effect causes only subpixel shifts, which are surely tolarable.

- The regular connectivity of the raster limits the degree of the Voronoi vertices. On a 3D discrete grid only 6 neighbours are possible, limiting the number of Voronoi edges joining at the same vertex. If there are more co-spherical points (which is unavoidable on a tightly filled integer raster), the procedure splits the vertices with degree higher than 6 into a cluster of neighbouring vertices.

- The integer resolution of the raster and the tight packing of the border cracks make it impossible that, during the label propagation, all boundary elements are represented in the set of propagating labels. The reason of this problem lies in the initialization, where some voxels may have more than one neighbouring cracks, while only one of them can be used for the initial labeling. Consequently the influence regions of the unrepresented cracks will be missing, locally changing the approximative Voronoi Diagram. This problem is especially disturbing in the case of very thin (1 voxel wide) structures.

The above mentioned problems seem to cause significant deviation in the neighbourhood of the generating points, i.e. near to the object boundary. The original reasoning was that this is exactly the part of the VD which has to be pruned anyway during the skeleton regularization procedure. The generalization of the 2D pruning however proved to be much harder than we originally expected. The basic reason for this is the much more complex topology of the 3D VD. If we regard the VD as a graph (of the Voronoi edges and vertices in any dimensions), the 2D Voronoi graph is planar, while the 3D graph in general is not. This causes serious problems if we want to formulate a recursive algorithm similar to the 2D case. The problem can also be formulated from the Delaunay tetrahedralization point of view. In the 2D case one can always identify triangles having two sides on the border and the third one through the object, as long as triangle deletion is possible without changing the object topology. This makes the selection of the triangles to be pruned very simple at every stage of the procedure. In 3D, however, the analogous case (3 sides of a tetrahedron on the surface and 1 within the object) happens only as an exception.

These problems make the study of the topological structure of the 3D VD unavoidable. In this case the structure of the outermost Voronoi surfaces has special significance, and the above mentioned approximation errors make any rigorous analysis impossible. In order to proceed with the study of the spatial and topological structure of 3D Voronoi Diagrams resulting from large medical objects, an exact 3D VD generation algorithm had to be found.

## 3 Voronoi Diagram Generation by Partitioning

While the proposed algorithm has no practical justification in 2D (the known 2D algorithms will perform much faster), we first formulate the basic concepts of the new procedure in 2D for simplicity, and give the generalization to any dimensions at the end of the section.

The worst case complexity of the known algorithms for 3D VD generation is far from linear. Therefore it seems reasonable to partition the original point set into small subsets, generate the VD of these subsets and merge the results. Such a partitioning is in principle possible using the following locality property of the VD:

Let $\mathcal{P} = \{P_i \in \mathbf{R}^2 \mid i = 1 \ldots n\}$ be the set of generating points. The Voronoi Diagram of an arbitrary region of the plane $\mathcal{S} \subset \mathbf{R}^2$ over the set $\mathcal{P}$ can be defined as a function mapping every point $s$ in $\mathcal{S}$ to the set of its nearest generating point(s):

$$\mathcal{V}_\mathcal{S}[\mathcal{P}] : \mathcal{S} \hookrightarrow 2^\mathcal{P} \mid r \in \mathcal{S} \to \{p \in \mathcal{P} \mid \forall \hat{p} \in \mathcal{P} \;\; \delta(p, r) \leq \delta(\hat{p}, r)\} \tag{1}$$

$2^\mathcal{P}$ is the set of all subsets of $\mathcal{P}$ and $\delta(x, y)$ is the Euclidean distance in the plane. Normally there is only one generating point belonging to an arbitrary point $r \in \mathcal{S}$, i.e. $|\mathcal{V}_\mathcal{S}[\mathcal{P}](r)| = 1$.

We select now an arbitrary region $\mathcal{S} \subset \mathbf{R}^2$, and collect all the points in the generating set $\mathcal{P}$ having an influence region in the VD $\mathcal{V}_{\mathbf{R}^2}[\mathcal{P}]$ overlapping with $\mathcal{S}$

$$\mathcal{Q} = \bigcup_{s \in \mathcal{S}} \mathcal{V}_{\mathbf{R}^2}[\mathcal{P}](s) \tag{2}$$

The locality property states that $\mathcal{V}_\mathcal{S}[\mathcal{P}] = \mathcal{V}_\mathcal{S}[\mathcal{Q}]$, i.e. the VD generated by only the "nearby" points $\mathcal{Q}$ is identical with the original VD generated by the complete point set $\mathcal{P}$ as long as we restrict ourselves to the selected region $\mathcal{S}$.

To prove this property we show that for all $s \in \mathcal{S}$ $\mathcal{V}_\mathcal{S}[\mathcal{P}](s) = \mathcal{V}_\mathcal{S}[\mathcal{Q}](s)$. Let $p \in \mathcal{V}_\mathcal{S}[\mathcal{P}](s)$. As $\mathcal{S} \subset \mathbf{R}^2$, $p \in \mathcal{V}_{\mathbf{R}^2}[\mathcal{P}](s)$, and so $p \in \mathcal{Q}$ by the definition of $\mathcal{Q}$. Because of the way $p$ is selected

$$\forall \hat{p} \in \mathcal{P} \;\; \delta(p, s) \leq \delta(\hat{p}, s) \tag{3}$$

As $\mathcal{Q} \subset \mathcal{P}$, any $\hat{q} \in \mathcal{Q}$ is element of $\mathcal{P}$, i.e. $\delta(p, s) \leq \delta(\hat{q}, s)$, i.e.

$$p \in \mathcal{Q} \;\; and \;\; \forall \hat{q} \in \mathcal{Q} \;\; \delta(p, s) \leq \delta(\hat{q}, s), \tag{4}$$

resulting in $p \in \mathcal{V}_S[\mathcal{Q}](s)$. This holds for any $p$, so $\mathcal{V}_S[\mathcal{P}](s) \subset \mathcal{V}_S[\mathcal{Q}](s)$ follows.

On the other side let $q \in \mathcal{V}_S[\mathcal{Q}](s)$. We will prove that $q \in \mathcal{V}_S[\mathcal{P}](s)$, i.e.

$$q \in \mathcal{P} \ and \ \forall \hat{p} \in \mathcal{P} \ \delta(q, s) \leq \delta(\hat{p}, s) \tag{5}$$

As $\mathcal{Q} \subset \mathcal{P}$, $q \in \mathcal{P}$ is trivial. Suppose that the above condition is not fulfilled. It means, that $\exists \hat{p} \in \mathcal{P}$ so, that $\delta(q, s) > \delta(\hat{p}, s)$. There are two possibilities:

- $\hat{p} \in \mathcal{V}_{\mathbf{R}^2}[\mathcal{P}](s)$. Let then $\hat{q} = \hat{p}$.

- $\hat{p} \notin \mathcal{V}_{\mathbf{R}^2}[\mathcal{P}](s)$, then by definition $\exists \hat{q} \in \mathcal{V}_{\mathbf{R}^2}[\mathcal{P}](s)$ so that $\delta(\hat{q}, s) < \delta(\hat{p}, s)$ ( $< \delta(q, s)$ ).

In both cases we found $\hat{q} \in \mathcal{V}_{\mathbf{R}^2}[\mathcal{P}](s)$, i.e. $\hat{q} \in \mathcal{Q}$ so, that $\delta(\hat{q}, s) < \delta(q, s)$, which is a contradiction. As a result we see that $\mathcal{V}_S[\mathcal{P}](s) \subset \mathcal{V}_S[\mathcal{Q}](s)$, which together with the previous result proves the property.

Based on this locality, the following VD generation algorithm seems to be feasible:

- partition the plane into regions $\mathcal{S}_0 \ldots \mathcal{S}_n$, where $\bigcup_{i=0}^{n} \mathcal{S}_i = \mathbf{R}^2$

- generate the sets $\mathcal{Q}_0 \ldots \mathcal{Q}_n$ of nearby points

- generate the "local" Voronoi Diagrams $\mathcal{V}_{\mathcal{S}_i}[\mathcal{P}] = \mathcal{V}_{\mathcal{S}_i}[\mathcal{Q}_i]$

- obtain the complete VD by simply putting together the pieces $\mathcal{V}_{\mathcal{S}_i}[\mathcal{P}]$.

Operating in the discrete domain, the image raster suggests directly the plane partitioning. For an object defined on an $n \times n$ image raster we select the (closed) quadratic pixel regions (pixels) as $\mathcal{S}_1 \ldots \mathcal{S}_{n^2}$. The rest of the plane outside the image matrix is $\mathcal{S}_0$. Clearly $\bigcup_{i=0}^{n^2} \mathcal{S}_i = \mathbf{R}^2$. The basic problem is how the nearby point sets could be generated, as their definition actually contains the complete VD.

If we restrict ourselves to the image region $\mathcal{I} = \bigcup_{i=1}^{n^2} \mathcal{S}_i$, and we discard $\mathcal{V}_{\mathcal{S}_0}[\mathcal{P}]$ (which is surely acceptable in our application), label propagation techniques offer a solution to this problem. Let, for any $p \in \mathcal{P}$

$$\mathcal{R}_{\mathcal{V}_{\mathcal{I}}[\mathcal{P}]}[p] = \{x \in \mathcal{I} \mid p \in \mathcal{V}_{\mathcal{I}}[\mathcal{P}](x)\} \tag{6}$$

be its influence zone generated by the VD (restricted to the image $\mathcal{I}$). As $\mathcal{R}_{\mathcal{V}_{\mathcal{I}}[\mathcal{P}]}[p]$ is convex, its covering by the pixels $\{\mathcal{S}_i \mid i = 1 \ldots n^2, \ \mathcal{S}_i \cap \mathcal{R}_{\mathcal{V}_{\mathcal{I}}[\mathcal{P}]}[p] \neq \emptyset\}$ is a 4-connected region. We assume that $p$ is the center of a pixel side - crack - separating the object from the background. We label the 2 4-neighbour pixels of all $p \in \mathcal{P}$ and let the labels propagate independently on 4-connected paths of the image raster. By checking if the pixels intersect with the influence regions, we end up with the desired nearby point sets, as the set of all labels propagating onto the pixels.

The only remaining question is how one can check the intersection of the pixels with the influence regions. The first thing to observe is, that if $\mathcal{Q} \subset \hat{\mathcal{Q}} \subset \mathcal{P}$ then $\mathcal{V}_S[\hat{\mathcal{Q}}] = \mathcal{V}_S[\mathcal{Q}] = \mathcal{V}_S[\mathcal{P}]$. This means, during the intersection checking it is not necessary to be exact. We just have to make sure, that none of the generating points will be left out which have an influence region intersecting the pixel under investigation. Inclusion of (actually superfluous) points deteriorates the performance, but does not cause errors.

A simple way to perform the intersection check can be constructed as follows. Let $c_i \in S_i$ be any point in the $i^{th}$ pixel, and take any $p_i \in V_{R^2}[\mathcal{P}](c_i)$. The influence zone of any other generating point $\hat{p}$ can intersect with $S_i$ iff it has a common Voronoi edge with the influence zone of $p_i$ within the pixel $S_i$. This means that the perpendicular bisector between $p_i$ and $\hat{p}$ surely intersects the pixel $S_i$. Because of the special selection of $S_i$ (as a square) we only have to check, if the perpendicular bisector separates $p_i$ from the corners of the pixel.

Unfortunately this criterion still requires a priori knowledge about $V_{R^2}[\mathcal{P}]$, namely one of the nearest generating points. To perform the check without this knowledge, we need an alternative necessary condition for the intersection. The previous criterion already limited the plane subdivision to a cartesian pixel raster. In the following we will additionally assume that $c_i$ is the center of the pixel $S_i$.

Let now $p_i \in V_{R^2}[\mathcal{P}](c_i)$ selected as before, and $\hat{p} \in \mathcal{P}$, $\hat{p} \neq p_i$ any other generating point. In order to exclude generating points, which can be left out when generating $Q_i$ we are now looking for a criterion, that the perpendicular bisector of $p_i$ and $\hat{p}$ does not intersect the

$$\Delta_\epsilon(c_i) = \left\{ s \in R^2 \mid \delta(s, c_i) \le \epsilon \right\} \tag{7}$$

closed $\epsilon$-environment of $c_i$. Because of the selection of $p_i$

$$\delta(c_i, p_i) \le \delta(c_i, \hat{p}) \tag{8}$$

which means that always exists some $\alpha \ge 0$ such that

$$\delta(c_i, \hat{p}) = \delta(c_i, p_i) + \alpha \tag{9}$$

Now, from the triangle inequality for any $s \in \Delta_\epsilon(c_i)$

$$\delta(s, p_i) \le \delta(s, c_i) + \delta(c_i, p_i) \le \delta(c_i, p_i) + \epsilon \tag{10}$$

$$\delta(c_i, \hat{p}) \le \delta(c_i, s) + \delta(s, \hat{p}) \le \delta(s, \hat{p}) + \epsilon \tag{11}$$

Substituting first (9) and then (11) into (10) we have

$$\delta(s, p_i) \le \delta(c_i, p_i) + \epsilon \le \delta(c_i, \hat{p}) - \alpha + \epsilon \le \delta(s, \hat{p}) + 2\epsilon - \alpha \tag{12}$$

If we want to achieve that $\delta(p_i, s) < \delta(\hat{p}, s)$ for all $s \in \Delta_\epsilon(c_i)$, we just have to assure, that $2\epsilon - \alpha < 0$, i.e. $\alpha > 2\epsilon$. If we select the $\epsilon$-environment so that it contains the whole pixel $S_i$, i.e. $\epsilon > l/\sqrt{2}$ (where l is the length of the pixel side), the perpendicular bisector of $p_i$ and $\hat{p}$ will not intersect the pixel. The result is, that the point more distant from $c_i$ can be disregarded if $\alpha$ (which is the difference between the distances of $c_i$ and the two generating point) is large enough ($\alpha > \sqrt{2}l$).

During label propagation the nearest point is still unknown. In every intermediate stage we have an estimate, the "current nearest point". As the distance to the current nearest point can only decrease during the propagation procedure, the above criterion can be safely applied at any intermediate state, using just the current nearest point instead of $p_i$.

The generalization of the above procedure to nD is simple. Neither the proof of the locality principle nor the perpendicular bisector criterion was dependent on the dimension of the Euclidean space (the bisectors are now of course hyperplanes). All considerations about the threshold selection hold in nD, only the selection of the suitable $\epsilon$ should be adjusted to $\epsilon > l\sqrt{n}/2$, resulting the nD threshold $\alpha > l\sqrt{n}$. The connectivity type to be applied in the label propagation algorithm has to be selected according to the dimensionality too ($2n$).

## 4  Implementation and Examples

The implementation of the algorithm proposed by the previous section is straight-forward. The selection of the VD generation algorithm is not at all critical. As the examples below will illustrate, in all cases the maximal number of remaining generating points in the regions was below 100. Consequently, the most trivial algorithms will be fast enough. On the other side special care must be taken because of the large number of co-spherical points. Working on the integer raster does not allow us to ignore this problem, in contrast to most of the published algorithms. For our test implementation we selected the simplest possible way. We generate the Delaunay-tetrahedralization first by simply checking the sphere-inclusion property of the Delaunay tetrahedra for all possible quadruples of the generating points. The co-sphericity check in this case is simple, the high co-sphericity rate actually speeds up the calculation considerably. The Delaunay tetrahedralization is then converted to the VD.

The performance of our algorithm depends basically on the efficiency of the partitioning. In order to check how well the generating points can be partitioned on real data sets, we tested the method on two 3D brain data sets segmented from gradient-echo MRI data. To check the effect of different resolution, we performed the calculation on the data with the original matrix size ($256 \times 256 \times 128$) and on data compressed by a factor 2. Figure 2 shows the 3D visualization of the datasets used in the study. For the 3D rendering we used the ANALYZE [13] software package.

The number of generating points (corresponding to the border cracks of the brain objects) was 276,901 and 238,611 for case 1 resp. case 2 when using full resolution. The compressed datasets had 58,151 resp. 55,242 boundary points.

In case 1 the voxel in the full resolution dataset with the highest number of nearby generating points had 78 points, 99% of all voxels had less then 41 nearby generating points. Using the low resolution data, those numbers were 73 and 35 respectively. In case 2 the largest number of nearby generating points was 66 with 99% of the voxels having less then 32 points for the full resolution case, for the compressed data 79 resp. 29 resulted.

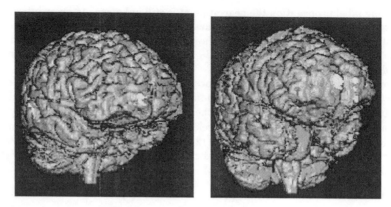

**Figure 2**: 3D rendering of the segmented brain datasets used in our test study.

We can see, that the partitioning provides satisfactory results on the data sets we want to process. They confirm our expectations too, that the number of the nearby generating points depends in principle on the shape of the objects, and the resolution plays a much less significant role.

## 5  Conclusions

Voronoi skeletons have proved useful tools for describing and manipulating 2D shapes. A Voronoi skeleton generation procedure in 3D would give us an appealing way to deal with the extremely complex problems of handling 3D shapes. While algorithms for generating approximative 3D Voronoi diagrams has been previously proposed, the 3D generalization of the regularization procedure is strongly obstructed by the unavoidable errors of the approximation nearby the object boundary.

In this paper we proposed an algorithm, which, through a divide and conquer approach, allows to generate the exact VD of several 100.000 generating points on the discrete image raster. Tests on real data sets showed, that satisfactory partitioning of the generating points can be achieved by a vector label propagation procedure.

While in our study we concentrated on the VD generation of points on the discrete image raster, this assumption is actually not necessary. It is also possible to use other space subdivision then the original voxel matrix. Especially, we can use a cartesian subdivision with smaller or larger resolution than our original image. The proposed algorithm actually consists of two steps. The first one is the partitioning, the second is the local VD generation. The finer the partitioning is, i.e. the better the resolution of the propagation, the smaller clusters can be possibly achieved for the VD generation. This means that the selection of the resolution for the label propagation actually decides, how much of the work should be done using label propagation, and how much should remain for VD generation. In general, the partitioning could be performed on inhomogeneously subdivided image space, as e.g. on octrees too. It would allow us to save unnecessary work on label propagation in sparsely populated areas, while the desired partitioning still can be achieved in the neighbourhood of dense centers. This way of proceeding would promise a substantial reduction of the large amount of computer memory needed by the present implementation.

The generation of the 3D VD allows us the necessary studies of the regularization procedure. Our future research must concentrate on the topological structure of the 3D Voronoi diagrams, and on the different pruning procedures, allowing the regularization of the 3D VD to a practically useful skeletonal description of 3D objects.

**Acknowledgment:**
Our intuitive understanding of the complicated anatomy hiding in 3D MRI data sets was substantially improved by the ANALYZE software package developed at the Mayo Clinic, Rochester MN. We are grateful to Prof. Richard A. Robb for offering research cooperation and making the software available. We would like to thank to Prof. F. Jolesz and Prof. R. Kikinis from MRI Division of the Brigham and Women's Hospital Boston for providing the segmented brain data used during this study.

## 6 References

[1] H. Blum, *A Transformation for Extracting New Descriptors of Shape*, from: Models for the Perception of Speech and Visual Form, W. Walthen-Dunn, ed. 1967, MIT Press 1967, Cambridge, MA.

[2] F. Klein, *Vollständige Mittelachsenbeschreibung binärer Bildstrukturen mit euklidischer Metrik und korrekter Topologie*, Dissertation ETH Nr. 8411, Zurich 1987.

[3] R.L. Ogniewicz and M. Ilg, *Voronoi Skeletons: Theory and Applications*, Proc. CVPR'92 pp. 63-69, IEEE Computer Society Press, 1992

[4] R.L. Ogniewicz, Discrete Voronoi Skeletons, Diss. ETH No. 9876 Zürich, 1992

[5] R.A. Dwyer, *Higher-dimensional Voronoi diagrams in linear expected time*, in: $5^{th}$ ACM Symposium on Computational Geometry, Saarbrücken, June 1989.

[6] J.D. Boissonat and M. Teillaud, *On the Randomized Construction of the Delaunay Tree*, Technical Report 1140, INRIA (France), 1989.

[7] E. Bruzzone, L. De Floriani and E. Puppo, *Reconstructing Three-Dimensional Shapes through Euler Operators*, in: Progress in Image Analysis and Processing, World Scientific Publishing Co., 1990.

[8] G. Székely, Ch. Brechbühler, O. Kübler, R. Ogniewicz and T. Budinger, *Mapping the human cerebral cortex using 3D medial manifolds*, Proc. VBC'92, Chapel Hill, October 1992, pp.130-144, SPIE Vol. 1808

[9] P.E. Danielsson, *Euclidean Distance Mapping*, CVGIP **14**, p. 227-248, 1980.

[10] J.C. Mullikin, *The Vector Distance Transform in Two and Three Dimensions*, CVGIP: Graph. Models **54**(6) pp. 526-535

[11] F.P. Preparata and M. I. Shamos, *Computational Geometry*, Springer-Verlag, Heidelberg, 1985.

[12] C. Arcelli and G. Sanniti di Baja, *Computing Voronoi diagrams in digital pictures*, Patt.Rec.Letters **4**(5) pp.383-389, 1986.

[13] R.A. Robb, *A software system for interactive and qualitative analysis of biomedical images*, in: K.H. Höhne, H. Fuchs, S.M. Pizer, *3D Imaging in Medicine*, NATO ASI Series, 1990, Vol. F60, pp.333-361

542

# HANDWRITTEN CHARACTER RECOGNITION
# USING DYNAMIC-RESOLUTION SHAPE ANALYSIS

GUIDO TASCINI   and   PRIMO ZINGARETTI

*Istituto di Informatica - Università di Ancona*
*Via Brecce Bianche I-60131 Ancona (Italy)*

ABSTRACT

The paper describes a character recognition method gathering Dynamic Resolution (DR) approach and character circumscription by the Minimum Rectangle (MR). Instead of extracting features from contours or skeletons the method extracts features primarily from the background regions bounded by character itself and its minimum bounding box. The information is integrated with features extracted from the profiles of the characters and with horizontal and vertical cut analysis. A "profile" is an ordered unidimensional vector of the vertical or horizontal minimum distances between a side of the MR and the character itself; a "cut" is a vertical or horizontal line segment delimited by the MR. The dynamic resolution allows to reconnect broken pieces and speeds up feature extraction. A balanced tree classifier based on feature tests is used to recognize characters. A validation stage follows a leaf node reaching. In case of failure, feature extraction and recognition is attempted again with a different resolution. The proposed method has been adopted to implement the core of a low-cost off-line character recognizer which classifies handwritten numerals and capital letters of the Roman alphabet.

## 1. Introduction

In the literature the *character shape recognition* approaches can be broadly classified into statistical and syntactical methods, while some recognition systems use combinations of both approaches. The recognition decision may be based on a distance comparison between the character and a reference model (template matching) or driven by a set of features extracted from the character (feature matching). Independently from the used approach, the recognition system may rely on a single decision or multiple decisions. In the latter case decisions from different recognition methods may be combined in parallel or sequentially [2].

The *feature matching* strategy is based on the hypothesis that a set of features can identifies a character, that is the differences among characters are more significant than the differences between the drawings of the same character. Features may derive both from processed properties of the characters and from more sophisticated properties using perceptual criteria. Moreover features can be binary or not. *Binary features* detect the presence or the absence of a characteristic in the unknown character; they easily lead to a decision tree but they do not produce alternative choices, which are very useful in the post-processing phase. As to the *non binary features*, they are developed many methods both for dividing the feature space into decision regions and to construct a suitable feature vector for the matching process [1, 2, 7]. Some common characteristics of the feature matching strategies are: the number of templates tends to increase with the character shape complexity; the cost of adding new features may increase exponentially and may become even ineffective due to complex interdependencies among features; changing the feature matching from a sequential to a binary search allows to decrease the computing cost.

In general, a pre-processing phase precedes the character shape recognition. The aim of *pre-processing* is twofold: character segmentation (separation of characters) and input data enhancement (noise reduction, stroke connection, slope correction, size normalization and others). As complex shapes can be recognized from a skeletonized or stylized drawing, then thinning techniques [3] (elimination of the border points that do not compromise character connection) play an important role in this phase and even more in the case of handwritten characters, where the thickness contains very little useful information.

The paper describes an innovative method to recognize handwritten characters using circumscription of the character by a Minimum Rectangle (MR) and a Dynamic Resolution (DR) approach.

Instead of extracting features from contours or skeletons the method extracts features primarily from the background regions bounded by character itself and its minimum bounding box [8]. The information is supplemented with features extracted from the profiles of the characters and with horizontal and vertical cut analysis. A "profile" is an ordered unidimensional vector of the vertical or horizontal minimum distances between a side of the MR and the character itself; a "cut" is a vertical or horizontal line segment delimited by the MR. The DR approach performs a shape modification of the character. In particular this modification happens in a dynamic way during the recognition process; that is, the partial or final result of the recognition strategy may suggest to modify resolution, going up or down on the 'pyramid' depending on the mismatching of data with the a-priori models.

The dynamic resolution allows to reconnect broken pieces and speeds up feature extraction. A balanced tree classifier based on feature tests is used to recognize characters. A validation stage follows a leaf node reaching. In case of failure, feature extraction and recognition is attempted again with a different resolution.

The proposed method has been adopted to implement the core of a low-cost off-line character recognizer which classifies handwritten numerals and capital letters of the Roman alphabet.

MR and its pertinent features are defined in section 2, and the DR approach is described in section 3. Finally, section 4 presents a brief overview of the prototypical recognizer we have implemented using the dynamic-resolution approach to handwritten character recognition.

## 2. The MR Region

In the following subsections, we will define the MR, and analyze in detail profiles and cuts.

### 2.1. MR Definition

Our approach to character shape recognition is based on the analysis of regions around the characters in addition to the information related to the character body. We define the area of interest where focusing analysis as the rectangle, named MR, that consists in the Minimum Rectangle circumscribing the character to be recognized.

The MR is calculated starting from the array containing a single character. Then, the MR definition process performs a region labelling by which a different label is assigned to each region.

The regions belonging to the background and enclosed in the MR allow to define new parameters. For example, some of these regions are *external* to the character and partially adjacent to MR, while other ones are totally surrounded by the character (*internal* regions). The right image of Fig. 1 shows the result of the application of the character circumscription process, at a level-2 resolution, to the input sample shown at its left. As

544

we can see, the character circumscription process generates two internal regions and four external regions for the processed character 'B'

While in the case of machine printed characters the regions resulting from the previous process are highly constrained, for handwritten characters these regions result variable in number, shape and position. A recognition process based on a rigorous classification of the above regions is bound to fail. For example let us consider the letter 'E'. The three quasi-horizontal segments can cross, exactly join or not reach at all the vertical segment, and besides any of them can be the larger one. Consequently the resulting regions can vary enormously as shown in Fig. 2.

Fig. 1. The character circumscription.

Fig. 2. Possible regions resulting from different writings of the letter 'E'.

Anyway, the analysis of the background regions of a training character set has been performed to identifying for each character the regions that are invariant about shape, dimension or position. For example it is often possible to discriminate between the characters 'U' and 'V' by evaluating the areas of the two low lateral regions of these characters; we can decide in favour of the 'V' whenever their sum is more than 30% of background area. We think this method is undoubtedly simpler than the study of the low profile curvature.

The results of this analysis allow to assert that the regions so obtained appear more stable and easy to handle than the usual stroke approach; this is due to the fact that most of the features characterizing a symbol are more stable if detected from the regions, and the advantage is reinforced by the possibility of varying the image resolution and of delaying the character thickness, as we will see in the next section.

Another relevant aspect of the approach is its insensibility to character size in that the character normalization is conceived as ratio to MR area. Furthermore, the features which are detectable from these regions result very sensible to character type.

Therefore, for each labelled region, we extracted many features. For example, the area and the coordinates of the extreme points in the four cardinal directions easy allow to deduce if a region is surrounded by the character or not.

## 2.2. "Profile" Analysis

The features above described are used to build a tree classifier based on feature tests to recognize characters. Many features have been extracted from labelled regions, but, often, they are unable to correctly discriminate characters; so they are integrated with features extracted from the profiles as well as with horizontal and vertical cut analysis.

The four profiles (left, right, top, down) of the character to the sides of MR are extracted. Each profile is an ordered unidimensional vector whose components represent the minimum distance of the character from the MR corresponding side. For example the left profile is constituted by all the minimum horizontal distances between the character and the MR left side, starting from the first row till the last one. Fig. 3 shows a '3' handwritten character, surrounded by its MR at the adopted lower resolution, with its left and right profiles. Many features can be extracted from profile analysis. For example an abrupt change (discontinuity) in the profile intensity may denote a "gulf".

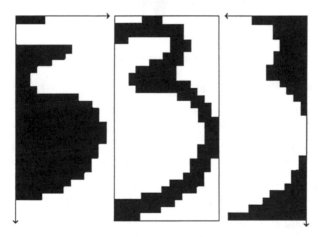

Fig. 3. Left and right "profiles" of a '3' handwritten character.

## 2.3. "Cut" Analysis

A "cut" is a horizontal or vertical line internal to the MR. The "cut" analysis supplies a suited set of features. In particular, it detects "gulfs", that is regions between two consecutive character-runs. Cut analysis is simply the analysis of a raster (a row or a column) of the MR. Starting from an extreme of the chosen raster, the process searches for a sequence of points (belonging to a gulf-region) situated between two series of points belonging to the character. If this gulf-region exists, the analysis evaluates if it extends as far as the nearer MR side which is parallel to the raster. This technique provides a lot of useful information. For example, if by applying a low-horizontal-cut (that is a cut in the lower half of the MR, as shown in Fig. 4) we detect a region which extends as far as the bottom side of the MR, then expected characters should be both 'A' and 'R'.

For computational reasons cut analysis is activated only by those characters which use specialized features to be differently classified or recognized.

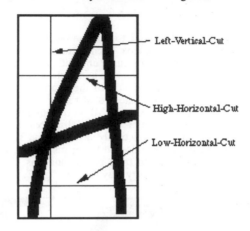

Fig. 4. Some "cuts".

## 3. The Dynamic Resolution Approach

The usual failures in character shape recognition are strictly related to the acquiring device resolution and to the input sample dimensions. Typical input resolution values vary from 75 to 300 dpi, while input handwritten character sizes range from 0.25 to 3 cm$^2$.

Our DR approach performs a character shape dynamic modification. From a digitized image it is built a quadtree [6] representation. This is obtained by partitioning the image in four square quadrants. Each quadrant, if not homogeneous (that is, with all pixels of the same colour), is partitioned again in four quadrants, and so on with a recursive process. This process stops if we reach homogeneous quadrants, which constitute the tree leaves, and in the worst case are represented by a single pixel at level 0. The quadtree so obtained is a compact image representation very useful to speed up the next processing. Besides, it is a hierarchical representation which allows to simulate a dynamic approach to the character resolution. In other words it is possible to go along a pyramidal structure whose levels may be implemented by rising from the leaves of the quadtree to an higher level: this is obtained by grouping n leaves in one with some homogeneity criterion, for instance the prevailing colour or the mean gray level. The result is a "working resolution" which varies in case of necessity.

After the previous step, the DR approach continues with a run-time binarization process. Binarization is applied as the information involved with gray level images is useless to our method for which black and white images are adequate. The starting threshold is selected by an automatic thresholding process [4] which is based on the histogram method [5], as the MR region has a bimodal gray-level intensity histogram. The binarization process along with the MR region allow to classify pixels as belonging to the character or to the background.

Apart from the input sample dimensions, which directly influence the number of levels in the quadtree representation (for example, a character of 80x140 pixels has a 256x256 image as the minimum circumscribing square, so requiring a quadtree with 9 levels), two other parameters may be used to vary the "working resolution". They are:

a) the quadtree level (L) at which we perform the feature extraction;

b) the minimum number (X) of pixels, at level 0, required to be black so that the common ancestor node, at a fixed quadtree level, can be considered black.

In particular, the possibility to work at a higher level in the quadtree structure constitutes a great improvement in that it fills up discontinuities and speeds up the processing. For example, the character 'A' shown in Fig. 5a (written using an orange felt pen) results, at level 0, as shown in Fig. 5b, after the automatic binarization process: its right stroke, in particular, is constituted by a lot of small disconnected regions. Instead, at level 1 of the quadtree structure the character is constituted by a unique connected region, as shown in Fig. 5c.

The above two parameters L and X are strictly correlated; anyway, they may produce different results in terms of character thickness and stroke connection. This different behaviour can be used to define both *invariant features* and *clue-features* useful in background region classification. We name invariant those features which do not change for relative small variations of L or X. They may be used to support the previously formulated hypotheses. Examples of invariant features may be: internal regions (holes), negative or positive gulfs, adjacency to a side of the MR, etc. Along with these invariant features we adopt clue-features to tune the system in a suitable resolution, in terms of L and X, for a fast and efficient character shape recognition. A typical clue-feature which leads to a higher resolution is the presence of "large regions", while coarse resolutions need in presence of the clue-feature "disconnected regions".

According to the second parameter, an original 256x256 image can be transformed to a 64x64 one by applying the following rule: a node at level L=2 in the quadtree (corresponding to a block of 4x4 pixels) becomes a black node if at least X of its 16 leaves are black. The parameter X greatly influences the character thickness. In particular, we can choose a value for X during a learning phase, and we can change the value of X during the validation phase in case of recognition failure.

a        b        c

Fig. 5. A noisy input sample (a), its binarization (b), and its recovery at quadtree level 1 (c).

Fig. 6 shows the results of resolution modifications by varying both L and X. Fig.6a shows the input sample, and Fig. 6b represents the result of the automatic binarization process (L=0). The three images in Fig. 6c represent the quadtree at level L=1 obtained with X=4, X=2 and X=1, respectively from left to right. In the same way, the three images in Fig. 6d represent the quadtree at level L=2 obtained with X=16, X=8 and X=1.

548

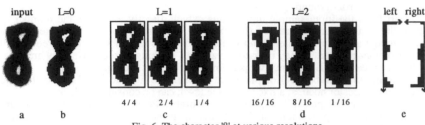

Fig. 6. The character '8' at various resolutions.

In the last case it becomes invisible the internal region of character '8', but analyzing its left and right profiles (Fig. 6e), which together represent an evident clue of the presence of large regions, it is easy to infer the adoption of a wrong resolution.

## 4. The Character Shape Recognition Strategy

In this section we describe a prototypical recognizer which uses a character-shape recognition strategy based on the analysis of features extracted from the MR region and on the DR approach.

Due to the chosen character set, constituted only by numerals and capital letters, input samples are usually disconnected. Moreover we were mainly interested in evaluating the performances and the robustness of the innovative character shape recognition approach, so we informed our writers to space out the characters. Consequently the recognizer can successfully perform the character segmentation without requiring recognition (external character segmentation).

The recognizer acquires images by a video camera, whose resolution is of about 75 dpi, connected to a digitalization board on a PC, or by an optical scanning device at resolution varying from 75 to 300 dpi. In either cases a pixel is stored using a 256 gray level scale in order to avoid loss of information. Classical preprocessing techniques, in particular spatial filtering with a 3x3 convolution kernel, are performed to reduce noise, and blocks, each containing only one character, are extracted from the acquired image.

The core module of the recognizer can be partitioned in the following seven steps: quadtree construction, binarization, resolution transformation, character circumscription, feature analysis, decision tree descent and result validation.

*Quadtree construction.* A full resolution (L=n) quadtree representation of the input sample, circumscribed in a square region, is built from the digitized image.

*Binarization.* A run-time automatic process, based on the histogram method, selects the best threshold at which the image will be binarized. Then, without losing information, this step updates the 1-bit field of each leaf node of the quadtree with the appropriate colour (white or black, 0 or 1).

*Resolution transformation.* Using the approach described in section 3, the input sample is reduced to a defined lower resolution by operating on the quadtree data structure; in particular they are chosen the parameters L and X at which the features will be extracted. The main results are the availability of a variable resolution (which allows the conjunction of strokes by increasing character thickness), and a simplified image description (which allows to increase the speed of successive algorithms).

*Character circumscription.* It detects the MR which allows to partition the background into regions that surround the character (external) or are enclosed by it (internal).

*Feature analysis.* As we have seen, the character inscribed in MR is analyzed using the typical features of a-priori character models. These models are related to the regions contained in MR, as well as to profiles and cuts. Regions may not be contour constrained and so they may be considered as more general features; that is, we can have an internal region like a hole, or a NW area as a NW quadrant.

The features are checked in a learning phase in order to obtain their occurrence probabilities. From these values we can compute the probabilities of the candidate models during the recognition phase, in which we descend along a decision tree (see next step). These features are based on regions with significant aspects. Some of these aspects are the followings: presence of more than one internal region; position of barycentre and extreme points of each internal region; regions with significant dimensions (greater than 10%); ratio "character area / MR area" (for 'I' about 50% ); regions with significant ratio "region area / MR area" ('U', 'V', 'L'); depth of central upper region (as in 'U', 'V', and 'Y' characters); difference between left and right parts of character-regions; difference between vertices (NW for 'S' and '5', or NE for 'Z' and '2'); SE region ('C' and 'G').

While region and profile features are computed in order to be used for character classification purpose, the cut analysis is activated only by those characters which use specialized features to be differently classified or recognized.

*Decision tree descent.* In a decision tree, the whole character set is partitioned in some sub-tree, which are recursively partitioned in sub-tree until a single character is reached. The feature test is the basis of the character-shape recognition process whose strategy consists in the visit of a decision tree.

In our case, the recognition process is performed descending a decision tree, where the features may be related to the profile shape, or detected by convenient cuts performed both horizontally and vertically on the character. At run-time, starting from the whole character set, the descent is performed on the basis of feature evaluations (tests). For example, if we adopt the decision tree represented in Fig. 7, the first two tests partition the whole set into three subsets so that: characters with at least an internal region are assigned to the first subset; characters with at least a gulf in the top profile are assigned to the second subset; all the other characters, that do not satisfy any of the previous two properties, are assigned to the third subset.

The prototypical recognizer uses the decision tree represented in Fig. 7. This is not the unique possible tree which can be successfully assumed with the adopted strategy. This one was chosen because it is constituted by balanced subsets, that is with almost the same number of elements. For example, after the execution of the first two tests, the whole set is subdivided into three large subsets each with 13, 11, and 16 elements respectively. Balancing, allowing to reduce the mean number of tests necessary to reach a leaf, is an important characteristic for execution time requirements. Exceptions to tree balancing happen when an element may interfere with the successive analysis of its brothers. For example the character 'W' is separated from its brothers because it needs of a special test based on a joined analysis of its top and down profiles.

Fig. 7 points out another characteristic of our decision tree: the elements belonging to the subsets originated from a father node may be more than the elements of the father itself. For example the root has 36 elements (26 Roman alphabet capital letter and 10 Arabic numerals) and its sons have 40 elements in all; so some characters may belong to more than one subset. For example the character '4', according to the writing style, may have an internal region (first subset) or not (third subset).

550

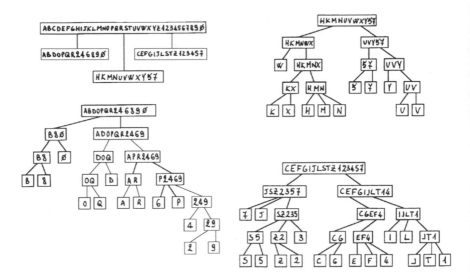

Fig. 7. The decision tree.

*Result validation.* The main disadvantage in adopting a decision tree approach is the lack of alternative results. If a post-processing context analysis should reject the decision adopted there are no indications how detecting another candidate-character. To overcome this problem we provided our recognizer of a result validation test by which a measure of confidence of the recognition is computed. This post-processing phase of handwriting recognition is performed to control and to increase the accuracy and the robustness of the recognition results. For each character, excluding the feature already used during the tree descent, they are tested 3-4 more characteristics. Each test returns a score which is totalized. If the final score is greater than a defined threshold then the candidate-character is accepted as recognized, else the core module is reactivated using a different resolution in the resolution transformation step.

For example, if the letter recognized is 'B', descending the tree the following features have been successfully analyzed: the character has at least 2 internal regions; they exist 2 internal regions; the 2 internal regions are not lateral; in the left profile there is not a central gulf. The confidence of the recognition is validated by analyzing the following other features: presence of a central gulf in the right profile (if it exists we add +30 otherwise -20); roundness of the lower edge (if a gulf is absent we add +30 otherwise -20); position of the lowermost point of the lower internal region (if it is nearly on the lower side of MR we add +20 otherwise -30); position of the uppermost point of the upper internal region (if it is nearly on the upper side of MR we add +20 otherwise -30). In practice, if an 'A' character is recognized as a 'B' this algorithm gives a very low scoring (-40) and then rejects the hypothesis.

This recognizer was checked on a set of 1200 characters: 1169 were recognized at the first iteration, other 18 characters were recognized at the second iteration and all the remaining 13 characters were recognized at the third iteration. To characterize the practical use of the recognizer it is necessary to define the constrains of character writing. In our case the main constrain is the following: the character has to be constituted by a single structure. Of course the Arabic numerals and the Roman alphabet capital letters are per se single-structured. Instead the acquisition noise may generate dummy holes and some separated strokes. For this purpose the variable resolution step was fundamental, and the connection of character point set became a weak constraint for our method.

In the immediate future the recognizer robustness will be statistically checked on a larger population of samples, and they will be included lower letters also. With the exception of the 'i' character, which can be treated separately, lower letters respect the continuity constrain, so good results are to be expected.

## 5. Conclusion

A method has been described to recognize isolated and broken handwritten numerals and capital letters. The method extracts features from background regions and from character profiles. In some cases it uses horizontal and vertical cut analysis. The background regions are bounded by the character and its minimum bounding box, named MR. The broken pieces of the character may be reconnected using a dynamic resolution approach which decreases the input image resolution. DR speeds up feature extraction by allowing, in some cases, computations with a rough scale. The characters are then recognized using a balanced tree classifiers, based on feature evaluations together with a validation stage which follows the reaching of a leaf. The feature extraction as well as the recognition is attempted again, with different resolutions in case of failure.

The promising results of the prototypical recognizer suggest to continue with this approach. The feature improvement will concern: firstly, a more rigorous analysis of the feature classification in terms of their discriminating, invariant and clue-aspect value; secondly, the analysis and the recognition of lower letters also; finally, the adoption of a Knowledge-Based System, as the generalized one proposed by Mai and Suen [2], with a recognition decision quantified by confidence measurements and using the same knowledge base for both training and recognition processes.

## 6. References

[1]  A. Belaid, J. P. Haton, "A syntactic approach for handwritten mathematical formula recognition", *IEEE Trans. Patt. Anal. Mach. Int.*, vol. PAMI-6, pp. 105-111, 1984.
[2]  C.Y. Suen, C.Nadal, R.Legault, T.A. Mai and L.Lam, "Computer recognition of unconstrained handwritten numerals", *Proc. IEEE*, vol. 80-7, pp.1162-1180, 1992.
[3]  N. J. Naccache and R. Shinghal, "SPTA: a proposed algorithm for thinning binary patterns", *IEEE Trans. Syst. Man Cybern.*, vol. SMC-14, pp. 409-418, 1984.
[4]  P. Puliti, G. Tascini, P. Zingaretti, "Region detection in grey-level images", in *Proc. 5th Int. Conf. on Image Analysis and Processing*, pp. 106-110, Sept. 1989.
[5]  A. Rosenfeld and A. C. Kak, *Digital Picture Processing*, vol. II, Academic Press, New York, 1982.
[6]  H. Samet, "The quadtree and related data structures", *ACM Comput. Surveys*, vol. 16 No. 2, pp. 187-260, 1984.
[7]  C. C. Tappert, C. Y. Suen and T. Wakahara, "The state of the art in on-line handwriting recognition", *IEEE Trans. Pattern Anal. Machine Intell.*, vol. PAMI-12, pp. 787-808, Aug. 1990.
[8]  G. Tascini, P. Puliti, P. Zingaretti, "Handwritten character recognition using background analysis", in *Character Recognition Technologies*, Proc. SPIE, vol.1906, San Jose, California, February 1993, pp. 126-133.

# LOGARITHMIC SHAPE DECOMPOSITION

REIN VAN DEN BOOMGAARD * and DANNY WESTER

*Department of Mathematics and Computer Science*
*University of Amsterdam*
*The Netherlands*

### ABSTRACT

This paper describes an algorithm to decompose an arbitrary shape into a union of convex subsets. These convex subsets are scaled versions of the shapes from a collection of "basis shapes". The basis shapes are very efficiently *logarithmically* decomposed. The algorithm to find the convex subsets of the shape to be decomposed makes use of the *generalized distance transform* and the *generalized medial axis*. With the new decomposition algorithm, a significant decrease in the computational complexity of the morphological erosion and dilation is obtained, ranging from a speedup factor of 3 to 15 for the test set of shapes.

## 1 Introduction

Mathematical morphology has proven to be a valuable tool in the description and analysis of shape [1]. In mathematical morphology quantitative shape description is based on shape deformation (e.g. the skeleton, the erosion curve [2] and the deformation described by partial differential equations [3, 4]). The basic operations for shape deformation as used in mathematical morphology are erosion and dilation where the shape under study is "probed" with a known shape (the structuring element). In practical applications there is often a need to use large structuring elements. In this paper the definitions and notation as introduced by Serra [1] are used and summarized in table 1.

The computational complexity of a brute force implementation of the erosion and dilation is linear in the number of pixels in the structuring element (its area) and thus quadratic in the size of the structuring elements (for 2D shapes). This observation explains the need for decomposition of large structuring element into a sequence of smaller structuring elements, such that the total number of pixels involved is significantly reduced.

---

*Work done in NWO/SION project 612-322-205: Model-controlled Image Processing.

Table 1: **Notation and Definitions** of the basic Morphological Set Operations, $X$,$Y$ and $S$ are sets.

| Name | Notation | Definition |
|---|---|---|
| Translation | $X_t$ | $X_t = \{x \mid x - t \in X\}$ |
| Complement | $X^c$ | $X^c = \{x \mid x \notin X\}$ |
| Transpose | $\check{X}$ | $\check{X} = \{x \mid -x \in X\}$ |
| Scaling | $kS$ | $kS = \{kx \mid x \in S\}$ |
| Union | $X \cup Y$ | $X \cup Y = \{x \mid x \in X \text{ or } x \in Y\}$ |
| Intersection | $X \cap Y$ | $X \cap Y = \{x \mid x \in X \text{ and } x \in Y\}$ |
| Power | $S^{\oplus k}$ | $S^{\oplus k} = S \oplus S \oplus \cdots \oplus S$ (k terms) |
| Area/No. of Elements | $\#(S)$ | $\#(S) = $ Area ($\mathbf{R}^n$) or No. of elements ($\mathbf{Z}^n$) |
| Minkowski Addition | $X \oplus S$ | $X \oplus S = \bigcup_{y \in S} X_y$ |
| Minkowski Subtraction | $X \ominus S$ | $X \ominus S = \bigcap_{y \in S} X_y$ |

Consider the task of eroding or dilating a shape $X$ with a structuring element $S$. Finding an optimal decomposition of $S$ seems to be an intractable problem, meaning that practical algorithms need to be based on some heuristics (e.g. restrictions on the shapes considered or restrictions on the resulting decomposition).

The simplest way to decrease the number of pixels in the structuring element $S$ is to simply leave some pixels out. Let $T$ be a subset of $S$ containing the boundary of $S$. Then $X \oplus S = X \oplus T$ in case the connected components of $X$ do not fit into the holes created in $S$. As an example, the intersection of $S$ with a regular grid containing just one pixels in every $2 \times 2$ neighbourhood (with the border added) reduces the number of pixels with nearly a factor 4. In case the objects to be dilated are everywhere more than 2 pixels wide, then the dilation with $T$ is equivalent with dilation using the original structuring element $S$. It depends on the application, of course, whether this naive approach can be used.

A very efficient decomposition technique is the dimensional decomposition in which a dilation with a 2D structuring element is replaced by a sequence of 1D dilations. In general any symmetric ($S = \check{S}$) polygonal set is equal to the dilation of all the edges in half its contour. Unfortunately this decomposition method is only valid in the continuous domain (except for those discrete polygons whose edges are aligned with the axes).

Algorithms for structuring element decomposition geared towards implementation on special purpose computers are described by Zhuang and Haralick [5] and Xu [6].

Perhaps the most well-known decomposition method for *convex* sets is the *linear decomposition* based on the fact that any convex set is divisible with respect to the dilation, i.e. $\alpha S \oplus \beta S = (\alpha + \beta)S$ iff $S$ is convex (see [7]). Thus a dilation with structuring element $kS$ can be implemented as $k$-times repeated dilation with $S$, i.e. $kS = S^{\oplus k}$. In general, in 2D space the number of pixels in $kS$ is $\mathcal{O}\left(k^2 \#(S)\right)$ whereas the number of pixels in the decomposition equals $k\#(S)$.

Starting from the linear decomposition Pecht, [8] has given an improved decomposition method. He has shown that for all structuring elements $S$ there exists a positive integer $m$ such that for all $k \geq m$: $(k+1)S = kS \oplus S = kS \oplus E(S)$, where $E(S)$ is the *extreme set* of $S$. For a convex polygon the extreme set $E(S)$ contains the vertices of the polygon. Assuming that $m = 1$ for structuring element $S$ we have that $kS = S \oplus E(S)^{oplus(k-1)}$, thus reducing the number of pixels to $\#(S)+(k-1)\#(E(S))$. In general $E(S)$ contains significantly fewer pixels than $S$ itself.

For convex sets the result of Pecht can be improved upon resulting in the *logarithmic decomposition* of sets. Again consider a set $S$ such that $S \oplus S = S \oplus E(S)$. Logarithmic decomposition is obtained by noting that for the set $2S$, Pecht's result can be used again: $2S \oplus 2S = 2S \oplus E(2S)$. Repeating the argument again for $4S$ and then for $8S$ etc. the decomposition of $16S$ is equal to $S \oplus E(S) \oplus E(2S) \oplus E(4S) \oplus E(8S)$. For the above decomposition the total number of pixels is reduced from $\#(S)+15\#(E(S))$ to $\#(S) + 4\#(E(S))$. Let S be the $3 \times 3$-square, then:

$$16S = \left\{ \vcenter{\hbox{$\vdots\vdots\vdots$}} \right\} \oplus \left\{ \vcenter{\hbox{$\vdots\ \vdots$}} \right\} \oplus \left\{ \vcenter{\hbox{$\vdots\ \ \vdots$}} \right\} \oplus \left\{ \vcenter{\hbox{}} \right\} \oplus \left\{ \vcenter{\hbox{}} \right\}$$

In this paper we introduce a decomposition algorithm that decomposes an arbitrary shape into a union of convex subsets. These convex subsets are chosen from a collection of "basis sets". These convex subsets, which can be quite large themselves, are very efficiently *logarithmically* decomposed. The algorithm to find the convex subsets of the shape to be decomposed makes use of the *generalized distance transform* and the *generalized medial axis*.

## 2    Logarithmic Decomposition of Convex Shapes

In the previous section, logarithmic decomposition has been briefly introduced as a generalization of the use of extreme points as introduced by Pecht [8]. A detailed theoretical treatment can be found in [9] whereas its practical use is discussed in [10], this subsection only considers logarithmic decomposition of 2D sets. Only continuous sets are considered to start with. Later on the decomposition of discrete sets is discussed.

Let $S$ be a *polytope* (i.e. a convex polygon). The extreme set $E(S)$ is the set of all vertices of the polytope. The *index-of-self-magnification* $\eta(S)$ is defined as $\eta(S) = \inf \{\alpha \mid \alpha S \oplus E(S) = (\alpha+1)S\}$. In [9] it is shown that for all $n$-dimensional sets an upperbound for $\eta(S)$ is the dimension $n$ (i.e. $\eta(S) \leq n$). A more accurate upperbound is given by the *index-of-symmetry* $\sigma(S)$. The index-of-symmetry equals

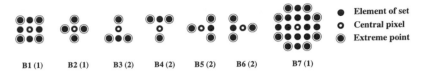

B1 (1)    B2 (1)    B3 (2)    B4 (2)    B5 (2)    B6 (2)    B7 (1)

Figure 1: **The 7 basis shapes used for decomposition.** The index-of-self-magnification is indicated in parentheses.

the smallest scaling factor $\alpha$ such that $\alpha S$ contains the transposed set $\check{S}$ (up to an irrelevant translation), i.e. $\sigma(S) = \inf\left\{\alpha \mid \exists\tau : \alpha S \subset \check{S}_\tau\right\}$. For 2D sets it is easy to show that $\eta(S) \leq \sigma(S)$. This means that instead of dilating $\sigma(S)S$ with $S$ we can dilate $\sigma(S)S$ with $E(S)$. For symmetric sets $\sigma(S) = 1$ and for triangles $\sigma(S) = 2$. In this sense triangles are the most non-symmetric polytopes in 2D.

Until now, the use of continuous sets is assumed. However, logarithmic decomposition can also be used for discrete sets. A *grid polytope* is a polytope whose vertices are (discretization) grid points. Let $S$ be a grid-polytope, then only for integer values of $\alpha$ it is true that $\alpha S$ is also a grid polytope.

Let $S$ be a discrete grid-polytope and let $\gamma = 1/\eta(S)$ then $kS$ (with $k > \eta(S)$) can be logarithmically decomposed according to the following algorithm (see [9]). Given the recurrence relations:

$$r_i = r_{i-1} + \lfloor \gamma r_{i-1} \rfloor, \quad S_i = S_{i-1} \oplus E(\lfloor \gamma r_{i-1} \rfloor S)$$

with starting conditions:

$$r_0 = \lceil \frac{1}{\gamma} \rceil, \quad S_0 = S^{\oplus r_0}$$

then, with $N = \max\{i \mid r_i \leq k\}$:

$$S^{\oplus k} = S_N \oplus E((k - r_N)S).$$

# 3 Decomposition of Arbitrary Shapes

In the new decomposition algorithm presented in this section, the shape $S$ is written as the union of convex sets $T_i$ $(i = 1, \ldots, n)$ such that $S = \bigcup_i T_i$. Then the dilation of a set $X$ with $S$ can be written as:

$$X \oplus S = X \oplus \left(\bigcup_i T_i\right) = \bigcup_i (X \oplus T_i).$$

For the erosion the duality $X \ominus S = (X^c \oplus S)^c$ leads to: $X \ominus S = X \ominus (\bigcup_i T_i) = \bigcap_i (X \ominus T_i)$. The sets $T_i$ are chosen to be scaled and/or translated versions of basis

Table 2: **Total number of pixels involved in the decomposition of the basis structuring elements** $kB_i$. The shapes $B_i$ are shown in figure 1. The number of pixels in the decomposition of $B_4$, $B_5$ and $B_6$ are equal to those tabulated for $B_3$.

| k | $\#(kB_1)$ | $\#_\ell(kB_1)$ | $\#(kB_2)$ | $\#_\ell(kB_2)$ | $\#(kB_3)$ | $\#_\ell(kB_3)$ | $\#(kB_7)$ | $\#_\ell(kB_7)$ |
|---|---|---|---|---|---|---|---|---|
| 1 | 9 | 9 | 5 | 5 | 5 | 5 | 21 | 21 |
| 2 | 25 | 13 | 13 | 9 | 13 | 10 | 69 | 26 |
| 4 | 81 | 17 | 41 | 13 | 41 | 16 | 249 | 34 |
| 6 | 169 | 21 | 85 | 17 | 85 | 19 | 541 | 42 |
| 8 | 289 | 21 | 145 | 17 | 145 | 22 | 945 | 42 |
| 10 | 441 | 25 | 221 | 21 | 221 | 25 | 1461 | 50 |
| 12 | 625 | 25 | 313 | 21 | 313 | 25 | 2089 | 50 |
| 14 | 841 | 25 | 421 | 21 | 421 | 28 | 2829 | 50 |
| 16 | 1089 | 25 | 545 | 21 | 545 | 28 | 3681 | 50 |
| 18 | 1369 | 29 | 685 | 25 | 685 | 28 | 4645 | 58 |

shapes. A finite number of basis shapes $B_j$ $(j = 1, \ldots, N)$ is considered, each of which is convex and chosen in such a way that its scaled versions $kB_j$ are efficiently logarithmically decomposed. The basis shapes $(B_1, \ldots, B_7)$ used in this paper are given in figure 1 with their index-of-self-magnification $(\eta)$. In table 2 the number of pixels in both the linear decomposition as well the number of pixels in the logarithmic decomposition of $kB_i$ are given. All subsets $T_i$ are thus characterized by the basis shape used (shape index is $\mathcal{J}_i$), its position $x_i$ and its size $k_i$. The task of the decomposition algorithm can now be formulated as determining the triples $\{k_i, \mathcal{J}_i, x_i\}$ for $i = 1, \ldots, n$ (note that the number of triples has to be found as well) such that:

$$S = \bigcup_{i=1}^{n} T_i = \bigcup_{i=1}^{n} (k_i B_{\mathcal{J}_i})_{x_i} .$$

Even with a finite number of basis shapes $(B_1, \ldots, B_N)$ to choose from, the number of different possibilities to choose the triples $\{k_i, \mathcal{J}_i, x_i\}$ is far too great $(\mathcal{O}\left(2^{N \#(S)}\right))$ to rely on a straightforward search for the optimal combination of triples.

Instead of brute force searching we have chosen to restrict the triples $\{k_i, \mathcal{J}_i, x_i\}$ such that $(k_i B_{\mathcal{J}_i})_{x_i}$ is a maximal "disk" in $S$ [11]. Let $B$ be a discrete grid polytope. Then $(kB)_x$ is a maximal disk in set $S$ iff no other scaled version of $B$ (say $(\ell B)_y$) exists which is also entirely within $S$ and contains $(kB)_x$. The set of centers of all maximal disks $(kB)_x$ in $S$ is called the generalized medial axis of $S$ with respect to shape $B$ (see figure 2). The size $(k)$ can be calculated with the generalized distance transform.

With this restriction the algorithm to select the largest convex subsets of $S$ within a family of basis shapes $B_1, \ldots, B_N$ is as follows:

Figure 2: **Generalized Medial Axis.** In a. the original set $S$ is depicted. In b. the generalized medial axis with respect to a diamond shape and in c. the medial axis with respect to a square shape are shown.

1. Initialize the decomposition. The approximation of $S$ thusfar is set to the empty set $(S' = \emptyset)$. There are no triples selected yet $(i = 0$, list $=$ empty).

2. Set $i = i + 1$. Select the triple $\{k_i, \mathcal{J}_i, x_i\}$ (if not in the selected list already) from the medial axis points (of all basis shapes) such that the number of pixels added to the approximation of $S$ *minus* the number of pixels needed in the logarithmic decomposition of $k_i B_{\mathcal{J}_i}$ is maximal (let the subtraction be equal to $W$).

3. If $W \leq 0$ (i.e. no profit anymore: we may stop): goto 7.

4. Add the selected triple to the list (list $=$ list $+ \{k_i, \mathcal{J}_i, x_i\}$).

5. Add the covered pixels to the approximation $(S' = S' \cup (k_i B_{\mathcal{J}_i})_{x_i})$.

6. Goto 2

7. Remove all redundant triples. A triple $\{k_i, \mathcal{J}_i, x_i\}$ is redundant in case the set $(k_i B_{\mathcal{J}_i})_{x_i}$ is a subset of the union of all other sets $(k_j B_{\mathcal{J}_i})_{x_j}$ with $j \neq i$.

   At this point not all pixels in $S$ need to be covered, i.e. $S$ is not necessarily equal to the union of all selected subsets $(S')$. Therefore the rest pixels $R = S \setminus S'$ need to be considered separately. This gives the following final decomposition of $S$:

$$S = R \cup \left\{ \bigcup_i (k_i B_{\mathcal{J}_i})_{x_i} \right\}$$

## 4 Experiments

In order to test the described decomposition algorithm several shapes have been decomposed. In figure 3 the test shapes are depicted with the resulting decomposition. For each shape the layout is as follows: the picture on the left shows the selected

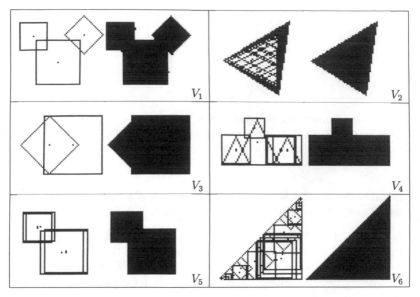

Figure 3: **Decomposition of Test Shapes.** For each shape the layout is as follows: to the left the selected medial axis points (in black) with the outlines of the corresponding basis shapes in grey and on the right the shape with the "left-over pixels" (see text) drawn in black.

medial axis points and the corresponding contours of the basis shapes and the picture on the right shows the original set with the left-over pixels (those pixels not covered in the logarithmic decomposition) in black. In table 3 for each of the test shapes the number of pixels in the original set, the total number of pixels in the decomposition, the brute force dilation time and the decomposition dilation time are given. Timing results were obtained on a SUN Sparc station by averaging over at least 10 dilation operations (on a $256 \times 256$ image).

Test shape $V_4$ clearly illustrates a disadvantage of the decomposition algorithm. In deciding which basis shape to choose only the number of pixels covered (relative to the number of pixels in the logarithmic decomposition) is taken into account. The largest basis shape with fits into $V_4$ is the upright triangle and thus is selected as the first subset. Because of this the algorithm prefers to use the triangle from that point onwards. It is evident however that in case only squares were selected the decomposition would have been much more efficient. Current research is looking at the possibility not only to consider the number of pixels in the selection criteria but also to consider the number of contours pixels covered by the selected shape. Note

Table 3: **Decomposition Test Results.** In the table below for each of the test shapes depicted in figure 3 the number of pixels in the set itself, the number of pixels in the decomposition of the set, the brute force dilation time and the decomposition dilation time are given.

| Shape | # | $\#_{ld}$ | $t$ | $t_{ld}$ |
|-------|------|-----|------|------|
| $V_1$ | 1849 | 65 | 3.79 | 0.41 |
| $V_2$ | 1153 | 83 | 2.46 | 0.65 |
| $V_3$ | 2138 | 56 | 4.43 | 0.38 |
| $V_4$ | 1434 | 68 | 3.06 | 0.47 |
| $V_5$ | 1484 | 35 | 3.05 | 0.27 |
| $V_6$ | 1891 | 99 | 3.88 | 0.67 |

that the selected triangle in shape $V_7$ shares only one side with original shape, whereas most maximal squares share at least half their boundary with the original shape. A criterion taking this into account would prevent the selection of the triangle.

Test shape $V_6$ illustrates that the choice of basis shapes is important. The large triangle is very poorly approximated by any of the shapes within the basis shape family. Further research is needed to select a shape family which performs best for a wide variety of shapes to be decomposed.

The second series of experiments described in this paper involves the decomposition of disks with varying radius. The center of the disk is chosen to coincide with the origin and the radius is from 1 to 31. The discrete disks were obtained by selecting only the grid points within the continuous disk. In figure 4.a both the straight forward as well as the decomposition dilation time are plotted as a function of the radius of the disk. Figure 4.b shows the total number of pixels involved in the logarithmic decomposition as function of the radius. Also shown are the functions $\pi r$, with $r$ the radius. In case the *continuous* disk is approximated with a symmetric polygon, this polygon can be decomposed by dilating all the edges from half its contour (see the introduction). Thus in case the approximation is very accurate (i.e. many edges in the polygon) the total length of half contour provides a lower bound on the number of pixels needed in the decomposition of the disk. Note that this line of reasoning only provides a very crude order estimation. As can be seen in the figure our decomposition algorithm approaches that minimum fairly well. Also note that in the case of a disk we cannot expect the logarithmic curve as a function of the radius as can be observed when decomposing a square. This is because the length of the straight edges in the polygonal approximation of the disk decrease as the radius increases.

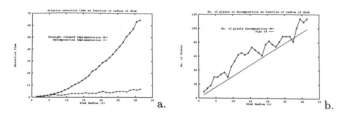

Figure 4: **Decomposition of Disks.** In a. the dilation time of both the straightforward as well as the decomposition implementation are shown. Note that whereas the straight forward implementation dilation time is quadratic in the radius (linear in the area) the decomposition implementation is almost linear in the radius of the disk. In b. the total number of pixels involved in the decomposition of a disk as function of the radius is plotted. Also shown is the lines $\pi r$ roughly indicating the number of pixels in the contour of the disk (see discussion in text).

# 5   Conclusions

A new algorithm is presented in this paper to decompose an arbitrarily shaped discrete shape into the union of the convex shapes taken from a fixed collection of basis shapes. These basis shapes are chosen to be efficiently logarithmically decomposable.

With the new decomposition algorithm efficient implementations of the morphological erosion and dilation operations with arbitrary structuring elements are made possible. For the test shapes considered in this paper the speed up factor (when comparing our new implementation with a straight forward implementation) ranged from 3 to 15. Preliminary experiments have already indicated that an extra speed-up of at least a factor 2 is obtained by optimizing the software (whereas our straight forward implementation is highly optimized, our new algorithm is not. Parts of it are still interpreted instead of compiled and run at full machine speed).

Future research will look into the optimal choice of a set of basis structuring elements. One of the examples presented in the previous section clearly indicated that in case none of the shapes in the set of basis shapes resembles the shape to be decomposed, the resulting decomposition is not particularly efficient. One of the criteria to guide that choice will be that one element from the basis should *not* be efficiently decomposable in the basis formed by all other shapes in the basis. For if this would be true, that particular shape could have easily well be left out of the basis in the first place.

A second item on the research agenda involves a more fundamental change in the decomposition algorithm. The algorithm presented in this paper can only decompose a shape into a union of (scaled) basis shapes. Consider the shape $S = \alpha B_1 \oplus \beta B_2$.

Because both $B_1$ and $B_2$ are efficiently decomposable, it would be profitable if the algorithm could handle this kind of (hierarchical) decomposition as well. Such an extension, however, will greatly increase the complexity of the algorithm.

# References

[1] J. Serra. *Image Analysis and Mathematical Morphology*. Academic Press, London, 1982.

[2] J. Mattioli and M. Schmitt. On the information contained in the erosion curve. In Ling Yi O, A. Toet, D. Foster, H.J.A.M. Heijmans, and P. Meer, editors, *Proceedings of the NATO Advanced Research Workshop "Shape in Picture"*, volume 126 of F, pages 177—196, Driebergen, The Netherlands, September 1992. Springer-Verlag.

[3] B.B. Kimia, A. Tannenbaum, and S.W. Zucker. Towards a computational theory of shape, an overview. In *Proceedings of the First European Conference on Computer Vision*, 1990.

[4] R. van den Boomgaard and A.W.M. Smeulders. Towards a morphological scale-space theory. In Ying Li O, A. Toet, D. Foster, H.J.A.M. Heijmans, and P.Meer, editors, *Proceedings of the NATO Advanced Research Workshop "Shape in Picture"*, volume 126 of F, pages 631—640, Driebergen, The Netherlands, September 1992. Springer-Verlag.

[5] X. Zhuang and R.M. Haralick. Morphological structuring element decomposition. *Comp. Vision Graphics and Image Processing*, (35):370—382, 1986.

[6] J. Xu. Decomposition of convex polygonal morphological structuring elements into neighbourhood subsets. *IEEE Transactions on PAMI*, (13):153—162, 1991.

[7] G. Matheron. *Random Sets and Integral Geometry*. John Wiley and Sons, New York, 1975.

[8] J. Pecht. Speeding up successive Minkowski operations. *Pattern Recognition Letters*, 3(2):113–117, 1985.

[9] R. van den Boomgaard. *Mathematical Morphology: Extensions towards Computer Vision*. PhD thesis, University of Amsterdam, March 1992.

[10] R. van den Boomgaard and R. van Balen. Methods for fast morphological image transforms using bitmapped binary images. *Computer Vision, Graphics and Image Processing, Models and Image processing*, 54(3):252—258, May 1992.

[11] D.A. Wester. Decomposition of structuring elements (in dutch). Master's thesis, Faculty of Mathematics and Computer Science, University of Amsterdam, 1993.

# ON DEFINING LENGTH AND WIDTH FOR
# BOTANICAL OBJECT DISCRIMINATION

G.W.A.M. VAN DER HEIJDEN

*DLO-Centre for Plant Breeding and Reproduction Research (CPRO-DLO),*
*P.O.Box 16, 6700 AA Wageningen, The Netherlands*
and
A.M. VOSSEPOEL

*Pattern Recognition Group, Faculty of Applied Physics, Delft University of Technology,*
*Lorentzweg 1, 2628 CJ Delft, The Netherlands*

### ABSTRACT

Shape parameters are often based on the ratio of size parameters. Size parameters can however be measured in several ways, as is illustrated for area and perimeter. Length and width are two other important size parameters. They can be defined in many ways, leading to different results. A systematic overview is presented of definitions of length and width, dividing the definitions into three groups: based on Euclidian geometry, based on arcs and derived from other parameters. It appears that the number of definitions is practically unlimited. Although one correct definition under all circumstances appears impossible, the behaviour of definitions for different types of objects is predictable. Also suitable definitions can be selected using the ratio of the between- and within-classes variation. This aspect is demonstrated for a number of botanical objects: pod of French bean, bulb of onion and root of carrot.

## 1. Introduction

Algorithms for shape analysis have been reviewed earlier [1,2]. Many algorithms are used for description of shapes with different topology. For shape comparison of objects differing not in topology but only in sizes or curvatures of segments, which is quite common for botanical objects, the group of scalar, boundary-based algorithms are most appropriate. Although Hausdorff distance [3] may offer a good alternative, prototypes of classes with natural variation are not readily available for applying this technique.

In applied image analysis literature, size and shape parameters are used for identification or discrimination of botanical objects, such as seeds, leaves or flowers [4,5,6,7,8,9]. For seeds of wheat, many shape parameters have been suggested such as different ratios of length, width and depth [4], and all kinds of size parameters such as height and length of brush, germ or seed [5]. Myers and Edsall [6] use 9 different parameters among which the major axis, which is defined as the maximum length of the seed through the centroid, the minor axis (perpendicular to the major axis through the centroid), the ratio between them, the "size" defined as 2*area/perimeter and compactness (something like shape factor). Besides these scalar parameters, they also use the first four magnitude components of the Fourier transform of the contour.

It is often considered advantageous to give descriptions that are not only invariant for translation and rotation, but for scaling as well. This is accomplished by taking ratios of size parameters that yield dimensionless shape parameters, and using size as a separate descriptor analogous to position and orientation. However, size parameters can be defined in several ways, leading to different results. This is especially true for the length and width of an object. Length and width are often defined on an ad hoc basis, without a proper consideration why a certain definition is chosen. There does not seem to be a consensus on one fitting definition for a family of objects. Even worse, it sometimes occurs that length and width are not properly defined, leaving the interpretation to the reader [7,8].

The purpose of this paper is to present an overview of possible definitions of length and width in a systematic way. This overview shows that it will be impossible to be exhaustive and to come to one unified definition of length and width: definitions are object-dependent. It is however possible to group definitions, and often it is also possible to predict the behaviour of definitions for a family of objects.

In the next paragraph some problems related to measuring well-defined size parameters such as area and perimeter in two-dimensional digitized binary images are discussed. In paragraph 3 a systematic overview of length and width definitions is given. In paragraph 4 a selection of length and width definitions are tested for their discriminating ability between various classes for a range of botanical objects. In paragraph 5 some conclusions will be given.

## 2. Consistency of size parameters

In two-dimensional discrete images, size parameters can be defined in different ways. This is illustrated in figure 1 for area (A) and perimeter (P).

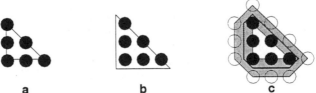

**a**          **b**          **c**

Figure 1: (a,b) triangular models ; (c) locus of perimeter positions before digitizing indicated in half-tone, with halfway contour.

If we know for certain that the original object (before digitizing) was a triangle, its area can be calculated as ½* length * width. The length of the triangle may be considered as the distance between the dots (in this case 2) yielding A=½*2*2=2, and a corresponding P=4+2√2=6.828 (cf. figure 1a). It is also possible to count the length of each pixel as one, in which case the length of the triangle is 3 yielding A= ½*3*3= 4.5, and P= 6+3√2=10.243. If one tries to draw the latter perimeter in the figure, one finds that the horizontal and vertical sides run between the pixel centres, whereas the diagonal side runs through the pixel centres, as is shown in figure 1b. This is quite unsatisfactory.

As was already shown by Thomson [10], the area of an object can be estimated accurately by counting points, i.e. the number of pixels is a good estimate of A, for the object concerned: 6. This method assumes that each pixel has been sampled by a Dirac delta function and that its boundary is halfway between the object pixel and its connected background pixel(s). The estimate is unbiased, and since it is simple and fast to calculate, it is frequently used in image analysis.

It is an interesting question what would be the corresponding perimeter P. In any case, we know that the contour before digitization is somewhere between the connected object boundary pixel centres (the inner contour) and the connected background boundary pixel centres (the outer contour). This locus is shown in figure 1c. If we assume 8-connected contours, a good candidate for P is halfway between the inner and the outer contour: P=4+4$\sqrt{2}$=9.656. P is also halfway between those of the P(inner)= 4+2$\sqrt{2}$=6.828 and P(outer)=4+6$\sqrt{2}$=12.485, with P(outer)-P(inner)=4$\sqrt{2}$. This value is constant, independent of size and shape. So a consistent estimate for P can be found by adding 2$\sqrt{2}$ to P(inner) or by subtracting 2$\sqrt{2}$ from P(outer). The only disadvantage of the halfway perimeter concept is that it encloses an area of half a pixel less than the number of object pixels. This is caused by the fact that the 8-connected candidate contour will always cut off 4 uncompensated pixel corners, as opposed to the 4-connected pixel boundaries (crack code). Of course, for increasing sampling density the bias decreases to zero [11].

Note that a lot of research has been done, mainly for determining unbiased estimates of the length of straight lines in a digitized image [12]. It appears that the formula for the length of straight lines can be applied for (circular) perimeters as well [11].

Other frequently used methods to measure A and P are based on polygonal approximations [13,14]. The object is viewed as a polygon and P is calculated as the sum of the lengths of all sides. To obtain P consistent with the pixel count definition of A, a length correction (in the order) of 2$\sqrt{2}$ can be applied.

The definition of A of a polygon with N vertices (x,y) is:

$$A = \frac{1}{2} \sum_{i=1}^{N} ( ( x_{i-1} . y_i) - ( x_i . y_{i-1} ) ) .$$

For the triangle in figure 1, the Euclidian area calculation is straightforward and yields A=2. This is in accordance with figure 1a, but inconsistent with the pixel count. The required area correction is $c/2+1$, where $c = \sum_{i=1}^{N} \max( |x_i - x_{i-1}|, |y_i - y_{i-1}|) .$

If the polygon description coincides with the Freeman-coded contour, $c$ is the number of contour pixels; in this case the corrections for A and P are exact. However, if one allows the boundary not to pass through all contour pixel centres, it is virtually impossible to reconcile exactly the polygon area and perimeter length with their pixel count equivalents.

## 3. Length and width

For the sake of simplicity, we will assume in this paper that object lengths and widths measured in a 2-D digitized image are representative of the length and width of (3-D) objects. Object length is ideally the length of its reconstruction in the real domain. As long as it is measured as a Euclidean distance between two pixels, the estimate error will be limited to approximately the size of one pixel. However, in some of our definitions of object length and width in a 2-D case, references are made to the arc length definition: object lengths x are defined in terms of arc length y. Now a different problem arises: arc length can be exactly calculated in the real domain, but after digitization, one has to rely on estimates based on all possible reconstructions of lines and arcs in the real domain [12,15].

When determining the length and width of a 2-D (or projected 3-D) object (8-connected set of pixels) in a 2-D image, the definitions of length and width can roughly be divided into three categories:
1. based on Euclidean geometry (one straight line segment);
2. based on arcs (curved segments);
3. derived from other parameters.

## 3.1 Definitions based on Euclidean geometry
The category, in which length and width are regarded as Euclidean, can be subdivided into several classes.

*3.1.1* The first class is based on the concept of projection: the length (width) is the size (distance between extremes) of the projected object along an axis. These projections are often called Feret-diameters [16] and therefore the symbol F is used to indicate definitions based on projections.
The Feret-diameter under angle $\alpha$ can be defined as:
$F_\alpha = x_{max} - x_{min}$
where $x_{max} = \max\{ x \mid (x, y) \in O_\alpha \text{ for any } y\}$
and $x_{min} = \min\{ x \mid (x, y) \in O_\alpha \text{ for any } y\}$
where $O_\alpha$ = connected object O rotated over angle $-\alpha$ with respect to the X-axis.
Length is often defined as the maximum Feret-diameter: $F_{max} = \max(F_\alpha)$ and width as the minimum Feret-diameter: $F_{min} = \min(F_\alpha)$.

Sometimes constraints are imposed, such as that length and width should be perpendicular. Then, having chosen one definition, the other one follows using $F_{\alpha + \frac{1}{2}\pi}$.

The definition of length as $F_{max}$ is a rather model free measure with a physical interpretation in the sense that $F_{max}$ is the smallest sieve diameter through which the object will always fit. Note that $F_{max}$ is in accordance with the intuitive notion of length for elliptic and tear-shaped objects, whereas for isosceles triangles with top angle smaller than 60°, it measures the length of the equal sides, and for rectangular objects it is equal to the diagonal (see figure 2).

Another definition follows from other information regarding the angle under which the Feret-diameter has to be determined. A preferred angle is the orientation of the symmetry-axis, if present. The symmetry-axis can be calculated or objects can be recorded in a fixed orientation with the symmetry-axis under angle $\alpha$ with respect to the grid. This definition of length ($F_\alpha$ ) can be very useful when speed is important or when most other definitions are not applicable. This is the case for a very broad leaf, where the length along the main nerve, i.e., the axis of symmetry, may be smaller than the width of the leaf.

Another group of Feret-lengths and widths are obtained by choosing two perpendicular Feret-diameters under some criterion, for example the two perpendicular Feret-diameters with minimum product: $(F_\alpha, F_{\alpha+\frac{1}{2}\pi})$: $\alpha = \arg_\alpha \{\min(F_\alpha * F_{\alpha+\frac{1}{2}\pi})\}$. This criterion yields the so-called minimum enclosing rectangle (MER), i.e. the one with minimum area. Here $\max(F_\alpha, F_{\alpha+\frac{1}{2}\pi})$ is the length (Lmer) and $\min(F_\alpha, F_{\alpha+\frac{1}{2}\pi})$ is the width (Wmer) of the MER. This definition of length is in accordance with the intuitive notion of length for elliptic and rectangular objects, whereas for isosceles triangles with top angle smaller than 60°, more equal MER's can be found. For tear-shaped objects the definition is simply counter-intuitive (see figure 2).

An alternative definition is obtained by maximizing the so-called aspect-ratio: length = $F_\alpha$ : $\alpha$ = $\arg_\alpha \{\max(F_\alpha/F_{\alpha+\frac{1}{2}\pi})\}$; the width is then $F_{\alpha+\frac{1}{2}\pi}$ .

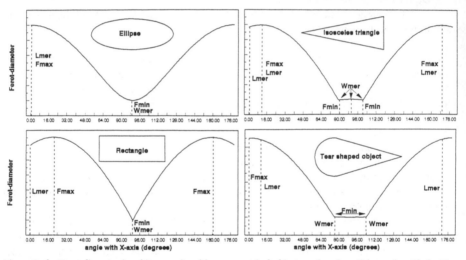

Figure 2: the Feret-diameter in arbitrary units of four geometrical objects as function of the angle with the X-axis.

3.1.2 The second class is based on the maximum length of a chord through the object, disregarding holes and gaps. The symbol LT (length through object) will be used for this.

$LT_\alpha$ is defined as the length of the largest horizontal chord through the object rotated over an angle $-\alpha$ with respect to the X-axis, i.e.

$LT_\alpha = \max(|x_p - x_q|)$ for $y_p = y_q$

where p=$(x_p, y_p) \in O_\alpha$ and q=$(x_q, y_q) \in O_\alpha$.

Also here length can be defined as LTmax = max{LTα} (=Fmax) and width as LTmin = min{LTα} (≠Fmin). Of course additional constraints can be imposed, such as position (e.g. through centre of mass), perpendicularity or orientation.

*3.1.3*    The third class is based on the length of the longest chord which can be drawn within the object without crossing holes or gaps. The symbol LW (length within object) will be used for this class.

LW is defined as the length of the largest horizontal chord within the object rotated over angle -α with respect to the X-axis, i.e.

$LW_\alpha = \max_\alpha( |x_p - x_q| )$ for $y_p = y_q$

where $p = (x_p, y_p) \in O_\alpha$  and $q = (x_q, y_q) \in O_\alpha$

and the whole segment [p,q] belongs to $O_\alpha$.

Note the analogy with the definition of convex hull. Also in this case, the maximum (minimum) LW may be chosen or some constraint, for example regarding the angle, may be imposed. Note that LW and LT are comparable to F . From their definitions, it can be seen that LT >= LW for all objects. If the object is convex, i.e. if for every pair of points p,q belonging to the object O, the whole segment [p,q] belongs to the object, it is straightforward from their definitions that $LW_\alpha$ and $LT_\alpha$ are identical for all α. Furthermore, one can easily see that $LT_\alpha <= F_\alpha$ since the definition of $LT_\alpha$ can be written in the same way as the definition for $F_\alpha$ with the additional restriction that $y_{min}$ and $y_{max}$ should be identical.

## 3.2 Definitions based on arcs

When regarding length as that of a curved segment, only one definition is known: the length of the skeleton. It has already been shown how the length of a skeleton (curve) in a two-dimensional digital image can be calculated. However, even without the problem of determining the length of a curve in a 2-D digital image, several problems remain:

* There are various thinning algorithms to obtain a skeleton.

* Defining the length of an object as the length of the skeleton is only valid if there is one clear main skeleton. i.e. branches can be properly pruned.

* Skeletons generally do not run from contour to contour. For instance the skeleton of an oval shape is a single relatively short line in the centre. Certainly, one will not consider this to be the length of the object.

A solution to these problems can be obtained when the skeleton is based on the chamfer distance transform [17]. The skeleton may contain several branchpoints which can be pruned using the following method: calculate using the chamfer distance transform for each endpoint the path distance to all other endpoints following the skeleton. Select the two endpoints which have the largest sum of the path distance between the points and the distances of the two points to the border. The skeleton-length can now be defined as the path distance between the two selected endpoints (SkL), and its extrapolated version is obtained by adding the distance values at the endpoints to this distance (SkLx).

Another advantage of using the distance transform for determining the skeleton is in measuring width. The width can be derived from the values of the distance transform. For instance, the width (SkW) may be defined as max{2*f(x,y) | (x,y) ∈ skeleton} where f(x,y) is the distance value at position (x,y). Also the average of f(x,y) over (part of) the skeleton may be defined as the width.

## 3.3 Definitions derived from other parameters

If length and width are derived from other parameters, many definitions are possible. A commonly used definition for the length of elongated objects is P/2. An unbiased estimate of P can be obtained using the corner-count method [12]. When measuring the length of objects with a known relationship between length, width and for example area and perimeter, the width can be taken into account by applying a correction factor [9].

Another definition of this type is to consider length as derived from the moments of inertia. In many applications the moments of inertia of an object are calculated to find the main direction of the object. The largest eigenvalue of the inertial moments matrix can also be used as an estimate of the length of the object. The length of the long axis (LAX) is equal to √(C*largest eigenvalue) and the length of the short axis (SAX) equal to √(C*smallest eigenvalue). For an ellipse C=16, for a rectangle C=12. The definition with C=16 which is called the long axis of the fitting ellipse, (LAX) is correct for purely elliptic objects; for other objects it is an approximation. Its main advantage is that it is less sensitive to outliers than most other methods, since it is based on the complete object. Its robustness makes it useful for the aspect ratio of an object (length/width).

A serious drawback for the parameter based definitions is that the relationship between the parameters is based on a model. The bias and accuracy depends on the deviation of the object from the model, the parameters used and the model used. For example when using the P/2, the object must have a smooth contour.

## 4. Experiments

The suitability of several definitions is tested for discriminating botanical objects. A subset of the definitions of section 3 are used (10 for length and 10 for width) which encompasses all categories (Table 1). They are tested for their ability to discriminate between classes (cultivars) of various botanical species. Of each class several objects are recorded and the criterium used for determining the discriminating power of a definition is the variation between classes divided by the variation within classes. This ratio is obtained by an analysis of variance.

The botanical objects used are:
1)  pods of French bean: 15 pods of 8 classes, total 120 objects.
2)  carrots: 12 classes, 3 replications, 10 carrots per replication, total 360 objects.
3)  onion bulbs: 32 bulbs of 35 classes, total 1120 objects.

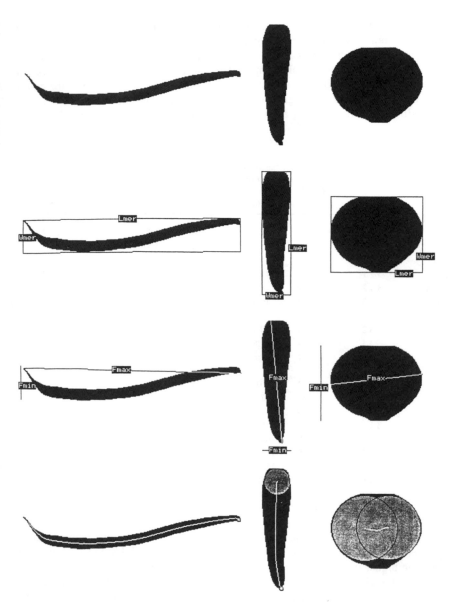

Figure 3: (a) examples of a binary images of French bean, carrot and onion. (b) minimum enclosing rectangle (MER) (c) maximum and minimum Feret-diameters (d) skeletons with circles indicating the distance from the skeleton endpoints to the border. This distance is added to the length of the skeleton SkL to obtain SkLx.

An example of the shapes of the recorded objects and the orientation in which they were recorded can be seen in figure 3. Pods of French bean are examples of long-narrow and curved objects. Likewise, carrots are ovate-like with the largest width near the top and onions are circular shaped. The images are processed to obtain correct binary images, which included automatic removal of the leaves at the top of the carrot and the onion. This caused straight contours at the top of these objects.

In figure 3b and 3c, the results of applying various definitions to these objects is shown.

Table 1: Mean (in pixels) and variance-ratio (ratio of variance between classes and within classes) of bean, carrot and onion are calculated for various definitions of length and width. The section refers to the text where the definition is introduced. The number of classes are: bean: 8, carrot: 12; onion: 35. The number of objects per class are: bean: 15 pods; carrots 30 roots; onions 32 bulbs.

| definition | section | BEAN | | CARROT | | ONION | |
|---|---|---|---|---|---|---|---|
| | | mean | F-ratio | mean | F-ratio | mean | F-ratio |
| LENGTH: | | | | | | | |
| Fmax | 3.1.1 | 335 | 44.9 | 164 | 2.3 | 132 | 10.9 |
| Fmin+$\pi/2$ | 3.1.1 | 335 | 45.1 | 164 | 2.4 | 130 | 11.2 |
| Lmer | 3.1.1 | 335 | 45.1 | 164 | 2.4 | 129 | 12.4 |
| $F_0/F_{\pi/2}$ | 3.1.1 | 334 | 45.4 | 163 | 2.4 | 129 | 11.9 |
| LTmax | 3.1.2 | 332 | 46.3 | 164 | 2.4 | 132 | 10.9 |
| LWmax | 3.1.3 | 297 | 14.8 | 164 | 2.4 | 132 | 10.9 |
| SkL | 3.2 | 351 | 50.2 | 148 | 2.4 | 53 | 5.0 |
| SkLx | 3.2 | 356 | 50.1 | 167 | 2.3 | 132 | 10.8 |
| LAX | 3.3 | 344 | 41.8 | 176 | 4.0 | 131 | 11.5 |
| P/2 | 3.3 | 354 | 49.8 | 177 | 2.2 | 191 | 12.4 |
| WIDTH: | | | | | | | |
| Fmax+$\pi/2$ | 3.1.1 | 52 | 10.0 | 34 | 6.3 | 112 | 17.3 |
| Fmin | 3.1.1 | 46 | 7.8 | 31 | 4.0 | 108 | 18.5 |
| Wmer | 3.1.1 | 46 | 7.9 | 31 | 4.0 | 109 | 17.6 |
| $F_0/F_{\pi/2}$ | 3.1.1 | 55 | 6.4 | 35 | 1.7 | 109 | 21.2 |
| LTmin | 3.1.2 | 25 | 64.3 | 30 | 4.1 | 108 | 18.3 |
| LWmin | 3.1.3 | 25 | 154.5 | 30 | 4.1 | 108 | 18.3 |
| SkW | 3.2 | 25 | 153.3 | 31 | 4.1 | 106 | 18.8 |
| SAX | 3.3 | 35 | 7.7 | 29 | 8.8 | 109 | 19.1 |
| A/Fmax | 3.3 | 20 | 139.2 | 23 | 4.5 | 85 | 18.5 |
| A/SkLx | 3.3 | 18 | 159.3 | 23 | 4.1 | 85 | 18.0 |

The overall means of the botanical objects for the 20 definitions are listed in table 1. From this table it can be seen that the curved length (SkLx and P/2) gives on the average higher values than the other length definitions. LAX gives higher or lower values than the Feret-diameters, depending on the shape of the object. LTmax and Fmax, which should be identical, differ slightly, which is due to the different algorithms used. All the length definitions of the first category are much alike. The width gives more differences. Especially with non-convex objects, such as the beans, a large difference is obtained between projection and other definitions. The definitions A/Fmax and A/SkLx give much smaller values than the other definitions, since this is an "average" width, whereas the others can be considered "maximum" width. The behaviour of SAX differs strongly over the different objects.

The F-ratio's which are an indication of the discriminating ability of each definition are also listed in table 1.

The correlations between the various definitions were calculated for bean, carrot and onion separately to enable grouping of definitions.

*French beans:*

Correlations between definitions of length are very high (all above 0.97) except for LWmax. The correlation for this definition with others is about 0.7. Its discriminating ability is less than that of the other definitions. This definition is unsuitable for curved narrow (non-convex) objects, since the observed length varies with the curvedness of the object. It is obvious that P/2 is a good discriminating length measure, together with the SkL and SkLx. Extrapolation of the skeleton to the contour has hardly any benefit, since the skeleton approaches the contour quite closely.

For the width remarkable results appear. The correlation coefficients show two groups: a group which is based on projections: Fmax+$\pi$/2, Fmin and Wmer, (correlation range 0.94-0.99) and to a less extent SAX and Fy (correlation ca. 0.8), and a group with LTmin, LWmin, SkW, A/Fmax and A/SkLx (correlation range within group 0.63-0.94). The correlations between the different groups range from 0.06 till 0.38. From the F-ratio's it is clear that the second group of definitions gives better results. This is in accordance with the expectation, since projections tell more about the curvedness of the object than about its actual width.

*Carrots:*

Correlations between definitions of length are very high, with a range 0.96 - 1.00 and many definitions having a correlation of 0.99 or higher. The discriminating power is also rather identical. Only LAX performs slightly better than the rest of the definitions. There is no explanation why this definition gives better results. Correlations between definitions of width are slightly lower (average of 0.9 ), with a negative exception for Fx. A reason for this may be that it is rather difficult to record the slightly bent and rather long carrots in a well-oriented way. The error made by not correctly orientating the root is length*sin($\alpha$), if this is larger than half the width, where $\alpha$ is the angle between the root and the Y-axis. The best results are obtained by dividing the area with a length-measure. Also the SAX gives good results. These three definitions give an overall (average) width measure, whereas the other definitions are based on the largest diameter under a certain angle. It appears that carrots can better be discriminated by using an average width than by calculating a maximum width. It is rather doubtful whether this conclusion may be extended to other similar objects.

*Onions:*

Notice that the length of the bulb in fact is perpendicular to the height of the bulb, i.e. horizontally. Correlations between all definitions of length are all very high

(0.94 - 1.00), except for P/2 (0.87 - 0.93) and SkL (0.24 - 0.37). It is clear that bulbs do not fulfil the model which is suitable for these two definitions. The discriminating power of SkL is also smallest. This definition is for circular objects very sensitive for small disturbances of the contour. Using the extrapolated version removes this sensitivity. The discriminating power of P/2 is quite high, indicating that, although it is not a good measure for length, it still can discriminate between the classes. All the definitions of width (i.e. the height of the bulb) have correlations between 0.93 and 1.00, with the exception of Fx (range 0.88 - 0.97). Fx, however, has the best discriminating power, which may be due to the manual alignment procedure. The high F-ratio of P/2 indicates, that for almost circular objects, less conventional definitions of length and width are also suitable for discrimination.

For each of the three types of objects, the correlations between length definitions and width definitions were between 0.10 and 0.65 with the main part between 0.30 and 0.50. This low correlation is an indication that the use of both definitions is valuable, whereas the aspect ratio (length/width) may be another helpful feature for discrimination.

## 5. Discussion and conclusion

We have given a systematic overview of possible definitions of length and width. Many more can be formulated by using our systematic approach as a basis. It appeared impossible to have one fitting definition of length and width suitable in all cases. It seems therefore necessary to choose a model for the kind of object under study and search for a definition which is correct and discriminating for the model. Having chosen a model (e.g. curved or convex objects), there is still some choice in definitions. Which (combination of) definition(s) is appropriate depends on the time required to measure length and width, the algorithms available and certainly also on aspects like consistency, robustness under translation, rotation and magnification, and the discriminating power of the method. On the other hand, if one does not have a model for the object, combinations of definitions of length and width might be used to choose a certain model. For example dividing the area by the Feret-width would yield the correct estimate for the length of a rectangle. By taking the square root of the sum of squares of length and width, the diagonal of the rectangle can be calculated. If the chosen model is correct, this should be equal to the Feret-maximum. Using this approach models may be discarded which are not in accordance with the object under study.

We are aware that the set of definitions of length and width and set of objects used in the experiment are only a small subset of all possible definitions and shapes. The purpose of the experiment was merely to demonstrate the differences between the various definitions, depending on the object under study. By choosing the right definition a lot of trouble can be avoided.

In any case, articles and especially software-packages should state which kind of definition for length and width is being used.

**References**

[1]  T. Pavlidis, "A review of algorithms for shape analysis", *Computer graphics and image processing*, vol. 7, pp. 243-258, 1978.

[2]  T. Pavlidis, "Algorithms for shape analysis of contours and waveforms", *IEEE Trans. Pattern Analysis and Machine Intelligence*, vol. 2, pp. 301-312, 1980.

[3]  D.P. Huttenlocher, G.A. Klanderman and W.J. Rucklidge, "Comparing images using the Hausdorff distance", *IEEE Transactions on Pattern Analysis and Machine Intelligence*, vol. 15, pp. 850-863, 1993.

[4]  W.L. Brogan and A.R. Edison, "Automatic classification of grains via pattern recognition techniques", *Pattern Recognition*, vol. 6, pp. 97-103, 1974.

[5]  P.D. Keefe and S.R. Draper, "An automated machine vision system for the morphometry of new cultivars and plant gene bank accessions", *Plant Varieties and Seeds*, vol. 1, pp. 1-11, 1988.

[6]  D.G. Myers and K.J. Edsall, "The application of image processing techniques to the identification of Australian wheat varieties", *Plant Varieties and Seeds*, vol. 2, pp. 109-116, 1989.

[7]  D.B. Churchill, D.M. Bilsland and T.M. Cooper, "Comparison of machine vision with human measurement of seed dimensions", *Transactions of the ASAE*, vol. 35, pp. 61-64, 1992.

[8]  M. Jay and F. Ferrero, "An integrated varietal identification approach using modern technology: application to pink carnation varieties", *Plant Varieties and Seeds*, vol. 2, pp. 63-71, 1989.

[9]  J.G. van de Vooren and G.W.A.M. van der Heijden, "Measuring the size of French beans with image analysis", *Plant Varieties and Seeds*, vol. 6, pp. 47-53, 1993.

[10]  E. Thomson, "Quantitative microscopic analysis, *J. Geol.*, vol. 38, pp. 193, 1930.

[11]  I.T. Young, "Sampling density and quantitative microscopy", *Analytical and Quantitative Cytology and Histology*, vol. 10, pp. 269-275, 1988.

[12]  A.M. Vossepoel and A.W.M. Smeulders, "Vector code probability and metrication error in the representation of straight lines of finite length", *Comp. Graphics and Image Processing*, vol. 20, pp. 347-364, 1982.

[13]  P.J. van Otterloo, *A contour-oriented approach to shape analysis*, Hemel Hempstead (UK): Prentice Hall, 1989.

[14]  Z. Kulpa, "Area and perimeter measurement of blobs in discrete binary pictures", *Computer Graphics and Image Processing*, vol. 6, pp. 434-451, 1977.

[15]  L. Dorst and A.W.M. Smeulders, "Length estimators for digitized contours", *Computer Vision, Graphics and Image Processing*, vol. 40, pp. 311-333, 1987.

[16]  L.R. Feret, *La grosseur des grains*. Zurich: Assoc. Intern. Essais Math 2D, 1931.

[17]  B.J.H. Verwer, "Improved metrics in image processing applied to the Hilditch skeleton", in *Proc. 9th Int. Conf. Pattern Recognition*, 1988, pp. 137-142.

# Compatibility Modelling for Graph Matching

Richard C Wilson and Edwin R Hancock
Department of Computer Science, University of York
York, Y01 5DD, UK

**Abstract**

This paper describes a new method for determining the compatibility coefficients required for performing graph matching by probabilisitc relaxation. Its novelty stems from the Bayesian modelling of graph topology corruption due to segmentation errors in the original image data. The corruption process leads to a very elegant relaxation scheme in which the compatibility coefficients are determined purely by the numbers of nodes and arcs in the graphs under match. We demonstrate the utility of the model in the fusion of pairs of remotely sensed infra-red images.

## 1. Introduction

Intermediate level recognition problems in machine vision are frequently formulated as relational graph matching tasks. Features extracted from image data are represented in terms of a scene graph which is then matched against a corresponding model graph. Unfortunately, this matching process is invariably frustrated by errors in the feature segmentation process which result in topological corruption of the scene graph. Under these conditions, the graph matching process can be viewed as a constraint satisfaction problem aimed at locating the maximally consistent interpretation of a topologically corrupted scene-graph; this can be accomplished by either graph-search [1,5,6] or by relaxation labelling techniques [7]. In the graph-search methods departures from consistency are handled by locating subgraph isomorphisms or by identifying maximal cliques [6]. The relaxation approaches share the common goal of optimising a global criterion of match; in the case of discrete relaxation the optimisation process is realised by symbolic label updating while in the case of probabilistic relaxation match probabilities are updated in the light of local support [3]. In both types of relaxation process, the main computational requirement is a means of gauging the quality and consistency of match.

In this paper it is the probabilistic relaxation method that concerns us. Here the model of consistency is captured by a series of compatibility coefficients whose role is to capture the constraints operating in the matching process. Renewed interest in the application of this technique to matching problems has recently been stimulated by the work of Li[10] who has presented an effective yet largely goal directed framework based around an attributed relational graph representation. The novelty of this work derives from the way in which the compatibility coefficients unify measurement and symbolic information through the use of binary relations. Some of the heuristic elements of Li's compatibility model have recently been overcome by Kittler, Christmas and Petrou [11] who have succeeded in establishing the method within a Bayesian framework in which the compatibilities are represented by well defined probability distributions for mixtures of measurements and symbols. In so doing they identify a number of benefits over the Bayesian framework previously employed by Kittler and Hancock[3] which imposes a rigid dichotomy between the roles of symbolic and measurement information in modelling compatibility.

Our aim in this paper is to return to the earlier framework of Kittler and Hancock [3] and to demonstrate that it is capable of handling the matching task provided that certain model refinements are adopted. Moreover, we will demonstrate that the dichotomy between measurements and symbols has certain tangible advantages in terms of its capacity to represent the different sources of uncertainty in the matching process. We observe that the main limitation of existing methods derives from their failure to directly model the processes by which the topology of the scene-graph becomes corrupted; this frequently results in heuristic matching algorithms of unnecessary parametric complexity which are not easily controlled.

In order to apply the Kittler and Hancock [3] evidence combining framework to the matching process requires a set of compatability coefficients which represent the topology of the graphs under match and capture the effects of segmentation error or occlusion. According to our philosophy these compatibilities are purely symbolic in their modelling role since they represent the topology of scene structure. The novel aspect of the work reported here is to present a methodology which allows the compatibility coefficients to be determined using a topological constraint corruption process. The entire set of compatibility coefficients required to implement the relaxation scheme is completely determined by the numbers of nodes and arcs in the scene graphs under match. This is an extremely desirable property since it obviates the need for an elaborate parameter estimation scheme.

The outline of this paper is as follows. Section 2 details the relaxation scheme used for graph matching. Section 3 develops the novel topological constraint corruption model required to compute the compatibility coefficients. Section 4 describes the experimental evaluation of the method, detailing how orientation and scale information can be used to compute initial probabilities for a matching application involving the fusion of aerial infra-red images. Finally, Section 5 offers some conclusions.

## 2. Relaxation Labelling

We are interested in matching tasks that can be abstracted in terms of relational graphs. The different images to be matched are given a graph representation in which the nodes are segmental entities and the arcs signify the existence of a topological relationship between two nodes. We use the notation $G = (V, E, R)$ to denote such graphs, where V is the set of nodes, E is the set of arcs and R is an incidence relation. If $(e, v) \in R$ then the arc e is said to be incident on node v. Our aim in matching is to associate nodes in two such graphs $G_1 = (V_1, E_1, R_1)$ and $G_2 = (V_2, E_2, R_2)$ using constraints provided by the arcs. Unmatchable entities are accommodated by augmenting the nodes in the model graph by a null label $\phi$.

In order to perform the matching task, the relaxation scheme must iteratively update the probability of node $J \in V_1$ matching node $j \in V_2 \cup \phi$. At iteration $n$ of the relaxation scheme this probability is denoted by $P^{(n)}(J \to j)$. According to our viewpoint the modelling role of the initial probabilities, $P^{(0)}(J \to j)$, is to capture uncertainties in the measurement information. In the matching domain this information is derived from the geometric properties of lines; uncertainties are produced by poor segmentation or geometric distortion. Probability updating is achieved using the standard Rosenfeld, Hummel and Zucker non-linear relaxation formula [8]

$$P^{(n+1)}(J \to j) = \frac{P^{(n)}(J \to j)Q(J \to j)}{\sum_{\lambda \in V_2 \cup \phi} P^{(n)}(J \to \lambda)Q(J \to \lambda)} \tag{1}$$

The crucial ingredient in this update formula is the support function $Q(J \to j)$. This combines evidence from the context conveying neighbourhood $\mathcal{G}_J$ of node $J$ for the match $J \to j$. This neighbourhood consists of the set of nodes connected to node J be arcs, i.e. $\mathcal{G}_J = \{I \in V_1 | (e, J) \in R_1 \Rightarrow (e, I) \in R_1\}$; it incorporates information conveyed by the nodes which interact directly with $J$ through sharing a common arc. There are many variants of the support function reported in the literature (see [3] for a review). Many of these are heuristic [8] and suffer from internal inconsistencies in their specification. Others make recourse to unsatisfactory assumptions such as the weakness of contextual information. Here we will use an internally consistent support function based on a Bayesian evidence combining framework [3]. It draws on constraints applying to the consistent labellings of pairs of nodes connected by an arc using a product-form support function; it is not restricted to conditions of weak context as is the case of the arithmetic average relaxation scheme applied by Kittler, Christmas and Petrou [11]. Details of its derivation are given in [3]. The computation of support is achieved by summing over the potential label assignments to the nodes in the neighbourhood and taking the product over nodes

$$Q(J \to j) = \prod_{I \in \mathcal{G}_J} \sum_{i \in V_2 \cup \phi} P^{(n)}(I \to i)R(I, J, i, j) \tag{2}$$

In our Bayesian framework the compatibility coefficient is specified by the mutual information measure

$$R(I, J, i, j) = \frac{P(I \to i, J \to j)}{P(I \to i)P(J \to j)} \tag{3}$$

The Bayesian ingredients of this formula are the single node prior $P(J \to j)$ and the conditional prior $P(I \to i | J \to j)$. It is the conditional prior that measures the consistency between the label match $I \to i$ at the node I and the match $J \to j$ at node J. According to our Bayesian framework, the prior probabilities model the role of purely symbolic information in the relaxation process. In Section 3 we will describe a model that can be used to compute the compatibility coefficients under conditions where the topology of the scene graphs is corrupted by noise and segmentation error.

## 3. Modelling Constraint Corruption

Application of the relaxation framework described in the previous section to the matching problem requires a probabilistic model of the graphs representing the different scenes.

In constructing this model we would like to capture some of the uncertainties caused by segmentation error. These uncertainties include noise contamination, fragmentation due to over segmentation and merging due to under segmentation. They are manifest in the scene graphs as topological corruption. Since the topology of the scenes is represented purely in terms of the labels assigned to nodes and the interconnectivity of the arcs, this corruption process is purely symbolic. It therefore falls into the modelling domain of the compatibility coefficients in our relaxation scheme.

Our adopted modelling philosophy is that the relaxation operations are aimed at locating correspondences between the nodes in graph $G_1$ and those in graph $G_2$. We take the view that the nodes in graph $G_1$ represent data that must be matched in the light of constraints provided by graph $G_2$. These constraints are provided by the arcs appearing in the model graph $G_2$. Imperfect segmentation will corrupt the pattern of binary constraints represented by the arc-set $E_2$. Segmental entities will invariably be lost through undersegmentation and extraneous entities will be introduced through oversegmentation effects. There will also be extraneous segments due to residual noise contamination. We would like to capture these effects in our probabilistic modelling of the label constraint process.

We have recently reported a methodology which lends itself to this purpose [4]. It is based on the idea of constraint corruption through the action of a label-error process. It can be viewed as providing a framework for softening the constraints represented by the arcs of graph $G_2$. In order to admit the possibility of erroneous or extraneous nodes we have augmented the scene model with the label $\phi$ which facilitates null matches of the nodes in the graph $G_1$ of the form $J \to \phi$. Because we admit the possibility of departures from consistency in the relaxation scheme we must potentially enumerate the computation of support over the complete combinatorial space of binary label configurations rather than over the arc-set alone. This implies that we must consider the possibility of match to any binary combination of augmented labels, i.e. $(j, i) \in V_2 \times V_2$, with small yet finite probability. For this reason, we must assign the probability mass to the $|V_2 \times V_2|$ terms entering the support function in equation 2 rather than to the $|E_2|$ configurations appearing in the arc-set. The specification of this distribution must capture departures from consistency.

The Bayesian basis for this constraint softening process is to compute the non-zero probabilities for each of the different combinatorial label configurations. Computation of these probabilities requires a model of the underlying constraint corruption process. In [4] we modelled this process in terms of memoryless label corruption; the parameter of this process being the probability of label errors p. Following the methodology described in [4] we adopt a binomial distribution of probability. Arcs drawn from the graph $G_2$ are uncorrupted and occur with total probability mass $(1 - p)^2$. Arcs with one node matched and one-node null-matched have total probability mass $2p(1 - p)$. Arcs in which both nodes are null-matched take the remaining probability mass, i.e. $p^2$. Matches involving non-null label pairs outside the arc-set $V_2$ are completely forbidden and therefore account for zero total probability mass. In each of the three cases listed above the available mass of probability is distributed uniformly among the label configurations falling into the relevant constraint class. The resulting distribution of joint probability is specified by the following rule

$$P(I \to i, J \to j) = \begin{cases} \frac{(1-p)^2}{|E_2|} & \text{if } (j,i) \in E_2 \\ \frac{p(1-p)}{|V_2|} & \text{if } (j,i) \in (V_2 \times \phi) \cup (\phi \times V_2) \\ p^2 & \text{if } (j,i) = (\phi, \phi) \\ 0 & \text{if } (j,i) \in V_2 \times V_2 - E_2 \end{cases} \qquad (4)$$

The single-label priors required in the computation of compatibility coefficients are obtained by summing the joint probabilities in the axiomatic way with the following result

$$P(I \to i) = \begin{cases} \frac{1-p}{|V_2|} & \text{if } i \in V_2 \\ p & \text{if } i = \phi \end{cases} \qquad (5)$$

With the joint priors and the single-object priors to hand the compatibility coefficients required to implement the relaxation scheme are specified by the following rule

$$R(I, J, i, j) = \begin{cases} \frac{|V_2|^2}{|E_2|} & \text{if } (j,i) \in E_2 \\ 1 & \text{if } (j,i) \in (\phi \times V_2) \cup (V_2 \times \phi) \\ 1 & \text{if } (j,i) \in \phi \times \phi \\ 0 & \text{if } (j,i) \in V_2 \times V_2 - E_2 \end{cases} \qquad (6)$$

This is a remarkable result: The graph-based constraint process is captured by a model which is entirely devoid of free parameters; it is specified purely in terms of the numbers of arcs and nodes in the model-graph. Moreover, the strength of the constraints elicited from the arc-set for the model graph is gauged by the ratio $K = \frac{|V_2|^2}{|E_2|}$. It is the connectivity structure of the model graph that determines this ratio. When the model graph is tree-like and $|E_2| \simeq |V_2|$, then $K \simeq |V_2|$; it is under these conditions that the constraints are strongest. Under conditions in which the graph is fully connected, i.e. $|E_2| = \frac{|V_2|(|V_2|-1)}{2}$, in which case $K \simeq 2$, then the constraints are much weaker. It is interesting to note that even in this latter case, the compatibility coefficient is never small enough to merit using the weak-context approximation of the support function; the approximation is only valid under conditions where $K \simeq 1$.

## 4. Experimental Evaluation

For the experimental aspects of this study we will be interested in matching road networks detected in aerial images captured at different altitudes. The strategy that we adopt in eliciting segmental entities for matching is to first process the raw data to extract line contours; in the data under study these predominantly correspond to man-made road networks in urban areas and are represented by intensity ridges in the available images. Contour extraction is achieved by applying orientational line detection kernels to the raw image and refining their output with a relaxation operator [2]. The refinement process enhances the connectivity of the extracted lines through the use of a model of local contour structure. Because the relaxation operator draws on an explicit dictionary model to represent this contour structure,

Figure 1: Aerial images

the detected lines are rich in important junction features. We abstract the matching process in terms of relational graphs in which the nodes represent junctions in the road network and arcs signify the existence of a connecting line contour.

### 4.1. Initial Match Probabilities

The remaining ingredient required to apply the relaxation formula to the feature matching process is a set of initial match probabilities between nodes. The role of the initial probabilities is to model transformational differences between the scenes under study, thereby complementing the topological constraint process which is modelled by the compatibility coefficients. The modelling of the initial probabilities draws on geometric information derived for the properties of the lines forming junctions in the scenes under match. Uncertainties introduced by poor image segmentation or by geometric distortion must therefore be captured by imposing appropriate probability distributions on the raw measurements.

Our philosophy in computing the initial match probabilities is to combine evidence from the lines that constitute the junctions under consideration. The calculation of initial probability is therefore based on the geometric properties of the lines which meet at junctions $J$ and $j$. In our graph-based description, the lines are represented by the arcs originating at the junctions $J$ and $j$, i.e. $\mathcal{L}_J = \{e_1 \in E_1 | (e_1, J) \in R_1\}$ and $\mathcal{L}_j = \{e_2 \in E_2 | (e_2, j) \in R_2\}$.

In order to compute the initial junction match probabilities we combine evidence in the form of arc-match supports. This evidence combination process is facilitated using the dictionary-based evidence combining formula described in [3]. In this application of the evidence combining formula the configuration of labels which define the lines associated with junction $j$ is regarded as a model for computing the initial match probabilities with junction $J$. Support is accumulated over the entire set of possible matching combinations between the line-sets $\mathcal{L}_J$ and $\mathcal{L}_j$ with all possible insertions of the null label $\phi$. Under the assumption of a uniform prior distribution for the candidate line matches appearing in the different combinations, the evidence combining formula for computing the initial junction match probabilities is

$$P^{(0)}(J \to j) = \frac{\sum\limits_{e_2 \in \mathcal{L}_j} \prod\limits_{e_1 \in \mathcal{L}_J} q(e_1 \to e_2)}{\sum\limits_{i \in V_2} \sum\limits_{e_2 \in \mathcal{L}_i} \prod\limits_{e_1 \in \mathcal{L}_J} q(e_1 \to e_2)} \qquad (7)$$

We use two properties of the lines to compute the arc match support $q(e_1 \to e_2)$; these are the line lengths ($l_{e_1}$ and $l_{e_2}$) and their angle difference in the two images $\theta_{e_1,e_2}$. The estimation of angle difference is unaffected by segmentation error in the rest of the image because it is a local property of the junctions. By contrast, the estimation of line-length is more vulnerable to segmentation error. The main factors contributing to this are the erosion of line endings, line fragmentation and junction drop-out. For this reason we can anticipate large disparities in the arc-lengths detected in the different scenes under match. We gauge the similarity of line length under scaling by the ratio of the line lengths, i.e. $S_{e1,e2} = \frac{l_{e_1}}{l_{e_2}}$. The problem of unreliable scale estimation is accommodated by summing over the possibilities of correct line segmentation and line segmentation error. As a result, the line-match support is equal to

$$q(e_1 \to e_2) = \left\{ (1-p)\rho(S_{e_1,e_2}, S) + p(1 - \rho(S_{e_1,e_2}, S)) \right\} \rho(\theta_{e_1,e_2}, \Theta) \qquad (8)$$

In the above expression $\rho(V_{e1,e2}, V)$ is an exponential probability distribution for the line-quantity $V$ (i.e. orientation or scale) defined in terms of its average value $V$ and its variance $\sigma_V^2$

$$\rho(V_{e_1,e_2}, V) = \exp\left[ -\frac{(V_{e_1,e_2} - V)^2}{2\sigma_V^2} \right] \qquad (9)$$

Our motivation in adopting the distribution of equation (8) has been to associate a constant segmentation error $p$ with pairs of wildly disparate lines; lines whose length are compatible under the image scaling acquire a probability $1 - p$. When substituted into the evidence combining formula (7), this model associates a support proportional to $(1-p)^3$ with correct matches and a support proportional to $p^3$ with spurious matches.

We stressed in Section 3 that our compatibility coefficient model which accommodates topological constraint corruption is entirely devoid of free parameters. It is only our initial probability model which accommodates the geometric transformations between scenes that requires the specification of parameters. There are four such parameters; these are the mean and variances of the orientation and scale required to transform between the scenes under match. In the work reported here we adopt an optimisation approach in the estimation of these parameters. We select the scale and orientation parameters to optimise an initial match criterion. We define this to be the sum of the line-match supports

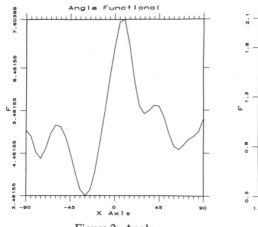

Figure 2: Angle

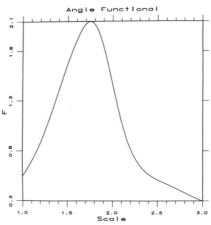

Figure 3: Scale

$$\mathcal{F} = \sum_{e_1 \in E_1} \sum_{e_2 \in E_2} q(e_1 \rightarrow e_2) \tag{10}$$

The optimal parameter values are computed by gradient ascent.

In order to transform between the low and high altitude images no net rotational transformation is required, However, there is a scaling factor of 1.73. These transformational parameters correspond to the global optimum of the matching functional whose orientation angle and scale projections are shown in Figures 2 and 3. It is worth commenting that the scale projection is unimodal. The orientation angle projection has a principal maximum with a number of suboptimal maxima. These suboptima are associated with the internal symmetry of the road network and are due to the fact that most T-junctions are right-angled.

### 4.2. Matching Experiments

In order to evaluate the performance of the relaxation scheme we have performed a number of experiments with the aim of posing tests of varying complexity to the matching algorithm. Our least demanding experiment involves matching a subregion of the low altitude image against the whole high altitude image; the low altitude image contains only 10% of the features contained within in the high altitude image. Here 67% of the low-altitude junctions are correctly matched and 20% are null matched; the fraction of junctions in the low altitude image for which a feasible match exists is 80%. This result not only illustrates the accuracy of the method, it also demonstrates that it is effective at matching subgraphs; this is a valuable property if the matching technique is to be used in situations where substantial occlusion is anticipated to be present. Our most demanding experiment involves matching

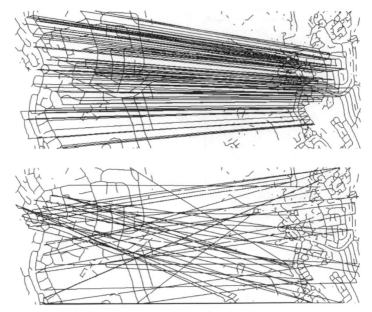

Figure 4: Results of matching

the whole low altitude image against the whole high altitude image; there are 351 junctions in the low altitude image while the high altitude image contains 394 junctions. In this case 64% of the junctions are matched correctly; 28% of the junctions are matched to the null category. The size of the data graph does not appear to limit the effectiveness of the technique.

The results of a typical matching experiment are shown in Figure 4. Although the figure is confused by the multitude of matches, the lines denoting correct matches shown in the top half of the figure define a conical envelope; those shown in the lower half of the figure are associated with incorrect matches and diverge from the envelope. It is worth noting that there is no pattern of organisation in the incorrect matches; they are distributed randomly across the scene. This is an encouraging observation since it means that the residual matching errors may be recoverable by a postprocessing operation. One strategy would be to cluster the transformational variables around the consistent matches provided by the relaxation process.

## 5. Conclusions

In conclusion, we have demonstrated how a Bayesian probabilistic relaxation scheme can be applied to scene matching problems in machine vision. The viewpoint adopted in the original derivation of the relaxation scheme imposes a strong dichotomy on the model components required to represent measurement information and symbolic constraints. In the matching problem the measurement process captures geometric effects present in the raw image data while the symbolic process captures the topology of the scene entities. We have presented novel models that can capture both components. Of particular note is our model of the topological constraint corruption processes operating in the scene graphs. This model is entirely devoid of free parameters; the compatibility coefficients required by the relaxation scheme are determined entirely by the numbers of nodes in the scene graphs under study.

## References

[1] N. Ayache and F. Lustman, "Efficient registration of stereo images by matching graph descriptions of edge segments", *International Journal of Computer Vision*, **1**, pp. 107-131, 1987.

[2] E.R. Hancock, "Resolving Edge-Line Ambiguities by Relaxation Labelling", *Proceedings of IEEE CVPR Conference*, pp. 300–306, 1993.

[3] E.R. Hancock and J. Kittler, "Combining Evidence in Probabilistic Relaxation", International Journal of Pattern Recognition and Artificial Intelligence, **3**, pp. 29–52, 1989.

[4] E.R. Hancock and J. Kittler, "Discrete Relaxation," *Pattern Recognition*, **23**, pp.711–733, 1990.

[5] R. Horaud , F. Veillon and T. Skordas, "Finding Geometric and Relational Structures in an Image", *Proceedings of First European Conference on Computer Vision*, pp. 374–384, 1990.

[6] R. Horaud and T. Skordas, "Stereo Correspondence through Feature Grouping and Maximal Cliques", *IEEE PAMI*, **11**, pp. 1168–1180, 1989.

[7] L. Herault, R. Horaud, F. Veillon and J-J. Niez, "Symbolic Image Matching by Simulated Annealing", *Proceedings of First British Machine Vision Conference*, pp. 319–324, 1990.

[8] A. Rosenfeld, R. A. Hummel and S .W. Zucker, "Scene labelling by relaxation operations", *IEEE*, **SMC-6**, pp. 420–433, 1976.

[9] R.C. Wilson and E.R Hancock, "Relaxation Matching of Road Networks in Aerial Images using Topological Constraints", *to appear in Sensor Fusion VI*, 1993.

[10] S.Z. Li, "Matching invariant to translations, rotations and scale changes", *Pattern Recognition*, **25**, pp. 583–594, 1992.

[11] J Kittler, W.J.Christmas and M. Petrou, "Probabilistic relaxation for matching problems in machine vision", *Proceedings of the Fourth International Conference on Computer Vision*, 666-673, 1993.

# Recognizing Facial Expressions

Yaser Yacoob & Larry Davis
Computer Vision Laboratory
University of Maryland
College Park, MD 20742

## ABSTRACT

An approach for analysis and representation of facial dynamics for recognition of expressions from image sequences is proposed. The algorithm utilizes optical flow computation to identify the direction of non-rigid motions that are caused by human facial expressions. A mid-level symbolic representation that is motivated by linguistic and psychological considerations is developed. Recognition results of six universal facial expressions, as well as eye blinking, are reported.

## 1  Introduction

In this paper we explore methods by which a computer can recognize human facial expressions [2]. We focus on the appearance of the face from its near frontal image projection, without considering the underlying anatomic and musculature models and actions.

Research in psychology has indicated that at least six emotions are universally associated with distinct facial expressions. Several other emotions, and many combinations of emotions, have been studied but remain unconfirmed as universally distinguishable. The six principle emotions are: happiness, sadness, surprise, fear, anger, and disgust (see Figure 1(a)).

Most psychology research on facial expression has been conducted on "mug-shot" pictures that capture the subject's expression at its peak [8]. These pictures allow one to detect the presence of static cues (such as wrinkles) as well as the position and shape of the facial features. Few studies have directly investigated the influence of the motion and deformation of facial features on the interpretation of facial expressions. Bassili [1] suggested that motion in the image of a face would allow emotions to be

The support of the Advanced Research Projects Agency (ARPA Order No. 6989) and the U.S. Army Topographic Engineering Center under Contract DACA76-92-C-0009 is gratefully acknowledged. The authors would like to thank the 35 volunteers who subjected themselves to the intrusive experiments on their facial expression.

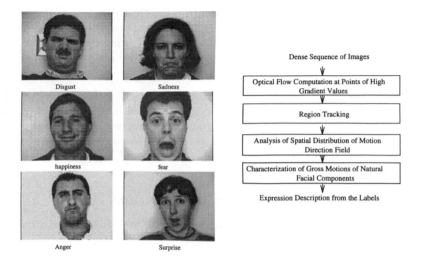

Figure 1: (a) Six universal facial expressions (b) The flow of the algorithm

identified even with minimal information about the spatial arrangement of features. The subjects of his experiments viewed image sequences in which only white dots on the dark surface of the person displaying the emotion are visible. The reported results indicate that facial expressions were more accurately recognized from dynamic images than from a single static image.

Before proceeding, we introduce some terminology needed in the paper. Face region *motion* refers to the changes in images of facial features caused by facial *actions* corresponding to physical feature deformations on the 3-D surface of the face. Our goal is to develop computational methods that relate such motions as *cues* for action recovery.

## 2 Overview of our approach

We chose not to model or analyze facial muscle actions, setting our work apart from [3-5]. Instead, we focus on the motions associated with the edges of the mouth, eyes, and eyebrows. Potential advantages of focusing directly on edges are:

- Edges are easier to compute than the identification of muscle parts through the observed deformations of the skin.

- Edges are more stable than face surfaces under projection changes. In comparison, the farther the face is from the frontal view, the harder it becomes to detect muscles.

- Motion is more accurately computed at image discontinuities than over smooth areas such as the muscles.

- Mapping the observed motion at edges into linguistic descriptions is relatively straightforward. In contrast, analyzing muscle actions requires the use of anatomic musculature models. Furthermore, the mapping of expressions into muscle actions is still not well developed; most of the available knowledge is applicable only to the synthesis of facial expressions.

Figure 1(b) describes the flow of computation of our facial expression system. The optical flow and feature tracking algorithms can be found in [6,7]. The correlation-based optical flow is computed at high gradient points, and the tracking locates the main facial features within rectangles throughout the sequence using a spatio-temporal approach. In this paper we focus on the mid and high level computations of the system.

## 3 Computing local motion representations

### 3.1 Psychological basis for recognizing facial expressions

Table 1 summarizes the results of Ekman and Friesen [2] on the universal cues for recognizing the six principle emotions. These cues describe the peak of each expression and provide a human interpretation of the static appearance of the facial feature. For example, a description such as "brows are raised" means that the viewer's interpretation of the location of the brows relative to other facial features indicates they are not in a neutral state but higher than usual. The viewer uses many cues to deduce such information from the image, among these are: the appearance of wrinkles in certain parts of the face, effect of the hypothesis of a high brow on the shape of the eyes (i.e., state of eyelids), etc. Unfortunately, the performance of humans in arriving at such descriptions is far better than what can be achieved, currently, by computers if only static images are considered. Notice that some of the linguistic expressions used to describe these cues appear very hard to model computationally-"upper lid is tense, tension or stress in the mouth, lip trembling" etc. These descriptions seem rather instinctive to humans.

Figure 2 summarizes the observations of Bassili [1] on motion based cues for facial expressions. The experiments of Bassili were intended to explore only the role of motion in facial expressions; therefore the face features, texture and complexion were unavailable to the experiment subjects. As illustrated in Figure 2, Bassili identified principle facial motions that provide powerful cues to the subjects to recognize facial expressions.

Bassili's results do not explicitly associate the motion patterns with specific face features or muscles since such information was unavailable to the experiment subjects. For example, a "surprise" motion is recognized by an upward motion in the upper part the face and a downward motion in the lower part of the face.

Table 1: The cues for facial expression as suggested by Ekman and Friesen

| Emotion | Observed facial cues |
|---------|----------------------|
| Surprise | brows raised (curved & high), skin below brow stretched, horizontal wrinkles across forehead, eyelids opened and more of the white of the eye is visible jaw drops open without tension or stretching of the mouth |
| Fear | brows raised and drawn together, forehead wrinkles drawn to the center upper eyelid is raised and lower eyelid is drawn up mouth is open, lips are slightly tense or stretched and drawn back |
| Disgust | lower lip is raised and pushed up to upper lip or is lowered and slightly protruding nose is wrinkled, cheeks are raised, lines below the lower lid, upper lip is raised lid is pushed up but not tense, brows are lowered, lowering the upper lid |
| Anger | brows lowered and drawn together, vertical lines appear between brows lower lid is tensed and may or may not be raised upper lid is tense and may or may not be lowered due to brows action eyes have a hard stare and may have a bulging appearance lips are either pressed firmly together with corners straight or down or open, tensed in a squarish shape nostrils may be dilated (could occur in sadness too) unambiguous only if registered in all three facial areas |
| Happiness | corners of lips are drawn back and up, cheeks are raised mouth may or may not be parted with teeth exposed or not a wrinkle runs down from the nose to the outer edge beyond lip corners lower eyelid shows wrinkles below it, and maybe raised but not tense Crow's-feet wrinkles go outward from the outer corners of the eyes |
| Sadness | inner corners of eyebrows are drawn up, upper lid inner corner is raised skin below the eyebrow is triangulated, with inner corner up corners of the lips are drawn or lip is trembling |

## 3.2 A dictionary for facial dynamics from image sequences

The dictionary of facial feature actions borrows from the facial cues of universal expression descriptions proposed in [2], and from the motion patterns of expression proposed in [1]. As a result, we arrive at a dictionary that is a motion-based feature description of facial actions. The dictionary is divided into: *components*, *basic actions of these components*, and *motion cues*. The components are defined qualitatively and relative to the rectangles surrounding the face regions, the basic actions are determined by the component's visible deformations, and the cues are used to recognize the basic actions based on motion detection by optical flow within these regions. Table 2 shows the components, basic actions, and cues that model the mouth. Similar tables were created for the eyes and the eyebrows.

## 3.3 Computing a mid-level representation

The dictionary allows us to convert local directional motion patterns within a face region into a linguistic, mid-level representation for facial actions. In addition to the basic actions the mid-level representation includes region and coordinated actions, defined as follows:

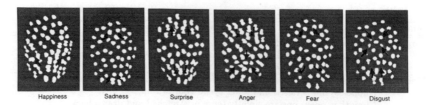

| Happiness | Sadness | Surprise | Anger | Fear | Disgust |

Figure 2: The cues for facial expression as suggested by Bassili

Table 2: The dictionary for mouth motions

| Component | Basic Action | Motion Cues |
|-----------|-------------|-------------|
| upper lip | raising | upward motion of an upper part of window |
|           | lowering | downward motion of an upper part of window |
|           | contraction | horizontal shrinking of an upper part of window |
|           | expansion | horizontal expansion of an upper part of window |
| lower lip | raising | upward motion of a lower part of window |
|           | lowering | downward motion of a lower part of window |
|           | contraction | horizontal shrinking of a lower part of window |
|           | expansion | horizontal expansion of a lower part of window |
| left corner | raising | upward motion of a left part of window |
|             | lowering | downward motion of a left part of window |
| right corner | raising | upward motion of a right part of window |
|              | lowering | downward motion of a right part of window |
| whole mouth | raising | upward motion throughout window |
|             | lowering | downward motion throughout window |
|             | compaction | overall shrinkage in mouth's size |
|             | expansion | overall expansion in mouth's size |

- Region actions: Basic actions within a rectangle surrounding a feature are combined to construct a region action. For example, the simultaneous raising of the upper lip and the lowering of the lower lip produce a region action corresponding to "mouth opening."

- Coordinated actions: Region actions that occur simultaneously at symmetric features (i.e., the eyes, and brows) can be combined to construct a coordinated action. For example, the raising of the right and left brows produces a "raising brows" coordinated action.

A temporal consistency procedure is applied to the mid-level representation to filter out errors due to noise or illumination changes (see [6]).

### 3.4 Computing basic action cues from optical flow

The flow magnitudes are first thresholded to reduce the effect of small motions probably due to noise. The motion vectors are then re-quantized into eight principle directions. The optical flow vectors are filtered using both spatial and temporal procedures that improve their coherence and continuity, respectively.

Statistical analyses of the resulting flow directions within each face region window provide indicators about the general motion patterns that the face features undergo. The statistical analyses differ from one feature to another, based on an allowable set of motions. The largest set of motions is associated with the mouth since it has the most degrees of freedom at the anatomic and musculature levels.

We measure the motion of the mouth by considering a set of vertical and horizontal partitions of its surrounding rectangle (see Figure 3(a)). The horizontal partitions are used to capture vertical motions of the mouth. These generally correspond to independent motions of the lips. The two types of vertical partitions are designed to capture several mouth motions. Single vertical partitions capture mouth horizontal expansions and contractions when the mouth is not completely horizontal. The two vertical partitions are designed to capture the motion of the corners of the mouth.

The partitions shown in Figure 3(a) use free-sliding dividers. For each possible partition, $P$, and for every side of $P$ we define the following parameters:

- $m$- the total number of points on this side of the divider.

- $c^q$- the number of points having a motion vector direction $q$ ($q = 1, 2, .., 8$).

- $p^q = c^q/m$- the percentage of points with motion vectors in direction $q$.

$p^q$ indicates the degree of clustering of the motion across the divider, while $c^q$ indicates the "strength," in count, of the motion in direction $q$. The confidence measure of the motion's homogeneity and strength that a divider creates in a direction $q$ is given by:

$$H^q = c^q \cdot p^q \qquad (1)$$

Within each type of partition, partitions are ranked according to the values $H^q$ (see [7]). The highest ranking partition in each type is used as a pointer into the dictionary of motions (see Table 2), to determine the action that may have occurred at the feature.

## 4 Recognizing facial expressions

### 4.1 Temporal considerations for recognizing expressions

We divide every facial expression into three temporal parts: the *beginning, epic* and *ending*. Figure 3(b) shows the temporal parts of a smile model. Since we use the outward-upward motion of the mouth corners as the principle cue for a smile motion pattern, these are used as the criteria for temporal classification also. Notice that Figure 3(b) indicates that the detection of mouth corner motions might not occur at the same frames in both the beginning and ending of actions, and that we require at least one corner to start moving to label a frame with a "beginning of a smile" label,

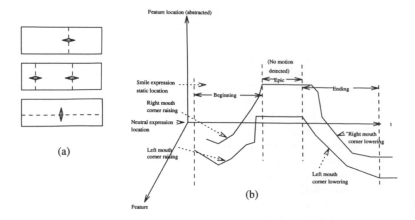

Figure 3: The temporal model of the "smile" expression

while the motions must completely stop before a frame is labeled as an epic or an ending.

Table 3 shows the rules used in identifying the onsets of the "beginning" and the "ending" of each facial expression. These rules are applied to the mid-level representation to create a complete temporal map describing the evolving facial expression. For a smile, the system locates the first frame, $f_1$, with a "raising mouth corners" action, and verifies that the frames following $f_1$ show a region or basic action that is consistent with this action (in this case it can be one of: right or mouth corner raised, or mouth expansion with/without some opening). It then locates the first frame $f_2$ where the motions within the mouth region terminate (verified with later frames, as before). Then, it identifies the first frame, $f_3$, in which an action "lowering mouth corners" is detected and verifies it as before. Finally, it identifies the first frame, $f_4$, where the motion is stopped and verifies it. The temporal labeling of the smile expression will have the frames $(f_1...f_2 - 1)$, $(f_2...f_3 - 1)$, and $(f_3...f_4)$ as the "beginning", "epic", and "ending" of a smile.

Due to noise in the optical flow, some temporal cues can only be deduced from changes in the windows tracking the facial features. Such changes are currently computed only for the mouth since the accuracy of measuring size changes of other face features was not sufficient. For example, an "anger" emotion is characterized by inward lowering motion of the eyebrows and by compaction of the mouth. The compaction may be hard to detect based on optical flow due to noise, aperture, or tracking inaccuracies. We measure the horizontal and vertical ratios of the window surrounding the mouth during the hypothesized start of an expression, and verify that some compaction in the window size occurred. Only if there is evidence that the mouth size decreased will the expression be accepted. Similar considerations are used to determine the exact ending of an expression.

Table 3: The rules for classifying facial expressions (B=beginning, E=ending)

| Expr. | B/E | Satisfactory actions |
|-------|-----|----------------------|
| Anger | B | inward lowering brows & mouth compaction |
| Anger | E | outward raising brows & mouth expansion |
| Disgust | B | upward nose motion & mouth expanded/opened & lowering of brows |
| Disgust | E | downward nose motion & raising of brows |
| Happiness | B | raising mouth corners or mouth opening with its expansion |
| Happiness | E | lowering mouth corners or mouth closing with its contraction |
| Surprise | B | raising brows& lowering of lower lip (jaw) |
| Surprise | E | lowering brows& raising of lower lip (jaw) |
| Sadness | B | lowering mouth corners & raising mid mouth & raising inner parts of brows |
| Sadness | E | lowering mouth corners & lowering mid mouth & lowering inner parts of brows |
| Fear | B | slight expansion and lowering of mouth & raising inner parts of brows |
| Fear | E | slight contraction and raising of mouth & lowering inner parts of brows |

### 4.2 Resolving conflicts between expressions

The system is designed to identify and recognize facial expressions from long video clips (i.e., clips including 3-6 expressions). We simplified the behavior model of our subjects by asking them to display one emotion at a time, and include a short neutral state between expressions.

Since the six expression classifiers operate on the whole sequence independently, the system may create conflicting hypotheses. Conflicts may arise when an ending of an expression is mistaken as the beginning of another expression. For example, the "anger" recognition module may consider the lowering of the eyebrows of the ending of a "surprise" expression as a beginning of an "anger" expression. To resolve such conflicts, we employ a memory-based process that gives preference to the expression that started earlier. Once conflicts are resolved, a new search for expressions that the system may have missed due to wrong hypotheses is performed.

## 5 Experiments

Our database of image sequences includes over 30 different faces. For each face several expressions were recorded, some expressions recurring. We requested each subject to display the emotions in front of the video camera while minimizing his/her head motion. Nevertheless, most subjects inevitably moved their head during a facial expression. As a result, the optical flow at facial regions was sometimes overwhelmed by the overall head rigid motion. The facial expression system detects such rigid motion and marks the respective frames as unusable for analysis.

The images were taken at 30 frames per second, and the number of frames per short sequence was 218 frames, double this number for long sequences; image resolution is 120x160 pixels. On a sample of 46 image sequences of 30 subjects (Figure 5(a)) displaying a total of 105 emotions, the system achieved a recognition rate of 86% for

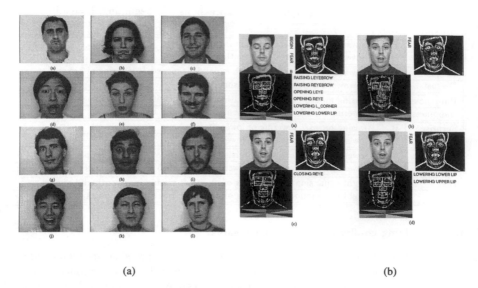

(a)                                                                                           (b)

Figure 4: Twelve faces (out of more than 35) used in experiments

smile, 94% for surprise, 92% for anger, 86% for fear, 80% for sadness, and 92% for disgust. Blinking detection success rate was 65%.

Table 4 shows the details of our results. Occurrences of fear, and sadness are less frequent than happiness, disgust, surprise and anger. Some confusion of expressions occurred between the following pairs: fear and surprise, anger and disgust, and sadness and surprise. These distinctions rely on subtle coarse shape and motion information that was not always accurately detected.

Table 4: Facial expression recognition results

| Expression | Correct | False Alarm | Missed | Confused | Rate |
|---|---|---|---|---|---|
| Happiness | 32 | - | 5 | - | 86% |
| Surprise | 29 | 2 | 1 | 2 | 94% |
| Anger | 22 | 1 | 2 | 2 | 92% |
| Disgust | 12 | 2 | 1 | 2 | 92% |
| Fear | 6 | - | 1 | 3 | 86% |
| Sadness | 4 | - | 1 | 1 | 80% |
| Blink | 68 | 11 | 38 | - | 65% |

Figure 5(b) shows four frames, the gap between each two frames being four frames. For (a)-(d) the upper left quarter shows the intensity image, the upper right quarter shows the gradient image, the rectangle in between displays the classification of facial expression, the lower left quarter shows the optical flow results, the rectangles around the face regions of interest and the mapping of colors into directions, and the lower right quarter shows the mid-level descriptions that were computed.

## 6 Summary

An approach for analyzing and classifying facial expressions from optical flow was proposed. This approach is based on qualitative tracking of principle regions of the face and flow computation at high intensity gradients points. A mid-level representation is computed from the spatial and the temporal motion results. The representation is linguistically motivated, following research in the psychology literature in [1,2].

We have carried out experiments on thirty subjects in a laboratory environment and achieved good classification of facial expressions. Further study of the system's components is being performed as well as expanding its capability to deal with non-emotion facial messages.

## References

[1] J.N. Bassili, "Emotion recognition: The role of facial movement and the relative importance of upper and lower areas of the face," *Journal of Personality and Social Psychology*, Vol. 37, 1979, 2049-2059.

[2] P. Ekman and W. Friesen, *Unmasking the Face*, Prentice-Hall, Inc., 1975.

[3] H. Li, P. Roivainen, and R. Forcheimer, "3-D motion estimation in model-based facial image coding," *IEEE PAMI*, Vol. 15, No. 6, 1993, 545-555.

[4] K. Mase, "Recognition of facial expression from optical flow," *IEICE Transactions,* Vol. E 74, No. 10, 1991, 3474-3483.

[5] D. Terzopoulos, and K. Waters, "Analysis and synthesis of facial image sequences using physical and anatomical models," IEEE PAMI, Vol. 15, No. 6, 1993, 569-579.

[6] Y. Yacoob, and L.S. Davis, "Computing Spatio-Temporal Representations of Human Faces" to be presented in *IEEE CVPR*, 1994.

[7] Y. Yacoob, and L.S. Davis, *Recognizing Human Facial Expression,* Technical Report, in preparation.

[8] A.W. Young and H.D. Ellis (Edited), *Handbook of Research on Face Processing*, Elsevier Science Publishers B.V., 1989.

# CONTINUOUS SYMMETRY FOR SHAPES

Hagit Zabrodsky and Shmuel Peleg
*Institute of Computer Science*
and
David Avnir
*Departmenet of Organic Chemistry*
*The Hebrew University of Jerusalem*
*91904 Jerusalem, Israel*

ABSTRACT

Symmetry is treated as a continuous feature, and the Symmetry Distance (SD) of a shape is defined to be the minimum distance required to move points of the original shape in order to obtain a symmetrical shape. This general definition of a symmetry measure enables a comparison of the "amount" of symmetry of different shapes and the "amount" of different symmetries of a single shape. The measure is applicable to any type of symmetry in any dimension. The Symmetry Distance gives rise to a method of reconstructing symmetry of occluded shapes. We extend the method to deal with symmetries of noisy and fuzzy data.

## 1 Introduction

One of the basic features of shapes and objects is symmetry. Symmetry is considered a pre-attentive feature which enhances recognition and reconstruction of shapes and objects [2]. Symmetry is also an important parameter in physical and chemical processes and is an important criterion in medical diagnosis. However, the exact

a.      b.      c.

Figure 1: Faces are not perfectly symmetrical.
a) Original image.
b) Right half of original image and its reflection.
c) Left half of original image and its reflection.

mathematical definition of symmetry [4, 6] is inadequate to describe and quantify the symmetries found in the natural world nor those found in the visual world (a classic example is that of faces - see Fig. 1). Furthermore, even perfectly symmetric objects loose their exact symmetry when projected onto the image plane or the retina due to occlusion, perspective transformations, digitization, etc. Thus, although symmetry is usually considered a binary feature, (i.e. an object is either symmetric or it is not symmetric), we view symmetry as a continuous feature where intermediate values of symmetry denote some intermediate "amount" of symmetry. We introduce a "Symmetry Distance" that can measure and quantify all types of symmetries of objects. This measure will enable a comparison of the "amount" of symmetry of different shapes and the "amount" of different symmetries of a single shape.

In Sect. 2 we define the Symmetry Distance and in Sect. 3 we describe a method for evaluting this measure. We then describe features of the symmetry distance including its use in dealing with occluded objects and with noisy data.

## 2 A Continuous Symmetry Measure - Definition

We define the **Symmetry Distance** (SD) as a the minimum effort required to turn a given shape into a symmetric shape. This is measured by the mean of the square distances each point is moved from its location in the original shape to its location in the symmetric shape. No a priori symmetric reference shape is assumed.

Denote by $\Omega$ the space of all shapes of a given dimension, where each shape $P$ is represented by a sequence of $n$ points $\{P_i\}_{i=0}^{n-1}$. We define a metric $d$ on this space as follows:

$$d : \Omega \times \Omega \to R$$
$$d(P, Q) = d(\{P_i\}, \{Q_i\}) = \frac{1}{n} \sum_{i=0}^{n-1} \|P_i - Q_i\|^2$$

This metric defines a distance function between every two shapes in $\Omega$.

We define the **Symmetry Transform** ST of a shape P, as the symmetric shape closest to P in terms of the metric $d$.

The **Symmetry Distance (SD)** of a shape P is now defined as the distance between P and it's Symmetry Transform:

$$SD = d(P, ST(P))$$

The SD of a shape $P = \{P_i\}_{i=0}^{n-1}$ is evaluated by finding the symmetry transform $\hat{P}$ of $P$ (Fig.2) and computing: $\boxed{\text{SD} = \frac{1}{n}\Sigma_{i=0}^{n-1}\|P_i - \hat{P}_i\|^2}$.

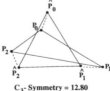

Figure 2: The symmetry transform of $\{P_0, P_1, P_2\}$ is $\{\hat{P}_0, \hat{P}_1, \hat{P}_2\}$. SD = $\frac{1}{3}\Sigma_{i=0}^{2}\|P_i - \hat{P}_i\|^2$.

$C_3$- Symmetry = 12.80

This definition of the Symmetry Distance implicitly implies invariance to rotation and translation. Normalization of the original shape prior to the transformation additionally allows invariance to scale (Fig. 3). We normalize by scaling the shape so that the maximum distance between points on the contour and the centroid is a given constant (in this paper all examples are given following normalization to 100). The normalization presents an upper bound of on the mean squared distance moved by points of the shape. Thus the SD value is limited in range, where SD=0 for perfectly symmetric shapes (see Appendix in [9]). The general definition of the Sym-

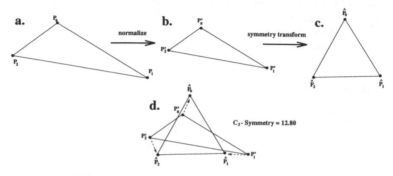

Figure 3: Calculating the Symmetry Distance of a shape:
a) Original shape $\{P_0, P_1, P_2\}$.
b) Normalized shape $\{P'_0, P'_1, P'_2\}$, such that maximum distance to the center of mass is one.
c) Applying the symmetry transform to obtain a symmetric shape $\{\hat{P}_0, \hat{P}_1, \hat{P}_2\}$.
d) SD $= \frac{1}{3}(\|P'_0 - \hat{P}_0\|^2 + \|P'_1 - \hat{P}_1\|^2 + \|P'_2 - \hat{P}_2\|^2)$
SD values are multiplied by 100 for convenience of handling.

metry Distance enables evaluation of a given shape for different types of symmetries (mirror-symmetries, rotational symmetries etc). Moreover, this generalization allows comparisons between the different symmetry types, and allows expressions such as "a shape is more mirror-symmetric than rotationally-symmetric of order two". An additional feature of the Symmetry Distance is that we obtain the symmetric shape which is 'closest' to the given one, enabling visual evaluation of the SD.

An example of a 2D polygon and it's symmetry transforms and SD values are shown in Fig. 4. Note that shape 4e is the most similar to the original shape 4a and, indeed, its SD value is the smallest. In the next Section we describe a geometric algorithm for deriving the Symmetry Transform of a shape. In Sect. 4 we deal with the initial step of representing a shape by a collection of points.

## 3  Evaluating the Symmetry Transform

In this Section we describe a geometric algorithm for deriving the Symmetry Transform of a shape represented by a sequence of points $\{P_i\}_{i=0}^{n-1}$. In practice we find the Symmetry Transform of the shape with respect to a given point-symmetry

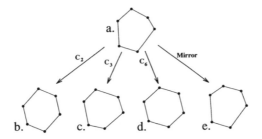

Figure 4: Symmetry Transforms and Symmetry Distances of a 2D polygon.
a) The 2D polygon.
b) Symmetry Transform of (a) with respect to $C_2$-symmetry (SD = 1.87).
c) Symmetry Transform of (a) with respect to $C_3$-symmetry (SD = 1.64).
d) Symmetry Transform of (a) with respect to $C_6$-symmetry (SD = 2.53).
e) Symmetry Transform of (a) with respect to Mirror-symmetry (SD = 0.66).

group. For simplicity and clarity of explanation, we describe the method by using some examples.

Following is a geometrical algorithm for deriving the symmetry transform of a shape $P$ having $n$ points with respect to rotational symmetry of order $n$ ($C_n$-symmetry). This method transforms $P$ into a regular n-gon, keeping the centroid in place.

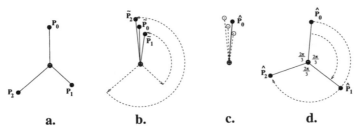

Figure 5: The $C_3$-symmetry Transform of 3 points.
a) original 3 points $\{P_i\}_{i=0}^2$.
b) Fold $\{P_i\}_{i=0}^2$ into $\{\tilde{P}_i\}_{i=0}^2$.
c) Average $\{\tilde{P}_i\}_{i=0}^2$ obtaining $\hat{P}_0 = \frac{1}{3}\sum_{i=0}^2 \tilde{P}_i$.
d) Unfold the average point obtaining $\{\hat{P}_i\}_{i=0}^2$.
The centroid $\omega$ is marked by $\oplus$.

## Algorithm for finding the $C_n$-symmetry transform:

1. *Fold* the points $\{P_i\}_{i=0}^{n-1}$ by rotating each point $P_i$ counterclockwise about the centroid by $2\pi i/n$ radians (Fig. 5b).

2. Let $\hat{P}_0$ be the average of the points $\{\tilde{P}_i\}_{i=0}^{n-1}$ (Fig. 5c).

3. *Unfold* the points, obtaining the $C_n$-symmetric points $\{\hat{P}_i\}_{i=0}^{n-1}$ by duplicating $\hat{P}_0$ and rotating clockwise about the centroid by $2\pi i/n$ radians (Fig. 5d).

The set of points $\{\hat{P}_i\}_{i=0}^{n-1}$ is the symmetry transform of the points $\{P_i\}_{i=0}^{n-1}$. i.e. they are the $C_n$-symmetric configuration of points closest to $\{P_i\}_{i=0}^{n-1}$ in terms of the metric $d$ defined in Sect. 2.

The common case, however, is that shapes have more points than the order of the symmetry. For symmetry of order $n$, the folding method can be extended to shapes having a number of points which is a multiple of $n$. A 2D shape $P$ having $qn$ points is represented as $q$ sets $\{S_r\}_{r=0}^{q-1}$ of $n$ interlaced points $S_r = \{P_{rn+i}\}_{i=0}^{n-1}$. The $C_n$-symmetry transform of $P$ (Fig. 6) is obtained by applying the above algorithm to each set of $n$ points seperately, where the folding is performed about the centroid of all the points.

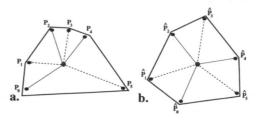

Figure 6: Geometric description of the $C_3$-symmetry transform for 6 points. The centroid $\omega$ of the points is marked by $\oplus$.
a) The original points shown as 2 sets of 3 points: $S_0 = \{P_0, P_2, P_4\}$ and $S_1 = \{P_1, P_3, P_5\}$.
b) The obtained $C_3$-symmetric configuration.

The procedure for evaluating the symmetry transform for mirror-symmetry is similar: Given a shape having $m = 2q$ points we divide the points into $q$ pairs of points and given an initial guess of the symmetry axis, we apply the folding/unfolding method as follows (see Fig. 7):

## Algorithm for finding the mirror-symmetry transform:

1. for every pair of points $\{P_0, P_1\}$:

    (a) fold - by reflecting across the mirror symmetry axis obtaining $\{\tilde{P}_0, \tilde{P}_1\}$.

    (b) average - obtaining a single averaged point $\hat{P}_0$.

    (c) unfold - by reflecting back across the mirror symmetry axis obtaining $\{\hat{P}_0, \hat{P}_1\}$.

2. minimize over all possible axis of mirror-symmetry.

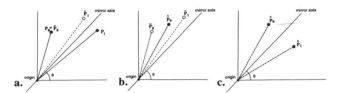

Figure 7: The mirror-symmetry transform of a single pair of points for angle $\theta$, where the centroid of the shape is assumed to be at the origin.
a) The two points $\{P_0, P_1\}$ are folded to obtain $\{\bar{P}_0, \bar{P}_1\}$.
b) Points $\bar{P}_0$ and $\bar{P}_1$ are averaged to obtain $\hat{P}_0$.
c) $\hat{P}_1$ is obtained by reflecting $\hat{P}_0$ about the symmetry axis.

The minimization performed in step 2 is, in practice, replaced by an analytic solution.

This method extends to **any** finite point-symmetry group $G$ in **any** dimension, where the folding and unfolding are performed by applying the group elements about the centroid.

Given a symmetry group G (having $n$ elements) and given a shape $P$ represented by $m = qn$ points, the symmetry transform of the shape with respect to G-symmetry is obtained as follows:

### Algorithm for finding the $G$-symmetry transform:

- The points are divided into $q$ sets of $n$ points.

- For every set of $n$ points:

  - The points are folded by applying the elements of the G-symmetry group.

  - The folded points are averaged, obtaining a single averaged point.

  - The averaged point is unfolded by applying the inverse of the elements of the G-symmetry group. A G-symmetric set of $n$ points is obtained.

- The above procedure is performed over all possible orientations of the symmetry axis and planes of G. Select that orientation which minimizes the Symmetry Distance value. As previously noted, this minimization is analytic in 2D but requires an iterative minimization process in 3D (except for the 3D mirror-symmetry group where a closed form solution has been derived).

## 4 Point Selection for Shape Representation

As symmetry has been defined on a sequence of points, representing a given shape by points must precede the application of the symmetry transform. Selection of points influences the value of SD and depends on the type of object to be measured. If a

600

shape is inherently created from points (such as a graph structure or cyclically connected points creating a polygon) we can represent a shape by these points (Fig. 8). This is the case when analysing symmetry of molecules ([10, 9, 7]).

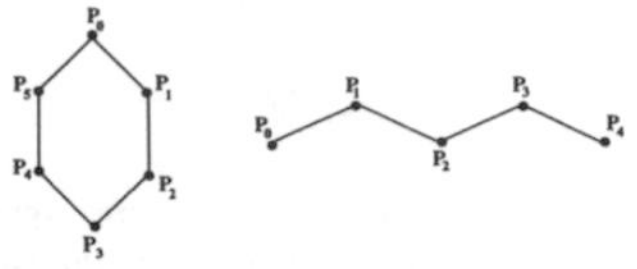

Figure 8: When measuring symmetry of shapes inherently created from points we represent the shape by these points.

There are several ways to select a sequence of points to represent continuous 2D shapes. One such method is selection at **equal distances-** the points are selected along the shape's contour such that the curve length between every pair of adjacent points is equal (Fig. 9).

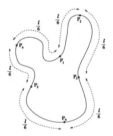

Figure 9: Point selection by equal distance: points are selected along the contour such that each point is equidistant to the next in terms of curve length. In this example six points are distributed along the contour spaced by $\frac{1}{6}$ of the full contour length.

In many cases, however, contour length is not a meaningful measure, as in noisy or occluded shapes. In such cases we propose to select points on a smoothed version of the contour and then project them back onto the original contour. The smoothing of the continuous contour is performed by moving each point on the continuous contour to the centroid of its contour neighborhood. The greater the size of the neighborhood, the greater is the smoothing (see Fig. 10). The level of smoothing can vary and for a high level of smoothing, the resulting shape becomes almost a circle about the centroid ([5]).

We use the following procedure for selection by smoothing:
The original contour is first sampled at very high density and at equal distances along the contour obtaining the sampled points $\{M_j\}$ (Fig. 11a). Following, each sampled point $M_j$ is replaced by the centroid $M_j'$ of a finite number of its neighboring sampled points. The "smoothed" shape is obtained by connecting the centroid points $\{M_j'\}$ (Fig. 11b). A second sampling of points is performed on the smoothed contour, where the points $\{P_i'\}$ are, again, selected at equal distances along the contour. The backprojection is performed by concidering each sampled point $P_i'$ as an interpolated point between two points of the smoothed shape $M_{j_1}'$ and $M_{j_2}'$ (Fig. 11c). The sample point $P_i'$ is backprojected onto the original contour at the point $P_i$ which is the interpolated point between the corresponding sampled points $M_{j_1}$ and $M_{j_2}$ on the original contour

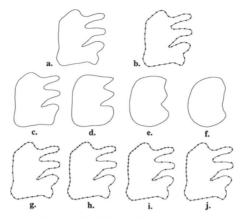

Figure 10: Selection by smoothing.
a) Original continuous contour.
b) Points are selected at equal distances along the continuous contour.
c-f) The smoothed shape is obtained by averaging neighboring points of (b). The amount of smoothing depends on the size of the neighborhood. The smoothed shapes (c-f) are obtained when neighborhood includes 5,10,15 and 20 percent of the points, respectively.
g-j) The sampling of points on the original shape using the smoothed shapes (c-f) respectively. Notice that fewer points are selected on the "noisy" part of the contour.

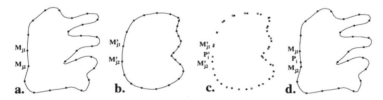

Figure 11: Selection by smoothing (in practice)
a) Continuous contour sampled at equal distances. Points $\{M_j\}$ are obtained.
b) Each sampled point $M_j$ is replaced by the centroid $M_j'$ of a finite number of its neighboring sampled points. The "smoothed" shape is obtained by connecting the centroid points $\{M_j'\}$
c) A second sampling of points is performed at equal distances on the smoothed contour obtaining points $\{P_i'\}$ (white points in Figure). The sample point $P_i'$ is concidered as an interpolation between the two points $M_{j_1}'$ and $M_{j_2}'$.
d) The sample point $P_i'$ is backprojected onto the original contour at the point $P_i$ which is the interpolated point between the corresponding sampled points $M_{j_1}$ and $M_{j_2}$ on the original contour.

(Fig. 11d). i.e. $P_i = (P_i' - M_{j_1})\frac{(M_{j_2} - M_{j_1})}{(M_{j_2}' - M_{j_1}')} + M_{j_1}$.
The ultimate smoothing is when the shape is smoothed into a circle. In this case,

equal distances on the circular contour is equivalent to equal angles about the center. For maximum smoothing we, therefore, use selection at **equal angles** (Fig. 12) where points are selected on the original contour at equal angular intervals around the centroid.

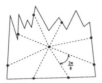

Figure 12: Selection at equal angles: points are distributed along the contour at regular angular intervals around the centroid.

## 5 Symmetry of Occluded Shapes - Center of Symmetry

When a symmetric object is partially occluded, we use the symmetry distance to evaluate the symmetry of the occluded shapes, locate the center of symmetry and reconstruct the symmetric shape most similar to the unoccluded original.

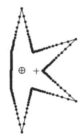

Figure 13: An occluded shape with sampled points selected at equal angles about the center of symmetry (marked by ⊕). The symmetry distance obtained using these points is greater than the symmetry distance obtained using points selected at equal angles about the centroid (marked by +).

As described in Sect. 4, a shape can be represented by points selected at regular angular intervals about the centroid. Angular selection of points about a point other than the centroid will give a different symmetry distance value. We define the **center of symmetry** of a shape as that point about which selection at equal angles gives the minimum symmetry distance value. When a symmetric shape is complete the center of symmetry coincides with the centroid of the shape. However, the center of symmetry of truncated or occluded objects does not align with its centroid but is closer to the centroid of the complete shape. Thus the center of symmetry of a shape is robust under truncation and occlusion.

To locate the center of symmetry, we use an iterative procedure of gradient descent that converges from the centroid of an occluded shape to the center of symmetry. Denote by *center of selection* the point about which points are selected using selection at equal angles. We initialize the iterative process by setting the centroid as the center of selection. At each step we compare the symmetry value obtained from points selected at equal angles about the center of selection with the symmetry value obtained by selection about points in the center of selection's immediate neighborhood. That point about which selection at equal angles gives minimum symmetry value is set to

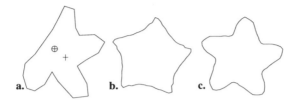

Figure 14: Reconstruction of an occluded shape.
a) Original occluded shape, its centroid (+) and its center of symmetry($\oplus$).
b,c) The closest $C_5$-symmetric shape following angular selection about the centroid (b) and about the center of symmetry (c). Selection about the centroid gives a featureless shape, while selection about the center of symmetry yields a more meaningful shape.

be the new center of selection. If center of selection does not change, the neighborhood size is decreased. The process is terminated when neighborhood size reaches a predefined minimum size. The center of selection at the end of the process is taken as the center of symmetry.

In the case of occlusions (Fig. 14), the closest symmetric shape obtained by angular selection about the center of symmetry is visually more similar to the original than that obtained by angular selection about the centroid. We can reconstruct the symmetric shape closest to the unoccluded shape by obtaining the symmetry transform of the occluded shape using angular selection about the center of symmetry (see Fig. 14c). In Fig. 15 the center of symmetry and the closest symmetric shapes were found for several occluded flowers.

The process of reconstructing the occluded shape can be improved by altering the method of evaluating the symmetry of a set of points. As described in Sect. 3, the symmetry of a set of points is evaluated by folding, averaging and unfolding about the centroid of the points. We alter the method as follows:

1. The folding and unfolding (steps 1 and 3) will be performed about the center of selection rather than about the centroid of the points.

2. Rather than averaging the folded points (step 2), we apply other robust clustering methods. In practice we average over the folded points, drop the points farthest from the average and then reaverage (see Fig. 16).

The improvement in reconstruction of an occluded shape is shown in Fig. 17. This method improves both shape and localization of the reconstruction. Assuming that the original shape was symmetric, this method can reconstruct an occluded shape very accurately.

## 6 Symmetry of Points with Uncertain Locations

In most cases, sensing processes do not have absolute accuracy and the location of each point in a sensed pattern can be given only as a probability distribution. Given sensed points with such uncertain locations, the following properties are of interest:

- The most probable symmetric configuration represented by the sensed points.

- The probability distribution of symmetry distance values for the sensed points.

### 6.1 *The Most Probable Symmetric Shape*

Fig. 18a shows a configuration of points whose locations are given by a normal distribution function. The dot represents the expected location of the point and the rectangle represents the standard deviation marked as rectangles having width and length proportional to the standard deviation. In this section we briefly describe a method of evaluating the most probable symmetric shape under the Maximum Likelihood criterion ([3]) given the sensed points. Detailed derivations and proofs are given in Appendix A.1. For simplicity we describe the method with respect to rotational symmetry of order $n$ ($C_n$-symmetry). The solution for mirror symmetry or any other symmetry is similar (see Appendix A.2).

Given $n$ ordered points in 2D whose locations are given as normal probability distributions with expected location $P_i$ and covariance matrix $\Lambda_i$:
$Q_i \sim \mathcal{N}(P_i, \Lambda_i)$ $i = 0 \ldots n - 1$, we find the $C_n$-symmetric configuration of points at locations $\{\hat{P}_i\}_0^{n-1}$ which is optimal under the Maximum Likelihood criterion ([3]).
Denote by $\omega$ the centeroid of the most probable $C_n$-symmetric set of locations $\hat{P}_i$:

Figure 15: Application example.
a) A collection of occluded asymmetric flowers.
b) Contours of the occluded flowers were extracted manually.
c) The closest symmetric shapes and their center of symmetry.
d) The center of symmetry of the occluded flowers are marked by '+'.

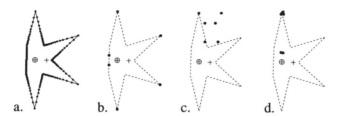

Figure 16: Improving the averaging of folded points
a) An occluded shape with points selected using angular selection about the center of symmetry (marked as ⊕).
b) A single set (orbit) of the selected points of a) is shown.
c) folding the points about the centroid (marked as +), points are clustered sparsely.
d) folding the points about the center of symmetry, points are clustered tightly. Eliminating the extremes (two farthest points) and averaging results in a smaller averaging error and better reconstruction.

$\omega = \frac{1}{n}\sum_{i=0}^{n-1}\hat{P}_i$. The point $\omega$ is dependent on the location of the measurements ($P_i$) and on the probability distribution associated with them ($\Lambda_i$). Intuitively, $\omega$ is positioned at that point about which the folding (described below) gives the tightest cluster of points with small uncertainty (small s.t.d.). We assume for the moment that $\omega$ is given. A method for finding $\omega$ is derived in Appendix A.1. We use a variant of the folding method which was described in Sect. 3 for evaluating $C_n$-symmetry of a set of points:

1. The $n$ measurements $Q_i \sim \mathcal{N}(P_i, \Lambda_i)$ are *folded* by rotating each measurement $Q_i$ by $2\pi i/n$ radians about the point $\omega$. A new set of measurements $\tilde{Q}_i \sim \mathcal{N}(\tilde{P}_i, \tilde{\Lambda}_i)$ is obtained (see Fig. 18b).

2. The folded measurements are *averaged* using a weighted average, obtaining a single point $\hat{P}_0$. Averaging is done by considering the $n$ folded measurements $\tilde{Q}_i$ as $n$ measurements of a single point and $\hat{P}_0$ represents the most probable

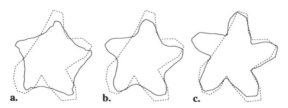

Figure 17: Reconstruction of an occluded almost symmetric shape.
The original shape is shown as a dashed line and the reconstructed shape as a solid line.
a) The closest symmetric shape following angular selection about the centroid.
b) The closest symmetric shape following angular selection about the center of symmetry.
c) The closest symmetric shape following angular selection about the center of symmetry and altered symmetry evaluation (see text).

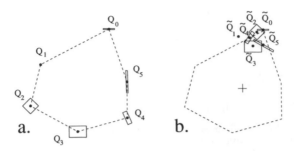

Figure 18: Folding measured points.
a) A configuration of 6 measuremented points $Q_0 \ldots Q_5$. The dot represents the expected location of the point and the rectangle represents the standard deviation marked as rectangles having width and length proportional to the standard deviation.
b) Each measurement $Q_i$ was rotated by $2\pi i/6$ radians about the centroid of the expected point locations (marked as '+') obtaining measurement $\tilde{Q}_0 \ldots \tilde{Q}_5$.

location of that point under the Maximum Likelihood criterion.

$$\hat{P}_0 - \omega = (\sum_{j=0}^{n-1} \tilde{\Lambda}_j^{-1})^{-1} \sum_{i=0}^{n-1} \tilde{\Lambda}_i^{-1} \tilde{P}_i - \omega$$

3. The "average" point $\hat{P}_0$ is *unfolded* as described in Sect. 3 obtaining points $\{\hat{P}_i\}_{i=0}^{n-1}$ which are perfectly $C_n$-symmetric.

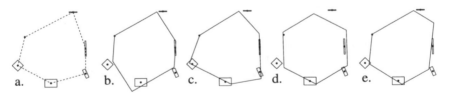

Figure 19: The most probable symmetric shape.
a) A configuration of 6 measured points.
b) The most probable symmetric shapes with respect to $C_2$-symmetry.
c) The most probable symmetric shapes with respect to $C_3$-symmetry.
d) The most probable symmetric shapes with respect to $C_6$-symmetry.
e) The most probable symmetric shapes with respect to mirror-symmetry.

When we are given $m = qn$ measurements, we find the most probable $C_n$-symmetric configuration of points, similar to the folding method of Sect. 3. The $m$ measurements $\{Q_i\}_{i=0}^{m-1}$, are divided into $q$ interlaced sets of $n$ points each, and the folding method as described above is applied seperately to each set of measurements. Derivations and proof of this case is also found in Appendix A.1.
Several examples are shown in Figure 19, where for a given set of measurements, the

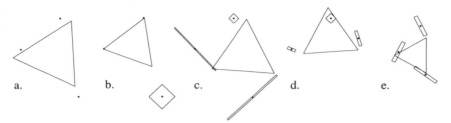

Figure 20: The most probable $C_3$-symmetric shape for a set of measurements after varying the probability distribution and expected locations of the measurements.
a-c) Changing the uncertainty (s.t.d.) of the measurements.
d-e) Changing both the uncertainty and the expected location of the measurements.

most probable symmetric shapes were found. Fig. 20 shows an example of varying the probability distribution of the measurements on the resulting symmetric shape.

**6.2** *The Probability Distribution of Symmetry Values*

Fig. 21a displays a Laue photograph ([1]) which is an interefrence pattern created by projecting X-ray beams onto crystals. Crystal quality is determined by evaluating the symmetry of the pattern. In this case the interesting feature is not the closest symmetric configuration, but the probability distribution of the symmetry distance values.

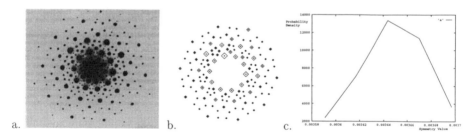

Figure 21: Probability distribution of symmetry values
a) Interference pattern of crystals.
b) Probability distribution of point locations corresponding to a.
c) Probability distribution of symmetry distance values with respect to $C_{10}$-symmetry was evaluated as described in Appendix A.3. Expectation value = 0.003663.

In Fig. 22 we display distributions of the symmetry distance value for various measurements. As expected, the distribution of symmetry distance values becomes broader as the uncertainties (the variance of the distribution) of the measurements increase.

608

Consider the configuration of 2D measurements given in Fig. 18a. Each measurement $Q_i$ is a normal probability distribution $Q_i \sim \mathcal{N}(P_i, \Lambda_i)$. We assume the centroid of the expectation of the measurements is at the origin. The probability distribution of the symmetry distance values of the original measurements is equivalent to the probability distribution of the location of the "average" point $(\hat{P}_0)$ given the folded measurements as obtained in Step 1 and Step 2 of the algorithm in Sect 6.1. It is shown in Appendix A.3 that this probability distribution is a $\chi^2$ distribution of order $n-1$. However, we can approximate the distribution by a gaussian distribution. Details of the derivation are given in Appendix A.3.

In Fig. 21 we display distributions of the symmetry distance value as obtained for the Laue photograph given in Fig. 21a. In this example we considered every dark patch as a measured point with variance proportional to the size of the patch. Thus in Fig. 21b the rectangles which are proportional in size to the corresponding dark patches of Fig. 21a, represent the standard deviation of the locations of point measurements. Note that a different analysis could be used in which the variance of the measurement location is taken as inversely proportional to the size of the dark patch.

## 7 Conclusion

We view symmetry as a continuous feature and define a Symmetry Distance (SD) of shapes. The general definition of the Symmetry Distance enables a comparison of

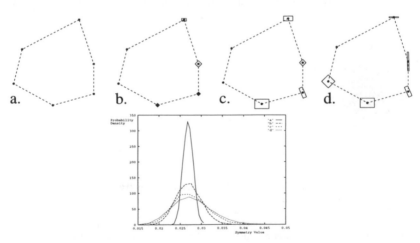

Figure 22: Probability distribution of the symmetry distance value as a function of the variance of the measured points.
a-d) Some examples of configurations of measured points.
e) Probability distribution of symmetry distance values with respect to $C_6$-symmetry for the configurations a-d.

the "amount" of symmetry of different shapes and the "amount" of different symmetries of a single shape. Furthermore, the SD is associated with the symmetric shape which is 'closest' to the given one, enabling visual evaluation of the SD. Several applications were described including reconstruction of occluded shapes, finding face orientation and finding locally symmetric regions in images. We also described how we deal with uncertain data, i.e. with a configuration of measurements representing the probability distribution of point location. The methods described here can be easily extended to higher dimensions and to more complex symmetry groups. Further extensions will deal with other symmetry classes such as planar symmetry (including translatory symmetry and fractals). Additional work has been done on evaluating reflective symmetry (and chirality) of graph structures ([7, 8]). Current work is expanding the method described here to deal with skewed and projected symmetries.

## Appendix

### A  Uncertain Point Locations

#### A.1  *The most Probable $C_n$-Symmetric Shape*

In Sect 6.1 we described a method of evaluating the most probable symmetric shape given a set of measurements. In this Section we derive mathematically and prove the method. For simplicity we derive the method with respect to rotational symmetry of order $n$ ($C_n$-symmetry). The solution for mirror symmetry is similar (see Appendix A.2).

Given $n$ points in 2D whose positions are given as normal probability distributions: $Q_i \sim \mathcal{N}(P_i, \Lambda_i)$, $i = 0 \ldots n - 1$, we find the $C_n$-symmetric configuration of points $\{\hat{P}_i\}_0^{n-1}$ which is most optimal under the Maximum Likelihood criterion ([3]).

Denote by $\omega$ the center of mass of $\hat{P}_i$:   $\omega = \frac{1}{n} \sum_{i=0}^{n-1} \hat{P}_i$.

Having that $\{\hat{P}_i\}_0^{n-1}$ are $C_n$-symmetric, the following is satisfied:

$$\hat{P}_i = R_i(\hat{P}_0 - \omega) + \omega \tag{1}$$

for $i = 0 \ldots \; n - 1$ where $R_i$ is a matrix representing a rotation of $2\pi i/n$ radians.

Thus, given the measurements $Q_0, \ldots, Q_{n-1}$ we find the most probable $\hat{P}_0$ and $\omega$. We find $\hat{P}_0$ and $\omega$ that maximize $\text{Prob}(\{P_i\}_{i=0}^{n-1} \mid \omega, \hat{P}_0)$ under the symmetry constraints of Equation 1.

Considering the normal distribution we have:

$$\prod_{i=0}^{n-1} k_i \exp(-\frac{1}{2}(\hat{P}_i - P_i)^t \Lambda_i^{-1}(\hat{P}_i - P_i))$$

where $k_i = \frac{1}{2}\pi \mid \Lambda_i \mid^{1/2}$. Having log being a monotonic function, we maximize:

$$\log \prod_{i=0}^{n-1} k_i \exp(-\frac{1}{2}(\hat{P}_i - P_i)^t \Lambda_i^{-1}(\hat{P}_i - P_i)$$

Thus we find those parameters which maximize:

$$-\frac{1}{2} \sum_{i=0}^{n-1} (\hat{P}_i - P_i)^t \Lambda_i^{-1}(\hat{P}_i - P_i)$$

under the symmetry constraint of Equation 1.

Substituting Equation 1, taking the derivative with respect to $\hat{P}_0$ and equating to zero we obtain:

$$\underbrace{(\sum_{i=0}^{n-1} R_i^t \Lambda_i^{-1} R_i)}_{A} \hat{P}_0 + \underbrace{\sum_{i=0}^{n-1} R_i^t \Lambda_i^{-1}(I - R_i)\omega}_{B} = \underbrace{\sum_{i=0}^{n-1} R_i^t \Lambda_i^{-1} P_i}_{E} \qquad (2)$$

Note that $R_0 = I$ where $I$ is the identity matrix.
When the derivative with respect to $\omega$ is zero:

$$\underbrace{(\sum_{i=0}^{n-1}(I - R_i)^t \Lambda_i^{-1} R_i)}_{C} \hat{P}_0 + \underbrace{\sum_{i=0}^{n-1}(I - R_i)^t \Lambda_i^{-1}(I - R_i)\omega}_{D} = \underbrace{\sum_{i=0}^{n-1}(I - R_i)^t \Lambda_i^{-1} P_i}_{F} \qquad (3)$$

From Equation 2 we obtain

$$\hat{P}_0 - \omega = (\sum_{j=0}^{n-1} R_j^t \Lambda_j^{-1} R_j)^{-1} \sum_{i=0}^{n-1}(R_i^t \Lambda_i^{-1} R_i)R_i^t P_i$$

Which gives the folding method described in Sect 6.1, where $R_i^t P_i$ is the location of the folded measurement (denoted $\tilde{P}_i$ in the text) and $R_i^t \Lambda_i^{-1} R_i$ is its probability distribution (denoted $\tilde{\Lambda}_i$ in the text). The factor $(\sum_{j=0}^{n-1} R_j^t \Lambda_j^{-1} R_j)$ is the normalization factor.

Reformulating Eqs. 2 and 3 in matrix formation we obtain:

$$\underbrace{\begin{pmatrix} A & B \\ C & D \end{pmatrix}}_{U} \underbrace{\begin{pmatrix} \hat{P}_0 \\ \omega \end{pmatrix}}_{V} = \underbrace{\begin{pmatrix} E \\ F \end{pmatrix}}_{Z}$$

Noting that $U$ is symmetric we solve by inversion $V = U^{-1}Z$ obtaining the parameters $\omega, \hat{P}_0$ and obtaining the most probable $C_n$-symmetric configuration, given the measurements $\{Q_i\}_{i=0}^{n-1}$.

Similar to the representation in Sect. 3, given $m = qn$ measurements $\{Q_i\}_{i=0}^{m-1}$, we consider them as $q$ sets of $n$ interlaced measurements: $\{Q_{iq+j}\}_{i=0}^{n-1}$ for $j = 0 \ldots q-1$.

The derivations given above are applied to each set of $n$ measurements separately, inorder to obtain the most probable $C_n$-symmetric set of points $\{\hat{P}_i\}_{i=0}^{m-1}$. Thus the symmetry constraints that must be satisfied are:

$$\hat{P}_{iq+j} = R_i(\hat{P}_j - \omega) + \omega$$

for $j = 0 \dots q-1$ and $i = 0 \dots n-1$ where, again, $R_i$ is a matrix representing a rotation of $2\pi i/n$ radians and $\omega$ is the centroid of all points $\{\hat{P}_i\}_{i=0}^{m-1}$. As derived in Equation 2, we obtain for $j = 0 \dots q-1$:

$$\underbrace{\left(\sum_{i=0}^{n-1} R_i^t \Lambda_{iq+j}^{-1} R_i\right) \hat{P}_j}_{A_j} + \underbrace{\sum_{i=0}^{n-1} R_i^t \Lambda_{iq+j}^{-1}(I - R_i)\,\omega}_{B_j} = \underbrace{\sum_{i=0}^{n-1} R_i^t \Lambda_{iq+j}^{-1} P_{iq+j}}_{E_j} \tag{4}$$

and equating to zero, the derivative with respect to $\omega$, we obtain, similar to Equation 3:

$$\underbrace{\sum_{j=0}^{q-1}\sum_{i=0}^{n-1}(I-R_i)^t\Lambda_{iq+j}^{-1}R_i)\,\hat{P}_j}_{C_j} + \underbrace{\sum_{j=0}^{q-1}\sum_{i=0}^{n-1}(I-R_i)^t\Lambda_{iq+j}^{-1}(I-R_i)\,\omega}_{D} = \underbrace{\sum_{j=0}^{q-1}\sum_{i=0}^{n-1}(I-R_i)^t\Lambda_{iq+j}^{-1}P_{iq+j}}_{F}$$

$$\tag{5}$$

Reformulating Eqs. 4 and 5 in matrix formation we obtain:

$$\underbrace{\begin{pmatrix} A_0 & & & & B_0 \\ & A_1 & & & B_1 \\ & & \ddots & & \vdots \\ & & & A_{q-1} & B_{q-1} \\ C_0 & C_1 & \cdots & C_{q-1} & D \end{pmatrix}}_{U} \underbrace{\begin{pmatrix} \hat{P}_0 \\ \hat{P}_1 \\ \vdots \\ \hat{P}_{q-1} \\ \omega \end{pmatrix}}_{V} = \underbrace{\begin{pmatrix} E_0 \\ E_1 \\ \vdots \\ E_{q-1} \\ F \end{pmatrix}}_{Z}$$

Noting that $U$ is symmetric we solve by inversion $V = U^{-1}Z$ and obtain the parameters $\omega$ and $\{\hat{P}_j\}_{j=0}^{q-1}$, and obtain the most probable $C_n$-symmetric configuration, $\{\hat{P}_j\}_{j=0}^{m-1}$ given the measurements $\{Q_i\}_{i=0}^{m-1}$.

### A.2  The Most Probable Mirror Symmetric Shape

In Sect 6.1 we described a method for finding the most probable rotationaly symmetric shape given measurements of point location. The solution for mirror symmetry is similar. In this case, given $m$ measurements (where $m = 2q$), the unknown parameters are $\{\hat{P}_j\}_{j=0}^{q-1}, \omega$ and $\theta$ where $\theta$ is the angle of the reflection axis. However these parameters are redundant and we reduce the dimensionality of the problem by replacing the 2 dimensional $\omega$ with the one dimensional $x_0$ representing the x-coordinate at which the reflection axis intersects the x-axis. Additionally we replace $R_i$ the rotation matrix with $R = \begin{pmatrix} \cos 2\theta & \sin 2\theta \\ \sin 2\theta & -\cos 2\theta \end{pmatrix}$ the reflection about an axis at an angle $\theta$ to the x-axis. The angle $\theta$ is found analyticaly (see [10]) thus the dimensionality of the problem is $2q + 1$ (rather than $2q + 2$) and elimination of the last row and column of matrix $U$ (see Sect 6.1) allows an inverse solution as in the rotational symmetry case.

**A.3** *Probability Distribution of Symmetry Values*

In this section we derive mathematically the probability distribution of symmetry distance values obtained from a set of $n$ measurements in 2D: $Q_i \sim \mathcal{N}(P_i, \Lambda_i)$  $i = 0 \ldots n - 1$ with respect to $C_n$-symmetry (see Sect. 6.2).

Denote by $X_i$ the 2-dimensional random variable having a normal distribution equal to that of measurement $\tilde{Q}_i$ i.e.

$$E(X_i) = R_i P_i$$
$$\text{Cov}(X_i) = R_i \Lambda_i R_i^t$$

where $R_i$ denotes (as in Sect. 3) the rotation matrix of $2\pi i / n$ radians.

Denote by $Y_i$ the 2-dimensional random variable:

$$Y_i = X_i - \frac{1}{n} \sum_{j=0}^{n-1} X_j$$

in matrix notation:

$$\underbrace{\begin{pmatrix} Y_0 \\ \vdots \\ Y_{n-1} \end{pmatrix}}_{\mathbf{Y}} = A \underbrace{\begin{pmatrix} X_0 \\ \vdots \\ X_{n-1} \end{pmatrix}}_{\mathbf{X}}$$

or $\mathbf{Y} = A\mathbf{X}$ where $\mathbf{Y}$ and $\mathbf{X}$ are of dimension $2n$ and $A$ is the $2n \times 2n$ matrix:

$$A = \frac{1}{n} \begin{pmatrix} n-1 & 0 & -1 & 0 & -1 & \cdots \\ 0 & n-1 & 0 & -1 & 0 & \cdots \\ -1 & 0 & \ddots & 0 & -1 & \cdots \\ & & & \ddots & & \\ & & \cdots & & & n-1 \end{pmatrix}$$

And we have

$$E(\mathbf{X}) = \begin{pmatrix} E(X_0) \\ \vdots \\ E(X_{n-1}) \end{pmatrix} \quad \text{Cov}(\mathbf{X}) = \begin{pmatrix} \text{Cov}(X_0) & & \\ & \ddots & \\ & & \text{Cov}(X_{n-1}) \end{pmatrix}$$

$$E(\mathbf{Y}) = AE(\mathbf{X}) \quad \text{Cov}(\mathbf{Y}) = A\text{Cov}(\mathbf{X})A^t$$

The matrix $A\text{Cov}(\mathbf{X})A^t$, being symmetric and positive definite, we find the $2n \times 2n$ matrix $S$ diagonalizing $\text{Cov}(\mathbf{Y})$ i.e.

$$SA\text{Cov}(\mathbf{X})A^t S^t = D$$

where $D$ is a diagonal matrix (of rank $2(n-1)$).

Denote by $\mathbf{Z} = (Z_0, \ldots, Z_{n-1})^t$ the $2n$-dimensional random variable $SA\mathbf{X}$.

$$
\begin{aligned}
E(\mathbf{Z}) &= SAE(\mathbf{X}) \\
\mathrm{Cov}(\mathbf{Z}) &= SA\mathrm{Cov}(\mathbf{X})A^t S^t = D
\end{aligned}
$$

Thus the random variables $Z_i$ that compose $\mathbf{Z}$ are independent and, being linear combinations of $X_i$, they are of normal distribution.

The symmetry distance, as defined in Sect. 3, is equivalent, in the current notations, to $s = \mathbf{Y}^t\mathbf{Y}$. Having $S$ orthonormal we have

$$
s = (SA\mathbf{X})^t SA\mathbf{X} = \mathbf{Z}^t\mathbf{Z}
$$

If $\mathbf{Z}$ were a random variable of standard normal distribution, we would have $s$ being of a $\chi^2$ distribution of order $2(n-1)$. In the general case $Z_i$ are normally distributed but not standard and $\mathbf{Z}$ cannot be standardized globally. We approximate the distribution of $s$ as a normal distribution with

$$
\begin{aligned}
E(s) &= E(\mathbf{Z})^t E(\mathbf{Z}) + \mathrm{trace}D^t D \\
\mathrm{Cov}(s) &= 2\mathrm{trace}(D^t D)(D^t D) + 4E(\mathbf{Z})^t D^t DE(\mathbf{Z})
\end{aligned}
$$

# References

[1] J.L. Amoros, M.J. Buerger, and M.Canut de Amoros. *The Laue Method*. Academic Press, New York, 1975.

[2] F. Attneave. Symmetry information and memory for patterns. *American Journal of Psychology*, 68:209–222, 1955.

[3] M. H. DeGroot. *Probability and Statistics*. Addison-Wesley, Reading, MA, 1975.

[4] W. Miller. *Symmetry Groups and their Applications*. Academic Press, London, 1972.

[5] F. Mokhatarian and A. Mackworth. A theory of multiscale, curvature-based shape representation for planar curves. *IEEE Trans. on Pattern Analysis and Machine Intelligence*, 14:789–805, 1992.

[6] H. Weyl. *Symmetry*. Princeton Univ. Press, 1952.

[7] H. Zabrodsky and D. Avnir. Measuring symmetry in structural chemistry. In I. Hargittai, editor, *Advanced Molecular Structure Research*, volume 1. 1993.

[8] H. Zabrodsky, S. Peleg, and D. Avnir. Continuous symmetry measures, IV: Chirality. In Preparation.

[9] H. Zabrodsky, S. Peleg, and D. Avnir. Continuous symmetry measures II: Symmetry groups and the tetrahedron. *J. Am. Chem. Soc.*, 115:8278–8289, 1993.

[10] H. Zabrodsky, S. Peleg, and D. Avnir. Continuous symmetry measures. *J. Am. Chem. Soc.*, 114:7843–7851, Sept 1992.

# AUTHOR INDEX

616